Apple Pro Training Series

Final Cut Pro 6 Beyond the Basics

Michael Wohl

Apple Pro Training Series: Final Cut Pro 6: Beyond the Basics
Michael Wohl

Published by Peachpit Press. For information on Peachpit Press books, contact:

Peachpit Press
1249 Eighth Street
Berkeley, CA 94710
(510) 524-2178
Fax: (510) 524-2221
http://www.peachpit.com
To report errors, please send a note to errata@peachpit.com
Peachpit Press is a division of Pearson Education

Editor: Bob Lindstrom
Apple Series Editor: Nancy Peterson
Contributing Writer (cameos): Serena Herr
Production Coordinator: Laurie Stewart, Happenstance Type-O-Rama
Technical Editors and Reviewers: Brendan Boykin, K.D. Gulko, Estelle McGechie, Mary Plummer
Copy Editor and Proofer: Darren Meiss, Dan J. Foster
Compositor: Chris Gillespie, Happenstance Type-O-Rama
Indexer: Karin Arrigoni
Cover Illustration: Kent Oberheu
Cover Production: Happenstance Type-O-Rama
Media Review: Eric Geoffroy

ISBN 10: 0-321-50912-9
ISBN 13: 978-0-321-50912-3
9 8 7 6 5 4 3 2 1
Printed and bound in the United States of America

Contents at a Glance

Table of Contents

Sound Editing

Visual Effects

Getting Started

Welcome to the official Apple Pro Training Series course for Final Cut Pro 6. This book is an in-depth journey into Final Cut Pro. The exercises will teach you the many advanced editing features of Final Cut Pro and will also show you how to perform the tasks you'll face daily in real-world editing projects.

Whether you're a newcomer or a working film and video editor, this book will enhance your Final Cut Pro knowledge while it advances your editing techniques.

The Methodology

This is, first and foremost, a hands-on course. Every exercise is designed to help you perform professional-quality editing in Final Cut Pro as quickly as possible. Each lesson builds on previous lessons to guide you through the program's functions and capabilities. If you are already very familiar with Final Cut Pro, you can go directly to a specific section and focus on that topic because every lesson is self-contained.

Course Structure

This book is designed to improve your skills both as an editor and as a Final Cut Pro operator. You will begin by learning editing techniques designed to streamline your workflow and allow you to handle tricky situations and effectively perform complex editing tasks. Then you'll focus on sound editing and mixing, using both Final Cut Pro and Soundtrack Pro. Next, you'll explore the world of effects, covering such diverse topics as compositing, filters, keyframing, nested sequences, and speed modification. Color correction techniques come next, providing a wealth of information about the goals and techniques of color correction in Final Cut Pro. Finally, you'll finish your studies with three lessons dealing with the "nuts and bolts" of Final Cut Pro workflows, including clip management, media management, and importing and exporting files.

The lessons are grouped into the following categories:

- Advanced Editing: Lessons 1–3
- Sound Editing: Lessons 4–5
- Visual Effects: Lessons 6–10
- Color Correction: Lessons 11–13
- Project Management: Lessons 14–16

In addition to the exercises, some lessons include "Project Tasks" that give you an opportunity to practice what you've learned before moving on to new material. Throughout the book, other valuable sections will guide you in evaluating your project before moving to the next editing stage.

Using the DVD Book Files

The *Apple Pro Training Series: Final Cut Pro 6: Beyond the Basics* DVD (included with the book) contains the project files you will use for each lesson as well as media files that contain the video and audio content you will need for each exercise. After you transfer the files to your hard drive, each lesson will instruct you in the use of the project and media files.

Installing the Final Cut Pro 6 Beyond the Basics Lesson Files

On the DVD, you'll find a folder titled Book Files, which contains two subfolders: Lessons and Media. These folders contain the lessons and media files for this course. Make sure you keep these two folders together in the Book Files folder on your hard drive. If you do so, Final Cut Pro should be able to maintain the original links between the lessons and media files.

1 Insert the *Apple Pro Training Series: Final Cut Pro 6: Beyond the Basics* DVD into your DVD drive.

2 Drag the Book Files folder from the DVD to your hard drive to copy it.

   The Media folder contains about 8 GB of media.

Each lesson will explain which files to open for that lesson's exercises.

Reconnecting Media

When copying files from the DVD to your hard drive, you may unintentionally break a link between a project file and its media files. If this happens, a dialog appears asking you to relink the project files. Relinking the project files is a simple process that's covered in more depth in the "Reconnecting Offline Files" section in Lesson 15. But should the dialog appear when opening a lesson, follow these steps:

1 Click the Reconnect button.

   A Reconnect Files dialog opens. Under the Files To Connect portion of the dialog, the offline file is listed along with its possible location.

2. In the Reconnect Files dialog, click Search.

   Final Cut Pro will search for the missing file. If you already know where the file is located, you can click the Locate button and find the file manually.

3. After the correct file is found, click Choose in the Reconnect dialog.

4. When the file is displayed in the Files Located section of the Reconnect Files dialog, click Connect.

   When the link between the project file and the media file is reestablished, Final Cut Pro will be able to access the media within the project.

Changing System Preferences

A few editing functions within Final Cut Pro use function keys also used by other programs, such as Exposé and the Dashboard. If you want to use the FCP editing shortcuts, you will need to reassign the function keys in these other programs.

1. From your Desktop, open System Preferences.

2. In the Personal section, click Dashboard & Exposé.

3. Reassign the keyboard shortcuts for F9, F10, F11, and F12 to other keys.

   Reassigning the shortcuts will allow Final Cut Pro to use these shortcut keys exclusively.

   At any time when using Final Cut Pro, you can return to System Preferences and change these key assignments.

System Requirements

Before using *Apple Pro Training Series: Final Cut Pro 6: Beyond the Basics,* you should have a working knowledge of your Macintosh and the Mac OS X operating system. Make sure that you know how to use the mouse and standard menus and commands, and also how to open, save, and close files. If you need to review these techniques, see the printed or online documentation included with your system. For the basic system requirements for Final Cut Pro 6, refer to the Final Cut Pro 6 documentation.

About the Apple Pro Training Series

Apple Pro Training Series: Final Cut Pro 6: Beyond the Basics is part of the official training series for Apple Pro applications developed by experts in the field. The lessons are designed to let you learn at your own pace. If you're new to Final Cut Pro, you'll learn the fundamental concepts and features you'll need to master the program. If you've been using Final Cut Pro for a while, you'll find that this book covers most of the new features found in Final Cut Pro 6.

Although each lesson provides step-by-step instructions for creating specific projects, there's room for exploration and experimentation. However, try to follow the book from start to finish, or at least complete the first three sections before jumping around. Each lesson concludes with a review section summarizing what you've covered.

Apple Pro Certification Program

The Apple Pro Training and Certification Programs are designed to keep you at the forefront of Apple digital media technology while giving you a competitive edge in today's ever-changing job market. Whether you're an editor, graphic designer, sound designer, special effects artist, or teacher, these training tools are meant to help you expand your skills.

Upon completing the course material in this book, you can become an Apple Pro by taking the certification exam at an Apple Authorized Training Center. Certification is offered in Final Cut Pro 6, DVD Studio Pro 4, Shake 4, and Logic Pro 7. Certification as an Apple Pro gives you official recognition of your knowledge of the Apple professional applications while allowing you to market yourself to employers and clients as a skilled, pro-level user of Apple products.

To find an Apple Authorized Training Center near you, go to www.apple.com/software/pro/training.

For those who prefer to learn in an instructor-led setting, Apple also offers training courses at Apple Authorized Training Centers worldwide. These courses, which use the Apple Pro Training Series books as their curriculum, are taught by Apple Certified Trainers, balancing concepts and lectures with hands-on labs and exercises. Apple Authorized Training Centers for Pro products have been carefully selected and have met Apple's highest standards in all areas, including facilities, instructors, course delivery, and infrastructure. The goal of the program is to offer Apple customers, from beginners to the most seasoned professionals, the highest-quality training experience.

Resources

Apple Pro Training Series: Final Cut Pro 6: Beyond the Basics is not intended as a comprehensive reference manual, nor does it replace the documentation that comes with the application. For comprehensive information about program features, refer to these resources:

- The Reference Guide. Accessed through the Final Cut Pro Help menu, the Reference Guide contains a complete description of all features.
- The Apple website: www.apple.com

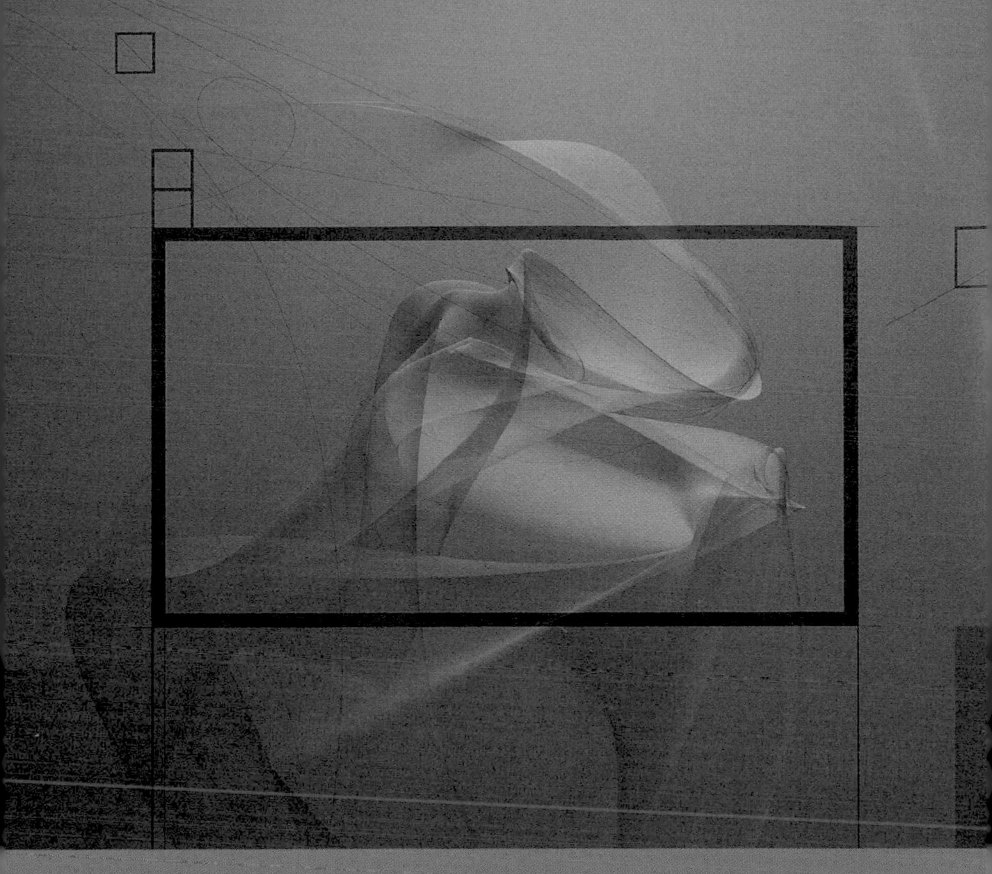

Advanced Editing

1

n Files Lesson Files > Lesson 01 > Timing.fcp

Media Poker and Blind Date

Time This lesson takes approximately 60 minutes to complete.

Goals Improve overall editing efficiency and effectiveness

Use Final Cut Pro's sophisticated editing tools

Improve timing with replace edits

Access used source clips quickly with Match Frame

Gang (synchronize) the Viewer and Canvas

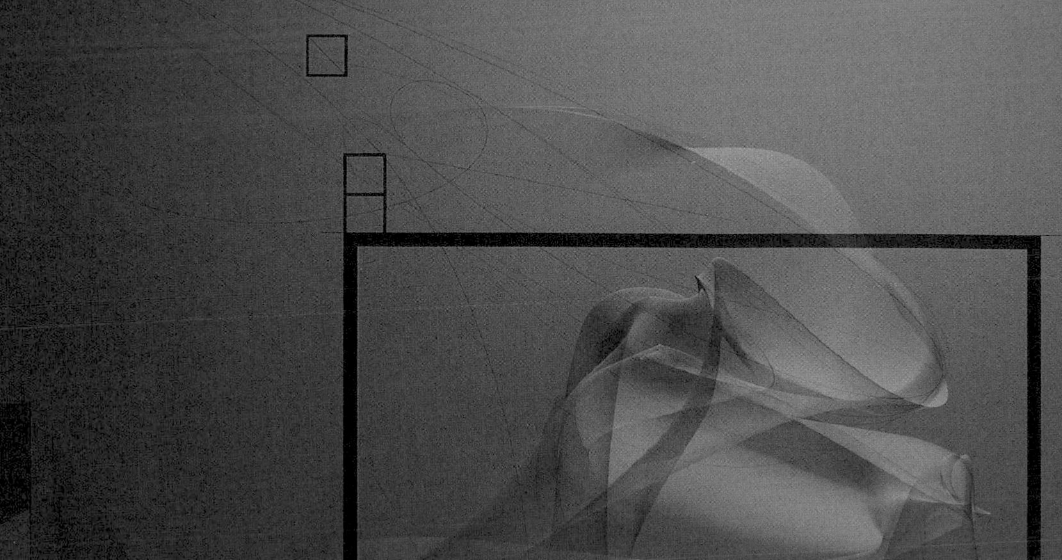

Lesson **1**

Accelerating Your Workflow

Although you can successfully edit projects in Final Cut Pro using only a few of the most basic tools, many other tools and techniques are available to speed your workflow and improve your final product. In most cases, these are compound tools or shortcuts that can perform several steps in a single action. Mastering these can significantly improve your editing experience and take you one step closer to that magical state when you can operate the software as fast as you can think.

In most cases, these methods aren't difficult to use. They simply require a more sophisticated approach to editing, in which you foresee all your editing objectives at once, like a chess master planning three or four moves in advance. For example, if you know that you want to cut back and forth between two close-ups in a dialogue scene, Final Cut Pro has commands—such as Match Frame and Gang Sync—specifically designed to accelerate that workflow.

As you grow more comfortable with these advanced techniques, they will become as familiar as three-point edits or the Blade tool, and you will find that they are equally as versatile. This lesson covers a selection of the most useful features frequently overlooked or underused by self-taught editors.

Going Beyond the Double-Click

You already know that you can double-click a clip in the Browser to open it, or drag and drop it from the Browser to the Viewer, or even select it and press Enter.

You also know that if you double-click a sequence clip in the Canvas or Timeline, it will open into the Viewer with sprocket holes displayed in the scrubber area to indicate that it's currently in use.

Clip opened from the Browser

Clip opened from a sequence

However, sometimes you want to quickly open a clip into the Viewer without going to the Browser, and without affecting the version of the clip currently in use in the sequence. For instance, you may have used a portion of a clip, cut away to another shot, and now want to use a different section of that first shot in another part of the sequence. Alternately, you might have applied some effects to a clip in the sequence, and you want to use the original, unfiltered clip in a different way. In another example, you might have a title or graphic that you want to reuse in more than one place in your sequence.

In any of these cases, you could hunt through the Browser or Effects tabs looking for the original master clip, but this can be time consuming, and it takes you out of the flow of the scene you're currently working on.

Using the Recent Clips Pop-Up Menu

One place to find clips quickly is in the Recent Clips pop-up menu in the Viewer window. This menu shows the last ten clips opened into the Viewer. Selecting a clip from the menu will automatically reopen it.

This is especially helpful when you want to reexamine a clip that you viewed briefly but chose not to use. You can also populate this menu all at once with a group of clips.

1 Open Lesson Files > Lesson 01 > **Timing.fcp.**

2 In the Viewer, click the Recent Clips pop-up menu.

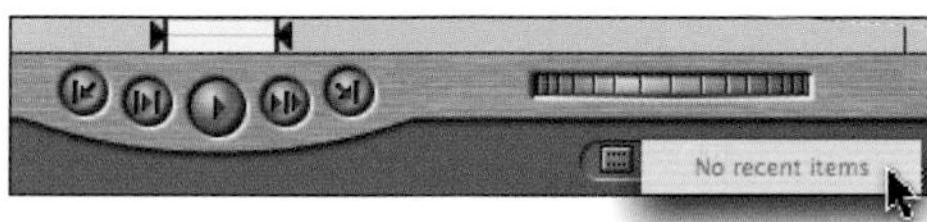

It indicates that there are no recent items opened.

NOTE ▶ If you have opened any clips prior to beginning this lesson, the menu might not be empty.

3 Select the five clips in the SloMo bin and drag all of them to the Viewer window.

The first of these clips is opened into the Viewer, but the other clips are automatically added to the Recent Clips pop-up menu.

4 Click the Recent Clips pop-up menu and choose **Fan Cards SloMo 20-S**.

The close-up of the cards is loaded into the Viewer, and the In and Out points are displayed based on the last time the master clip was opened.

Additionally, you can customize the number of clips listed in the menu.

1 Choose Final Cut Pro > User Preferences and click the General tab.

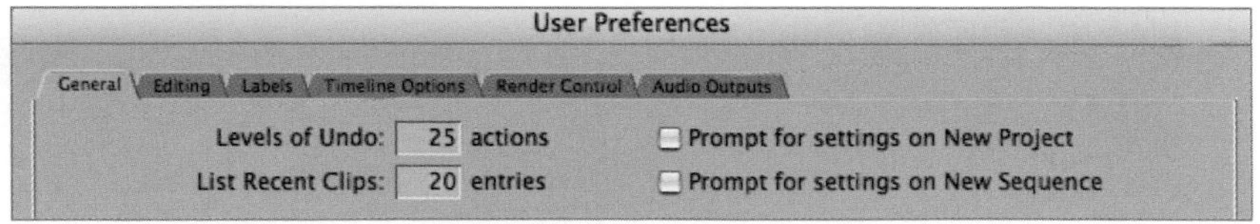

2 Set the List Recent Clips setting to *20* and close the window.

Now, the 20 most recently accessed clips will appear in the menu. They appear in the reverse order that they were opened. Twenty is the maximum value for this setting (which is just as well—with any more than that, it would lose its benefit as a shortcut).

Using Match Frame

Another tool that opens a recently-used clip is the Match Frame command. Match Frame automatically opens into the Viewer the master clip of the shot currently under the playhead, on the lowest Auto Select–enabled track.

The clip opens into the Viewer with the playhead parked on the same frame it was parked on in the sequence. Although this function may seem unimpressive, it is actually one of the handiest and most versatile shortcuts in Final Cut Pro. Throughout the rest of this chapter, you will employ the Match Frame command for a variety of purposes.

> **NOTE ▸** If there is no video clip under the playhead, or if Auto Select is disabled on the video tracks, Match Frame will open the audio clips at the playhead position.

1. In the Browser, double-click the *Match Frame* sequence (if it's not already open).
2. Park the playhead anywhere in the second clip (**Overhead ELS 17-S**).
3. In the Canvas, click the Match Frame button (or press F).

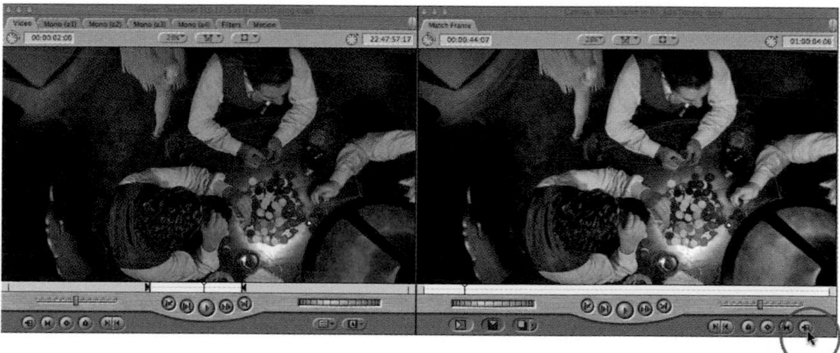

The unfiltered master clip is opened into the Viewer.

Note that the clip in the sequence has a Desaturate filter applied to it (making it appear black and white), but the clip in the Viewer—the original clip—has no filter applied. This was specifically done for this lesson to emphasize the difference between double-clicking a clip in the sequence and performing a Match Frame command. Also notice that there are no sprocket holes in the Viewer scrubber area. This also reinforces that the clip in the Viewer is not the same clip used in the sequence.

There is also a Match Frame button in the Viewer. Clicking this button (or pressing F while the Viewer is active) will attempt to move the Canvas play-head to the frame currently active in the Viewer.

If that frame appears more than once in the sequence, the first instance *after* the current sequence playhead position will be used. If that frame does not exist in the open sequence, Final Cut will just beep at you.

Viewing Master Clips in the Browser

Match Frame will work even if the master clip you are looking for doesn't exist in the Browser window. For example, you may have deleted the clip from the project after placing it in the sequence, or you may have opened more than one project and dragged a clip from Project 2 into a sequence in Project 1, and so on.

If the master clip does exist in the Browser window somewhere, however, Final Cut Pro can find it.

1 Position the sequence playhead over the first clip (**steadicam Opener 1-8**).

2 Choose View > Reveal Master Clip.

   The Browser window takes focus and opens the bin containing that master clip and selects the clip.

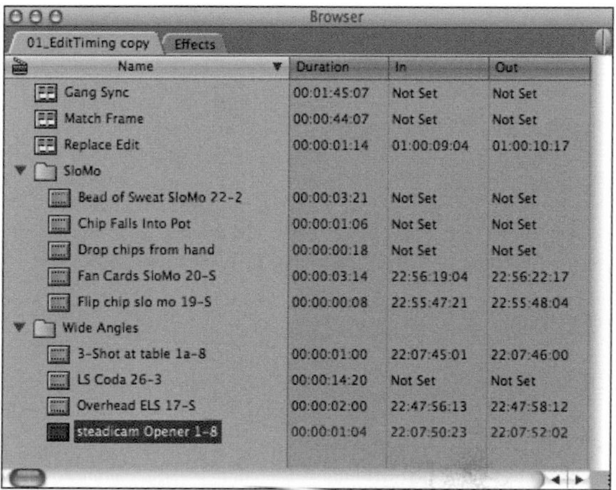

If the master clip does not exist in the Browser, Final Cut can automatically regenerate one for you.

3 Position the sequence playhead over the fourth clip (**MS Dawn & Paul 10-3**).

4 Chose View > Reveal Master Clip (or press Shift-F).

A dialog appears.

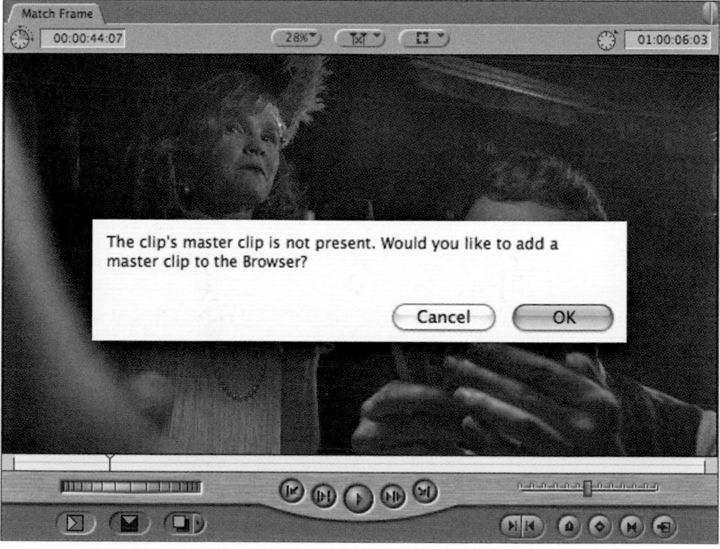

5 Click OK.

The master clip is added to the Browser and selected.

This technique can be useful when you have more than one version of a clip in the Browser and you have lost track of which clip the affiliate clip in the sequence refers to.

Matching to the Source File

In some cases, rather than opening the master clip associated with the clip you are viewing, you may want to Match Frame directly to the original source clip. For example, you might do this if some parameters were modified on the master clip and you want to return to the unmodified footage.

First, you'll perform a standard match frame. The raw version need not be opened into your project. Final Cut Pro will look to the hard disk for the source footage and open a new version of the clip.

1 Position the sequence playhead over the fifth clip in the sequence (**3-Shot at table 1a-8**).

   This clip has a filter applied to accentuate the shadows.

2 Choose View > Match Frame > Master Clip (or press F).

The master clip is loaded into the Viewer, but the filter effect is still applied. This is because, in this case, the filter was applied before the clip was edited into the sequence.

3 Press Q to make the sequence active.

 Pressing the Q shortcut key toggles focus between the Viewer and the Canvas.

4 Choose View > Match Frame > Source File (or press Option-Command-F).

Now the original version of the clip is opened into the Viewer.

Using the Replace Edit

Overwrite and insert edits are probably second nature to you, in which you determine the edit points based on the In or Out points of the clip or the sequence. But often, the important moment in a shot isn't the first or last frame you see. Instead, the edit may hinge on a frame that happens midway through the shot, such as a lover slamming a door, a policeman shooting a gun, or a judge banging her gavel.

The replace edit allows you to make an edit based on just such an *anchor* frame, in which the In and Out points are set automatically based on the existing structure of the sequence. The replace edit is an invaluable tool for replacing a wide shot with a close-up of the same action—but without changing the timing that was already established. In another situation, you might replace a shot with itself to adjust the timing of an edit that wasn't quite working.

There are countless occasions when a replace edit is just what you need. The following sections show a few examples of how you can use it.

Replacing One Shot with Another

One of the most obvious uses of the replace edit is exchanging a shot with a different angle of the same action—without modifying the timing already established in the sequence; for example, if you have a wide shot and you instead decide to use a close-up.

1 Double-click the *Replace Edit* sequence to open it into the Canvas and Timeline.

2 Play the sequence.

   This is a slightly different version of the same scene.

3 Step frame by frame through the fifth shot, **3ShotFavorPaul**, and position your playhead on the exact frame where the chip falls into the pile (at approximately 06:14).

This will be the anchor frame in the sequence. You do not need to set any In or Out points, just leave the playhead parked there.

4 In the Viewer, click the Recent Clips pop-up menu and choose **Chip Falls Into Pot.**

NOTE ▶ If that clip does not appear in your Recent Clips pop-up menu, double-click it in the SloMo bin in the Browser.

5 Play the clip and park the playhead on the frame exactly where the same action happens (at approximately 47:09).

This is the anchor frame in the Viewer.

6 Drag the clip to the Canvas and drop it on Replace in the Edit Overlay.

7 Play the sequence again.

The shot is replaced, but the timing remains perfectly intact.

A replace edit doesn't base the edit on standard three-point editing rules in which In or Out points determine a clip's resulting position in the sequence. Instead, a replace edit uses the current frame in both Viewer and Canvas to define the edit.

Final Cut Pro will grab as many frames as are needed before and after the anchor frame to fill the duration of the clip in the sequence. If there are not enough frames before or after, the replace function will not work.

1 Reposition the sequence playhead on the same anchor, where the chip lands in the pile (06:14).

2 In the Recent Clips pop-up menu, choose **Drop chips from hand.**

3 Find the frame where the chip lands in the pile (23:04:48:16).

4 In the Viewer, drag the clip to the Canvas and drop it on Replace in the Edit Overlay (or press F11).

An error dialog warns you that there is insufficient content, which means that there aren't enough frames to replace all of the frames of the shot in the sequence.

Although the clip in the sequence is 17 frames long, and the clip in the Viewer is 18 frames long, the replace edit must match the position of the playhead in the Viewer with the playhead in the sequence. When it does that, there are not enough frames remaining after the chip hits the pile to replace the similar frames in the sequence.

This is the most common problem that editors new to the replace edit function encounter. If you moved the playhead back a few frames in the Viewer, the replace edit would work, but you would no longer be properly lining up the chip landing action.

Replacing Using In and Out Points

Although no In and Out points are necessary to use the replace edit, you can use sequence In and Out points to limit the effect of the replace action.

1 Play forward through the new clips in the sequence, until the other poker player drops his chip into the pile.

2 Park your playhead directly on the frame where the chip hits the pile (approximately 10:08).

3 Press M to add a marker on that frame.

NOTE ▶ Although the marker isn't required, it will help ensure that you perform the edit on exactly the correct frame. While you're learning to master the replace edit, adding markers can help you keep track of anchor frames.

In this case, rather than replace the entire wide shot, you want to replace only the second half of it, without manually recalculating the precise timing already established in the sequence.

4 Enter –5 (minus five) to move the playhead backward five frames.

5 Press I to set an In point.

6 Press the Down Arrow to move to the next edit point, then press Left Arrow to step back one frame.

7 Press O to set an Out point.

8 Press Option-M to navigate to the marker you set in step 3.

This returns your playhead to the anchor frame.

9 **Drop chips from hand** should still be open in the Viewer; if it's not, use the Recent Clips pop-up menu to open it.

10 If the Viewer playhead is not already parked on the frame where the chip lands in the pile, position it there (48:16).

11 Perform the replace edit.

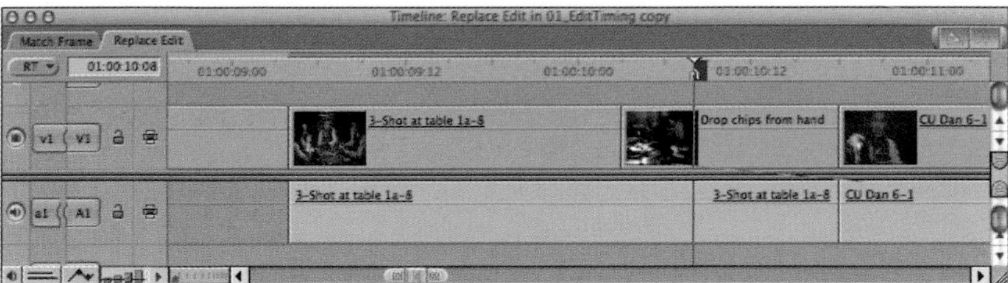

In this case, the replace edit lines up the playheads, but limits the edit to the In and Out points set in the sequence. (In this case, you could even have omitted the Out point, and the end of the clip would have been used.)

Marks in the Viewer will always be ignored.

Replacing a Shot with Itself

Another common use for the replace edit is to quickly adjust the timing of a shot by temporarily loading a clip into the Viewer, adjusting the timing, and replacing the shot on top of itself.

1 Press End to jump to the end of the *Replace Edit* sequence.

2 Back up a few shots and watch the edit.

  In the last shot, the girl's dialogue was edited to speed up the edit. This is frequently done with an *OTS* (over the shoulder) shot, but the timing seems slightly off. The girl makes a strong shrugging gesture that ought to coincide with the moment when she says, "...keep it DOWN?"

3 Play this part of the sequence again and find the frame right where she says, "down," (approximately 41:15).

  This will be your anchor in the sequence.

4 Press F to perform a Match Frame, opening the master clip into the Viewer.

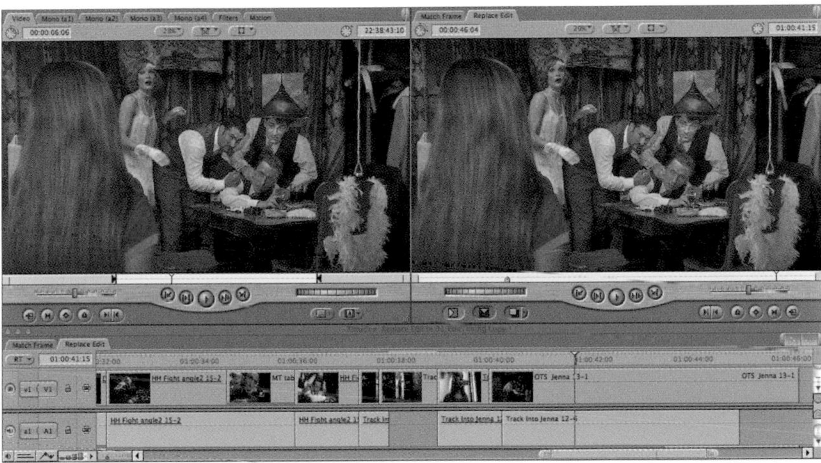

5 In the Viewer, move the playhead to the apex of her shrug action (approximately 22:38:42:20).

6 Perform a replace edit (F11).

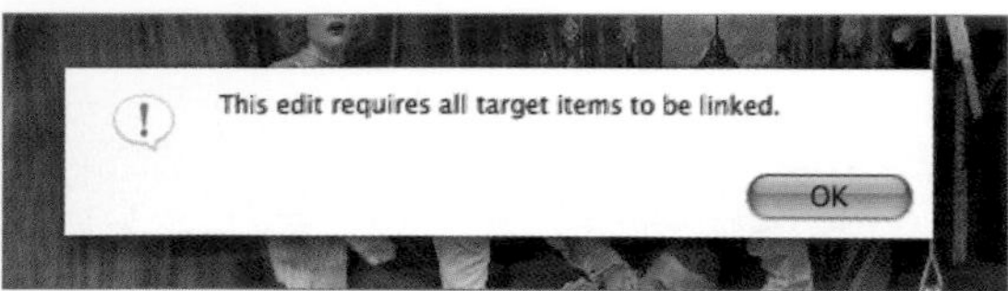

An error dialog appears warning that all target items need to be linked. This is because the audio under the playhead is from a different clip than the one you are replacing.

7 Click the a1 Source control to untarget that track, so only the video track is targeted.

8 Perform the replace edit again.

Nothing appears to be different in the Timeline, but the clip has replaced itself, and the timing of the shot has been improved.

9 Play the end of the sequence.

The shrug now lines up with the dialogue, and the edit feels much more natural.

Ganging the Playheads

One of the most common editing situations you'll encounter is when you have multiple angles of the same action, and over the course of the scene, you cut back and forth between those shots. The most familiar example of this is a typical dialogue scene, in which you have matching OTS shots or matching *singles* showing two sides of a conversation.

When building such a sequence, you can take advantage of the Final Cut Pro Gang Sync feature, which locks the playhead position of the Viewer to that of the Canvas and Timeline. That way, as you play forward (or backward) in one window, the playhead moves by the same number of frames in the others.

Once you establish a place where the Viewer and Canvas are in sync, you can lock that position, *ganging* the playheads together. As long as the action in both the sequence and the Viewer follows the same timing, you can freely edit pieces of the clip in the Viewer into the sequence and trust that they will always remain in sync.

Although this may seem confusing in theory, it is extremely easy to do in practice and can be a huge timesaver.

1. Open the *Gang Sync* sequence.

2. Play the scene to get familiar with it.

   This sequence has been roughed together, but it is fairly obvious that more editing is required to make full sense of the story. Because, like most dialogue scenes, the performance in each of the shots has (nearly) identical timing, this is a perfect opportunity to take advantage of the Gang Sync feature.

3 Position the sequence playhead anywhere over the second clip (**MCU Caroline**).

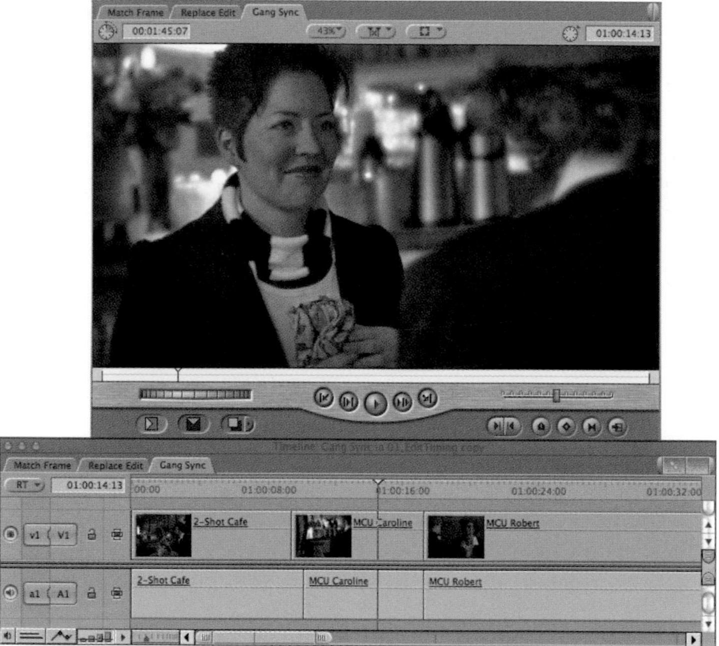

4 Press F to perform a Match Frame, opening the master clip into the Viewer.

At this point the Canvas and Viewer are obviously in sync (they are showing the exact same frame), so this is a good time to gang their playheads together.

5 In either the Canvas or the Viewer, click the Playhead Sync pop-up menu and choose Gang.

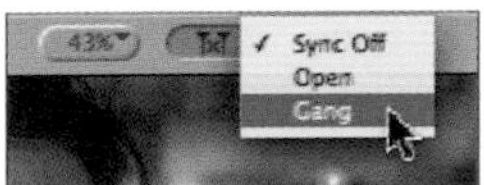

The icon in the Playhead Sync pop-up menu changes to show two parallel playheads, indicating the Gang state.

6 Play the sequence until just after the man says, "I just had a feeling," (at approx 21:00).

This is an appropriate point to cut back to the OTS shot of Caroline.

7 Set an In point in the sequence.

The Viewer playhead has been moving along with you, so it is already in the exact position for the In point.

8 Press Command-1 to make the Viewer window active.

TIP You can also press Q to toggle between the Viewer and Canvas windows.

9 Press I to set an In point in the Viewer.

10 Play forward until she finishes her line and the man says, "or something," and set an Out point there (at approximately 10:23:03:20)

11 Perform an overwrite edit.

12 Press \ (backslash) to play around the edit you just made.

You'll see that the timing of the edit is near-perfect.

Because of the ganged playheads, you could make the edit just about anywhere and be assured that the clips will remain in sync and the timing will be accurate. Here's another example of that.

1 Return to the beginning of the sequence and position your playhead anywhere over the first clip.

2 Press F to perform a Match Frame, opening the master clip into the Viewer.

   Whenever you open a new clip into the Viewer, the Gang setting will be turned off.

3 Click the Playhead Sync pop-up menu and choose Gang.

4 Press Q to make the Canvas window active, and play through the first 30 seconds of the sequence until just after the man says, "Thanks," as the server delivers the coffee. Try to ensure that you see a frame or two where the coffee cup is visible.

5 Set an In Point there (at approximately 31:20).

6 Play forward until just before he says, "What brings you down to the Mission?", at approximately 42:15.

7 Mark an Out point there.

8 Press Q to switch to the Viewer.

9 Press O to set a matching Out point in the Viewer.

Because the playheads are ganged, the playhead in the Viewer has been moving along with you, but it is very easy to make a common mistake at this point. The Viewer still contains the old In point, and if you just perform the edit at this point, the rules of three-point editing will cause the Out you just set to be ignored. To get the results you desire, you must clear the Viewer In point. Then the Out will be used, and the In will be automatically backtimed.

10 Press Option-I to clear the In point in the Viewer.

11 Overwrite the clip into the sequence.

12 Play around the edit to see the results of your work.

Skipping the time-consuming steps of lining up the action in both Viewer and Canvas for each edit will speed your workflow dramatically. However, this method is not magic. If the performance in the two shots was different, even by a small amount, the new edit wouldn't be picture-perfect.

Nonetheless, ganging your playheads is a great way to take advantage of the similar timing in your shots, and it allows you to make a quick rough cut with little effort. This way you can rough your shots into the sequence with incredible speed, and you can use the Trim tools described in the next lesson to finesse and clean up the edits with frame-by-frame precision.

Lesson Review

1. What happens when you drag multiple clips into the Viewer?
2. What is the maximum number clips you can show in the Recent Clips pop-up menu?
3. Does Match Frame load a clip from the Timeline into the Viewer?
4. How do you Match Frame to the clip's source file (instead of the master clip)?
5. When is a replace edit useful?
6. True or false: Replace edit observes three-point editing rules.
7. True or false: Replace edit will work as long as the new clip is longer than the clip being replaced.
8. True or false: Gang Sync locks the Canvas playhead to the Timeline playhead.
9. Gang Sync is most useful with what kind of footage?

Answers

1. The first clip is loaded into the Viewer, and the rest are placed into the Recent Clips pop-up menu.
2. 20.
3. No. Match Frame loads the master clip of a Timeline clip into the Viewer.
4. Press Option-Command-F.

5. When you want to perform an edit based on a frame between a clip's In and Out points.
6. Partially true: In and Out points in the Canvas are observed, but Viewer In and Out points are always ignored.
7. False: Even if the new clip is longer, there must be adequate frames before the playhead position to accommodate the In point, and after the playhead to accommodate the Out point.
8. False: Gang Sync locks the Canvas playhead to the Viewer playhead (the Canvas and Timeline playheads are *always* locked together).
9. Scenes in which you cut back and forth between multiple angles of the same action.

2

Lesson Files	Lesson Files > Lesson 02 > Trimming.fcp
Media	Poker
Time	This lesson takes approximately 120 minutes to complete.
Goals	Improve overall editing efficiency
	Trim clips from the keyboard
	Utilize the Trim Edit window
	Use dynamic trimming
	Utilize multitrack trimming
	Perform asymmetrical trim edits

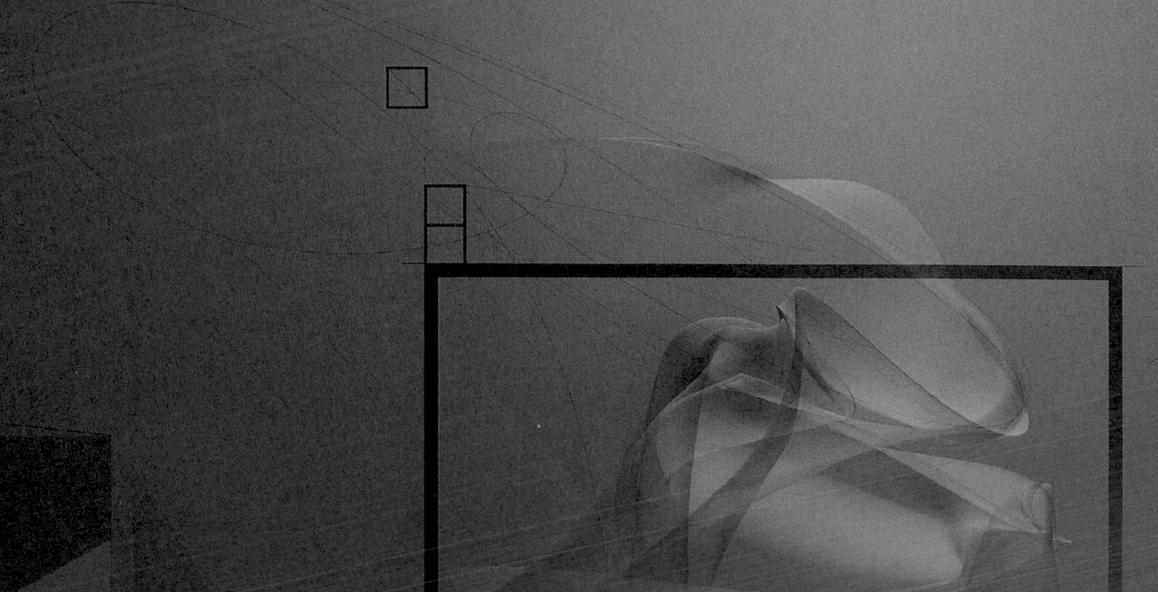

Lesson **2**

Trimming Edits

For many endeavors, the first 80 percent of the job takes only 20 percent of the time. That is to say, the last little bit of work—the finessing, refining, polishing, and so on—typically uses up a vast majority of the hours required to complete a project. Editing is a perfect example of this.

Roughing out a sequence or assembling the basic scene typically happens very quickly. In short order, you can watch your program and get a feel for how it will look. But that doesn't mean you're finished. You'll likely spend far more time tweaking and adjusting each of the edits in your show than you spent assembling that rough cut. This is what trimming refers to: the painstaking, detail-oriented, mind-numbing work of ensuring that each edit is perfect.

In some ways, trimming is a very different art than assembling. It uses a different part of your brain and requires that you pay attention to different aspects of the footage than those that preoccupied you during the rough cut. An individual trimming task may seem unimportant; and yet, if one edit is off by a mere five frames, it can disrupt the flow of a scene, which in turn can sour an entire sequence and, by extension, undermine the flow and feeling of the whole show.

The Dynamic Art

Like most aspects of Final Cut Pro, using the trimming tools is not difficult to do, but understanding how and when to employ the myriad controls can be daunting.

Most trimming follows a predictable pattern: First, you *ripple* one or both sides of the edit point to get the timing to seem natural. Then, you *roll* the edit point, looking for the transitional moment that best hides the cut. Often, you roll the video or audio elements separately to create a split edit. Because these techniques are highly subjective (and typically gauged by nothing more than "feel"), it's very common to explore a variety of approaches before settling on one.

The best and most crucial advice about trimming is to *make your edit decisions while the video is playing*. It can be useful to study the symmetries or contrasting compositions of the frames at your edit point, but there is no substitute for experiencing the scene in exactly the way the audience will: moving by at 24 frames per second (or whatever your chosen frame rate may be). Good edits are invisible; bad edits are jarring. It's nearly impossible to sense how successful an edit is until you see it in context.

The creators of Final Cut Pro understood this and developed a vast array of playback controls that facilitate playing your sequence in a wide range of contexts. Furthermore, there are many techniques and tools designed specifically for making edits while the sequence is playing. This chapter will familiarize you with these controls, get you thinking dynamically, and teach how you can make all of your edits on-the-fly. This type of editing is not only efficient and accurate, it is also exhilarating and fun.

Understanding Basic Trimming

The basis of all trimming is the Ripple and Roll functions. In order to master all of the more advanced types of trimming covered throughout this lesson, you must have a complete and thorough understanding of these basics.

1 Open Lesson Files > Lesson 02 > **Trimming.fcp**.

The *1. Basic Trimming* sequence should be open.

2 Play the sequence.

These two shots contain a simple action—the woman putting the glass down on the table—that serves as the cut point. This is a very typical edit, and it has a very typical problem. The timing is slightly off, so there is an overlap of action.

3 Press the Up Arrow or Down Arrow to move the sequence playhead to the edit point.

4 Press \ (backslash) to play around the edit.

Play Around is an essential tool to use while trimming, and you can customize how far before and after the current position it will play.

5 Choose Final Cut Pro > User Preferences, then click the Editing tab.

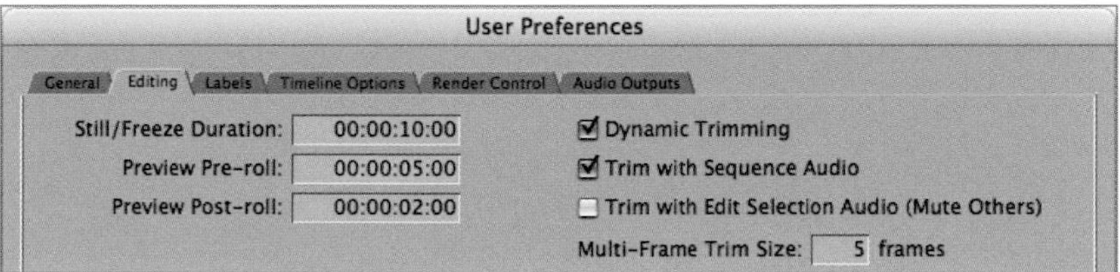

The Preview Pre-roll and Preview Post-roll settings default to 5 seconds before and 2 seconds after the current position. Although for slower-moving shows a 5-second pre-roll is useful, it can be far too long for quick-cut shows, and if it crosses over multiple edits, the pre-roll can prove more distracting than helpful.

6 Change the Preview Pre-roll value to *2:00* and click OK.

7 Play around the edit again.

The shorter pre-roll allows you to more sharply focus on the edit point. And when you watch the edit, what do you see? The glass is placed on the table in the first shot and then again in the second shot.

In fact, it doesn't quite touch the table in the first shot, but the woman's action of reaching toward the table is quite clearly repeated in the second shot.

This is a perfect time to whip out the Ripple tool.

8 Press RR to select the Ripple tool, and drag the outgoing clip to the right about five frames.

9 Play around the edit.

Now, the glass is clearly placed on the table in the first clip. Although this makes the timing of the edit worse, it will make it easier to fix quickly and accurately because you can match that specific action in both shots.

This task will be made even easier if you display the audio waveforms.

10 Press Command-Option-W to show audio waveforms in the Timeline.

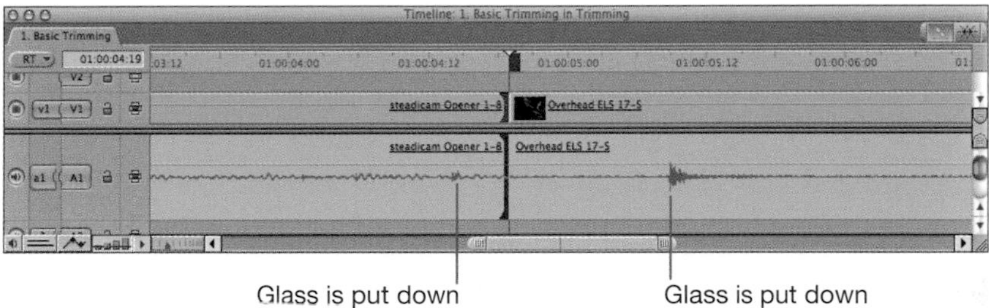

The waveform when the glass hits the table is visible in both shots.

11 Ripple the outgoing clip until the frame where the glass hits the table is the last frame in the shot (approximately four frames).

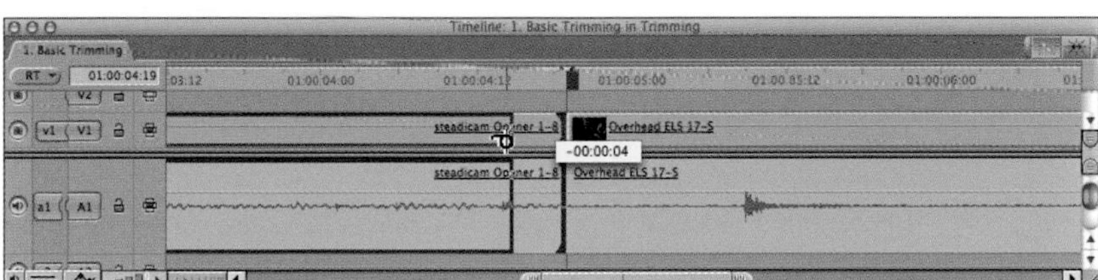

12 Ripple the incoming clip to line up precisely with the action (approximately 14 frames).

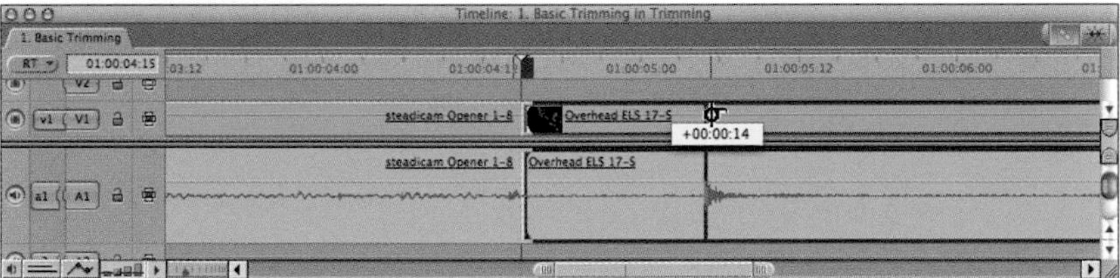

13 Play around the edit.

The timing of the edit should be just about perfect, but putting the cut precisely on the apex of the action draws unnecessary attention to the edit. This is easily alleviated with the Roll tool. Because you've already established accurate timing, you can roll the edit as far as you want in either direction, and the timing within the scene will remain correct.

14 Press R to select the Roll tool.

15 Drag the edit to the left about five to seven frames.

16 Play around the edit.

17 Drag the edit to the right about 10 to 12 frames and play around the edit there.

Either position could work. Only the specific nature of the scene you are cutting can inform this decision. In this example, if the action of putting the glass down was significant, you might choose to see it in the lower-angle shot by rolling the edit to the right. The overhead angle of the second shot takes the emphasis off that particular action, so rolling the edit to the left diminishes its significance.

TIP Don't get distracted by the different audio levels in the two takes, you can (and probably would) replace the sound with foley during the sound mix.

Trimming from the Keyboard

Dragging the edges of clips is great if you want to get a tactile feel for the way trimming works, but it is probably the most inefficient way to trim. Because it is so important to make these decisions while the video is playing, the less often you have to stop playback to make the edit, the better. This is why learning a handful of essential keyboard shortcuts can vastly improve your performance.

Trimming from the keyboard is very easy. In fact, there are really only four keys you need to add to your arsenal of memorized shortcuts:

- V—Select edit
- U—Toggle edit type (ripple/roll)
- [(left bracket)—Trim one frame left
-] (right bracket)—Trim one frame right

That's it! Of course, you'll also use a few shortcuts you already know. Most important is the \ (backslash) key to play around the edit you're manipulating and see the work you've done.

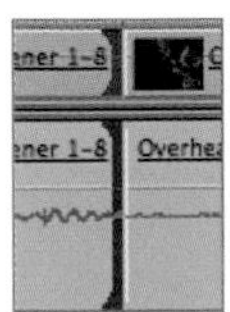

Ripple outgoing

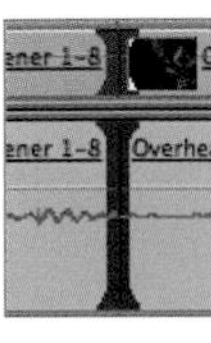

Roll

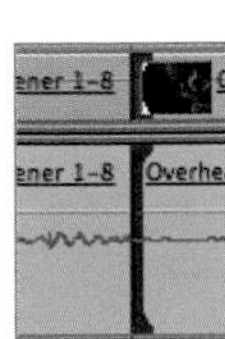

Ripple incoming

It's also vital that you can tell at a glance whether an edit is selected as a roll, a ripple outgoing, or a ripple incoming.

1 In the Browser, double-click the *2. More Trimming* sequence and play it.

This is the same card game footage you've already seen but with a little more of the sequence incorporated. As you watch it, look for edits that might need trimming. You'll probably zero in quickly on the last two edits, both of which clearly need work.

2 Press the Up or Down Arrow keys to navigate to the second-to-last edit.

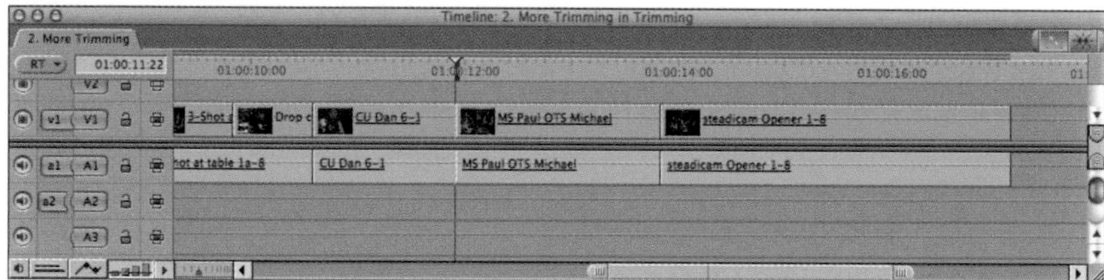

3 Press \ (backslash) to play around the edit and figure out what you're going to do to fix it.

The problem is that the action of the cards hitting the table is missing. The cigar-chomping fellow starts to slap his cards onto the table, but in the next shot, the cards are already there. A few frames need to be added, and it's up to you to decide whether to add them to the outgoing clip or to the incoming clip. Both solutions could work.

4 Press V to select the edit.

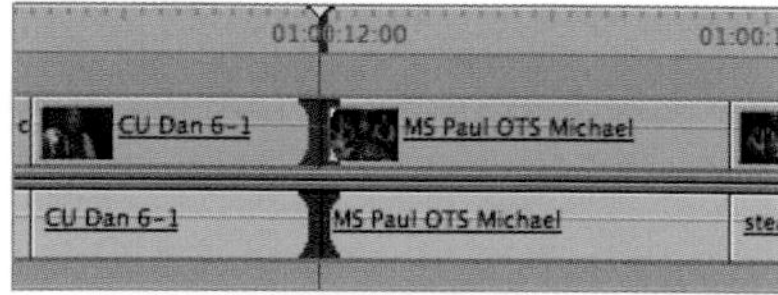

By default, selecting an edit always selects it as a roll. This is good because a roll is generally less destructive than a ripple. On the other hand, you generally want to ripple your edit to fix the timing before you roll it.

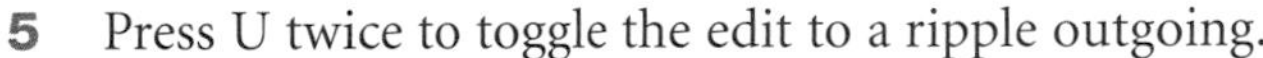

5 Press U twice to toggle the edit to a ripple outgoing.

Each time you press U, the way the edit is selected cycles among three states: roll, ripple incoming, and ripple outgoing. If you'd like, press U a few more times to see the state change. Make sure you return to the ripple outgoing selection.

6 Press] (right bracket) a few times to add frames to the outgoing clip.

If you press Shift-], you will add five frames instead of one. You can even customize your system so Shift-] will add up to 99 frames by changing the Multi-Frame Trim Size setting in the Editing tab of User Preferences.

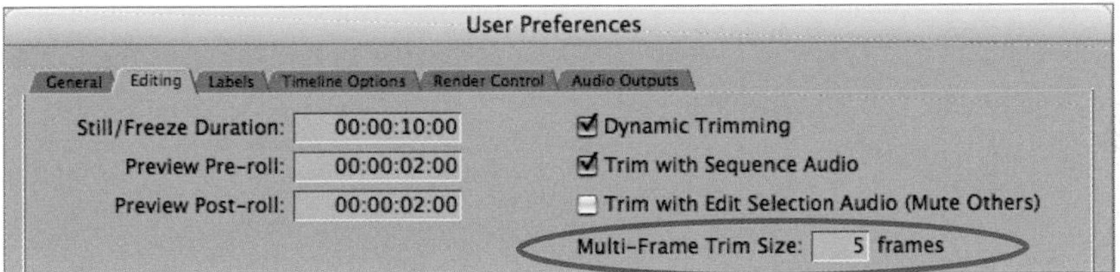

You can also simply hold down the right bracket key (]) and the edit will move along in near-real time.

7 Play around the edit (press \) and keep adding frames and playing around until the timing feels right (about 15 frames). If you go too far, press the left bracket key ([) to move the edit point left.

Once you get the timing right, you can stop, but it's wise to keep working to make sure you've made the best edit possible. For example, in the shot you're lengthening, you can't actually see the cards hit the table, but the incoming shot doesn't show the expression on the actor's face. It will be up to you to decide what's important.

Because you established the timing using the ripple, you can roll to just about any position and the timing will remain accurate. However, rolling to different positions will produce different effects.

8 Press U to toggle the edit to a roll.

9 Press the bracket keys to experiment with different edit positions, and play around the edit frequently to "feel" the new edit.

TIP The technique employed in the first exercise is a great way to ensure accurate timing. That is, you added and removed frames from both shots until the action happened precisely on the edit, then rolled it for a less obvious cut. In this case, we are assuming you can accurately guess at the timing, even though the cards hit the table offscreen.

Extending Edits

Now that you're comfortable with the trimming shortcuts, one more shortcut should further encourage you to make your editing decisions while the video is playing.

Rather than tapping the bracket keys a few times, playing around the edit, and then repeating this process over and over again, you can play the sequence and automatically roll the edit point to the current playhead position in one step. This is called an extend edit, and the keyboard shortcut is E.

1 With the edit still selected as a roll, press L to play the sequence forward, then after the cigar-chomper sits back and settles in his chair (at approximately 13:05), press K to stop playback.

2 Press E to roll (or *extend*) the edit to the current playhead position.

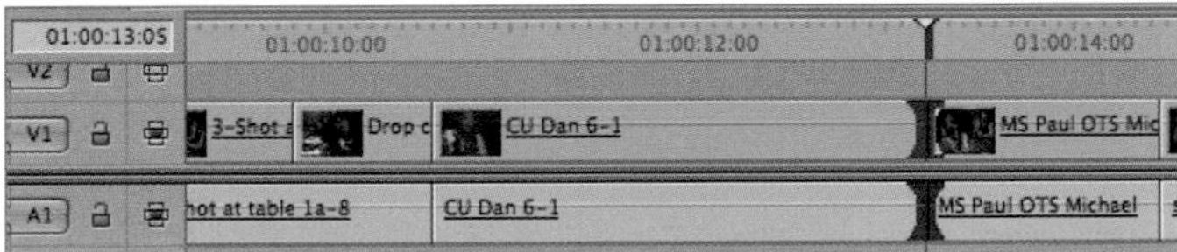

3 Play around the new edit.

The result is interesting. Much more emphasis is put on the reaction of the cigar-chomper. The next shot might feel too short, but that can be fixed later.

The beauty of the extend edit is that it enables you to make your edit decision entirely while playing. In fact, you don't even have to stop playback to use it.

4 Press J to play the sequence backward, then while it's playing, press E to roll the edit back to an earlier position.

5 Play around the new edit.

Don't panic if you don't get the edit exactly right. You can always undo, or just play in the other direction and extend again. Eventually, you'll get a feel for the technique and you'll be comfortable rolling your edits on-the-fly. Extend will always operate on the selected edit and only performs a roll. If the edit is selected as a ripple, pressing E will have no effect.

Extend works best with longer clips. The one concern is that extend will allow you to roll one edit right over another.

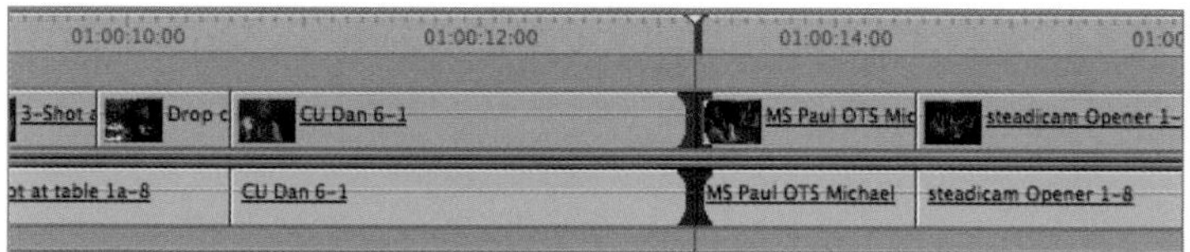

Before

After

This allows you to completely eliminate a clip in your sequence. But even if you do such an edit (and you didn't intend to), you can always undo it and return to the previous state.

Using Numerical Trimming

As you get even more comfortable with trimming, and when you're doing quite a bit of it, you'll be able to watch an edit and immediately have a sense of how many frames it needs to be adjusted. In this case, rather than tapping the bracket keys repeatedly, you can simply enter a number to perform a trim by a precise number of frames.

The best aspect of numerical trimming is that no special mode or field entry is necessary. As soon as you type a number, or press the + (plus) or – (minus) key, Final Cut Pro automatically interprets that entry as a trimming instruction and applies the edit based on the current selection. If the edit is selected as a roll, the numbers will perform a roll edit. If the edit is selected as a ripple, you'll get a ripple edit. It's entirely context sensitive. You'll see later that you can do the same thing with the Slip and Slide tools, and even with selected clips.

1 Press Shift-E to move the playhead to the next edit in the sequence.

Notice that the edit selection moves along with you, so you don't need to reselect the edit point. This is because Final Cut Pro anticipates that you will employ the common workflow of roughing all of your shots into the sequence, then walk through them one by one, finessing each with the trim tools.

2 Play around this edit.

In this case, there is a tiny amount of overlapping action: The cards hit the table twice. This means you must subtract some frames from one or the other side of the edit.

3 Press U to toggle to a ripple outgoing edit.

4 Type –7.

An information box appears in the Timeline, identifying the type of edit and the value you entered.

5 Press Enter (or Return) to perform the edit.

6 Play around to see how you did.

If you're not happy with the edit, type a new number. You don't need to bother typing the plus sign. Any positive number will move the edit to the right, and any negative number will move it left.

You can also press U to toggle to ripple incoming and adjust that side of the edit.

7 Once you've got the timing right, switch to a roll, type *10*, then press Enter.

8 Play around the edit.

9 Type *–20* to move 10 frames before the original edit.

10 Play around again.

And so on. You can continue to explore different positions for the edit until you find one that best tells the story of these particular shots. It's also important to occasionally step back and play a longer section of your sequence. For example, if you had moved the previous edit significantly to the right, moving this edit to the left would result in a very short clip in between. You need to look at the big picture to get a sense of the overall pacing of the scene.

Splitting Edits

Another way you can improve your edits with trimming is to use the Roll tool to offset the audio and video so they don't change at the same time, thereby creating a *split* edit. Remember, one of the fundamental goals of editing is to convey new information in a new shot without drawing undue attention to the change in framing required by an edit. In other words, you make the edits invisible. One of the most effective ways to do this is to split your edits.

An edit can be split in two ways. The audio can lead the video, creating a *J cut*, or the video can lead the audio, commonly called an *L cut*.

J cut

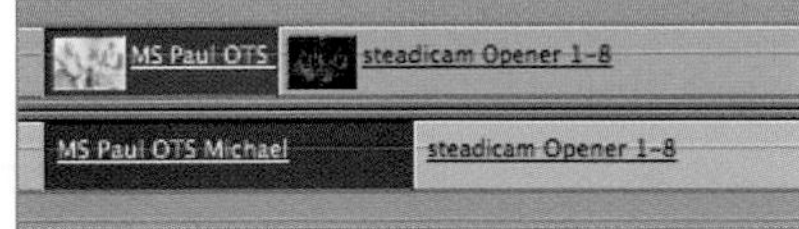

L cut

J cuts tend to be much more common than L cuts, and for a good reason. In the real world, hearing a noise often prompts you to turn your head to see the source of the sound. If a viewer hears an offscreen sound in a film, she instinctively wants to turn her head to see what caused the noise. If the editor creates such a trigger with an audio cut, then follows it with a video cut, the whole transition is hidden from the viewer, who is busy reconciling the sound and the picture.

1 Open and play the *3. Split Edits* sequence.

   This is another version of the same scene with a few more clips added.

2 Press A to make sure you have the Selection tool selected.

3 Find the section where the cigar-chomping guy says, "Hey! What was that?" and position your playhead somewhere near the edit between **CU Paul 2-3** and **CU Dan 6-2** (around 20:00).

   This is a perfect moment when a split edit can dramatically improve the scene.

4 Option-click to override linked selection and select only the video edit.

5 Play the sequence, and just after you hear the word, "Hey," press E.

The edit is rolled to the playhead position.

6 Play around the edit.

The idea is to mimic that sense of turning your head. So try it a few times until it feels like the sound of his voice triggers the cut.

After you have successfully split the edit, you will see that you also have shortened the following clip (**CU Dan 6-2**) to a mere 10 frames or so, which is clearly too short. However, this is easily remedied by splitting the following edit too.

7 On track V1, Option-click the next edit.

8 Enter *10*, and press Enter (or Return) to move the edit forward 10 frames.

9 Option-click the next edit on track V1.

10 Play the sequence, and just as the guy takes the cigar out of his mouth, press E.

11 Back up a few edits and watch this part of the sequence.

The improvement should be quite evident. You can probably see how you can quickly walk through almost any scene and split nearly every single edit in your show. And you should. Splits edits are just as appropriate for documentaries or training videos as they are for dramatic scenes.

Using Splits to Tighten Scenes

One of the side benefits of splitting edits is that it allows you to conserve time. It's a truism that every show is too long, and if there's a way to shorten a scene, even by just a few frames here and there, it's generally worth it. The goal isn't to suck all the air and quiet spaces out of your scenes, but rather to keep the pace active and realistic. Remember, a quiet reaction can produce a dramatic moment that is just as potent as a line of dialogue, but the time between those beats can often be compressed with no noticeable detriment to its effect.

1 Press RR to select the Ripple tool.

2 On the first edit you split, click the outgoing edge of **CU Paul 2-3**.

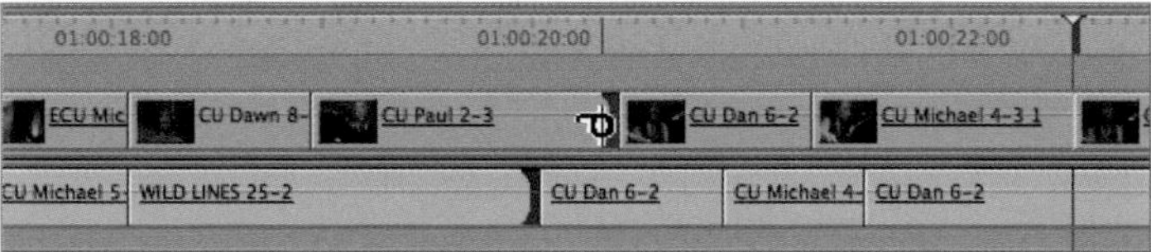

This time you want to select both audio and video because rippling just the video would cause downstream clips to move out of sync.

3 Press Command-Option-W to turn on audio waveforms.

4 Drag the edit to the left, until just after the end of the waveform representing the previous line of dialogue.

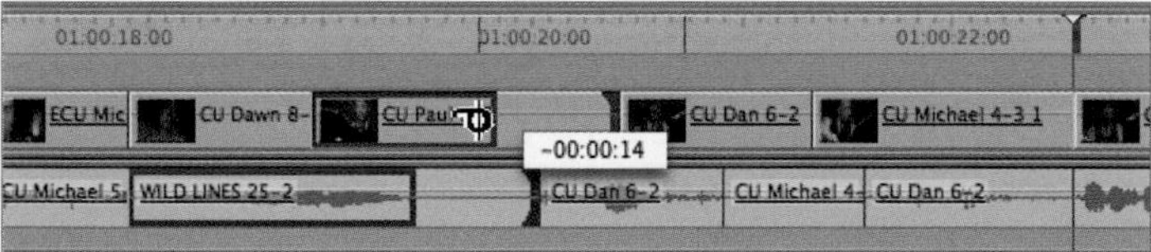

5 Play around the edit.

This trim makes another subtle improvement. The timing still feels natural, and the scene is half a second shorter. The next couple of edits are already pretty tight, but there's some definite dead space before the cigar guy says, "What was that?"

In the original scene, that pause made sense because the actor took the cigar out of his mouth and looked around. But now that you've split the edits, we're looking at the other player's reaction, and it seems strange that he waits so long to make his accusation.

6 Press ' (apostrophe) two or three times until the edit between **CU Michael 4-3** and **CU Dan 6-2** is selected.

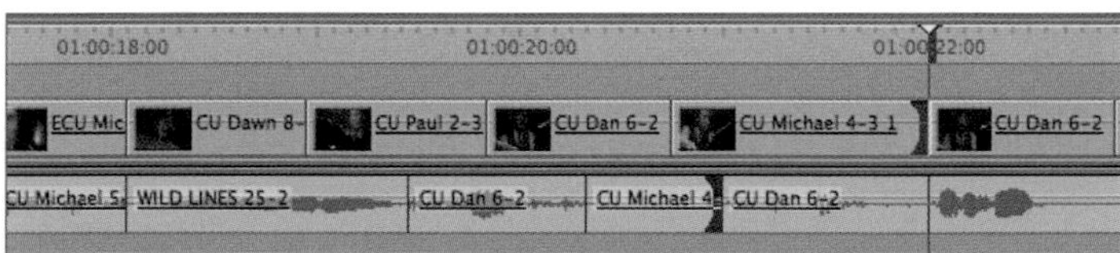

Currently, the outgoing side of the edit is selected, but the dead space is in the incoming clip.

7 Press U twice to toggle the edit to a ripple incoming.

It would be ideal if he started talking just before you cut back to him, utilizing the same strategy you exercised when you first created the split edits. And because you can see the audio waveforms that represent his dialogue, it's fairly easy to make that needed trim.

8 Press Shift-] (right bracket) repeatedly, watching each time to see when the audio waveform begins just before the cut.

9 Play around the edit and finesse it as you see fit.

Using Slip and Slide

Ripple and roll are powerful tools that allow you to perform multiple steps in a single operation. (Think about how many steps it would take to make split edits using the Razor Blade and track selection tools!) In that sense, slip and slide are even more impressive. These tools allow you to perform *two* roll or ripple edits in a single operation. Both tools have no effect on the overall length of a sequence.

Slipping Clips

Slip simultaneously performs a ripple edit on both the incoming and outgoing edges of the same clip. This has the effect of changing the In and Out points of a clip in a sequence without modifying its duration or changing any of the surrounding clips.

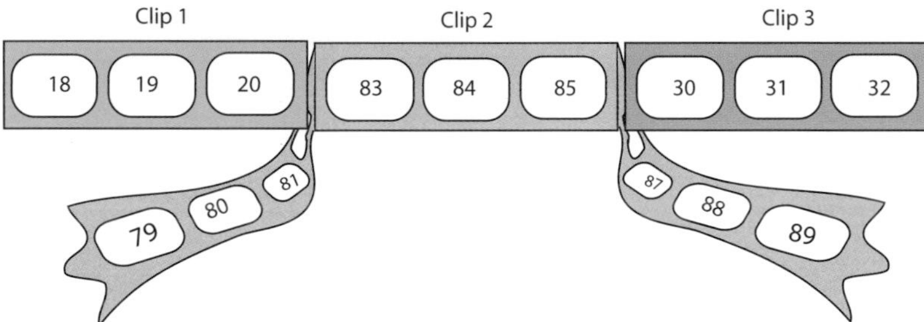

It's as if the media for the clip is *slipped* underneath the clip's position in the sequence.

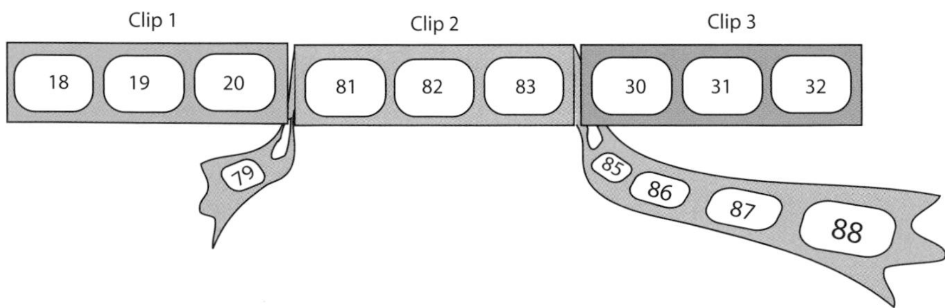

So, for example, in the preceding figures, clip 2 has been slipped by two frames. Its position in the sequence hasn't changed, and clips 1 and 3 have not been affected, but different frames from clip 2's source footage are being used.

This is exactly what would happen if you rippled the incoming edge of the clip by two frames and then rippled the outgoing edge by the same amount.

1 Open and play the *4. Slip & Slide* sequence.

  Again, a few additional clips have been added to the same sequence.

2 Navigate to around 22:00 where **CU Dawn 8-2** begins.

In this shot, the woman is supposed to give an incriminating look to her cohort, but in the current edit, she's not looking at anything in particular.

3 Press S to select the Slip tool.

4 Click the clip and drag to the left about 10 frames.

As you drag, feedback in the Canvas shows you the new In and Out points for the clip. Look for the frames where she turns to her left.

Sliding Clips

Slide is similar to slip, but it is generally used for a very different purpose. Sliding a clip is similar to the effect of rolling both its starting and ending edits by the same number of frames, although with a slide, the clip in the center is left untouched.

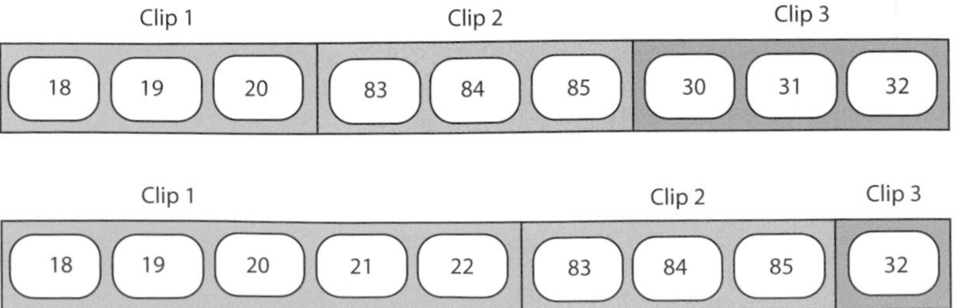

While slip changes the content within a shot, slide changes the two shots surrounding a shot but leaves the shot itself unchanged. When sliding, you change the timing of a shot without changing the rest of the sequence This is most often employed on cutaways or b-roll footage.

1 Press SS to select the Slide tool.

2 Drag the **CU Dawn 8-2** clip to the left by about five frames.

The Canvas shows a two-up display, but this time it shows the two frames that are changing—the last frame of the preceding clip and the first frame of the following one.

If you watch the Canvas, you can gauge how far to drag the clip by looking at the frame on the right (the clip following the one you are sliding). When the man looks screen-right, he is looking at the woman, and this makes a perfect cut point.

3 Play around the new edit.

If you click a clip with the Slip or Slide tool, you can drag to perform the edit, but when you release the mouse, the clip won't stay selected. You can press the bracket keys to slip and slide one frame at a time, or directly enter a number; but, in order to use these keyboard shortcuts, you need the clip to remain selected.

1 With the Slide tool still active, hold down Shift and click the **CU Dawn 8-2** clip.

Holding down the Shift key enables you to select the clip. After it is selected, you can slide it using keyboard shortcuts.

2 Press the left and right bracket keys ([and]) to slide the clip left and right.

As you might expect, holding down Shift allows you to slide five frames (or by whatever number is set in the User Preferences, as described earlier in this lesson).

TIP It is very important to know which tool is currently active. After a clip is selected, the active tool determines what happens when you use the trimming keyboard shortcuts.

Furthermore, you can also slip or slide numerically.

3 Press S to activate the Slip tool.

4 Type *–20*, and press Enter (or Return).

The clip is slipped by 20 frames.

Performing Advanced Techniques

By now, you probably appreciate how powerful and essential these trimming tools are. Trimming is one of the most intensive aspects of the editing process, but with mastery of the tools it can be easy, and even fun. Still, no matter how you splice it, you're going to be trimming for quite a long time on each project. Although simple tasks like those in the preceding exercises are straightforward, you are likely to encounter more complicated scenarios. Fortunately, Final Cut Pro is capable of far more sophisticated trimming techniques, and it includes a special interface just for trimming: the Trim Edit window.

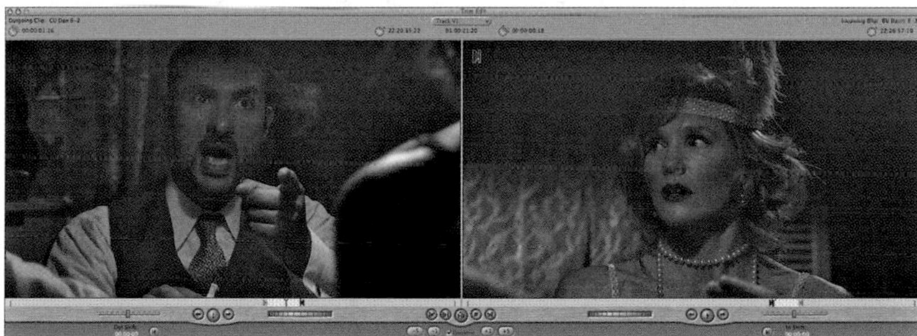

Using the Trim Edit Window

The Trim Edit window is like a zoomed-in view on a single edit point. The left side of the window shows the outgoing clip, and the right side shows the incoming clip. The scrubber bars under each clip display provide essential information not available in the Timeline, such as how many frames are available beyond the current In or Out points.

You can also view the sections of either clip that lie beyond the edit points, which can be invaluable in determining the precise positioning of an edit. The J, K, and L keys not only control playback of each clip; when dynamic trimming is enabled, those keys perform trims.

1 From the Browser, open *5. Advanced Trimming.*

   A few more clips have been added to the sequence.

2 Navigate to around 25 seconds into the sequence, where the players all get up from the table.

All of these edits can be improved with a bit of trimming.

3 Using the Selection tool, double-click the edit point at 25:18, between **CU Paul 2-3** and **HH Fight angle2 15-2**.

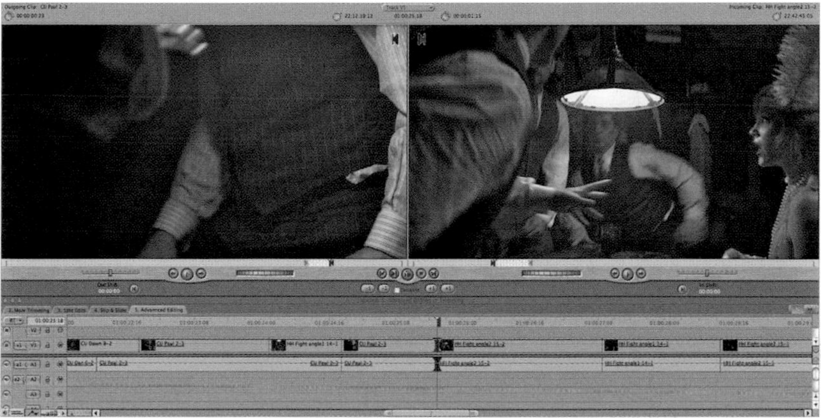

Double-clicking an edit point selects it and automatically opens the Trim Edit window. By default, that window opens directly on top of the Viewer and the Canvas, and because it looks so similar, you might not even notice anything happened.

Double-clicking the edit in the Timeline with the Selection tool selects the edit as a roll. If you double-click with the Ripple tool, the Trim Edit window will still open, but the edit will be selected as a ripple (based on whichever side you clicked). You can also press Command-8 to open the Trim Edit window. The nearest edit to the playhead will be selected as a roll.

In the Trim Edit window, the green bars above the video windows indicate which type of edit is selected. Currently, both sides are lit up green.

4 Press U three times to cycle through the edit selection states and observe the green bars in the Trim Edit window.

TIP You can also click the Trim Edit window directly to select the edit type. Clicking either window selects that side of the edit as a ripple, and clicking in the middle selects a roll. The cursor will change to indicate which edit type will be selected depending on your cursor position.

With the J, K, and L keys, you can navigate the clips in the Trim Edit window, but the side they control is based on the edit type. If the edit is set to ripple outgoing, the J, K, and L keys will always control the outgoing clip. If it's set to ripple incoming, those keys will control that clip. When the edit is set to a roll, the keys will control whichever side your cursor is positioned over.

5 Position the cursor anywhere over the outgoing (left) clip. Do not click.

6 Press L or J to play the clip.

The clip on the left plays.

7 Press K (or Spacebar) to stop playback.

8 Position the cursor anywhere over the incoming (right) clip. Do not click.

9 Use J, K, and L to navigate through that clip.

This can be a little confusing, because nothing else in Final Cut Pro works merely because your cursor happens to be placed in one quadrant of the screen. Once you get the hang of it, however, you'll find it is a quick and efficient way to work.

10 Press Spacebar.

Unlike in the Viewer or Canvas, in the Trim Edit window, pressing Spacebar performs the play around function, and regardless of the global looping setting, play around *always* loops.

11 Press Spacebar again to stop playback.

Part of the reason that playback always loops in the Trim Edit window is to enable you to make edits while the video is playing. As you make each adjustment, you can immediately see the result when the section is looped.

12 Press Spacebar again to begin looping.

13 Press the left bracket key ([) a few times until you eliminate the pause after they all stand up (about 10 frames).

Try a few frames, then watch the loop play; then try a few more frames, and so on.

14 When the edit looks good, go a few extra frames just to make sure. Then, trim in the other direction until you're happy with the edit. Press Spacebar again to stop the looping playback.

15 Click the Go to Next Edit button to advance the selection to the next edit.

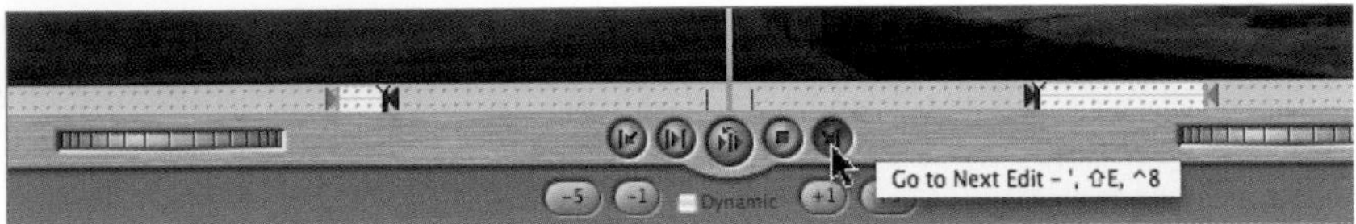

The tooltip lists three different shortcuts that also perform this task. Pressing Down Arrow also works. Most importantly, observe that the edit stays selected, and the Trim Edit window stays open. This can really help speed your trimming workflow, but it does also beg the question: How do you get rid of the Trim Edit window?

A close button is available in the upper-left corner, like in any window, and the standard keyboard shortcut (Command-W) will work as well. The window will also close automatically if you simply move the playhead off an edit point. The Trim Edit window can only exist if an edit point is selected.

16 Click anywhere in the Timeline ruler to deselect the edit point.

The Trim Edit window closes.

17 Double-click the edit (at 27:09 between **HH Fight angle2 15-2** and **HH Fight angle1 14-1**) to reopen the Trim Edit window.

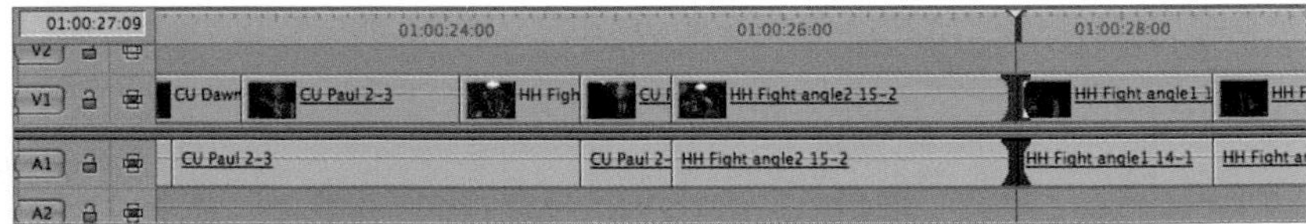

18 Press Spacebar to play around this edit and assess what needs fixing. Press Spacebar again to stop playback.

Perhaps you observed that a bit of overlapping action occurs at the edit point: The man being forcibly seated in the chair starts sitting, then sits down again. This means that there are extra frames, and you will need to ripple one side or the other of this edit to correct the timing.

19 Press U twice to set the edit to ripple outgoing.

20 Use the J-K-L keys and the arrow keys to find the frame where the man appears to reach the nadir of his sitting action (about 22:42:46:22). This will be the new Out point for that shot.

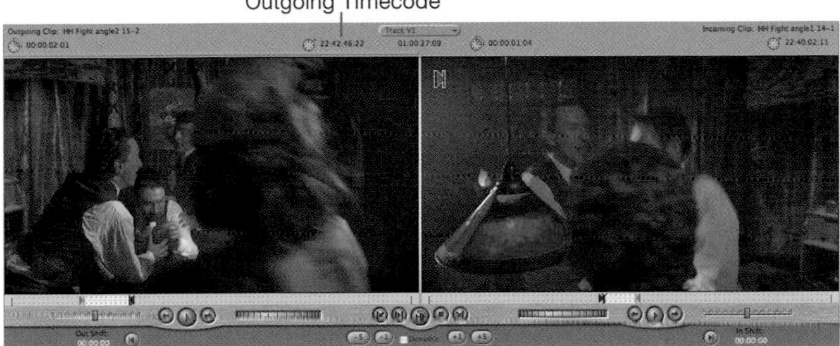

Just finding the frame doesn't perform the edit, however. Once you are parked on the correct frame, you must mark a new In or Out point. Because you are modifying the outgoing clip in this case, you need to confirm the frame you are on as the new Out point.

21 Press O to set the Out point.

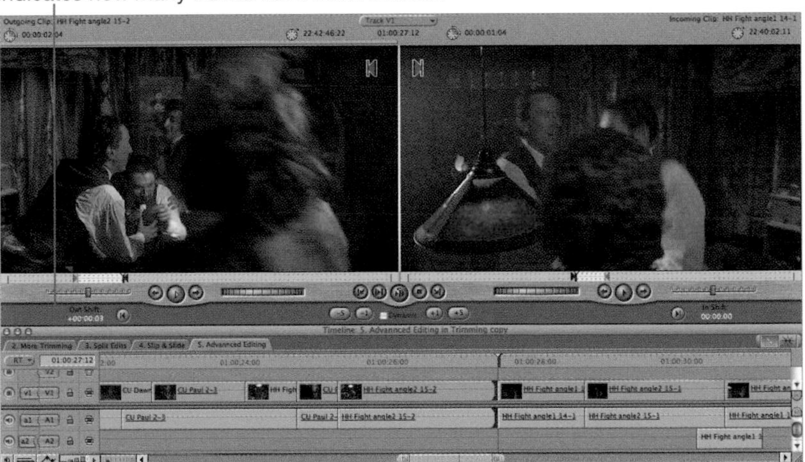

The trim is applied. The Trim Edit window displays the *out shift*, indicating how many frames have been modified during the trim operation.

22 Press Spacebar to play around the edit again.

Now the timing is worse, but this will make it easier to line up the action precisely.

23 Press U twice to change the edit to a ripple incoming.

24 Use the J-K-L keys to find the approximate frame where the man is completely seated in this shot (22:40:02:18).

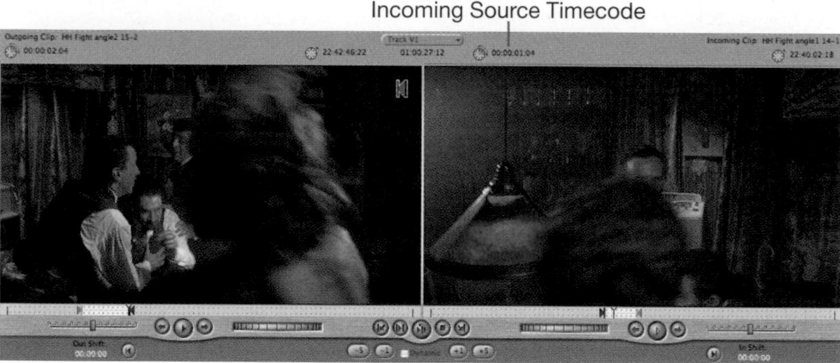

This is a very typical edit in that it's difficult to tell exactly which is the perfect frame because the action happens offscreen. Remember that trimming is all about experimenting with different edit positions to gauge which one feels right.

25 When you have found a frame you think might be correct, press I to set a new In point.

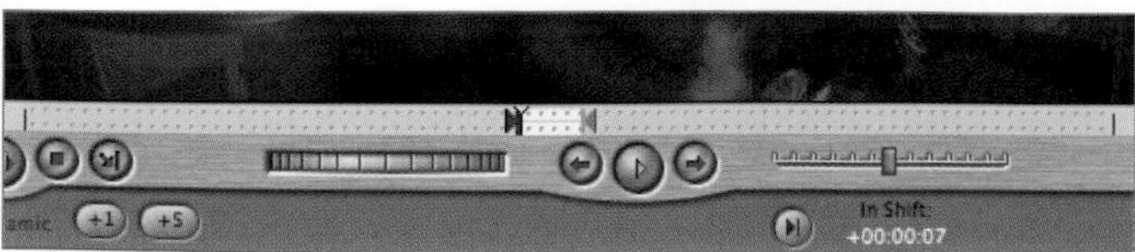

26 Play around the edit (press Spacebar).

27 Press the bracket keys to experiment with different edit positions.

TIP You can also enter a specific number of frames, just as you did when trimming in the Timeline.

When you think you have the correct timing for the edit, it's time to switch to a roll edit and find the best placement.

28 Press U twice to toggle the edit selection type to a roll.

29 Position your cursor over the outgoing (left) clip. Do not click.

30 Use the J-K-L keys to find a frame when the man is halfway down in the chair (around 22:42:46:18).

31 Press O to perform the trim.

The edit is rolled to the new position.

32 Play around the edit.

33 Experiment with other edit positions to find an edit you are most happy with.

Working in the Trim Edit window provides additional information to help you make trimming decisions. Being able to see the frames after the Out point in the outgoing clip and before the In point in the incoming clip can provide essential information that is not available in the Timeline.

Trimming Dynamically

Once you've got the hang of trimming this way, you will find it can be extremely fast, especially when you learn all the keyboard shortcuts and get used to looping the playback while you are making editing decisions. However, another step can be eliminated to further speed your workflow.

Currently, you use the J-K-L keys to find a new edit position, then press I or O to confirm the edit. Final Cut Pro has a way to skip that step, so that as soon as you choose a frame, pressing K automatically sets the edit. This is called *dynamic trimming.*

1 Press Down Arrow to move the edit selection to the next edit in the sequence.

The Trim Edit window remains open, and the edit type remains set to roll.

2 Play around the edit and assess what needs to be done.

In this case, rather than overlapping action that indicates extra frames, there are missing frames. The man gets up from the chair in the outgoing clip, and on the other side of the cut, he's already crashed into the woman.

To fix this edit, you will follow the same procedure you used in the previous examples, only this time you will employ dynamic trimming.

3 In the bottom center of the Trim Edit window, select the Dynamic checkbox.

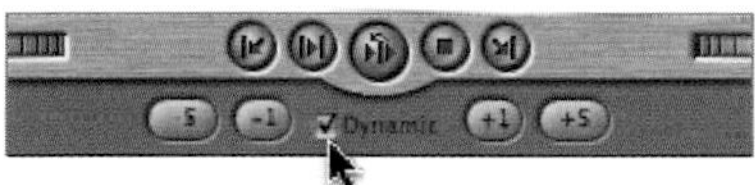

TIP The Dynamic Trimming setting can also be selected in the Editing tab of User Preferences.

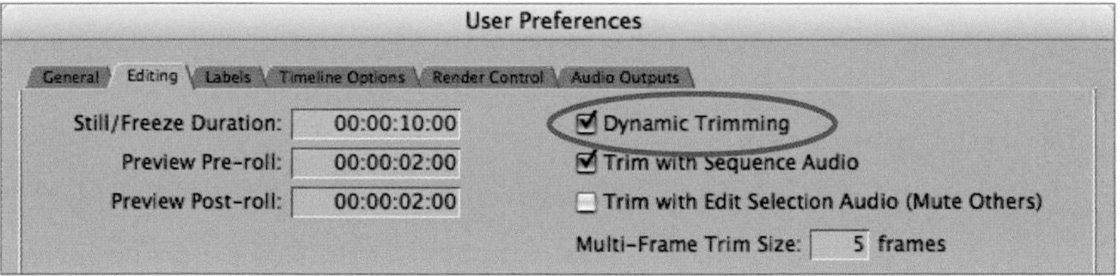

Selecting this setting has only one tiny effect, but it completely changes the way you work. When this setting is enabled, every time you press K to stop playback (when using the J-K-L keys) the edit is performed.

4 Press U twice to switch to a ripple outgoing edit.

5 Press L to play the outgoing clip forward, and as soon as the man touches the woman under the arm, press K to stop (around 22:40:03:21).

That's it. The edit has been performed! If you don't like the frame you landed on, just use the J-K-L keys to choose a new frame.

When you're still getting used to dynamic trimming, it can be fairly intimidating, but there's really nothing to fear. If you go too far forward, press J to go backward. If you go too far backward press L to go forward again. Every time you press K to stop, the edit moves along with you. In the worst case, if you get yourself really confused, you can always undo.

Additionally, if you're pressing J and L to play back and forth and you want to stop without affecting the edit, just press Spacebar. This will stop playback and leave the edit point unchanged, just as if you had pressed the Esc (escape) key.

It's also helpful sometimes to back up before playing forward, in order to give yourself more time to make the edit.

6 Press J to play backward; then, without pressing K, press L to play forward.

7 Again, try to find the exact frame where the man touches the woman's side, and press K to stop and perform the edit.

8 Play around the edit and keep working until you are happy with the edit.

Don't be confused by the audio jump-cutting (the woman's scream might get cut off). You can easily solve that by splitting the edit or rolling the whole edit to a new position once you've gotten the timing right.

Dynamic trimming is just one more way to help you follow that one essential rule advised at the very beginning of the chapter: Whenever possible, make your edits while the video is playing.

Trimming Across Multiple Tracks

Although there are many ways to trim edits, it is a very straightforward process: ripple to get the timing right, roll to position the edit. You can trim by dragging in the Timeline, using keyboard shortcuts, working in the Trim Edit window, or using dynamic trimming to make the process even more fluid.

But there are some cases when trimming gets a tiny bit more complex. In Final Cut Pro, you can trim one edit per track at the same time. This means that if you have a section of a sequence with many tracks, you can (and in many cases should) trim an edit on each of the tracks. Otherwise, you run the risk of knocking items out of sync.

1 Press ' (apostrophe) to move the edit selection to the next edit.

2 Play around the edit.

In this case, there is some overlapping action, but there is also an extra audio clip on track A2 (the woman saying, "No, wait!"). The editor carefully arranged it so that the woman's voice overlaps the edit, and her word, "wait," adds a percussive emphasis to the action of the man hitting the chair.

Your job is to fix the timing of the edit while keeping intact the relative timing of the A2 clip. To do this, you must trim that extra clip along with the main edit.

3 If necessary, use the U key to select the edit as a ripple outgoing.

4 On track A2, Command-click the edit at the head of the clip.

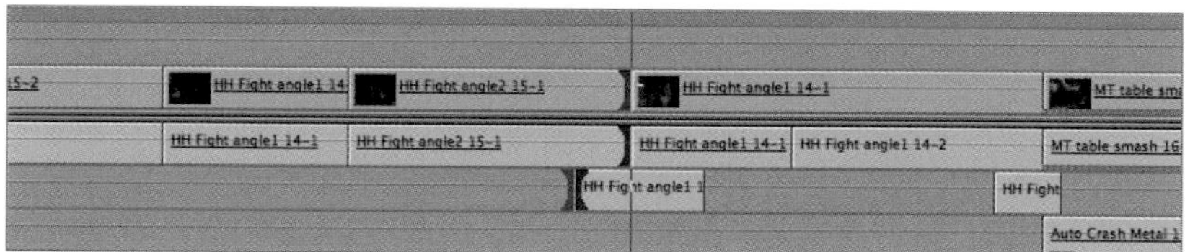

This adds the edit on that track as part of the selection. Right away, you should notice that the edit on tracks V1 and A1 is selected as a ripple outgoing, and the edit on track A2 is selected as a roll. Nothing prevents you from making this sort of complex selection (or selecting an edit containing a gap), and in some cases it may be just what you want, but in this case it will prove to be a problem.

5 Type *–12*, and press Enter.

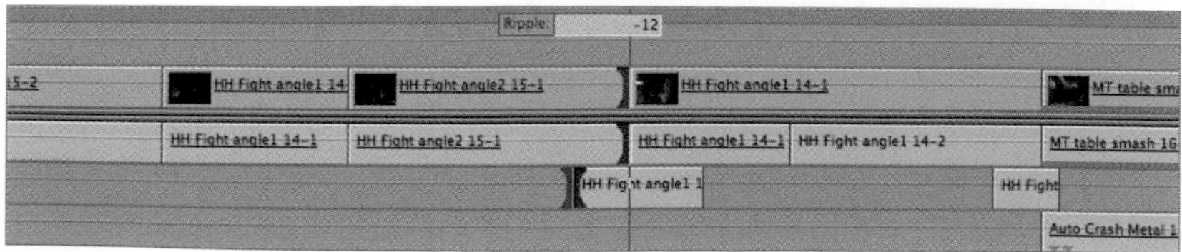

The trim is applied, and as you might expect, the clips on tracks V1 and A1 are rippled, and the clip on track A2 is rolled.

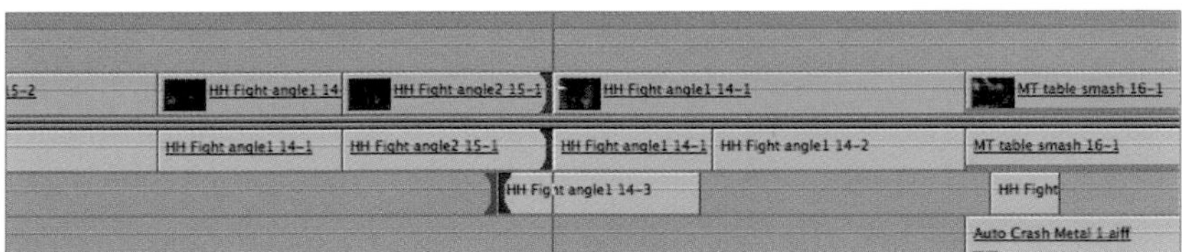

6 Play around the edit.

At first it may seem that you have no additional concerns. Sure, the A2 clip got longer, but there were no undesired sounds in that earlier section, so no harm appears to have been done. The timing of the main edit has been fixed, and the scream stayed in sync with his rear hitting the chair.

But by rolling the clip on that track, and rippling the clips on the other tracks, you inadvertently allowed the clips that appear later in time (on track A2) to go out of sync.

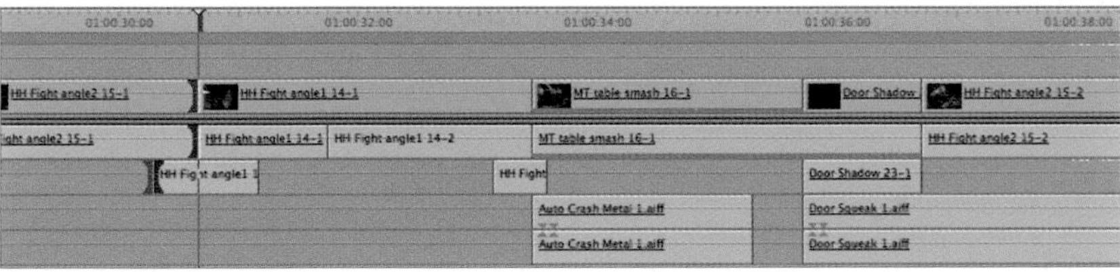

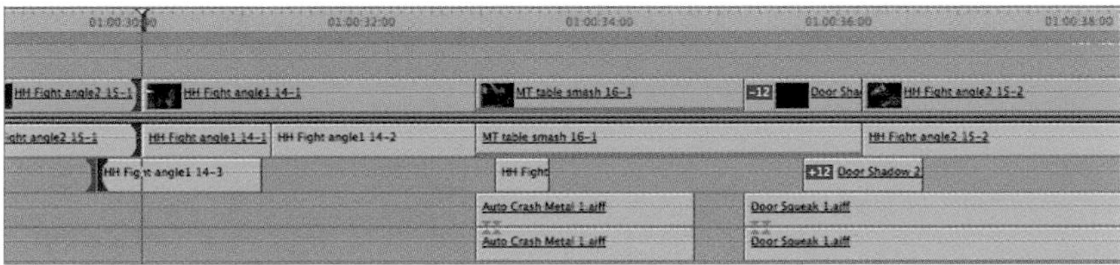

In this case, it is imperative that you ripple all the tracks to ensure that everything downstream of the edit remains in sync.

7 Press Command-Z to undo the last edit.

8 Press RR to select the Ripple tool.

9 On track A2, Command-click the outgoing side of the edit to select that edit as a ripple outgoing.

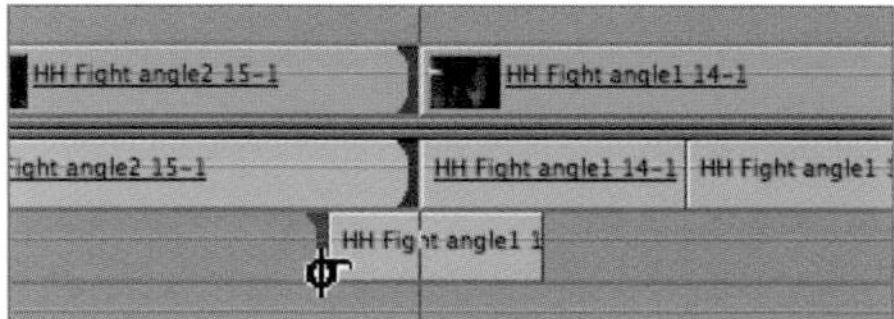

It may seem strange to be trimming a gap, but in this case, it's exactly the right thing to do. Essentially, you are instructing Final Cut Pro to make the gap longer or shorter just as you would do with a clip.

10 Type *–12* and press Enter.

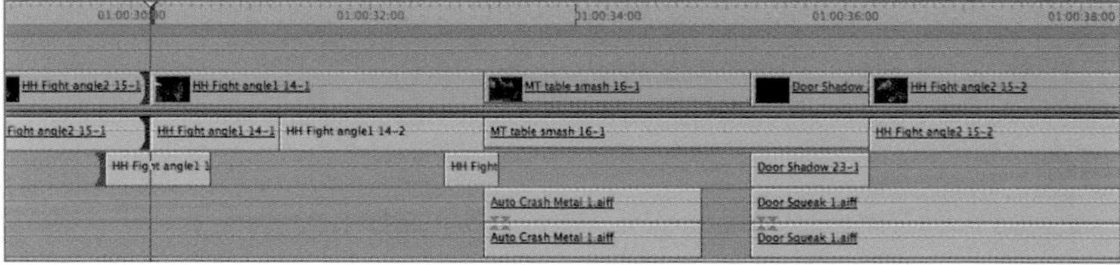

11 Play around the edit.

The edit has been trimmed, and the downstream clips retain their original timings relative to the clips on the other tracks.

Trimming Asymmetrically

Once you understand that every track in your Timeline can be trimmed simultaneously (as long as you select just one edit per track), even more complex possibilities arise.

In certain instances, you may actually want to trim a clip on one track in one direction (such as ripple incoming) and another track in a different direction (such as ripple outgoing). In such a case, it may still be critical to trim both tracks by the same number of frames to maintain a particular sync relationship. So it is ideal to do the trim as a single operation.

This may seem incredibly complicated, but it's not as bad as it sounds. In practice, it's even fairly intuitive. It's called asymmetrical trimming.

1 In the Timeline, click any blank area to deselect the current edit.

2 Play over the next video edit, where the man's head is slammed onto the table.

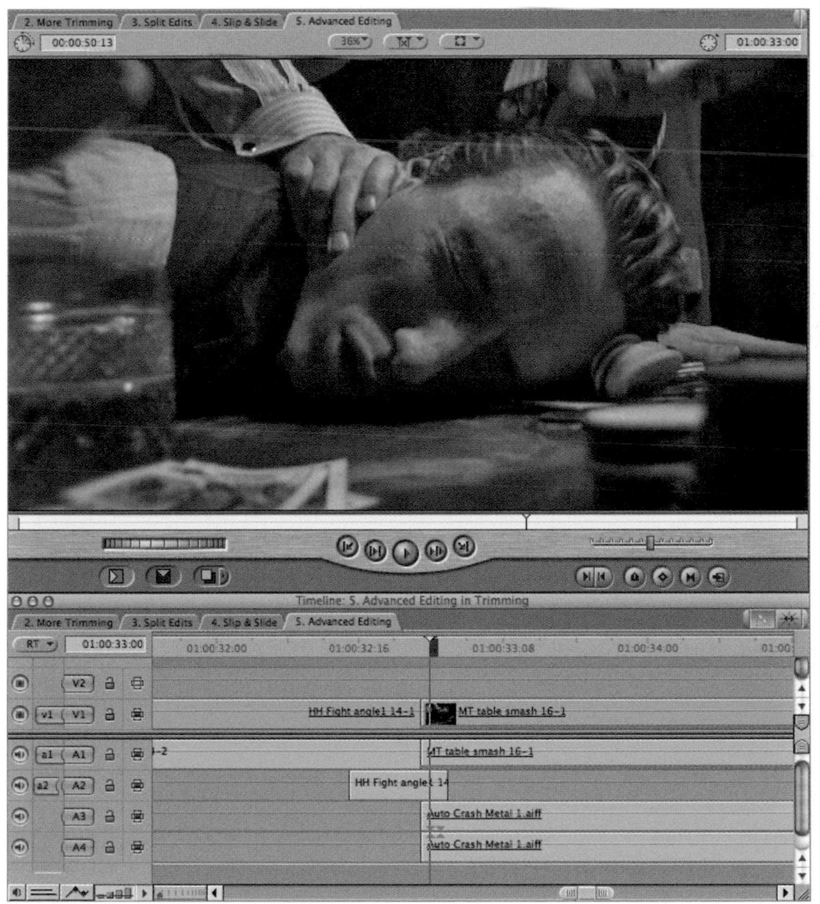

In this edit, the incoming clip (**MT table smash 16-1**) begins with the man's face already on the table. A few frames have to be added to the head of that shot to perfect the timing.

In this case, some extra audio clips have already been laid in: another scream from the woman on track A2 and a sound effect for the table smash on tracks A3 and A4.

3 Press RR to select the Ripple tool (if it's not already selected).

4 Press Shift-L to turn off linked selection.

5 Click the incoming edge of the edit between **HH Fight angle1 14-1** and **MT table smash 16-1.**

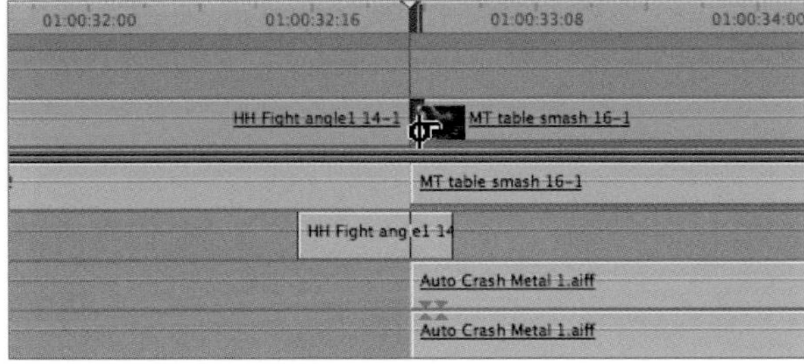

6 Command-click the incoming edge of the audio edit directly beneath the video.

Command-clicking is how you add tracks to an edit selection.

For this edit, the timing of the audio on track A2 doesn't need to be precise, so you can ignore it. The sound effect on tracks A3 and A4, however, must line up precisely with the action in the video.

Furthermore, you don't actually want to modify the sound effect clip. Instead, you want to keep it where it is, which you can do by rippling the outgoing edge of the preceding gap.

7 Command-click the outgoing edge of the edit on track A3.

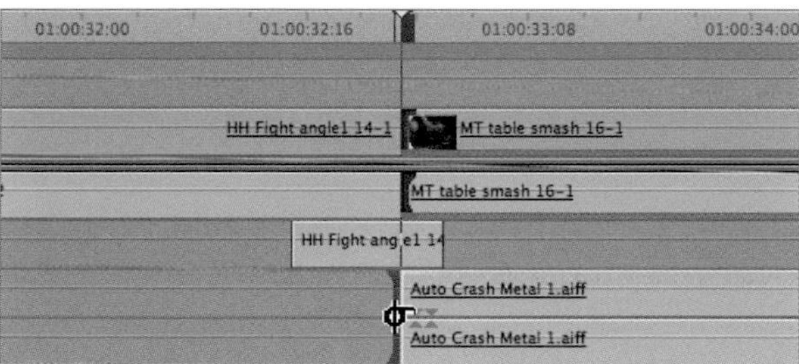

The edit on track A4 is automatically selected because the sound effect is a stereo pair. Now you have an asymmetrical edit selection.

8 Drag the edit on track V1 to the left by about six frames.

The incoming edge of the edit on tracks V1 and A1 is trimmed, and the outgoing edge of the edit on tracks A3 and A4 is trimmed. The edits move in opposite directions. The result is that the sound effect remains in sync with the action in the video.

9 Play around the edit to see the results.

Although asymmetrical trimming is fairly rare, it can be a real time-saver in certain situations. The sound effect example here is one frequently encountered case; another is when a lower third title is used over an interview.

It is common to have an interview subject's name appear one second or so after the interview clip begins. Once that title has been positioned, asymmetrical trimming can help to keep the lower third in position even when trimming the head of the interview clip is required.

The remaining edits in this sequence all need additional trimming. Experiment using the various trimming techniques covered in this lesson.

Lesson Review

1. What is the most important advice about trimming?
2. Which is generally done first: Rippling or rolling?
3. How do you control the amount of pre- and post-roll used when performing a play around function?
4. What five keys are essential to trimming from the keyboard and what are their functions?
5. True or false: Extend edit can ripple an edit in either direction.
6. What is a split edit?
7. Why are split edits used?
8. Is a slip edit the same as two ripple edits or two roll edits?
9. How do you open the Trim Edit window?
10. In the Trim Edit window, which side of the edit do the J-K-L keys affect?
11. When dynamic trimming is enabled, what changes?
12. How are edits added to an edit selection?

Answers

1. Make your trimming decisions while the video is playing.
2. Rippling is typically done before rolling.
3. In the Editing tab of the User Preferences window.
4. V selects the nearest edit; U toggles the edit selection type; the bracket keys ([and]) perform the trim one frame at a time; and \ (backslash) plays around the current playhead position.
5. False. Extend edit *rolls* an edit in either direction.
6. A split edit is an edit where the audio and video edits happen on different frames.
7. Split edits significantly soften the jarring nature inherent in a cut, thereby making an edit point more "invisible."
8. A slip edit is the same as two ripple edits of the same amount on the beginning and end of the same clip.
9. Double-click an edit point or press Command-8.
10. It depends on the type of edit selected: In a ripple, the J-K-L keys will always control the clip on the selected side of the edit. In a roll, they will control the side where the cursor is located.
11. Pressing K performs the edit.
12. By Command-clicking an edit point.

3

Lesson Files	Lesson Files > Lesson 03 > Multicam.fcp
Media	Turn to Stone and Broken Fists_multicam
Time	This lesson takes approximately 60 minutes to complete.
Goals	Create multiclips from multiple camera footage Control the view of multiclips in the Viewer Edit multiclips on-the-fly Control audio and video of multiclips separately Rearrange, add, and delete angles from a multiclip Adjust sync of angles within a multiclip Apply filters to multiclip angles and move them to another angle

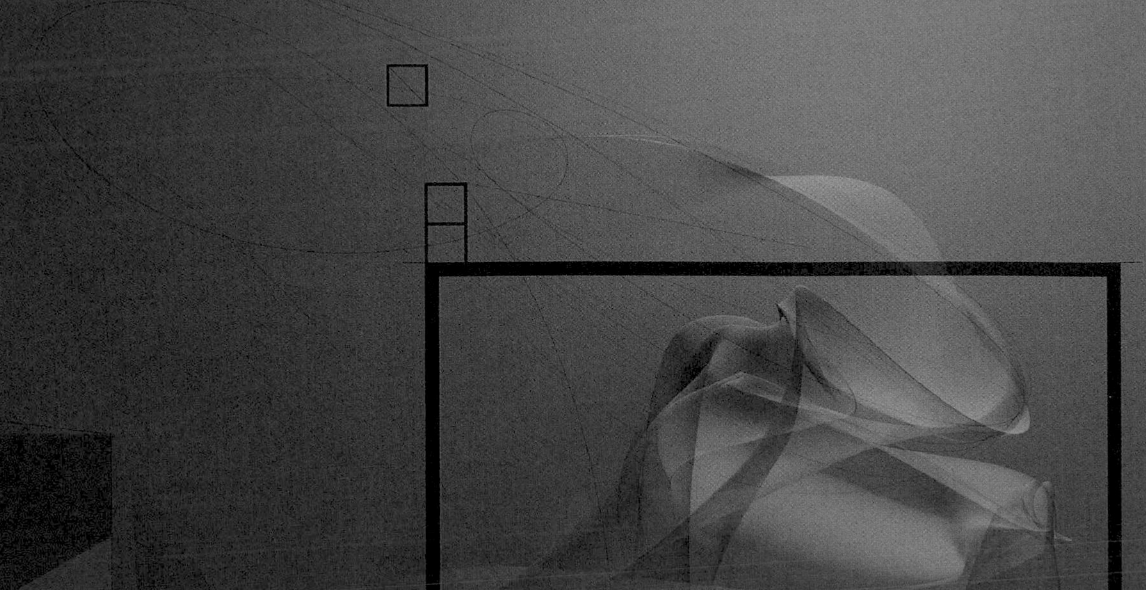

Lesson **3**

Multicamera Editing

Although traditional filmmaking is done with a single camera, some types of productions use more than one camera operating at the same time. Most often this *multicamera* technique is used when documenting a live event, such as a concert, theatrical performance, or sporting event. Shooting with multiple cameras is essential in these instances; otherwise there would be no way to edit the footage without automatically jump-cutting. Multiple cameras are also frequently used for complicated stunts or for action that is difficult to stage or repeat, such as improvisational performances.

Of course, sacrifices must be made when shooting with more than one camera. Framing options are severely limited if you are going to avoid showing other cameras in the shots, and lighting must be unnaturally even to ensure that all angles get an acceptable image. This explains the very formulaic and artificial look employed by many television sitcoms and soap operas in which three cameras are operated simultaneously and the show is edited on-the-fly using a broadcast switcher.

Editing Multicamera Footage

Although there are some limitations for the production team, editing multicamera source is especially easy. When multiple cameras are capturing the same action at the same time, you can effortlessly cut from one angle to the other without worrying about matching the timing. Not only will audio be in sync from angle to angle, but so will any action that happens simultaneously in all the shots. In many ways, multicamera setups are an editor's dream, except that the limited camera angles often mean that you may not have the exact close-up or insert that will most clearly tell the story.

Because multicamera content is such a special situation, Final Cut Pro has a special feature designed to take advantage of multicam footage and simplify editing such footage.

Using the Multiclip

Final Cut Pro can group multiple clips into a *multiclip*. A multiclip can hold up to 128 *angles* in a single clip; when the multiclip is used in a sequence, you can toggle between each of the angles to choose which one is currently visible.

Although you can create and use multiclips in a variety of ways, this chapter will focus on a recommended workflow that takes advantage of special features in Final Cut Pro and also serves the creative needs of multicam editing.

Creating a Multiclip

Although you can collect any group of clips into a multiclip, the feature is primarily designed for clips that are synchronous—especially clips that were photographed in a multiple-camera situation.

However, though the clips may all contain the same content, you must synchronize them manually in Final Cut Pro. This means that you identify some element that will link the clips together, such as matching timecode, a slate clap, or even a flashbulb going off.

1 Open Lesson Files > Lesson 03 > **Multicam.fcp**.

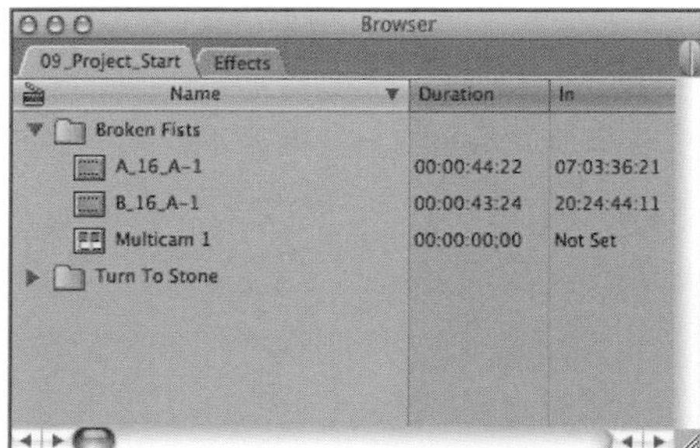

This project contains two sets of clips, each of which was created in a multicamera environment.

2 In the Browser, double-click **A_16_A-1** in the Broken Fists bin.

3 In the Viewer, set an In point at the frame where the slate closes (07:03:36:21).

TIP When looking for the frame where a slate closes, you should always step through the frames one at a time, moving backward and forward until you're sure you have found the exact frame where the clap stick has closed.

4 Double-click **B_16_A-1** to open it in the Viewer.

5 Set an In Point at the frame where the slate closes in this clip (20:24:44:11).

6 In the Browser, select both clips and choose Modify > Make Multiclip.

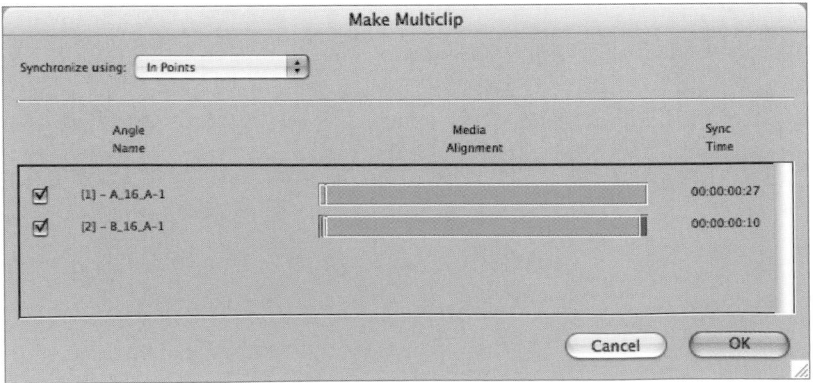

The Make Multiclip window appears. You can see which sections of the clips overlap based on the sync point.

7 Verify that the "Synchronize using" pop-up menu is set to In Points and click OK.

A new clip appears in the Browser named **A_16_A-1 [1]-Multiclip.**

8 Double-click the multiclip to open it in the Viewer.

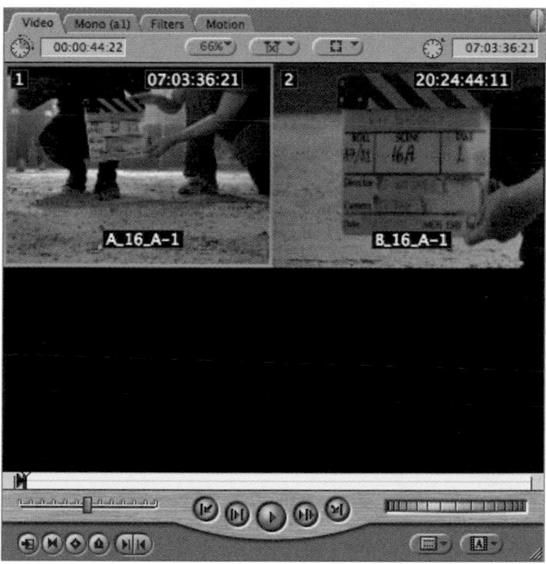

9 Play the clip.

Both angles play simultaneously.

10 While the clip is playing, click each of the two angles in the Viewer.

The active angle has a blue border around it. Notice that the multiclip name changes in the Browser to reflect the currently selected angle.

Editing with a Multiclip

Linking the clips together gets you prepared, but editing the multiclip in a sequence is where the real fun starts.

1 Click Angle 1.

2 Set an In point just before the woman stands up, at approximately 07:03:54:00.

3 Set an Out point after the action ends, at around 07:04:20:10.

4 Double-click the *Multicam 1* sequence to open it in the Canvas and Timeline.

5 Option-drag the clip from the Viewer into the Canvas as an overwrite edit.

NOTE ▶ You must press Option as you drag because clicking the clip in the Viewer changes the active angle.

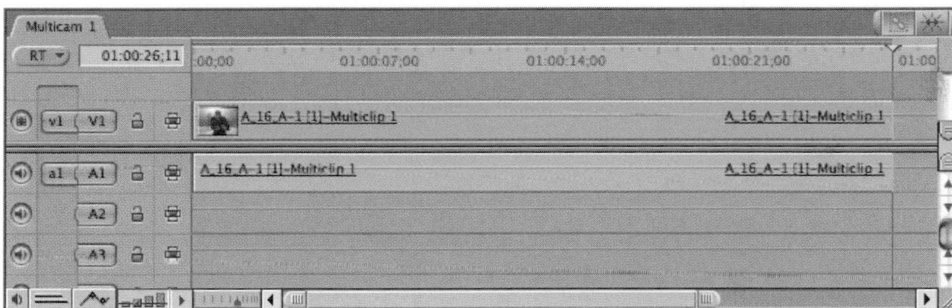

After the multiclip is edited into the sequence, it looks like any other clip. But don't be fooled. It has special features that allow you to switch angles—even while it's playing back. However, to enable those features, you must first set two controls.

6 Check to make sure Linked Selection is turned on.

7 Set the Playhead Sync mode to Open.

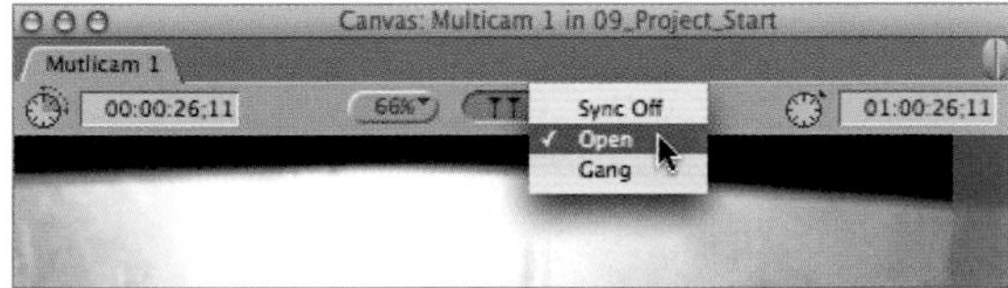

The clip at the playhead position in the sequence will be opened into the Viewer. If you choose another option from the Playhead sync pop-up menu, you can still change angles. However, you will not be able to simultaneously play the multiclip in the Viewer and Sequence.

8 In the Timeline, click the RT menu and verify that a checkmark is next to Multiclip Playback.

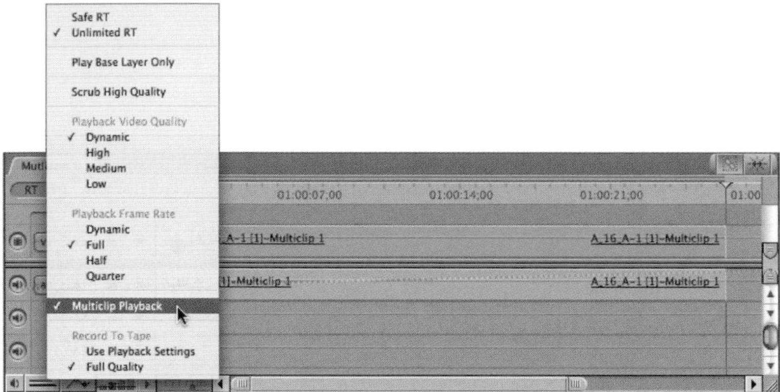

9 Play the sequence and, while it plays, click back and forth between the angles in the Viewer.

Each time you click, you are creating a virtual edit point, temporarily indicated by a blue marker in the Timeline.

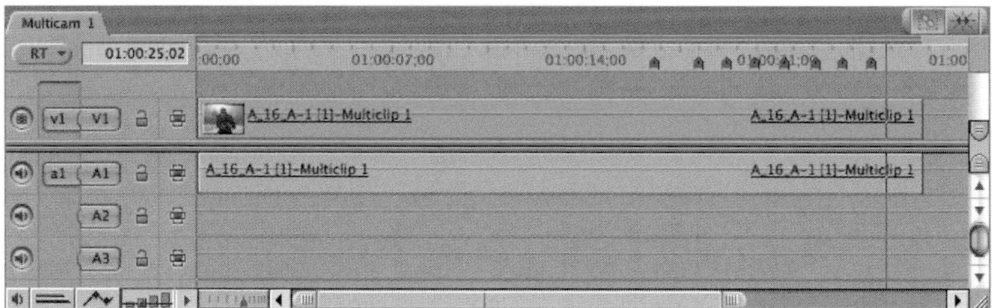

When you stop playback, the blue markers automatically turn into edit points.

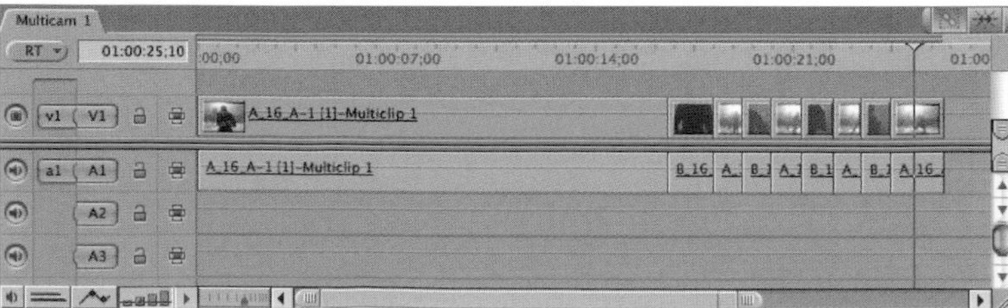

You can continue to improve your sequence by modifying these edits. If you roll any edit point, both clips will remain in sync, but rippling, slipping, or sliding edits or clips will cause the affected clips to move out of sync.

NOTE ▶ Be sure that the Canvas or Timeline window is active. If the Viewer window is active, the multiclip edits will not work.

Collapsing a Multiclip

After your angles have been selected, you may want to prevent further angle changes by collapsing the multiclip. When you collapse a multiclip, it is replaced by the active angle of the multiclip. This is useful when you send a sequence to a colorist or effects artist and you want them to focus only on the angles you chose during editing. Collapsing multiclips also improves performance because less video is streaming from disk. Because the collapsing is not permanent, you can uncollapse the active angle at any time and return to the full multiclip, even after you close and reopen a project.

1 Press Command-A to select all the clips in the sequence.

2 Choose Modify > Collapse Multiclip(s).

The angles are converted into ordinary clips based on the master clips to which they refer.

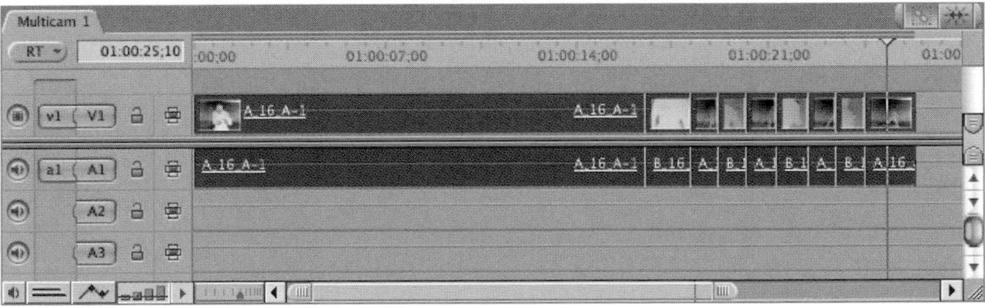

3 To switch a clip back to the multiclip format in order to change its angle, select the clip and choose Modify > Uncollapse Multiclip(s).

Working with Many Angles

The previous example was very simple, involving only two angles, but Final Cut Pro can accommodate many angles in a single multiclip, and the editing process quickly can get more complex.

1 Open the Turn To Stone bin and select all nine clips.

2 Control-click any of the selected clips and choose Make Multiclip from the shortcut menu.

The Make Multiclip window appears.

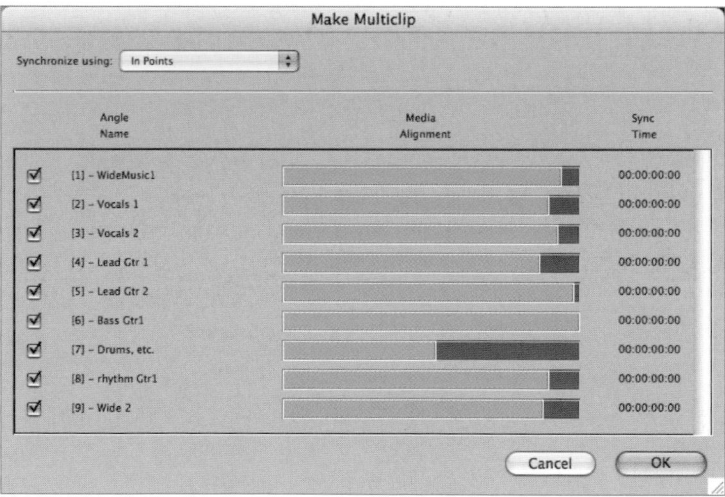

NOTE ▶ You can also Control-click the bin and choose Make Multiclip to create a multiclip that includes all the clips in the bin.

In this case, all these clips share identical timecode, so you can sync to that, rather than syncing to an In point set on a slate clap as you did previously.

3 In the "Synchronize using" pop-up menu, choose Timecode.

The Make Multiclip window displays the way the various clips overlap. Some of the clips are significantly shorter than others. Selecting one of these angles in an area where there is no media will just display black.

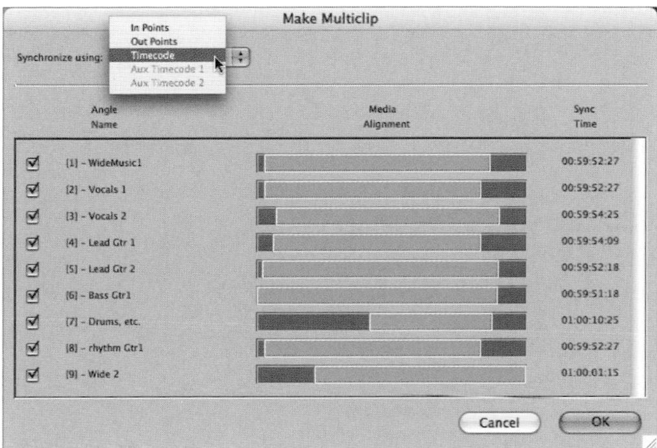

4 Click OK.

The new multiclip is created in the Turn To Stone bin.

Multiclip names always start with the name of the angle currently selected, but you can modify the rest of the name, just like changing any other clip name.

5 In the Browser, select the multiclip, then click it to edit the name.

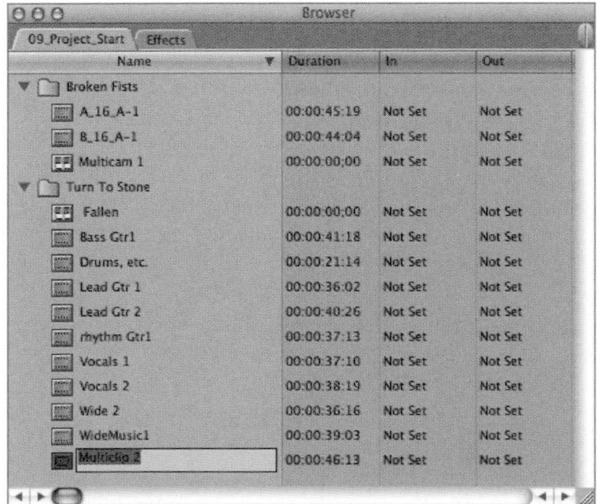

When the clip name appears, only the editable part is visible.

6 Rename the multiclip *Fallen Multi* and press Return.

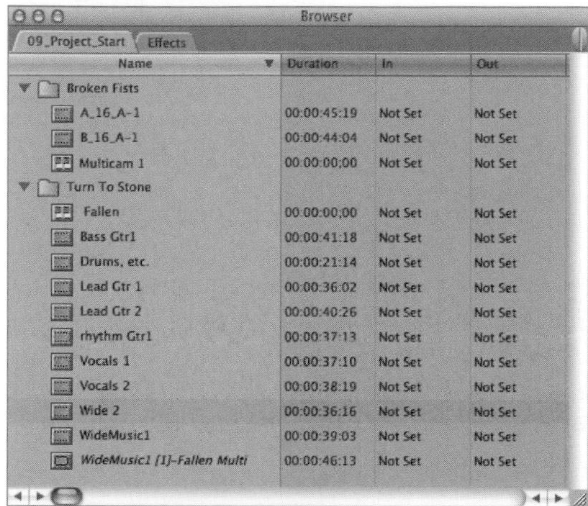

The new name still includes the current angle, but it now ends with your customized name.

7 Double-click the multiclip.

The Viewer displays the **Fallen Multi** multiclip.

8 Choose View > Show Multiclip Overlays to display the clip names and timecodes in the Viewer.

9 Shuttle through the clip until you can see video in all four angles.

10 In the Viewer, click the View button and choose Multiclip 9-Up.

Although this looks impressive, it's a lot of information for you to monitor, and a lot of data for your computer to display at one time. In most cases, working in 4-Up is more manageable, but which of the four clips will you monitor? This choice is controlled by the order of the angles, and you can modify that order in a number of ways, as you'll see in the next section.

Setting Angle Order

The order of the clips initially is based on the value in the Angle field of each clip. The Angle field number can be entered when logging clips, or at any time in the Browser or Clip Properties windows.

1 Double-click the Turn To Stone bin.

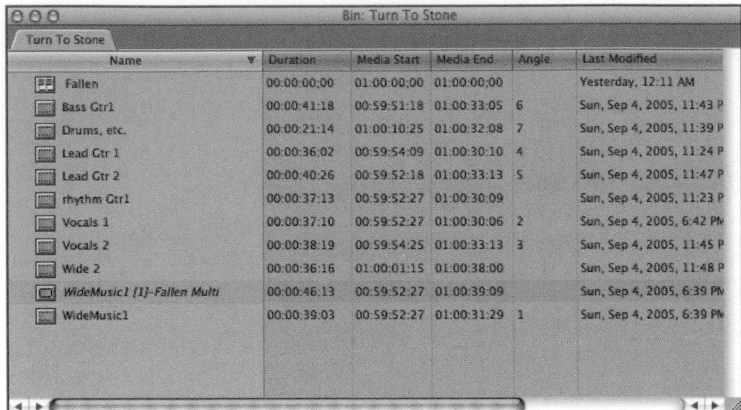

Bin: Turn To Stone

Turn To Stone

Name	Duration	Media Start	Media End	Angle	Last Modified
Fallen	00:00:00;00	01:00:00;00	01:00:00;00		Yesterday, 12:11 AM
Bass Gtr1	00:00:41:18	00:59:51:18	01:00:33:05	6	Sun, Sep 4, 2005, 11:43 P
Drums, etc.	00:00:21:14	01:00:10:25	01:00:32:08	7	Sun, Sep 4, 2005, 11:39 P
Lead Gtr 1	00:00:36:02	00:59:54:09	01:00:30:10	4	Sun, Sep 4, 2005, 11:24 P
Lead Gtr 2	00:00:40:26	00:59:52:18	01:00:33:13	5	Sun, Sep 4, 2005, 11:47 P
rhythm Gtr1	00:00:37:13	00:59:52:27	01:00:30:09		Sun, Sep 4, 2005, 11:23 P
Vocals 1	00:00:37:10	00:59:52:27	01:00:30:06	2	Sun, Sep 4, 2005, 6:42 PM
Vocals 2	00:00:38:19	00:59:54:25	01:00:33:13	3	Sun, Sep 4, 2005, 11:45 P
Wide 2	00:00:36:16	01:00:01:15	01:00:38:00		Sun, Sep 4, 2005, 11:48 P
WideMusic1 [1]-Fallen Multi	00:00:46:13	00:59:52:27	01:00:39:09		Sun, Sep 4, 2005, 6:39 PM
WideMusic1	00:00:39:03	00:59:52:27	01:00:31:29	1	Sun, Sep 4, 2005, 6:39 PM

The Angle field is visible to the right of the Media End field.

Final Cut Pro works hard to determine how to arrange clips that don't have a value in that field. If the clip name is identified with an *A* followed by a number (such as A2 or A11), that number will be used to set the Angle number. Otherwise, the first number that appears in the clip name will be identified as the angle number. (For example, a clip titled **CUGuitar_7_01** would be identified as Angle 7.) If no number is identified, the reel name and the media file name are consulted.

If two clips have the same angle number and are included in the same multiclip, they appear in the order they were sorted in the Browser window at the time the multiclip was made, and they push other angle numbers down the list. (So if there are two Angle 5 clips, Angles 6 and 7 will become Angles 7 and 8.)

2 Close the Turn To Stone bin.

3 In the Viewer window, Command-drag one of the angles to rearrange it in the 9-Up display.

The other clips move to make room for the new clip.

4 Arrange the clips so that the first four clips are **Bass Gtr1**, **Lead Gtr 1**, **Vocals 1**, and **WideMusic1**.

5 Choose View > Multiclip Layout > Multiclip 4-Up.

Now, the first four clips are visible, and you can play the sequence and switch among them on-the-fly. The other angles are still viewable; you just have to scroll them into view.

6 Position the mouse pointer in the lower-right corner of the Viewer window.

A small, boxed arrow appears.

7 Click the arrow to move Angles 5 and 6 into the 4-Up display.

Each time you click that arrow, another row of angles is revealed. You can scroll up through the rows by clicking the similar arrow in the upper-right corner of the display.

Deleting and Adding Angles

After a multiclip has been created, you can change its number of angles by dragging into or out of the Viewer.

1 Scroll the view so that Angles 1 through 4 are visible.

2 Click the **Bass Gtr1** angle to make it active.

3 Command-click the **Vocals 1** angle and drag it out of the Viewer window.

   This angle is removed from the multiclip.

NOTE ► You cannot delete the active angle.

4 In the Turn To Stone bin, select the **Vocals 1** clip and drag it into the Viewer. Continue to hold down the mouse button until the overlay appears.

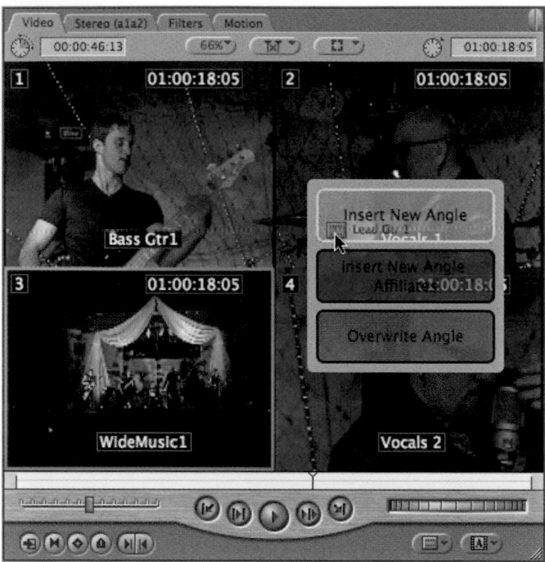

5 Drag the clip onto Insert New Angle and release the mouse button.

The angle is added back into the multiclip.

Alternatively, you could have overwritten one of the existing angles or added a new *angle affiliate,* which would add the angle to the multiclip currently in the Viewer and would also add that angle to any other versions of that multiclip. You would do this, for example, when adding an angle to a multiclip that was already used in a sequence and that was divided into multiple edits.

Offsetting Sync

If one of the angles in your multiclip is out of sync with the other angles, you can correct it in the Viewer window, as long as you have some way of determining how many frames out of sync it is.

This sort of error can occur if the timecodes or In points you used to sync the multiple angles were incorrect at the time you created the multiclip. In this example, the timecode value was set incorrectly on one of the source clips.

1 In the Viewer, navigate to frame 00:59:54:20.

2 Find the **Lead Gtr 1** angle.

Notice that the timecode visible on the DAT player in the video reads 00:59:54:24. Somehow the timecode for this clip was marked four frames too early, making the clip out of sync with the other angles (and with the accompanying audio).

3 Press Control-Shift and drag the mouse pointer over that angle to the left until the timecode display in the video reads 00:59:54:20.

That angle has now been properly synced with the rest of the multiclip.

Editing the Multiclip

Remember that you must first put a multiclip into a sequence in order to edit it.

1 In the Turn To Stone bin, double-click the *Fallen* sequence.

  The sequence opens in the Canvas and Timeline. Make sure the Playhead Sync menu is set to Video + Audio.

2 In the Viewer, click **Bass Gtr1** to make that angle active.

3 Play the clip until the camera pulls out and settles on the opening wide shot for that angle. Set an In point there (at approximately 00:59:54:15).

4 Press the Down Arrow to advance the playhead to the end of the clip.

5 Set an Out point there.

  Because this footage is only used to illustrate the multiclip technique, just the first 30 seconds or so of the song have been included.

6 Option-drag the clip into the Canvas and perform an overwrite edit.

Preset Multiclip Button Bars

Final Cut Pro provides a preset button bar configuration to assist with multiclip editing. This provides shortcuts to the most common multiclip controls such as turning on multiclip display, switching the Viewer to 4-Up view, and even switching and cutting between angles.

You can further customize the button bars to suit your personal multiclip editing style if, for example, you often use the 9-Up display or frequently switch audio and video angles together.

1 Choose Tools > Button Bars > Multiclip.

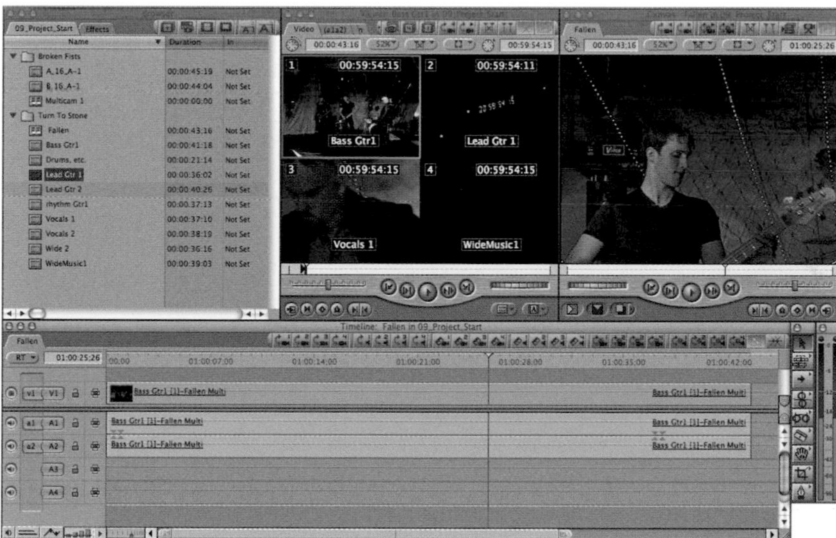

Dozens of buttons are added to the Viewer, Canvas, and Timeline windows. These buttons can be used to configure Final Cut Pro for multiclip editing and even to perform the edits.

2 Set the Playhead Sync mode to Open.

3 Switch focus to the Timeline or Canvas and play the sequence.

4 Instead of using the Viewer to cut between angles, click the green buttons in the Timeline button bar to cut between Angles 1 through 4. For this example, just make a few edits.

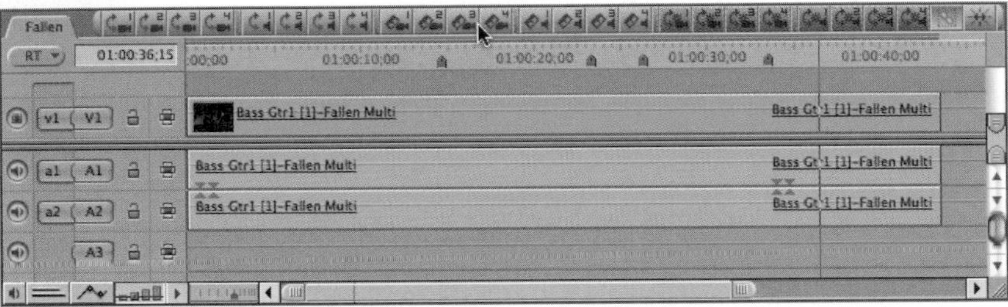

The temporary blue markers appear whenever you click one of the angle buttons and, when playback is stopped, the markers are converted to edits.

As you can see, there are buttons to perform a variety of other actions, such as cutting the audio separately from the video (see "Separating Audio and Video" in this lesson) and switching between angles with effects on them (see "Applying Effects to Multiclips" in this lesson).

Switching Angles

After your multiclip has been divided into separate clips, you may change your mind and want to choose a different angle for a segment. This is called *switching* angles.

1 In the Timeline, Control-click the second clip.

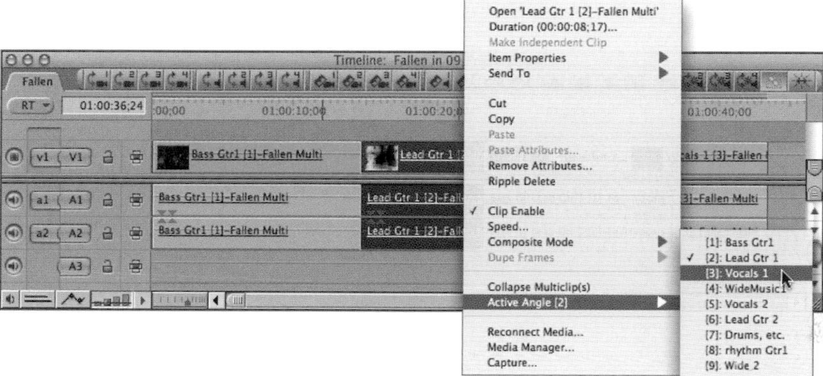

2 Choose Active Angle > Vocals 1 from the shortcut menu.

That segment is changed to display the **Vocals 1** angle. (You can also use the buttons in the button bar to switch angles.)

3 Deselect all clips, then position the playhead over the third clip in the Timeline.

If a clip is selected, the buttons will switch the angle of that clip. If nothing is selected, they will apply to the clip under the playhead.

4 In the Timeline button bar, click the Switch Video to Angle 2 button.

Alternately, you can step through the different angles in order by clicking the Switch Video to Next Angle or the Switch Video to Previous Angle buttons in the Canvas or Viewer button bars.

Using the Keyboard

You can work with multiclips most efficiently when you program keyboard shortcuts that help you quickly perform tasks at the touch of a key (or two).

Final Cut Pro has a keyboard layout specially designed for multiclip editing. This layout transforms the number keys so you can quickly switch and cut between angles.

To use this keyboard layout, choose Tools > Keyboard Layout > Multicamera Editing. Although no obvious changes occur, your keyboard has been transformed into a multiclip editing console:

- Pressing the 1 through 0 keys (0 serves as angle 10) automatically switches the current video angle to the angle of the number you press.
- Pressing Option in combination with a number key switches the audio to the angle number selected.

- Pressing Command in combination with a number key *cuts* the multiclip, switching the new angle to the number chosen. This is equivalent to clicking the images in the Viewer.
- Pressing Shift in combination with a number key switches the video to the new angle number along with any applied effects.

One advantage to using keyboard shortcuts is that you can press keys to perform quick cuts or switches while the video is playing. Another advantage is that you can cut or switch among up to ten angles at once.

If you forget what shortcuts are available in the Multicamera Editing keyboard layout, the tooltips on the button bar provide a quick reminder.

Separating Audio and Video

So far in this lesson, you've been cutting or switching multiclip angles with linked audio and video, or just changing the video (when using the buttons or keyboard shortcuts). So you've probably realized that you can switch the audio and video angles separately.

This is exactly what you would want to do with the current footage, in which the prerecorded version of the band's song is attached to only one of the clips. All of the other video tracks include scratch audio, which is great for ensuring that all the clips are in sync but not ideal for a finished soundtrack.

When you edit a multiclip by clicking images in the Viewer, the affected channels are controlled by the setting in the Playhead Sync menu.

1 In the Viewer, click the Playhead Sync menu button and choose Audio > All.

This setting can also be found in the View menu in the Multiclip Active Tracks submenu.

2 In the Viewer, click the **WideMusic1** angle.

A green border indicates which angle is providing the audio; a blue border indicates the selected video angle. These are referred to as the *active* angles.

NOTE ► If the Viewer switches to the Audio tab, click back to the Video tab to select the desired angle.

3 Make sure that the Playhead Sync mode is set to Open and that Multiclip Playback is chosen.

4 Make the Timeline or Canvas window active and play the sequence.

5 As it plays, click between the different angles in the Viewer.

   This time, only the green box moves and, correspondingly, the edits you make in the sequence affect only the audio tracks.

Switching Audio and Video Separately

In addition to cutting audio tracks independently from the video, you can switch audio and video separately for clips that are already edited into the sequence.

1 In the Timeline, position the playhead over the first clip in the sequence.

2 Click the Switch Audio to Angle 4 button or press Option-4.

The Timeline displays the different names for the audio and video tracks of that clip.

3 Control-Option-click the audio tracks for the second clip and choose Active Angle > WideMusic1 from the shortcut menu.

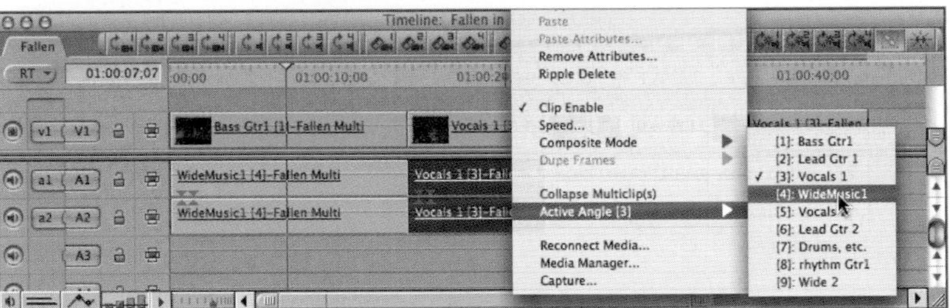

The clip's audio is now set to **WideMusic1**, although the video is still set to **Vocals 1**.

4 Choose View > Multiclip Active Tracks > Video + Audio.

This resets the active angle settings back to all tracks in preparation for the next exercise.

Applying Effects to Multiclips

You can apply filters, speed changes, and other effects to multiclips, just like ordinary clips, but you must determine whether you want the effect applied to an individual angle or to the whole multiclip, regardless of which angle is currently active.

After a filter or effect has been applied, you also must account for that effect when switching angles on the multiclip.

1 In the Effects tab, open the Video Filters bin and then open the Image Control bin.

2 Drag the Desaturate filter to the last clip in the Timeline. Continue to hold down the mouse button until the overlay appears.

   The overlay provides two choices: Apply to Source Angle or Apply to Multiclip.

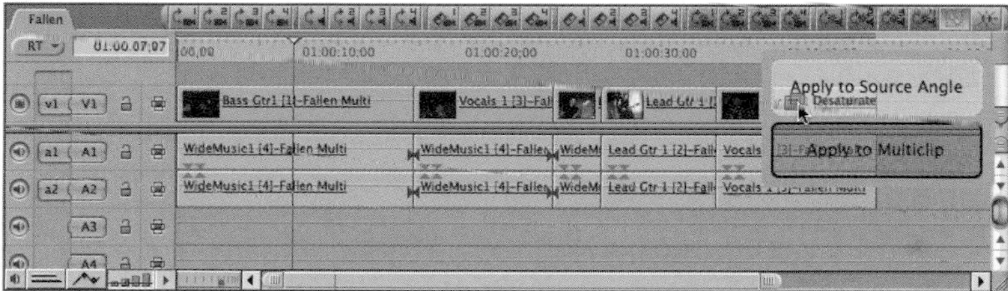

3 Drag the clip onto Apply to Source Angle and release the mouse button.

4 Move the playhead so you can see the effect of the filter in the Canvas.

   When a filter is applied to an individual angle, only that angle is affected. Switching to a different angle will leave that filter on the angle that is no longer in use, and the newly selected angle will be unfiltered.

   If you choose Switch Video with Effects, the filter is applied to the new angle.

5 In the Timeline button bar, click the Switch Video with Effects to Angle 4 button, or press Shift-4.

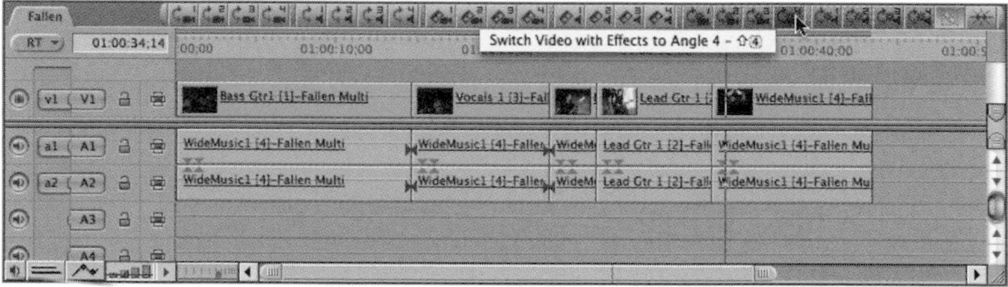

The angle is switched, and the filter is applied to the new angle. Other effects, such as speed and motion effects, can also be moved from angle to angle in the same manner.

Lesson Review

1. What is a multiclip?
2. How do you create a multiclip?
3. How do you drag and drop a multiclip into the Timeline or Canvas from the Viewer?
4. What are two settings you must activate before live multiclip editing is possible?
5. What does it mean to collapse a multiclip?
6. How do you rearrange multiclip angles in the Viewer?
7. How do you control which tracks are affected by multiclip edits?
8. Can filters and effects be applied to multiclips?

Answers

1. A multiclip is a special type of clip that contains between 2 and 128 angles, any one of which can be used at one time.
2. Select the clips in the Browser and choose Modify > Make Multiclip.
3. You must press the Option key to drag and drop a multiclip in the Viewer.
4. In the RT menu, turn on the Multiclip Editing setting and set the Playhead Sync mode to Open.
5. Converting a multiclip back into individual clips after it has been edited in a sequence.
6. Press Command while dragging the angles to rearrange them in the Viewer. Command-dragging an angle out of the Viewer deletes it from the multiclip.
7. Choose the video and/or the specific audio tracks listed in the Playhead Sync menu.
8. Yes.

Cameo

Flying High (in High Def)—Brian Terwilliger

FOR MODERN TRAVELERS, THE ROMANCE OF flying has devolved into a scramble through a crowded airport, a slow anxious dance through security, and a cramped middle seat.

"That isn't flying," says indie filmmaker and pilot Brian J. Terwilliger. "That's like getting on a big bus. There's just nothing beautiful or sensational or romantic about it."

But Terwilliger has resurrected all three adjectives in a high-definition, feature-length documentary with an unlikely star—the Van Nuys Airport—and a strikingly odd name—*One Six Right*—which refers to the famous coordinates of its main runway.

A movie starring an airport might not suggest romance, but it has struck a chord with hundreds of thousands of viewers who have seen the film projected in HD during a recent 12-city theatrical tour or on one of over 50,000 DVDs sold. They've been moved by the emotional testimonies of Van Nuys–based pilots and by the stunning aerial footage of restored vintage planes in flight over and around the airport.

"I made the film to capture an emotion," says Terwilliger. "You don't have to be a pilot or an aviation nut to get it. If you're passionate about anything, you will probably be able to relate to this film. Love stories of any kind are about someone you didn't know when you walked into the theater. Two hours later, you're crying or emotionally moved by the character. In this case, believe it or not, it's an airport."

The genesis of the film was simple. "I really had no agenda other than wanting to relay a feeling—what I loved about flying and what I loved about the airport. But while I knew the feeling that I wanted the audience to be left with at the end of the film, I had no idea about how to get there."

After three years of trying to raise the money, Terwilliger decided to produce a 5-minute DVD teaser trailer to jumpstart investment.

After scoring donations of crew time and the loan of a Sony F900 camera, Terwilliger purchased a Power Mac G5 with Final Cut Pro and DVD Studio Pro. Then he taught himself to use the applications, cut the trailer from HD footage, and pressed 1000 DVDs.

"Less than 6 weeks later, I had raised all the money I needed from 12 investors," he says. "I know it's cliché," Terwilliger continues, "But if you believe in a project, it has to be your priority. You have to say to yourself, 'Till death do us part, I am making this film.' The sacrifices I had to make personally, professionally, and financially included taking a second mortgage instead of a paying job."

Fully budgeted, Terwilliger shot the rest of the film over the next few months in HD (1080p). The 49 production days included 4 aerial shoot days and 85 interviews. Then he and editor Kimberley Furst used the Mac to edit 120 hours of footage in DVCAM in 54 weeks.

"I wasn't thinking workflow or ease of use when I shot HD, I was thinking of making the best quality product I could," says Terwilliger. "You have all these options, and I almost never take the cheapest path. I always take the best path, and then get the cheapest price. If you stay true to that, each and every time, the cumulative result is awesome."

Terwilliger used Final Cut Studio far more than he had planned. In addition to editing, he used Final Cut for basic color correction, Cinema Tools for frame rate conversion, and Compressor and DVD Studio Pro for the SD DVD release. "The glass masters were made straight from the output of DVD Studio Pro," he says.

"The film has actually caused a small problem," he says. "People now come in to Van Nuys Airport from the East Coast for no other reason than to enter into their logbook that they landed on runway One Six Right. And if they get diverted to One Six Left, a parallel runway, they refuse to land. They go around, enter the traffic pattern, and come back until they get their clearance."

For more information, see www.onesixright.com. This profile includes excerpts from "Runway Romance," by Joe Cellini, copyright Apple, Inc.

Sound Editing

4

Lesson Files — Lesson Files > Lesson 04 > SoundEditing.fcp

Media — One Six Right and Golfer

Time — This lesson takes approximately 75 minutes to complete.

Goals

- Sweeten dialogue to improve clarity and tone
- Use normalization to automate level settings
- Control dynamic range using compression
- Reduce noise using Soundtrack Pro
- Perform equalization to finesse frequency levels
- Remove hums caused by electrical interference
- Add ambiance and sound effects to bring a scene to life
- Perform subframe audio adjustments
- Integrate music into your sequence

Lesson 4

Sound Editing

Although working with audio employs many of the same tools you use when cutting video, it requires a very different mindset. Aside from the obvious difference of focusing on hearing instead of vision, sound carries a subtler element of the program than images. Sound conveys the emotional tone of a scene, whether it is through music or the inflection of spoken words. It can be said that if seeing is believing, then hearing is feeling.

Because of this fundamental difference, some people tend to excel at editing and mixing sound while others are perfect picture editors. Hollywood understands this and traditionally hired specialists to handle the sound editing tasks. However, increasingly, the picture editor is asked to do at least a large portion of the sound work herself. If you're put in this situation, understand that you will need to change your perspective to excel at sound editing and focus on feeling more than meaning.

Understanding the Sound Editing Process

Although some sound work is done in tandem with the video edit—such as finessing timing or splitting edits—the bulk of sound editing tasks are generally deferred to the end of the process, after picture has been locked. Picture editing is an iterative task; you cut and review and cut and review, and continue refining and finessing the edit until everyone agrees that it's done (or that the air date is upon you). Cutting sound is much less amenable to repetitive tweaking. Each fade and filter is tied to a specific point in time, and trimming a clip by even a few frames can undermine the intended result of an effect.

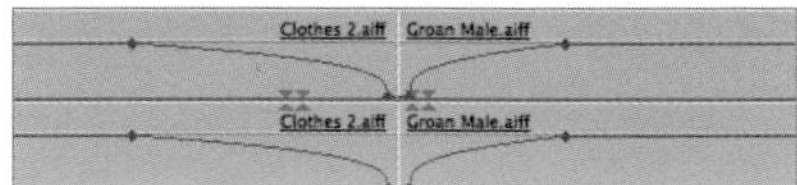

Fade before Trim

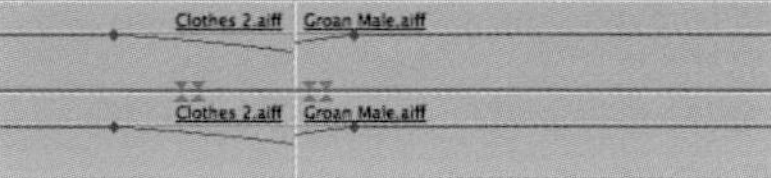

Fade after Trim

By delaying sound editing until the picture is finished, each sound clip can be faded, filtered, and mixed to perfection once and only once.

Sound elements generally are divided into three categories: dialogue, effects, and music. Working with each requires different techniques and different tools. This chapter takes you through each of these categories and teaches you the essential tasks required to make the best use of them.

Cleaning Dialogue

Dialogue is any spoken language used in your program, including interviews, narration, singing, and character dialogue. With rare exceptions, dialogue is meant to be clearly heard and understood by the listener. Unfortunately, the realities of production often result in poorly recorded dialogue that must be cleaned, or *sweetened*, to improve its clarity.

Final Cut Pro and Soundtrack Pro provide a wealth of tools specifically designed to address common dialogue problems. Mastering these tools can help you create better-sounding audio.

It may be helpful to review the basic components of sound before delving into details about how to adjust them. Think of an audio signal as a specific frequency transmitted at a specific amplitude. In more common parlance, this means a given *pitch* at a certain *volume*. This is important to understand because when you are adjusting audio, you are typically adjusting the frequency or the amplitude (or a combination of the two). If you can identify an issue as a frequency problem or an amplitude problem, you'll likely resolve it more quickly.

Normalizing Audio

You make amplitude adjustments all the time by adjusting the volume (or *gain)* of an audio clip. Such adjustments modify the level uniformly across the entire clip. *Boosting* the volume makes a sound louder, but if you go too far, the loudest sections will distort, or *clip*. *Attenuating* quiets the sound, but when overdone, the quietest audio may become inaudible.

Deciding how much to adjust a clip's level can be tricky. First of all, some pitches can seem louder than others—even at equal gain settings—and original recording conditions can vary enormously, so each track may need individual settings.

Normalization is an automated process that adjusts a clip's gain so that its loudest points are at their maximum volume without clipping. This may require either boosting or attenuating the signal. Normalization is a way to quickly create a relatively uniform volume level across a range of clips (provided that they were all recorded in similar environments).

1 Open Lesson Files > Lesson 04 > **SoundEditing.fcp**.

   This sequence uses footage from *One Six Right,* director Brian J. Terwilliger's documentary about the Van Nuys Airport (www.onesixright.com).

2 Play the first few clips of the *1. Normalize* sequence.

Pay particular attention to the levels in the audio meters. You'll notice that the average level of the first two clips is about –32 dB, and the loudest point hits about –26 (where he says "realization").

3 Position your playhead over the first clip in the sequence.

4 Choose Modify > Audio > Apply Normalization Gain.

The Apply Normalization Gain window appears.

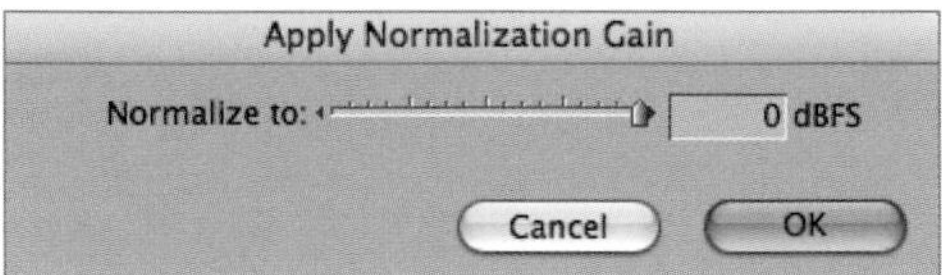

Setting this to 0 dBFS (decibels full scale) attempts to place the loudest point in your clip at maximum volume without distorting. However, because sound waves are so variable, it is very difficult to guarantee that some brief peaks won't break the barrier and create pops or clipping. For this reason, it is much safer to lower the slider by a few decibels.

5 Set the Normalize slider to –8 and click OK.

6 Play the sequence again and observe the audio meter.

Now, the whole clip plays much louder.

7 Double-click the first clip (**HD-96 1 6**) and, in the Viewer, click the Filters tab.

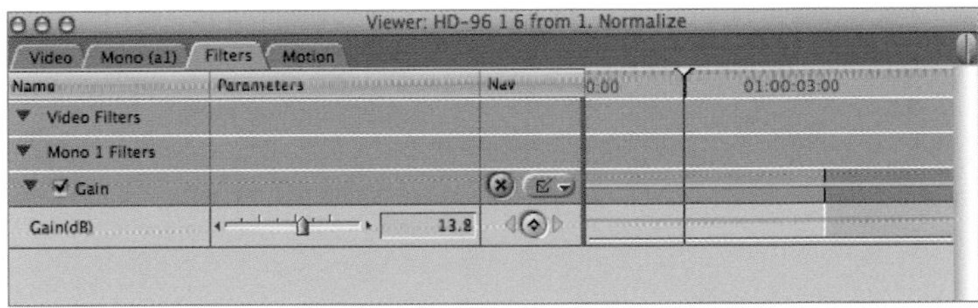

When you add normalization gain, a Gain filter is automatically applied to the clip, and Final Cut Pro calculates the proper setting to achieve normalization. Adding normalization gain to a clip with the Gain filter already applied does not add a new filter, it simply resets the filter's settings to create a new normalization goal.

Because the setting is applied as a filter, you can still use the level controls to remove a pop, create a fade-in or fade-out, or further modify the overall volume level of the clip. You can also remove the normalization by removing the filter.

8 In the Filters tab, select the Gain filter and press Delete.

The clip is returned to its original state.

Normalizing a Group of Clips

In the real world, normalization is typically performed on a group of clips to create a seemingly uniform volume, regardless of discrepancies in the individual shots.

1. Play the whole sequence, paying special attention to the audio levels.
2. Press Command-A to select all of the clips, then choose Modify > Audio > Apply Normalization Gain.
3. Set the slider to –12 and click OK.
4. Play the sequence.

   Now the levels have been unified to a typical dialogue level.

   NOTE ► See Lesson 5, "Sound Mixing" for more information on volume settings.

Controlling Dynamic Range

Because most clips contain a variety of loud and soft sections, simple level adjustments such as normalization are sometimes inadequate to achieve your desired goals. The difference between a clip's quietest audio level and its peak level is called *dynamic range*. A clip with a wide dynamic range has both very quiet and very loud parts. A clip with more limited, narrower dynamic range plays at a largely uniform volume.

A wide dynamic range can intensify the emotional impact of a scene, but too much dynamic range can make it difficult to set a proper audio level. For example, imagine a shot where someone intermittently whispers quietly and yells loudly. If you set the level high enough to hear the whispers, the yelling will peak and distort. If you lower the level so the screams aren't too loud, the whispers become inaudible.

Fortunately, you can *compress* the dynamic range and bring the level of the peak closer to the average level of the clip.

1. Open the *2. Compression* sequence and play it.

   This sequence repeats the same clip three times. The first version is unadulterated, the second has been normalized, and the third will be used to demonstrate the Final Cut Pro Compressor/Limiter filter.

2. Select the third clip and choose Effects > Audio Filters > Final Cut Pro > Compressor/Limiter.

3. Double-click the clip to open it into the Viewer, and click the Filters tab.

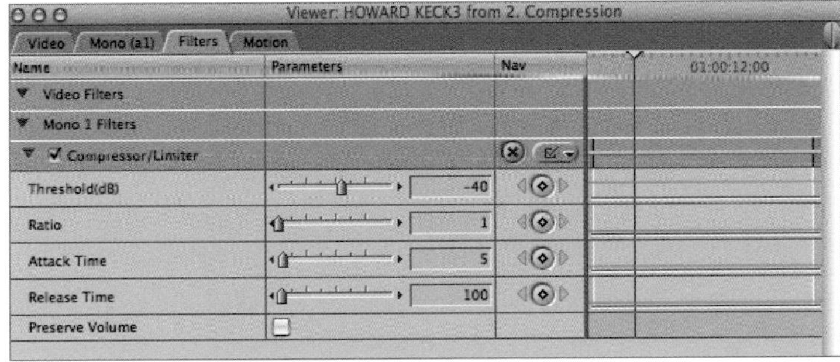

   To compress the dynamic range, you must define the target maximum level using the Threshold(dB) slider and define how aggressively the area above that level is reduced using the Ratio slider. The other two sliders—Attack Time and Release Time—affect how quickly the effect is applied and removed. You can ignore them for now.

   The best way to apply Final Cut Pro audio filters is to adjust them while looping playback, so you can hear in real time how the filter changes affect the clip.

4. In the Timeline, position the playhead over the third clip, then press X to mark the clip (setting an In point at its beginning and an Out point at its end).

5 Choose View > Loop Playback (or press Control-L).

6 Press Shift-\ (backslash) to Play In to Out.

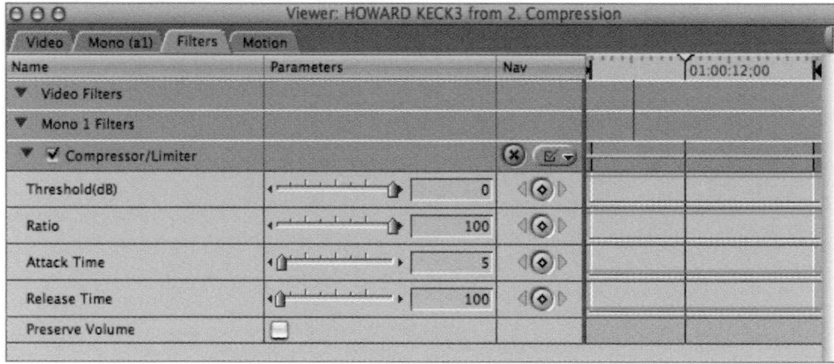

7 In the Filters tab in the Viewer, raise Threshold(dB) to 0 dB and Ratio to 100.

By setting Ratio at its highest value, the effect of the filter will be plainly apparent, but not until you lower Threshold(dB) to the level of the actual audio in the clip.

If you look at the audio meters while the clip plays, you can see that the average level is around –30 dB, but some of the quieter words are as low as –40 dB, and some of the loudest are as high as –23 dB.

Your goal is to reduce that dynamic range using the Compressor filter so that the quietest and loudest parts all occur at roughly the same level. This is done by attenuating the loud parts until they are the same volume as the quiet parts. Once that's done, you can raise the overall level to whatever volume you prefer.

8 Lower the Threshold(dB) slider slowly and listen carefully.

You should begin to hear an effect when you near –30 dB. The further you go, the quieter the whole clip seems to be. If you watch the audio meters, you can see the dynamic range being reduced.

9 Set Threshold(dB) to approximately –42 dB.

10 Lower Ratio to 1.

At a ratio of 1, the filter has no effect, but you can raise it slowly until you achieve your desired effect.

11 Select the Preserve Volume checkbox.

When this checkbox is enabled, the clip level is gained up to compensate for the amount of applied compression. The result is that the more compression you apply, the louder the clip.

12 Drag the slider to slowly raise Ratio from 1 to 4.

You can now hear how significantly the compression is affecting the clip.

13 Set Ratio to 2.

14 Play the entire sequence.

The difference between the second and third clips may seem subtle at first, but it is very significant. Watch the meters as the clips play. In the second clip, the level ranges from –24 to –6; in the third clip, it ranges from –18 to –12. Although the clips appear to have a similar "loudness," the second clip is much closer to peaking. If you added some music or sound effects, it would be nearly impossible to avoid some spikes that would clip and distort.

Separating Signal from Noise

Another basic sound concept is the difference between signal and noise–that is, the distinction between the recorded sounds you *want* people to hear and the extraneous elements that were accidentally recorded. In a dialogue track, the signal is obviously the voice, and the noise is any sound other than the voice. This could be environmental noise, such as traffic or an air conditioner, or it could be people talking or clanking dishes in the café where your interview was recorded.

Ideally, the signal is significantly louder than the noise, but sometimes poor recording technique will leave you with a track that contains similar volume levels for both signal and noise.

If the noise is isolated to audio frequencies that don't overlap much of the signal, you can attenuate the unwanted frequencies, rendering the desired frequencies easier to hear (see "Removing Hums" later in this lesson). If, however, both signal and noise span across the frequency spectrum (the most common scenario), you need to use a tool such as a noise gate.

A noise gate attenuates sections in which the audio is relatively quiet, such as the moments between your talent's words or sentences when the background noise can be heard. The result is a reduction in noise level that leaves the signal unaffected. This is, in effect, the opposite of a compressor, and, in fact, this type of filter is often called an *expander*. Final Cut Pro has an Expander/Noise Gate filter that can accomplish this effect, but if you're willing to venture into Soundtrack Pro, there are several additional expanders, including a specialized feature just to remove unwanted noise.

1 Open and play the *3. Background Noise* sequence.

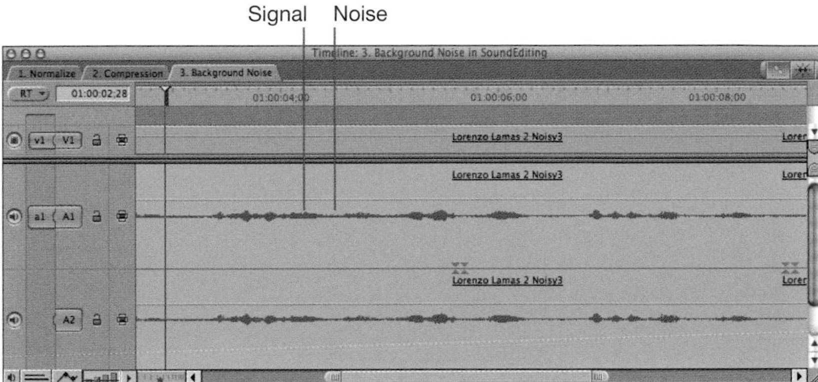

This clip obviously has quite a bit of background noise that is reducing the clarity of the interview subject's dialogue. You can even see this in the waveforms.

2 Select the clip and choose File > Send To > Soundtrack Pro Audio File Project.

A dialog appears, asking for a new filename.

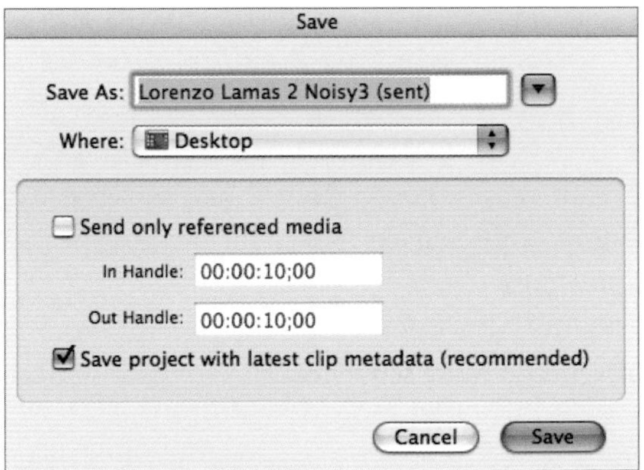

For this exercise, you can save the file to the desktop, but in the real world, you would want to save this file to your Final Cut Pro Documents folder or wherever you store Final Cut Pro project files.

3 Keep the default clip name and checkbox settings and click OK.

NOTE ► This procedure enables you to keep the audio from the original clip unchanged and use Soundtrack Pro to modify a duplicate copy that you are naming and saving here. Final Cut Pro will automatically put this new, modified version of the clip and its audio into your sequence when you return from Soundtrack Pro.

When you click OK, Soundtrack Pro opens automatically with the selected clip loaded into a new project. Soundtrack Pro has a variety of tools that remove background noise, but the noise reduction feature yields the best results with the least effort. To use this feature, you will specify a *noise print,* a section of audio used to identify the frequency and amplitude of the offending sounds and then use the Reduce Noise command to control how much noise to eliminate.

4 Drag the mouse in the green area of the clip display to select a portion of the audio where the waveform appears basically flat.

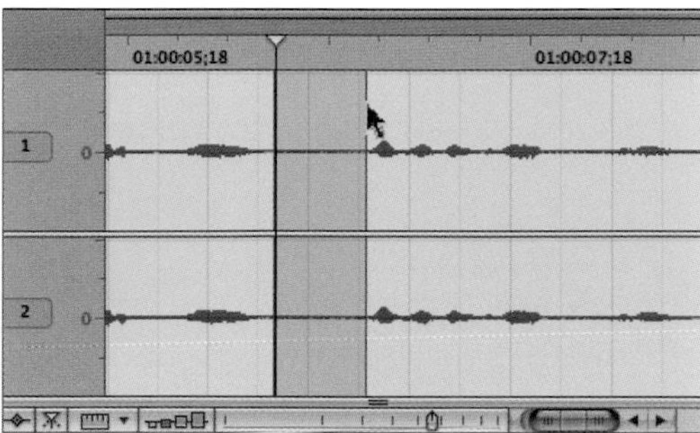

The longer the section you choose as a noise print, the more effective noise reduction will be. Near the end of the clip, there is a good section to use.

5 Press the Spacebar to play the selected section.

By default, the playback will loop. Make sure you have not accidentally selected part of a word. When you are sure you have selected only the background noise, press the Spacebar to stop the looping playback.

6 Choose Process > Noise Reduction > Set Noise Print.

7 Click anywhere in the green area of the audio clip to deselect the section of the clip.

This allows you to apply the noise reduction to the entire clip. If you made a different selection before step 8, you would be applying the noise reduction only to that new selection.

8 Choose Process > Noise Reduction > Reduce Noise.

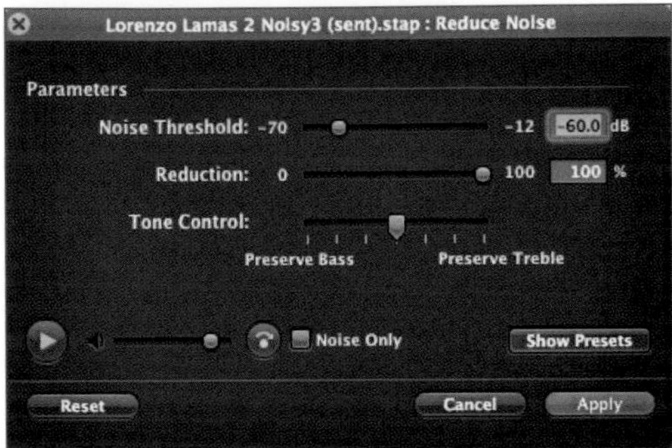

The Reduce Noise window appears. This works similarly to the Compressor filter in Final Cut Pro. The Noise Threshold setting identifies the peak volume level of the noise. The Reduction slider determines how much to attenuate that noise. The Tone Control allows for a small degree of frequency adjustment.

9 Click the Preview Play/Pause button and adjust the volume slider to a comfortable level.

10 Drag the Reduction slider all the way to 100%.

This allows you to easily hear the results of the effect.

11 Select the Noise Only checkbox to hear only the sound you are eliminating.

Selecting this checkbox can be very helpful to ensure you are not accidentally removing too much of the signal along with the noise.

12 Deselect the checkbox again to turn off Noise Only.

13 Adjust the Noise Threshold slider until you can hear the effect of the filter, then back it off slightly and begin to adjust the Reduction slider.

14 When you are happy with the results, click Apply.

Remember, the goal is not to remove all background noise, but to improve the clarity of the signal by reducing the noise. Also note that noise reduction works quite well on some clips and not so well on others. If the signal-to-noise ratio is too low (that is, the signal and noise are at similar volumes, and/or the signal and noise frequencies are very similar) you may not be able to eliminate the noise. In those cases, your best course of action is to re-record the track.

15 Press Command-S to save your work.

16 Choose File > Close Project.

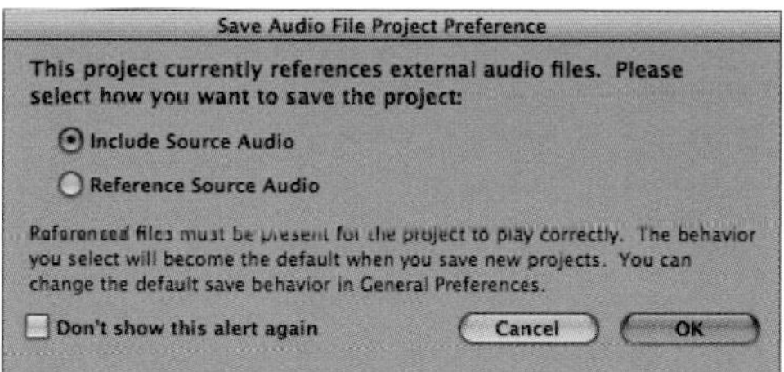

The Save Audio File Project Preference dialog appears, asking whether you want to embed the audio file into the Soundtrack Pro document, or to reference the original clip.

17 Select Include Source Audio, and click OK.

When you return to Final Cut Pro, the audio will be updated automatically.

Controlling Audio Frequencies

Almost everyone has some experience modifying audio frequencies on home or car stereos using an *equalizer* (EQ) or just a tone knob. If the low frequencies (or *bass*) are too loud, the thumping vibrations can overpower the more delicate high frequencies (or *treble*). On the other hand, if the treble is too loud, the sound can be piercing or "tinny." Most audio sounds best when the frequencies have been balanced or equalized. This is done by boosting or attenuating the frequency levels individually.

The most familiar tool for adjusting audio frequencies is a 3-band EQ, which lets you independently control the high, mid, and low frequencies. Adding more "bands" or control points allows more customized shaping of the sound.

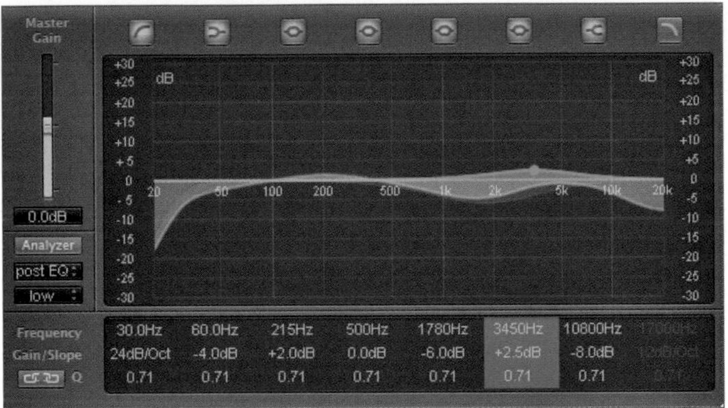

The Soundtrack Pro Channel EQ

TIP Because audio mixing is additive, it is generally better to attenuate the frequencies you don't want rather than boost the ones you do.

1 In Final Cut Pro, open and play the *4. Equalization* sequence.

   This is a typical audio track that can be improved with some minor EQ work. Final Cut Pro has a few equalization filters, but those in Soundtrack Pro have more intuitive interfaces.

2 Select the clip and choose File > Send To > Soundtrack Pro Audio File Project.

3 Save the new audio file to the destination of your choice.

4 In Soundtrack Pro, choose Process > Effects > EQ > Channel EQ.

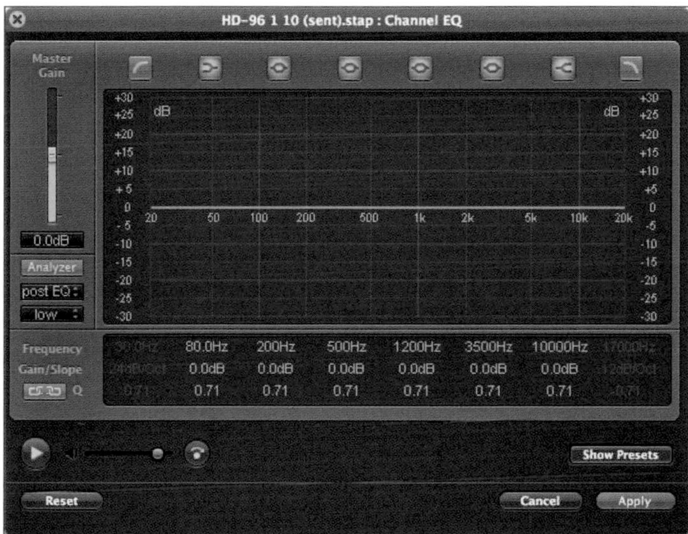

The Channel EQ window opens.

The horizontal scale represents frequency, and the vertical scale represents the amplitude. To equalize your sound, simply click the horizontal frequency line and drag it up or down.

5 Click the Play button so you can preview your changes in real time, then experiment with changes to the equalization graph.

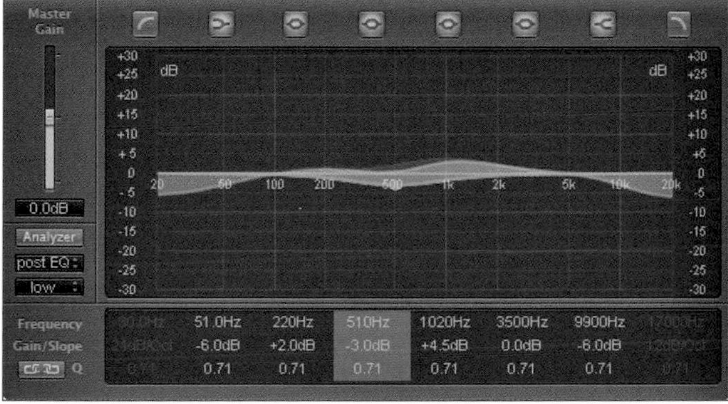

There are no "correct" settings. This figure represents one possible approach.

Correcting Highs and Lows

One of the other common frequency-related tasks is the elimination of very low or very high frequencies to remove a low rumbling from poor mic handling or the high whining sound of mic feedback.

A High Pass filter eliminates the lower frequencies, allowing everything above a designated pitch to *pass through* unaltered. A Low Pass filter does the opposite, removing sounds above a specified frequency.

Both Final Cut Pro and Soundtrack Pro have pass filters; however, there are also roll-off buttons built into the Channel EQ that perform a similar service by adding a steep reduction of the lowest and highest frequencies.

1 Click the Bass Roll-off button.

The low frequencies are eliminated from the clip.

2 Click Apply to add the effect to the clip, then save and close the project to return to Final Cut Pro.

Removing Hums

Some noise doesn't fit so neatly at the top or bottom of the frequency spectrum. For example, the hum introduced by electrical interference has a very specific frequency based on the rate of the alternating current. In the United States, the interference manifests as a 60-Hz hum.

To eliminate this sort of noise, you can employ a parametric equalizer, which boosts or attenuates frequencies within a definable and graduated range.

Because that 60-cycle hum is so common, Final Cut Pro has a filter specifically designed to remove it.

1 Open and play the *5. Hum* sequence.

   That familiar noise is impossible to miss.

2 With the playhead anywhere over the clip, choose Effects > Audio Filters > Final Cut Pro > Hum Remover.

3 Double-click the clip to open it into the Viewer and click the Filters tab.

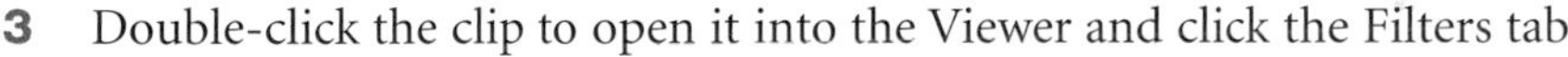

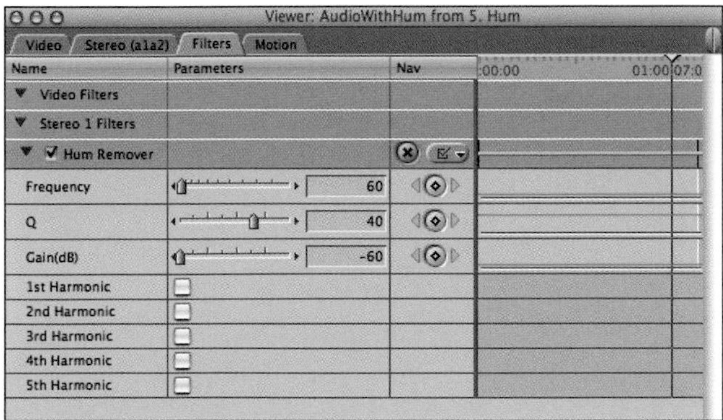

4 Press Shift-\ (backslash) to Play In to Out.

   Although the filter is applied, you can still hear the hum because in addition to the noise at 60 Hz, you can hear its *harmonics* (other frequencies that resonate along with the offending sound).

5 Experiment with selecting and deselecting the harmonic checkboxes.

You'll find that more than one combination of selections will remove the hum. Depending on the clip you're trying to fix, you may not want to remove certain harmonics.

Although this filter is designed to remove the hum commonly caused by electrical interference, other narrow-frequency noise can be removed exactly the same way. The hum filter is really just a notch filter (an equalizer targeting a single frequency range) preset to 60 Hz. You can change the particular narrow-frequency band by changing the Frequency setting of this filter, or by employing a generic notch filter or parametric EQ in Final Cut Pro or Soundtrack Pro.

Integrating Sound Effects

One of the signature aspects of professional filmmaking is the painstaking attention paid to the sound. Amateur editors often don't realize that the audio recorded on the set is only a starting point. Production microphones are specifically engineered to record human voices, and the directional shotgun mics and close-mounted lavalier mics do very little to record any of the other complex elements—such as footsteps, hand props, and ambient noise—that comprise the environmental sound of the scene.

Proper sound design requires reconstructing all of these elements and even adding sounds that weren't there at all. Almost everything that moves on screen requires a corresponding sound element. This includes titles and graphics, as well as objects and actions within a shot. In the real world, almost nothing that moves is silent (and if it does, it scares us!) If a car drives by outside the window, a failure to include its sound will subtly pull your audience out of the story.

Sound design is a very important creative task; the sounds you choose can have an extraordinary impact on the feelings a scene evokes. For example, putting the sounds of children playing behind an interview subject can give a subtle cue to the audience that he is friendly and active in the community. Replacing that background sound with the deep hum of a walk-in freezer will make him seem less friendly and less connected to the world around him.

And this brings up an important point. Sound design is not reserved just for narrative, dramatic films. Documentaries, corporate training videos, even wedding videos are immeasurably improved by thoughtful sound design.

1 Open and play the 6. *Sound Effects* sequence.

   You will bring this scene to life by adding a variety of sound effects. The first task is to identify where sound elements should be added. This process is called *spotting*.

2 Play the sequence again, and think about what sounds could be added.

3 While the sequence plays, press M to add markers wherever a sound might go.

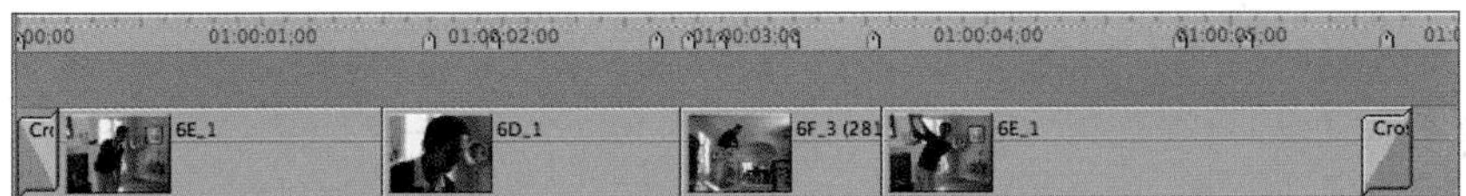

   Obviously, the impact of the golf club hitting a golf ball needs a sound, but there is quite a bit more to be added. As the sequence opens, the man rubs his hands on the golf club grip, and rocks his legs back and forth; during the swing, his clothes move; at the end of the swing, his foot scuffs the ground; and then, of course, he walks away.

   Every one of those elements needs a sound effect to make the scene feel truly real. Final Cut Studio comes with a huge library of sound effects for this purpose. You can browse and preview those sound effects in Soundtrack Pro, but to save time, you'll find a group of them already imported into a bin in the project.

Constructing Ambiances

In the world of sound effects, it is very common to combine multiple sounds to create a single "effect," or, in this case, an ambiance. One trick to combining ambient sounds is to pay attention to the frequencies used in each element. If too many sounds use the same frequencies, the result will sound muddy and vague. If, however, you combine some low-frequency sounds with some highs, both will be clearly audible and the sound will feel more defined.

1 In the Browser, expand the Golf Sounds bin.

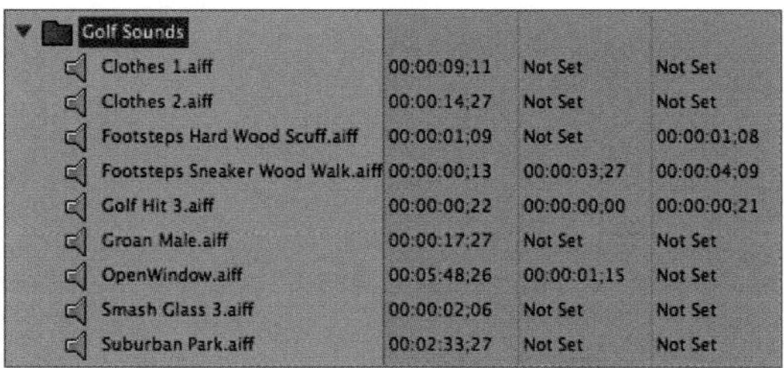

This bin contains all of the sounds used in this project. In addition to the clothes, footsteps, and golf hit, there are some tracks that can serve as an ambiance track.

2 Open and play **OpenWindow**.

3 Set an In point anywhere after the initial fade-in has completed (about 2 seconds in).

4 In the Timeline, set the a1 audio target track to track A3.

5 Press End to bring the playhead to the end of the sequence, then press O to set an Out point.

6 Press Home to move to the head of the sequence, then press F10 to overwrite the ambiance track into the sequence.

Although this element helps to establish the environment, there's room for improvement. It sounds more natural than absolute silence, but because it is so constant, it doesn't give much sense of place or texture.

The **OpenWindow** sound has a nice mid-to-low frequency hum to it (along with a higher-frequency hiss that you may or may not decide to remove using a Low Pass filter). To add something without muddying the sound, it would have to either be very low-pitched or very high-pitched.

7 Open and play **Suburban Park.aiff.**

This sound provides more of a sense of place and time of day (there are birds singing, not crickets chirping) and, conveniently, those bird sounds are high-pitched and won't compete with the audio frequencies in the **OpenWindow** shot.

8 In the Timeline, set the a1 target to track A4 and the a2 target to track to A5.

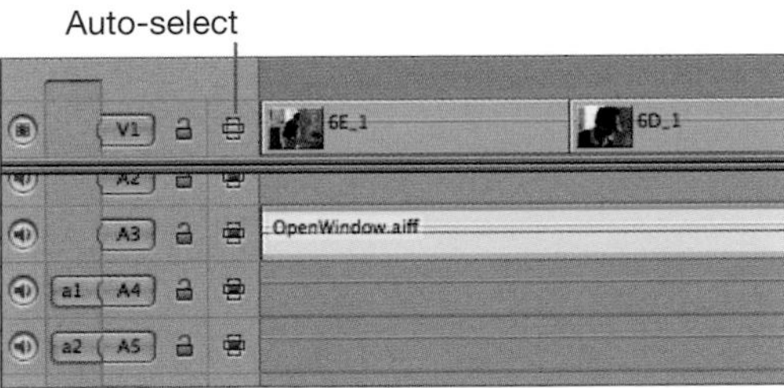

9 Click the Auto Select control for track V1 to disable it.

10 With the playhead positioned anywhere over **OpenWindow**, press X to set In and Out points at the head and tail of the clip.

11 Press F10 to edit the **Suburban Park** clip onto tracks A4 and A5.

12 Play the sequence.

The birds add a nice touch, but those chirps at the end are overpoweringly loud. We don't want to suggest that our golfer has a sparrow caged in his living room. It would be better if we could find a section of the bird track without those loud chirps.

13 In the Timeline, double-click the **Suburban Park.aiff** clip to open it into the Viewer.

Be sure you see the sprocket holes in the Viewer scrubber area to confirm that you are editing the version from the sequence.

14 Press Shift-Z to zoom the entire length of the **Suburban Park** clip to fit in the Viewer.

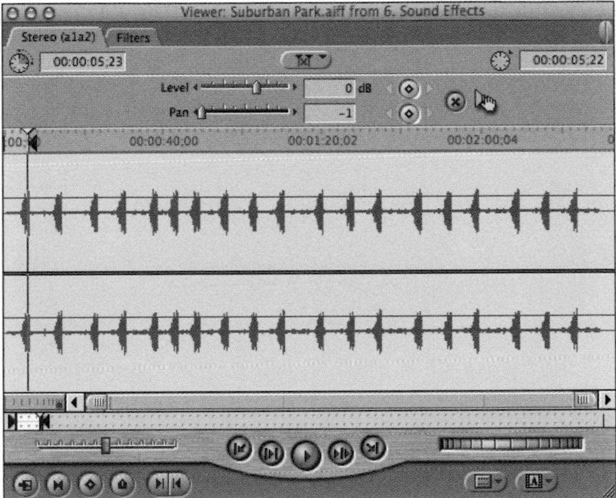

The waveform clearly shows where the loud chirps appear. If you have any doubt, play the clip and watch the playhead move through the waveform.

15 Shift-drag the Out point until the In and Out points are safely located between loud chirps (after the second chirp and before the third).

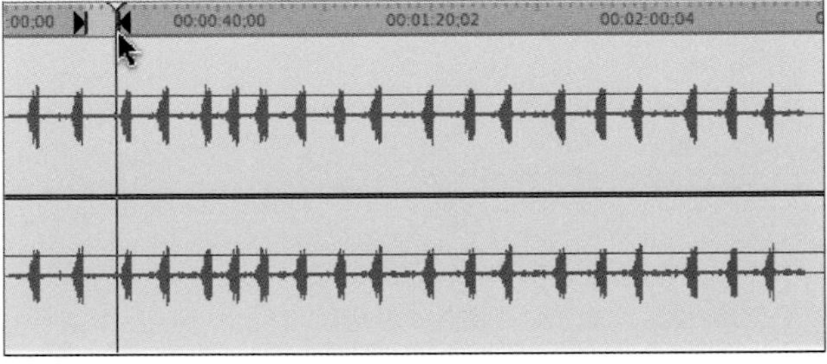

Holding down Shift locks the In and Out points together, allowing you to perform a slip edit, just as you would when using Slip tool in the Timeline.

16 Play the sequence to hear how your ambiance is taking shape.

Of course, it will be critical to set the relative levels of these two clips, but as long as they're not overpowering now, you can defer that task until the rest of the sound effects have been laid in.

Editing Subframe Audio

The next step is to add the sound of the golf club hitting the ball. Such a task is often as simple as dropping in a sound effect that lines up with the correct frame in the sequence, but sometimes a sound may not line up precisely at the start of a frame.

1 Open and play **Golf Hit 3.aiff.**

If you zoom in, and position your playhead over the moment of impact, you'll see that the actual sound occurs midway through the frame.

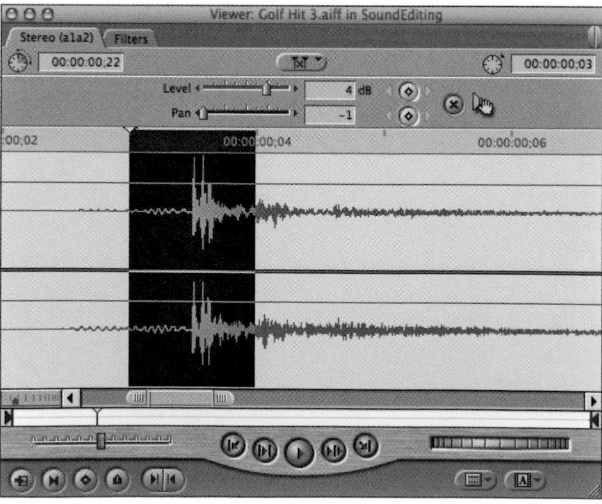

Sound is recorded in much finer gradations than video frames. There may be as many as 800 to 2,000 sound samples for each frame of video. Final Cut Pro allows you to make audio adjustments down to 1/100th of a frame.

2 Shift-drag the playhead until the beginning of the playhead lines up precisely with the initial impact of the sound.

Now the sound begins precisely at the start of the frame.

Holding down Shift allows you to override the frame boundaries and establish a new beginning for your frames. However, in order to lock the playhead into this new position, you must mark a new In point.

3 Press I to mark a new In point.

After you set this In point, each surrounding frame will adjust itself to match, so each frame still has a constant duration. You can clear the In point now so that you can use the few frames of buildup sounds.

4 Press Option-I to clear the In point.

5 In the Timeline, position the playhead on the precise frame where the club appears to hit the ball (at approximately 02:27).

6 In the Viewer, click the Add Marker button to place a marker on the frame where the sound begins.

7 Drag the **Golf Hit 3** clip into the Timeline to tracks 6 and 7 (using the drag handle in the upper-right corner of the Viewer window). Align the marker with the playhead position.

NOTE ► You may need to toggle off snapping by pressing N.

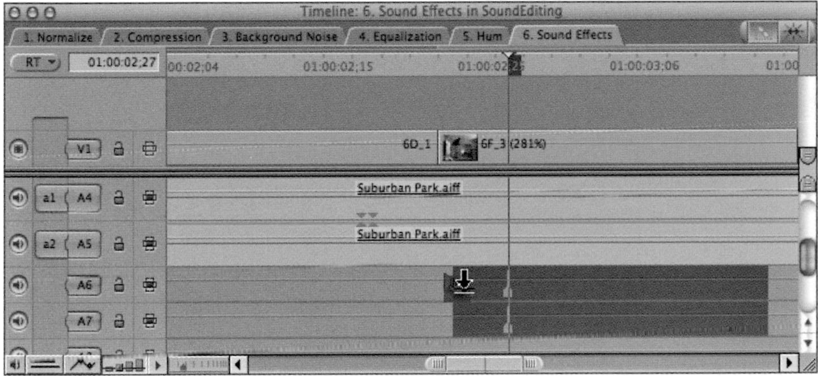

8 Press \ (backslash) to play around the edit.

TIP In the Timeline, you can use clip markers as snap points by directly clicking the marker when you select the clip. However, when dragging a clip from the Viewer into the Timeline, markers will not behave as snap points.

Sound effects such as the footsteps at the end of the sequence also can be dropped in using this technique. You will probably have to mark each footfall individually, and you should be thankful there's only two. Because of the wide variance in footwear, ground surface, and gait, it is actually quite rare to use pre-recorded footsteps. It is much more common to record new footsteps timed precisely to the video playback. This process is called *foley*.

Enhancing the Scene

For "extra credit," take a few minutes to lay in the remainder of the sound effects. Be aware, however, that the hard part (and, some would say, the fun part) of the job has already been done for you. Choosing the sounds from your own library is where the creative aspect of sound design really occurs.

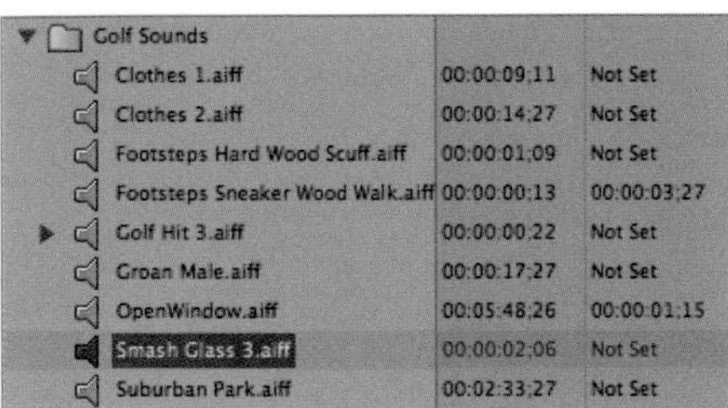

You may notice that the Sound Effects bin contains a breaking glass effect. If you are wondering why, think about the content of the scene. Here is a guy driving a golf ball inside his house. You have to ask yourself, where is that ball going to go? Sometimes the sound effects you add contribute story elements that are not otherwise apparent in the shot. Sound is nearly always just as vital to your story as the images.

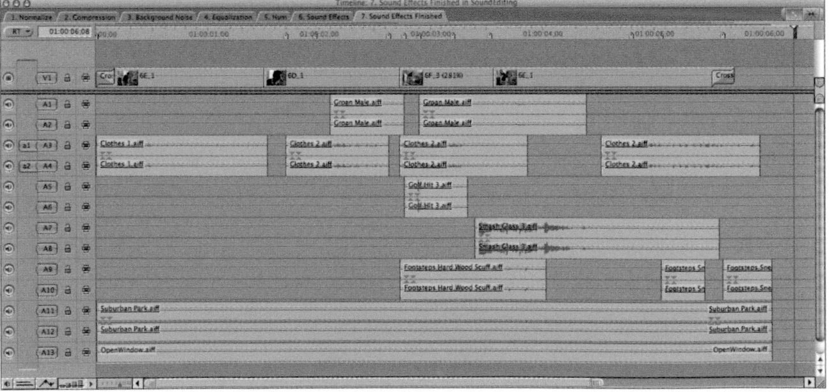

To examine one possible finished version of the scene, open and play the *7. Sound Effects Finished* sequence.

Adding Music

Music has incredible power to add emotion to a scene. But it's not a cure-all. First of all, smothering a scene with music should never be done *instead* of the dialogue and sound effects work described previously. Music should always be added after the other stages are complete. You may be surprised that plenty of scenes need no music, or very little.

Second, music can wield a very broad brush. Although the right music can bring emotional aspects of a scene to the fore, the wrong music can alienate and confuse your audience. Using clichéd music to evoke suspense, or sadness, or triumph may offer an immediate sense of clarity about the dramatic tone of a scene, but the cliché quickly wears thin and your audience will disengage from the story. Good music, like a well-written character, is complex and subtle and unique.

Finally, it is imperative that your music supports the story, and not the other way around. If a scene doesn't seem to work when you mute the music track, it probably needs to be recut (or removed entirely). If your story is taking a backseat to the music, then what you have is a music video, and the artistic credit should go to the musicians, not the filmmakers.

Having said that, music is amazingly powerful, and when used appropriately, it can be an incomparable element of the overall work.

1 Open and play the *8. Look Ma* sequence.

   This scene desperately needs music to glue together the interviews and make it feel complete.

2 Expand the Look Ma music bin in the Browser, then open and play the **Two Maidens Holding Pearls** clip.

   The sequence already has In and Out points set.

3 Press F10 or drag the audio drag handle onto the Overwrite Edit Overlay in the Canvas.

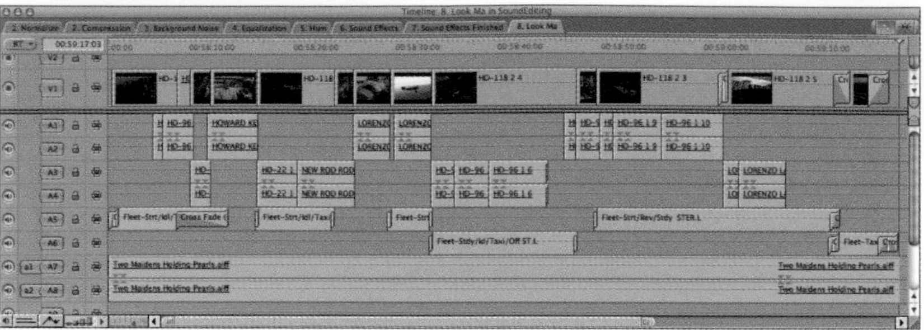

The clip is laid in on the target tracks.

4 Play the sequence.

The music works for a while, but it does get a little repetitive. Plus, the scene changes tone midway through: The interviewees begin by talking about how overwhelming a pilot's first solo flight can be, but then they describe the moment of epiphany every pilot goes through. This is exactly the sort of emotional change in a story that music can subtly reinforce.

5 Mark an In point just after the man says, "It's up to you," (around 58:39).

6 From the Look Ma Music bin, open and play **Red Plane**.

7 In the Viewer, mark an In point just as the piano melody begins (around 26:10).

8 Press F10 to overwrite the clip into the sequence.

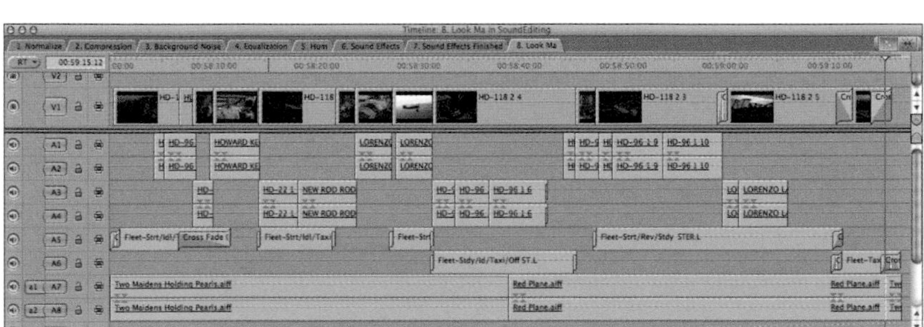

9 Play around the edit.

Well, it sounds fairly ridiculous as a straight cut, but a crossfade will smooth it out nicely.

10 Control-click the edit between the two music clips and choose Add Transition 'Cross Fade (+3 dB)' from the shortcut menu.

Unfortunately, the crossfade undermines the sense of transformation conveyed by the beginning of the piano. This is partly because the piano is still fading in at the cue point.

11 Control-click the Transition and choose Transition Alignment > End On Edit from the shortcut menu.

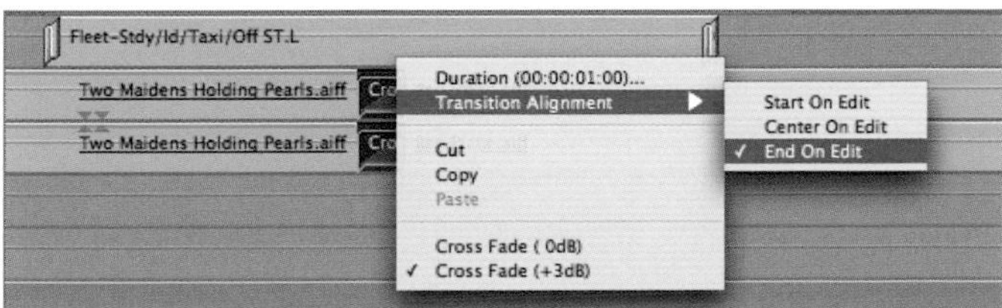

This ensures that the transition is complete before the melody kicks in. However, the transition is still too blatant because it is too short.

12 Drag the left edge of the transition by about 7 seconds until it lines up approximately with the beginning of the dialogue (visible on tracks 3 and 4).

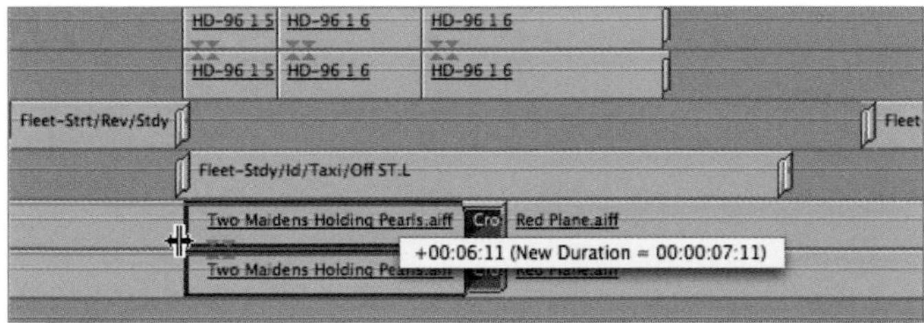

13 Play across the transition.

This is a vast improvement, allowing the musical transition to support and reinforce the transition occurring in the narration. The melody kicks in right on cue, and the guitar fade-out doesn't draw undue attention to itself.

14 Play the entire sequence.

Everything works except for a small problem at the end.

15 Delete the piece of **Two Maidens Holding Pearls** at the end of the sequence.

Of course, your work isn't done. There's still the essential work of setting all the levels for all of the sound elements in your program. That process is covered in Lesson 5, "Sound Mixing."

Lesson Review

1. What is normalization?
2. How can you remove the normalize effect?
3. What is dynamic range?
4. What does compression do?
5. Does compression make a clip louder or softer?
6. What is a noise print?
7. What does an equalizer do?
8. Does a High Pass filter remove or preserve the high frequencies?
9. How do you change an audio clip's frame boundaries?
10. Why would you want to change a clip's frame boundaries?

Answers

1. An automatic level adjustment designed to maximize volume without clipping.
2. Delete the Gain filter from the clip.
3. The difference between a clip's lowest level and its peak level.
4. Attenuates the loudest portions to reduce dynamic range.
5. Compression makes a clip louder only when the Preserve Volume setting is enabled.
6. In Soundtrack Pro, the noise print identifies and samples the area of your track considered "noise."
7. An EQ allows different frequency bands to be boosted or attenuated independently.
8. A High Pass filter preserves frequencies *above* a designated frequency threshold.
9. Shift-drag the playhead in the viewer's Audio tab.
10. To adjust audio timing at the subframe level.

5

n Files	Lesson Files > Lesson 05 > SoundMixing.fcp
Media	One Six Right
Time	This lesson takes approximately 120 minutes to complete.
Goals	Complete a full audio mix in Final Cut Pro
	Smooth edits using a variety of fade methods
	Adjust audio levels across multiple clips
	Record keyframes live using automation
	Create perspective effects using level and pan
	Export multitrack mixes to Soundtrack Pro

Lesson **5**

Sound Mixing

After sound is edited, the final task is creating the *mix* in which all the audio elements are combined and their volumes set to maximize the editor's control over the point of focus. Your choice of which sound elements are in the foreground and which are in the background is another essential storytelling tool that enables you to precisely guide an audience through the story.

Final Cut Pro contains a wide array of robust audio mixing tools—including an audio mix window, dynamic mute and solo controls, and full automation—that allow you to animate audio levels on-the-fly. In addition, it seamlessly integrates with the dedicated audio tool, Soundtrack Pro.

In Soundtrack Pro, you can complete your mix with even more control: *bussing* tracks to streamline filtering workflow, customizing audio fades, and creating mixes in surround sound. After your mix is complete, you can export it back to Final Cut Pro for final output.

Mixing in Final Cut Pro

For many shows, you may not need Soundtrack Pro. The sophisticated audio mixing tools in Final Cut Pro—both in the Timeline and in the Audio Mixer window—may be all you need to speed your workflow and execute every mixing decision.

Fading In and Out

A critical aspect of mixing is that every single audio clip in your sequence should begin with a fade-in and end with a fade-out, even if the fades are only a few frames long.

Hard-cutting an audio clip—any audio clip—can create unwanted audio interference, such as a pop or click. Often you may not hear anything wrong as you're creating the final mix; but such hard cuts may still rear their ugly heads (and tails) when the audio is compressed for DVD, the web, or portable playback devices.

Fortunately, adding fades can be quick and easy, especially if done at just the right stage: after all editing is completed, but before you create your main mix.

1. Open Lesson Files > Lesson 05 > **SoundMixing.fcp**.

   The *Audio Fades* sequence should already be open. This lesson uses footage from Brian J. Terwilliger's documentary, *One Six Right* (www.onesixright.com).

2. Play the sequence.

   Although there are no obvious errors, it is still advisable to smooth the head and tail of each clip, just in case. Begin working on the dialogue tracks.

3. On tracks A1 and A2, select the incoming edit of the first dialogue clip **HD-96 1 3.**

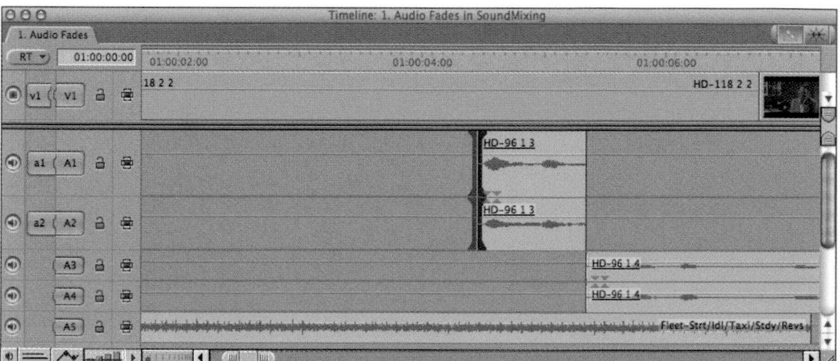

4 Press Command-Option-T to add the default audio transition (a +3 dB cross fade).

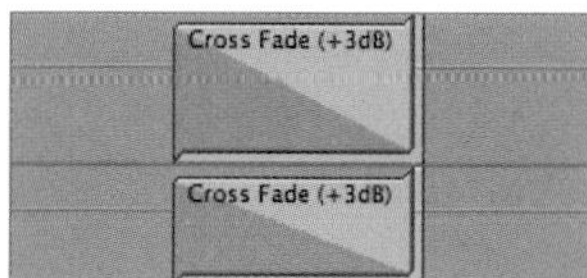

The cross fade transition is applied to the edit. In this case, the default duration is longer than the clip duration, so the transition covers the entire clip.

5 Double-click the transition.

The Duration dialog appears.

6 Type *4*. Press Tab, and then click OK.

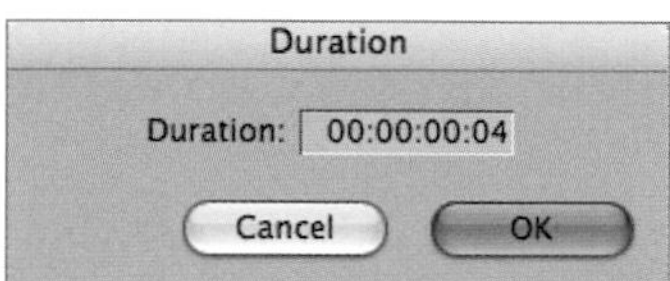

You've changed the length of the transition to four frames.

The default transition is the Cross Fade (+3dB), which is designed specifically for fading between two constant volume sources, such as music. This is sometimes referred to as a *constant power* cross fade because it slightly boosts the volume of both clips to prevent an audible dip in volume at the center point of the fade.

However, a constant power cross fade serves little benefit when fading to or from silence, and depending on the clip, can produce a more abrupt, less natural–sounding fade.

For fading to and from silence, Final Cut Pro offers an alternative: the Cross Fade (0dB), also known as a *constant gain* cross fade. This fades the two elements in a linear fashion.

TIP The enormous variety of sounds you will encounter means that the 0 dB and +3 dB cross fades can both be used in a wide range of scenarios. If you're ever in doubt, try them both and listen to the results.

7 Control-click the transition and choose Cross Fade (0dB) from the shortcut menu.

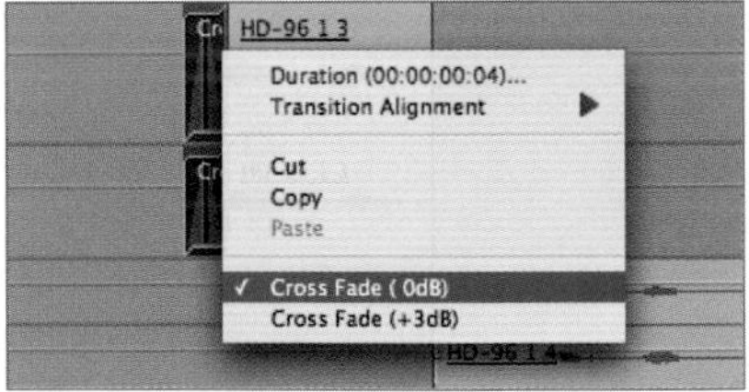

The transition is updated.

This short, 0 dB transition is very handy, and you may use it quite a bit while mixing your projects. So why not save a copy of it for repeated use?

8 Drag the transition to the Browser, and place it in the Favorites bin of the Effects tab.

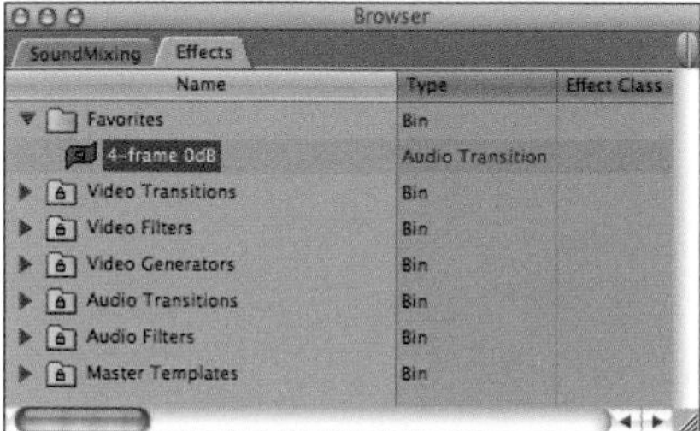

9 In the Browser, rename the transition *4-frame 0dB.*

You can make this new custom transition the default transition by Control-clicking it and choosing Make Default from the shortcut menu; but for this lesson, leave the default transition as it is.

10 In the Timeline, Option-drag the 4-frame transition to copy it from the head of the first clip to the end of the clip.

NOTE ▶ If you have difficulty copying the first transition, add a default transition to the second edit, change its duration to four frames, and then Option-drag it to each of the remaining edits.

11 Option-drag the transition again to add it to the beginning and end of each of the other clips on tracks A1 and A2 and on tracks A3 and A4.

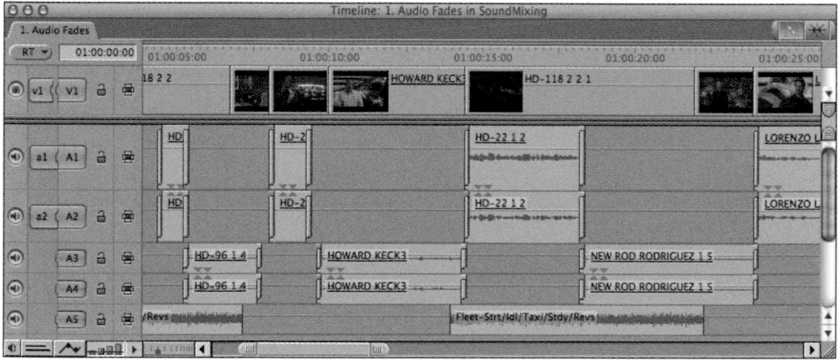

12 Play the sequence and listen for errors.

In some cases, even the 4-frame fade might cut off the beginning or end of the audio.

13 Navigate to around 8 seconds into the sequence and play around that edit.

The interview subject's line "You don't know when it's gonna happen" is cut off, so all you hear is "gonna hap."

14 Control-click the transition and choose Transition Alignment > Start on Edit from the shortcut menu.

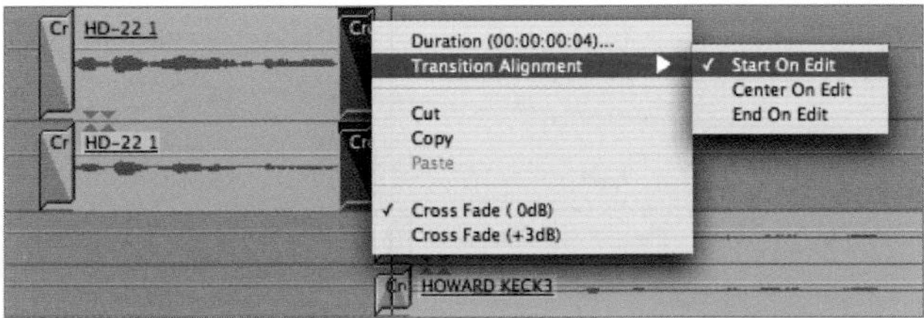

Beginning the transition on the end of an edit ensures that you'll retain all of the frames you meticulously included during the trimming process. Similarly, if a sound is cut off at the head of a clip, you would set the transition alignment to End On Edit.

Using Audio Keyframes to Fade

Another method for quickly applying a short fade-in and fade-out to each of your clips is to keyframe the audio level for a single clip, then paste those attributes onto all the other clips.

If you previously set specific audio levels on any of the clips, this method would obliterate those settings, so you should only paste attributes before independently finessing the levels.

NOTE ▸ Gain filter settings, such as those applied using the Normalize command, will not be affected.

1 Play the sequence.

The sound effect used for the plane has been properly placed to match all of the shots, but the way it cuts in and out draws unneeded attention to the edits.

2 Zoom in to fill the screen with the first sound effect as seen in the figure below.

3 Press Option-W to turn on clip overlays.

4 Option-click the audio level overlay (the pink line) to add keyframes, and position the keyframes to create a short fade-in and fade-out for the clip.

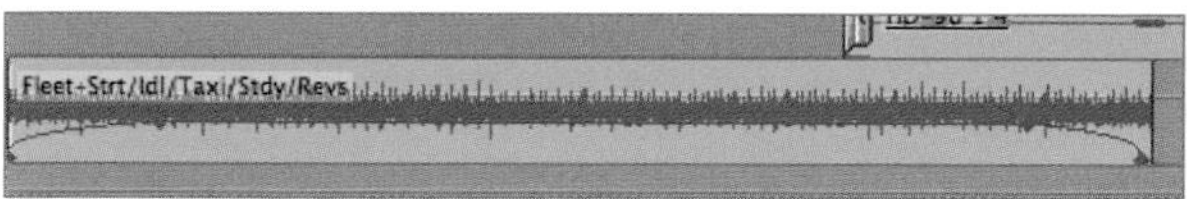

Be careful not to modify the overall level of the clip.

5 Select the clip and press Command-C to copy it to the clipboard.

6 Press Shift-Z to zoom the window to fit, then select all of the sound effects on tracks A5 and A6.

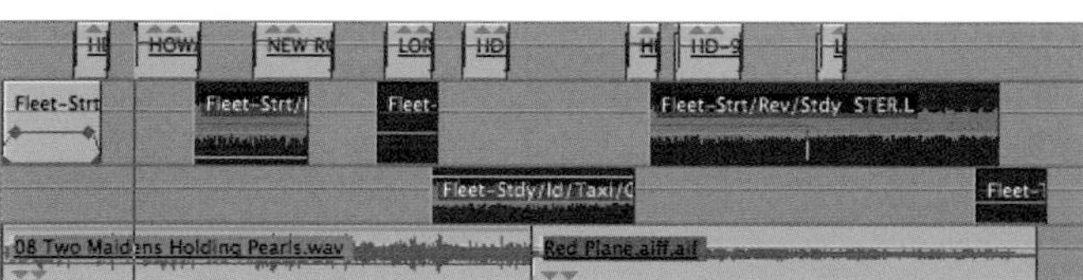

7 Press Option-V to Paste Attributes.

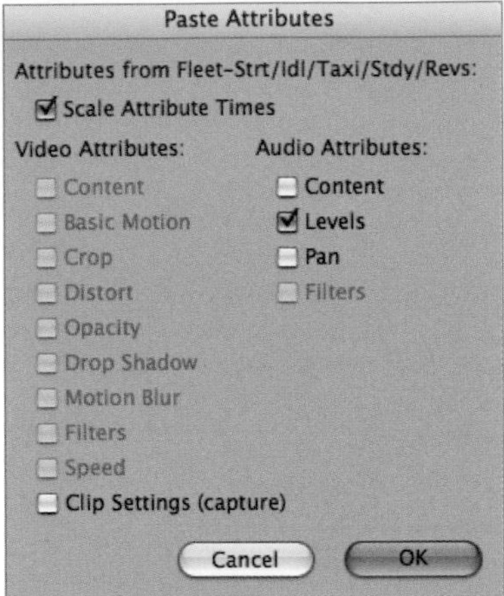

The Paste Attributes dialog appears.

8 Make sure Scale Attribute Times is selected, then select the Audio Attributes Levels checkbox and click OK.

The fade-in and fade-out is applied to each of the remaining clips.

Solo and Mute Controls

While playing this sequence, you have probably noticed that the music on tracks A7 and A8 was not audible. This might seem strange since the clips are enabled and the level settings are not turned all the way down.

It is very useful—often essential—to temporarily turn on and off individual components of the audio to focus on the rest. For this sequence, the music tracks were *muted* because adding the dialogue and effects fades would be much more difficult if the music was playing.

1 In the lower-left corner of the Timeline, click the Audio Controls button.

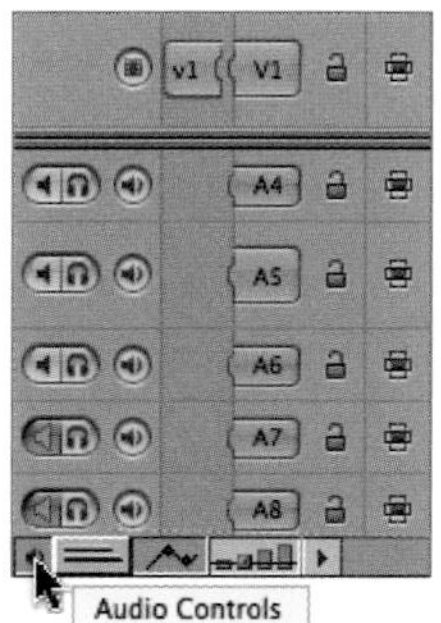

This adds two controls to the Timeline track header area. The first control is the mute button, which excludes that track from playback. When a track is muted, the speaker turns yellow. In this sequence, tracks A7 and A8 are muted.

The second control is the solo button, which effectively mutes all of the other tracks. You can *solo* multiple tracks to hear more than one track at a time. When a track is soloed, the headphone icon turns red, and all the other tracks display a mute icon with a yellow background.

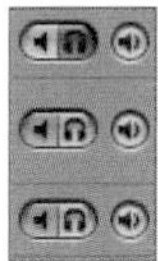

Muting a track is fundamentally different from turning off the Track Visibility control. When a track is muted, it will still be included when you export a file or lay it off to tape. Clicking the Track Visibility control to disable the track essentially removes that track from the sequence entirely.

One of the most useful aspects of the mute and solo buttons is that they can be enabled while the sequence is playing—which reinforces their essential role in audio mixing. Often, you want to hear just the dialogue or just the effects tracks without the distraction of the other audio elements. Soloing those tracks is the perfect solution.

2 Play the sequence.

3 In the Timeline patch panel, click the solo button for tracks A1, A2, A3, and A4.

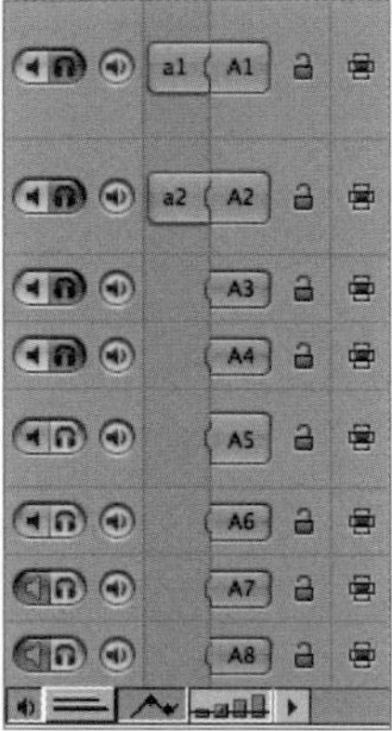

The music and sound effects are muted. The mute buttons for those tracks are inverted and turn yellow. Because tracks A7 and A8 are already manually muted, they appear a different color.

4 Click the solo buttons for tracks A5 and A6.

Now those tracks are added to the mix.

5 Click the solo buttons for tracks A7 and A8.

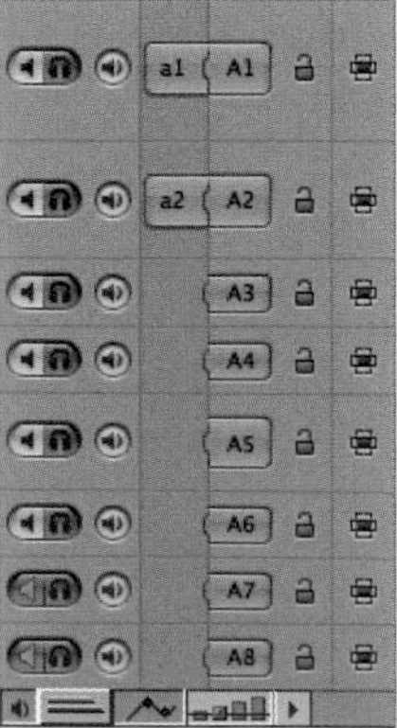

It is possible for a track to be muted and soloed at the same time. The mute overrides the solo, and the mute button appears in a slightly different color. This can be very helpful if you have a large number of tracks and, while a number of them are soloed, you want to temporarily mute one or two without changing the solo set you are working with.

When every track is soloed, the effect is the same as soloing no tracks at all.

6 Option-click any of the solo buttons.

All of the tracks are unsoloed. This works only when either all of the tracks or none of the tracks are soloed. If none of the tracks are soloed, Option-clicking will solo all of them.

7 Click the mute buttons for tracks A7 and A8 to unmute the tracks.

Engaging the Button Bar

Final Cut Pro provides three preset collections of buttons targeted for common workflows. One of these is used specifically for audio editing.

1 Choose Tools > Button Bars > Audio Editing.

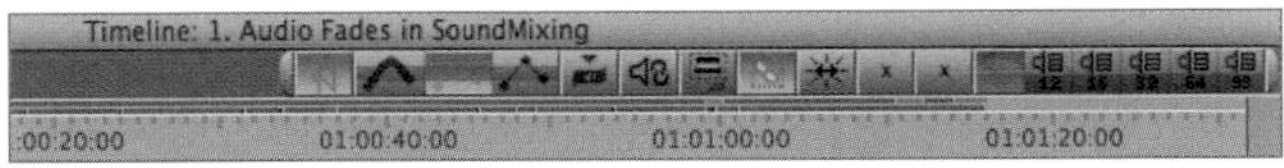

Audio editing buttons are added to the button bars in the Timeline, the Canvas, and the Browser. These buttons allow quick access to many common functions.

If you position your mouse pointer over the different buttons, a tooltip appears that identifies the button and displays any keyboard shortcuts associated with that command.

A group of buttons is located at the right edge of the Timeline button bar. These buttons control how many tracks Final Cut Pro attempts to play in real time. By default, Final Cut Pro attempts to play eight tracks. Playing any additional tracks will require rendering.

2 Open the *2. Ready for Mix* sequence.

All of the fades are applied to this sequence.

At some places where cross fades occur, the audio render bar shows a red section. When playing across those sections, you will hear a beeping sound.

Cross fades and some filters have an increased track processing "cost," so to play this sequence without rendering you must increase the number of available real-time tracks.

3 Click the Real-Time Audio Mixing: 12 Tracks button.

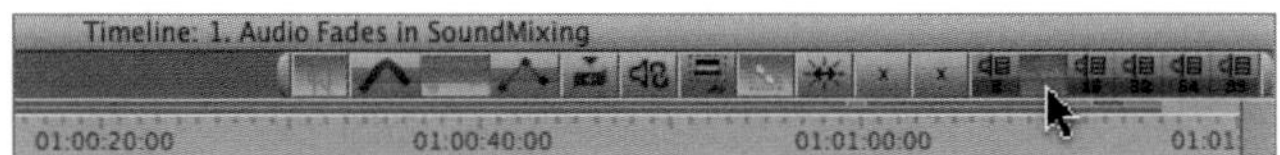

The red area in the sequence render bar disappears.

NOTE ▶ If you're wondering why you shouldn't always leave the number of real-time tracks set to the maximum (99 tracks), it's because the more processor power you allocate to audio mixing, the less you'll have for real-time video effects. By leaving this setting at the lowest required value, you'll preserve as much processing power as possible for picture.

Setting Audio Levels

Momentarily, you'll dive into the Audio Mixer window, where you can animate all of your audio levels on-the-fly, dynamically adding fades and keyframes. But before you do, remember that there are several other ways to adjust audio levels that are sometimes more efficient than using the Mixer.

1 Play the *2. Ready For Mix* sequence.

It's probably apparent to you that the plane sound effect is a little too loud, and it competes with the dialogue tracks. You could individually adjust each of those sound effects clips, but because they are so similar to one another, you can adjust all of their levels simultaneously.

2 Select all of the clips on tracks A5 and A6.

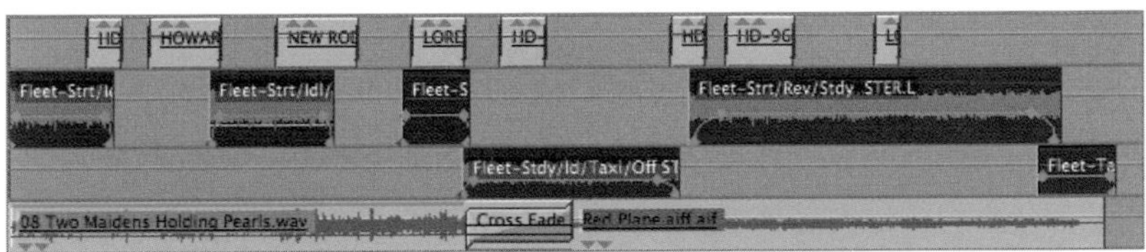

3 Choose Modify > Levels, or press Command-Option-L.

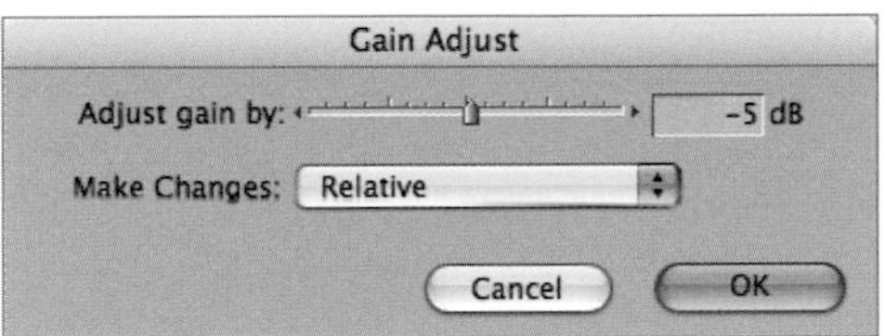

The Gain Adjust dialog appears.

In this dialog, you can modify the audio level of all the selected clips in one operation. You can choose to set an absolute level for all the clips, or to make a relative adjustment so that each clip's level is boosted or attenuated from its current setting.

4 Set the "Adjust gain by" slider to –5, leave Make Changes set to Relative, and click OK.

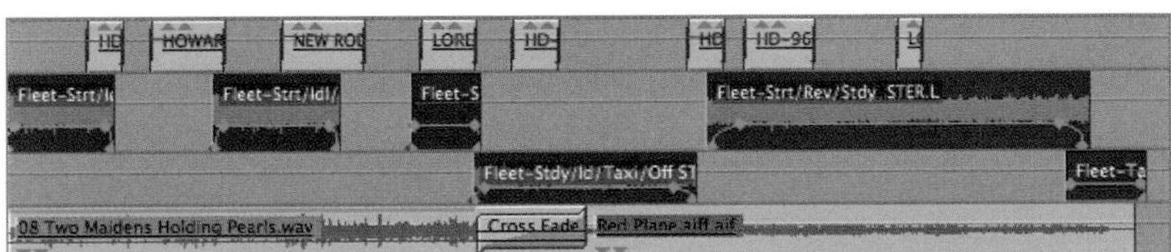

Each clip is attenuated by 5 dB. Notice that the fade-ins and fade-outs are not affected. If you set Make Changes to Absolute, any keyframes would be eliminated.

NOTE ▸ Although this dialog uses the term *gain*, it is the clip level that is modified, not the gain filter as described in the "Normalizing Audio" section in Lesson 4.

5 Play the sequence.

If you are still not happy with the level of the sound effects, you can also make 1 dB or 3 dB adjustments using the keyboard.

6 While the sequence is playing, press Control-+ (plus) to boost the gain by 1 dB. Press Control-– (minus) to lower it by 1.

Or, you can press Control-] (right bracket) or Control-[(left bracket) to boost or attenuate the level by 3 dB.

These commands will affect all selected clips, or if no clips are selected, they will apply to the clip currently under the playhead.

What Is a Good Level?

Proper audio levels vary dramatically depending on your intended output format and exhibition location. A good sound mix for an iPhone video is very different from one intended for a movie theater. However, there are a few essential things to keep in mind:

- Understand dynamic range—Dynamic range is the difference between your minimum level and your peak levels. If you want your music or explosions to feel especially loud, rather than turning them up, turn down your dialogue track. The dialogue tracks should be set to your target "average level," which typically is –12 dB for television viewing, or –20 dB for theatrical exhibition. If your average level is too high, there's no room to get louder. On the other hand, if your dialogue is too quiet, a home viewer will turn up the volume to hear it, and when the music comes on at full blast, the neighbors wake up, which definitely spoils the movie.

- Furthermore, different exhibition formats are capable of handling different dynamic range settings. For example, an airplane safety video will be watched in a loud environment through cheap speakers, so don't expect those speakers to handle much dynamic range.

- Know your exhibition environment—Before locking your sound mix, it is critical that you hear it in the same environment as your audience. If you create your entire mix in your bedroom listening to headphones and then show it to an audience at a film festival theater, you're going to be in for some big surprises, and so is your audience. If you mix your show on a professional sound stage and most viewers are going to watch it on their iPods, you'll run into similar problems. Different speakers are capable of playing back different frequency ranges. You may be monitoring on a set that can play those crisp high or beefy low tones, but if your exhibition equipment doesn't have the same playback capability, your audience will never hear any of those tones.
- Never exceed 0 dB—Digital video formats have no *headroom*. If an audio signal exceeds 0 dB, it will distort on playback. Because sound has such variance in loudness, it's always better to play it safe and set your absolute maximum ceiling for peaks (not average) of around –3 dB to –6 dB. That leaves a little headroom for unexpected spikes or for unforeseen peaks created by later transcoding or translations that may modify your clip without your control (such as uploading a file to YouTube).
- Trust your ears (sometimes)—Apparent volume can vary significantly from actual volume. Human ears are specially attuned to certain frequencies. In general, a higher-pitched sound "feels" louder than a lower-pitched one at the same measurable volume level. It's important to acknowledge this in your mix; don't turn up the siren sound effect so loud that it hurts just because you want to see it reach –12 on the audio meter. On the other hand, don't ever turn up a sound so that it risks peaking, even if it sounds relatively quiet to your ears. If any sound hits that 0 dB mark, you're likely to hear a click or buzz rather than the sound that you intended.

The Audio Mixer Window

The Final Cut Pro Audio Mixer window offers another way to view the audio tracks in your sequence. But unlike the horizontal track arrangement seen in the Timeline, you view the tracks in vertical strips.

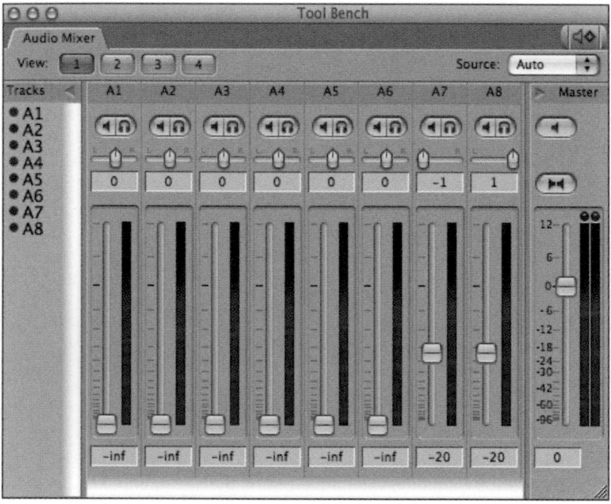

One advantage to the Audio Mixer is that each track's level can be monitored independently, while you can simultaneously observe the overall audio level of the show. The other primary benefit of the Audio Mixer is that you can adjust audio levels while the sequence is playing, even adding keyframes on-the-fly for level changes and fades.

1 Choose Window > Arrange > Audio Mixing.

   The windows rearrange, and the Audio Mixer window opens. Each vertical slider in the Mixer window represents a track in your sequence. There will always be one slider for each track in the sequence.

   TIP You can open the Audio Mixer window without changing your window layout by choosing Tools > Audio Mixer or pressing Option-6.

2 Press Spacebar to play the sequence.

As the sequence plays, the meter beside each slider displays the audio level for its track. The sliders also move to reflect the level settings of each clip. On the right, the master slider displays the overall output level. The number of meters reflects the number of audio outputs in the sequence. By default, sequences are set to stereo output.

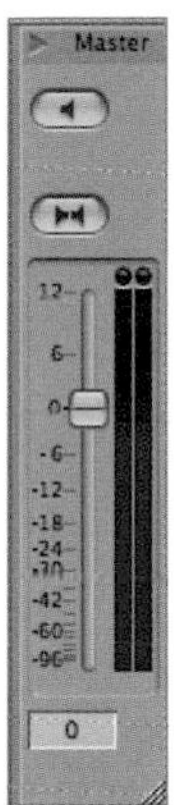

Above each slider is a pan control and mute and solo buttons identical to those in the Timeline.

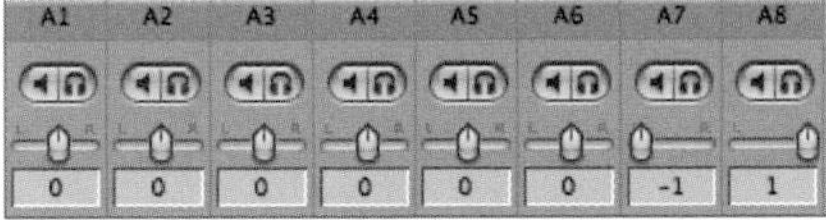

Setting Up Views in the Audio Mixer

When using eight or more tracks, it may be difficult to monitor everything at once, so Final Cut Pro enables you to create four different views, each of which can display a custom selection of tracks in the Audio Mixer.

One common technique is to create one view just for dialogue tracks, one for effects, and one for music. The fourth view can be reserved for viewing all the tracks at the same time.

1 In the track list on the left, click the black circle to hide tracks A5, A6, A7 and A8.

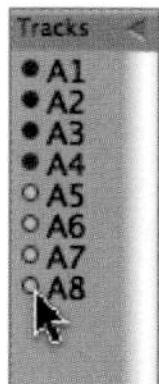

The mixer view now shows only the dialogue tracks.

2 Click the View 2 button.

3 In the track list, hide tracks A1 through A4 and tracks A7 and A8.

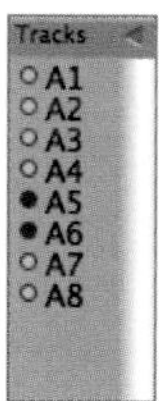

This view now shows only the effects tracks.

4 Click the View 3 button.

5 Hide all but tracks A7 and A8.

View 3 now shows just the music.

6 Click each of the View buttons and observe the different collections of tracks.

NOTE ▶ Limiting the visible tracks in a view does not mute them; it only hides the sliders to allow you to better focus on a particular aspect of your mix.

TIP The view settings illustrate one reason for organizing your audio tracks efficiently. For example, if you put sound effects and dialogue on the same tracks, it makes the mixer far less effective.

Mixing On-the-Fly

By now, you should understand the value of making editing decisions while watching your program, rather than while playback is paused. Audio mixing is another task that benefits immensely from that same ethic.

Be aware that anytime you adjust an Audio Mixer slider while a clip is playing, you change the level for that clip. There are two ways to employ this technique. By default, changes affect the level over the whole duration of the clip. Or, if you enable audio keyframe recording, every adjustment you make with the slider is recorded and applied to the clips in real-time. This process is often called *automation*.

Automation is especially useful for adjusting the level of music as it plays under dialogue.

1 In the button bar of the Audio Mixer window, click the Record Audio Keyframes button.

2 Set the Audio Mixer to View 3.

3 Play the sequence.

As it plays the first time, think about what you want to do with this sequence. In this case, the first piece of music has a good level, but the second piece seems to overpower some of the interviews.

4 Play the sequence again, and position your mouse pointer over the slider on track A7.

Because the clips on A7 and A8 are stereo pairs, changing one slider automatically changes the other.

5 As the sequence plays, listen to the mix. At the point where the music is too loud, pull the slider down slightly. After the last line of dialogue—"Look ma, no hands!"—quickly pull the slider all the way up to 0.

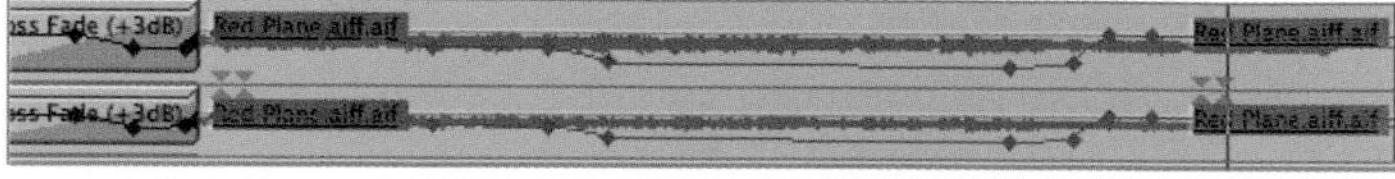

You have just added a few keyframes to the **Red Plane** clip, instantly mixing the sequence on-the-fly.

6 Play the sequence again and listen to your work.

The levels reflect the changes you just made. If you don't like what you did, don't fret. There are many ways to get rid of those keyframes.

First, you could use undo, but an even simpler solution is just to play the sequence again and make different adjustments with the slider. Each time you move the slider, new keyframes replace any that occurred at the same points in time. If you don't move the slider for a while, any existing keyframes remain intact.

Controlling Keyframe Frequency

There are times when you want every fine adjustment made with sliders to be recorded, and there are times when you want to record only the fewest number of keyframes. To accommodate both situations, Final Cut Pro provides a keyframe recording frequency with three settings.

In the previous example, you recorded keyframes with the default Reduced setting. When Record Audio Keyframes is set to Reduced, Final Cut Pro applies keyframes only as often as is necessary to smoothly reproduce your slider adjustments. In the real world, this setting works for nearly every situation.

1 Choose Final Cut Pro > User Preferences, and click the Editing tab.

2 Set the Record Audio Keyframes pop-up menu to All, and click OK.

3 Play the sequence again, and make a series of adjustments to the audio sliders.

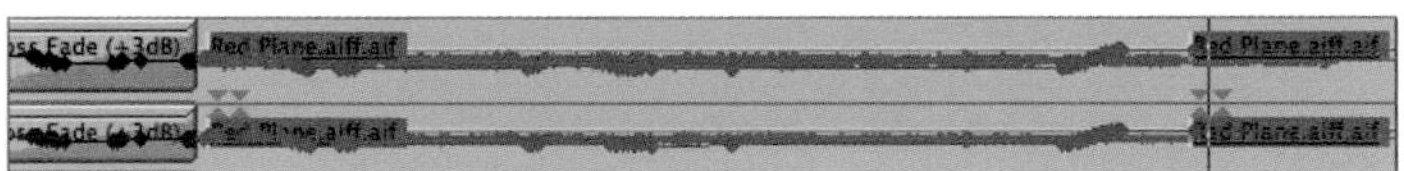

When Record Audio Keyframes is set to All, a new keyframe is added every time the slider is moved. Although this can be precise, the larger number of keyframes produced does make later adjustments more difficult.

You can also change the keyframe recording frequency using the buttons in the Timeline button bar.

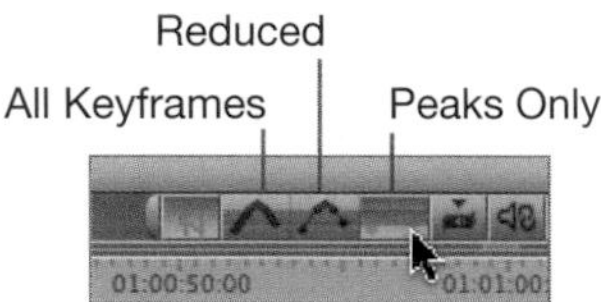

4 Click the Peaks Only button.

5 Play the sequence again and adjust the slider.

There is no need to delete or reset the old keyframes. Recording new keyframes will automatically overwrite any existing ones.

When Record Audio Keyframes is set to Peaks Only, the fewest possible keyframes are added to replicate the movements you made with the slider.

6 Click the Reduced keyframe setting in the Timeline button bar.

Resetting All Keyframes

If you get in a situation where you just want to start fresh and eliminate all the keyframes you have recorded, you have two choices: You can play the sequence and use your mouse to hold the slider in place, thereby erasing any previously applied keyframes; or you can double-click the clip in question, and in the Audio Viewer click the Reset button.

Creating Perspective

One of the characteristics of successful sound design is the thoughtful implementation of perspective. If a visual event requiring a sound effect occurs on the right side of the frame or outside of the right side of the frame, use the pan controls to put the corresponding sound there. Similarly, if a noise-generating object is moving toward or away from the camera, be sure to change the level accordingly.

Perspective is just as important for dialogue as it is for effects. The audio level for a close-up should seem slightly louder than a shot of the same person talking in a *wide*. Be careful not to overdo it; your goal is not to replicate reality, but to subtly suggest the change in perspective that occurs when the camera moves or when an edit changes the viewer's point of view.

1 In the Audio Mixer, click the View 2 button to hear the sound effects.

2 Click the solo button for track A6.

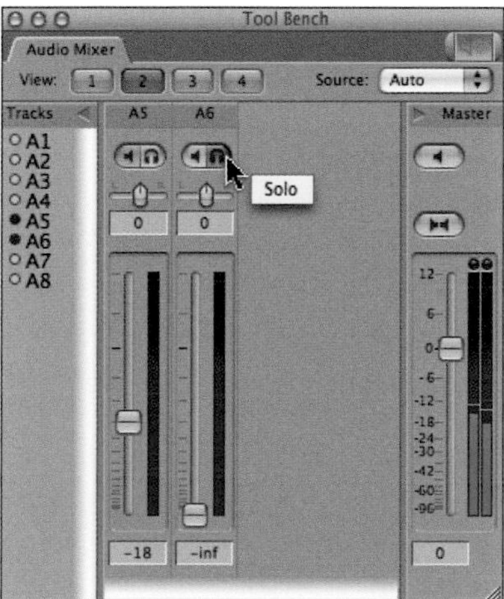

3 Navigate the playhead to approximately 31 seconds and play.

This shot begins very close to the plane, and over time it moves farther away and toward screen right.

It may be helpful to mark the clip so you can play across just this section of the Timeline while you finesse this shot.

4 With your playhead positioned anywhere over the **HD118 2 4** clip, press X to mark it.

5 Press Shift-\ (backslash) to Play In to Out.

6 At beginning of the clip, raise the A6 slider to about the middle of its range then, as the plane moves farther away, slowly lower the slider to about the one-third point.

Remember that you don't want the sound to fade out completely, but rather to go from slightly louder to slightly quieter. It will likely take you a few tries to get it right.

7 Repeat steps 5 and 6 until you are happy with the fade.

When the fade is working correctly, you can tackle the pan settings. Just as with levels, adjusting the pan slider while the clip plays will automatically record the changes you make.

8 Play from In to Out, and while the clip plays, slowly move the pan slider away from the center point and slightly toward the right.

Because the plane doesn't actually move that far to the right, you only want to make a subtle adjustment, but even a tiny change has an impact that can bring your audience into the scene.

9 Play from In to Out again.

If you're not happy with your pan automation, do it again; remember that every time you move the slider, you erase any keyframes from the previous attempt.

10 When you think you have it right, click the solo button to unsolo track A6, and listen to the effect in combination with the rest of the mix.

11 For extra credit, go through the rest of the sound effects shots and apply similar perspective adjustments.

Finishing Your Mix

The sound mix is typically completed in four stages. First, set the dialogue levels, ensuring that they are all at a uniform volume (usually –12 or –20); then set the sound effects levels to make them feel natural and integrated into the scene; then set the music levels, fading them in and out so as not to overwhelm the rest of the mix; and finally, play all tracks at the same time and hear how each element interacts with the others.

Remember to spread your sounds across the frequency spectrum. If you add music with a heavy bass track on top of a scene that already has a significant low-end ambiance track, you risk getting a muddy sound from both tracks. You're much better off choosing a different song.

Mixing in Soundtrack Pro

Although Final Cut Pro has everything you need to successfully finish your mix, many sound professionals crave more audio-specific controls, filters, and options than even the most full-featured video editor can cram in. Fortunately, Final Cut Studio comes bundled with Soundtrack Pro, a program tailored specifically to the audio needs of film and video postproduction.

For example, Final Cut offers 2 types of audio transitions, but Soundtrack Pro has 16—not to mention its 68 filters compared to 32 in Final Cut Pro.

Soundtrack Pro offers *bussing*, which allows you to group tracks to simultaneously apply effects and automate them. It also includes full surround sound mixing, so instead of just panning from left to right, you can pan sounds in three-dimensional space. Because Soundtrack Pro is dedicated to audio, it has an efficient workflow and many additional niceties and shortcuts that simplify and speed up your audio editing.

An exploration of all of these amazing features is beyond the scope of this book (for a more complete exploration, see *Apple Pro Training Series: Soundtrack Pro 2* by Martin Sitter). However, as a Final Cut Pro editor, it is still important for you to be comfortable moving between the two programs.

Sending to a Soundtrack Pro Multitrack Project

It is a well-known fact that a film, like any creative work, is never finished. At some point you simply must abandon it. (That paraphrased quote is attributed to artist Leonardo da Vinci, or to poet Paul Valery, both of whom died long before the film medium was invented.) So it's a good idea to use sending out your audio for the final mix as the milestone for forbidding yourself from making additional edits. However, if you must make changes, there are ways to reconcile them.

Assuming that your picture is locked, and you've been diligent, your tracks have been organized into D, M & E (dialogue, music and effects) and you are ready to move to Soundtrack Pro.

1. Open and play the *3. Ready For Soundtrack* sequence.

   This is another version of the *Look Ma No Hands* sequence. The fades haven't yet been added, and the levels of the sound effects and music are very rough.

2. Select the sequence in the Browser and choose File > Send To > Soundtrack Pro Multitrack Project.

A Save dialog appears. You are saving a Soundtrack Pro project file which, like a Final Cut Pro project file, contains only pointers to the actual media and is therefore very small. It is wise to save such files in the same location that you save your Final Cut Pro project files.

3 Navigate to the destination of your choice and click Save.

Soundtrack Pro opens and displays a Timeline nearly identical to the one in Final Cut Pro. Audio levels, pan settings, and cross fades are all present.

One notable difference is that Soundtrack Pro stores both channels in a single track, compared to the two separate tracks in Final Cut Pro.

You can also rename tracks in Soundtrack Pro, which provides a huge organizational benefit, especially in complex projects that can quickly grow to include dozens of tracks.

4 Click the name area of track A1 & A2 and rename it *Dialogue 1*.

5 Click the name area for the next track and rename it *Dialogue 2*.

6 Rename tracks A5 and A6, *FX1* and *FX2*, respectively, and rename track A7 & A8 *music*.

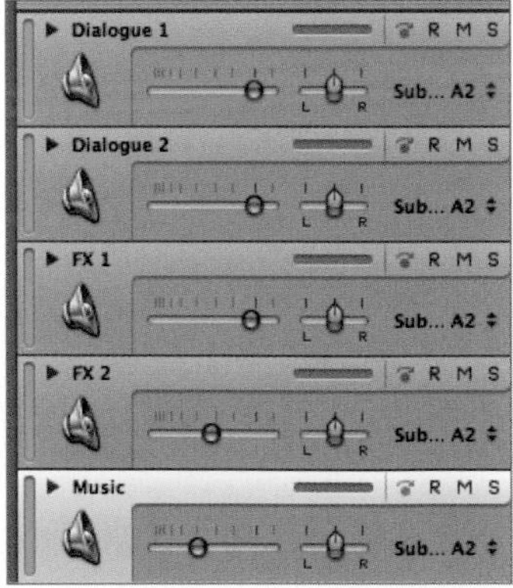

7 Press Spacebar to play the sequence.

TIP You'll find that many of the familiar Final Cut Pro keyboard shortcuts also work in Soundtrack Pro, including J, K, and L for multi-speed playback; I and O (as well as their Shift and Option key modifiers) to control In and Out points; Shift-Z to zoom the Timeline to fit in the window; N to toggle snapping; M for markers; and so on.

Performing Basic Mixing Tasks

In Soundtrack Pro, you can do the same mixing tasks that you earlier performed in Final Cut Pro. Some of these are easier to do in Final Cut Pro, because there are fewer options; others are easier or faster in Soundtrack Pro.

Muting and Soloing

The mute and solo controls are vital to effectively mix any multitrack project. On most projects, you will frequently turn on and off groups of tracks to focus on one aspect at a time.

Soundtrack Pro tracks can be muted and soloed either in the Timeline track area or in the mixer window.

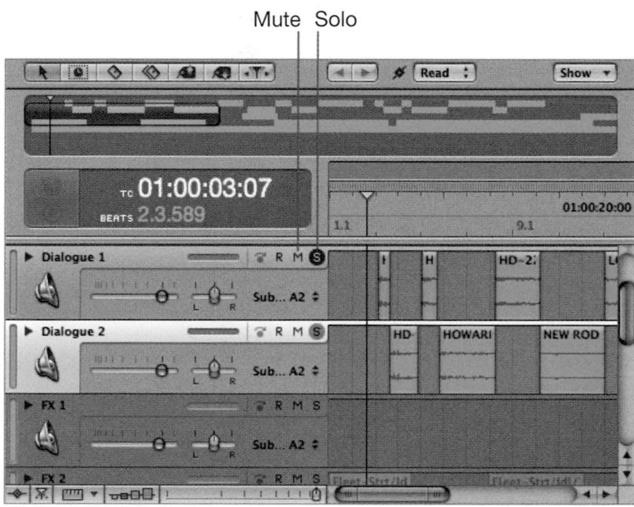

1 Click the solo button for the Dialogue 1 and Dialogue 2 tracks.

2 Play the sequence.

The tracks are successfully soloed.

3 Click the solo buttons again to unsolo those tracks.

Adding Fades

Sound designers could talk for hours about fades. Fortunately, applying them in Soundtrack Pro takes almost no time at all.

1 Press Home to bring the playhead to the beginning of the sequence. Press Command-+ (plus) to zoom in, if necessary, until the first few dialogue clips fill the Timeline.

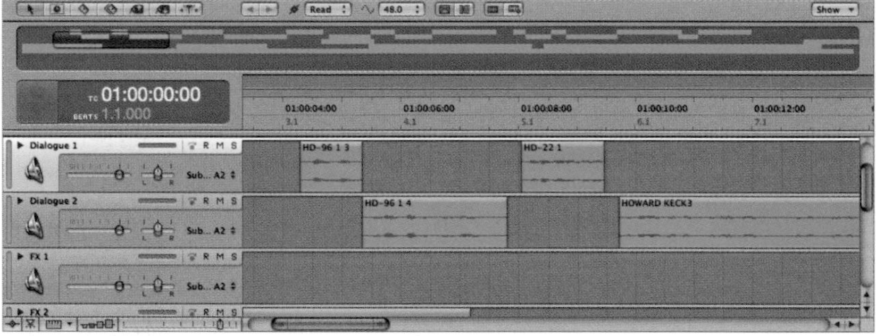

2 Position your mouse pointer over the upper-left corner of the first clip (**HD-96 1 3**).

The pointer changes to the Add Fade pointer.

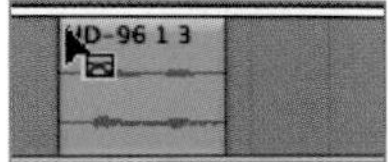

3 When the pointer appears, drag to the right, and extend the fade to the first bump in the waveform.

4 Double-click the fade.

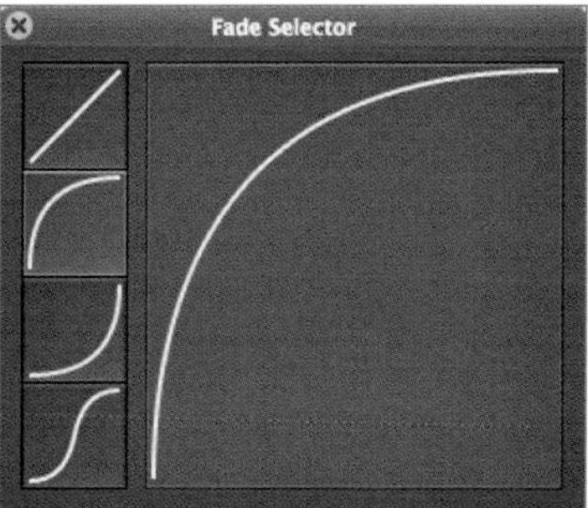

The Fade Selector Heads-Up Display (HUD) appears, allowing you to choose one of four fade patterns.

5 Click the various patterns to apply them to the fade on the clip, then click the Close button to close the HUD.

Soundtrack Pro allows you to set either side of a cross fade to a different fade pattern.

6 Press Shift-Z to zoom the entire scene into view, then scroll down until you can see the Music track.

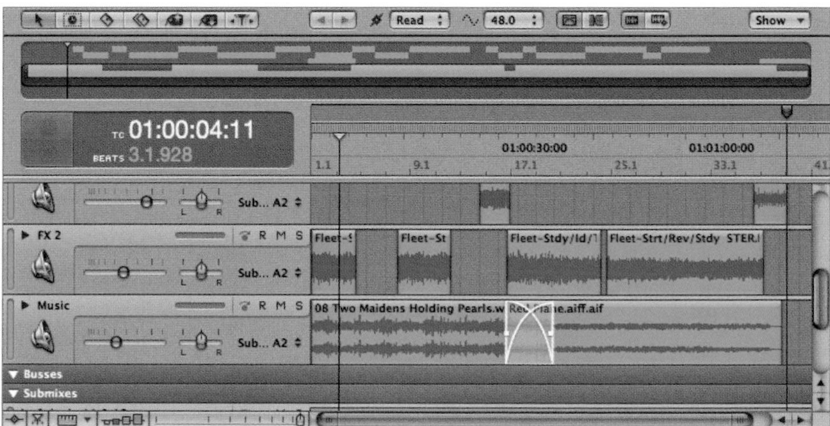

7 On the Music track, double-click the cross fade to open the HUD.

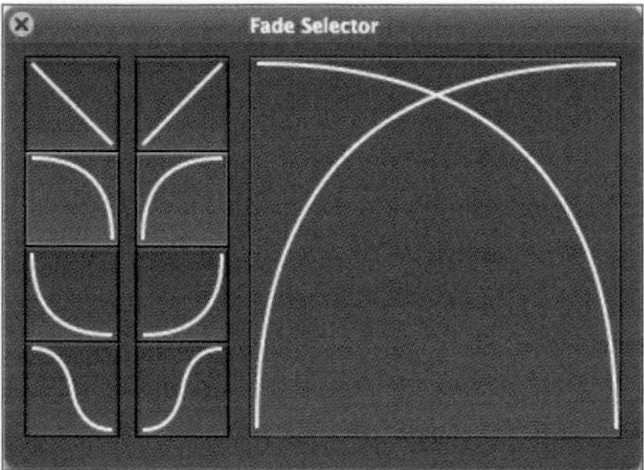

Now, the HUD shows both sides of the fade.

8 Experiment with different fade selections, then close the HUD.

Adjusting Levels

Just like in Final Cut Pro, Soundtrack Pro has a mixer window in which you can set and monitor levels, and automate level changes by dragging sliders while a sequence plays.

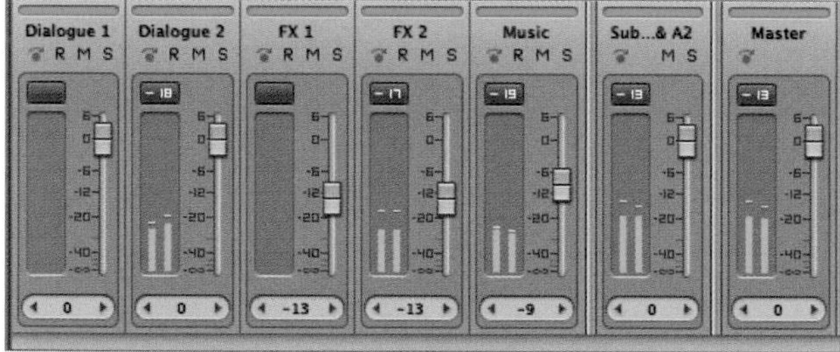

Moving a slider changes the values on the associated track. You can also change levels in the Timeline area. Volume and pan sliders are located under the track label for each track.

Positioning the pointer over either slider displays a tooltip that shows the current value.

The Timeline can also display graphs (known as *envelopes*) that show how levels change over time.

1 In the upper-left corner of the FX 2 track, click the disclosure triangle.

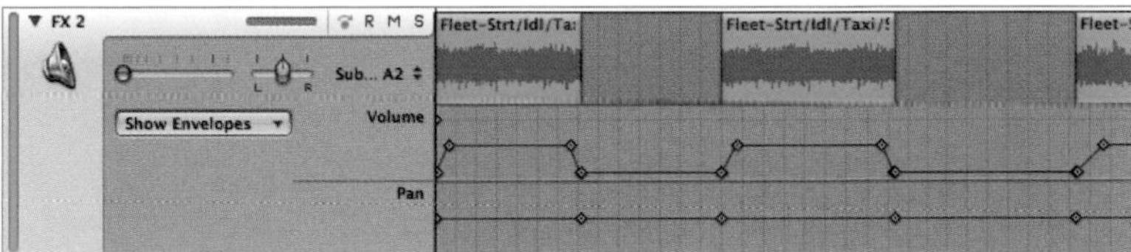

The envelopes for both volume and pan are displayed.

Adjusting the volume slider affects the clip currently under the playhead.

2 Position the playhead over the first clip. Drag down the volume slider to approximately –33 dB.

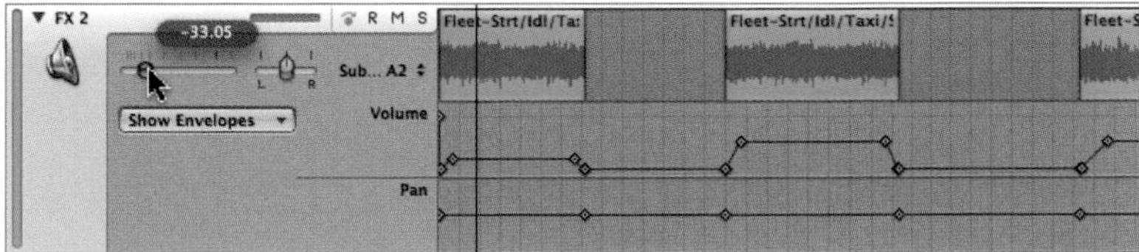

3 Play the sequence to hear the results.

You can continue dragging to finesse the level setting while the sequence plays.

NOTE ▶ When keyframes are added to the level envelope, adjusting the slider will affect only the segment under the playhead.

Automating Level Changes

Of course, you can also add keyframes on-the-fly in Soundtrack Pro, and there are even multiple modes (Latch and Touch) that produce slightly different results. Latch mode adds keyframes as you adjust the slider and, after the last keyframe, the level remains constant. Touch mode does the same thing, except after you release the slider, the level jumps back to wherever the level was before you first dragged the slider. Touch mode is helpful for doing quick *ducks* or boosts in a mix where you don't want to disturb the other levels.

1. In the upper-left corner of the mixer, set the Automation Mode pop-up to Latch.

   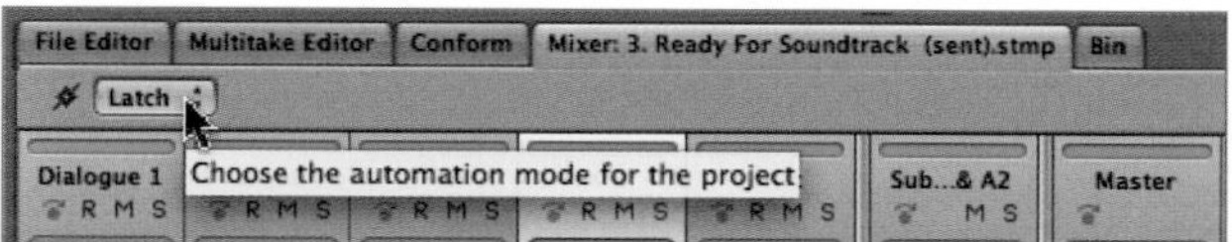

   This enables keyframe recording. It's not necessary to expand the tracks in the Timeline, but doing so allows you to see the keyframes as they appear.

2. Click the disclosure triangle to the left of the music track's label to display the level and pan envelopes.

3. Position your pointer over the mixer slider for the music track, then play the sequence and drag the slider to adjust the levels of the music track as it plays.

   The keyframes are added while the sequence plays.

4. In the Timeline, drag a marquee around the keyframes, and press Delete.

   The keyframes are removed from the clip.

Soundtrack Pro offers countless other tools and techniques to aid and improve your mixing experience. The filters and audio processing techniques (some of which are discussed in Lesson 4) provide enormous flexibility for sound design and sound mixing.

Integrating Changes from Final Cut Pro

Remember when you exported your sound and intended to lock the picture and stop making changes in Final Cut Pro? Now you want to make more changes, don't you? Tsk tsk.

Well, rest assured that you're not alone. This is the dirty little secret of desktop editing: filmmakers wind up recutting their projects after every screening or airing. Every batch of DVDs has a slightly different cut, and the poor sound mixer has to face the miserable task of conforming the audio mix again and again to match changes made to the edit.

Fortunately, Soundtrack Pro has the invaluable Conform feature, which compares two projects, automatically finds discrepancies, and fixes them for you.

1 In Final Cut Pro, open and play the *4. Trimmed* sequence.

   This is a sequence nearly identical to the one you sent to Soundtrack Pro, but a few edits have been made: The first clip has been trimmed so it now starts with the first line of narration; two of the edits midway through have been trimmed slightly; and one clip has been removed.

2 In the Browser, select the *4. Trimmed* sequence, and choose File > Send To > Soundtrack Pro Multitrack Project.

   The Save dialog appears.

3 Leave everything at its default setting, navigate to the destination of your choice, and click Save.

Soundtrack Pro is brought forward, and a new tab is added that contains the new mix.

4 Choose File > Conform Projects.

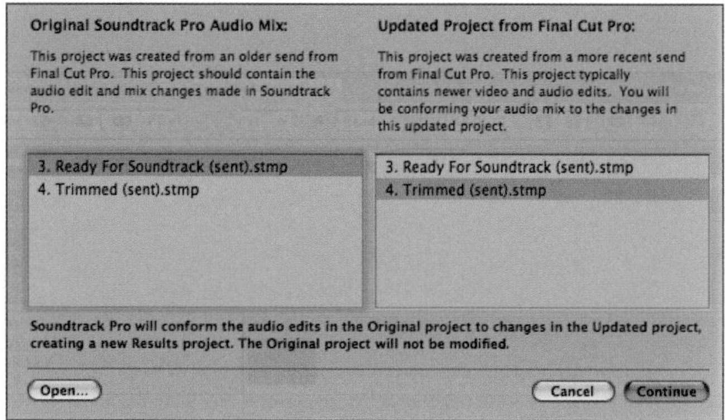

The Conform sheet appears.

5 From the list on the left, select the first project, **3. Ready For Soundtrack (sent).stmp.**

This indicates the project you have been working on in Soundtrack Pro.

6 From the list on the right, select the new version, **4. Trimmed (sent).stmp**, then click Continue.

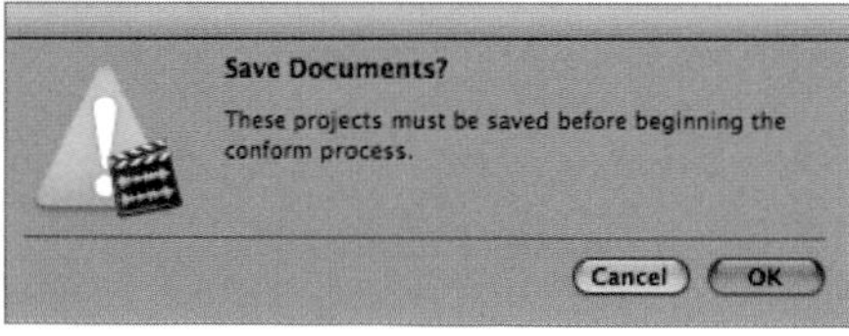

A save warning appears.

7 Click OK.

The conform progress bar appears as the projects are compared.

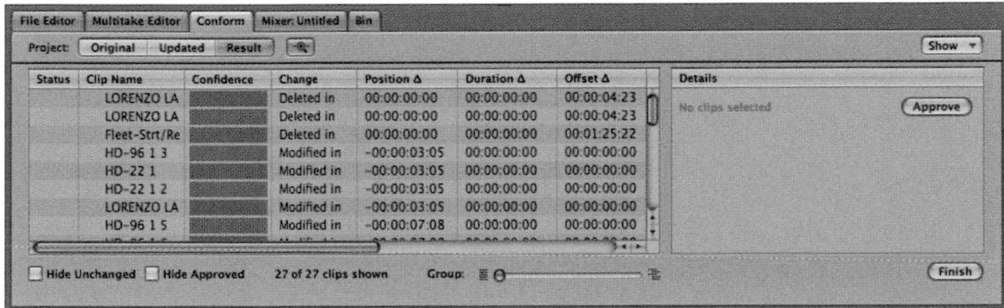

Once the comparison is complete, the Conform tab displays all of the changes identified between the two projects.

8 Select the first item in the Conform list.

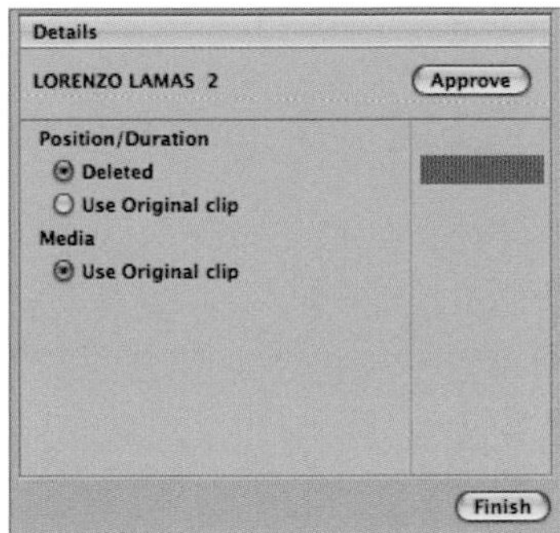

The right side of the window provides more information about the change and gives you the opportunity to approve the changes or to retain the original settings.

9 Leave the settings at the default settings and click Approve.

You may not have noticed, but a new Soundtrack Pro project was also automatically created as part of the Conform process. It appears as a new tab in the Timeline area.

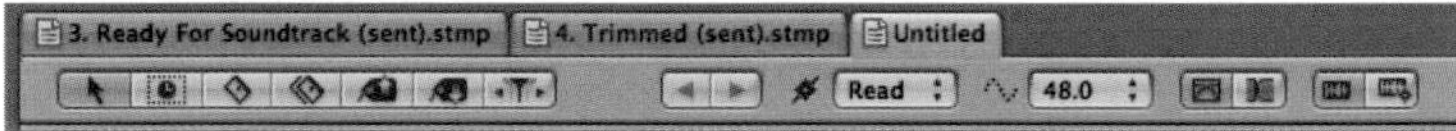

10 Choose File > Save to save the new version of the project.

11 In the Save dialog, name the project *Conformed* and save it to the directory of your choosing.

12 Select the Hide Approved checkbox.

13 In the Conform tab, press Command-A to select all remaining items in the list.

14 Click the Approve button to accept all of the changes at once.

TIP If at any point you realize that a change was incorrect, you can select it in the list, click Edit, and revert to your original settings.

15 In the lower pane, click the Mixer tab to return to the mixer view.

TIP Close old projects to ensure that all future changes are made in the conformed project.

This process saves countless hours spent matching the old and the new edits by hand. After it's done, you can continue working on the mix in Soundtrack Pro.

Returning to Final Cut Pro

So after you are finished with your sound mix, it's time to move back to Final Cut Pro in preparation for final output.

1 In Soundtrack Pro, choose File > Export.

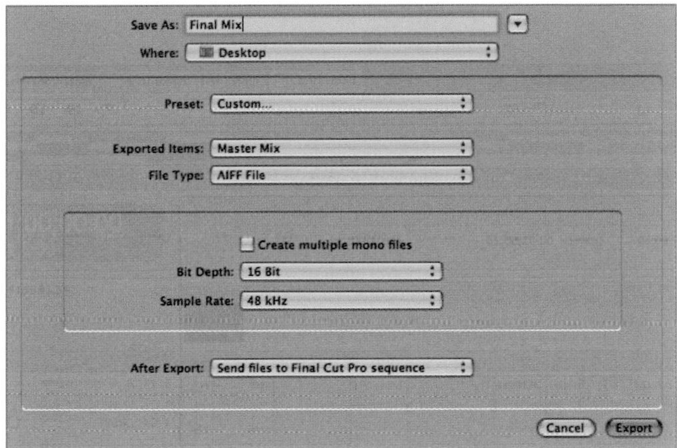

The Export dialog opens. In this example, you made only one stereo mix. As you get more comfortable in Soundtrack Pro, you will learn how to create submixes and surround mixes, any of which can be exported in the same way.

2 Name the file *Final Mix*. Leave all of the settings at their defaults, except After Export. Set it to "Send files to Final Cut Pro sequence." Click Export.

The mix is exported to an XML file, and Final Cut Pro is automatically brought forward with the Import XML dialog.

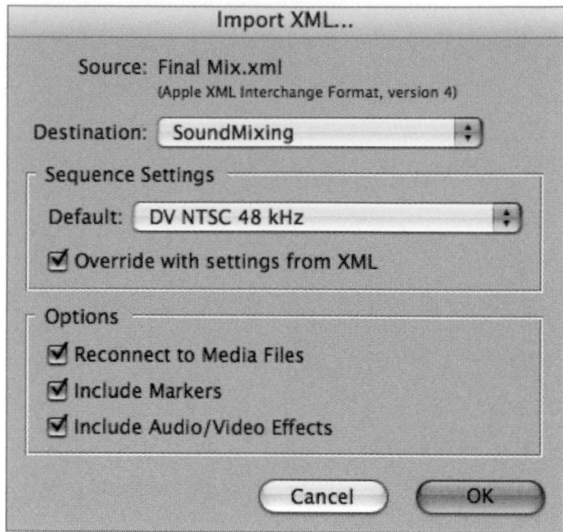

3 Leave all the settings at their default values, and click OK.

A Save dialog appears, asking you to save a project.

4 Navigate to the directory of your choice and click Save.

NOTE ▶ You may safely disregard any non-critical error warnings.

A new sequence named *Final Mix* is added to the Final Cut Pro project.

5 Double-click the sequence.

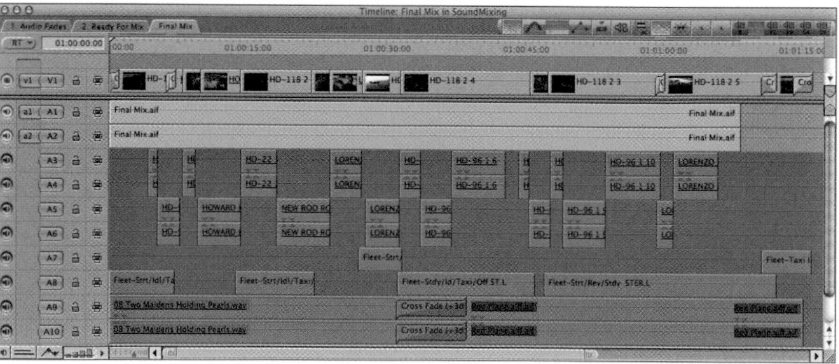

The sequence contains all of the clips from the original sequence you previously exported. Two new audio tracks have been added to tracks A1 and A2, and these contain the finished mix you exported from Soundtrack Pro. All the other audio tracks have been moved down and disabled.

Lesson Review

1. When should a clip be hard-cut (and no fade effect applied)?
2. True or false: If a clip is soloed, all other clips must be muted.
3. Are muted clips included or excluded from an exported mix?
4. How many tracks can be displayed in the Audio Mixer window?
5. What is automation?
6. What missing features prevent finishing your mix in Final Cut Pro?
7. Name three Soundtrack Pro features that are not found in Final Cut Pro.
8. Must "perspective" effects be performed in Soundtrack Pro?
9. Can track labels be renamed in Soundtrack Pro?
10. How can changes from Final Cut Pro be incorporated into an existing Soundtrack Pro project?
11. How do you return your final Soundtrack Pro mix to Final Cut Pro?

Answers

1. Never.
2. False. More than one clip can be soloed.
3. Muted clips are included in an export operation.
4. The Audio Mixer window will show up to 99 tracks—the same as can be displayed in a single sequence in the Timeline.
5. The act of recording audio keyframes on-the-fly.
6. None. Final Cut Pro has all tools needed for a professional final mix.

7. More audio transition types; twice as many filters and effects; bussing and submixing; surround mixing; two automation modes; automatic conforming.
8. No, perspective effects can be performed in Final Cut Pro using level and pan controls.
9. Yes.
10. Using the Soundtrack Pro Conform feature.
11. Choose "Send files to Final Cut Pro sequence" from the After Export pop-up menu in the Export dialog.

Cameo

Black Snake Moan—Billy Fox

BILLY FOX HAS USED VIRTUALLY EVERY electronic editing system known to man.

In fact, the award-winning editor—whose recent credits include *Black Snake Moan*, *Pride*, *Four Brothers*, and *Hustle & Flow*—has a secret: "I've never cut film," he says. "At a recent meeting at Paramount, I told them that, and they thought it was just hilarious."

Fox's story is one of those interesting cases where the technology developed to meet the individual, rather than the other way around.

As a teen in San Diego, he hung out at the CBS affiliate TV station where his father was general manager. At 16, he got a job there, editing at nights. By the time he was 23, he was at NBC, editing sports and news on a CMX 340 and, later, a Lightworks system.

Over the next 15 years, Fox cut everything from music videos and commercials to *Wings* and nine seasons of *Law & Order* (for which he received two Emmys and nine Emmy nominations). But, by the mid-1990s, he realized what he really loved was drama.

"When I started out, there was this giant river between electronic editing and film," says Fox. "I wanted to do long form, but how was I going to make that jump? They were two different worlds, and people did not cross-pollinate."

Fortunately for Fox, the technological landscape shifted, and electronic editing began to make inroads to film. "You just saw the waters recede," remembers Fox, "to the point where today, there isn't any divide there at all."

Fox cut his first four films on Avid systems, but chose Final Cut Pro to edit *Black Snake Moan* and *Pride*.

"The things that really put it over the top for me, funny enough, were Soundtrack Pro and Motion," says Fox, who runs 20 tracks of audio when he edits and has been known to create his own opening titles in Motion. "We stay 24-frame all the way: sound, picture, visual effects. When it comes time to show the movie to the studio, we don't conform a workprint, we don't make a temp dub. We make a high-def QuickTime file and take it straight to the theater."

The benefit is not just time-savings, says Fox, it's an invaluable improvement in the normal film workflow, where a picture must be locked two weeks before the screening so the sound and effects departments can work on the temp dub. Meanwhile, "I'm still cutting away, so at the screening I'm looking at an old cut of the movie, and sometimes it's hardly relevant. The audience is seeing the movie you made two weeks ago. Major decisions are based on their reaction, and you're thinking, 'Wait, that scene's completely different, it plays much better now.'"

At the *Black Snake Moan* screening, "Paramount loved it," Fox says. "They said, 'When did you guys lock picture?' I said, 'Well, we were cutting it yesterday.' They were blown away."

The digital workflow also speeds collaboration. "When it's time to show scenes to the director or composer, we actually use iChat and send a QuickTime file so they can give us instant feedback or do a quick music cue on it," says Fox.

Fox says changes in tools and workflow have given him more control over the final picture, sound, and grading. "It's such a creative, non-constricting environment," he says. "You can show the colorist—on his 50-foot screen—a high-def QuickTime version of the color correction that you and the director have already temped in, and get right to work. What's happening editorially these days is so exciting."

Plus, reduced travel: "These last four movies I've done right here at home," Fox says with obvious enjoyment.

Composer Scott Bomar (on couch) confers with writer/director Craig Brewer while editing *Black Snake Moan*.

Visual Effects

6

Lesson Files	Lesson Files > Lesson 06 > Compositing.fcp
Media	Surf Video
Time	This lesson takes approximately 90 minutes to complete.
Goals	Use motion parameters to transform clips Create motion effects using the onscreen controls in the Canvas Reset attributes Apply composite modes to clips Copy and paste attributes from one clip to another Arrange multiple clips into a single composition Use the Crop and Distort tools Work with multilayered Photoshop files Construct Travel Matte effects

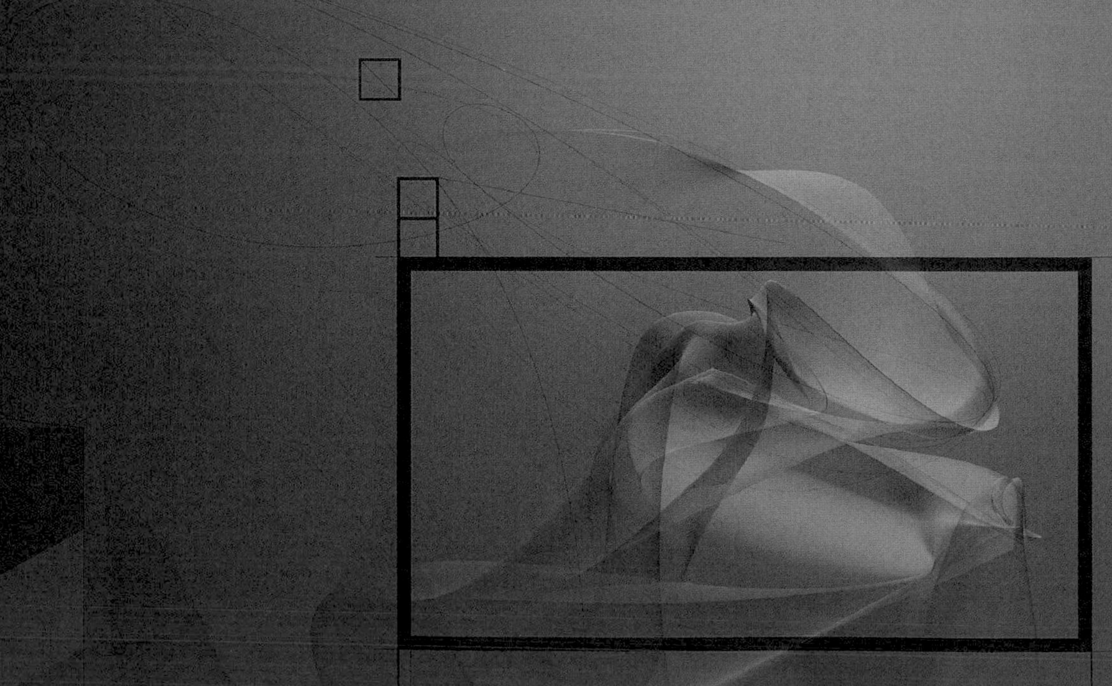

Lesson **6**

Advanced Compositing

Compositing is a general term that describes the act of combining multiple images onscreen at the same time. The result is called a *composition*. In Final Cut Pro, to composite images, you stack clips on multiple tracks at the same point in the Timeline. Compositing typically begins by modifying the scale, position, rotation, and other similar parameters of the clips involved.

Such parameters in Final Cut Pro geometrically transform images in your sequences. Using motion parameters such as Scale, Rotation, Center, and Crop, you can create anything from a simple split screen to a multilayered motion graphics sequence that integrates video and imported graphics. By mastering the manipulation of these parameters, you can create exciting visuals, as well as solve simple, everyday editing problems.

In this lesson, you will learn the fundamentals of motion properties and then create a finished composition—an opening sequence for a program about surfing culture. You also will learn how to quickly reshape, distort, reposition, crop, and superimpose video clips; save time by reusing motion settings; and refine your effects for professional results.

Launching a Project

To begin, you'll open a project file and change the window layout to one best suited for this kind of motion graphics work.

1. Open Lesson FIles > Lesson 06 > **Compositing.fcp**.

2. Double-click the *Surf Intro* sequence to open it into the Timeline, if it's not already open.

3. Choose Window > Arrange > Two-Up.

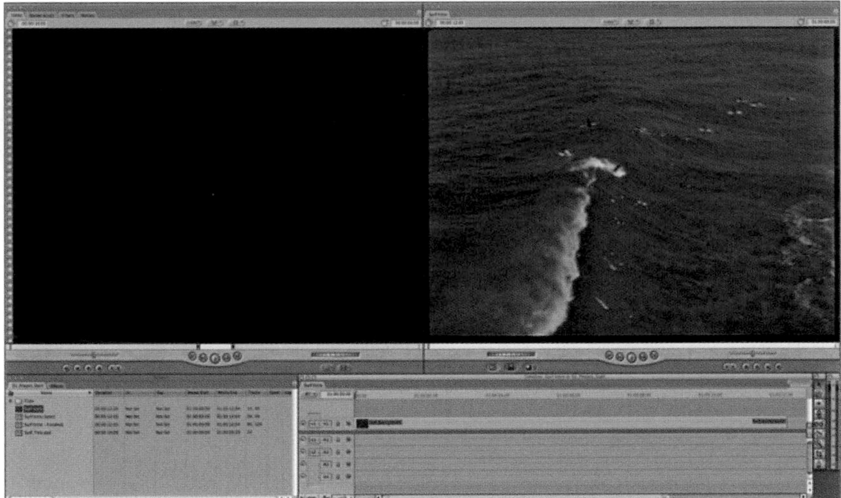

By default, the Final Cut Pro standard window layout maximizes the area available for the Timeline by shrinking the Viewer and Canvas and making room for the Browser. Although this is an excellent layout for editing, you may find that the two-up window layout is more useful for working on effects because it increases the size of the Viewer and Canvas while reducing the Timeline's width. Motion graphics and compositing tasks involve more activity in the Viewer and Canvas adjusting parameters and onscreen controls, and less activity in the Timeline. So, this redistribution of screen real estate makes sense.

If your computer's display is big enough, you may want to increase the height of the Timeline so you can view more video tracks.

4 Move the playhead to the border between the Timeline and the Viewer or Canvas. When it turns into the Resize pointer, drag up the border to simultaneously resize all four windows in the interface.

You'll find that different compositing tasks emphasize different parts of the interface. Some tasks require more room in the Canvas, others need more room in the Timeline or the Viewer. With the Final Cut Pro window resizing controls, you can quickly make room where you need it and keep your workspace organized.

5 To make even more room for your video clips in the Timeline, drag down the divider between the video and audio tracks.

Using RT Extreme Settings

With a few exceptions, most of the effects you'll be using in this book will play in real time on current Macintosh systems. You should be aware, however, that Final Cut Pro includes a few options to optimize real-time playback performance on your computer. These settings are located at the top-left of the Timeline in the Real-Time Effects (RT) pop-up menu.

Clicking the RT pop-up menu reveals the following options:

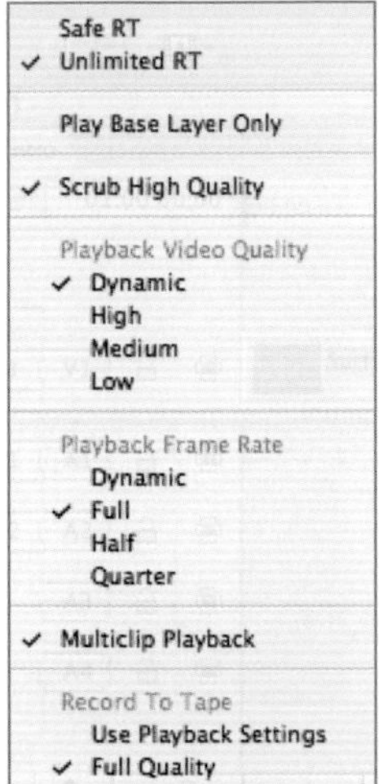

These settings allow you to maximize the real-time performance of your computer; the following settings are especially important:

- Safe RT restricts Final Cut Pro to displaying only those effects that can be played in real time at the current frame rate of your project. Sections of your Timeline that exceed your computer's capabilities are not displayed, and they are identified by a red render bar at the top of the Timeline ruler. By using Safe RT, you avoid the likelihood of your playback being interrupted by dropped frames (stuttering playback).
- Unlimited RT frees Final Cut Pro to attempt the processing and playback of effects combinations that exceed the guaranteed capabilities of your computer. In other words, if you're piling on more effects than your Mac can reasonably handle, it'll try to process them anyway. Sections of your sequence that trigger this behavior are identified by an orange render bar at the top of the Timeline ruler. Unlimited RT playback may result in dropped frames as your Mac attempts to keep up with the processing demands placed upon it.

- In both the Playback Video Quality and Playback Frame Rate sections, choosing Dynamic allows Final Cut Pro to dynamically reduce and increase the resolution and/or frame rate of the Canvas to continue real-time playback of effects. For consistency, if you want to fix the quality at which your images play back onscreen, you can choose one of the resolutions or frame rates that appear below in the RT pop-up menu. Lower resolutions and frame rates exchange image quality for increased real-time playback capabilities when you're working with effects-intensive projects.

In the current project, the Browser contains a project file that shows Unlimited RT in action.

1 Double-click the *Unlimited RT Demo* sequence to open it into the Timeline.

   Depending on your computer's capabilities, the three sections of the sequence containing effects should have orange render bars.

   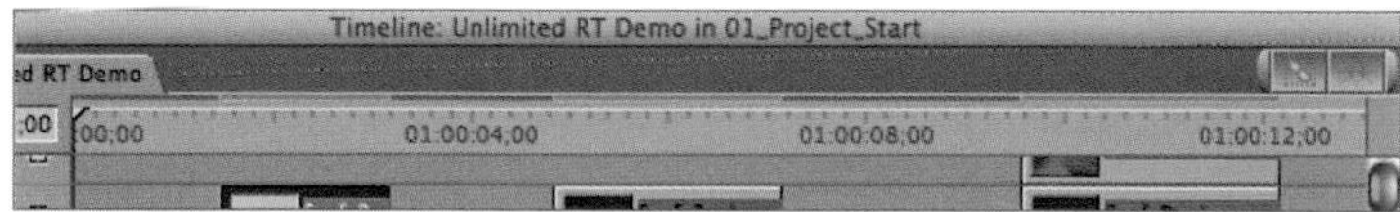

2 Play the sequence, and watch the results in the Canvas.

   As the sequence plays, you should observe that playback is smooth in the sections of the sequence with no effects, and you see varying numbers of dropped frames in each orange bar–marked Unlimited RT section. This is an exceptionally useful mode in which to work because you can see real-time previews of your compositions regardless of the type or quantity of effects you use. This defers the need to render a sequence until you have to see the final, full-resolution result.

   NOTE ▶ The results of this exercise will vary depending on your Mac's speed, number of processors, and graphics card.

3 Position your mouse over the orange area of the render bar to activate the tooltip.

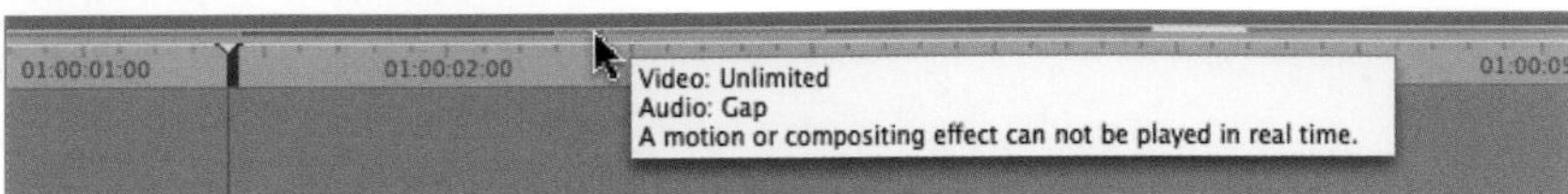

The tooltip indicates what effect is requiring Final Cut Pro to activate Unlimited RT mode.

4 Position your mouse pointer over several areas of the render bar to see other indications that the Render Bar tooltip can display.

Raw media files are indicated as such, as are areas that have already been rendered.

5 In the Timeline, Control-click the Unlimited RT Demo tab and choose Close from the shortcut menu.

Monitoring Canvas Playback Quality

One last note before you get started: The image quality of effects in the Canvas will vary depending on the effects you've applied and your computer's ability to keep up with the processing demands of Final Cut Pro.

Clips in the Timeline identified with green, yellow, dark yellow, or orange render bars are displaying *approximations* of their final appearance. This is useful for quickly seeing the results of your work, but when your project is complete you should always render these sections to verify the appearance of the final effect.

Effects in these color-identified sections of the Timeline are always rendered prior to being printed to video or edited to tape unless you override this behavior by opening the RT pop-up menu and choosing the Record to Tape > Use Playback Settings option. Video exported to QuickTime or that uses Compressor is always rendered at full quality.

Reviewing Motion Basics

Before diving into the Surf lesson, take a moment to review the most common ways you can transform clips. These techniques will be used extensively in later exercises.

1 Double-click **Surf_Background** in the Timeline to open it into the Viewer, and click the Motion tab.

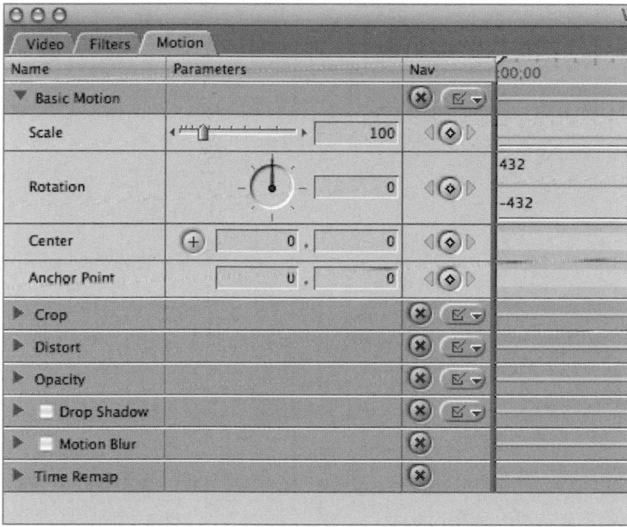

The Motion tab contains motion parameters associated with every video clip. The controls in this tab are separated into groups, which you can open or close by clicking the disclosure triangles to the right of each group name. By default, the Basic Motion parameters are exposed, revealing the Scale, Rotation, Center, and Anchor Point controls.

2 Drag the Scale slider to the left, until it's set at around 60.

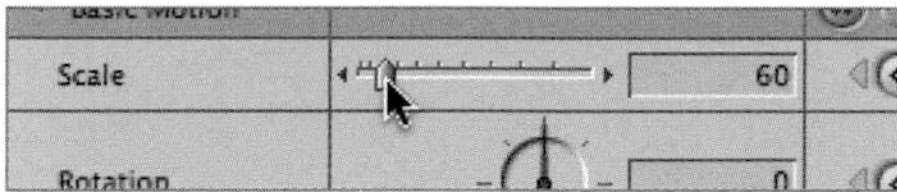

As you make this adjustment, you can see the clip shrink in the Canvas.

The Scale parameter is a simple percentage, which can be adjusted from 0 (which makes the image non-existent) to 1000. Be aware that enlarging an image beyond 100 will result in a softening of the image.

3 In the Canvas, click the View pop-up menu, and choose Image+Wireframe.

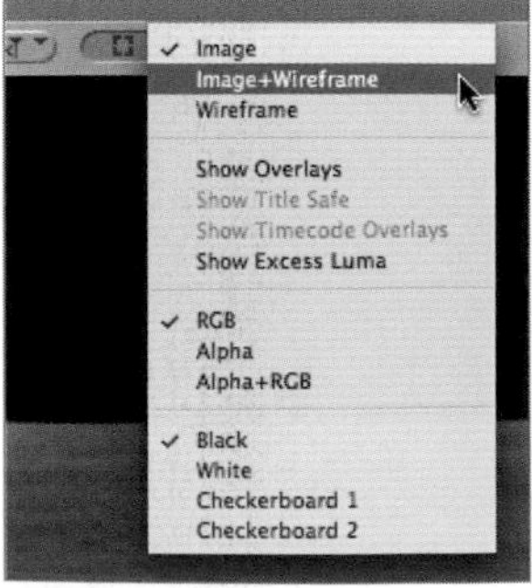

This option makes a wireframe appear over the selected clip in the Canvas. If you don't see the wireframe, either the playhead isn't over the selected clip, or no clip is selected. To select a clip, click it in the Canvas or in the Timeline.

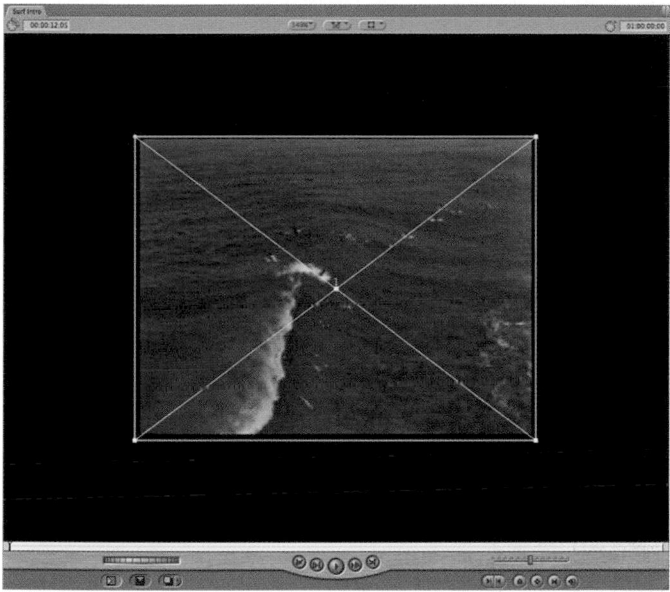

TIP Double-clicking a clip, either in the Canvas (in Wireframe mode) or in the Timeline, opens that clip into the Viewer.

Wireframes serve two purposes. First, they let you know which clips are selected. Second, they provide you with onscreen controls to graphically adjust most of the motion parameters (displayed in the Motion tab of the Viewer) in the Canvas.

4 In the Canvas, move the pointer directly over one of the corner handles of the wireframe.

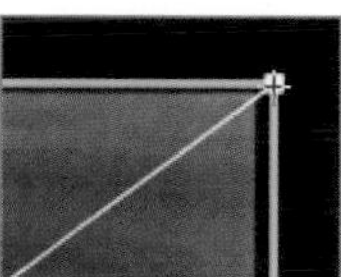

5 When the arrow turns into a crosshair, drag the corner point toward the center of the Canvas to shrink the clip.

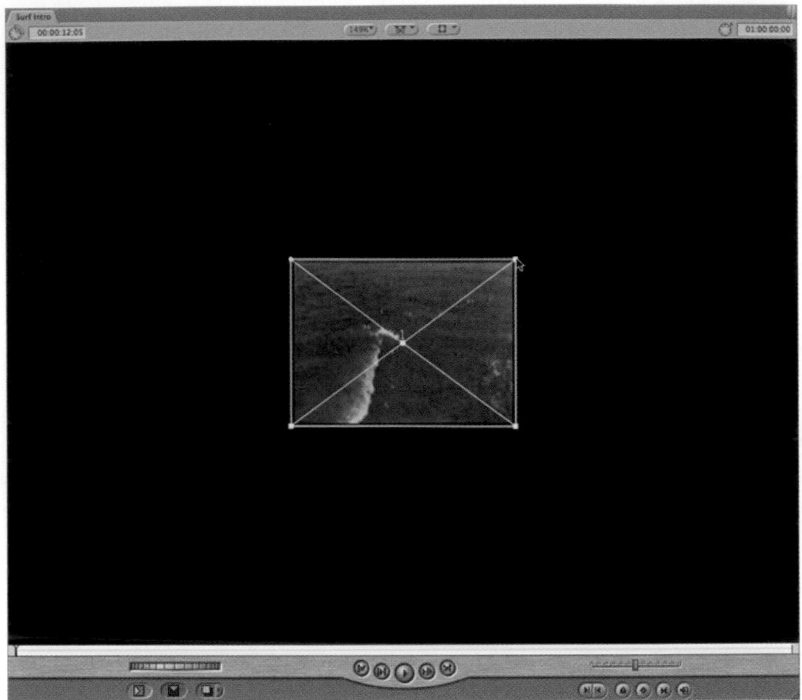

TIP If your pointer changes to the Window Resize pointer instead of the crosshairs, dragging will resize the windows rather than resize the clip. Be sure to see which pointer is active before dragging.

As you drag the clip's corner, notice how the Scale parameter updates in the Motion tab of the Viewer. By default, resizing is done proportionally, around the center of the clip.

6 Shift-click one of the wireframe corners, and drag it up and to the left.

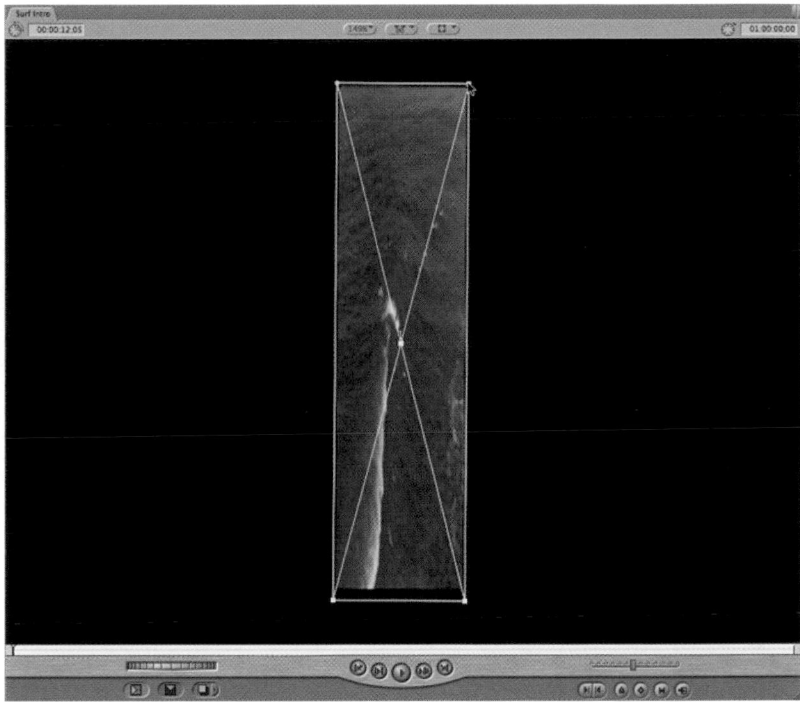

By pressing the Shift key while you resize an image in the Canvas, you can resize it freely, squeezing or stretching it out of its original proportions by simultaneously adjusting the Aspect Ratio parameter (currently hidden in the Distort parameter group in the Motion tab of the Viewer).

7 Position your pointer over any edge of the clip.

The Rotate pointer appears.

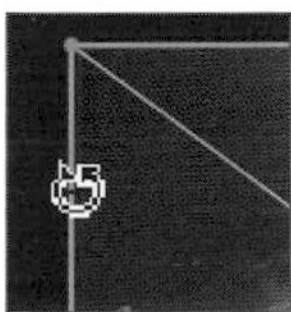

8 Drag the edge of the clip to rotate it.

9 Position your pointer anywhere over the body of the clip.

The Rotate arrow changes to a Move pointer (a crosshair with arrows on each end).

10 Drag the clip to change its position in the Canvas.

Notice that the Center Point control in the Viewer updates to reflect the new value.

11 Shift-drag the clip from anywhere in the body of the object, left to right or up and down.

Pressing Shift constrains clip movement to horizontal or vertical directions.

For every action you make in the Canvas, the values in the Motion tab are updated. And similarly, modifying the values in the Motion tab automatically updates the Canvas (assuming the Canvas is currently parked on the clip open in the Viewer).

Both methods have their benefits. If you want to set precise numerical values, it is far easier to use the Motion tab, but if you want to observe the intuitive feedback and get a general feel for the effect, dragging in the Canvas is superior.

Resetting Attributes

Before you continue, it's critical to know how to undo all of these changes and reset the clip to its native state. Aside from manually returning each parameter to its default settings, there are two ways you can restore a clip's attributes.

1 Click the Reset button, located in the Motion tab of the Viewer to the right of the Basic Motion section header.

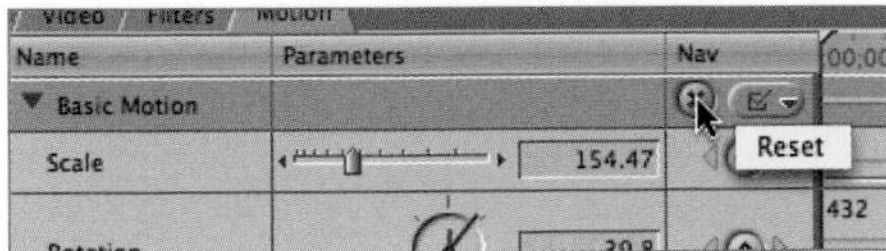

This button resets all the controls in the Basic Motion section. Unfortunately, it doesn't restore the Aspect Ratio parameter located in the Distort parameter group. Fortunately, another method for resetting a clip's parameters is more comprehensive.

2 In the Timeline, Control-click the **Surf_Background** clip, and choose Remove Attributes from the shortcut menu.

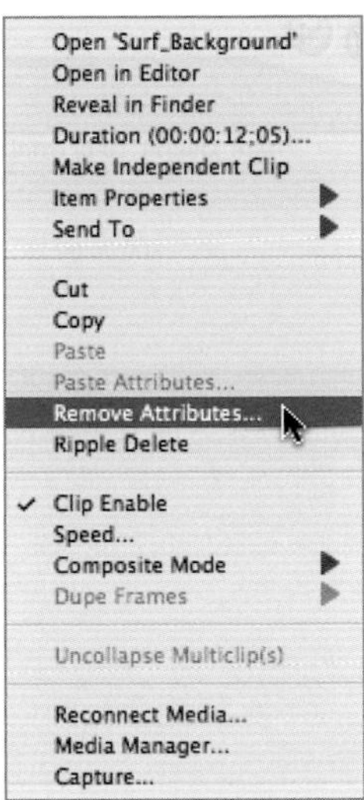

3 In the Remove Attributes dialog that appears, select the parameter groups you want to restore to their default settings and click OK. By default, the Distort setting is already selected.

The image is now returned to its default size and position, ready for you to create your first composition.

The Remove Attributes dialog displays checkboxes for every parameter group, filter, and speed setting that can be applied to a group. If you want to immediately set a clip to its default state, this is the way to do it.

TIP You can also use the Remove Attributes dialog to remove attributes from multiple clips at once. For instance, one clip may have a filter and another clip may have an altered motion setting. Simply select all clips with effects, Control-click, and choose Remove Attributes from the shortcut menu. Then select the attributes you want to remove from all of the clips.

Creating a Multilayered Show Opener

In this exercise, you'll build on the previously described techniques to create an intro for a video program on surfing, imaginatively titled *Surf*. As is typical for many show opens, a wealth of unused B-roll was made available from the shoot, providing you with the opportunity to create a multilayered composition of surfing shots. A designer has also provided a multilayered Photoshop file that you will use as the actual title and logo for the show.

The final composition will consist of a background clip, four foreground clips, and four graphics layers on top of that. In the process of marrying all of these elements together, you'll combine many compositing techniques used to create motion graphics for video.

Previewing the Final Composition

Before you get started, take a look at the final product to orient yourself.

1 Double-click the *Surf Intro - Finished* sequence to open it into the Timeline.

2 Press the Spacebar to play the sequence.

NOTE ▶ If your computer is dropping too many frames to keep up with all the effects in this sequence, make the Timeline or Canvas the active window, and choose Sequence > Render All > Both (Option-R) to render the sequence prior to playing it.

As you work on the exercises in this lesson, feel free to refer to the finished version of the project by clicking back and forth between the *Surf Intro* and *Surf Intro - Finished* tabs in the Timeline or Canvas. This should help guide your adjustments.

Editing Superimposed Video Layers

The first thing you need to do is edit in the clips you want to use in this composition. Because you'll be superimposing clips throughout the lessons in this book, a small refresher on the subject is probably in order to ensure that you can perform this step as quickly as possible.

1 Click the *Surf Intro* tab.

There's a single item in the Timeline: the **Surf_Background** clip that happens to be the placeholder clip from your imaginary original program.

You need to superimpose the clips that you'll arrange in the middle of this composition.

2 In the Browser, open the Clips bin.

There are two ways to edit superimposed clips into a sequence.

3 Press Home to move the playhead to the beginning of the sequence, then drag the **Surf_Shot_02** clip into the Canvas and drop it onto the Superimpose Edit Overlay.

A new video track is created above track V1, and the clip is edited into it. You can also superimpose the clips by using keyboard shortcuts.

NOTE ▶ To use the F9 through F12 keyboard shortcuts to make edits in this next step, you need to disable these keyboard shortcuts in the Dashboard and Exposé panels of the System Preferences window.

4 With the Timeline active, press Home to move the playhead back to the beginning of the sequence in the Timeline. Press Command-4 to make the Browser active, use the arrow keys to select the **Surf_Shot_01** clip, and press the Return key to open that clip into the Viewer. Press F12 to edit the selected clip into the sequence with a superimpose edit.

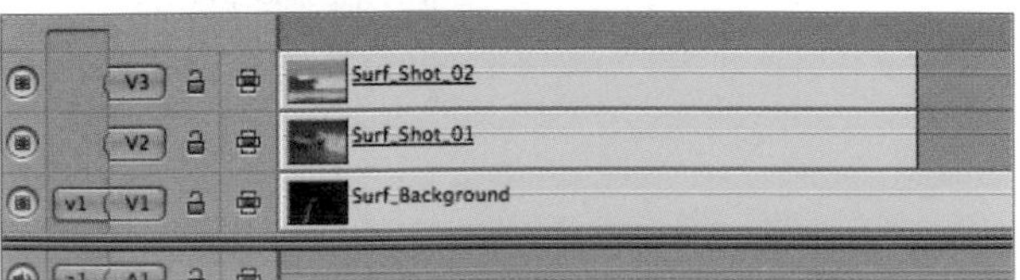

Notice that **Surf_Shot_01** has been superimposed over the track indicated by the source/destination controls, which is still track V1. The first clip you edited in, **Surf_Shot_02**, moved up to a new video track to make room. This demonstrates that superimposed clips are always edited into a sequence above the destination track. If there are clips already in the track above, they're all moved up one track to make room.

The second method of superimposing clips in the Timeline is a more hands-on technique (for those of you who prefer to keep your hands on the mouse).

5 Drag the **Surf_Shot_03** clip to the beginning of the Timeline and drop it into the gray area above track V3.

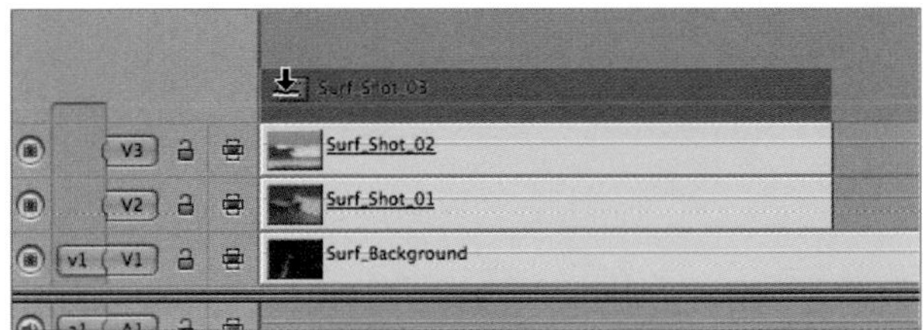

A new video track is created, and the clip is edited in above the other clips. One advantage to dragging a clip into place is that it spares you the step of changing the source/destination track pairing when you want to add a clip to the very top of a growing stack of clips.

NOTE ▶ In this latest method, the clip will snap, if snapping is turned on, so you can use the beginning of the clip in the Timeline or the playhead for precise alignment. Like most of the GUI direct manipulation functions, this very intuitive method is faster if you're using a graphics tablet as your interface.

6 Drag the **Surf_Shot_04** clip to the top of the superimposed stack of clips. These are all of the video clips you'll be using for this opening sequence.

Cropping Images

Cropping allows you to cut off part of the top, bottom, and sides of an image. You might do this to hide unwanted edges of an image, to eliminate all but just the portion of a clip you want for your composition, or to open up room for other images.

If you look closely in the Canvas in the following figure, you'll notice a thin black border at the edges of the image.

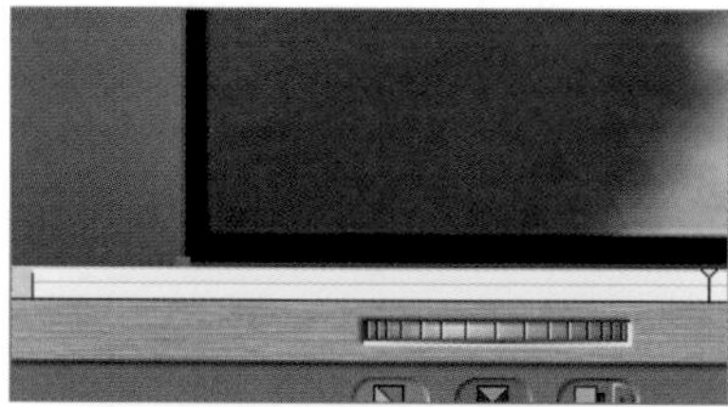

Borders such as these along one or more edges of the frame are a common occurrence in video from a variety of sources. Many camcorders commonly record these black borders along one side of the frame. Some video capture cards introduce similar borders. In other cases, the equipment used to telecine film to video may introduce such borders.

In this exercise, you'll trim these unwanted borders from clips that are resized and superimposed into the overall composition. You'll also crop into some of the images to make room for other elements. Along the way, you'll turn on features in the Canvas that make it easier for you to perform these and other compositing tasks.

1 Move the playhead to the beginning of the sequence, and from the View pop-up menu, choose Show Overlays. If you don't see the title safe boundaries, choose Show Title Safe from the View pop-up menu.

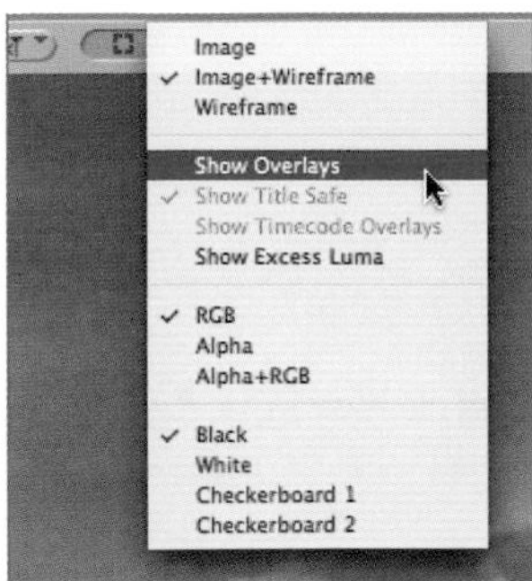

The title safe boundaries appear in the Canvas.

As you create compositing layouts for broadcast video programs, it's typical to refer to the title and action safe boundaries of the picture. Most home televisions display a video image by overscanning it. In other words, approximately 10 to 20 percent of the outer parts of the image is "cut off" behind the bezel of the television, to provide a "full-screen" image. This overscan hid the fact that older television tubes had significant distortion due to the curves at the edges of the screen. These problems are less severe or alleviated altogether with modern flat-screen and flat-panel TVs.

However, to give guidance to the motion graphics designer, the outer boundary indicates the action safe area, which is the area you can reliably expect will be cut off by most televisions (consisting of the outer 10 percent). The inner boundary indicates the title safe area (which excludes the outer 20 percent of the picture) that should be visible and undistorted on virtually every television.

In this image, you can see a common aspect found in many captured clips: a thin black border. Some video clips have this along only one side, and others clips have more (such as footage that originated on film and was telecined to video). Compared to the outer action safe boundary, you can assume that this part of the picture will be outside the area that anyone will see on television. On the other hand, if you intend to resize the image to fit within a composition (as in this example), you can't let these borders show.

2 In the Timeline, double-click **Surf_Shot_04** to open it into the Viewer. Click the Motion tab, and then click the disclosure triangle next to the Crop parameter group.

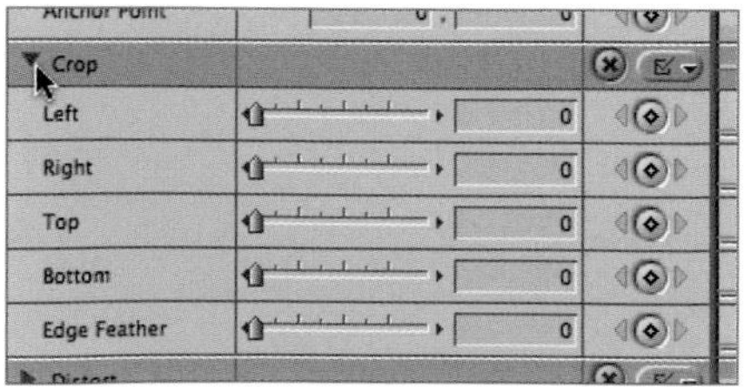

3 Drag the Left slider to the right until you've cropped the image all the way to the action safe boundary.

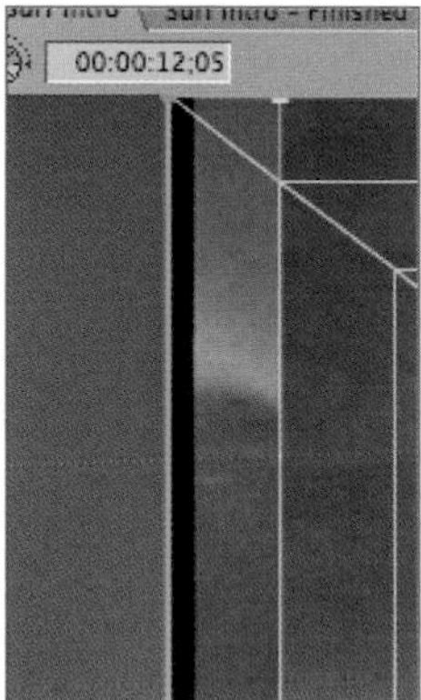

As you crop the top image, notice that the area being cropped is indicated by a separate crop wireframe, and the images that appear underneath start to peek through.

The sliders are really useful when you need to make precise adjustments. However, there's a tool you can use to crop images directly in the Canvas that's a little more interactive.

4 Click the Crop tool.

5 In the Canvas, move the pointer to the right edge of the image. When the pointer turns into the Crop pointer, drag the edge to the left, all the way to the action safe boundary, to crop it.

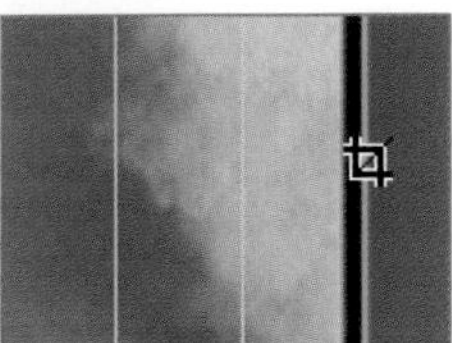

This would be useful if you just wanted to exclude the unwanted border around the image prior to shrinking it, but you actually want to crop in to isolate the surfer within the frame.

6 From the Zoom menu at the top of the Canvas, choose Fit All.

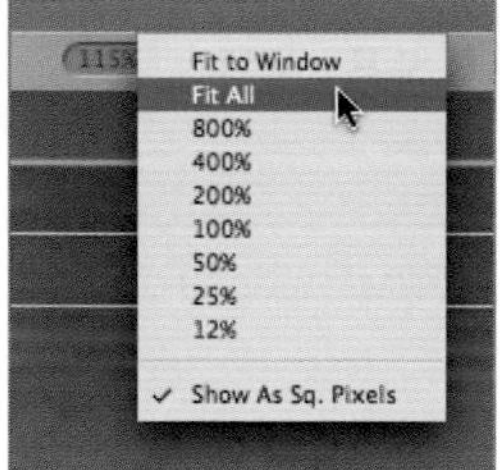

The image in the Canvas shrinks to display more gray border around the image. This makes it easier to manipulate the outer edges of wireframes located at the edge of the frame. You could also do this by reducing the magnification of the image, but Fit All is an automatic operation.

7 In the Canvas, scrub through **Surf_Shot_04** to get a sense of where the surfer goes in the frame.

In this clip, the surfer moves from his position at the right of the frame to a point just about halfway through the frame, before he "cuts back."

8 Use the Crop tool on the right edge of **Surf_Shot_04** to drag the crop wireframe to touch the surfer at the beginning of this motion, and drag the crop wireframe at the left edge of the clip to touch the surfer at the end of

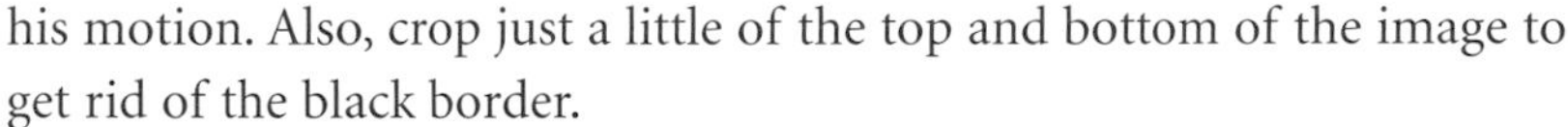
his motion. Also, crop just a little of the top and bottom of the image to get rid of the black border.

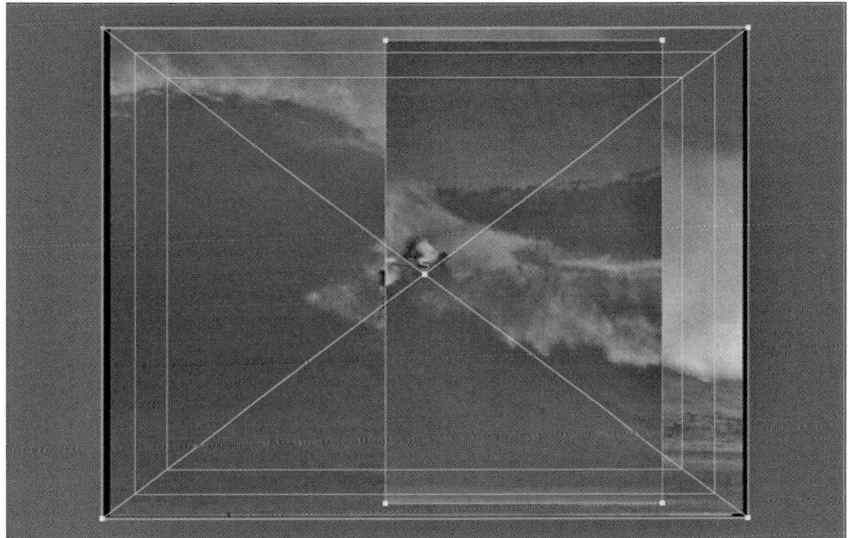

Next, you'll crop each superimposed clip to isolate the greatest area of motion. With so many clips in the Canvas, however, operating on the wireframe of a layer underneath can be difficult, so you should solo each video track containing the clip you want to work on.

9 Option-click the Track Visibility control for track V4.

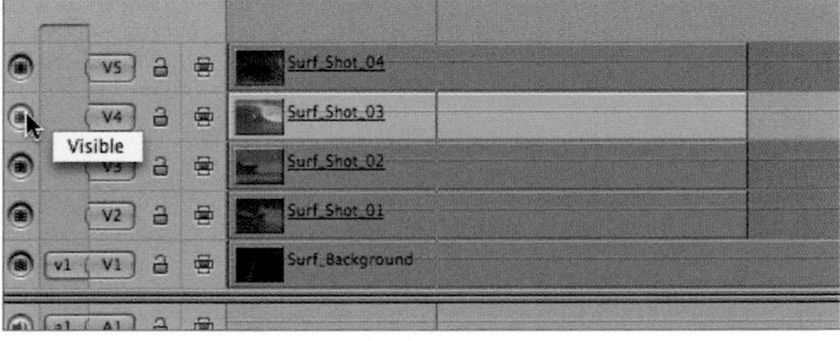

This control turns off the visibility of every other video track, leaving just the clips in the track you Option-clicked visible. Option-clicking the same Track Visibility control a second time makes all of the tracks visible again.

10 In the Canvas, click the clip.

Notice that selecting the clip in the Canvas also highlights it in the Timeline. The opposite also works. Selecting a clip in the Timeline also highlights that clip in the Canvas. This is a good way to select clips that may appear underneath other clips in a multilayered composition, as well as to select multiple clips for simultaneous operations.

So far, you've been individually cropping each side of an image. You can also crop two adjacent sides at once using the corner crop handles.

11 Move the Crop tool to the upper-right corner of the selected clip in the Canvas, and drag down and left to crop the top and right sides at the same time.

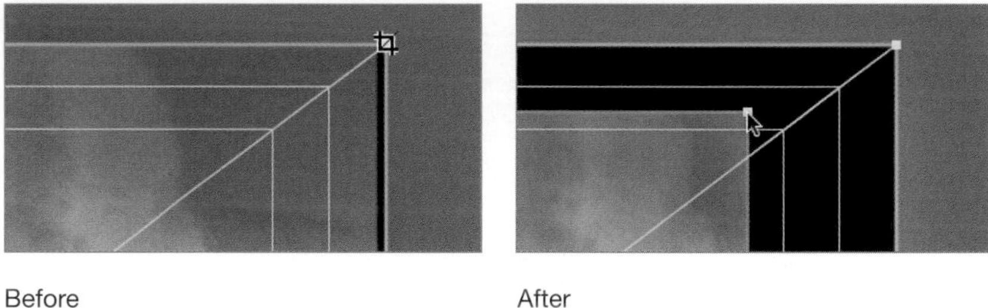

Before After

12 Using the corner crop handles, crop all four sides of **Surf_Shot_03** to isolate and center the surfer within a smaller region.

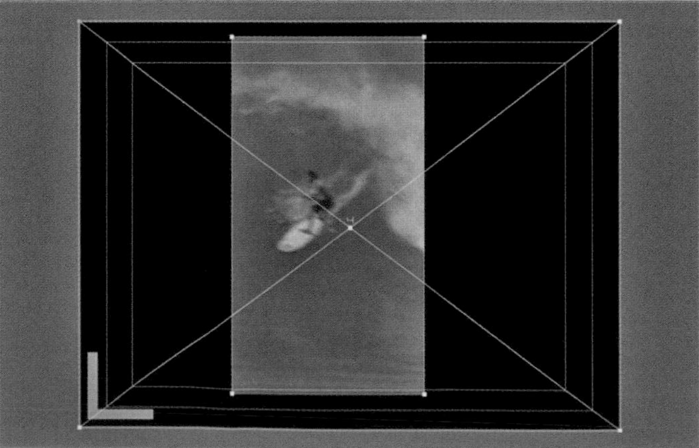

Because the **Surf_Background** clip is also hidden, you can clearly see the background of the sequence, which defaults to black. Sometimes, to more clearly see what you're doing, it helps to choose a different background, strictly for display purposes.

13 In the View pop-up menu in the Canvas, choose Checkerboard 1.

14 In the Canvas, click **Surf_Shot_02** to display the wireframe, and crop the four sides to similarly isolate the surfer's movement within a smaller frame. (This time, crop the top and bottom a little closer.)

As you make this adjustment, you can see the clip image against a checkered background.

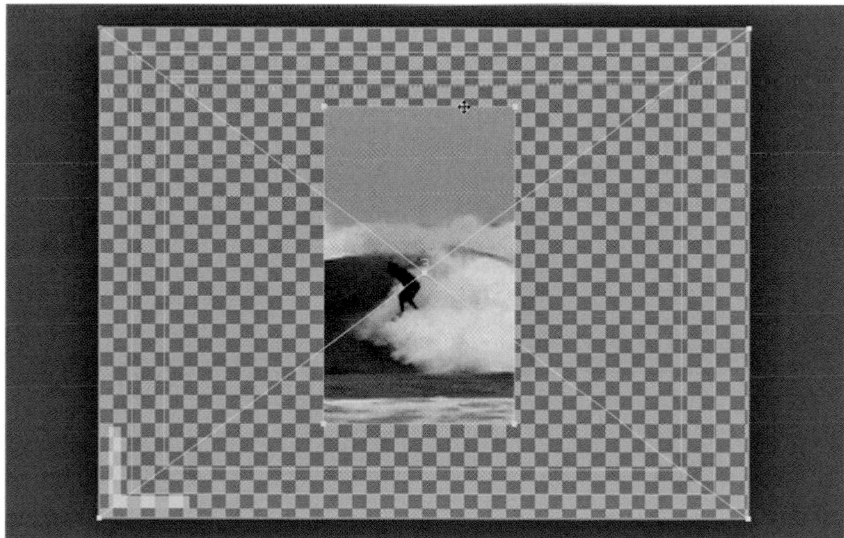

As with the resizing operations you performed, there are also keyboard shortcuts you can use to alter the behavior of the Crop tool.

15 Option-click the Track visibility control for track V3 to return all tracks to visibility.

Another way to isolate a clip is to use the solo command.

16 Select the clip on track V2 and press Control-S to solo it.

17 In the Canvas, click the isolated clip to display its wireframe, then press Command while you drag the left side of the image to crop both sides evenly.

NOTE ▸ You can also press Shift-Command while dragging an edge with the Crop tool to crop all four sides proportionally to the clip's aspect ratio.

18 Press Command and drag down the top edge of the clip to crop the top and bottom of the clip by the same amount.

19 Press Control-S to unsolo the clip, re-enabling all of the clips in the Timeline.

Resizing and Repositioning Clips

Now that you've cropped each of the superimposed clips, it's time to arrange them horizontally in the Canvas. In the process, you'll control the selection of clips using onscreen controls in the Canvas and items in the Timeline.

1 Press Home to return the playhead to the beginning of the sequence.

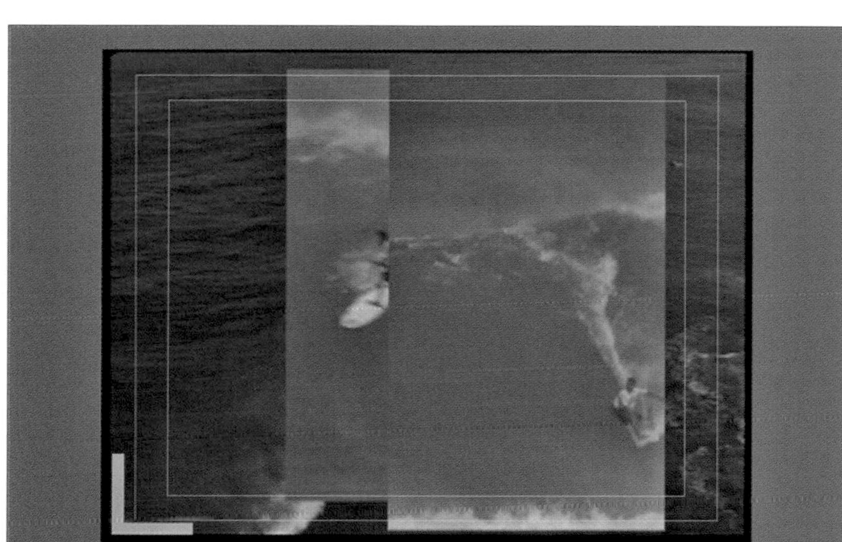

As you can see, the topmost clip is **Surf_Shot_04**. Clip ordering in the Canvas depends on the track order in the Timeline—clips in higher-numbered video tracks appear in front of clips in lower-numbered video tracks.

2 Double-click **Surf_Shot_04** to open it into the Viewer, and click the Motion tab, if necessary, to view the clip's motion parameters.

It's not necessary to open a clip into the Viewer to transform it in the Canvas, but looking at its settings in the Motion tab while you make adjustments lets you see the numeric value of the changes you're making.

3 Press the A key to switch to the default Selection tool, and drag one of the four resize handles (the outer corners, not the inner crop handles) toward

the center of the clip until the value of the Scale parameter is around 56. It's not necessary to be exact.

4 Double-click **Surf_Shot_03** to open it into the Viewer, and drag one of its resize handles toward the center of the clip until the value of the Scale parameter is around 70. It's not necessary to be exact.

TIP ▶ When you open a clip into the Viewer, whichever tab was open for the previous clip remains open but it is updated to reflect the settings of the newly-opened clip.

At this point, the clips underneath the top two clips in the Timeline are getting obscured. It's time to move the top two clips into position.

5 Open **Surf_Shot_04** in the Viewer, then Shift-drag the clip to the left until the first value in the Center parameter is about –147.

NOTE ▶ You may have to release the mouse button periodically to let the Center parameter in the Motion tab update to its current position.

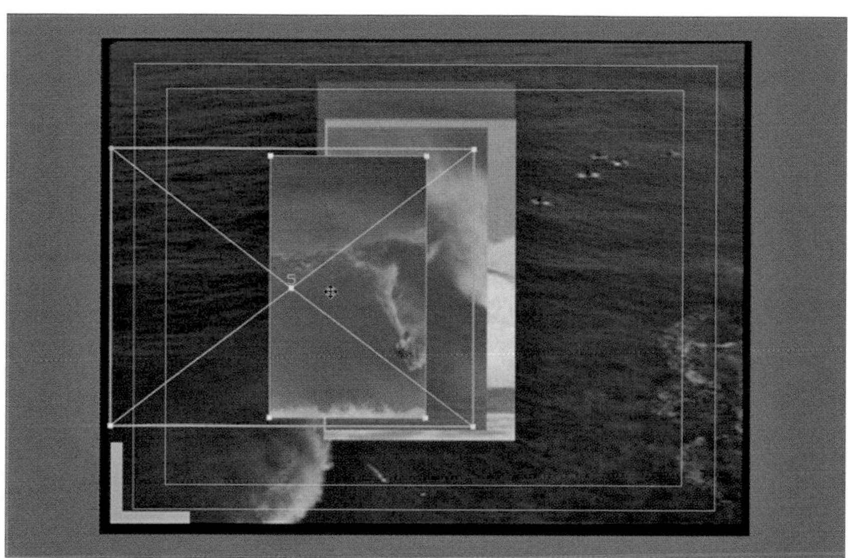

6 Select **Surf_Shot 03** in either the Timeline or Canvas, and Shift-drag it to the right to roughly match this position:

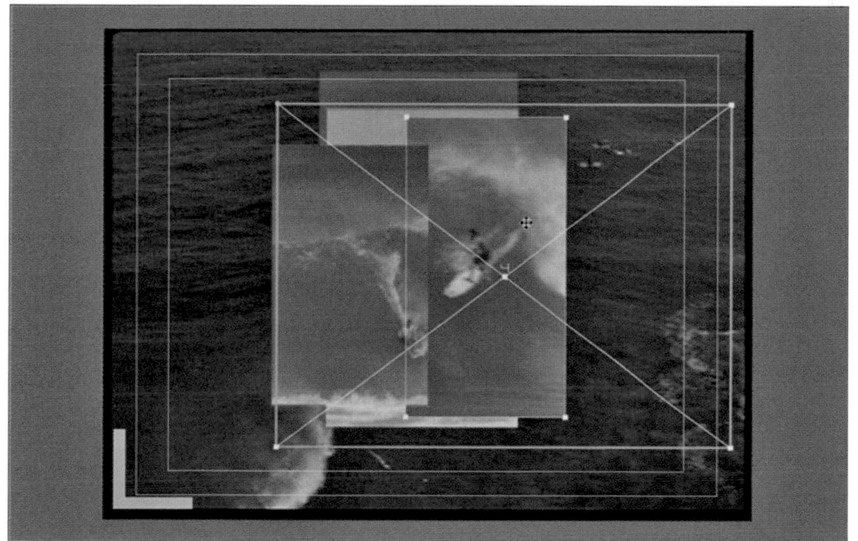

Double-click **Surf_Shot_03** to open its settings in the Viewer. If you look at the Motion tab, you'll see that the Center parameter's value is about 85.

At this point, the onscreen controls of the two front clips are obscuring those of the clips below them. Fortunately, you can still select any clip in the Canvas by selecting it in the Timeline.

7 Move and resize the remaining two clips until your composition in the Canvas resembles this:

TIP Refer to the *Surf Intro - Finished* sequence to see how your version compares at this point to the finished project.

Positioning Clips Precisely in the Canvas

From time to time, you'll find yourself wanting to nudge a clip's position in the Canvas one pixel at a time. Other compositing applications typically use the arrow keys for this function. In Final Cut Pro, the arrow keys are used to navigate and position clips temporally in the Timeline. However, selecting a clip and then pressing Option with an arrow key lets you nudge a clip spatially in the Canvas.

1 Select **Surf_Shot_03** in the Canvas.

2 With the Canvas active, press Option-Down Arrow repeatedly to more closely align the top and bottom of this clip with the superimposed clip appearing all the way to the left.

   This step will only work with the Canvas selected.

Distorting Images

The settings in the Distort parameter group of the Motion tab are useful for many purposes. By adjusting the Aspect Ratio slider, you can mix 4:3 and 16:9 material in the same sequence. By using the corner parameters or the Distort tool in the Tool palette, you can warp an image by its corner handles to create artificial perspective, to make an image fit into a design, or to fit the clip into a composite (such as making a graphic look like a sign on a wall by matching the perspective of the wall).

In this exercise, you'll use the Distort tool to add some angles to your design.

1 In the Tool palette, click the Crop icon and hold down the mouse button. When the related tools appear, select the Distort tool and release the mouse button.

   TIP You can also press the D key once, or the C key twice, to change to the Distort tool.

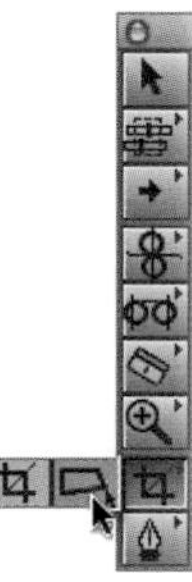

2 Select **Surf_Shot_04**, then drag each of the four corner handles (not the inner crop handles) to warp the image so that it looks like this:

Using the Distort tool, you can independently drag each corner handle to create a wide range of effects.

3 Select **Surf_Shot_03**, and Shift-drag the upper-left corner to the left using the Distort tool.

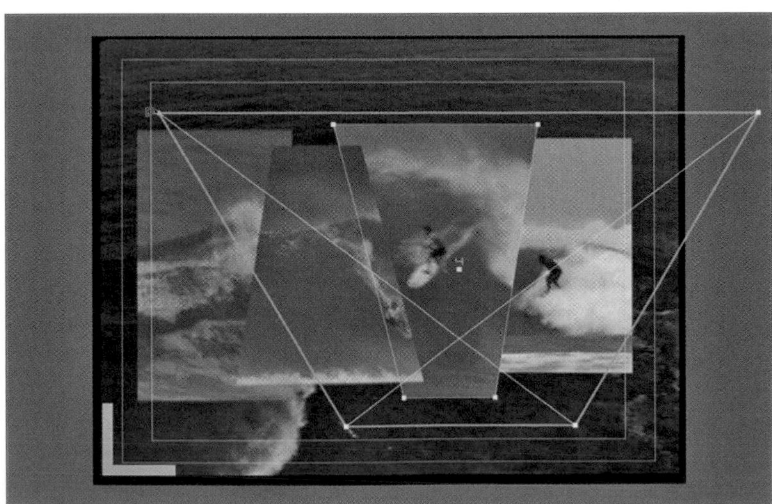

The top corners move outward simultaneously as the bottom corners move inward, simulating a perspective shift, as if the clip were tilting.

4 Use the Distort tool to warp **Surf_Shot_02** and **Surf_Shot_01** to look like this:

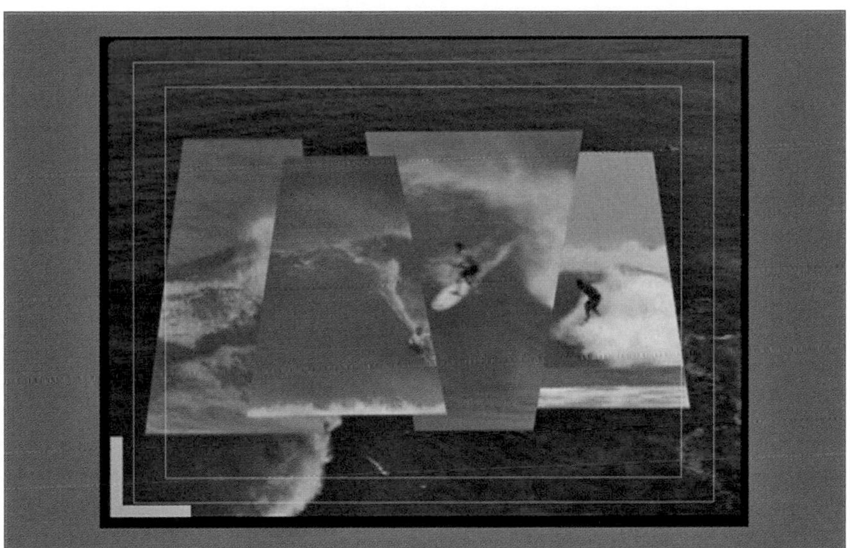

Changing the Clip Timing

At this point, the layout is starting to take shape, but it's a little static. An easy way to add some life to the composition is to stagger the introduction of each of the clips so they appear one at a time. You can then take advantage of their pre-edited durations to have them fade out, one at a time, making room for the title graphic to be added later.

1 Drag to select all of the superimposed clips above the **Surf_Background** clip in the Timeline.

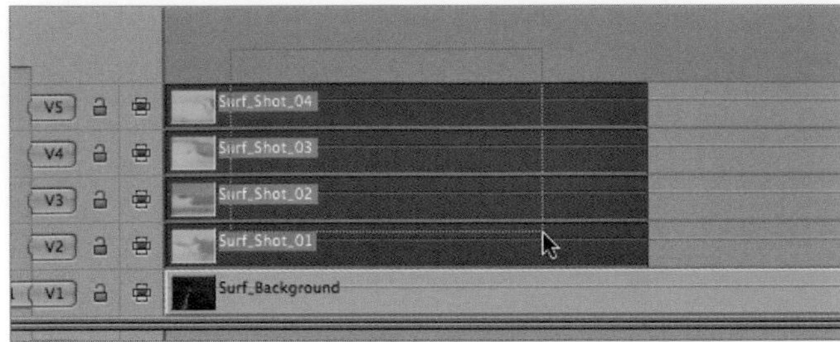

2 Type *1.* (1 period) so that a special indicator appears at the top of the Timeline. Press Return.

The period is a placeholder for two zeros, so you've specified that the selected clips should move 1 second forward.

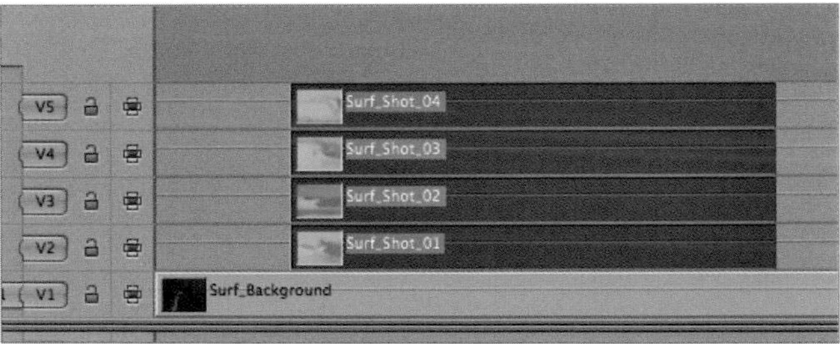

3 Command-click **Surf_Shot_01** to deselect it while leaving the clips above selected. Then type *+15* and press Return to move the selected clips forward 15 frames in the Timeline.

4 Keep moving the clips forward in staggered fashion, deselecting the bottom clip by Command-clicking it, and shifting the remaining selected clips forward by 15 frames until the sequence looks like this:

5 Control-click the end point of each clip, and choose Add Transition 'Cross Dissolve' from the shortcut menu.

NOTE ▶ If your default transition is not set to Cross Dissolve, you can set it to be the default by Control-clicking on the Cross Dissolve transition in the Effects tab.

After you've added a dissolve to the end of each clip, your sequence should resemble this:

6 Play the sequence from the beginning.

Each clip should appear 15 frames later than the previous one, dissolving away in the same staggered order.

Experimenting with Composite Modes

Whenever two objects overlap in a video composite, you can mix the images in a variety of ways. The simplest is for one image to completely obscure another, or you can attenuate the opacity of the top image to create transparency.

Additionally, you can mix the pixels of the two images together in a mathematical equation, such as adding or subtracting the values together. The results of such combinations can be significantly different than either of the images looked originally. Such operations are called composite modes, and Final Cut Pro has several to choose from.

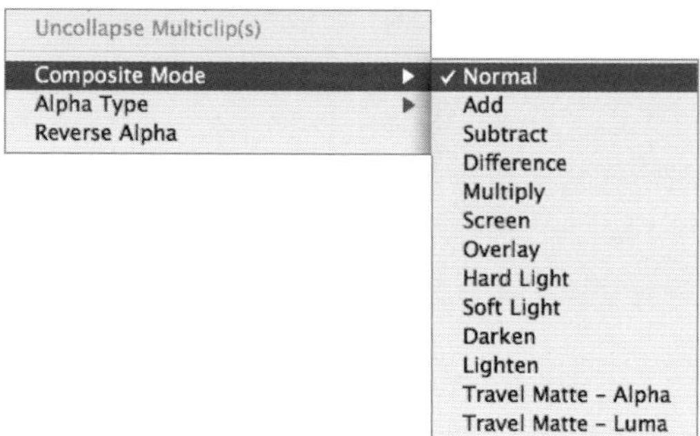

Some composite modes have an overall darkening effect, and some have an overall lightening effect. Some invert color values, and others do a combination of things. Composite mode effects tend to have seemingly unpredictable results, and in most cases the best procedure is to experiment and try different ones.

The composite modes that behave the most predictably are Multiply and Screen. A Multiply effect will only combine the dark portions of the clip, leaving the lighter areas unaffected. Drop shadows are traditionally applied using a Multiply mode, so that the shadow appears to darken the background, without having any impact on the lighter areas.

Conversely, the Screen mode adds only the lightest areas of the clip. Typically, effects like lightning bolts or explosions are combined using a Screen effect so that the background clip is illuminated without affecting the darker areas of the clip.

Overlay does a sort of combination of Multiply and Screen, affecting the darkest and lightest areas of an image without affecting the midrange values.

Composite modes are easy to apply and fun to experiment with.

1 Select **Surf_Shot_01** in the Timeline.

2 Choose Modify > Composite Mode > Add.

The Add composite mode tends to make the composition brighter. You can moderate the effect by changing the foreground clip's opacity.

3 In the Timeline, click the Clip Overlays control to display the opacity overlays.

4 Adjust the overlay for **Surf_Shot_01** to about *50%*.

5 Control-click **Surf_Shot_02** and choose Composite Mode > Difference from the shortcut menu.

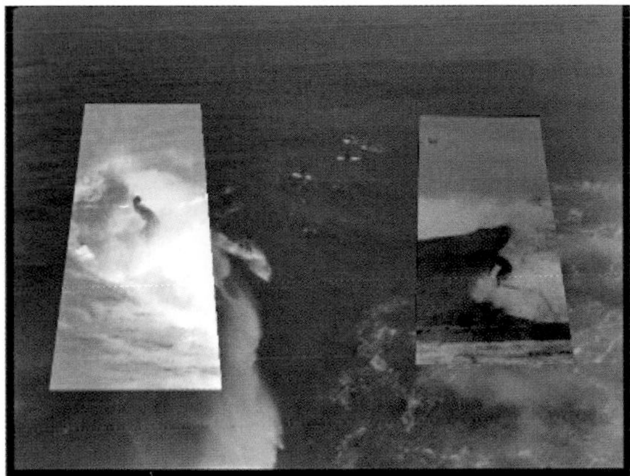

Difference is one of the most unpredictable composite modes.

6 Control-click **Surf_Shot_03** and choose Composite Mode > Screen from the shortcut menu.

As you can see, each of the modes has a unique and interesting effect. Experiment with the different modes yourself, and don't forget to see how opacity changes moderate the effect.

Adding Graphics from a Layered Photoshop File

Now it's time to add the title graphics. In this project, the title graphics have been created as a layered Adobe Photoshop file. Final Cut Pro can import files from any version of Photoshop. However, Final Cut Pro supports only those features available in Photoshop 3. Opacity settings, composite modes (only those available in Photoshop 3), layer order, and layer names are imported; but newer features appearing in versions of Photoshop 4.0 and later, such as layer effects and editable text, are not supported.

Layered Photoshop files are imported like any other media file, but the way they appear inside your project is quite different.

1 Choose File > Import > Files, and select **Surf_Title.psd** from the Media > Surf Video folder.

   NOTE ► If you have trouble finding the **Surf_Title.psd** file, it's also inside the Clips bin in the Browser.

   As you can see, instead of being imported as a clip, the layered Photoshop file has been imported as a sequence.

2 In the Browser, double-click **Surf_Title.psd**.

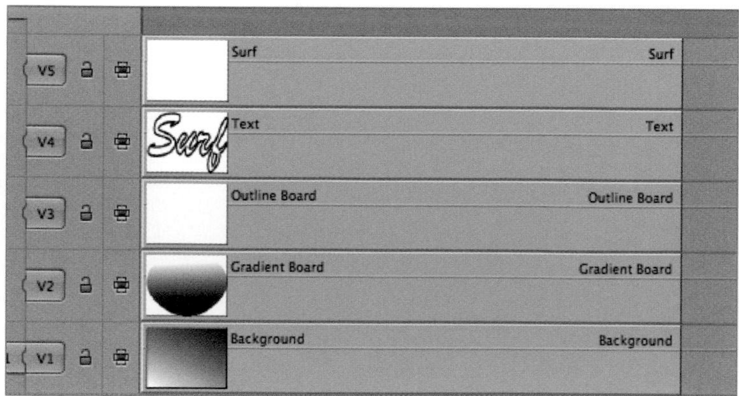

Like any sequence, it opens in the Timeline. There, each layer of the Photoshop file has been translated into a still image on an individual video track.

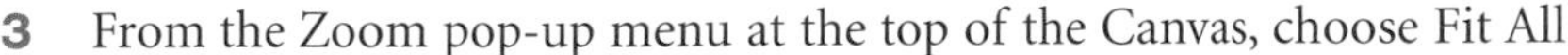

3 From the Zoom pop-up menu at the top of the Canvas, choose Fit All.

You can see that the graphic itself is quite large. It's fairly typical for motion graphics artists to provide artwork at a larger size than it will eventually be used. That way, you don't have to enlarge any clips beyond 100 percent and risk softening the image if it is later decided to enlarge the graphics.

4 Turn off the Track Visibility control for track V1, which contains the background clip.

You can tell from the checkerboard background that the top four layers have a built-in *alpha channel.* An alpha channel is a fourth image channel—in addition to the red, green, and blue channels—that defines regions of transparency in an image.

5 From the View pop-up menu, choose Alpha.

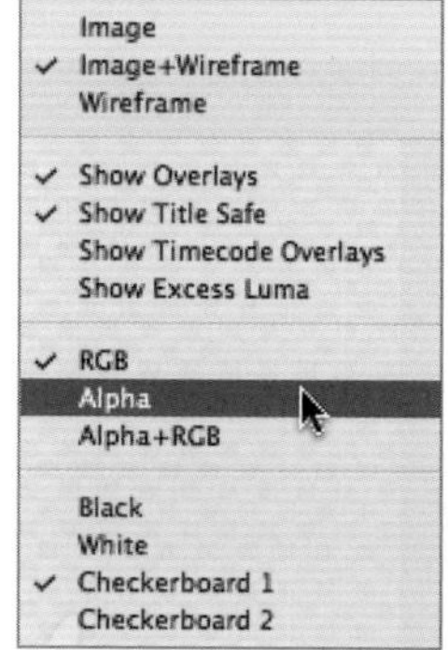

This sets the Canvas to display the alpha channel as a grayscale image.

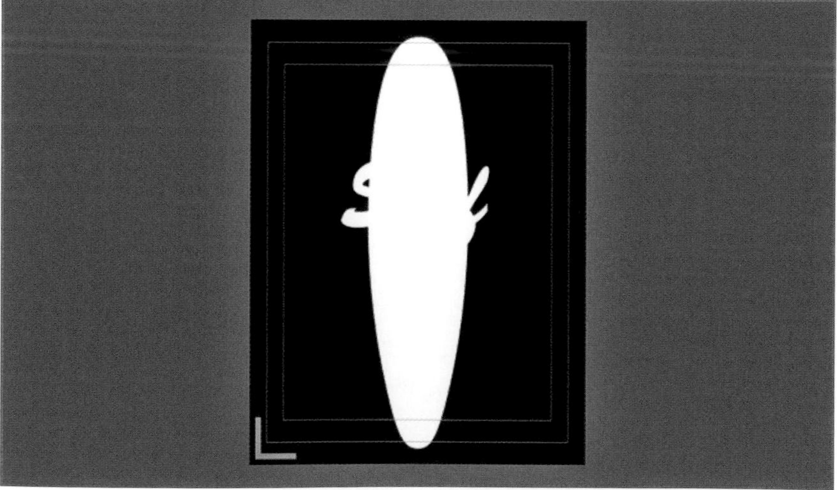

White areas of the alpha channel are 100 percent solid; black areas are 100 percent transparent. Gray areas of an alpha channel (if there are any) represent the semi-translucent values in between, with light-gray areas being more translucent than dark-gray areas.

6 From the View pop-up menu, choose RGB to display the image.

Adding the Logo to the Composition

In your composition, you need only the top four images, so you'll copy and paste these into the sequence you've been working on.

1 Drag to select the clips in tracks V2 through V5, then press Command-C to copy them.

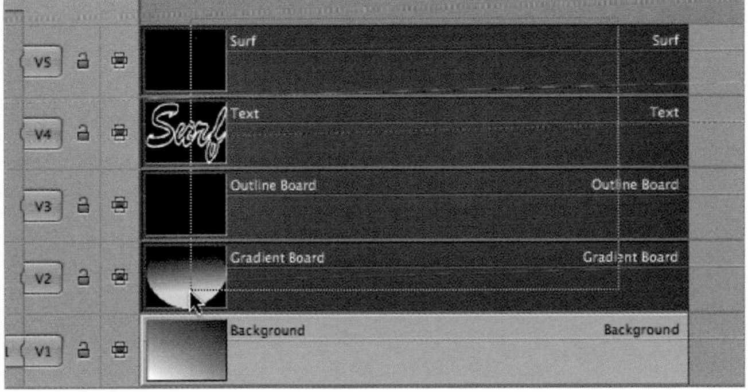

2 At the top of the Timeline, click the Surf Intro tab.

If you simply pasted these clips into your Timeline, the default behavior would be to paste them into the same tracks from which they originated, starting at the position of the playhead. Unfortunately, this would overwrite the existing clips in your sequence. You can override this behavior by using the Auto Select controls in the Timeline header.

The Auto Select controls let you determine which tracks in the Timeline are affected by operations such as filters, edits, and copying and pasting.

3 Control-click the gray area above the top video track in the Timeline and choose Add Track from the shortcut menu.

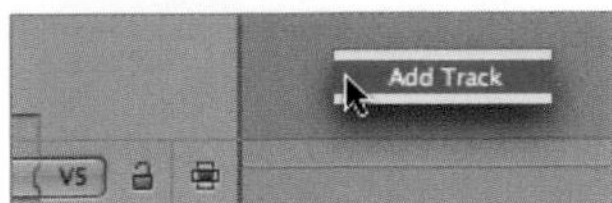

4 Option-click the Auto Select control for track V6.

Option-clicking an Auto Select control turns on that control and turns off all the other Auto Select controls, effectively "soloing" it. Option-clicking a soloed Auto Select control turns back on all the other Auto Select controls.

5 Move the playhead to 01:00:03:00, and press Command-V to paste the copied clips to track V6 (and above).

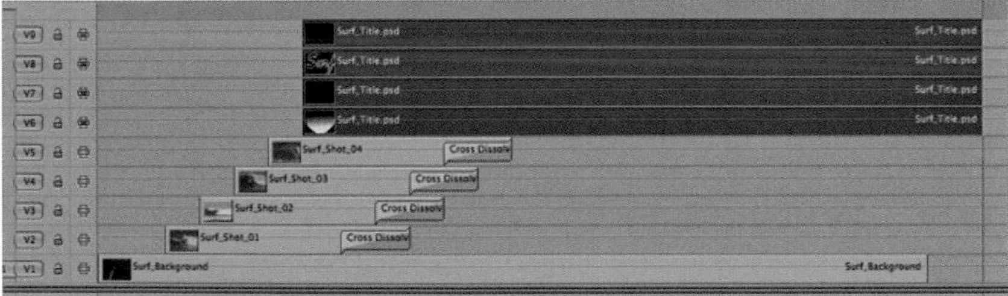

All of the superimposed graphics you copied are pasted into your composition sequence, with the bottommost graphic layer appearing in the Auto Select–enabled track, and all the other superimposed graphics clips appearing above it, automatically making new video tracks.

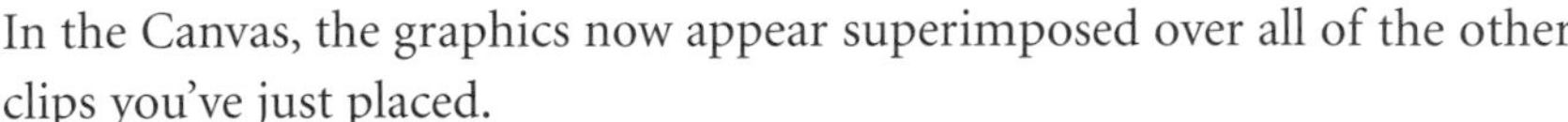

In the Canvas, the graphics now appear superimposed over all of the other clips you've just placed.

Rotating the Surfboard

Next, you'll want to rotate the surfboard so that it's horizontal.

1 Press Shift-Command-A to deselect all the clips in the Timeline, and then select the clip in track V6 so that you're selecting only the surfboard graphic (not the text).

2 Press A to switch to the Selection tool, then move the pointer to the inner corner of the upper-right wireframe handle.

3 When the arrow becomes the Rotate pointer, drag in a circular motion to rotate the clips in the Canvas.

You can freely rotate any clip about its anchor point, but there's a keyboard shortcut that's really handy when you want to rotate a clip in 45-degree increments.

4 Press the Shift key. With the Rotate pointer, drag the inner corner of a wireframe handle. Notice how the graphic snaps vertically, diagonally, and horizontally. Drag the surfboard logo's gradient layer so that it's horizontal.

5 On track V7, select the surfboard outline and press the Shift key while dragging its rotation onscreen control to match the orientation of the surfboard logo gradient layer you rotated in step 4.

Creating Transparency

Now that the surfboard is correctly oriented, you need to make the center semitransparent to let some of the surfing action show through. Although opacity has no onscreen controls in the Canvas, there are still two ways of making opacity adjustments.

1 On track V6, double-click the clip to open it into the Viewer. Click the Motion tab, and click the disclosure triangle next to Opacity.

   This is the Opacity slider, which lets you make uniform opacity changes to an entire clip. If the clip already has an alpha channel, the Opacity slider affects only the visible areas. Opacity is a percentage from 0 (transparent) to 100 (solid).

2 Drag the Opacity slider to the left until the value field reads *30*.

As you drag the slider, you can see the middle of the surfboard become increasingly transparent.

3 Check that the Clip Overlays control is active.

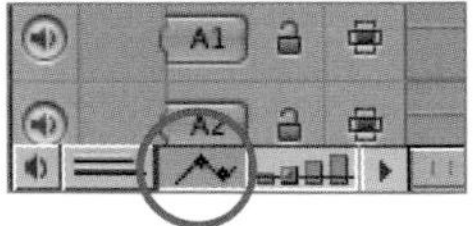

The Clip Overlays control toggles the visibility of the opacity and audio level overlays that appear respectively over video and audio clips in the Timeline. The opacity overlay provides another means of controlling clip opacity.

If you look at the opacity overlay for the clip in track V6, you can see that its opacity is lower than the other clips, because you've already made an opacity adjustment to that clip.

4 Move the pointer directly over the opacity overlay for the clip in track V6. When the pointer turns into the Resize pointer, drag up until the tooltip that appears shows a value between 45 and 50.

When you release the mouse button, the Canvas updates to show the new opacity setting. Unlike the Opacity slider in the Motion tab, the opacity overlays do not allow interactive adjustments to the image in the Canvas. The overlays are generally more useful for keyframing dynamic opacity changes, which you'll learn in a later lesson, or when you simply need to make a quick opacity change and you don't want to open the clip in the Viewer.

Copying Attributes

The last task to complete the title is to move and resize the text component of the title graphic and add drop shadows to the four superimposed video clips. For both of these exercises, you'll be applying the same settings to multiple clips. To make this process faster, you'll use the Paste Attributes command.

Adjusting the Text Layers

Now that you've moved the surfboard, you need to transform the text of the title graphic to fit the new layout.

1 Select the clip in track V9, and drag it into the Canvas so that it fits at the center of the surfboard graphic.

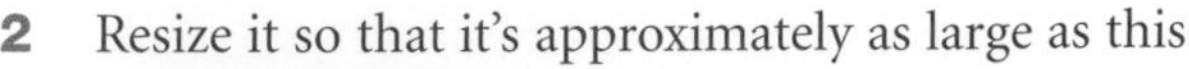

2 Resize it so that it's approximately as large as this:

When you move the top clip, you can see that the black outline was actually created with a second graphic layer underneath, which is now offset. You could copy and paste the values from the top clip's Motion tab to the corresponding parameters in the bottom clip, or you could drag the bottom clip in the Canvas to approximate the size and position of the top clip. But there's an easier way.

3 Select the clip in track V9, and press Command-C to copy it.

4 Control-click the clip in track V8, and choose Paste Attributes from the shortcut menu.

5 In the Paste Attributes dialog, select Basic Motion, then click OK.

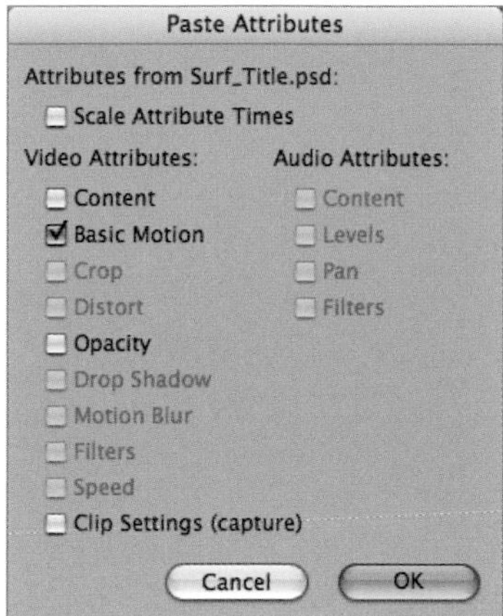

The clip in track V8 is transformed to match the scale and position of the clip you copied. As you can see, Paste Attributes is the opposite of the Remove Attributes command you learned earlier. It allows you to paste the attributes from any copied clip into the Motion parameter settings of another.

Adding Drop Shadows

Now you'll finish off the composition by adding drop shadows to the superimposed video clips and adding transitions to the In points of all the graphics layers in tracks V6 through V9.

1 Move the playhead to the beginning of **Surf_Shot_04**.

2 Double-click **Surf_Shot_04** to open it into the Viewer. Click the Motion tab, and click the disclosure triangle next to the Drop Shadow parameter group.

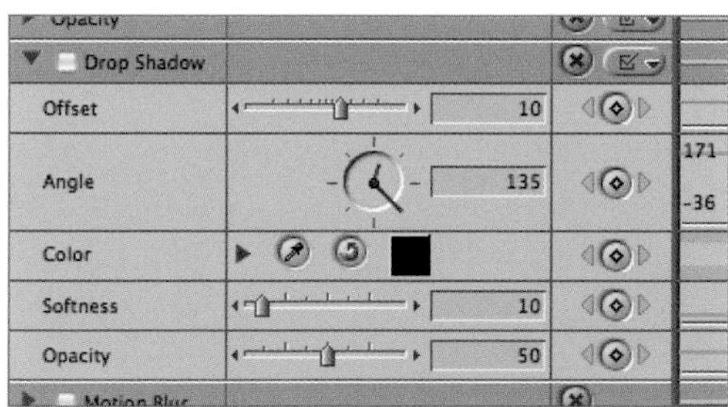

Unlike most of the parameter groups (with the exception of Motion Blur), the Drop Shadow group can be turned on and off as a whole, because all the parameters within this group adjust the same effect.

3 In the parameter group header, select the Drop Shadow checkbox.

A drop shadow immediately appears underneath the selected clip. Drop shadows give the illusion of depth to objects within a composition.

4 To lighten the drop shadow a bit, drag the Softness slider to 50 and the Opacity slider to 30.

Now that you've customized the settings of one drop shadow, you don't have to go through all of these steps for the drop shadows in the remaining three clips. You can use Paste Attributes just once.

5 Make sure that **Surf_Shot_04** is selected in the Timeline, and press Command-C to copy it.

6 Select **Surf_Shot_03**, **Surf_Shot_02**, and **Surf_Shot_01**. Control-click them and choose Paste Attributes from the shortcut menu.

7 In the Paste Attributes dialog, select the Drop Shadow checkbox, and click OK. (Don't select any other parameters.)

The drop shadow parameters are automatically copied to every selected clip in the Timeline.

8 In the Browser, click the Effects tab. Open the Video Transitions > Iris bin, and drag the Oval Iris transition to the beginning of every clip on tracks V6 through V9.

9 Press Home to move the playhead to the beginning of the sequence. Then play the sequence to see how you've done.

Creating a Travel Matte

A common effect is to use the shape of one image to serve as a matte for another—for example, having the video of the surfers visible inside the letters of the text.

This effect is called a *traveling matte* (or shortened to *travel matte* in FCP parlance). It's called *traveling* because the matte shape can change or move, effectively causing the video playing through it to potentially travel across the screen.

Of course the matte doesn't have to move to be considered a travel matte; to qualify, one image must be used to limit which portion of another image is displayed.

In Final Cut Pro, travel mattes are considered a composite mode, because they are yet another way of combining two images that occur at the same time and space.

1 Double-click the *Travel Matte* sequence to open it into the Canvas and Timeline.

   Track 1 contains a modified version of the Surf title, and Track 2 is disabled.

2 Click the Track Visibility control on Track 2 to turn on track visibility.

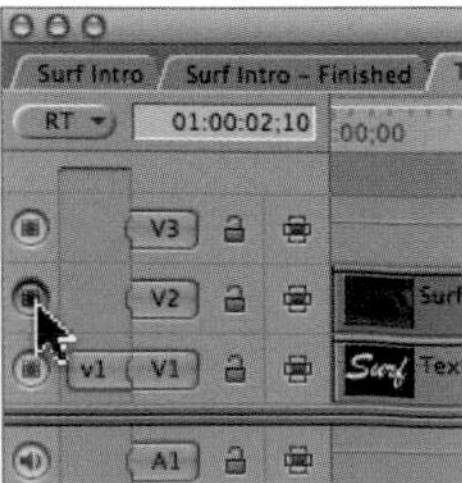

The **Surf_Shot_04** clip obscures the Surf title.

3 Control-click **Surf_Shot_04** and choose Composite Mode > Travel Matte - Alpha.

The Surf title now acts as a matte, defining which areas of the other clip are visible.

There is one tricky aspect to creating travel matte effects in Final Cut Pro: rather than applying the matte to a background image, you must apply the background image to the matte, which may seem counterintuitive.

The clip acting as the matte must be on the track *below* the clip that is to show through the matte, and it is the upper clip that must be set to the Travel Matte composite mode.

In the previous example, the Surf title's alpha channel (previously created in Photoshop) is acting as the matte. Alternately, you could matte a shot with another image's *luminance* (the levels of brightness or darkness). The affected clip will show through the light areas of the shot on the track below it. Every clip has some luminance values, so any clip can be used in this way. Depending on the clip you use, this can create some really bizarre effects. One great way to use this feature is to use one of the Final Cut Pro Generators as the matte.

1 In the Timeline, skip to the second copy of **Surf_Shot_04**.

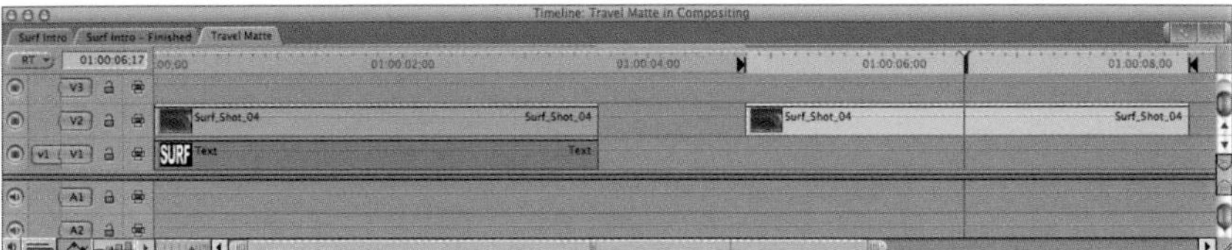

2 Position your playhead anywhere over the clip and press X to set an In and Out point around the clip.

3 In the Viewer, click the Generators pop-up and choose Render > Cellular.

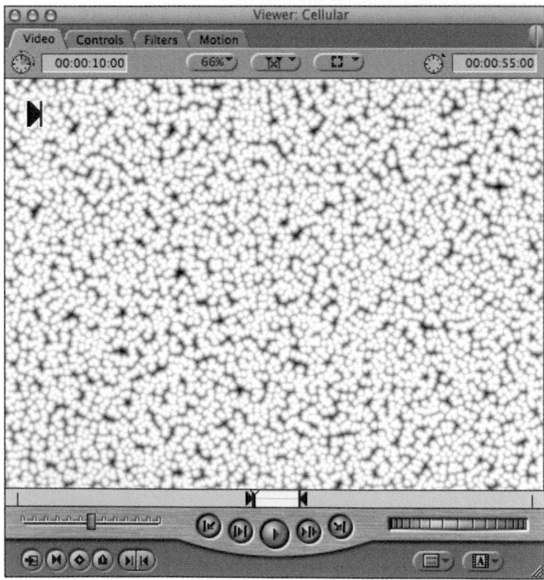

The Cellular generator is loaded into the Viewer.

4 Switch to the Controls tab and drag the Size slider to 64 (the maximum value).

5 Click the Overwrite button or press F10 to edit the generator into the sequence.

6 In the Timeline, Control-click **Surf_Shot_04** and choose Composite Mode > Travel Matte - Luma from the shortcut menu.

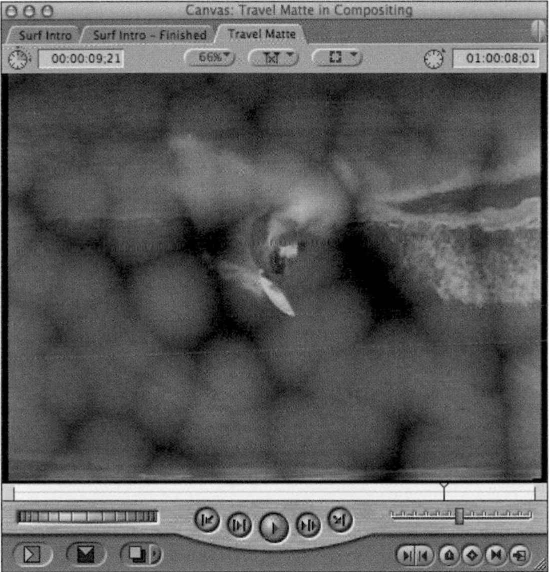

7 Play across the clip to see how the luminance value of the Cellular clip mattes the **Surf_Shot_04** clip.

NOTE ▶ You may need to render the clip (Option-R) to play it back in real time.

Lesson Review

1. Where are each clip's motion parameters located?
2. What motion parameters can you manipulate with the Selection tool using the onscreen controls in the Canvas?
3. What two motion parameters can you manipulate in the Canvas using separate tools?
4. How can you copy the motion effects settings from one clip to another?
5. How do you create a drop shadow for a clip?
6. What is a composite mode?
7. What kind of clips can have a composite mode applied?
8. How do you import a multilayered Photoshop file, and how does it appear within Final Cut Pro?
9. What is a travel matte effect?
10. In a travel matte effect composite, is the matte placed above or below the clip to be matted?

Answers

1. In the Motion tab, whenever that clip is open in the Viewer.
2. Scale, Rotation, and Center.
3. Crop and Distort each have separate tools.
4. Copy the clip with the settings you want to copy, then use the Paste Attributes command on the clip you want to paste these settings into.
5. In the Motion tab, select the Drop Shadow checkbox, and adjust the Offset, Angle, Color, Softness, and Opacity settings to create the desired shadow effect.
6. Composite modes determine how two clips that overlap in time and space are displayed. Various mathematical equations are used.
7. Every clip can have a composite mode applied.

8. Photoshop files are imported using the File > Import > Files command. They appear within Final Cut Pro as sequences, with each layer of the Photoshop file superimposed on its own video track.
9. A travel matte effect uses one clip to determine which areas of another clip are visible.
10. The matte goes below the clip to be matted, and the upper clip gets the travel matte composite mode applied.

7

Lesson Files	Lesson Files > Lesson 07 > Filters.fcp
Media	Surf Video, Motocross, and Misc
Time	This lesson takes approximately 120 minutes to complete.
Goals	Apply filters to clips
	Customize filter effects
	Modify effects by changing the order of multiple filters
	Control filter timing using filter Start and End points
	Apply filters to multiple clips at once
	Save favorite filters
	Control which effects are displayed in the Effects tab
	Reduce camera shake with SmoothCam

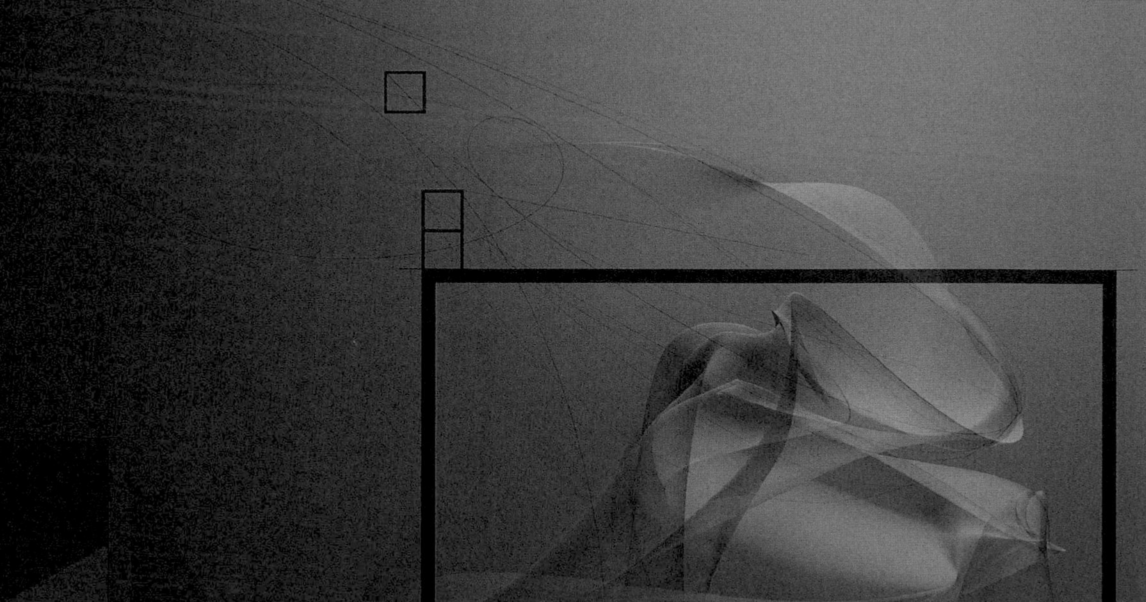

Lesson **7**

Mastering Video Filters

Filters are an easy way to create myriad effects from the subtle to the sublime. Many filters serve strictly utilitarian functions such as correcting color or screen direction errors made during production. Others can stylize an image with painterly effects or glows; distort an image with blurs or pond ripples; overlay timecode numbers, borders, or other data; turn areas of the image transparent; and create a wide range of other effects.

The Final Cut Pro video filter system is a flexible and versatile architecture allowing for third-party plug-ins and even scripting directly in the program. Best of all, using filters is simple, easy, and quick to do.

This lesson deals exclusively with video filters. Final Cut Pro also has audio filters designed to create effects with your sound. Those are covered in Lesson 4, "Sound Editing."

Applying Filters

Filters can be applied to clips in a wide variety of ways to accommodate diverse workflows and editing styles. Most editors employ different methods in different situations—dragging and dropping in one case, using the menus in another, and copying and pasting in a third.

One important distinction is whether you are applying the filter to a clip in the Browser or to a clip in a sequence. Modifying a clip in the Browser means that every occurrence of that clip used (from that point forward) will have the filter applied. Applying the filter to a clip in a sequence will modify only that one instance.

Applying Filters to a Browser Clip

If you want every instance of a clip to be filtered, apply the effect to the master clip in the Browser.

1 Open Lesson Files > Lesson 07 > **Filters.fcp**.

2 Double-click **Surf_Background** to open it into the Viewer.

3 Choose Effects > Video Filters > Image Control > Desaturate.

The clip turns black and white.

4 Drag the clip from the Viewer to the Canvas to overwrite it into the open *Applying Filters* sequence.

The clip in the sequence has the Desaturate filter applied.

If you later use any portion of this same clip, the filter will also be applied. However, any changes you make to the master clip, such as deleting the filter or modifying the filter's parameters, will *not* propagate to the affiliate clips in the sequence. Similarly, changes made to any of the instances in the sequence will not affect any other instance or the master clip in the Browser.

Applying a Filter to a Clip in a Sequence

If you want a filter to be applied to only one use of a clip, after it's been edited into a sequence, all you have to do is park the sequence playhead anywhere over the clip and choose the filter from the Effects menu.

1 In the Browser, double-click the *Surf Clips* sequence.

2 Make sure the playhead is parked on the second clip (**Surf_Shot_02**).

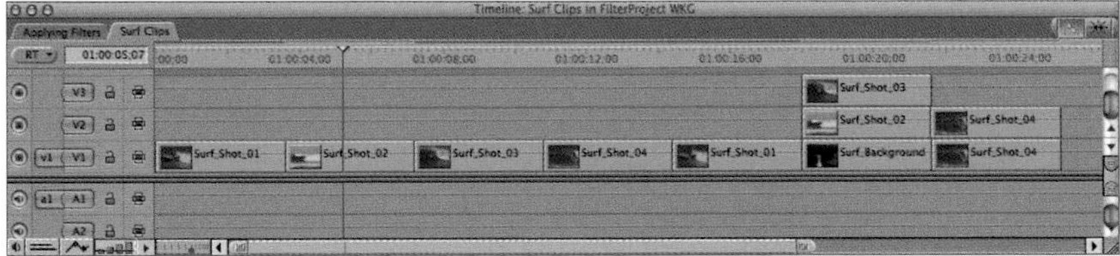

3 Choose Effects > Video Filters > Distort > Ripple.

The filter is applied to the clip. This works because of the Timeline's Auto Select feature.

Auto Select off Auto Select on

However, if a clip is selected in the Timeline, Auto Select is overridden and the filter is applied to the selected clip.

4 Select the fourth clip (**Surf_Shot_04**).

5 Choose Effects > Video Filters > Perspective > Mirror.

The filter is applied to the selected clip, rather than the one under the playhead. You won't be able to tell until you play the sequence or move the playhead to the fourth clip.

6 Play the sequence until you can see the Mirror effect.

It is very easy to get confused in a situation like this, where a filter is successfully applied, but is applied to the wrong clip. If you ever apply a filter and don't notice any effect, always check which window is active and which clips are selected.

Using Auto Select with Multiple Tracks

If there is more than one clip under the playhead, the filter will be applied to any clip under the playhead, on a track where Auto Select is active.

1 Click outside the track area, or press Shift-Command-A, to deselect all.

2 Position the playhead over the three stacked clips near the end of the Timeline.

3 Turn off Auto Select for track V2. Make sure Auto Select is on for tracks V1 and V3.

4 Choose Effects > Video Filters > Channel > Invert.

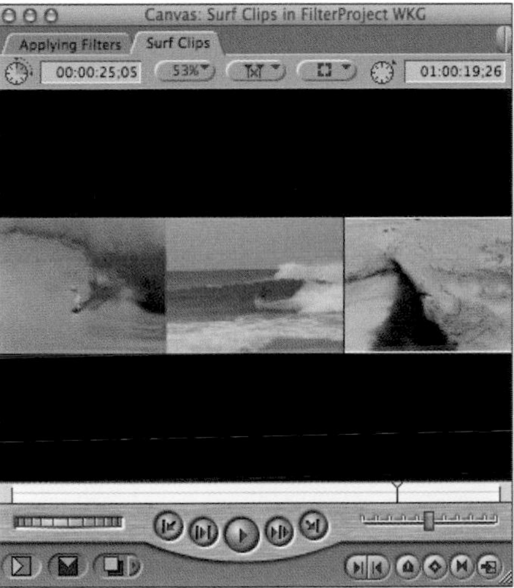

The filter is applied to the clips on the tracks where Auto Select is enabled.

You can also double-click a clip in the Timeline to open it into the Viewer. If the Viewer is the active window, choosing a filter from the Effects menu will apply the filter to that clip.

Always double-check whether the Viewer contains the version of the clip in the Browser or the version of the clip from the sequence.

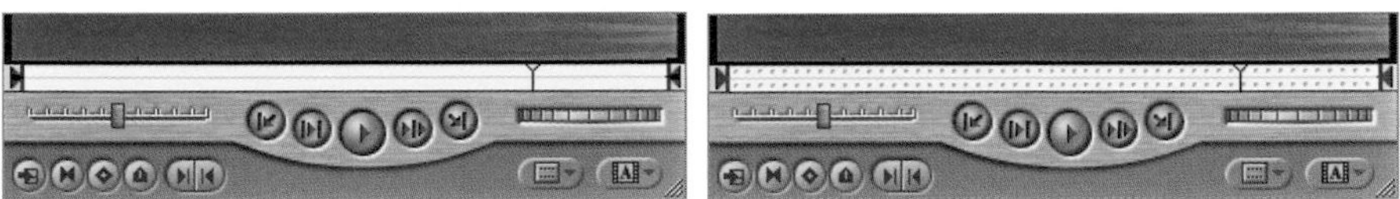

Clip from Browser Clip from sequence

The sprocket holes visible in the scrubber bar are the clearest indication that the clip in the Viewer is from an active sequence.

Applying a Filter with Drag and Drop

In most cases, using the Effects menu is the quickest, most efficient method of applying filters, but there is another way, which allows you to see more precisely what is happening.

The Effects tab in the Browser is an exact mirror of the contents of the Effects menu.

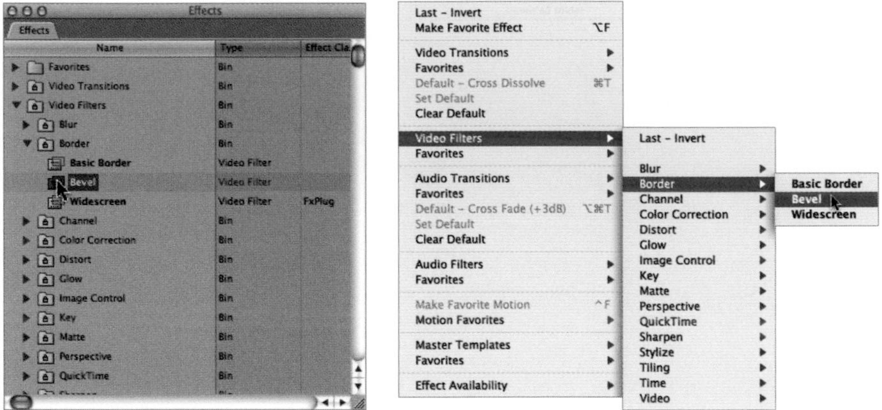

Objects in the Effects tab can be dragged directly to clips in any of the other windows. (You cannot drag a filter onto a clip in the Browser, but if you open the clip, you can drag a filter from the Effects tab directly to the Viewer.)

Applying a Filter to Multiple Clips

Often, you will use a particular effect on more than one clip in your sequence. If you plan ahead, you can do this in one simple step.

1 Select the third, fourth, and fifth clips in the *Surf Clips* sequence.

2 From the Effects bin, open the Image Control bin (inside the Video Filters bin) and drag the Desaturate filter to the selected clips in the Timeline.

NOTE ▶ Remember to move the playhead so you can see the effect of the filter.

The filter is applied to all of the clips. Unfortunately, if you don't like the default parameters, you will need to open up each of the three clips and modify their settings individually, undermining the time saved by applying the filter simultaneously. However, if you adjust the settings first, you can apply the modified version of the filter to the clips and be done quickly.

3 Click the Effects tab. Click the disclosure triangles to open the Video Filters bin and the Border bin.

4 Double-click the Basic Border filter.

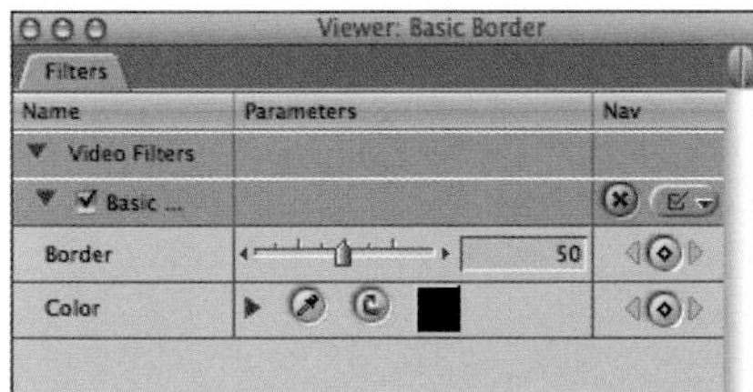

The filter opens into the Viewer, exposing its parameters.

5 Click the Color swatch and change the color to red.

Now the filter is modified and ready to be applied to the clips in the sequence.

NOTE ► Changing this version of the filter affects all future uses of the filter.

6 Make sure the same three clips are still selected in the Timeline.

7 In the Viewer, click the title bar of the filter and drag it onto the selected clips.

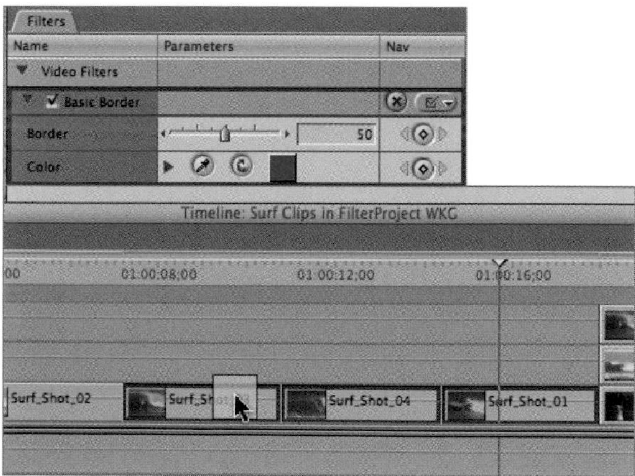

The Border filter is applied on top of the Desaturate filter on all three clips.

NOTE ► Additional changes made to the filter in the Viewer will *not* affect the clips in the Timeline.

Copying and Pasting Filters

Although applying a filter to multiple clips works in some instances, it's often difficult to set a filter's parameters without seeing how they look when applied to a clip. For that reason, in the event you want to apply one filter to multiple clips, it is often more prudent to apply the filter to one of the clips, tweak the settings, then paste the filter onto the remaining clips.

1 Double-click the *Bike Jumps* sequence.

  The playhead should be parked over the first clip.

2 Choose Effects > Video Filters > Stylize > Add Noise.

3 Press Return to open the clip into the Viewer.

  Notice the sprocket holes in the scrubber bar, which indicate the clip is from an active sequence.

4 In the Viewer, click the Filters tab.

5 Set the following parameters (leave the others at default):

Amount: .75

Type: Pink Noise (TV static)

Blend Mode: Add

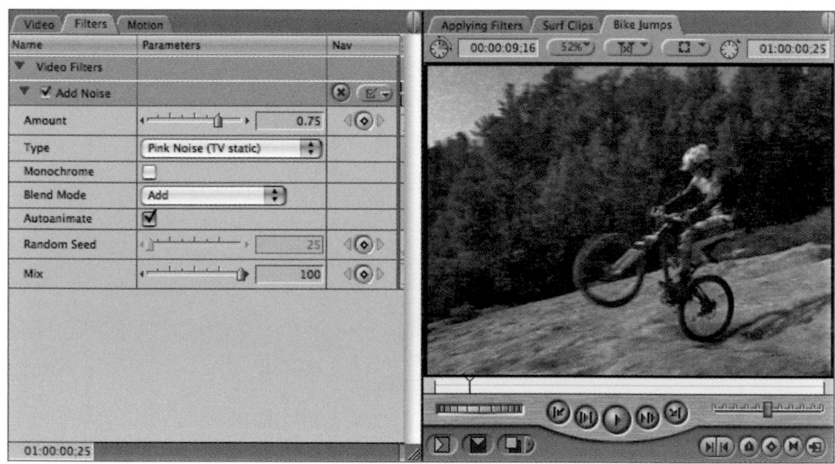

You should see the effect of the changes in the Canvas. If you aren't seeing the effect, check that the sequence playhead is over the first clip.

6 To see exactly how the filter is affecting the clip, select and deselect the checkbox next to the filter name a few times. Make sure to leave it selected when you're done.

Now that the filter is adjusted, you can apply it to the other clips in the sequence.

7 Select the second and third clips in the Timeline.

8 In the Viewer, click the title bar of the filter (the name) and drag it onto the selected clips.

The filter will be applied. Remember, however, that changes made in the Viewer at this point will only affect the clip in the Viewer.

Alternately, you can copy the clip with the filter applied and paste just the filter effect onto other clips.

9 Select the first clip in the sequence.

10 Choose Edit > Copy, or press Command-C.

The clip is copied to the clipboard.

11 Select the last two clips in the sequence.

12 Choose Edit > Paste Attributes, or press Option-V.

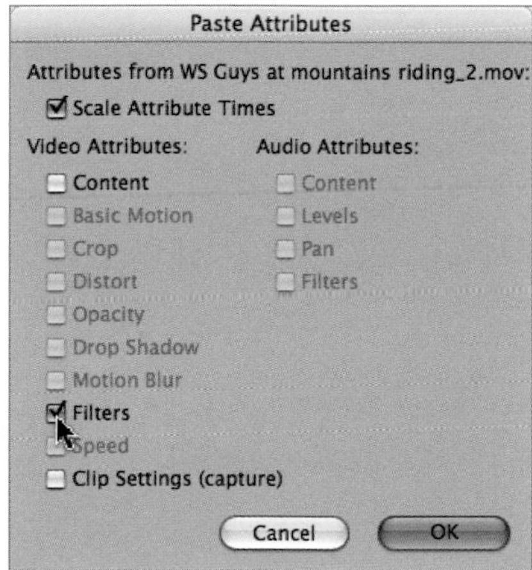

The Paste Attributes window opens.

13 Select the Video Filters box and leave all the other boxes deselected. Click OK.

The filter is applied to the selected clips.

Although this process will save you plenty of time, it does have one significant drawback: If you change your mind about the filter settings, you will need to open each of these clips and modify the parameters individually.

There are two solutions to this problem. The first is to *nest* the clips into a subsequence and apply the filter just once, so that any changes you make will automatically affect all the clips. (For more information on nesting, see Lesson 9, "Nesting Sequences.")

The other solution is more clunky but also more flexible.

1 Double-click the last clip in the sequence.

2 In the Viewer, click the Filters tab (if it's not already visible).

3 Change the Type to Gaussian Noise (Film Grain), and lower the Amount to .3 (period 3).

If you are not seeing the change in the sequence, make sure the playhead is parked on the clip you are modifying.

4 In the Timeline, select the last clip and press Command-C to copy it to the clipboard.

5 Press Command-A to select all of the clips in the sequence.

6 Choose Edit > Remove Attributes.

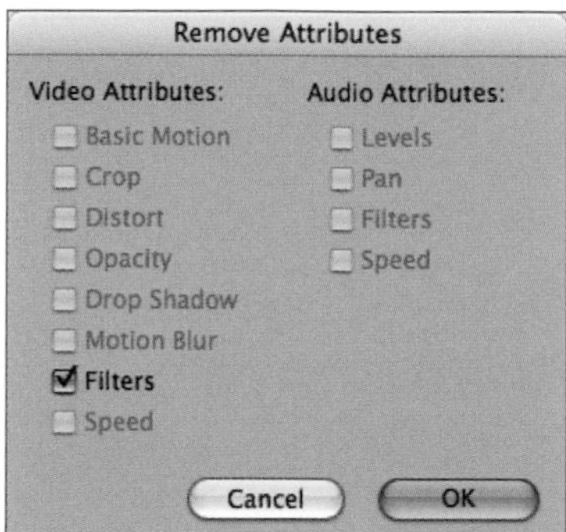

The Remove Attributes window appears. The only setting that should be active is the Video Filters because none of these clips have any other attributes applied.

7 Click OK.

This action removes the filter from all of the clips in the sequence, including the last one, but because you previously copied the clip with the new settings to the clipboard, you are prepared to reapply that filter to all of the clips in one step.

8 If the clips are not all still selected, press Command-A to select all of the clips again.

9 Choose Edit > Paste Attributes, or press Option-V.

The Paste Attributes window appears.

10 Select Video Filters and make sure that none of the other settings are selected.

NOTE ► Scale Attribute Times doesn't apply in this case, so it doesn't matter whether it is selected or not.

The Add Noise filter (with the new settings) is reapplied to all of the clips in the sequence.

Applying a Filter to a Portion of a Clip

You can also apply a filter to a section of a clip, rather than to the entire clip. This can be helpful if you have a clip that includes multiple elements, and you want to filter only one portion.

1 Deselect all the clips by clicking in the inactive area of the Timeline or by pressing Shift-Command-A.

2 In the Toolbar, select the Range Select tool (or press G three times).

3 In the Timeline, click the second clip (**SERIES_JUMPS**) at approximately 02:15, where the first biker just clears the hilltop, and drag to the right until the two-up display in the Canvas shows the first biker just landing (at approximately 01:26:30:15).

The Canvas displays the Start and End points of the selection as you drag.

4 Choose Effects > Video Filters > Time > Echo.

The filter is applied only to the selected range.

NOTE ▶ You may need to render the sequence (Option-R) to see the effect play in real time.

Instead of using the Range Select tool, you can also use In and Out points and the Auto Select feature to specify which part of the clip you want to apply the filter to.

1 Find the place in the third clip (**WS Guys at mountains riding_2-1**) where the biker's shadow completely passes the rock on the left edge (at around 05:00) and set an In point there.

2 Set an Out point approximately 1 second later when the rock on the left has completely left the frame.

3 Make sure that nothing is selected and that Auto Select is enabled for track V1.

4 Choose Effects > Video Filters > Glow > Bloom.

5 The filter is applied only to the area between the In and Out points and only on the Auto Select–enabled tracks.

You can also limit a filter's effect using keyframes. With this technique, you can create gradual changes to individual filter parameters, which results in much more complex and dynamic effects. For more information on keyframing filters, see Lesson 8, "Animating Effects."

Modifying Filters

Nearly 180 filters are available to create a breathtaking variety of effects (and scores more third-party filters are available as plug-ins). What's more, each of those filters has multiple parameters that can dramatically vary its result.

Changing Parameters

In order to modify any filter, you must open it into the Viewer window, but as you learned in the last example, it's usually important to monitor the filter's effect as you adjust. For this reason, it is generally easiest to apply a filter to a clip that is already in a sequence, then immediately double-click the clip to open it into the Viewer.

1 Double-click the clip to which you applied the Bloom filter.

2 In the Viewer, click the Filters tab.

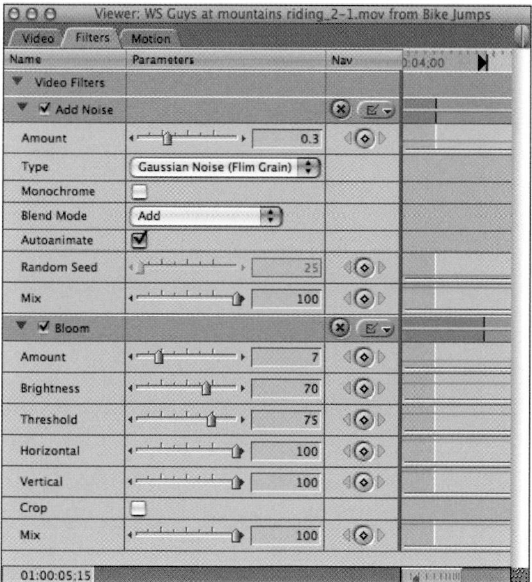

3 Make sure that the Canvas is displaying a frame in the area affected by the filter.

4 Disable the Add Noise filter, and click its disclosure triangle to hide the parameters.

5 In the Bloom filter, lower the Amount slider to 3, and lower the Threshold setting to about 65.

6 Adjust the Mix slider to reduce the visibility of the effect to your liking.

7 Toggle the Bloom filter on and off to clearly see how it is affecting the image.

Adjusting a Filter's In and Out Points

Remember that this filter is applied only to a portion of the clip because you set an In and Out point in the sequence when applying it. You can modify which section of the clip the filter is applied to in the area to the right of the filter parameters in the Filters tab.

1 Choose Window Arrange > Two-Up or simply expand your Viewer window so you can see the controls to the right of the parameter sliders.

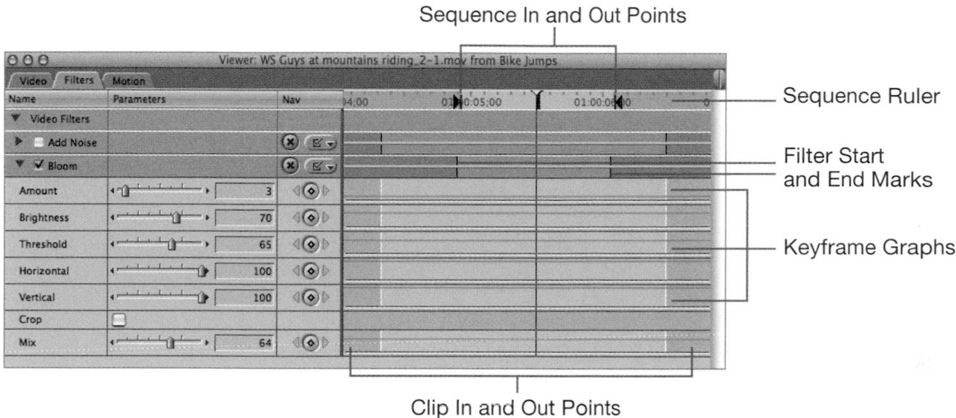

This area is another view of the Timeline in which the clip is currently active. Keyframe graphs can be created and manipulated here for instances when you want to modify a filter's parameters over time. (Keyframing effects are discussed in Lesson 8.)

You can probably see the In and Out points that correspond directly to the marks in the Timeline and Canvas. Also, the timecode in the ruler is the sequence timecode, and the playhead is the sequence playhead. If you drag the playhead around you'll see it move in the Timeline and Canvas, too.

White vertical lines in each of the keyframe graphs indicate the clip's In and Out points in the sequence. You can use the same zoom tools you use in the Timeline to zoom in and out on this mini-Timeline area.

2 Press Shift-Z to make sure the clip is zoomed to fit the window.

3 Clear the In and Out points by pressing Option-X or by Control-clicking the ruler area and choosing Clear In and Out points from the shortcut menu.

You'll see that there are still two black vertical lines in the area below the ruler and above the keyframe graphs. These lines indicate the boundaries where the filter takes effect.

4 Drag the left line for the Bloom filter to the left to start the filter effect earlier in the clip.

You can also move the filter's start and end time together, effectively slipping the filter within the clip.

5 Move the pointer anywhere over the area between the filter Start and End points.

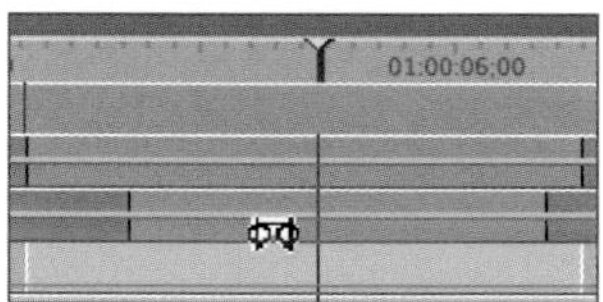

The pointer turns into a Slip pointer.

6 Drag to the right, moving both Start and End points later in the clip.

Resetting Parameters

As you get more comfortable experimenting with filters, you may occasionally get to the point when you want to start over and restore the filter to its default settings. Fortunately, this is just one click away.

1 To the right of the filter name, click the Reset button.

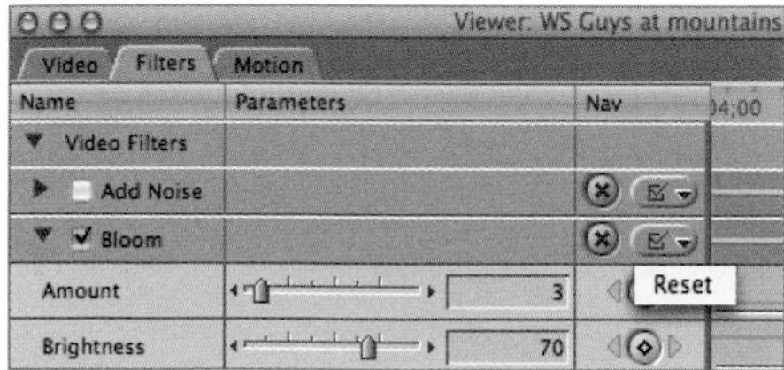

2 Readjust the filter's settings to create a unique look.

Deleting Filters

Because filters require so much experimentation, it is also very common to audition several filters before finding the exact look you are seeking.

You can temporarily disable a filter by deselecting the checkbox next to the filter's name in the Filters tab. Selecting and deselecting this checkbox is a great way to examine the effect of a filter. This can be especially useful when using subtler effects such as the noise you applied in the previous exercise.

You can also easily remove a filter altogether.

1 In the Filters tab, select the Bloom filter by clicking the name.

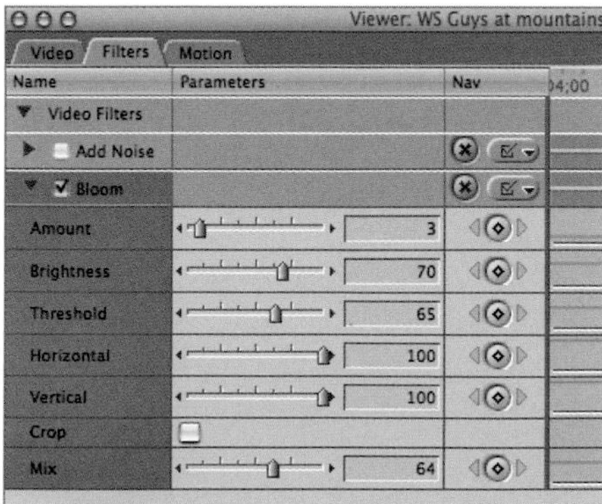

2 Press Delete.

The filter is removed from the clip.

TIP You can also use Edit > Cut, Edit > Copy, or Edit > Clear to remove or move filters. As long as another clip's Filters tab is active, you can paste whatever effects are currently stored on the clipboard.

Controlling Filter Order

You will quickly realize that the real fun and magic of filters comes from combining different effects for especially unique looks. However, it is very important to control the order in which the filters appear.

Filters are applied to each clip in the order they appear in the Filters tab, from top to bottom. In some cases, the order will have no effect, but in other cases, the order will dramatically change the look of the clip.

1 In the Timeline, click the *Surf Clips* tab to make that sequence active.

2 Position the playhead over the third clip (**Surf_Shot_03**) so it is visible in the Canvas, then double-click it to open it into the Viewer.

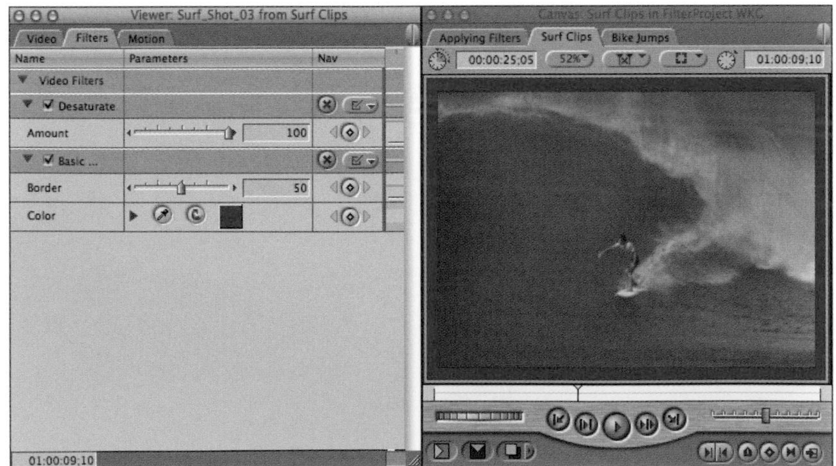

NOTE ► When the Filters tab is active in the Viewer, Final Cut Pro will keep that tab visible, even when opening a new clip into the Viewer. This can be helpful if you are modifying filters on different clips, but it can also confuse you, especially if you have two clips with the same filter applied. Always check the name of the clip in the Viewer title bar to ensure you are modifying the correct clip.

This clip has two filters applied. A Desaturate filter removes the color from the shot, and then a red border is applied. If the Basic Border filter was applied before the Desaturate filter, the red color would be reduced to gray.

3 Click the name area of the Basic Border filter and drag it to the top of the window, above the Desaturate filter.

Now, the red border is being desaturated.

4 Choose Effects > Video Filters > Distort > Whirlpool.

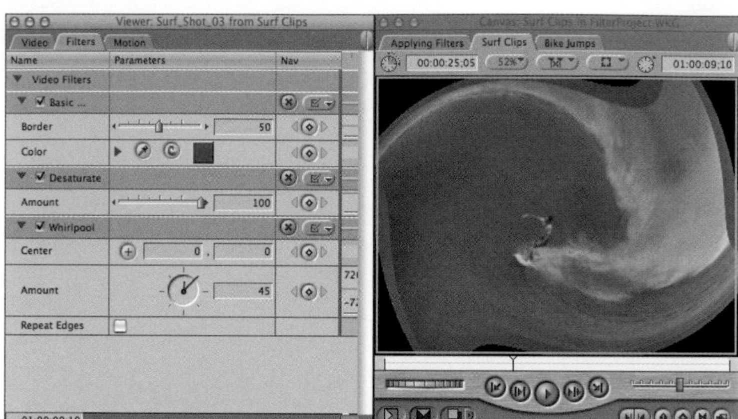

Because the distortion is happening after the border effect, the border itself is distorted. If you want the distorted image to have a border around it, you must change the filter order.

5 Drag the Basic Border filter to the end of the filter list in the Filters tab.

The entire window becomes highlighted, indicating that the effect will be added to the end of the list.

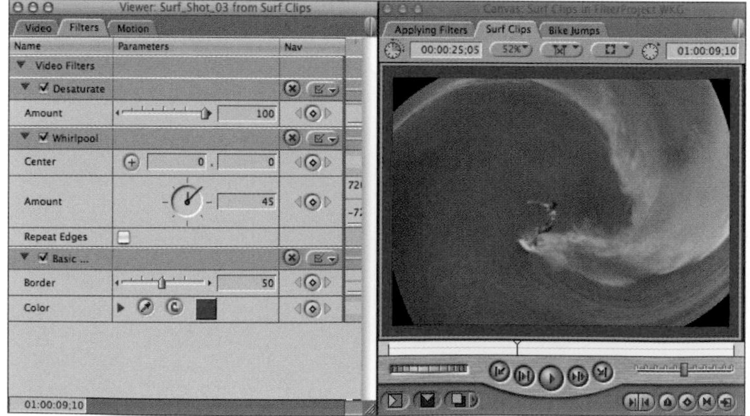

The whirlpool effect is now contained within the border effect.

Moderating Filter Effects

You may have noticed that some filters (such as the Bloom filter used earlier in this lesson) have a Mix slider below the other attributes.

This slider controls how much of the overall effect to apply or, to put it another way, how much of the filtered clip should be *mixed* with the original. This is an enormously helpful way to temper the effect of the filter without having to decrease the actual parameter values.

Controlling Filter Effect Amount

For filters that don't have a Mix slider, there is still a way to accomplish a similar effect.

1 Select the second clip (**Surf_Shot_02**).

2 Choose Edit > Remove Attributes, or press Option-Command-V.

The Remove Attributes dialog appears.

3 Ensure that the Filters checkbox is selected and click OK.

Now the clip has no filters applied to it.

4 Shift-Option-drag the clip onto track V2 to create a duplicate.

NOTE ▸ Be sure to release the Option key *before* releasing the mouse, otherwise you will perform an insert edit on track V2.

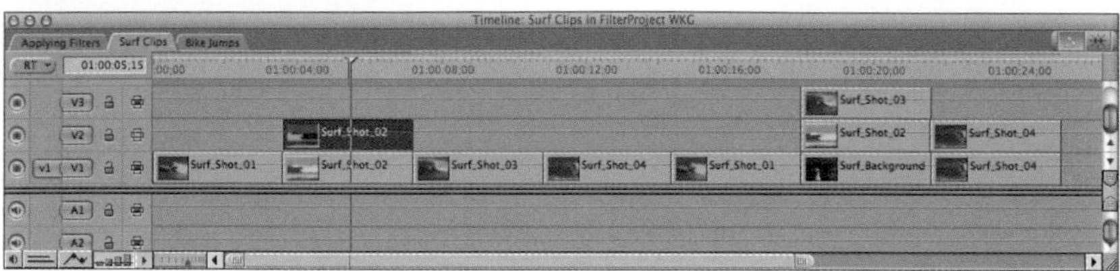

5 Be sure that only the top version of the clip is selected, and choose Effects > Video Filters > Stylize > Posterize.

This filter limits the number of colors available and is a great tool for creating stylized high-contrast looks. It looks most effective when you severely limit the number of available colors.

6 Double-click the filtered clip to open it into the Viewer.

7 Click the Filters tab and set the value for all three settings (Red, Green, and Blue) to 3.

This creates a very interesting look but also makes the overall image a bit too illegible. A Mix slider would come in handy, but alas, no such slider exists in this filter.

8 In the Viewer, click the Motion tab and expand the Opacity controls.

9 Lower the Opacity to about 40.

This reduces the visibility of the filtered image, revealing the unaffected version beneath it and providing the equivalent of the Mix slider.

Masking Filter Effects

You can use a similar procedure to limit an effect to a specific area of the clip. In this case, rather than adjusting the upper clip's opacity, you use a matte filter on the V2 clip to mask certain areas of the image.

For example, rather than applying this posterize effect to the entire clip, you could choose to limit it, so that just the surfer is posterized, and the rest of the shot appears unfiltered.

1 Raise the Opacity to about 75.

2 In the Viewer, click the Filters tab.

3 Choose Effects > Video Filters > Matte > Mask Shape.

A rectangular matte is applied, limiting the posterize effect.

4 Set the Shape to Oval.

5 Click the Center point control, then click in the Canvas on the Surfer's foot.

TIP For best results, you may want to shuttle through the clip to set the center point on a frame that approximates the middle of the surfer's movement throughout the shot. In this example, the sequence playhead is at 01:00:06:02.

6 Lower the Horizontal Scale slider to about 35.

7 Choose Effects > Video Filters > Matte > Mask Feather.

8 Set the Soft slider to about 75.

9 Press \ (backslash) to play around the clip and see the results of your work.

NOTE ▶ When using filters, you should set your sequence to Unlimited RT, although you may still need to render the clip (Command-R) to play the clip in real time.

You can also invert the filter's effect, so that the entire image is posterized except for the circle around the surfer.

10 In the Mask Shape filter, select the Invert checkbox.

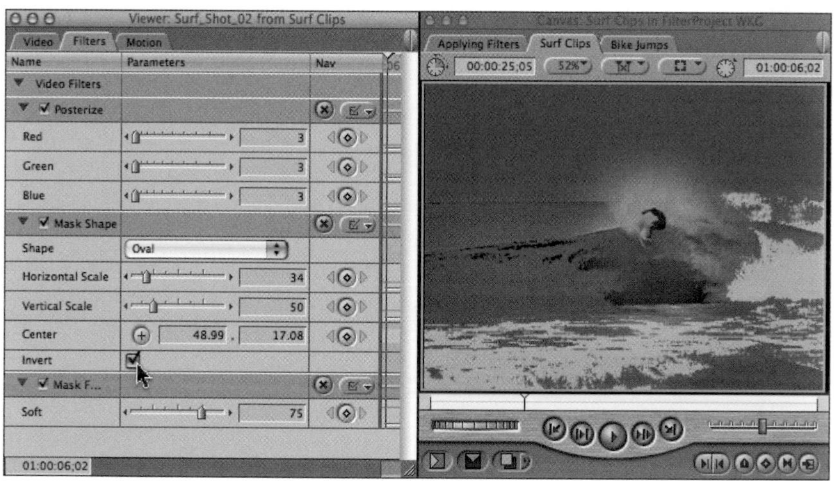

The effect is inverted.

This masking technique can work on any set of filters, but the Final Cut Pro masking features are somewhat limited. The Four-Point and Eight-Point Garbage Mattes give more precise control than the Mask Shape filter does, allowing you to create a custom-shaped mask, but there are no Bezier or B-spline controls built into Final Cut Pro. There are third-party filters that provide such functionality and allow much more fine control over the shapes of your mattes. Motion also has robust masking tools that can be used in conjunction with Final Cut to perform the same effects.

Furthermore, in this example, the surfer mainly stays in the same small area of the frame; but in many cases the subject will move around, creating an additional challenge. You can manually keyframe the mask to accommodate such movement. However, Final Cut Pro doesn't contain any sort of effective motion tracking to automate the process. Shake, Motion, and third-party plug-ins all offer such functionality. For more information on motion tracking, please refer to *Apple Pro Training Series: Motion 3*.

Managing Filters

Now that you know how to make good use of the Final Cut Pro filters, take a step back and learn how to manage and organize your filters to maximize your productivity.

Final Cut Pro can access filters from a variety of sources. There are built-in filters, filters provided by QuickTime, FxPlug filters such as those included in Motion, third-party filters created for Final Cut Pro, and even some third-party filters created for After Effects.

With all these sources of effects, there can be quite a bit of overlap, with multiple filters that create near-identical effects, and even multiple filters with the same names.

Final Cut Pro tries to eliminate any confusion by providing a set of recommended effects, which hides any FxPlug filters if an identically named built-in filter exists.

1 Choose Effects > Effect Availability > All Effects.

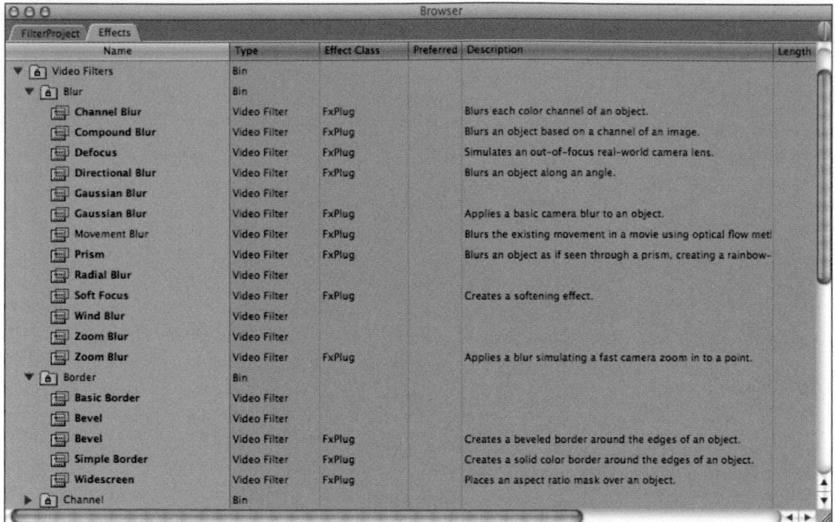

Name	Type	Effect Class	Preferred	Description	Length
Video Filters	Bin				
Blur	Bin				
Channel Blur	Video Filter	FxPlug		Blurs each color channel of an object.	
Compound Blur	Video Filter	FxPlug		Blurs an object based on a channel of an image.	
Defocus	Video Filter	FxPlug		Simulates an out-of-focus real-world camera lens.	
Directional Blur	Video Filter	FxPlug		Blurs an object along an angle.	
Gaussian Blur	Video Filter				
Gaussian Blur	Video Filter	FxPlug		Applies a basic camera blur to an object.	
Movement Blur	Video Filter	FxPlug		Blurs the existing movement in a movie using optical flow met	
Prism	Video Filter	FxPlug		Blurs an object as if seen through a prism, creating a rainbow-	
Radial Blur	Video Filter				
Soft Focus	Video Filter	FxPlug		Creates a softening effect.	
Wind Blur	Video Filter				
Zoom Blur	Video Filter				
Zoom Blur	Video Filter	FxPlug		Applies a blur simulating a fast camera zoom in to a point.	
Border	Bin				
Basic Border	Video Filter				
Bevel	Video Filter				
Bevel	Video Filter	FxPlug		Creates a beveled border around the edges of an object.	
Simple Border	Video Filter	FxPlug		Creates a solid color border around the edges of an object.	
Widescreen	Video Filter	FxPlug		Places an aspect ratio mask over an object.	
Channel	Bin				

Every effect is now displayed in the Effects tab and in the Effects menu. FxPlug filters are labeled as such in the Effect Class column and also have a text description of the filter's effect in the Description column.

With so many duplicates, it may seem wise to just choose Only Recommended Effects and forget about the others, but this prevents you from taking advantage of many benefits available only in the FxPlug versions of the duplicate filters. In many cases, the FxPlug versions are newer filters and have additional or different parameters.

For example, look at the parameters available in a filter as simple as Gaussian Blur.

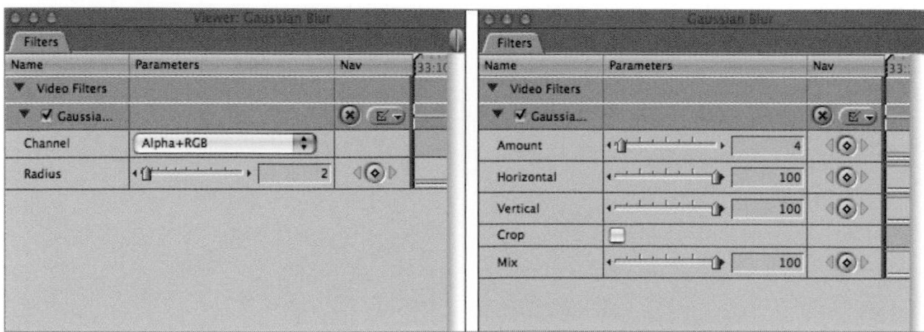

Built-in version FxPlug version

For one thing, all of the FxPlug filters contain the Mix setting, described earlier in this lesson. Plus, in the Gaussian Blur filter, the FxPlug version allows you to separately control horizontal and vertical blurring, greatly increasing the versatility of the effect.

But not all FxPlug filters are superior. For example, the built-in Invert filter allows you to invert individual color and alpha channels; the FxPlug version can only invert the entire image.

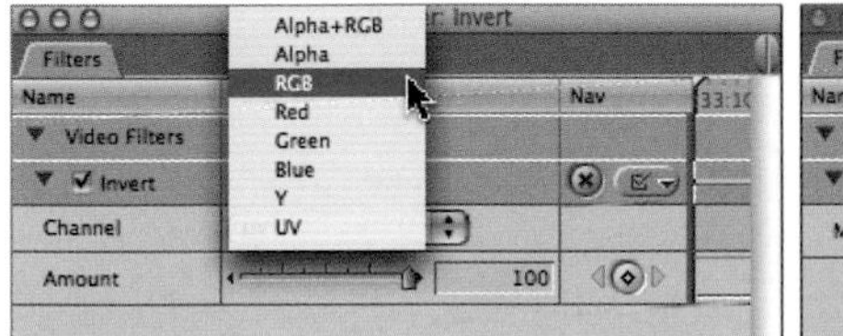

Built-in version

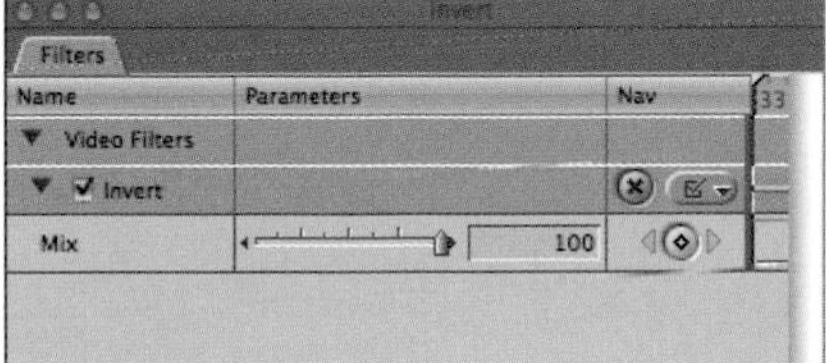

FxPlug version

Preferred Effects

So what are you to do? Fortunately, Final Cut Pro also provides a way to customize which filters are displayed, allowing you to designate some effects as preferred, and then limit the display so only preferred effects are shown. The downside to this is that you need to walk through every single effect and choose whether or not it should be preferred—and thus displayed—which can be quite a time-consuming process.

1 In the Effects tab, click in the Preferred column—a checkmark notes the selected effects—for each of the effects you want to display.

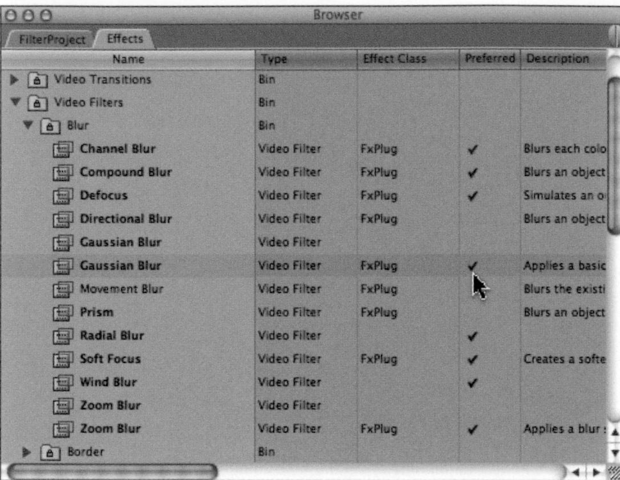

2 When you have marked all the effects you want to include, Control-click in any empty space in the Name column of the Effects tab and, from the shortcut menu, choose Show My Preferred Effects.

NOTE ▸ Although this section has focused exclusively on video filters, the recommended and preferred effects settings also affect all other classes of effects found in the Effects tab.

Creating Favorite Filters

As you work on more and more projects, you'll discover interesting ways to use filters to create unique effects. If you have a particular filter with specific settings you really like, use often, or need to reuse frequently for a specific client or project, you can save it as a favorite.

Favorite filters are stored in the Favorites bin in the Effects tab, and are then available in the Favorites submenu of the Effects menu.

You can create a favorite filter in a number of ways.

1 Click the Effects tab.

2 Expand the Video Filters and the Border bins.

3 Drag the Basic Border filter to the Favorites bin at the top of the window.

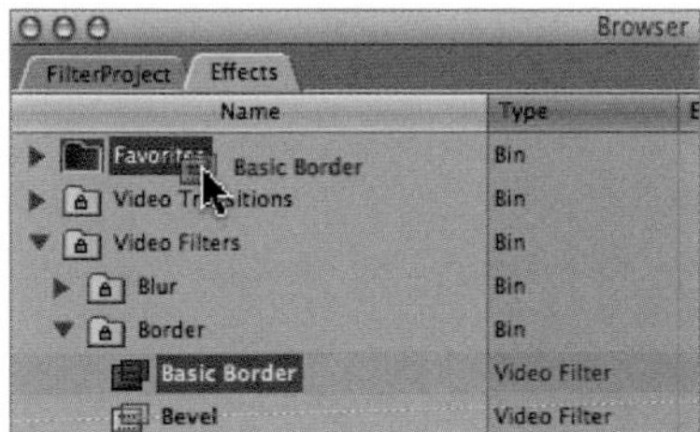

4 Expand the Favorites bin and rename the effect *Blue Border 25*.

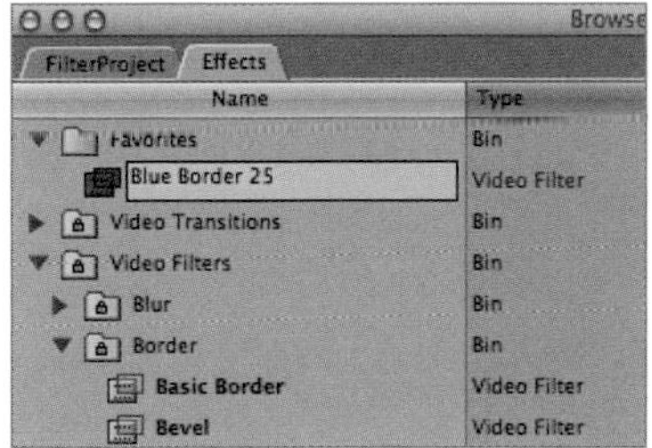

5 Double-click the filter to open it into the Viewer and set the Border to *25* and the color to your favorite hue of blue.

That filter is now ready to use with those preset attributes.

However, you often won't realize you want to save a favorite filter until after you have applied it to a clip in a sequence.

1 Open the *Bike Jumps* sequence.

2 Position the playhead over the first clip (**WS Guys at mountains riding_2**), which should have the Add Noise filter that you customized earlier.

3 Make sure no clips are selected and that Auto Select is active for track V1, then choose Effects > Make Favorite Effect (or press Option-F).

4 Look in the Favorites bin in the Effects tab.

The Add Noise filter is there.

5 Rename the filter *Custom Noise* or something similar that will help you remember what makes this effect special.

Effects saved in the Favorites bin will stick around between projects. You can even move them from one Final Cut Pro system to another as described in "Moving and Preserving Favorites" later in this lesson.

Creating Filter Packs

Often, an effect is composed of several different filters, and if you create a custom effect this way, you can save that, too. These saved filters will retain their settings, and the order in which they were applied.

1 Click the *Surf Clips* sequence tab.

2 Position the playhead over the last two clips in the sequence.

The upper clip has been scaled down and feathered using controls in the Motion tab, but has no filters applied. The bottom clip has three filters applied: HSV Adjust, Light Rays, and Replicate.

3 Make sure that nothing is selected and that Auto Select is disabled for track V2 and enabled for track V1.

4 Choose Effects > Make Favorite Effect, or press Option-F.

A sub-bin has been added to the Favorites bin, and inside that sub-bin are the three filters that created the glowing replicated effect used in that composition. This is commonly called a *filter pack*.

NOTE ▶ Do not double-click to open the filter pack into its own window. Doing so will alphabetize the filters and change the order in which the filters are listed, rather then preserving the order in which they were originally applied.

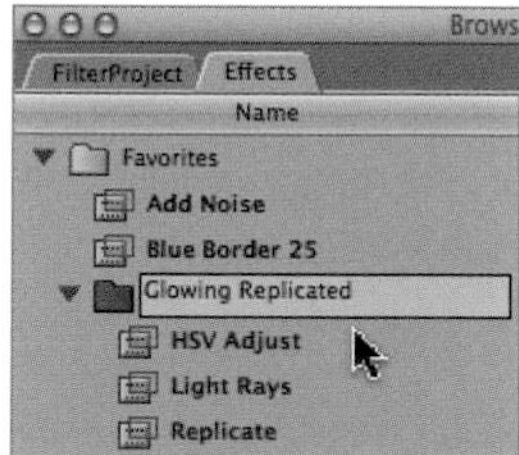

5 Rename the Surf Clips (Filters) bin to *Glowing Replicated*, or some other descriptive name.

To apply this filter pack to another clip, drag it from the Effects tab of the Browser onto one or more selected clips in the Timeline.

TIP Filter packs are easiest to apply by dragging them from the Effects tab of the Browser. When using the Effects menu, you can select only one favorite filter at a time from the filter pack, so you need to click into the menu several times to apply multiple filters.

Organizing the Favorites Bin

When you rely on a lot of custom favorites, you may want to spend some time organizing the contents of your Favorites bin so that you can quickly and easily locate what you need. For example, if you regularly work with four different clients on recurring shows, and specific filters are used for each show, you can create a hierarchy of sub-bins, one for each client.

1 In the Effects tab of the Browser, Option-double-click the Favorites bin icon to open the bin as another tab in the Browser.

2 Press Command-B, or Control-click the bin and choose New Bin from the shortcut menu, to add new bins as needed.

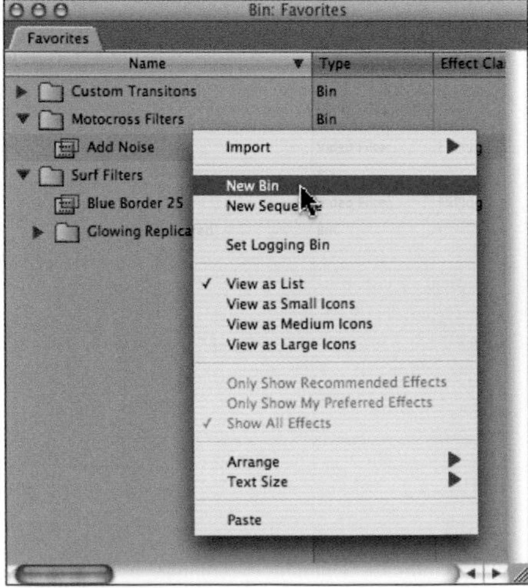

Once you've created a hierarchy of bins in the Favorites bin, you can organize the contents however you like. In particular, because there are so many other types of effects that you can store in the Favorites bin (transitions and motion effects, for example), you may want to create sub-bins for each.

NOTE ▶ Although you can store favorite filters, transitions, and motion effects in the same bin, filters are the only type of favorite settings you can apply to a clip as a group. When the effects in a given bin are of different types (filter, transition, or motion), you must apply each effect individually.

3 Close the Favorites tab.

Moving and Preserving Favorites

As you build up a collection of favorites, you will need to take special steps to preserve them, in case you need to reinstall the software on your computer or move your setup to a new computer.

When you save a filter, motion, or transition to the Favorites bin, that information is stored in the Final Cut Pro preferences file. If you reinstall your system, move to a new system, or delete the preferences file as a part of regular system maintenance or troubleshooting, you unfortunately will lose all your favorites!

However, it's very easy to save all of your favorite filters and effects in a project file that can be moved around and opened on different computers.

1 Create a new project by pressing Shift-Command-N.

2 Select the tab for the new project and drag it out of the Browser so it appears in its own window. This enables you to see it and the Effects tab side by side.

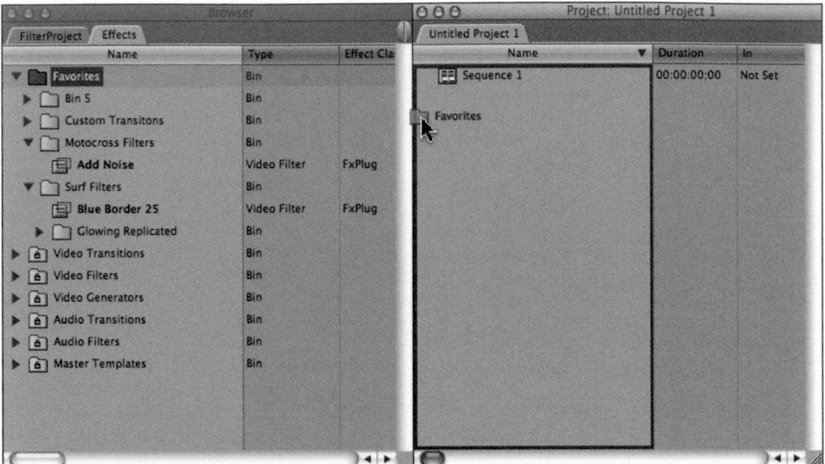

3 Drag the Favorites bin from the Effects tab into the new project.

4 Save and close the new project, naming it *Favorite Effects* or something similar.

You can then copy this project onto a portable drive or even email it to yourself so you can open it on another Final Cut Pro system, When you do, all of your favorite effects will be available on the new system.

Using Specific Filter Categories

Throughout this lesson you have been learning how to apply, modify, and manage filters, but no time has been spent discussing the specific filters and when they might be employed. Although most filters are very flexible and can be used in a wide variety of circumstances, it may be helpful to mentally group the filters into a few basic categories.

Not all of the groupings listed here correspond directly with the way filters are grouped in the Final Cut Pro Effects tab. In some cases, the groupings in the program are simply wrong, and in others they might serve more than one purpose. Either way, as long as you understand how to use the various filters, finding them won't be too much of a problem.

Understanding Corrective Filters

Many filters are designed specifically to solve mistakes made during production or to improve the look of an image to create a desired result. Such corrective filters are generally used in situations when you want to hide the fact that a filter is in use at all.

Blur and Sharpen

Blur filters are commonly employed to help control the point of focus in a scene. By blurring a portion of a shot or certain elements within a composition, you subtly guide the viewers' focus to the area that is in focus. Some specific blur filters, such as Defocus, Zoom Blur, Prism, and Soft Focus, are designed to simulate similarly named effects that can be created photographically.

Sharpening filters can be used to improve the visibility of edges in an image that lacks sharp focus.

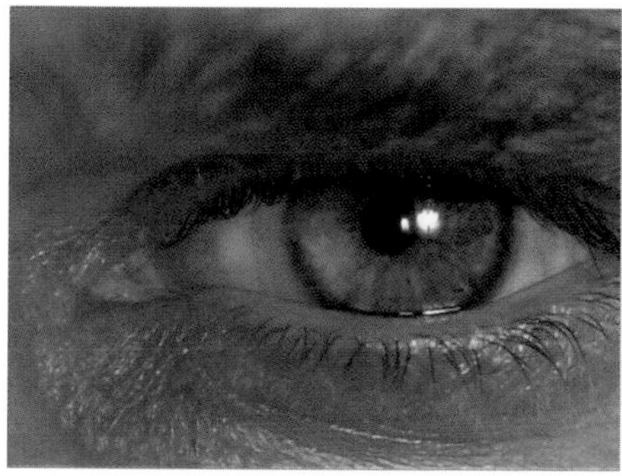
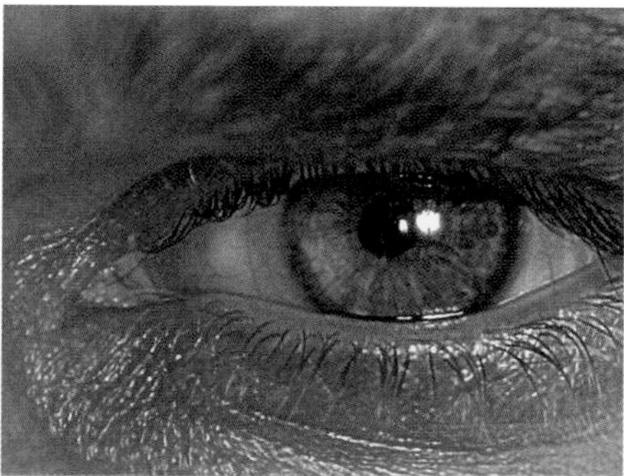

Some of the stylize edge detection filters can be helpful sharpening tools, although for a subtle effect they must be mixed back in with the original.

Noise Filters

Blurs can also be used to reduce unwanted noise in an image. The Channel and Compound Blur filters affect individual color or luminance channels of an image, which may be especially useful if the noise you are trying to eliminate resides primarily in one of these channels. Anti-Alias (found in the Stylize category) can also be effective at reducing noise.

In other cases, adding noise can be helpful in matching shots that were shot in different environments or with different equipment. Adding noise can also help when seamlessly mixing a computer-generated image into other shots that were created photographically.

The Reduce Banding filter (found in the Image Control section) adds a tiny bit of noise to your image to help mask color banding that can occur from inadequate digital sampling.

Image Control and Color Correction Filters

Another category of corrective effects comes in the form of filters designed to overcome exposure, white balance, color, or lighting problems in otherwise useful shots. These filters can generally be divided as follows:

Filters that affect the luminance:

- Brightness
- Brightness & Contrast
- Contrast
- Gamma
- Gamma Correction

Filters that affect the color:

- Channel Mixer
- Channel Offset
- Color Balance
- Color Reduce
- Desaturate

- Desaturate Highlights
- Desaturate Lows
- Sepia
- Tint

Filters that do a combination of these things:

- Color Corrector
- Color Corrector 3-Way
- Levels
- Proc Amp
- HSV, YIQ, and YUV Adjust filters.

All of these filters provide subtly different tools to control the same basic aspects. Some are more inclined toward subtle results, and some create more exaggerated effects. In general, you can only correct an image so far before noise is introduced in dark areas, clipping occurs in bright areas, and color becomes unnatural.

For more information on such filters, see Section IV of this book, "Color Correction."

Flop Filters

Screen direction mistakes are very common and, in many cases, can be easily solved editorially. Screen direction refers to the left-to-right or right-to-left movement or the eye-line of the subjects within a scene. If a car chase shows three shots of the car moving from right to left, and then suddenly there's a shot where the car is going from left to right, it will appear that they are heading back where they came from.

The Flop filter can easily address this problem.

1 Double-click the *Screen Direction* sequence and play it.

   Notice that in the first, third, and fourth shots, the bikers are moving from right to left, but in the second shot, they are moving from left to right.

Although this scene is not part of a narrative in which such a screen direction would significantly confuse the audience, it still disrupts the flow of action. If this was part of a race sequence, it could be very confusing if some of the shots show movement in the wrong direction.

2 Select the second clip and choose Effects > Video Filters > Perspective > Flop.

The orientation of the shot is reversed and the bikers are now moving in the same direction in all of the shots.

Be aware that this filter won't work in situations where written words appear in the shot (the words will appear backward) or in situations when the geography of the scene is clearly established (if someone is leaning against a wall, the wall will suddenly be on the wrong side, and so on).

De-Interlacing and Flicker Reduction Filters

Another problem that occurs with regularity is that scan lines in NTSC, PAL, and interlaced HD footage become visible, creating comb-like artifacts in your images.

This can occur for a number of reasons, ranging from mismatched field order settings to creating a freeze-frame effect on an image that contains significant horizontal movement.

In such cases, the De-interlace filter will eliminate the fields in the offending shot, either by duplication or interpolation.

In some cases, usually due to transcoding one format to another, the scanline order can become inverted or offset. The Shift Fields filter can switch between odd and even interlacing by moving the entire image up or down by a single line.

Lastly, in some cases, interlacing and frame rate conversions can introduce an apparent flicker that is invisible when the playhead is parked, but becomes apparent when the clip is played. The Flicker filter can reduce this effect by blurring together adjacent scan lines.

Image Shake Filters

Camera shake is a fact of life with handheld camera work and, to some degree, it has become a signature style of certain genres. However, there are times when you just wish a shaky shot was a bit less bumpy.

The Final Cut Pro SmoothCam filter can remove a certain amount of camera shake. In order to do this, it must first perform an analysis of the clip to be smoothed.

1 In the Browser, double-click **Driving_02** and play it.

2 Choose Effects > Video Filters > Video > SmoothCam.

The Viewer is outlined with a red warning border and the Background Processes window appears. This window indicates the progress of the SmoothCam analysis and provides controls to abort or pause the process.

As the window's name implies, this process goes on in the background, which means that while it works, you can continue working on other things, including marking and playing the clip that is being analyzed. However, you cannot see the results of the filter until the analysis is complete.

3 While you are waiting for the analysis to complete, Control-click the column header area in the Browser and choose Show SmoothCam from the shortcut menu.

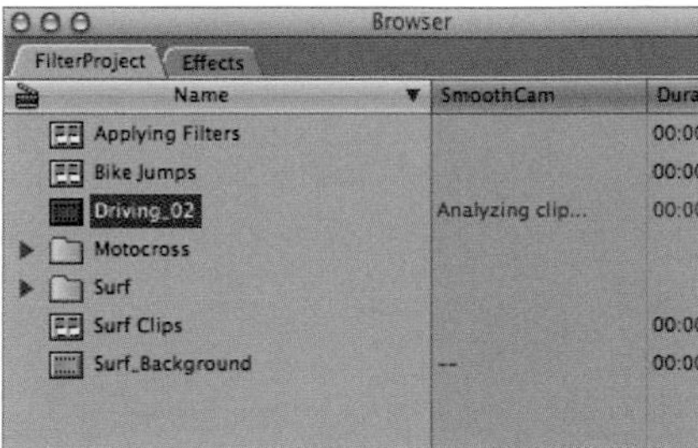

The SmoothCam column appears and indicates the status of the clip being analyzed.

4 Once the analysis is complete, tear out the Viewer Filters tab so you can see both the Filters tab and the Video tab simultaneously.

5 Set Auto Scale to 0.

6 Play the clip.

You can see that the car and the cable car remain perfectly steady in the middle of the frame, but the edges of the frame jump around like crazy, as the filter compensates for the camera movement in the shot.

Unfortunately, with a clip that has as much camera shake as this clip does, you would have to zoom in quite far to avoid seeing the shake.

7 You can adjust the Translation, Rotation, and Zoom settings depending on how much movement your clip has.

The higher the values, the more compensation Final Cut Pro will make. The lower the values, the more shake will remain in your clip, but the less you will have to zoom in to keep the frame full.

NOTE ► Once a clip analysis has been performed, changes made to the clip, including changes to the filter settings, will not require re-analysis.

Using Utility Filters

Another class of filters is typically used for special situations or in combination with other effects. This category of filters includes mattes, which enable you to mask out part of an image; keying filters, which allow you to identify a portion of the shot (usually by color) and make that section transparent; and timecode display filters, which print a timecode window on top of your video image.

Matte Filters

You already used a simple matting technique to limit the effect of a filter earlier in this lesson. Mattes are also commonly used to mask out equipment or unwanted elements of a frame (hence the name "garbage matte"—a matte used to hide the visual garbage).

Because mattes make part of the frame transparent, they are frequently used in compositing scenarios, where other elements are used to fill in the missing spaces.

However, one of the most commonly used mattes is not used for compositing at all: the widescreen matte masks off the top and bottom of an image to create a more cinematic aspect ratio (though sometimes it's used just to hide a boom microphone that keeps dipping into the frame).

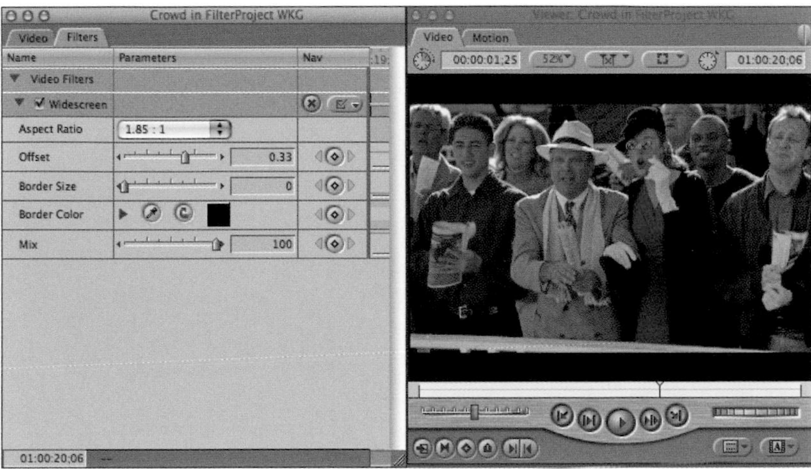

Keying Filters

One of the most common special effects techniques is to shoot a subject against an all-green or all-blue backdrop in order to isolate the subject and later put him in a different environment. *Keying* is the act of removing those blue or green sections of the frame and turning them transparent. Final Cut Pro has several robust keying filters, and there are widely respected third-party plug-in keying filters available as well.

Keying is a very specialized task, and successful results require that the footage is lit properly and that the shooting format contains adequate color information.

Timecode Display Filters

There are times when you need to see timecode numbers burned right into your video image.

Typically, this is used when passing files between people to ensure that everyone is perfectly clear about specifically when various elements begin and end. For example, when exporting audio to go to a sound mixing facility, it is customary to also send along a *window dub* of the edited show (a copy of the video with the timecode visible in a window onscreen), so the sound mixer can ensure that his audio mix is always in perfect sync with the video.

To some degree, this is a legacy technique, carried over from days of yore, before all video files had timecode data embedded. Still, there's nothing like seeing the numbers right there in front of you to ensure that they're accurate. Final Cut Pro has both a Timecode Generator filter (which displays numbers that the filter generates based on your input settings) and a Timecode Reader filter, which displays the exact timecode numbers from the embedded timecode values in each clip.

Using Non-Corrective Filters

Most of the video filters in Final Cut Pro fall into the category of non-corrective. These are filters that modify the image in ways that are not subtle or realistic. There are several subcategories for such effects.

> **NOTE ▶** For this section, you can examine many of the examples described in the *Filter Examples* sequence. Track V2 contains the filtered clip and Track V1 shows the raw clip. Toggle visibility for track V2 to quickly see a before-and-after effect.

Distortion Filters

These filters displace pixels to simulate the effect of the image flowing like water, or the image being projected onto an uneven surface.

Distort > Scrape Filter

Distort > Pond Ripple Filter

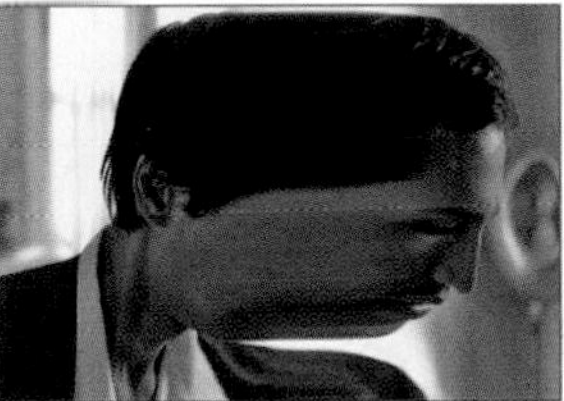

Distort >Cylinder Filter

Several distortion filters (Bump Map, Displace, and Refraction) require an input image or video clip, which is applied as a texture or projection surface.

To use one of these filters, just drag a still image, video clip, or generator onto the Map Image target.

Name	Parameters	Nav
▼ Video Filters		
▼ ✓ Bump Map	893020	
Map Image		
Luma Scale	0	
Direction	10	
Outset	10	
Repeat Edge		

Stylization Filters

The next most common types of effects are created using stylization filters. These filters modify the pixels of a clip to simulate a painterly effect, or group pixels together based on color value or luminance. Common effects such as Diffuse, Posterize, Find Edges, and Solarize fall into this category.

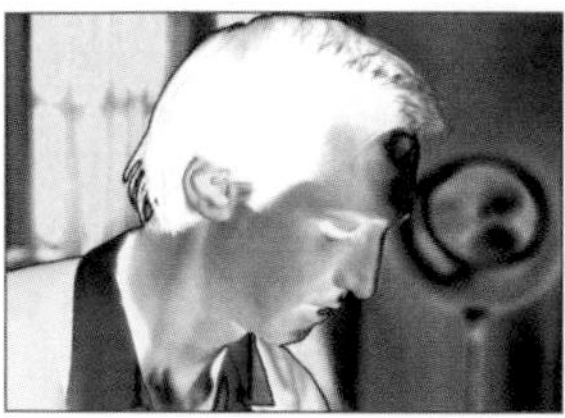

Stylize > Solarize Filter

Stylize > Diffuse Filter

Stylize > Line Art Filter

At low settings, these filters can be quite subtle, but very quickly they can become highly abstract. Filters such as Slit Scan, Slit Tunnel, Stripes, and Target (the last two are found in the Distort category) are particularly extreme, turning your image into an abstract mess but providing hours of entertainment.

Stylize > Slit Scan Filter

Tiling and Perspective Filters

Two more filter categories that are undeniably fun are the Tiling and Perspective filters. Tiling takes part of your image and repeats it. This includes such filters as Mirror (found in the Perspective group), Replicate (found in the Stylize category), and Kaleidoscope.

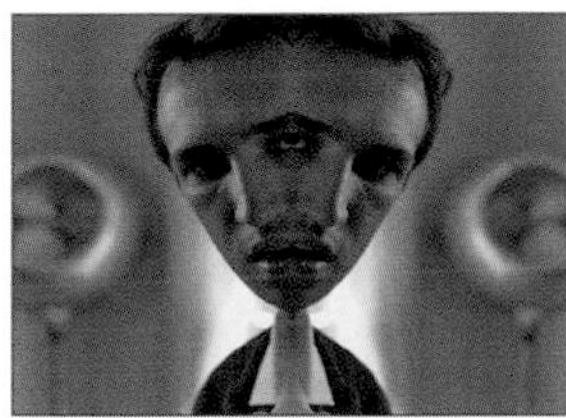

Perspective > Mirror Filter

Stylize > Replicate Filter

Tiling > Kaleidoscope Filter

Similar to these are the Perspective filters, which allow you to move the imaginary screen upon which your clip is projected. These include Rotate, Curl (similar to a page peel), and the versatile Basic 3D.

Perspective > Basic 3D Filter

> **NOTE ▸** The Drop shadow in the figure is not part of the Basic 3-D filter, but rather a setting in the Motion tab.

Although Final Cut Pro doesn't have any actual 3D capabilities (you have to use Motion for those), the Basic 3D filter can do a pretty good job of simulating the most common 3D effects.

Glow Filters

Used in small quantities, these popular filters can simulate the subtle bloom of overexposed film, but a more generous helping quickly transforms an image into a burst of light.

Glow > Dazzle Filter

Time Adjustment Filters

Most of the filters previously described work by modifying the pixels of the image in geographic space, but one category of filters works by mixing the surrounding frames in time.

You used one of these, the Echo filter, earlier in the lesson. Other time-based filters include Strobe, Trails, and Scrub, which allow you to mix your video in time the way a DJ scratches a record.

Using Other Filters

There are many other filters that don't neatly fit into the categories described in the preceding sections. Some have multiple uses, and others do very specific and unique things, such as Camcorder (which overlays a blinking Record light to simulate the viewfinder of a consumer video camera).

The best advice is to get in there and experiment. And remember, each filter can yield widely different results depending on the settings used, and the combination of various filters can often surpass the sum of the individual effects.

Lesson Review

1. Does Auto Select override a manual selection?
2. Does pasting attributes on a clip that already has the same filter applied modify the existing filter settings or does it apply a second copy of the filter?
3. How can you remove filters from multiple clips?
4. Does it matter what order you use to apply filters?
5. How can you apply a filter to a portion of a clip's duration?
6. How can you apply a filter to a portion of a clip's image?
7. Which are superior: built-in filters or FxPlug filters?
8. What is a "filter pack?"
9. What is the SmoothCam filter used for?
10. What is the sacrifice SmoothCam requires?

Answers

1. Manual selections in the Timeline override Auto Select.
2. Pasting attributes will add an additional filter to the recipient clip.
3. Use Remove Attributes.
4. Yes, filters affect a clip in the order they are applied, so a red border will turn gray if a Desaturate filter is applied after it.
5. Use the Range Select tool (GGG) or set In and Out points before you apply the filter.
6. Create a duplicate copy of the clip and apply a matte filter to the top clip.
7. Neither type of filter is inherently superior. Each case is different.
8. A group of filters saved as a single favorite, which appears in the Favorites bin as a subfolder and can be applied, *en masse*, to another clip.
9. For reducing camera shake.
10. You must zoom in on the clip to accommodate for the smoothing effect.

8

Lesson Files	Lesson Files > Lesson 08 > AnimatingEffects.fcp
Media	HoopinUSA
Time	This lesson takes approximately 120 minutes to complete.
Goals	Animate objects and parameters over time
	Keyframe motion parameters in the Canvas
	Keyframe motion and filters in the Viewer
	Modify and manipulate keyframes in the Timeline
	Save and reapply keyframed effects

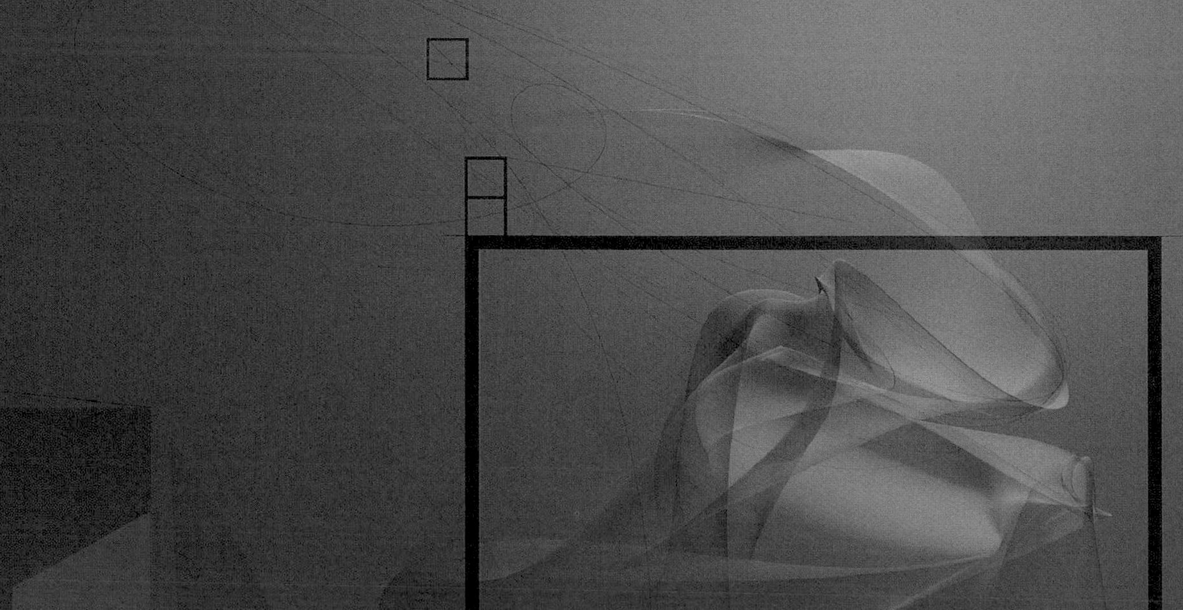

Lesson **8**

Dynamic Effects

The video medium is engaging because it moves. If you want your effects to be compelling, they need to be dynamic. When you want an object to move across the screen, or a title to appear or disappear over time, or if you want an effect to occur gradually, you need to instruct Final Cut Pro to make such changes.

The mechanism for these instructions is called animation, or *keyframing*. A keyframe is simply an indicator that says, "Make this effect happen at this point in time." When you set two keyframes, Final Cut Pro interpolates the changes between them. For example, to create a common one-second fade-in, you set two opacity keyframes. On frame 1, set the opacity to 0, and 30 frames later, set it to 100%. Final Cut Pro automatically makes each of the 29 frames in-between increasingly opaque, resulting in the familiar fade effect.

Keyframing Basics

Keyframing is tricky because it requires you to think about two things at the same time. Whenever you set a keyframe you must always answer two questions: What is the parameter value, and when does it occur in time?

You'll be surprised at how easily you can forget to answer one of these questions, and if you do, your clever and exciting effect won't work. Furthermore, it's critical to understand that setting one keyframe doesn't actually create a change over time. It's not until you add a second keyframe (at a different value) that the animation will occur.

Keyframes are easiest to understand and manipulate when you picture them on a graph, so Final Cut Pro generates such graphs in no less than six different places:

- You can keyframe opacity and audio levels in the Timeline.

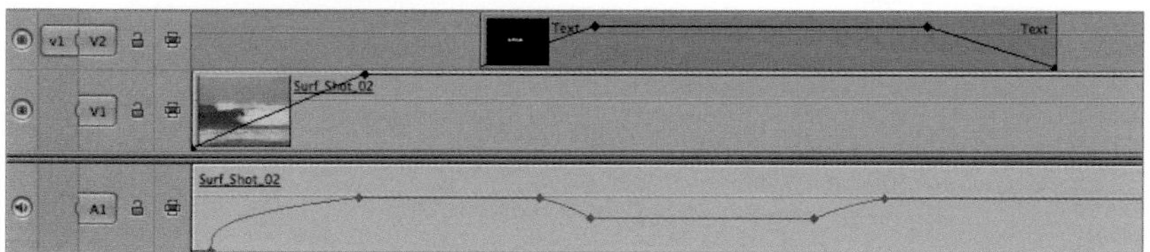

- You can keyframe audio levels and pan settings in the Audio tab of the Viewer.

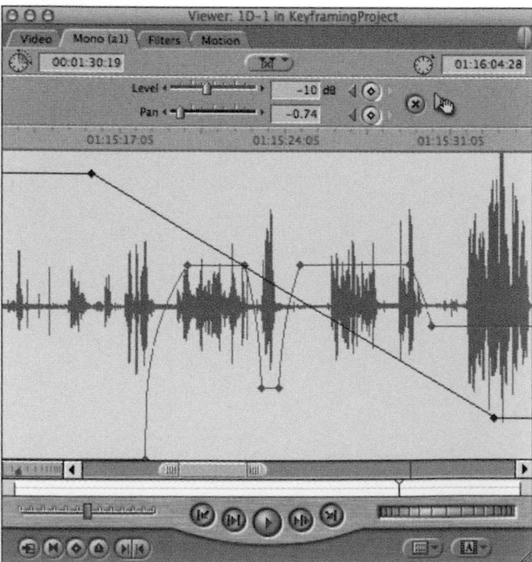

- You can keyframe filter parameters in the Filters tab.

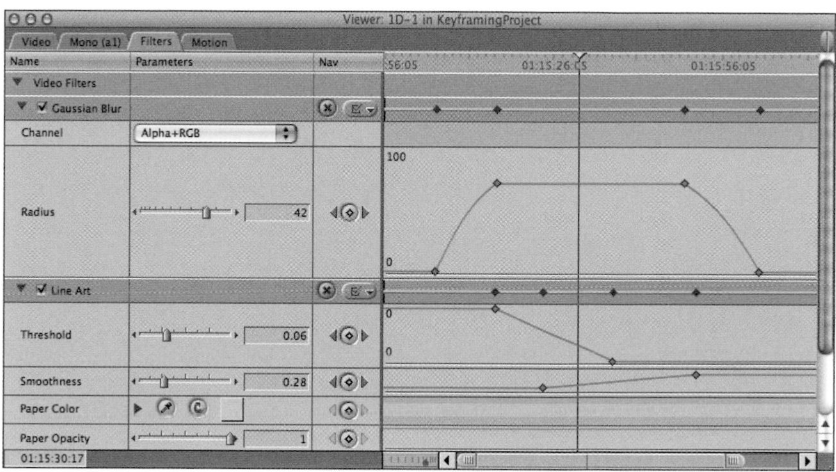

- You can keyframe motion parameters in the Motion tab.

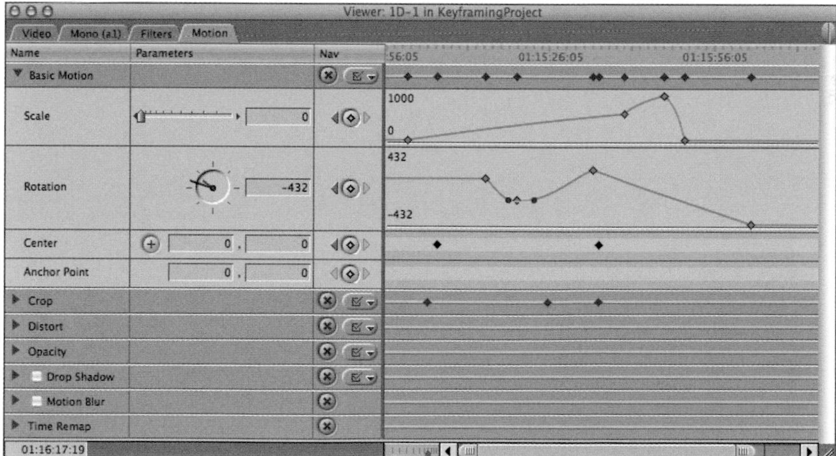

- You can animate a clip's position in the Canvas.

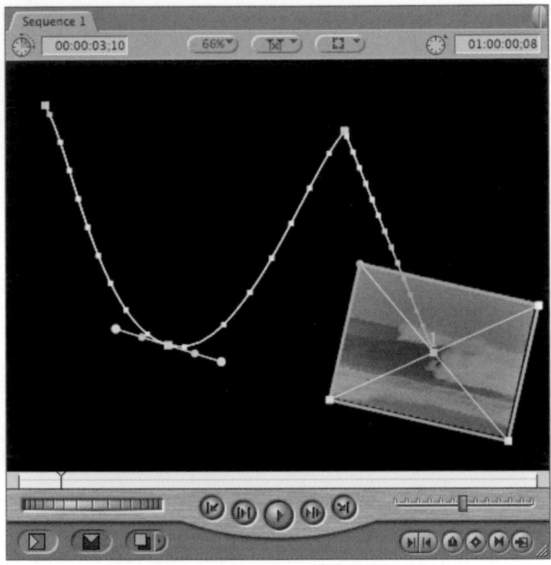

- And you can display any filter or motion parameter in a special optional keyframe graph in the Timeline.

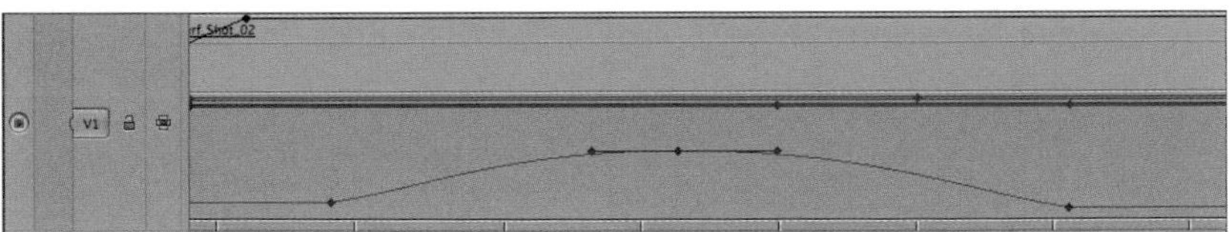

Fortunately, keyframes work exactly the same in all of these places, so once you grasp the basics, you'll quickly become comfortable creating dynamic effects of all types.

Keyframing in the Canvas

Although animating objects in the Canvas is one of the more difficult methods of keyframing, it is a good place to start because moving objects around the screen is such a common effect, and the keyframe graph in the Canvas is the easiest to understand.

1 Open **AnimatingEffects.fcp**.

The *Logo Animation* sequence automatically opens into the Canvas and Timeline.

2 Choose Window > Arrange > Two-Up.

This arranges your interface to maximize the Canvas window, which will make it easier to perform keyframing there.

3 In the View pop-up menu, choose Image+Wireframe.

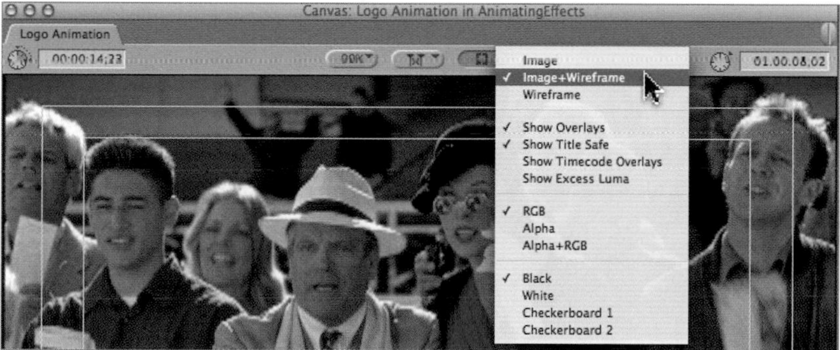

4 Set the Zoom level to 50%.

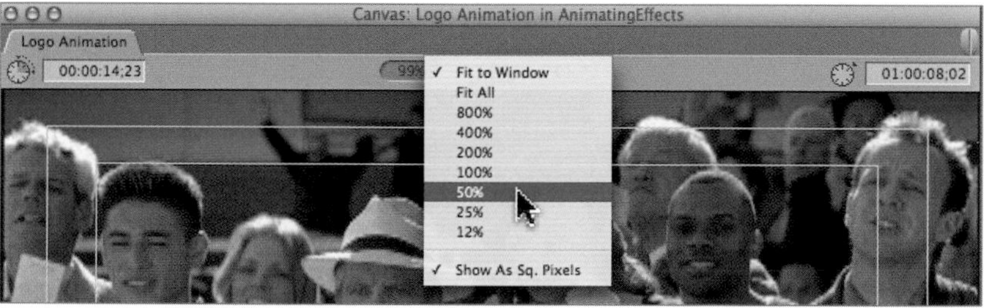

This will ensure that a small pasteboard area (in gray) surrounds the visible frame.

5 Type *10.00* to move the sequence playhead to exactly 10 seconds.

6 In the Canvas, drag the WRAC logo to the lower-right corner, so the edge of the object lines up precisely with the action safe boundary.

NOTE ▶ If you accidentally select the clip on track V1, you can directly select the logo clip in the Timeline.

This is the position where the logo will land at the end of the animation.

TIP The action safe and title safe boundaries are controlled by choosing Show Title Safe in the View pop-up menu in the Canvas.

7 In the Canvas, click the Add Motion Keyframe button.

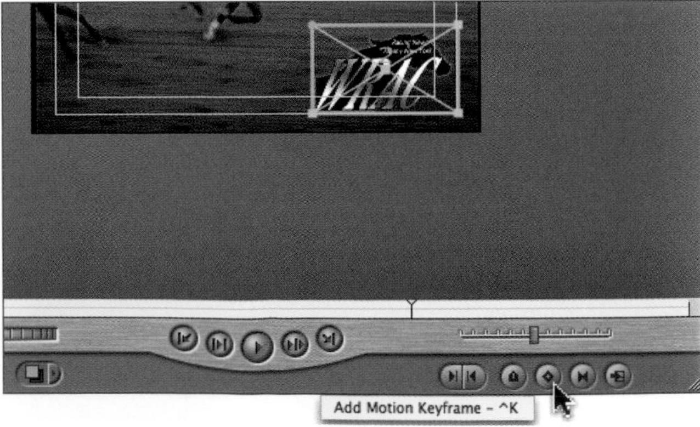

The object's wireframe turns green. A green wireframe indicates that the playhead is parked on a keyframe. Remember, setting the first keyframe doesn't create an animation; rather, it's as if you have pinned the logo to that part of the screen at that point in time.

8 Press the Up Arrow three times to move the sequence playhead to the beginning of the WRAC logo.

Although the logo hasn't moved, the wireframe is no longer green. You are now ready to set your second keyframe.

9 Drag the WRAC logo straight up until it is just past the frame boundary. Hold down Shift to constrain the movement to a straight line.

You will notice that several things happen automatically. First of all, the clip's center point turned green. This indicates that a keyframe for the clip's Center Point parameter has automatically been added.

You do not need to explicitly add the second keyframe. Because you told Final Cut Pro that the logo must be at the lower-right corner by 10 seconds in, putting it somewhere else at a different point in time forces Final Cut Pro to create an animation.

Second, you will see the dotted line indicating the path that the object will follow. This is the clearest indication that you have successfully built an animation.

10 Play the sequence to see your animated effect.

Although it may seem strange to set the end before the beginning, it's actually a very smart way to work. The object will only be at its starting position for one frame, but the ending composition is what your viewer will see for the duration of the scene. This is why it's important to establish its *ending* position at the beginning of the process.

Furthermore, in this example (and in many real-world scenarios), the object begins offscreen. If you began by setting the first keyframe when the object is out of sight, locating the object to drag it to the final position would be difficult.

Modifying the Path

The dotted line provides a clear indication of the animation you created. If you modify that path, you'll change the logo's movement.

1 Press Option-K as necessary to move the playhead to the first keyframe.

2 Click the middle of the path and drag it to the left.

This adds a new keyframe, and forces the logo to move along a new path. It also automatically curves the path (which may or may not be desirable).

3 Play the sequence again.

The speed indicators along the path indicate how fast or slow the object will move. The closer the dots are, the slower the clip moves.

This is where it becomes very important to track both aspects of a keyframe: the parameter value, and when it occurs in time.

4 Press Command-Z to undo the change you made to the clip's path.

5 Press the Up Arrow to move the sequence playhead to the previous edit.

6 Drag the logo to the center of the Canvas.

You'll see that there are several differences this time. The path is not automatically curved. (Don't worry. You can curve it later, if you want.) Additionally, the speed indicators are now closer together before the new keyframe, and farther apart after it.

7 Play the sequence.

The clip moves at a moderate speed between the starting position and the second keyframe and then moves much more quickly to its final resting place.

In the first example (when you grabbed the path), you defined the parameter value, identifying where the clip should be located, but you hadn't planned when you wanted it to be there. In the second case, you first picked a point in time, then decided where the object should be.

Both are valid ways of working, depending on whether the position or the time is your priority.

Smoothing Your Path

One other difference between those two methods was that in the first case, the path defaulted to a curve; in the second, it defaulted to create a corner point.

You can toggle this setting in the shortcut menu for each keyframe.

1 Make sure the Logo clip is selected, then Control-click (or right-click) the middle keyframe and choose Linear from the shortcut menu.

The path becomes curved.

2 Use the Bezier handles to adjust the shape of the curve.

TIP You may want to zoom into the Canvas to better control the curve.

3 Press the Command key and drag one of the handles.

This allows you to modify one side of the curve, but it constrains both handles' lengths to reciprocal movement. If you lengthen or shorten one length, the other changes by the same amount, even though its position doesn't change.

4 Hold down Shift-Command and drag one of the handles.

This allows you to independently control one side of the curve.

5 Control-click the middle keyframe and choose Make Corner Point from the shortcut menu.

The path is returned to its original shape.

Moving the Path

In some cases, you may create a path that you like but need to move to a different location in the Canvas. You could move each individual keyframe, but that is time consuming, and it would be very difficult to maintain their relative positions.

For these reasons, there is a way to move the entire path in one step.

1 Ensure that the playhead is placed at the In point of the clip.

2 Shift-Command and drag the logo to the left.

The path is moved as a single entity.

Deleting Keyframes

There are two ways to remove keyframes in the Canvas.

1 Control-click the middle keyframe and choose Delete Point from the shortcut menu.

The keyframe is removed.

The other way to delete a keyframe offers more flexibility.

2 Press Command-Z to undo step 1 and restore the middle keyframe.

3 Move the sequence playhead to frame 09:05 (so it is parked on the keyframe).

4 In the Canvas, Control-click the Add Keyframe button.

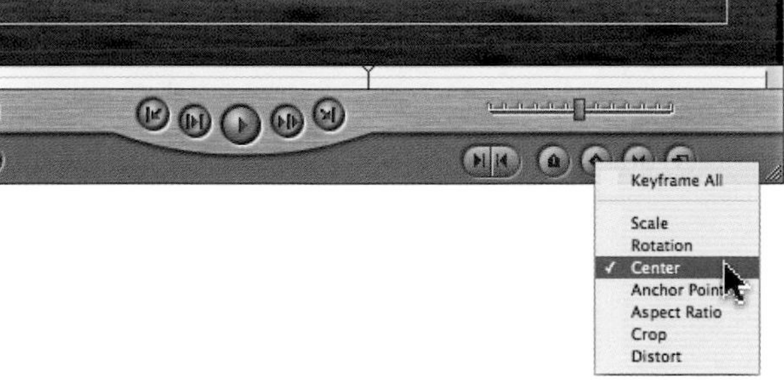

The shortcut menu shows all of the parameters currently keyframed at that point in time. In this frame, only the center point is keyframed.

5 Click Center to remove the checkmark and delete the keyframe.

Controlling Acceleration

In addition to setting a path's shape, you can control how fast or slow the clip will move as it moves to and from each keyframe.

1 First, return the logo to the location at the bottom right.

2 Shift-Command-drag the logo to the right, until its right edge aligns with the action safe boundary.

3 Control-click the first keyframe (the one in the gray pasteboard area) and choose Ease In/Ease Out from the shortcut menu.

4 Control-click the second keyframe and choose Ease In/Ease Out from the shortcut menu.

Notice that this affects the relative spacing of the dots along the path.

5 Play the sequence.

The clip slowly leaves its starting position, reaches a cruising speed, and then slows down as it settles into the second position.

This enables you to simulate the real-world phenomena of inertia and momentum, or to put it more simply, it makes your movement feel more organic.

NOTE ► You can also use the inner blue dots on the Bezier handles for any keyframe to control a clip's acceleration as it approaches and leaves that point. However, in most cases, it is not possible to achieve specific results this way.

Keyframing Other Parameters

Keyframing an object's center point in the Canvas is intuitive and straightforward. However, you can also animate a variety of other parameters in much the same way.

1 Open the **HoopinUSA** clip and play it.

In this exercise, you will animate scale, rotation, and other attributes to create this dynamic composition.

2 Open the *Complex Ani Start* sequence.

All of the clips are already placed in the Timeline, but they have not been animated. To begin, you will create the animation for one of the hula-hoopers and then apply that movement to the other clips.

Remember that it is generally easier to work backward: figure out where you want the clip to end and then figure out where it should start.

3 Move the playhead to frame 10.

This will be the point at which the clip will resolve in its final position.

4 Select **Steven1**, scale it down to about one-third of its size, and position it at the middle of the left edge, similar to the following figure:

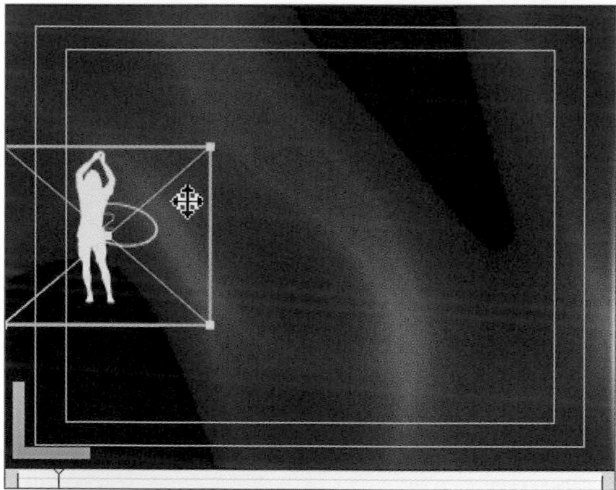

NOTE ▶ It is not critical that your settings precisely match those pictured here.

5 Click the Add Keyframe button (or press Control-K).

The clip's keyframe turns green.

6 Press Home to move the sequence playhead to the first frame.

7 Rotate the clip to turn the dancer completely upside down, and scale up the clip as large as you can.

8 Press Command-– (minus) a few times to zoom out the Canvas to about 12%.

9 Continue enlarging **Steven1** until it is much larger than the Canvas window, and center it to resemble the following figure:

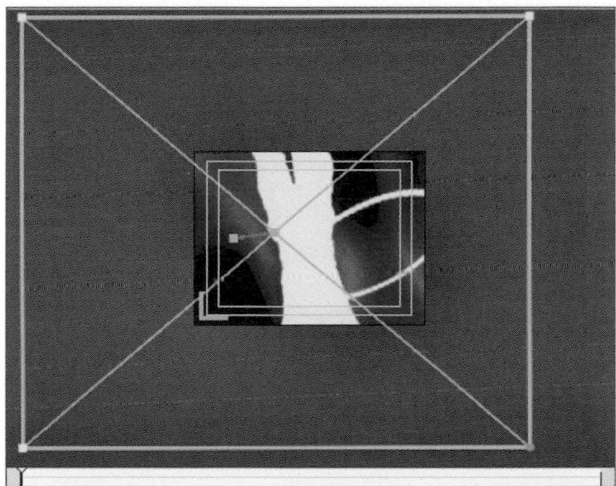

With these three adjustments, you have automatically keyframed the rotation, scale, and position parameters. You can tell when you're parked on a keyframe because parts of the clip's wireframe turn green; but it can be tricky to know exactly which parameters have keyframes on the current frame. There is one place where you can be absolutely sure.

10 Control-click the Add Keyframe button.

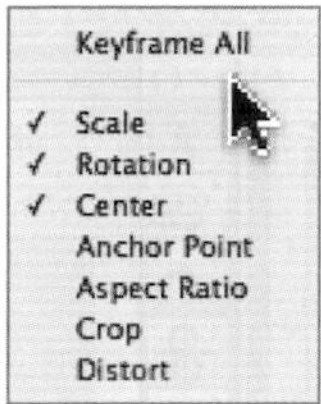

There are checkmarks next to the parameters that are keyframed on the current frame.

11 Play the sequence.

NOTE ▸ You may need to render the clip (Option-R) to play it at full frame rate.

You can see that the effect is partially complete, but to match the finished version, the rotation is supposed to be completed before the object settles into position.

12 Position the sequence playhead on frame 5.

13 Rotate the clip so Steven is right-side up and move Steven so he is centered in the frame.

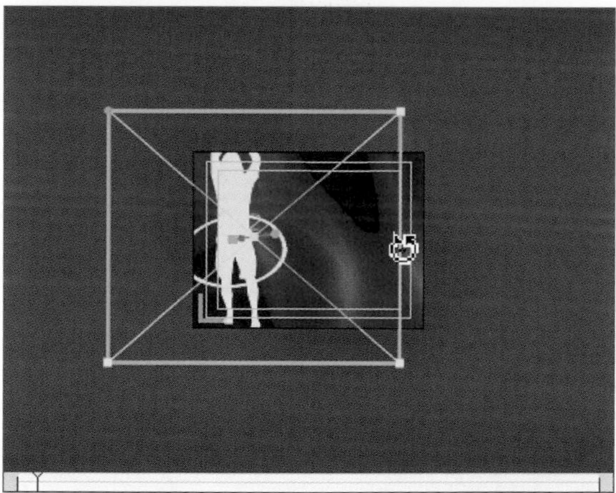

A keyframe is created for the rotation and center point parameters, but the scale parameter is left alone.

14 Step through the first 10 frames of the sequence to see exactly how the animation works.

NOTE ▸ You may want to press Shift-Z to zoom the Canvas window to fit the video so you can see the image more clearly.

Unfortunately, because this is such a short animation, it looks a little bit funny that the rotation happens in the center of the frame and then Steven zips over to his position when the animation is complete. This is due to the extra center point keyframe you added in step 13. It seems that, in this case, it would be better to eliminate that keyframe.

You learned earlier to delete keyframes by Control-clicking them, but there's another, more flexible method you can use on any type of motion keyframe.

15 Position the playhead on frame 5 where the offending keyframe resides.

16 Control-click the Add Keyframe button and, in the shortcut menu, choose Center to remove the checkmark and delete the keyframe.

The keyframe is removed, and now Steven glides from his starting position to his ending position in one smooth movement, although his rotation still ends halfway through the move. Perfect!

Copying and Pasting Keyframes

Now that the animation is set for one hula-hooper, you need to animate the rest of the hula-hoopers. Although they don't have exactly the same animation as **Steven1**, they all have nearly the same animation, so you can save time by applying the animation you just made to the rest of the hula-hooper clips.

1 Select **Steven1** and press Command-C to copy it to the clipboard.

2 On track V2, Option-click the Track Visibility control twice.

The first click solos that track, and the second click unsolos it, enabling all of the other tracks.

You were focused on the Canvas earlier in the exercise, but for the next few steps you'll be working in the Timeline, and it will be helpful to make the Timeline as large as possible.

3 Drag the divider between the Timeline and the Canvas windows upward until the Timeline is as large as possible.

4 Press Shift-Z to fit the entire Timeline into view.

You may also need to adjust the track height so at least tracks V1 through V9 are visible.

5 Select the clips on tracks V3 through V9.

6 Press Option-V to paste the attributes to this group of clips.

7 In the Paste Attributes dialog, select Basic Motion and click OK.

Now each of the clips has the same motion path, which is not exactly what you want. In this example, the clips will all begin in the same place, but each should end in a unique position.

When you drag the clips into new positions, it's critical that you do so on the correct frame. You must first set the center on the second keyframe for each of the clips.

To do this, you will use the Final Cut Pro keyframe navigation tools to jump directly to the correct frame.

8 Press Shift-Command-A to deselect everything.

9 Press Home to bring the playhead to the head of the sequence.

10 Select **Anah1** on track V3.

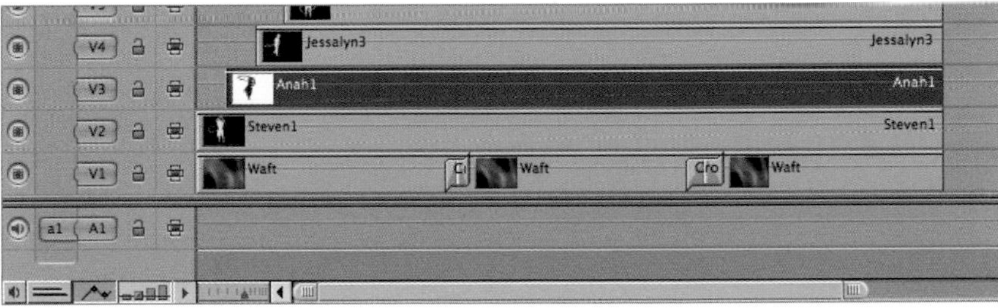

11 Choose View > Next > Keyframe or press Shift-K.

The playhead automatically jumps to the first frame of the **Anah1** clip. Because there is a keyframe there, the playhead ignores the keyframes in the other clips because they are not selected.

TIP Pressing Shift-K jumps to the next keyframe. If you want to move to the previous keyframe, press Option-K.

12 Press Shift-K twice.

The playhead moves to the third keyframe, which is exactly where you want to reposition Anah.

NOTE ▶ Because keyframes have already been added to this clip, if you moved Anah to a different position on any other frame, you would add yet another keyframe, and the clip would still move to that position on the left before moving to the place you chose.

13 Drag **Anah1** to the upper-right corner.

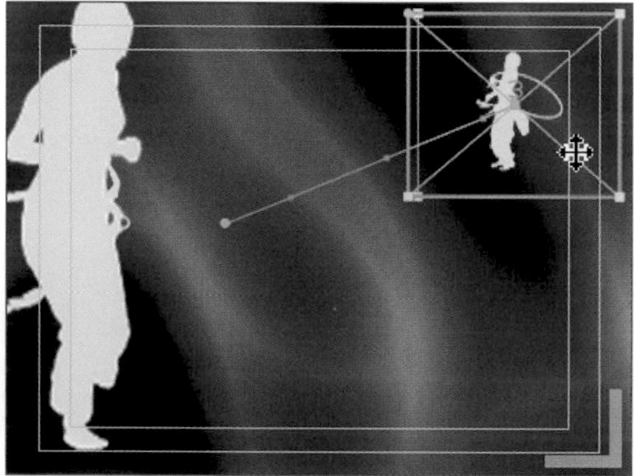

14 Select **Jessalyn3**.

15 Press Shift-K.

16 Drag Jessalyn to the bottom center.

17 Use the same procedure to position the rest of the clips into the remaining slots, as shown in this figure:

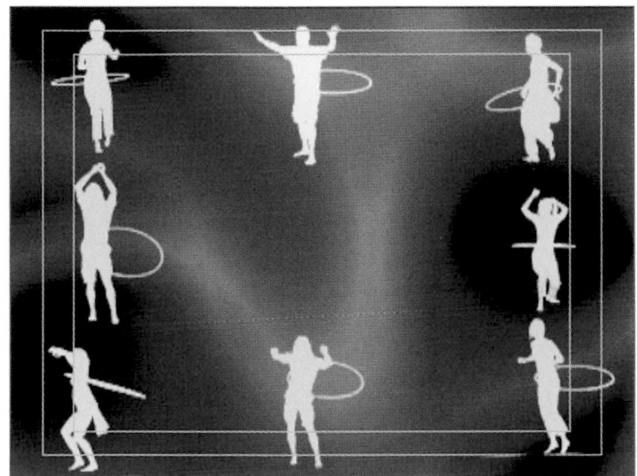

It really doesn't matter which dancer goes into which slot, as long as each goes to a different location. However, be very careful never to skip the step of moving the playhead to the second keyframe for each clip.

18 Render and play back the sequence to see what you have built.

Keyframing in the Viewer

Although keyframing in the Canvas can be quick and easy, the more complex your animations become, the more you'll find yourself wishing for more precise control and for more specific feedback on each parameter. The Canvas lets you achieve approximate settings, but if you want to guarantee specific numeric values, you'll have to use the Viewer.

For example, when dragging those clips to their positions, how do you know if they are accurately lined up? In the Viewer, you can see the precise numerical value of each setting.

1 In the Canvas or the Timeline, double-click **Christabel1**.

The clip opens into the Viewer. Notice the sprocket holes to indicate you are editing the version from the sequence (and not the master clip from the Browser).

2 Switch to the Motion tab.

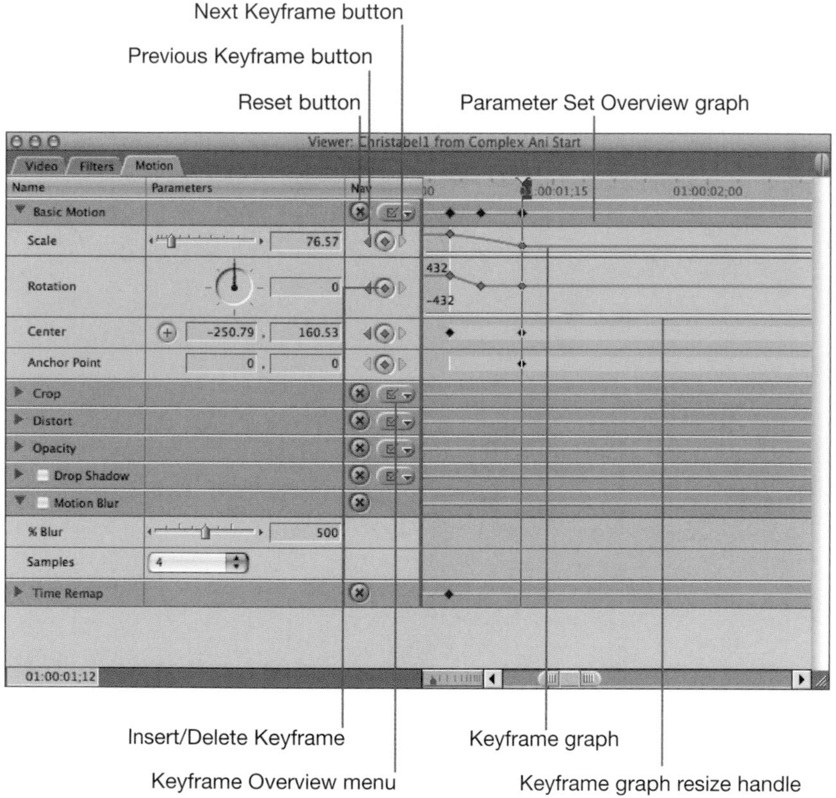

Here, you can see the numerical values for each of the parameters you manipulated, and you can see the graph for the keyframes you created.

NOTE ▶ The Center parameter has no graph because its graph is represented in two dimensions in the Canvas.

You can manipulate the keyframes directly in the graph, or you can position the playhead on a particular frame and use the sliders and dials. It is very important to remember that adjusting a slider *always* changes the current frame—not the value of the keyframe you may be looking at.

By default, the graphs are a little small, so it's helpful to expand them.

3 Drag the line beneath the Rotation graph downward.

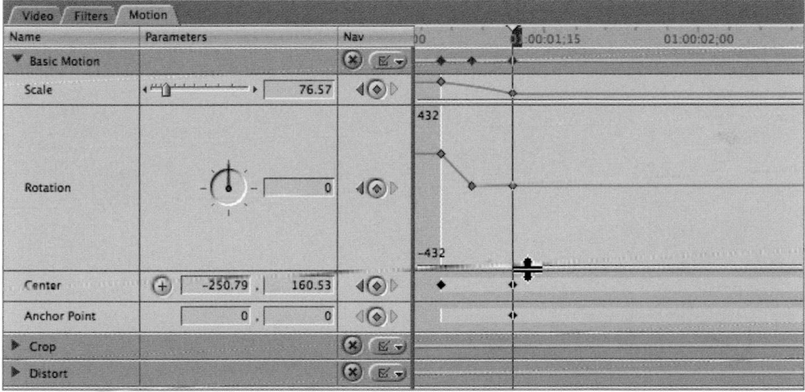

It's also important to zoom in or out on the keyframed area of the clip. Pressing Command-+ (plus) and Command-– (minus) will zoom in and out on the ruler area, respectively.

Each parameter has its own Add Keyframe button, and if you are parked on a keyframe, the corresponding button is colored green. Furthermore, the Previous Keyframe and Next Keyframe buttons (on either side of the Add Keyframe button) will dim if there are no more keyframes in that direction.

Each group of parameters has an overview bar showing the keyframes for the parameters within each group.

4 Click the Keyframe Overview pop-up menu for Basic Motion to select which parameters to display in that overview graph.

5 Deselect Rotation.

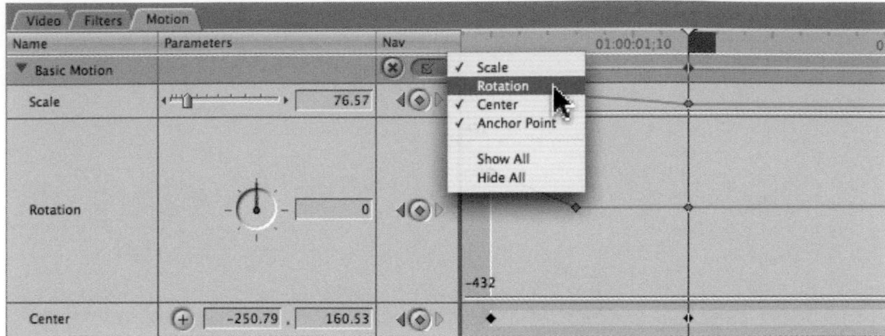

The rotation keyframes are no longer displayed in the overview graph.

The overview graph is visible even when the parameter group is collapsed, which allows you to simplify your view and see only information vital to the current operation.

6 Click the disclosure triangle to hide the Basic Motion parameters.

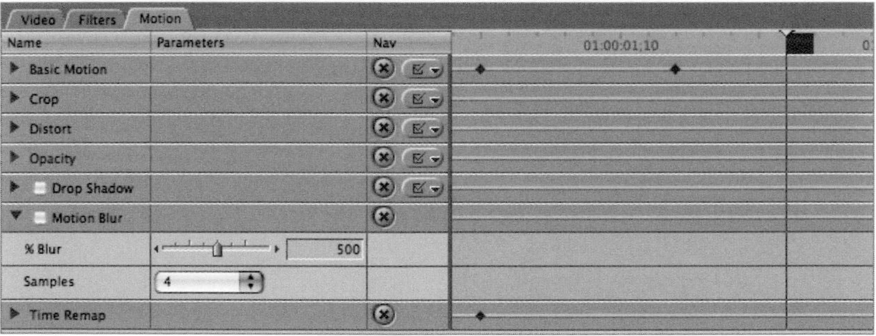

TIP You can restore all default values and delete all keyframes for every parameter within each group by clicking the Reset button.

7 Click the disclosure triangle to view the Basic Motion parameters again.

When manipulating keyframes in the Canvas, you used Ease In/Ease Out to create organic, smooth motion. You can apply similar smoothing to the keyframes here.

8 Control-click the second keyframe in the Rotation parameter and choose Smooth from the shortcut menu.

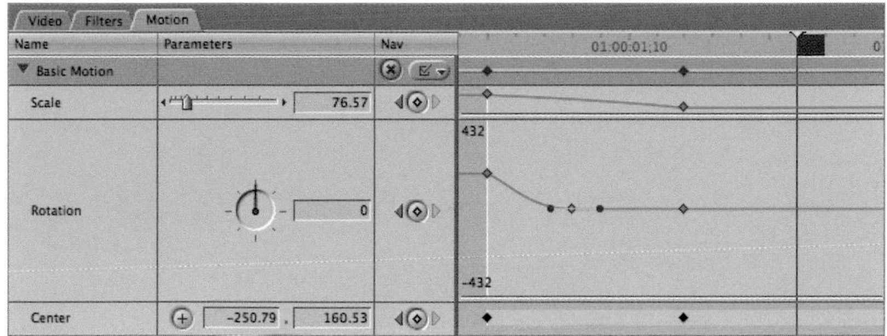

A Bezier handle appears, and the keyframe path automatically becomes curved. If you don't modify the Bezier handle, this should approximate a smooth "ease" effect in which the parameter reaches the value gradually.

9 Play the sequence to see the effect of the Smooth setting.

TIP Some parameters already have curved paths because they automatically follow a nonlinear path.

In the case of Scale, objects that scale linearly appear to slow down as they get larger. The built-in curve is an attempt to override this and create scaling effects that *appear* more linear. You can override the built-in curve by making the keyframes "smooth" and manipulating the Bezier handles to create the exact path you desire.

Audio Levels has a similar built-in curve because the decibel (dB) metric by which levels are gauged is inherently nonlinear. That is, 3 dB sounds twice as loud as 0 dB and 12 dB sounds four times as loud.

Using Motion Blur

Many of the advanced compositing tools in Final Cut Pro are designed to make your digitally generated effects seem more natural. Like the Smooth and Ease settings you've been using, Motion Blur is another way to more naturally simulate the real world. When objects move quickly, we expect them to appear blurry. This is partially because traditional film cameras capture at the relatively slow rate of 24 frames per second. But even the naked eye can only capture movement so fast (hence the expression, "it was all a blur," when something happens very quickly).

When you move objects digitally—such as the zooming, scaling, and rotating hula-hoopers in this composition—there is no blur at all. Final Cut Pro interpolates each frame, always seeking to deliver the sharpest, most accurate interpolation of the frames between keyframes.

If you want a more realistic look for movement (as opposed to a more accurate one), enable Motion Blur. Every clip has a Motion tab, and every Motion tab has a Motion Blur section. However, be aware that Motion Blur is a processor-intensive effect; turning it on can significantly slow your workflow.

1 Make sure the sequence playhead is positioned over one of the first ten frames of the clip open in the Viewer (**Christabel1**).

2 Select the checkbox to enable Motion Blur in the **Christabel1** Motion tab.

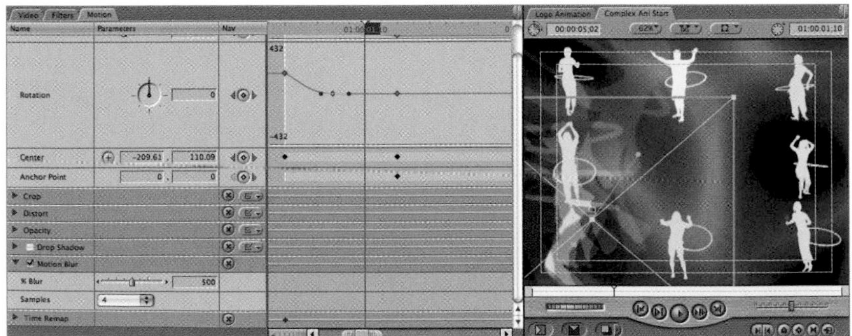

3 Expand Motion Blur and set % Blur to 25 and Samples to 16.

4 Play (rendering if necessary) to see the resulting effect.

The way Motion Blur works is that, rather than actually blurring the clip, Final Cut Pro displays increasingly faint images of the preceding frames, so its movement appears to smear across the frame.

The higher the % Blur, the more frames are drawn, and the higher the number of samples, which increases the blur effect.

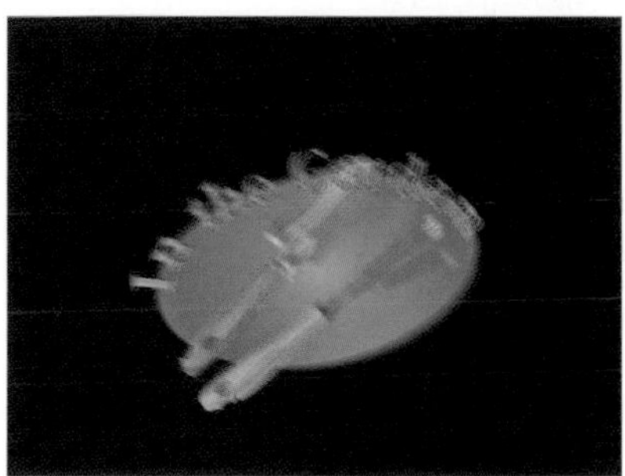

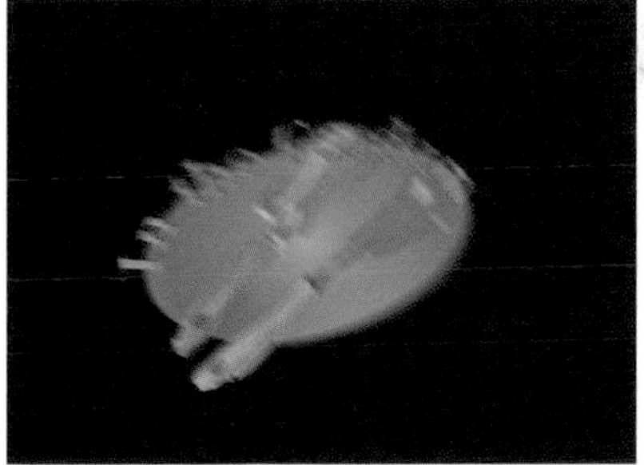

Animating Keyframing Filters

Filter parameters can be animated using exactly the same method as the motion effects you have been keyframing throughout this lesson.

1 In the Timeline, Option-click the Track Visibility control for track V10.

This solos that track and makes it easier to isolate the effect of the filter you will animate.

2 Select the **HoopinUSA.tif** clip on track V10.

3 Choose Effects > Video Filters > Glow > Light Rays.

Light Rays is a popular effect, especially for text, but the filter's promise isn't truly realized until you animate the parameters a bit.

4 Double-click the clip to open it into the Viewer. Click the Filters tab.

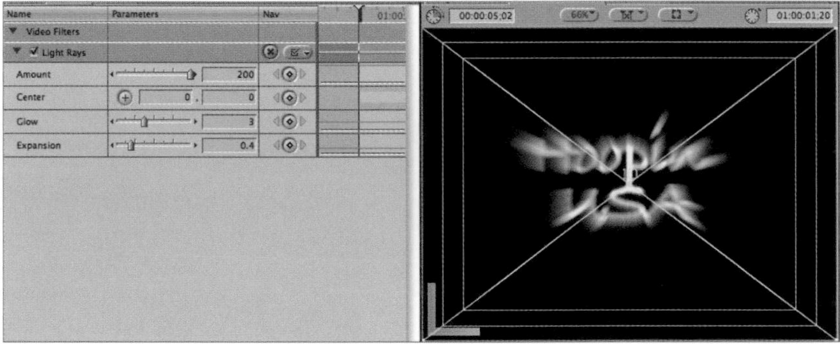

Remember, whenever you keyframe you not only need to set the value of the parameter you want to animate but also choose the frame in which you want to apply it.

5 Press the Up Arrow to move the playhead to the first frame of the clip.

6 Click the Center point control in the Filters tab, then click anywhere in the Canvas—but don't let go of the mouse!

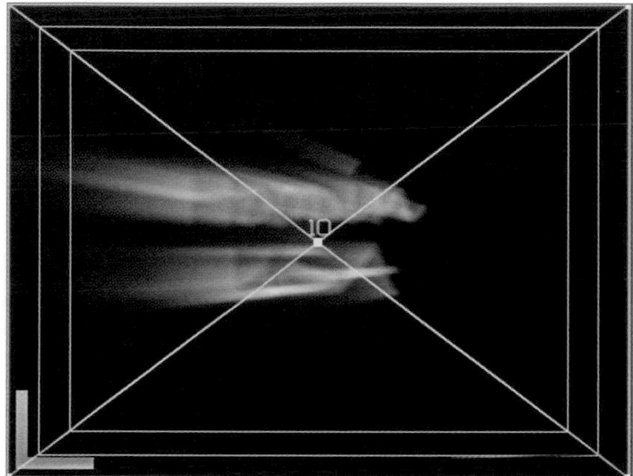

7 Drag the point around, from the left edge to the right edge of the screen.

This previews how the parameter will look when you animate it.

8 Choose a point to the right of the words, so the light rays are pointing to the left.

9 In the Filters tab, click the Insert Keyframe button for the Center parameter.

Light Rays		
Amount		200
Center	268.3	-3.02
Glow		3
Expansion		0.4

This sets your starting point for the parameter.

10 Press Shift-O to move the playhead to the Out point of the clip.

11 Click the Center point control and choose a point to the left of the words in the Canvas.

Because you already set a keyframe for this parameter, setting a different value on a different frame automatically creates a second keyframe. No motion path is drawn in the Canvas (those only appear for a clip's center point), but the Filter tab in the Viewer shows the two keyframes.

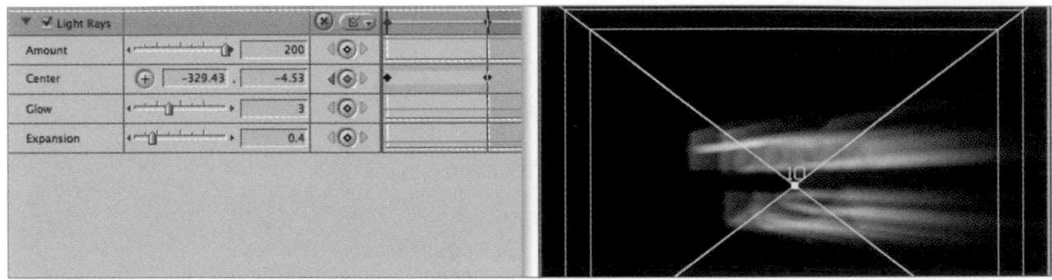

12 Render the sequence and press \ (backslash) to Play Around Current so you can see the animated effect.

Because the Light Rays effect distorts the image so much, adding a second copy of the clip on the track above allows you to see the light rays but still read the text.

13 Click the Track Visibility control for track V11.

V11 actually contains a subsequence containing a copy of the text used as a travel matte. (For more information on travel mattes, see Lesson 6, "Advanced Compositing.")

14 Render and play the sequence.

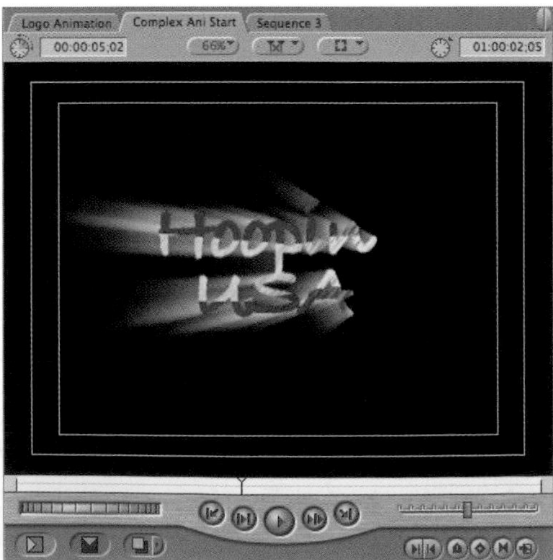

Keyframing in the Timeline

In addition to keyframing in the other windows, you can view, create, and modify keyframes directly in the Timeline. Clip opacity levels and audio volume settings are both adjusted so frequently that Final Cut Pro can display keyframe graphs for these parameters right on top of the clip objects in the Timeline tracks.

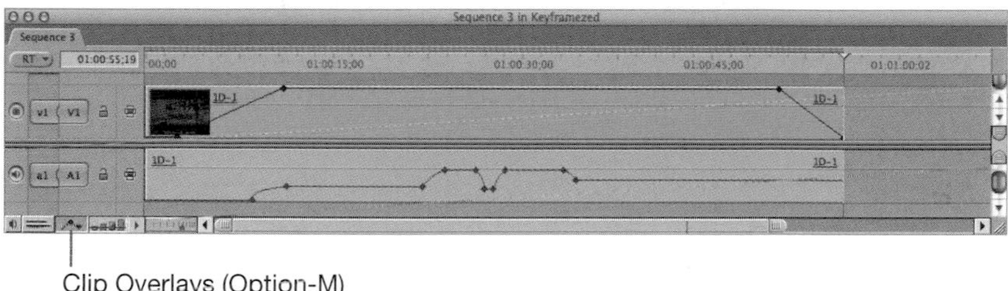

To display these overlays, you must turn them on in the Timeline.

1 Open the *Timeline Graph* sequence.

  This is another copy of the *Hoopin USA* sequence, with most of the work already done for you. Before it is completed, however, a few additional keyframes must be created, beginning with a fade-in effect for each of the silhouette clips.

2 Click the Clip Overlays control (or press Option-W) to turn on clip overlays.

  A black line appears on each of the tracks, representing that clip's opacity.

3 Zoom in on the beginning of the sequence.

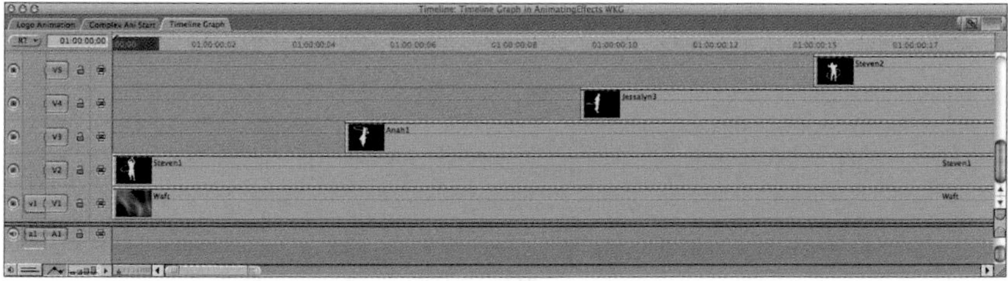

4 Option-click the opacity overlay (black line) for **Steven1** twice to add two keyframes as shown in the following figure.

By adding two keyframes at once, it will be easier to create the fade-in effect.

5 Drag down the left keyframe to the lower-left corner of the **Steven1** clip.

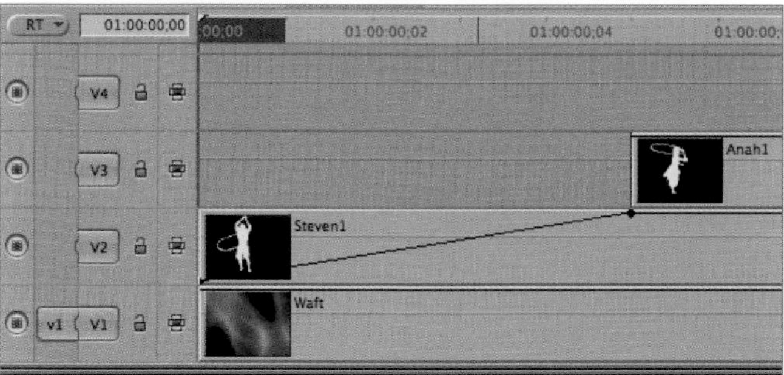

This creates a fade-in effect as the opacity transforms from 0% to 100% opaque.

6 Step through the frames where the keyframe graph changes to see the fade-in effect.

7 Control-click the second keyframe and choose Smooth from the shortcut menu.

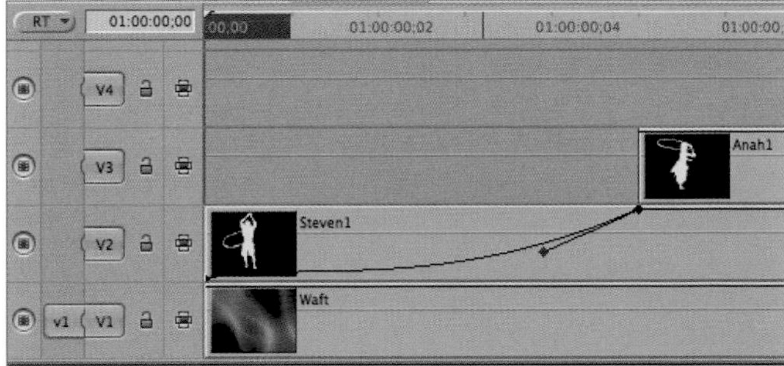

8 Adjust the Bezier handle to create a slight convex angle to the curve (as shown in the preceding figure), thus creating a more gradual fade-in.

You can employ all the same keyframe manipulations as in the other windows.

TIP Clicking keyframes that are very close to the edge of a clip in the Timeline is often difficult because the Selection tool defaults to selecting the edge of the clip, rather than the keyframe. If you want to ensure that you can select a keyframe, switch to the Pen tool (P).

Now that the fade-in effect is perfected on this one clip, you can apply an identical fade-in to each of the other clips.

1 Press Shift-Z to zoom the Timeline to fit, then press Shift-T several times until the tracks are at the shortest track height.

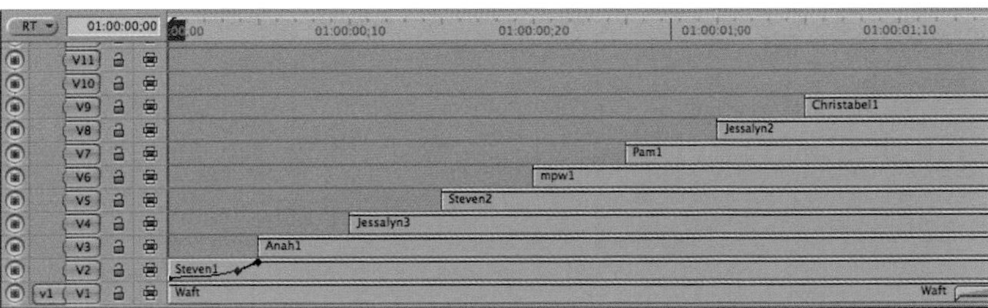

This allows you to see more tracks in the Timeline.

2 Select the **Steven1** clip and press Command-C to copy it to the clipboard.

3 Select the clips on tracks V3 through V9 and press Option-V to paste the attributes.

4 In the Paste Attributes dialog, select Opacity and make sure none of the other parameters are selected. Click OK.

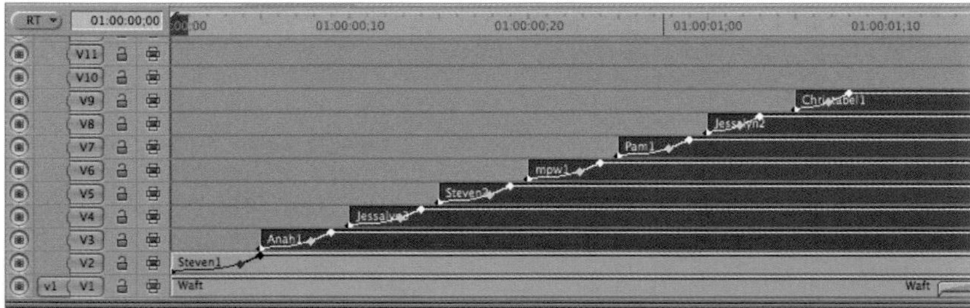

Now each of these clips has a fade-in effect applied, but if you look closely, you'll notice that the fade-in appears to get shorter and shorter on each of the clips.

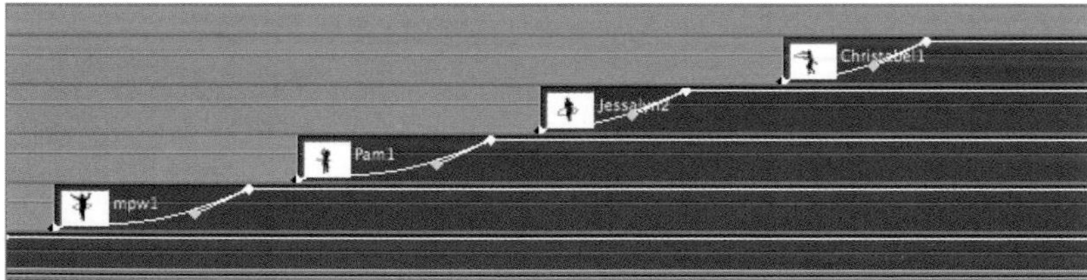

Scaling Attribute Times

When copying and pasting keyframed effects to clips of different lengths, you have to choose whether the keyframes should be set using absolute frames (for example, the fade-in takes exactly five frames) or whether they should be set as a percentage of the clip (for example, the fade-in occupies exactly three percent of the duration of the clip).

This decision is based on the setting of the Scale Attribute Times checkbox at the top of the Paste Attributes dialog.

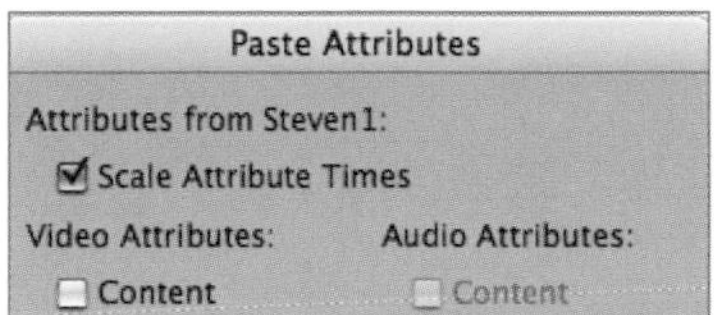

If the checkbox is selected (the default), keyframes will be pasted as a percentage. This is why the shorter clips received shorter fade-in effects.

1. Select the clips on tracks V3 through V9 and press Option-V to paste the attributes.
2. In the Paste Attributes dialog, deselect the Scale Attribute Times checkbox, select the Opacity checkbox, and click OK.

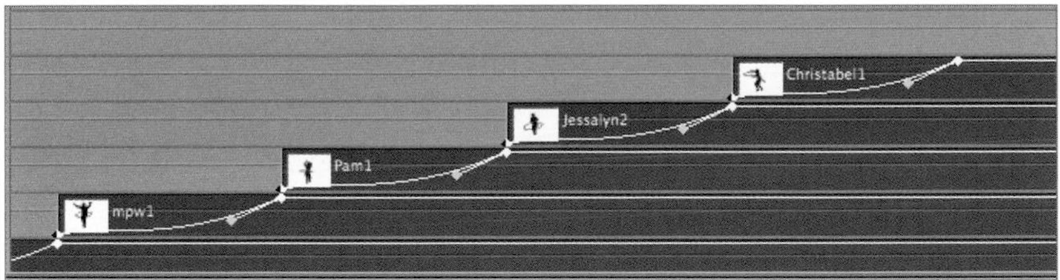

Now the fade-in lasts exactly the same number of frames in each clip. This choice works in this situation, but it can cause trouble in the case of a fade-out effect.

3 Zoom in to the end of the Timeline and add a fade-out to the **Steven1** clip.

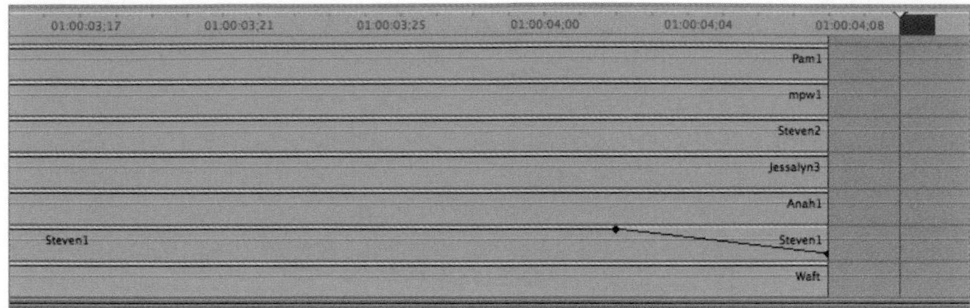

4 Copy the clip, select **Anah1**, and press Option-V to paste the attributes.

5 In the Paste Attributes dialog, deselect Scale Attribute Times, select the Opacity checkbox, and click OK.

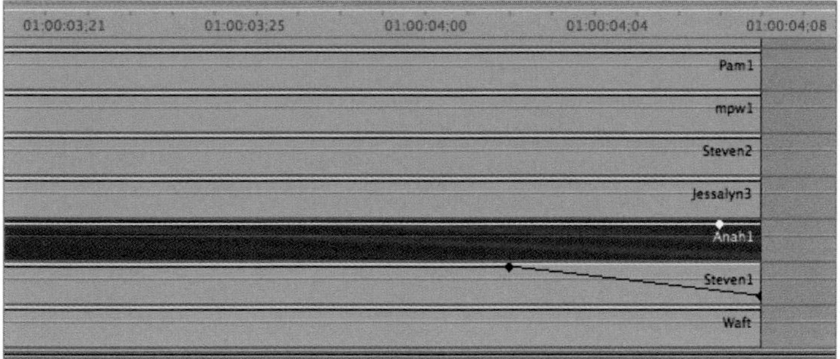

In this case, because the Anah clip is shorter than the Steven clip, the keyframes are cut off, destroying the intended fade-out effect.

6 Press Command-Z to undo the Paste Attributes command.

7 Press Option-V to paste the attributes again, and this time leave Scale Attribute Times selected. Select the Opacity box and click OK.

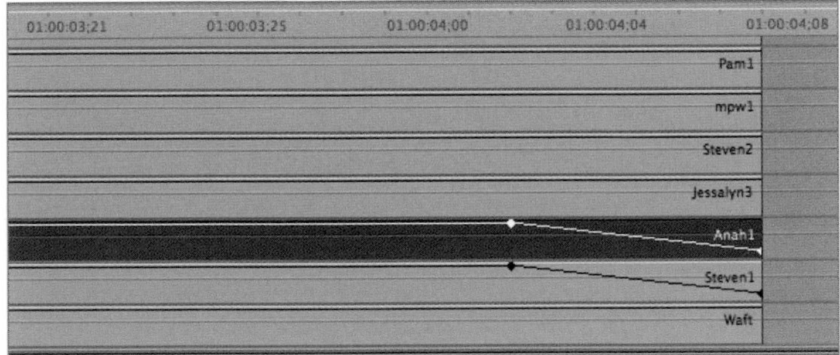

Now the fade-out is correctly scaled so that it ends exactly on the last frame of the clip.

Keyframing Audio Levels

Just as you adjust video clip opacity, you can modify audio levels by adding and changing keyframes directly in the Timeline tracks once the clip keyframes are turned on.

For more information on setting audio levels, please see Lesson 4, "Sound Editing."

Displaying Keyframe Bars

But wait, there's more! Not only can opacity and audio levels be animated in the Timeline, you can actually view any parameter from any filter or motion effect, although in a somewhat limited way.

1 Turn off clip overlays in the Timeline.

2 Click the Clip Keyframes control.

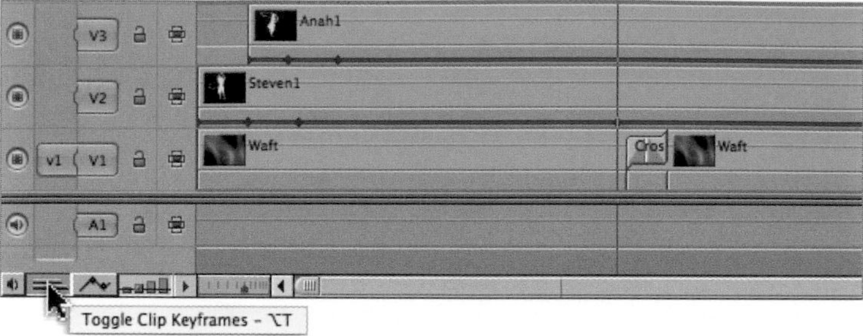

A blue line appears beneath each of the clips in the Timeline.

3 Control-click the Clip Keyframes control.

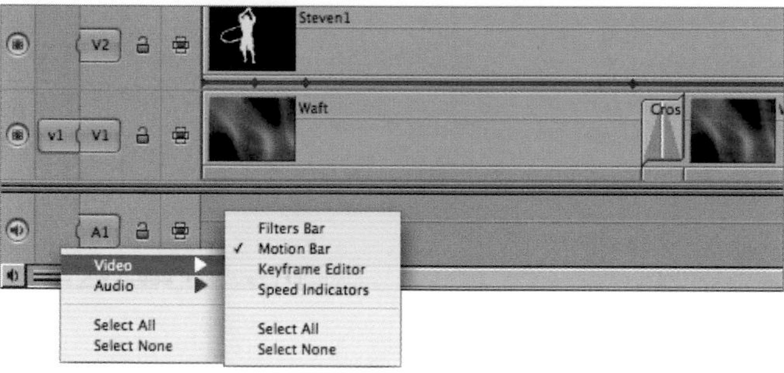

The Clip Keyframes settings shortcut menu appears.

In the Clip Keyframes shortcut menu, you can customize exactly what happens when you turn on clip keyframes. You can display filter keyframes, motion keyframes, a keyframe graph, and speed indicators for video clips, as well as similar audio clip parameters.

Currently, this sequence is set to display only the motion bar (the blue line). It is an overview of all motion parameters, collapsed into a single bar. The primary advantage to seeing keyframes in the Timeline is that you can compare clips to compare when their effects occur. For example, if you wanted one clip to begin fading out on the exact frame where another clip begins scaling down, you could see (and align) all of those keyframes at once.

Customizing Keyframe Bars

The trouble is, if you have a lot of keyframes, this simple display can quickly become a mess. So in most cases, rather than displaying all keyframes, it makes sense to limit which parameters are visible for any given clip.

1 Control-click the blue line beneath the **Hoop Landing** clip (on track V12).

A shortcut menu appears, listing all of the parameters for that clip. If you poke around the menu, you can see which parameters are active (indicated by a checkmark) and which are hidden from view.

By default, just about all the parameters are selected, so the blue bar is showing every single keyframe for every single parameter. If two parameters have keyframes on the exact same frame, you will not know which keyframe you are looking at (or manipulating), which can be problematic.

2 From the shortcut menu, choose Hide All, then choose Basic Motion > Scale.

Now only one parameter's keyframes are visible for that one clip.

TIP The Keyframe Overview menu for each parameter set in the Motion tab is live-linked to this shortcut menu. Turning a parameter on or off in either place will change the other.

3 Control-click the Clip Keyframes control and choose Video > Filters Bar from the shortcut menu.

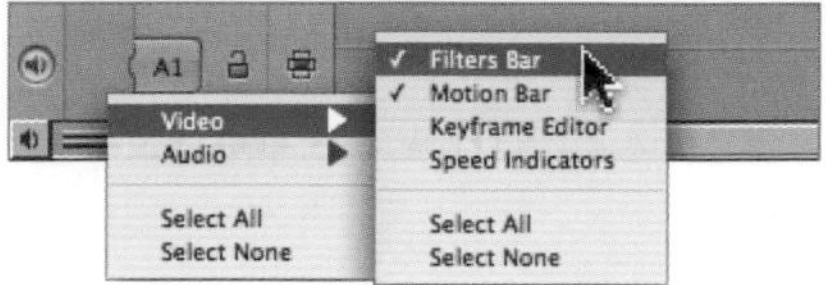

A green bar appears, displaying keyframes for any clips with filters applied. The **HoopinUSA.tif** clip has the Light Rays filter applied, and there is a keyframe visible near the beginning of the clip that begins the movement of the light rays across the screen.

4 Control-click the green bar to check which parameters' keyframes are displayed for that filter.

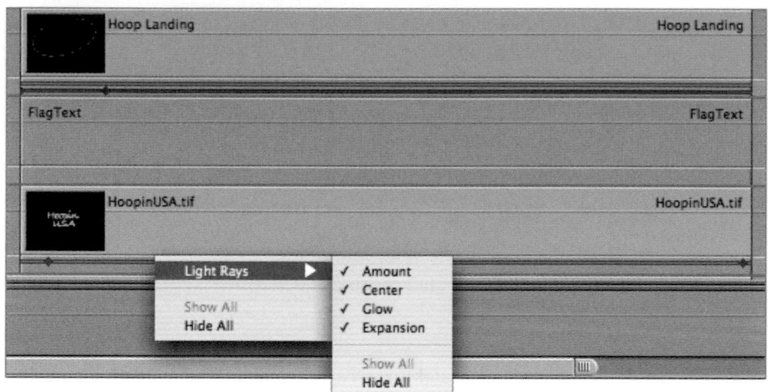

5 From the shortcut menu, choose Hide All, then choose Light Rays > Center.

The filter bar is restricted to display keyframes from that one parameter.

In this example, the goal is to align the beginning of the light rays' movement with the end of the hula-hoop's scaling animation. Being able to see the keyframes in the Timeline makes this very easy.

6 Drag the green keyframe to the right to align it with the second keyframe in the **Hoop Landing** clip.

7 Render and play the sequence to see the result of the effect.

The light rays' movement now precisely corresponds with the hula hoop completing its scale animation.

NOTE ► Because many of these effects happen so quickly, you may need to step through the sequence frame by frame or play it in slow motion to see the results of the steps you've completed.

Editing Keyframe Graphs in the Timeline

The keyframe bars allow you to compare the timing of keyframes across effects and across clips, but you can only change a keyframe's position in time; you cannot change its value. If you need to see an entire parameter graph in the Timeline, you can do so, but for only one parameter (per clip) at a time.

1 Control-click the Clip Keyframes control and choose Video > Keyframe Editor from the shortcut menu.

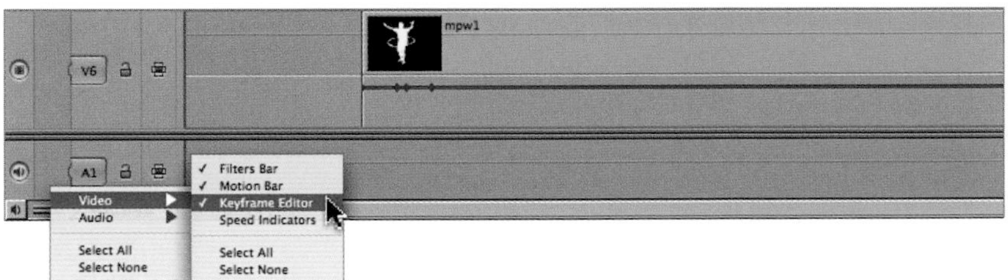

More space is added beneath each of the clips (so each track takes up quite a bit of space), but no keyframe graph will be visible until you specify which parameter graph you want to see.

2 Scroll your Timeline view so you can see the head of the sequence and see the **Steven1** clip in track V1.

3 Control-click in the area beneath the blue filter bar and choose Basic Motion > Scale from the shortcut menu.

The scale graph is displayed for that clip. Only one graph can be displayed at a time, so if you choose another parameter, its graph will replace this one.

You can increase the size allocated for the graph on a track-by-track basis.

4 Click the right-most edge of the track header area for track V1 and drag upward.

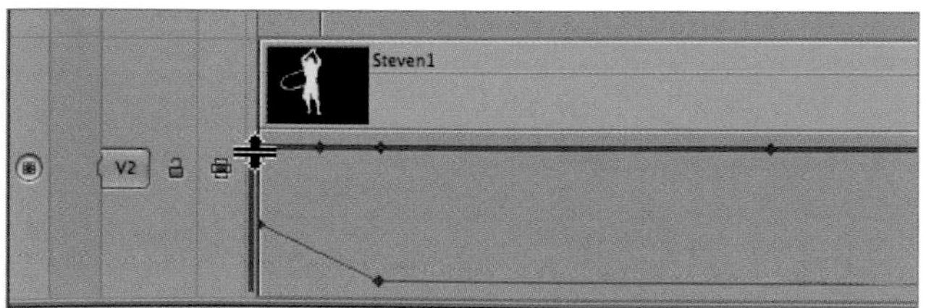

As you increase the size of the graph, the entire track area gets larger.

This graph is identical to the one in the Motion tab (except that it's much bigger), and changing values in one place automatically updates the other. You can do all of the same keyframing operations here as in the other graphs.

The main advantage to accessing a keyframe graph here is to compare this graph with a graph on another clip. You can compare the relative slopes of various parameter animations and adjust them to make them more or less similar.

5 Click the Clip Keyframes control to hide the keyframe controls.

Saving Favorite Motion Effects

As you are now well aware, animating effects can be a painstaking, time-consuming process. Fortunately, many motion graphics projects utilize repetition and consistency across their varied elements, so it's likely you'll use the same effects multiple times. For this reason, you can save and reapply keyframed effects to other clips in Final Cut Pro.

You already know how to save a customized filter as a favorite (see Lesson 7, "Mastering Video Filters"). If there are keyframes in that filter, those keyframes will be saved as part of the favorite. You can also save the settings in any clip's Motion tab—keyframes and all. So if you created a particular way that a clip flies across the screen—or a combination of scaling, rotation, cropping, distorting, or any of the other parameters in the Motion tab—you can save the entire effect as a favorite and later apply it to other clips in the same project, or in an entirely different project.

1 In the Timeline, select **Steven1**.

2 Choose Effects > Make Favorite Motion (or press Control-F).

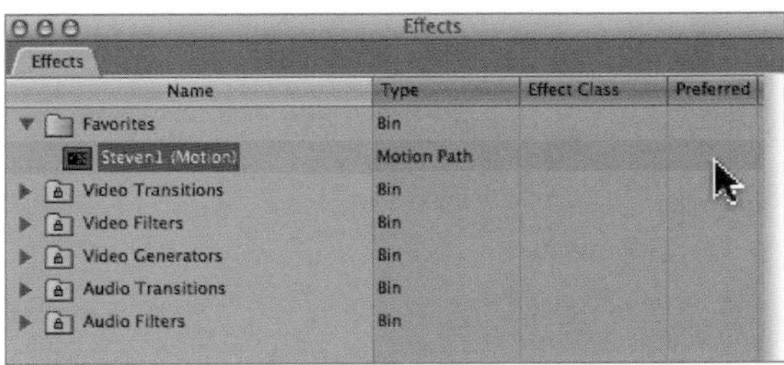

A favorite motion object is added to the Favorites folder in the Effects tab.

3 Name the favorite motion *Scale Rotate & Fade In (10Frame).*

4 In the Timeline, select **Anah1**.

5 Choose Effects > Motion Favorites > Scale Rotate & Fade In (10Frame).

The Anah clip is updated with the settings from the saved motion.

NOTE ▶ Motion Favorites are all-or-nothing. If you apply a Motion favorite, all of the settings from the original clip's Motion tab are assigned to the new clip. There is no way to pick and choose which settings to apply. For that style of effect, use Paste Attributes.

Lesson Review

1. What is a keyframe?
2. Which windows permit keyframing?
3. How do you change a corner point to a smooth point?
4. What is Ease In/Out?
5. How do you delete a keyframe?
6. How do you navigate to a keyframe?
7. What is Motion Blur and where can you enable it?
8. How are filters animated?
9. What parameters' keyframe graphs can be viewed in the Timeline?
10. How do you grab a keyframe that is positioned too close to a clip's In or Out point?
11. What does Scale Attribute Times do, and where is it set?
12. How can a clip's motion or filter keyframes be viewed in the Timeline?
13. How can a motion effect be saved for use at a later time?

Answers

1. A mark to indicate that a parameter must be at a specific value on a specific frame.
2. The Canvas, the Timeline, and all of the tabs in the Viewer window.
3. Control-click a keyframe and choose Smooth from the shortcut menu.
4. Ease In/Out automatically sets the acceleration of an animation to slow down as it approaches and leaves a keyframe.
5. Control-click the keyframe and choose Delete or Clear from the shortcut menu, or in some cases, just drag it off the graph. In the Canvas, you can also park on the keyframe and deselect it from the Add Motion Keyframe shortcut menu.
6. Shift-K and Option-K will take you to the next or previous keyframe for the selected objects. In the Viewer, you can also use the Previous Keyframe and Next Keyframe buttons.
7. Motion Blur simulates the visual smearing of an object when it is moving quickly. It can be enabled and configured in the Motion tab for any clip.
8. Animate filters by opening the Filters tab and using the keyframe controls to the right of the parameter settings.
9. Any parameter can be viewed in the Timeline using the Clip Keyframes' keyframe editor (albeit only one at a time, per clip). Clip opacity and audio levels can be viewed directly on top of the clips in the timeline by turning on clip overlays.
10. The Pen tool can be used to select keyframes in the Timeline when the Selection tool is erroneously selecting the clip edge.
11. Scale Attribute Times is located in the Paste Attributes dialog, and it controls whether keyframes are pasted with an absolute or a relative duration.
12. Keyframe bars for both motion and filters can be displayed in the Timeline by activating the Clip Keyframes control.
13. Select the clip containing the motion and choose Effects > Make Favorite Motion, or press Control-F. The motion settings will be saved in the Favorites bin of the Effects tab.

9

n Files	Lesson Files > Lesson 09 > Nesting.fcp
Media	Motocross
Time	This lesson takes approximately 90 minutes to complete.
Goals	Create a nested sequence by editing one sequence into another
	Convert clips into a nested sequence using the Nest Items command
	Apply effects to nested sequences
	Modify individual clips in a nested sequence
	Use nesting to override the default Final Cut Pro render order
	Mix sequence frame sizes to create scaling effects
	Use nesting to manage long-format shows

Lesson **9**

Nesting Sequences

When working with complex sequences involving multiple tracks, you may want to treat a group of clips as a single object. For example, you may wish to apply a single filter to multiple items, or to scale or rotate several clips at once. Final Cut Pro's nesting features can efficiently accomplish such complex tasks.

Furthermore, nested sequences also allow you to quickly add effects and perform tasks that would otherwise be time consuming or impossible any other way. Learning to manage nested sequences will enable you to create powerful effects, as well as improve your overall workflow and flexibility within Final Cut Pro.

Understanding Nested Sequences

You can treat any sequence as a clip and edit it into another sequence by dragging and dropping it into the Canvas or Timeline. The embedded sequence is called a *nested* sequence, and the sequence it is embedded into is often referred to as the *parent* sequence.

You can also select a group of clips already in a sequence and turn it into a nested sequence—replacing the group of items with a single item.

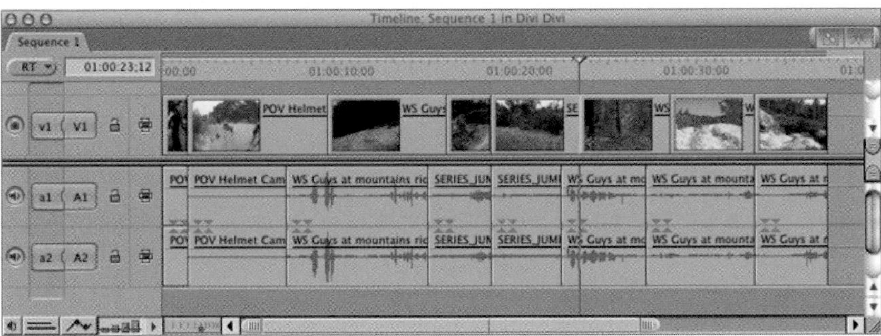

Un-nested

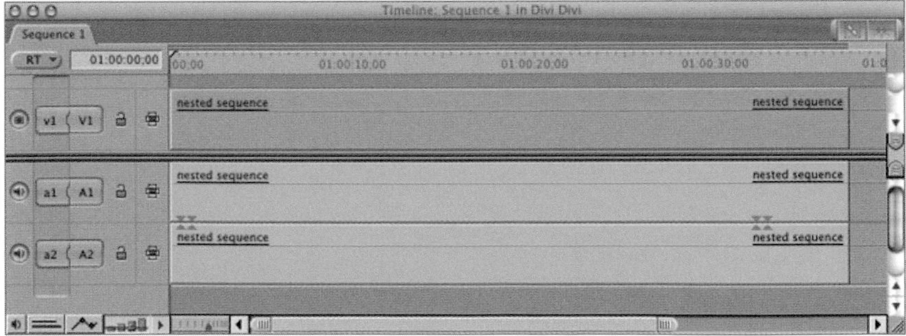

Nested

Using Basic Nesting

First you will edit one sequence into another.

1 Open Lesson Files > Lesson 09 > **Nesting.fcp**.

The *Bike Jumps* sequence should be open in the Timeline. If it's not, double-click it in the Browser to open it into the Timeline.

2 Play the sequence to get familiar with it.

The sequence contains three clips on V1 and a title clip on track 2.

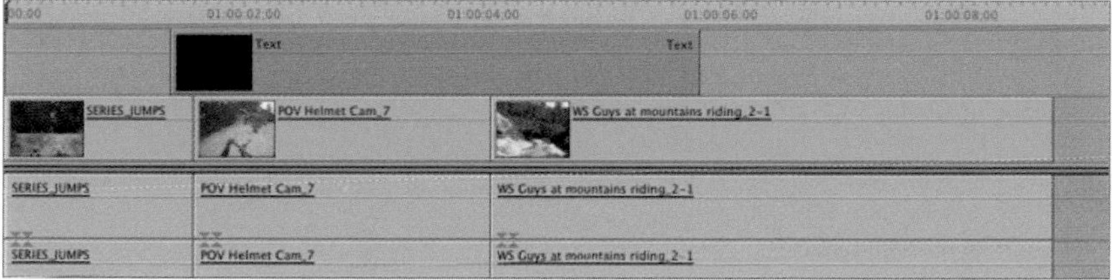

3 In the Browser, double-click *Motocross Sequence.*

It opens as a second tab in the Timeline.

4 Press Home to ensure that the sequence playhead is at the beginning of the sequence.

5 Press N to activate snapping if it is not already activated.

6 In the Browser, select the *Bike Jumps* sequence.

7 Drag it into the Canvas and drop it as an Insert edit.

You have now nested the *Bike Jumps* sequence inside *Motocross Sequence*. You can see that the color of the new item is slightly different than ordinary clips in the Timeline; this helps identify which items in your sequence are nested.

When you play *Motocross Sequence*, clips nested in the *Bike Jumps* sequence will play as they were originally edited. Even the title from video track 2 of the *Bike Jumps* sequence will be visible.

Understanding Live Links

The link between a nested sequence and its parent sequence remains live: When you make changes inside a nested sequence, those changes take effect when you play the parent sequence. Any changes made to clips or other items inside a nested sequence are automatically updated in the parent sequence.

1 In the Timeline, click the *Bike Jumps* tab.

2 Double-click the title clip on track V2 to open it into the Viewer.

3 Position your sequence playhead anywhere over the title clip to see the results of changes you make in the Viewer.

4 In the Viewer, click the Controls tab. Type *Motocross Madness!* in the text box and press Tab or click anywhere outside the text box to update the Canvas.

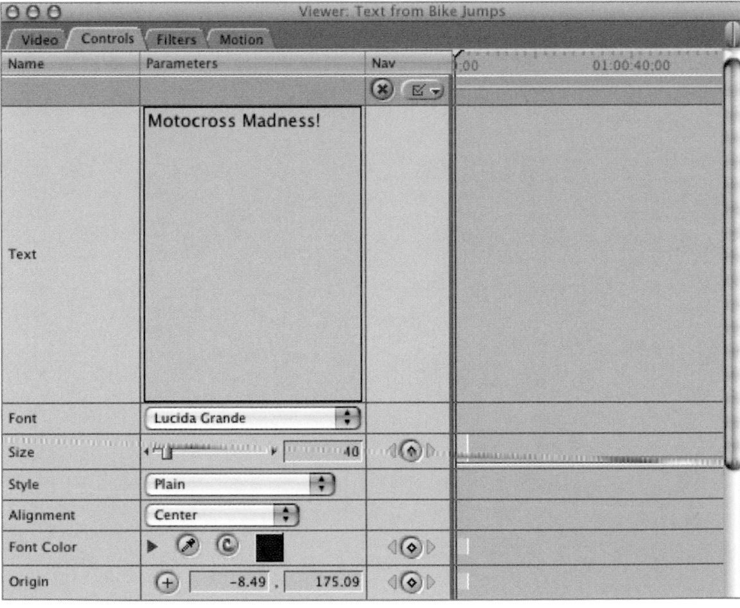

The Canvas reflects the change. If your playhead isn't over the area of the title, drag it there to confirm that the text has been updated.

5 In the Timeline, click the *Motocross Sequence* tab.

6 Scrub the playhead through *Motocross Sequence* until you see the section where the title should appear.

Notice that the text has been updated here as well.

Whenever you change the title clip from the *Bike Jumps* nested sequence in the Controls tab of the Viewer, the changes continue to update live in *Motocross Sequence*, the parent sequence.

Applying Effects to Multiple Clips

You can use nesting to apply a single effect to multiple items at once. This saves time by eliminating the need to individually apply a filter or transformation to each clip. If you later decide to change the parameters of the effect, the changes will affect all clips simultaneously.

In this example, you will tint all of the clips inside the nested sequence red.

1 Be sure that *Motocross Sequence* is open in the Timeline.

2 In the Timeline, select the *Bike Jumps* nested sequence.

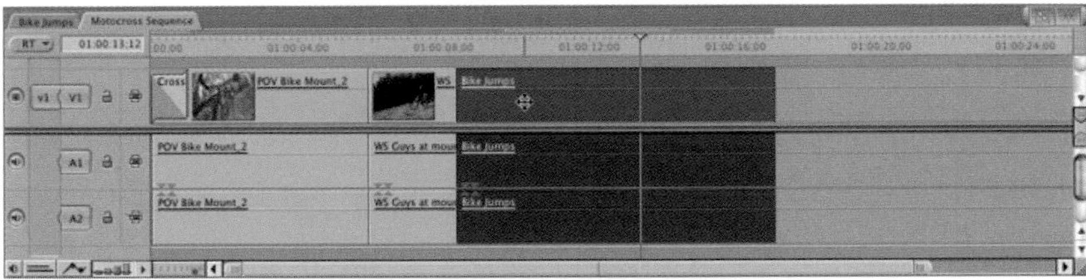

3 Choose Effects > Video Filters > Image Control > Tint.

The tint effect is applied to every clip in the *Bike Jumps* nested sequence.

The filter is applied to the nest and not the individual clips contained in the nest. Open the nested sequence in the Viewer to modify the parameters of the filter.

Ordinarily, double-clicking a clip in the Timeline opens it in the Viewer. But when you double-click a nested sequence, it opens in the Timeline and Canvas as a new tab, just as any sequence does when you double-click it in the Browser.

4 In the Timeline, select the *Bike Jumps* nested sequence (if it's not already selected).

5 Press Enter, choose View > Sequence, or Control-click the nested sequence and choose Open in Viewer from the shortcut menu.

The *Bike Jumps* sequence is now displayed in the Viewer as if it were an individual clip.

6 In the Viewer, click the Filters tab.

The Tint filter controls should be visible.

7 Set the color of the tint to a pale red by clicking the color selector and adjusting the color settings.

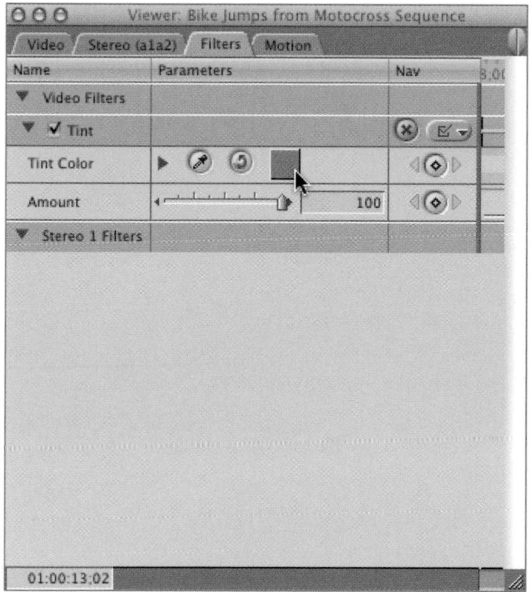

8 Play *Motocross Sequence*. Notice that the new reddish tint affects the entire *Bike Jumps* segment.

You could accomplish the same results by applying the tint filter to each individual clip. However, if your client decided that she preferred a blue tint instead of red, you would then have to open and modify the clips individually. With nested sequences, you can modify filter settings and apply those changes to all clips at once.

Applying Complex Geometric Settings

Some effects can only be achieved by using nested sequences. For example, by combining multiple clips into a single element in the Timeline, you can apply geometric attributes such as scale, rotation, and movement to all of the clips as a single unit.

1 In the Browser, double-click the *Split Screen* sequence to open it into the Timeline.

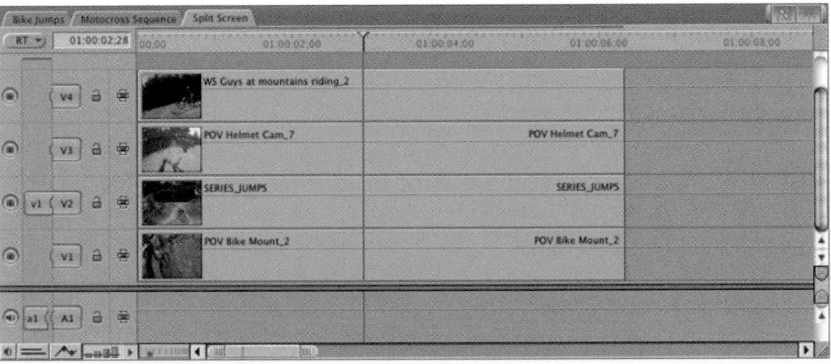

The *Split Screen* sequence contains four clips scaled down to 50% and arranged into quadrants in the Canvas so that all four images are visible onscreen at the same time.

NOTE ▶ If your system is powerful enough, you may be able to play the sequence without rendering. If the Timeline displays a red line in the render bar area, you might not have selected Unlimited RT in the Real-Time Effects pop-up menu in the Timeline. Selecting Unlimited RT and Dynamic quality, instead of Safe RT, will allow you to play more effects in real time.

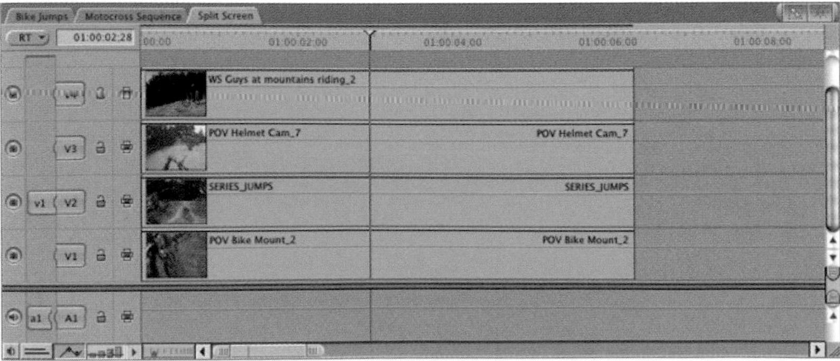

2 If necessary, render your sequence by pressing Option-R.

3 Play the sequence.

The four video clips play simultaneously.

Earlier in this lesson, you created a nested sequence by dragging one sequence into another. In the following steps, you will spin the four elements around a single anchor point, and then shrink the whole image to a single point, revealing a new image.

4 Select the four clips in the Timeline.

5 Choose Sequence > Nest Item(s) or press Option-C.

The Nest Items dialog appears.

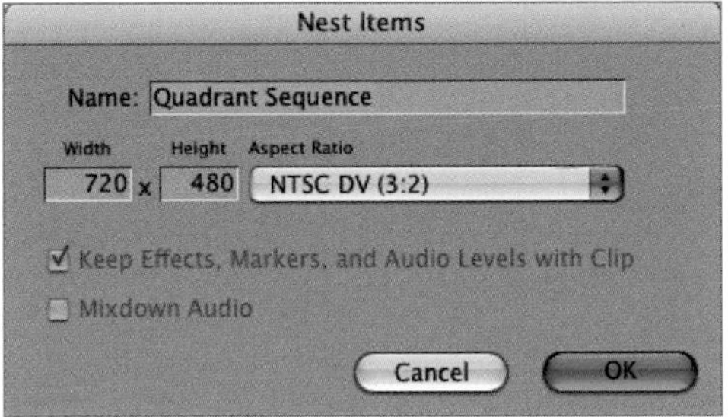

6 In the Name box, type *Quadrant Sequence.* Leave the other settings at their default values and click OK.

Now, instead of four clips on four tracks, the parent sequence contains one item, *Quadrant Sequence*. The image in the Canvas does not change.

The Nest Items command automatically puts the new nested sequence on the lowest available track. If a clip already occupies the lowest track, the next available higher track will be used. In some cases, Final Cut Pro will generate a new track to make space for the item. The following figures show an example in which V2 becomes the location of a nested sequence created from clips on V1 through V4.

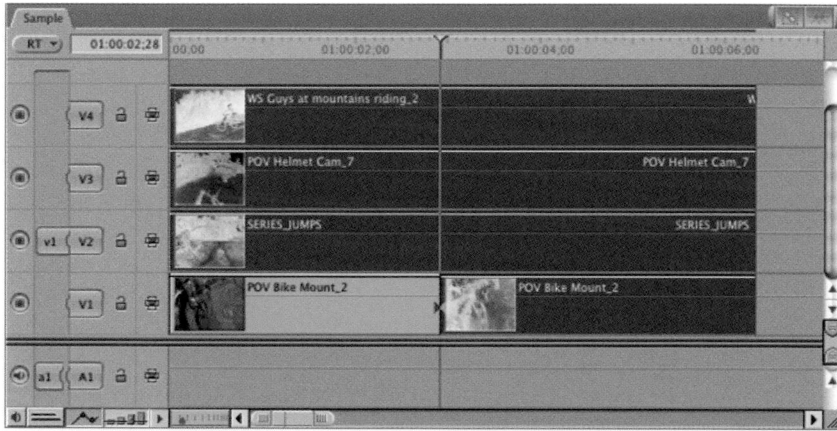

Un-nested

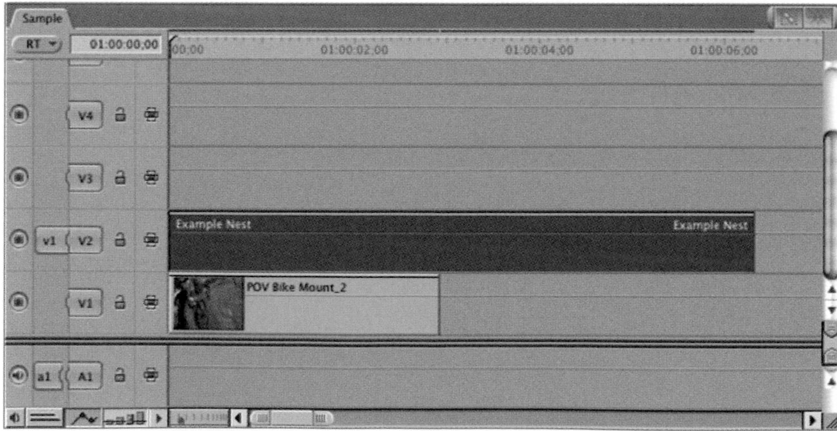

Nested

Nest Items also adds a new sequence in your project. You can use this sequence like any other. Any changes you make to the nested *Quadrant Sequence* will modify the parent *Split Screen* sequence.

Apply Motion Parameters

All four clips are now neatly contained in a nest, so you can modify the Motion parameters of the nest without affecting the individual motion parameters of the clips within. For example, nesting these clips is particularly useful if you want to rotate all four clips as a group while maintaining their individual X/Y positions and rotation values.

1 Open *Quadrant Sequence* into the Viewer by selecting it in the Timeline and pressing Enter.

2 In the Viewer, click the Motion tab.

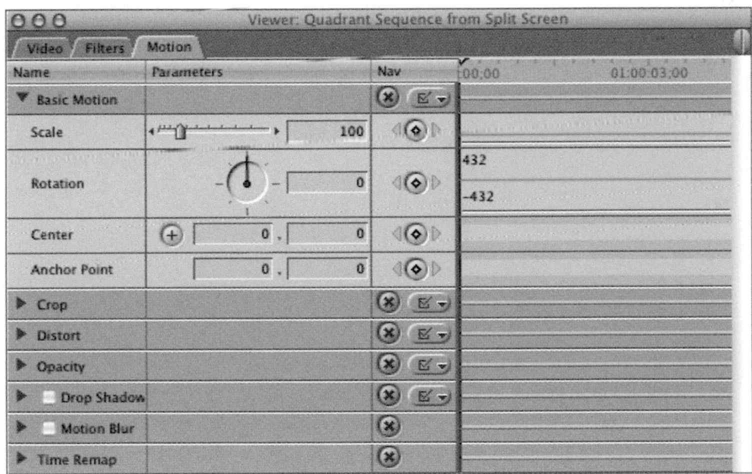

3 Press Home to bring your playhead to the beginning of the sequence in the Viewer.

4 Click the Add Keyframe button for the Rotation parameter.

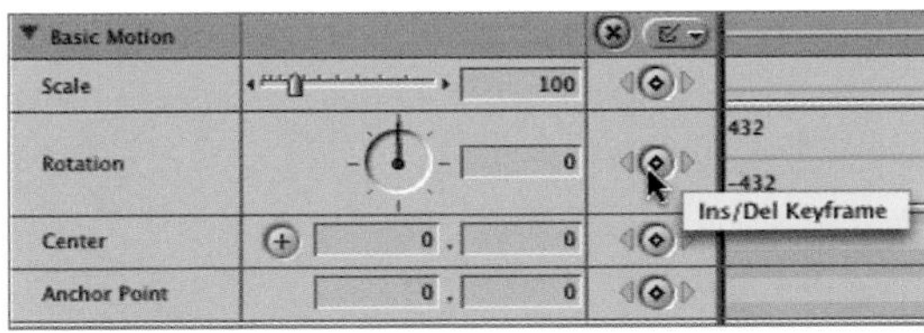

5 Move the playhead 6 seconds into the sequence in the Viewer by typing *+600* or you can type *6* and then type a single period. Press Enter.

6 Set the Rotation value to *1440* degrees (four rotations) and press Enter.

A second keyframe is automatically added.

When you play this sequence, the four videos will spin in unison around a common center point. Setting similar Rotation parameters for each clip individually would have resulted in each clip spinning around its own center point.

7 With your playhead on the last Rotation keyframe, in the Motion tab of the Viewer, type *–500* and press Enter.

This moves the playhead 5 seconds earlier.

8 Add a keyframe for the Scale parameter (leaving the value at 100).

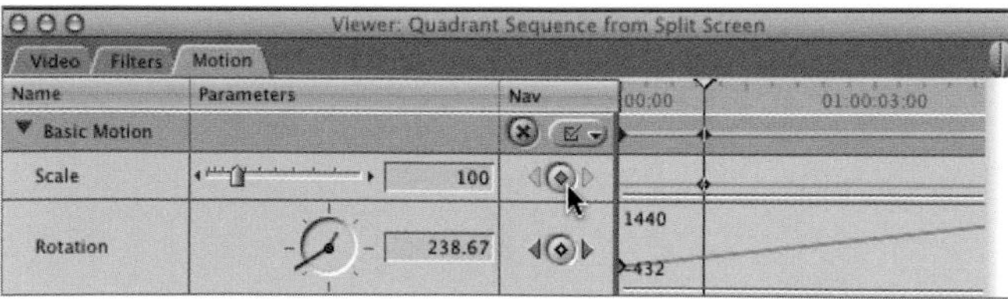

9 Move the playhead forward 5 seconds again so it lines up precisely with the Rotation keyframe.

10 Set the Scale parameter to *0* and press Enter, which will shrink the nest over time until it is invisible.

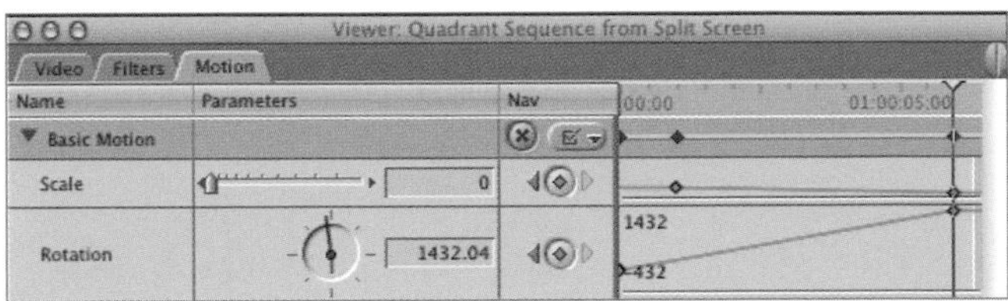

11 Play the sequence.

The four clips spin around a single center point and then vanish into the distance.

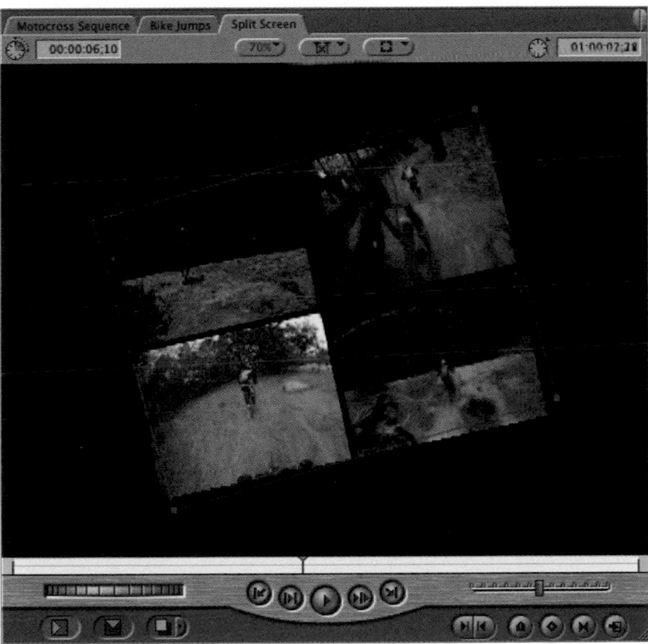

Add a Background Element

At this point, the clips vanish into a black field. You can use this effect as a transition, revealing another clip as the spinning clips disappear.

1 In the Timeline, Shift-drag *Quadrant Sequence* from track V1 onto track V2. Pressing Shift as you drag prevents the clip from moving left or right.

2 Drag **Blue Background** from the Browser into the Timeline, dropping it on track V1 directly underneath *Quadrant Sequence*.

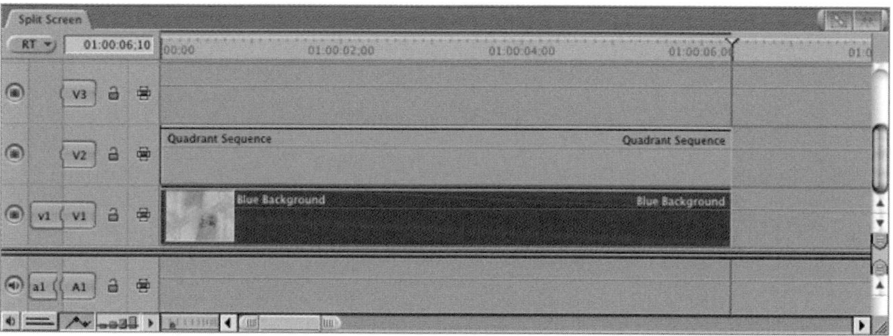

Now when the four clips scale down, **Blue Background** is revealed.

3 Play back the sequence.

Adjust the Anchor Point

In the **Blue Background** clip, the bike icon is slightly off center. To integrate the four quadrant clips with the background clip, you'll alter the anchor point of the nested sequence so that the clips spin around and vanish into that bike icon.

1 In the Canvas, move the playhead near the end of the sequence and park on a frame where the background bicycle graphic is visible. Note the approximate position of the bicycle.

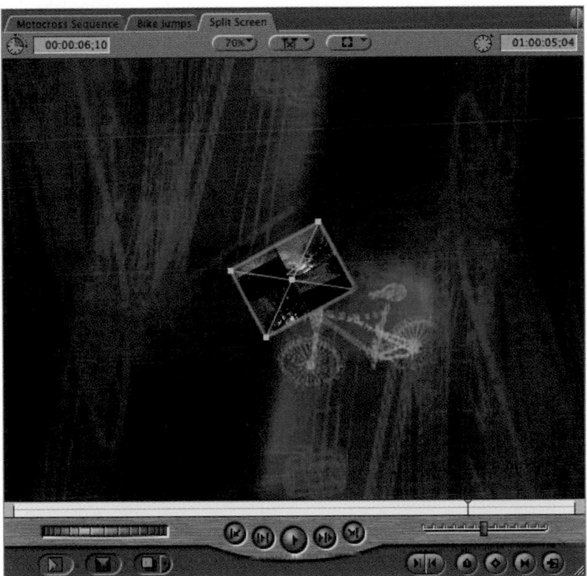

2 Select the Distort tool (D) and press Home to bring the playhead to thc beginning of the sequence.

3 Click the Canvas View button and choose Image+Wireframe from the pop-up menu. Place the pointer over the center point of *Quadrant Sequence* in the Canvas and drag it to the approximate position of the bicycle.

This modifies the clip's anchor point, the point around which the object rotates and scales. What you see onscreen may be confusing. Final Cut Pro displays a representation of the change in the motion path, based on the rotation and scaling keyframes you set.

4 Render, if necessary (Option-R), and play the sequence.

To finesse this effect, you can apply a drop shadow or motion blur to *Quadrant Sequence*, smooth out the scaling and rotational movement by applying Ease In/Ease Out settings, crop the black lines at the edges of the clips, or alter the timing of the four clips within so that they reach the apex of their jumps as they scale down and vanish.

Changing the Render Order

Effects in Final Cut Pro are rendered in a specific order. Filters are applied in the order they are listed in the Filter tab of the Viewer, from top to bottom. Rearranging the render order can change the results. For example, if you apply a Mask Shape filter after applying a Blur, the edge of the matte will be sharp, but the image behind the matte will be blurred. If you apply the matte first and then add the Blur, the edge of the matte will blur along with the rest of the image.

Blur before Mask Shape

Mask Shape before Blur

Furthermore, filters are rendered before motion parameters. This is easy to remember, because the Filters tab appears to the left of the Motion tab in the Viewer. So if you apply a distort filter, such as Wave or Ripple, and then reduce the size of the image, the filter will be applied before the scale operation. The distortion effect is limited to the clip's original size, so the effect may end abruptly at the edges of the clip.

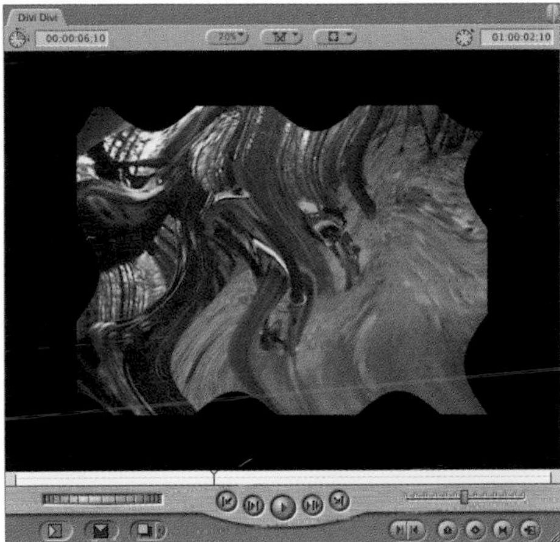

If you scale the clip first and then nest it within another sequence, applying this filter to the nested sequence will produce the desired effect.

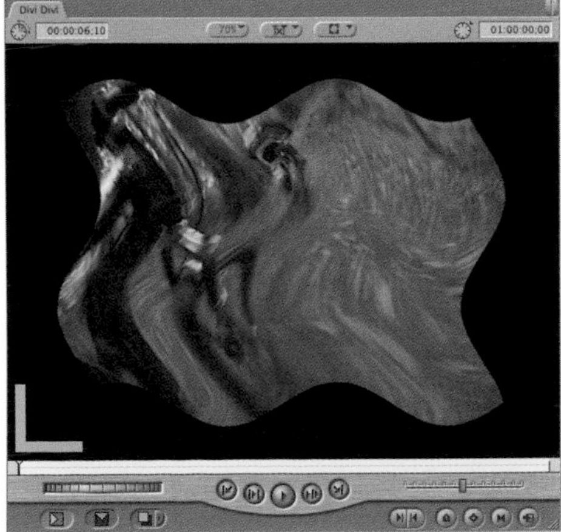

However, nesting is the only way to apply a scale effect (which is a Motion parameter) before the Ripple filter. This exercise demonstrates how to accomplish this.

1 Create a new sequence and name it *Render Order*.

2 To make the effect more visible, set the Canvas background color to white using the Canvas View pop-up menu. Be sure the Selection tool is active.

3 Edit the clip **POV Bike Mount_2** into the new *Render Order* sequence.

4 With the Canvas in Image+Wireframe mode, use the Selection tool to drag one of the corner points and scale the clip down to approximately 80 percent of its original size.

5 Double-click **POV Bike Mount_2** and select the Motion tab in the Viewer.

6 Select the checkbox to activate Drop Shadow.

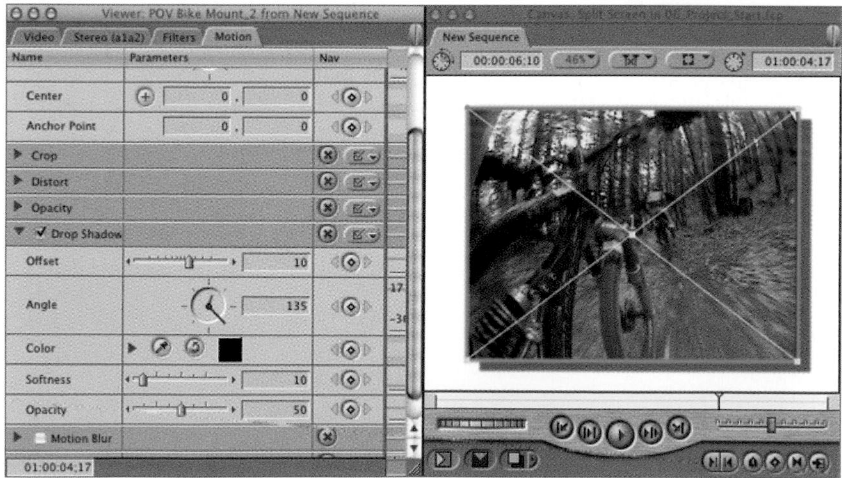

7 Select the clip in the Timeline and choose Sequence > Nest Items, or press Option-C.

8 Name the new sequence *POV Bike Mount Nested Sequence* and click OK.

9 Select the nest in the Timeline, then choose Effects > Video Filters > Distort > Ripple to apply a ripple effect to the nested sequence.

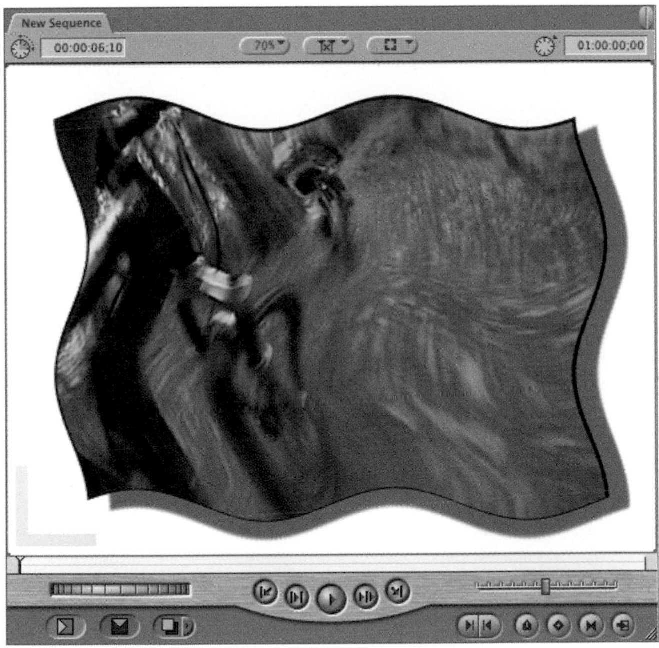

Applying the filter to the nested sequence allows the filtering effect to be processed after the motion parameters are applied. In this case, you can see how the drop shadow is distorted along with the image.

Reordering Motion Effects

You can also use nesting to reorder effects within the Motion tab. In an earlier exercise, you changed an anchor point that affected both scaling and rotation. Now, you'll change the anchor point for the scaling, but leave rotation alone, by applying a second nesting operation.

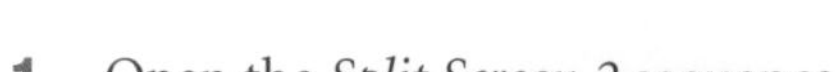

1 Open the *Split Screen 2* sequence.

This sequence is just like the *Split Screen* sequence you modified earlier. The rotation has already been applied to *Quadrant Sequence*, but the Scale and Anchor Point settings have not yet been modified.

2 Select *Quadrant Seq* and choose Sequence > Nest Items.

3 In the Nest Items dialog, name the nested sequence *Rotating Quadrant Sequence* and set its frame size to *1140×760*.

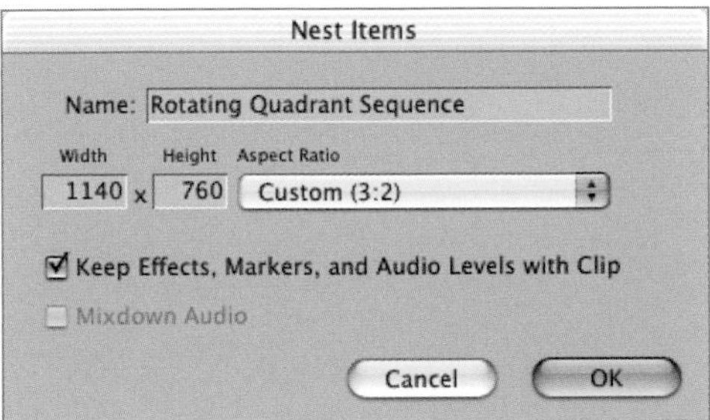

Increasing the nested sequence frame size allows the clips plenty of room to rotate in virtual space without bumping into the edge of the frame.

4 Click OK.

Although *Quadrant Sequence* is already a nested sequence, you can nest it again. There is no limit to the number of times you can nest a sequence.

5 Open *Rotating Quadrant Sequence* into the Viewer and click the Motion tab.

6 Set a keyframe value of *100* in the Scale parameter at 01:00:01:00.

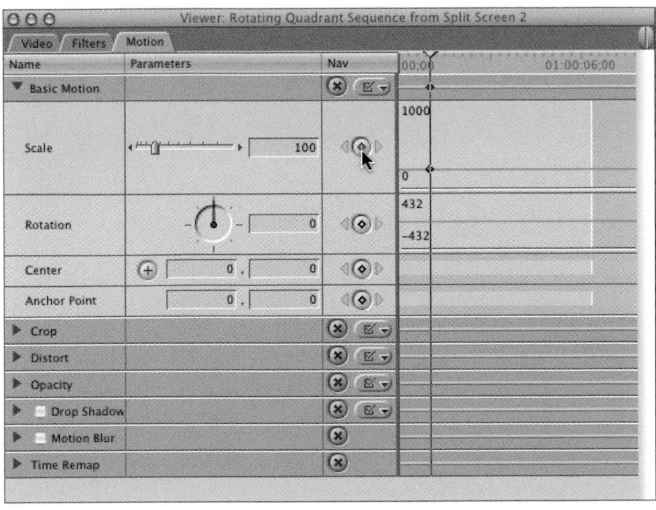

7 Set a second keyframe at 01:00:06:00 with a value of *0*.

8 Temporarily set the opacity for the nested sequence to 20%, so you can see where to drag the anchor point.

9 Press Home or drag the playhead to the beginning of the sequence.

10 Select the Distort tool and drag the center point of *Rotating Quadrant Sequence* to the approximate position of the bicycle.

11 In the Motion tab of the Viewer, set Opacity back to 100%. Render, if necessary, and play back your sequence.

The sequence will rotate around the center point of the four quadrants, but when it scales down, it will vanish into the center of the bike logo.

Mixing Sequence Sizes

In the Nest Items dialog, you can modify the frame size for newly created nested sequences. Changing the frame size further expands the creative possibilities of nesting.

For example, if you want to build a background composed of multiple video images and pan across that background, you can construct a sequence with a large frame size and nest it into a standard, NTSC-sized sequence.

1 Open the *Stacked* sequence from the Browser.

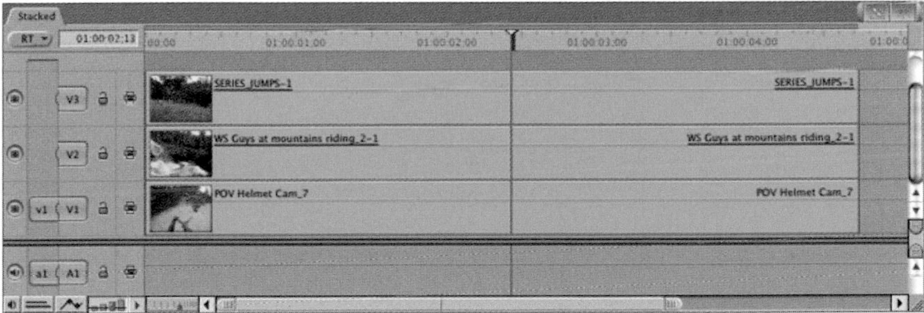

This sequence contains three clips that are stacked one on top of another. All are full-frame, standard DV resolution.

2 Select the three items and choose Sequence > Nest Items.

3 In the Nest Items dialog, set the Aspect Ratio pop-up menu to Custom, then define the new frame size as *2160×480*.

This frame size is three times the width of a standard NTSC DV frame.

4 Name the new sequence *Wide Sequenc*e and click OK.

5 Double-click *Wide Sequence.*

A new Timeline tab appears.

The Canvas displays the wide sequence, reduced to fit into the viewable area, so that you can see your nonstandard frame size.

6 Set your Canvas background back to Black and then set the Canvas view to Image+Wireframe mode.

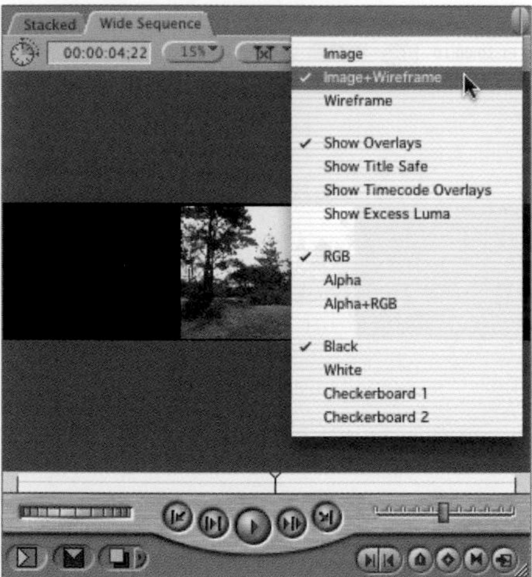

7 With the Selection tool, select the clip in track V3 in the Timeline. In the Canvas, drag it to the left.

8 In the Timeline, select the clip in track V2. Again, in the Canvas, drag this selected clip to the right of the frame. Press Shift to constrain the lateral movement.

All three clips now appear side-by-side in the Canvas window.

9 From the Generator pop-up menu in the Viewer, open a new text generator.

10 Target track V3 and place the Timeline playhead in the center of the clips. Drag the **Text** clip from the Viewer to the Canvas and drop it as a superimpose edit.

This action places the text on a new track above the existing clips.

11 In the Timeline, double-click the text from track V4 to open it into the Viewer.

It has now updated to the sequence size.

12 In the Controls tab in the Viewer, change the text to *Motocross*.

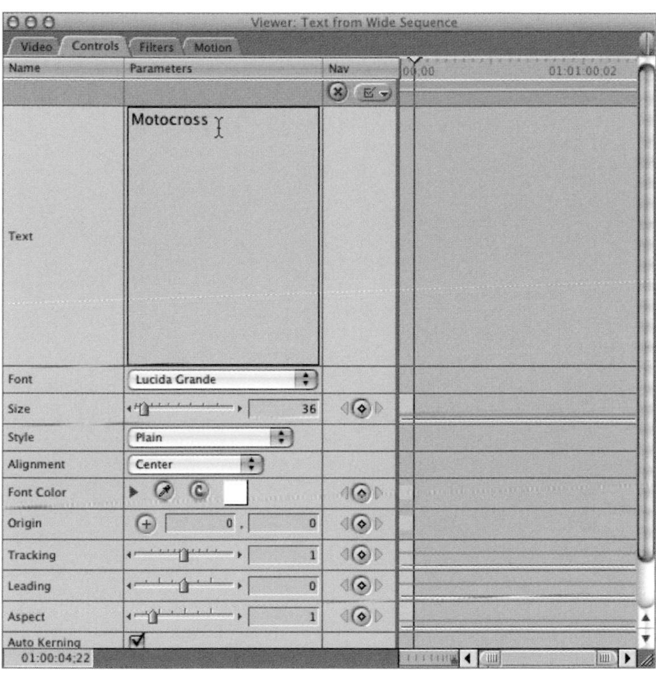

13 Set the text color to your liking. Set the font Size to *100*.

The Canvas updates to reflect your changes.

14 In the Controls tab in the Viewer, use the Origin control to adjust the text so that it is centered across the three images.

15 In the Canvas, click the Stacked tab. Currently, the *Wide Sequence* is scaled down to view the entire sequence in the 720x480 frame size. Open the *Wide Sequence* into the Viewer and scale to 100 percent under the Motion tab.

16 Set the Canvas Scale pop-up menu to Fit All so that you can see the entire wireframe boundary box of the nested sequence inside the *Stacked* parent sequence.

It may help to think of this view as looking through the standard-sized window of the *Stacked* parent sequence into the wider nested sequence below it.

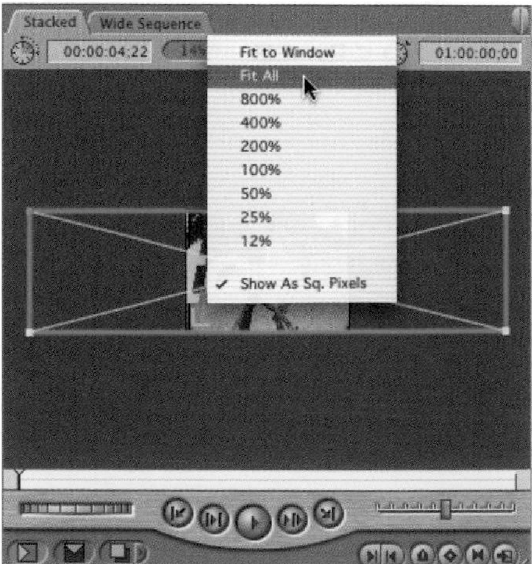

17 In the Canvas, drag the wireframe for the nested *Wide Sequence* to the right, until its left edge aligns with the visible area of your sequence.

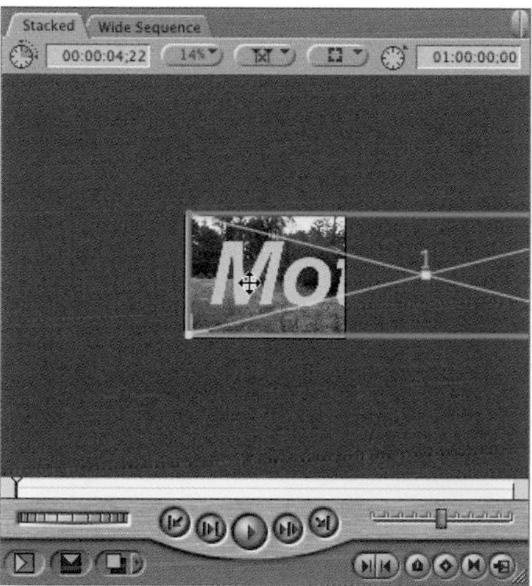

18 Press Home to move the playhead to the beginning of the sequence. Then, with the nest still selected, add a keyframe by clicking the Add Motion Keyframe button in the Canvas, or by pressing Control-K.

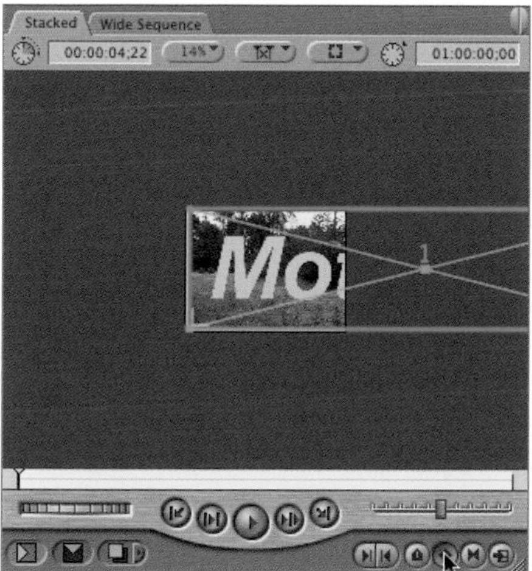

The wireframe for the nest turns green to indicate that a keyframe has been created.

19 Move the playhead to the last frame of the sequence.

20 In the Canvas, drag the nested sequence to the left until the right edge of the visible image aligns with the right edge of the boundary box.

A new keyframe is automatically added, and a motion path appears in the Canvas.

21 Set the Canvas back to Fit to Window. Render (Option-R), if necessary, and play the sequence.

Using Nesting as an Editing Tool

Although Final Cut Pro doesn't prevent you from building hours of program material in a single sequence, it's not the most efficient or practical way to work. When editing long-format shows such as TV programming or feature films, most editors break the program into sections (often called scenes, reels, or segments) and treat each one as a separate sequence. When individual segments are complete, they can be edited into a single main sequence for viewing and output.

When editors nest a scene or segment into a longer main sequence, some will call the main sequence a *master* sequence, instead of a *parent* sequence, and sometimes call the nested sequence a *subsequence.*

The differences in terminology are strictly a matter of preference. In Final Cut Pro, a master sequence is identical to a parent sequence, and a subsequence is identical to a nested sequence. The terms are often used interchangeably in everyday industry practice; we will use them interchangeably in this section to help you get used to the terminology.

Nesting allows you to quickly rearrange entire segments to experiment with scene order. You can manipulate the sequences as if they were a series of clips, trim nested sequences using the trimming tools, and add transition effects using In/Out points and Bezier handles. Nesting facilitates flexibility because you can modify the contents of individual subsequences, and the parent sequence will update to reflect the latest edits.

1 Create a new sequence named *Master Sequence* and open it.

2 Drag the *Stacked* sequence from the Browser directly into the Timeline.

The *Stacked* sequence is now nested in the master sequence.

Mark a Sequence with In and Out Points

By setting an In or Out point in a sequence before you nest it, you define which portion of the sequence will be included in the master sequence. As when editing a single clip, the portions that fall outside the In and Out points become handle frames to accommodate transition effects, such as a cross dissolve, or for trimming of the edit points in the Timeline.

1 Double-click the *Bike Jumps* sequence to open it in the Timeline.

2 Set an Out point at the end of the title on track V2.

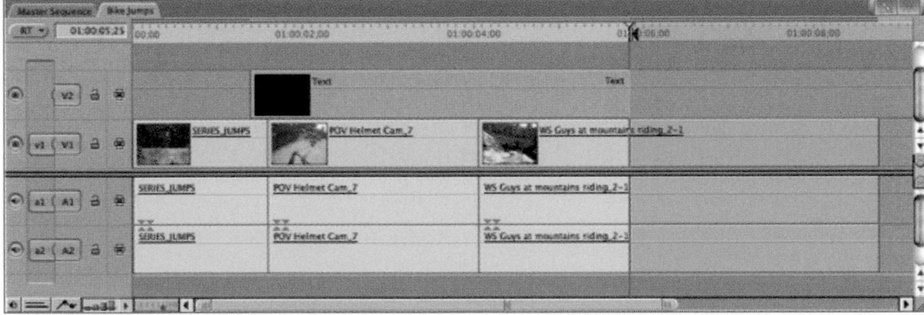

3 In the Timeline, click the *Master Sequence* tab to bring it to the foreground. Press the Down Arrow or End key to make sure your playhead is at the end of the sequence, one frame past the nested *Stacked* subsequence.

4 Edit *Bike Jumps* into *Master Sequence* by dragging it from the Browser to the Canvas or Timeline.

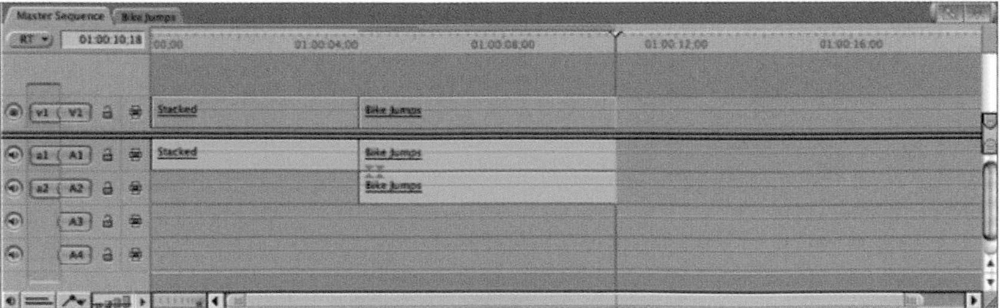

Now the master sequence contains two subsequences: *Stacked* and *Bike Jumps*. Because nested subsequences follow all the standard rules of three-point editing when edited into master sequences, the *Bike Jumps* sequence ends in its master sequence at the Out point you designated inside the *Bike Jumps* sequence.

Editing Within the Nested Sequence

Imagine that these are the first two scenes of the finished program. You can continue to make editorial changes to clips inside the individual subsequences, and the master sequence will be updated automatically.

1 Place the playhead at the end of *Master Sequence.*

2 Press M to add a sequence marker.

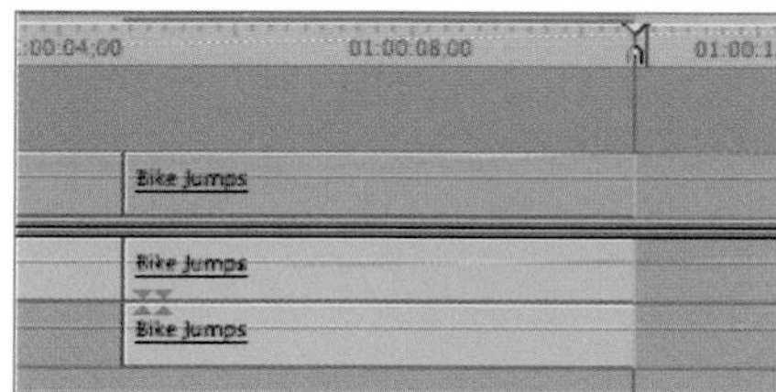

This marker will be used to illustrate how editing changes in the nested sequences affect the parent sequence.

3 In the Browser, double-click the *Stacked* sequence to open it into its own Timeline tab.

4 Drag the clip **SERIES_JUMPS** from the Browser and edit it in at the end of *Wide Sequence.*

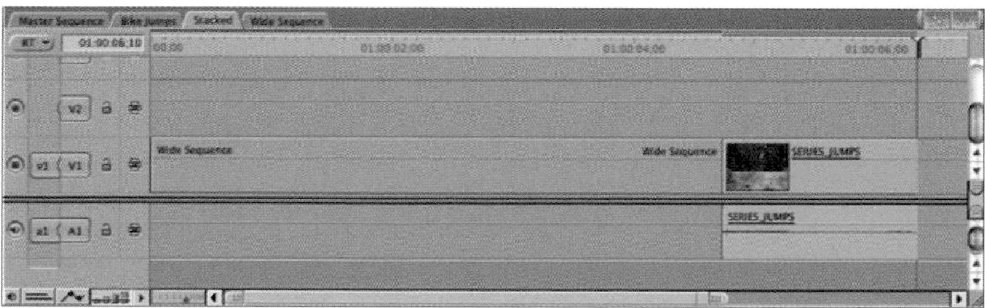

5 Switch back to *Master Sequence.*

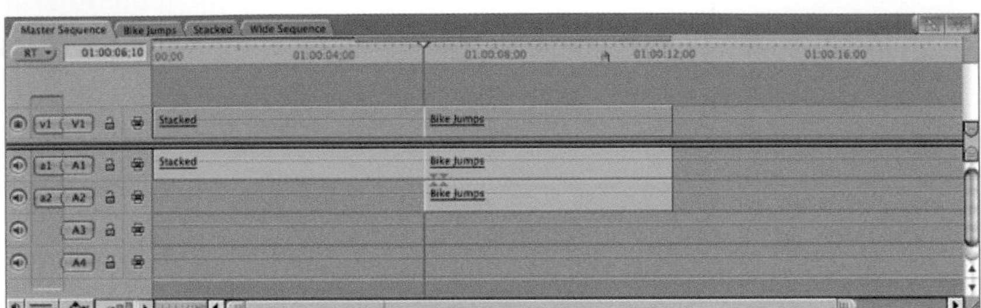

When you added the clip to *Stacked* as an insert edit, the master sequence was affected. To make room for the new clip, the sequence rippled to the right, and the entire master sequence became longer, as you can see by the marker you added.

If you add, delete, or trim individual clips inside a nested subsequence (or even another nested sequence) *that has no In or Out points set in it,* the master sequence will ripple to the right or left, making the master sequence shorter or longer. Again, the editorial changes you make within the nested subsequences are automatically updated in the parent, but only as long as you have not set an In or Out point in the nested subsequence.

Using an Alternate Behavior

However, one behavior is different from the behavior of nested subsequences with no In or Out points: If you set an In or Out point in the nested subsequence *before editing it into the master,* you will achieve somewhat different results.

1 In the Browser, double-click the *Bike Jumps* sequence.

2 Drag the **SERIES_JUMPS** shot from the Browser into the Timeline to add it to the end of this sequence.

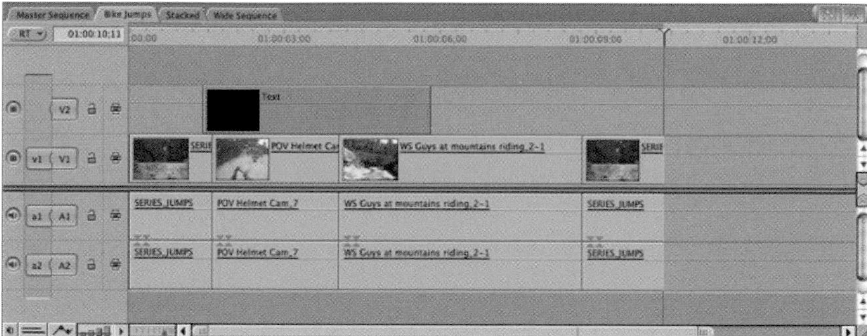

Although this action lengthens this subsequence here, the Out point set earlier still defines the sequence's length within the master sequence.

3 Bring *Master Sequence* to the front.

Notice that nothing in *Master Sequence* has changed. Of course, you can manually ripple the nested *Bike Jumps* subsequence in the master, just like any clip, to reveal more of its content.

4 Using the Selection tool in the master sequence, drag the right edge of the *Bike Jumps* subsequence to make it longer.

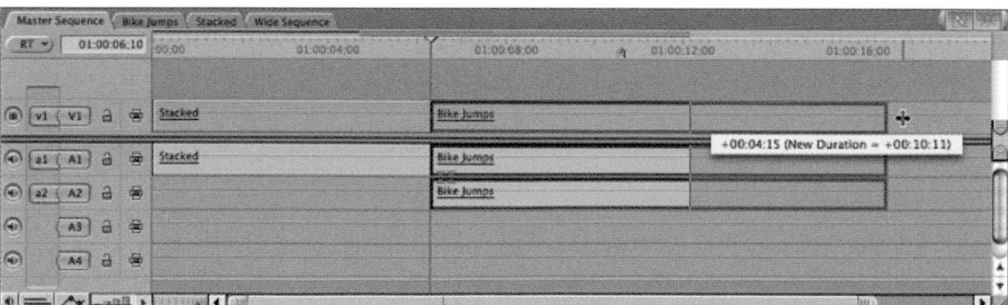

The additional content in the subsequence is now visible in *Master Sequence*.

Editing the Content of a Subsequence

In all of the examples so far, you have been nesting several clips and treating them as a single item to add effects or edits to a group of clips at one time. Occasionally, you may need to perform the reverse technique to un-nest individual items in a nested sequence. This is necessary when making an Edit Decision List (EDL), which is a text list of all of the In and Out points for all of the clips in your sequence. If your master sequence contains a nested sequence composed of multiple clips, the EDL will mistakenly represent that nested sequence as a single clip. This may cause serious problems if you are using the EDL to re-create your sequence on another system.

1 Close all of your open sequences by closing the Canvas window.

2 In the Browser, double-click *complex sequence*.

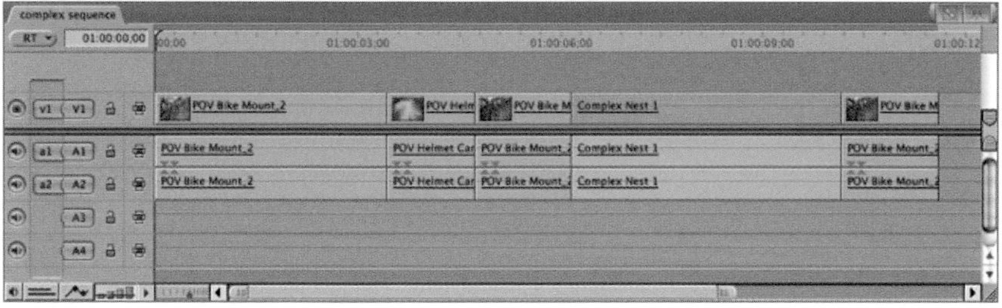

This sequence contains a series of clips, as well as a nested sequence.

The nested sequence *Complex Nest 1* is also located in the Browser. You will replace *Complex Nest 1* with the clips that comprise it, in its parent sequence.

3 Make sure snapping is enabled (N).

4 In the Browser, select the *Complex Nest 1* sequence and drag it over the Timeline. Position it directly over the existing instance of the same nest, but do not release the mouse button yet.

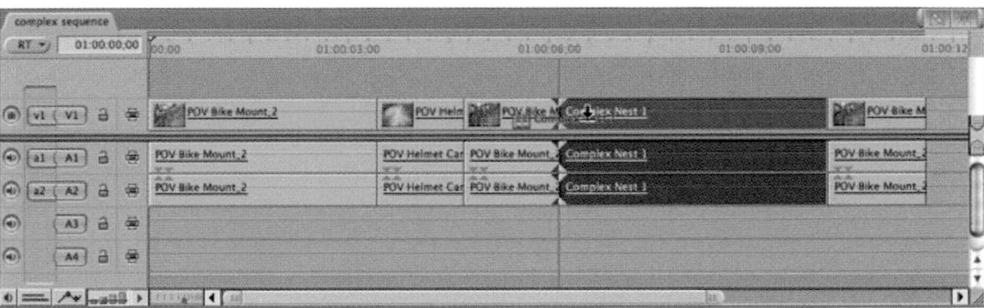

5 Press and hold the Command key.

The Timeline overlay identifies the individual clips in the sequence.

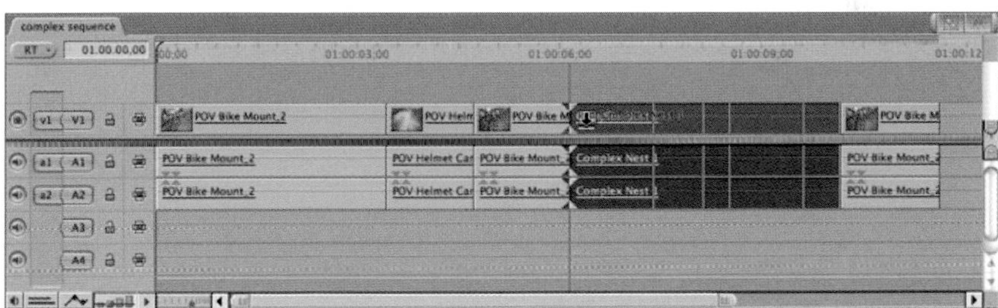

6 Make sure you are performing an overwrite edit (not an insert edit) by placing the pointer in the lower section of the Timeline track. Release the mouse button to drop the five clips originally edited into *Complex Nest 1* as an overwrite edit.

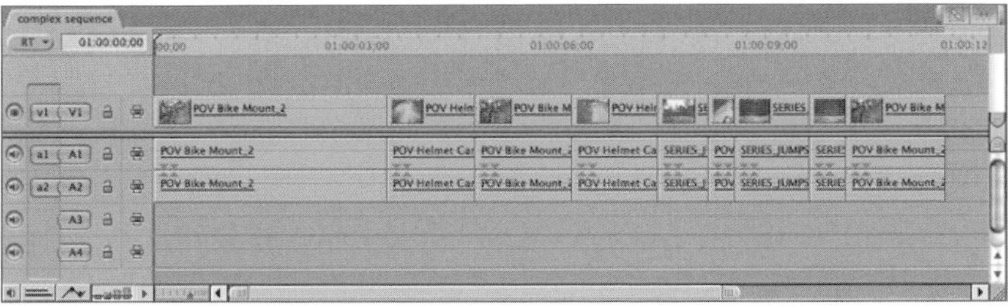

The nested sequence has been replaced by its original clip contents. You have un-nested the sequence, and your EDL will accurately reflect all of the individual clips used to build the master sequence.

NOTE ▶ After you complete this operation, there is no live link between the sequence and the individual clips. From this point forward, changes made will not affect the others.

Nesting is incredibly versatile. For audio-intensive projects, you can use nesting to combine groups of sounds to approximate the bussing features of audio-specific tools. For example, you might make a nest of different sound effects tracks and then control the overall volume with a single slider. Or you might use nesting to output a sequence with Timecode Print filters applied to nests so that both sequence and source timecode are burned in when output to tape. As you become more adept at nesting, you will find countless ways to use it. Nesting is one of the fundamental tools for exploring the true depth and flexibility of Final Cut Pro.

Lesson Review

1. Identify two ways of nesting a sequence.
2. Can you apply filters to a nested sequence?
3. If you adjust the Rotation parameter of a nested sequence with four composited layers, what happens to those layers?
4. If you edit three sequences within a fourth sequence and change the In and Out points of each nested sequence, what happens if the overall duration of one of the sequences you nested changes?
5. If you edit three sequences within a fourth sequence without setting their In and Out points, what happens if the overall duration of one of the sequences you nested changes?
6. How do you edit the content of a sequence into a Timeline without nesting it?

Answers

1. Edit a sequence inside of a second sequence, and select one or more clips in the Timeline and choose Sequence > Nest Items.
2. Yes. Filters affect every clip within a nested sequence to which they're applied.
3. The layers all rotate together as if they were a single clip.
4. Nothing. Setting the In and Out points of a nested sequence locks its duration.
5. The nested sequence with the changed duration gets longer or shorter, rippling the position of the other nested sequences that come after it.
6. Drag a sequence into the Timeline, and before you release the mouse button, press the Command key. When the edit points between each clip in the sequence appear, release the mouse button.

10

esson Files — Lesson Files > Lesson 10 > SpeedFX.fcp

Media — Golfer and Misc

Time — This lesson takes approximately 60 minutes to complete.

Goals
- Apply basic speed manipulations to clips
- Learn to read the speed indicators in the Timeline
- Add and manipulate keyframes using the Time Remap tool
- Manipulate time keyframes in the motion bar
- Customize the Clip Keyframes control
- Create freeze frames using variable speed controls
- Play part of a clip backward
- Smooth speed keyframes to create gradual changes
- Save a speed setting as a favorite

Lesson **10**

Variable Speed

Speed effects are among the most common and versatile effect types in Final Cut Pro. Basic speed changes, such as slow motion, can be employed for dramatic effect, and increasing playback speed can simulate time-lapse photography.

The real fun happens when you employ variable speed effects (often called *time ramping*) to vary a clip's speed during playback. For example, a shot can begin playing in slow motion, speed up, and then return to another playback speed near the end of the shot. A speed-varied shot can slow to a freeze frame or play in reverse. Final Cut Pro displays time remapping data in several ways. Learning how to read time controls is essential to mastering the variable speed tools.

Using Basic Slow Motion

Before delving into variable speed effects, it's important to review how Final Cut Pro handles constant speed changes such as slow motion.

1. Open Lesson Files > Lesson 10 > **SpeedFX.fcp.** The sequence *Golfer 1* should be open in the Timeline. Play the sequence.

2. Select clip **6E_1** (the third clip) and choose Modify > Speed.

3. Select the Frame Blending box if it's not already selected.

   Frame blending generates new frames by blending the surrounding frames to create a smoother slow-motion effect.

4. Set the Speed to *50* percent and click OK.

   In the Timeline, you can see that slowing down the clip rippled it to the right and made it longer.

5 Click the Clip Keyframes control to turn on clip keyframes.

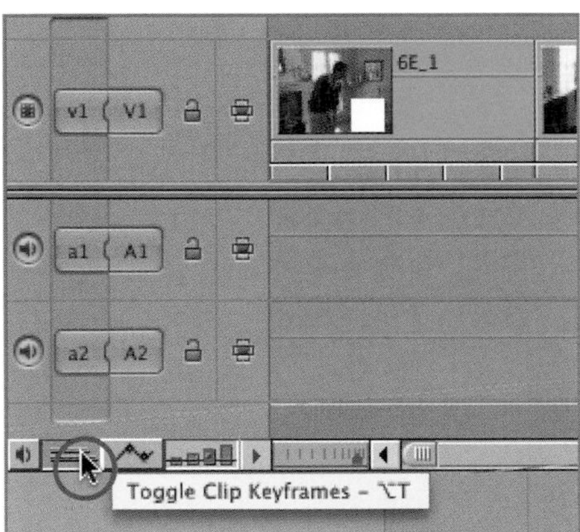

The Clip Keyframes control turns on speed indicators, which are located beneath clips in the Timeline. Notice that the tic marks beneath **6E_1** are farther apart than they are in the surrounding clips. The distance between the tics indicates the clip speed. The farther apart the tics, the slower the clip will play back.

6 Render and play your sequence.

NOTE ▸ If you play the sequence using Unlimited RT instead of rendering, you can see a preview version of the effect. However, frame blending will not be applied until you render the sequence.

You may notice that even with frame blending enabled, **6E_1** still appears to have a strobing or stuttering quality. The fourth clip (**6F_3**) was actually photographed in slow motion. You can see the difference between the two clips. Creating slow motion in-camera will always produce a smoother result than an effect applied in postproduction.

Understanding Variable Speed Effects

The Modify Speed window can be used to speed up or slow down clip playback, or even to make a clip play backward, but to make a clip change speed while it's playing requires an entirely different workflow.

In this exercise, you'll slow down only one portion of a clip.

1 Double-click the *Dancer* sequence to open it into the Timeline.

   This clip contains a single shot of a dancer leaping across an empty stage.

   NOTE ► This clip was filmed in slow motion, so when played at standard speed, it still appears in slow motion. This should not interfere with your ability to further manipulate its playback speed.

2 Select the clip, play the sequence, and set a marker just as the dancer begins her big leap (around 3:20).

3 In the Tool palette, choose the Time Remap tool (or press S three times).

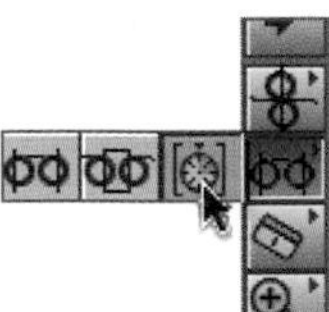

4 Click the clip at the frame where you added the marker to set a speed parameter keyframe.

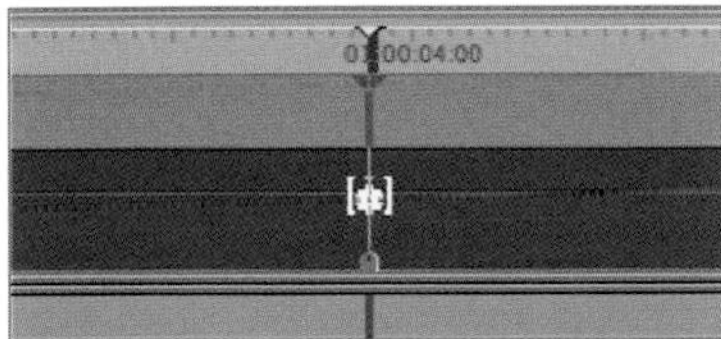

Although this action doesn't actually change the speed of the clip, setting this keyframe prepares the clip so that the speed changes you make will affect the clip from this point forward.

The word *Variable* appears next to the clip's name in the Timeline to indicate that speed keyframes have been applied.

5 Using the Time Remap tool, hold down the mouse button as you position the tool near the right edge of the clip. Turn off snapping (N) if necessary. You might see the tool turn into an arrow near the right edge, but if you click and hold, a tooltip appears.

6 While continuing to hold down the mouse button, drag the Time Remap tool to the left until the tooltip indicates that Speed Left equals approximately 50%.

The clip will play at normal speed until the dancer begins her leap (where you set the first keyframe), and then switch to slow motion for the duration of the shot.

7 In the Timeline, click the Clip Keyframes control.

8 Play the sequence to see the results of your work.

In the speed indicator, notice that the tic marks spread out during the section of the clip that is in slow motion. Also, the blue motion bar indicates where keyframes have been set.

Creating a Freeze Frame

Variable speed effects can be used to make a clip play at normal speed, then stop and hold on a particular frame. This is sometimes used to introduce characters in title sequences and trailers.

1 Double-click the *Freeze Frame* sequence to open it into the Timeline.

   This is another copy of the same shot. This time you will create a freeze frame at the apex of the dancer's leap.

2 Play the sequence and stop playback when the dancer is in mid-leap (at approximately 4:07).

3 Choose the Time Remap tool and click at the current playhead position to add a single speed keyframe.

4 Enter +2. (plus 2 period) to move your playhead forward 2 seconds.

5 Add a new keyframe by clicking with the Time Remap tool at the new playhead position.

The clip still plays at normal speed, but you've prepared it to create the freeze-frame effect.

6 Turn on clip keyframes.

The Clip Keyframes control aids in performing keyframing operations in the Timeline. In addition to displaying speed indicators and a motion bar, a keyframe editor also appears and can display speed keyframes for manipulation directly in the Timeline.

Although the Clip Keyframes control itself simply toggles the visibility of Timeline controls on and off, you can make it more useful by customizing the controls it displays and which keyframes are visible.

7 Control-click the Clip Keyframes control and deselect Video > Filters Bar from the shortcut menu. Leave the other three selections selected.

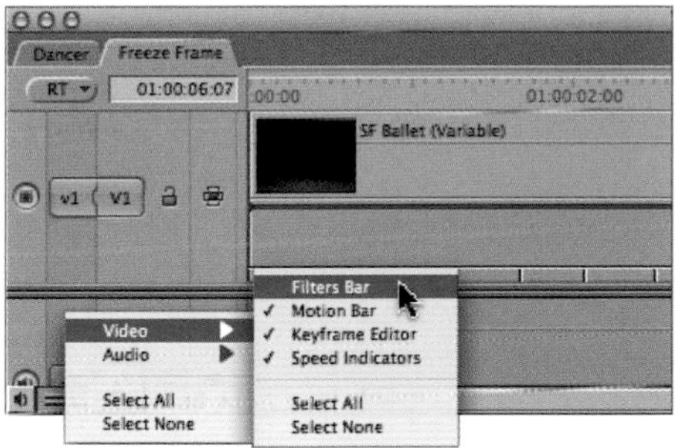

8 Control-click the Clip Keyframes control again and choose Audio > Select None from the shortcut menu.

Now the variable speed effects settings are the only ones visible in the Timeline tracks.

NOTE ▶ Variable speed effects cannot be applied to audio clips.

9 Control-click the blue motion bar under the clip and choose Hide All from the shortcut menu.

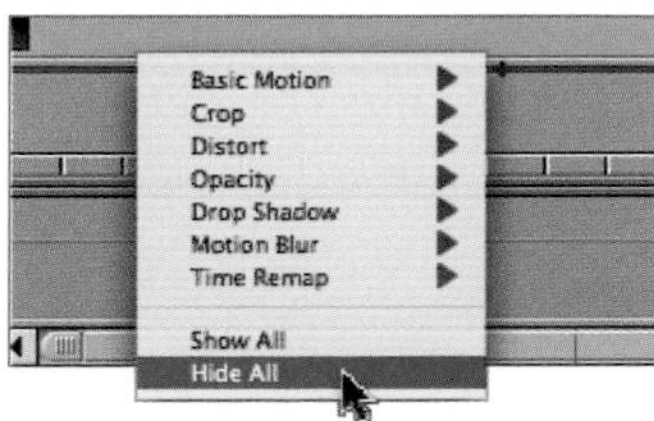

By default, keyframes for all parameters are visible. After you choose Hide All, no keyframes are displayed in the motion bar.

In this menu, you can choose which keyframes are displayed in the motion bar. You can have multiple parameters displayed simultaneously, but you will not be able to tell them apart by looking at the motion bar. In this case, you want to view only the speed keyframes.

10 Control-click the blue motion bar and choose Time Remap > Time Graph from the shortcut menu.

Now only speed keyframes are displayed in the motion bar. But, in addition to seeing the keyframes displayed on the blue bar, you can also display a keyframe graph, right there in the Timeline.

11 Control-click the area below the blue motion bar and above the tic marks of the speed indicator, and then choose Time Remap > Time Graph from the shortcut menu.

In this shortcut menu, you can choose which keyframe graph will be displayed in the Timeline's keyframe editor. You can only view one parameter graph at a time. Graphs for all parameters are always visible in the Motion pane of the Viewer.

When the keyframe editor is visible, a small, new control appears at the right edge of the track headers: This thin bar controls the height of the keyframe graph.

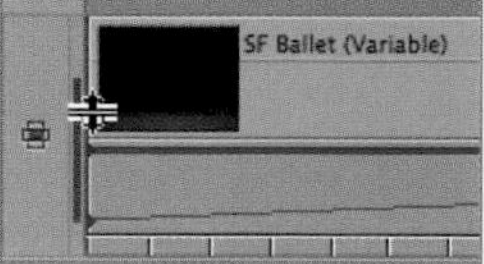

12 Drag the thin, vertical black bar upward to increase the height of the graph, which will give you more room in which to manipulate the time remap keyframes.

The graph represents the progression of the frames over time:

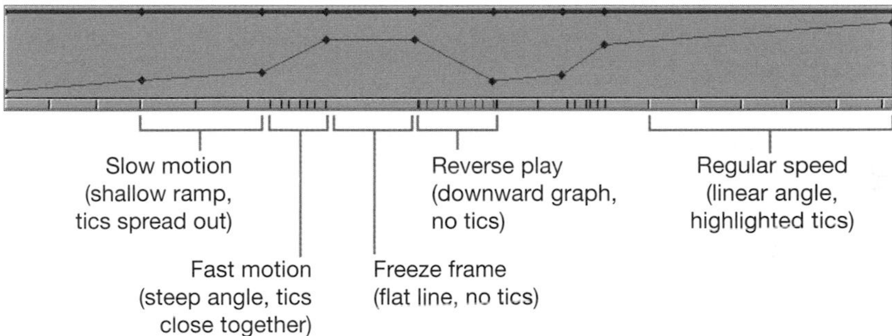

- A steady upward trajectory indicates forward play at regular speed.
- Downward trajectory means backward playback.
- The steepness of the line indicates the relative speed (steeper is faster).
- A perfectly flat line indicates no movement at all (freeze frame).

Next, you will set the second speed keyframe to display the same frame as the first, thereby creating a freeze-frame effect.

13 Press Option-K to navigate your playhead to the previous keyframe.

14 Choose View > Match Frame > Master Clip, or press F.

This loads the source clip into the Viewer, parked on the identical frame. You'll use this as a visual reference for setting the speed keyframe.

15 Make sure snapping is turned on. Using the Time Remap tool, hold down the mouse button with the pointer positioned on the second keyframe in the Timeline. Do not click in the keyframe graph; click the clip, itself.

The tooltip appears.

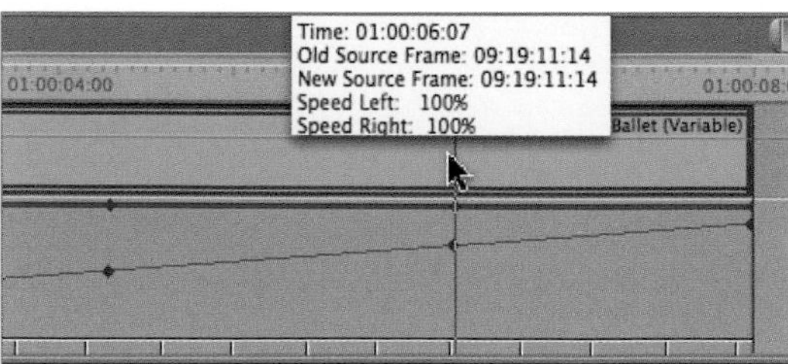

The Canvas displays the frame assigned to the place in time where you clicked. As you drag the Time Remap tool, the Canvas updates to display the new frame you are assigning to that time position.

16 Drag to the left until the frame in the Canvas matches the exact frame displayed in the Viewer. As you drag, match the source timecode in the Canvas to the current timecode position in the Viewer (09:19:09:14).

The keyframe graph and speed indicator can also assist you in identifying when you have achieved the freeze frame. The keyframe graph will display a horizontal line, and the speed indicators will not contain any tic marks for the duration of the freeze.

To finalize the effect, you must reset the remaining portion of the clip to regular speed.

If you have trouble setting the speed value to a precise number, you can use the keyboard modifiers Shift and Command to restrict the movement of the Time Remap tool. Hold down Shift to constrain movements to 10 percent increments, or hold down Command to restrict movements to 1 percent increments.

17 Using the Time Remap tool, click the last frame of the clip and drag it to the left until the tooltip reads Speed Left: 100%.

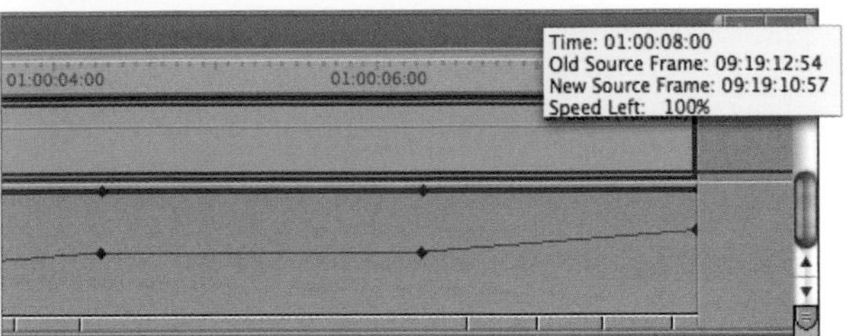

18 Play your sequence and view the freeze-frame effect.

Modifying Existing Speed Keyframes

Once you've applied speed keyframes, you can modify their positions in time to alter the variable speed effect. For example, you can alter clip speed to play in fast motion leading up to the freeze frame.

The Time Remap tool normally does what its name implies: it remaps, or moves, a particular clip frame to the current position in sequence time where you click the tool. It then speeds up or slows down other frames in front of and behind that particular frame to execute this remap.

When you Option-click using the Time Remap tool, however, you move the current frame to a different position in time. Frame rates speed up and slow down on either side of this repositioned frame to compensate for the move.

To reflect this difference, a tooltip displays the Old Time and New Time, rather than the old and new Source Frame. In both cases, you are modifying the speed of the clip, so the Speed Left and Speed Right information is still visible.

1 Use the Time Remap tool to Option-click the clip at the first keyframe position. (Click the clip at the keyframe postion, not the graph.)

   A tooltip appears.

NOTE ▶ Clicking or Option-clicking the clip with the Time Remap tool sets a new keyframe if one was not there already. When adjusting settings for an existing keyframe, turn on snapping to avoid accidentally adding a new keyframe.

2 Drag the keyframe to the left until New Time reads approximately 01:00:02:00.

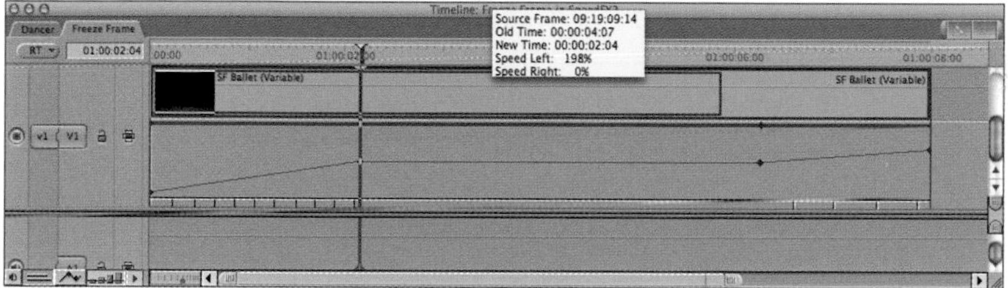

As you can see, using the Option key with the Time Remap tool allows you to extend this freeze frame for 2 additional seconds. However, to accomplish this, the beginning frames that were playing normally are now squeezed together in time to play back at approximately 200%. This is reflected in the Timeline by the speed indicator, which shows the tic marks positioned very close to each other.

3 Play the sequence to see the results of your work.

This may be a desirable effect, but if not, you can use the Time Remap tool (without pressing the Option key) to drag the speed keyframe on frame 1 to the right until the tooltip indicates that Speed Right is 100%. This returns that portion of the clip to normal speed, effectively forcing the clip to begin at a later point in time (after the dancer has already appeared onstage).

When creating freeze frames, you need to check how the output looks on an interlaced, external monitor to be sure that no field artifacts are visible in the frozen frame. If you select a frame that contains fast, horizontal movement, the freeze frame might look good on your computer screen, but it will flicker when displayed on a TV monitor.

If you see flicker in the freeze frame, choose a frame that doesn't contain lateral movement. If you must choose a frame that contains movement, you can eliminate the flickering effect by applying the De-Interlace filter to the range of the clip that includes the freeze frame. Be aware, however, that removing interlacing from a clip can have a negative effect on slow-motion effects, amplifying the strobe or stutter effect mentioned earlier in the lesson.

Applying Complex Speed Effects

Once you have mastered the basics of variable speed effects, you can make increasingly complex effects using many keyframes. You can even switch between forward and backward play.

1 Close all of your open sequences. Open the *Complex Speed* sequence and watch it once.

   This is another unaltered version of the dancer clip.

2 Identify the frame where the dancer begins her big leap (around 03:17).

3 Set a keyframe at that point by clicking the clip with the Time Remap tool.

4 Control-click the keyframe graph and choose Time Remap > Time Graph from the shortcut menu.

5 Find the frame where her first foot hits the ground (around 04:18).

6 Option-click that frame and drag it to the left, compressing the time between the two keyframes to approximately 236%.

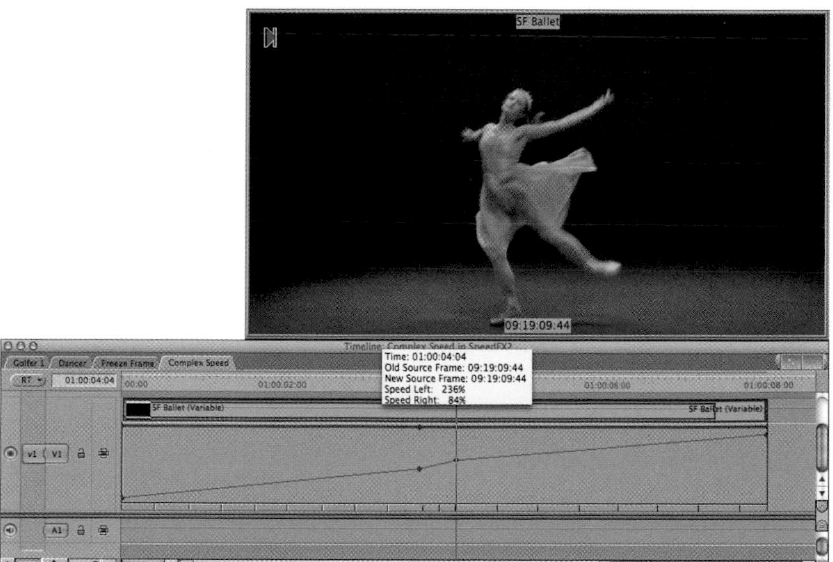

7 Move the playhead to around 5:00. Using the Time Remap tool, drag to the left (without holding down the Option key) to create a new keyframe with a Speed Left value of approximately –150%.

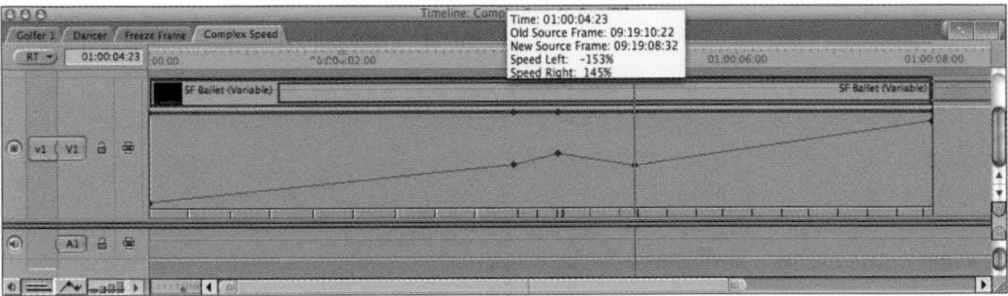

You have just set the clip to play backward between the second and third keyframes. The speed indicator displays red tic marks for the duration of reverse playback. Notice that the keyframe graph displays a downward slope.

8 Move the playhead forward to around 7:00 and, using the Time Remap tool, drag to the left (do not hold down the Option key). Watch the Canvas and stop dragging when the frame appears where her foot touches the ground at the end of the big leap.

This adjusts the speed between keyframes three and four to about 70%.

9 Play your sequence.

You can continue adding additional keyframes to extend that short head turn for great comic effect.

Making Gradual Speed Changes

The speed effects you have created thus far transition abruptly from one speed to another—the clip plays at one speed until it reaches a new keyframe and then suddenly switches to a different speed. This creates dramatic effects, but you can further improve your speed effects by controlling the ramping velocity of the speed changes.

1 Control-click the middle keyframe in the keyframe graph and choose Smooth from the shortcut menu.

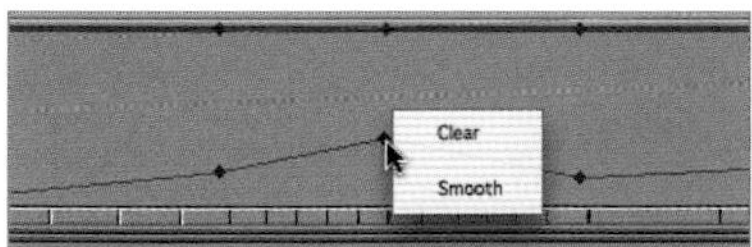

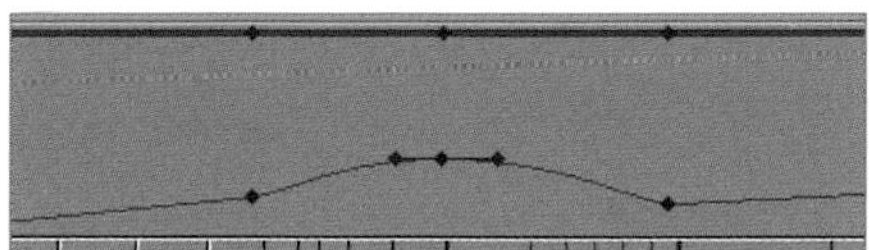

The transition from forward to reverse speed now occurs gradually, creating a subtler and more natural-looking effect. The Bezier handles that appear when you choose Smooth allow further manipulation of the transition.

NOTE ► Be careful when manipulating these handles. Small movements can have dramatic effects and may completely alter the subtlety of the speed settings you just established. Adding Bezier handles can distort your graph in an unanticipated way, often creating a short downward movement that results in a brief moment of unintended backward playback

2 Zoom in to get a closer look at the keyframe you are about to manipulate. You may also want to increase the track height.

3 Drag the Bezier handle points towards the keyframe to reduce the duration of the transition.

Be careful to keep the handles completely horizontal. By default, moving one handle automatically moves the other.

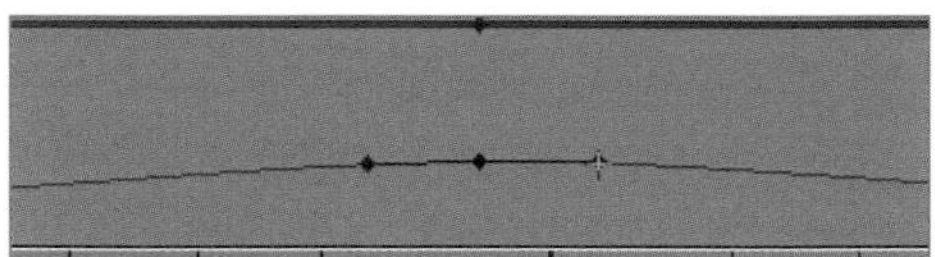

Lengthening the handles adds time to the transition between speed settings. Experiment with different settings to find the transition that feels most natural to you.

After you smooth a keyframe, the Speed tooltip reports the Speed Left and Speed Right as Variable.

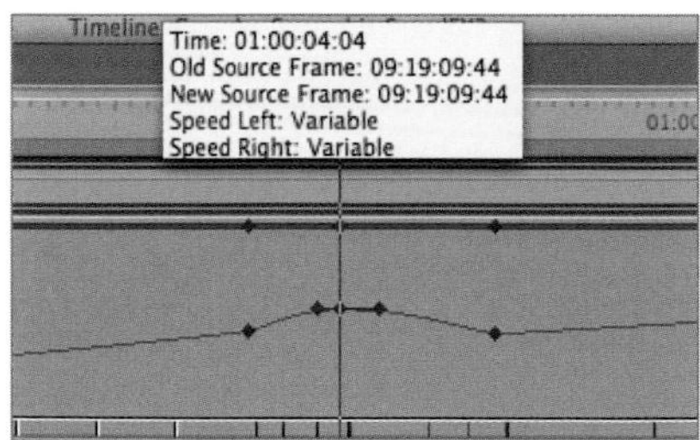

This makes it impossible to apply additional changes to the keyframe values. Because of this, do not apply smoothing to your keyframes until your speed value changes are final. Of course, you can always Control-click the smoothed keyframe and set it back to a corner point, if necessary.

4 Apply the smoothing effect to all keyframes in the sequence.

You don't need to adjust Bezier handles, because the default settings provide adequate smoothing.

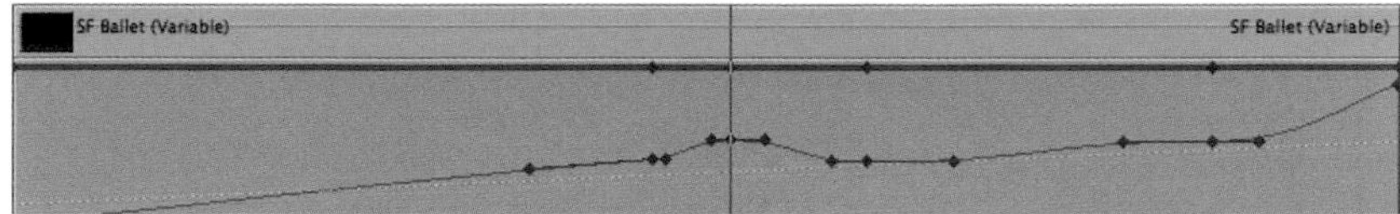

5 Play the finished sequence.

Using the Motion Viewer

The speed effects and controls used in the Timeline are also visible in the Time Remap section of the Motion tab in the Viewer.

1 Press A to select the Selection tool, and then in the *Complex Speed* sequence, double-click **SF Ballet** to open it into the Viewer.

2 Click the Motion tab. Click the disclosure triangle to display the Time Remap parameters.

The graph displayed here is identical to the graph visible in the Timeline. Viewing this graph in the Motion tab allows you to compare it to keyframes applied in other motion parameters.

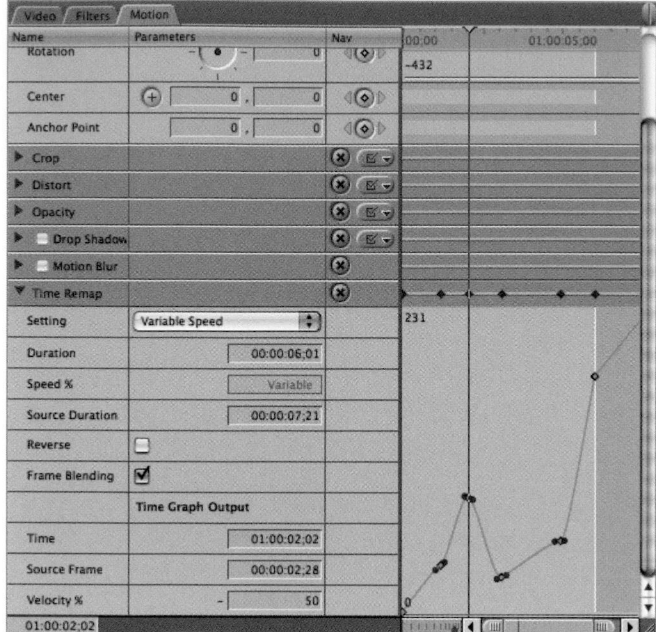

The Motion tab allows you to see numerical values for each of the frames you are manipulating. This can aid your precision when applying variable speed effects.

TIP If you Control-click the Timecode fields and change the view to sequential frames, you may be better able to identify where a particular keyframe is taking place in your shot.

One particularly useful control in the Motion tab is the Reset button that removes all speed keyframes.

3 Click the Reset button for the Time Remap section of the Motion tab.

The keyframes are removed, and the clip's speed is reset to 100%.

Copying and Saving Speed Effects

Speed effects are recorded in the Motion tab, so you can copy or save a clip's speed settings just as you can copy and save any motion setting.

1 Open the *Copy Clip* sequence.

2 Play back the sequence.

The first clip has a variable speed effect applied to it, and the second clip plays at regular speed.

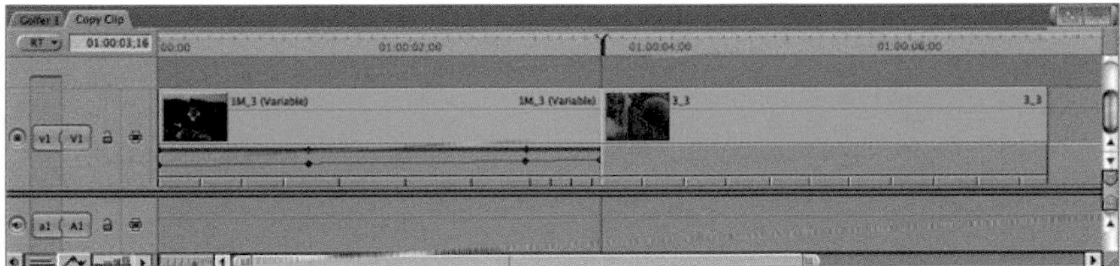

3 Select the first clip and choose Edit > Copy (or press Command-C).

4 Select the second clip and choose Edit > Paste Attributes (or press Option-V).

The Paste Attributes dialog appears.

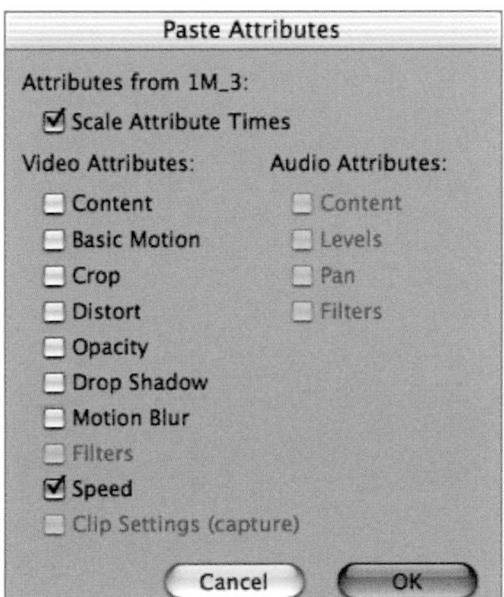

5 Select the Speed box and click OK.

If you are pasting attributes to a clip of a different length, selecting the Scale Attribute Times box will scale your keyframes to fit the length of the new clip.

You can save the speed settings so they'll be available to use on other clips.

6 Select the first clip and choose Effects > Make Favorite Motion.

Make Favorite Motion stores all motion settings (Scale, Distortion, Drop Shadow, Variable Speed, and so on) that are currently applied to the clip in the Motion tab.

7 In the Browser, click the Effects tab and open the Favorites bin.

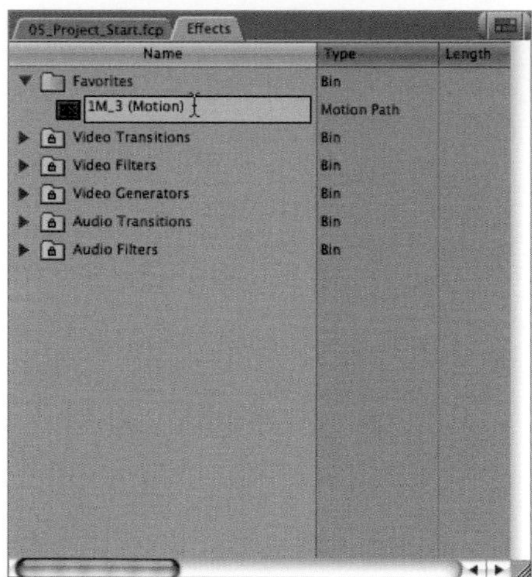

8 Rename **1M_3 (Motion)** to *Golfer speed* and press Enter.

The custom effect also appears in the Effects > Motion Favorites submenu. You can now apply this setting to any clip in any sequence.

Lesson Review

1. How can you make simple, linear changes to the speed of a clip?
2. How can you make variable speed changes to a clip in the Timeline?
3. What's a good way to soften the strobing that occurs in a slow-motion clip?
4. How do you identify a clip's speed using the speed indicators?
5. How can you make a change from one speed to another more gradual?
6. Can you save a speed effect as a favorite?

Answers

1. Select the clip, choose Modify > Speed, and specify the percentage at which you want the clip to play.
2. Use the Time Remap tool, or turn on the keyframe graph in the Timeline, reveal the time graph, and manipulate the keyframes.
3. Turn on frame blending.
4. Tic marks that are farther apart indicate slow motion; tic marks that are closer indicate fast motion; and no tic marks means a freeze frame.
5. Choose the Smooth command in a keyframes shortcut menu in the Motion tab or the keyframe graph of the Timeline.
6. Yes.

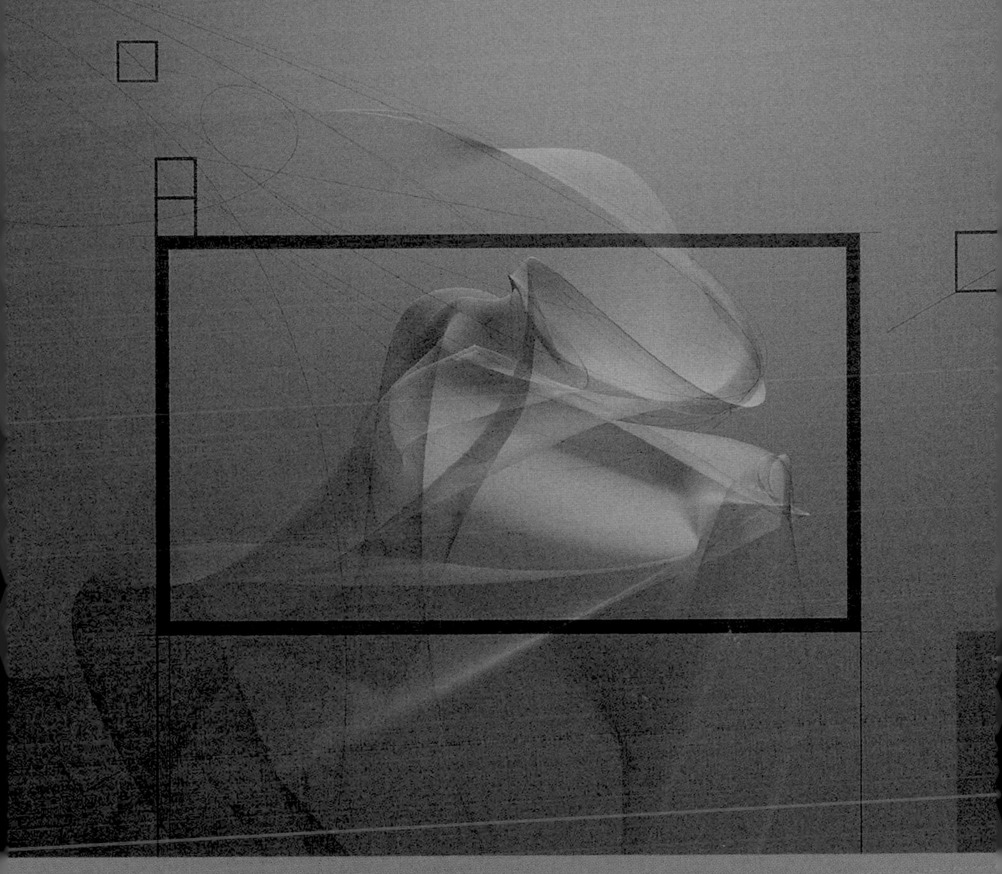

Color Correction

11

Lesson Files Lesson Files > Lesson 11 > Contrast.fcp

Media Dance Correction Example

Time This lesson takes approximately 60 minutes to complete.

Goals Break down a video image into its components

Incorporate video scopes in the grading process

Use the Color Corrector 3-way filter

Modify the contrast of an image

Understand contrast, blacks, mids, whites, highlights, and grayscale

Lesson **11**

Controlling Contrast

Color correction is a process for enhancing a video image. It is sometimes called *finishing*, because it's typically the last step in finalizing the image. A color correction artist, or *colorist*, is charged with molding raw, photographed images into something fantastic. In some cases, color correction involves using broad strokes to dramatically change the look of a film. Other times, it's used for more subtle tasks, such as smoothing variations in exposure and lighting or fixing the occasional mistake. Color correction means different things depending on the project, but its success always depends on the skill of the colorist. Like good editing, good color correction often goes entirely unnoticed in the final product.

Professional colorists spend years honing their skills and their eye for color. It's essential to learn to really *see* the video image—to grasp subtle color nuances and appreciate the subconscious effects of manipulating color balance and contrast.

There are fundamental principles that you will apply to correct the first shot of any scene. In this lesson, you'll begin with the first and most essential task of all: controlling the contrast.

Understanding Contrast

The term *contrast* is thrown around a lot and means different things to different people. For the sake of simplicity, consider that contrast represents the number of steps from the darkest to the lightest tone in your image.

Regardless of the colors involved, an image can range from deep, solid blacks, through varied mid-gray tones, to light, pure whites.

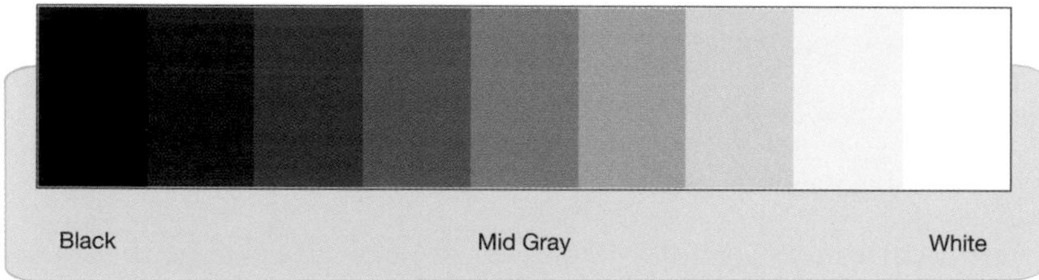

In this exercise, you'll examine the contrast in two different images, with the help of the Final Cut Pro video scopes.

Getting Started

1 Open Lesson Files > Lesson 11 > **Contrast.fcp**.

2 Choose Window > Arrange > Color Correction to change the window layout and automatically open the Video Scopes tab.

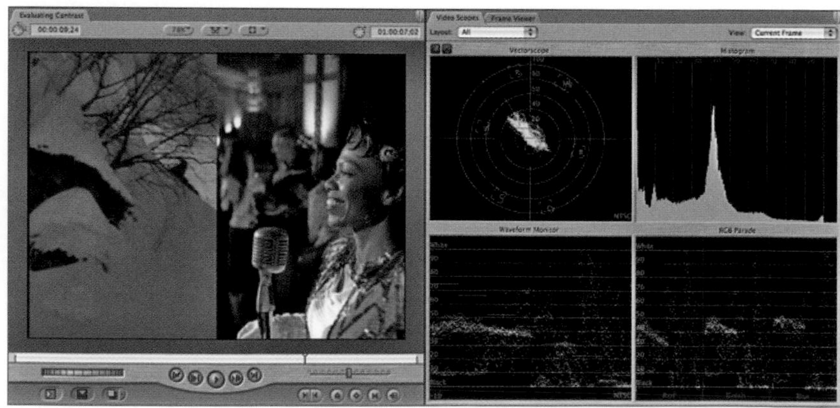

In the Video Scopes window, you can control the brightness of both the *traces* (the representation of the video data) and the gauges. These controls can be very helpful, especially when trying to identify small areas of activity.

3 In the upper-left corner of the Video Scopes window, click the Traces Brightness button (on the left).

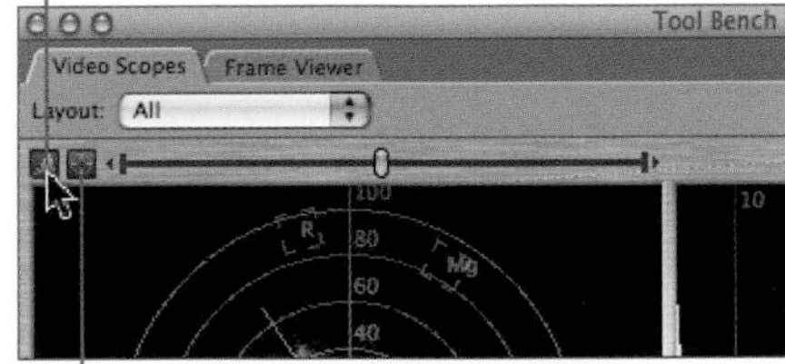

A slider appears beside the two buttons.

4 Drag the slider to brighten the display.

5 Click the Scales Brightness button.

The slider now changes the brightness of the gauges.

6 Adjust the brightness to your liking.

In the real world, you will make frequent adjustments to these two values, based on the specific needs of the content you are color correcting.

7 Click the Scales Brightness button again.

The slider disappears.

8 Click the Layout pop-up menu and choose Waveform to switch to that view.

9 Make sure that the View pop-up menu is set to Current Frame.

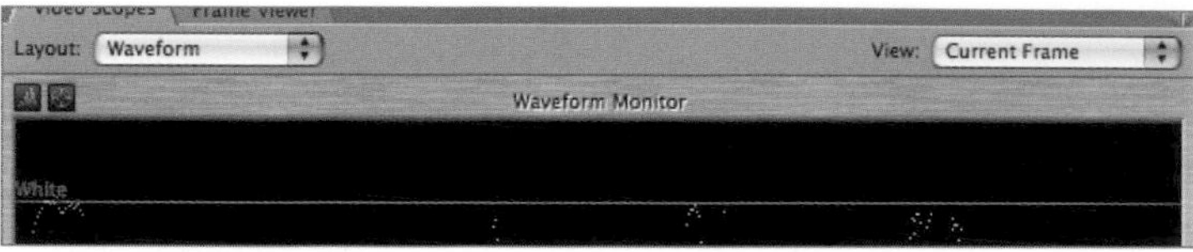

10 Open the Exercise 1 – Evaluating Contrast bin and double-click the *Evaluating Contrast* sequence.

Evaluating the Values in an Image—Highlights vs. Shadows

You first need to break down the image into shadows, midtones, and highlights. In the Final Cut Pro color correction controls, these regions are referred to as *blacks*, *mids*, and *whites*.

This may sound obvious, but learning to perceive which color values of an image fall into which of these zones is the basis for all the color correction work to follow, and it is a valuable skill to develop.

1 Scrub through the first clip in the *Evaluating Contrast* sequence.

To focus on the brightness levels in the image, you can eliminate the color.

2 Select the **Dance_Club.mov** clip, then choose Effects > Video Filters > Image Control > Desaturate.

The image is *desaturated*. In other words, the chrominance of the image has been eliminated, conveniently leaving the luminance for your evaluation.

3 Scrub through the desaturated image, and pay careful attention to the darkest and lightest areas of the image.

The different levels of brightness should really leap out at you. In particular, notice how some areas that may have seemed darker because of their colored tint, like the almost sepia glow in the windows and interior highlights, are now revealed to be very close to white.

Judging Contrast Ratios

For purposes of color correction, one of the most important characteristics of an image is its *contrast ratio*: how much difference there is between the blackest black and the whitest white. You can quickly judge the contrast ratio by looking at the height of the graph displayed in the Waveform Monitor.

1 Scrub through the desaturated image again, this time watching the graph in the Waveform Monitor.

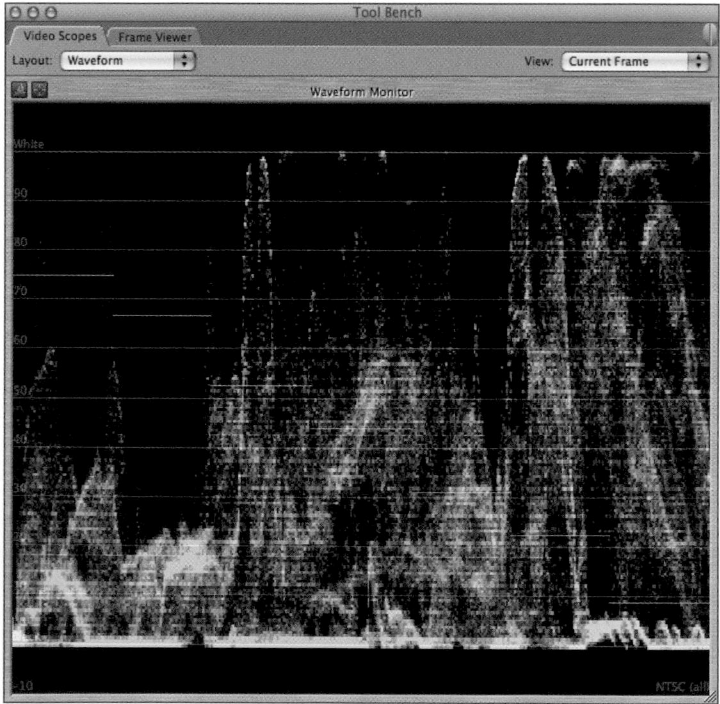

As you can see, there are large portions of the image that fall into the blacks down around 0 percent, but there are also numerous graph spikes up in the whites at 100 percent luminance. This is the widest possible contrast ratio, and it accounts for the crispness of the image.

2 Move the playhead to the **Skier.mov** clip, and play through it to get a sense of the colors and brightness.

3 Select the **Skier.mov** clip, and choose Effects > Last - Desaturate.

TIP Because the Desaturate filter was the last one you applied, it appears at the top of the Effects menu in case you want to apply it again.

4 Move the playhead to 01:00:04:11, and look at the Waveform Monitor.

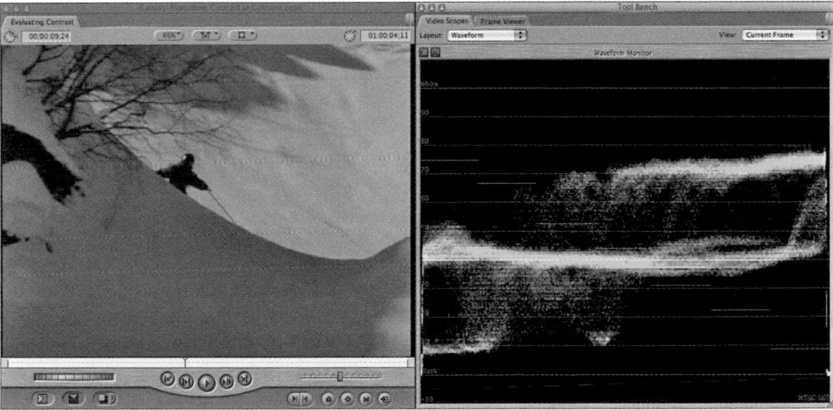

You may already have noticed, and the waveform confirms, that the whitest white in the image tops out around 80 percent, landing it firmly in the mids. Also, the darkest black (the rocks at the left of the frame), don't really fall all the way to 0 percent.

The result is an image that looks somewhat murky, with washed-out shadows and lackluster highlights. This is the result of a narrow contrast ratio.

5 Press the Down Arrow key to navigate to the next cut, which is actually both clips superimposed using a split screen.

   Once again, look carefully at the areas of light and shadow in the image, and try to imagine what it looks like without any color.

6 Select both clips, and choose Effects > Last - Desaturate.

   Although you may have had difficulty seeing the difference between both images' contrast ratios when jumping between the two clips, the split screen makes that difference readily apparent.

The blacks in the **Skier.mov** clip aren't nearly as deep as those in the **Dance_Club.mov** clip, nor are the whites as light. The graph in the Waveform Monitor shows this more dramatically.

NOTE ► You may need to adjust the traces brightness, as described earlier, to see all the detail in the Waveform Monitor.

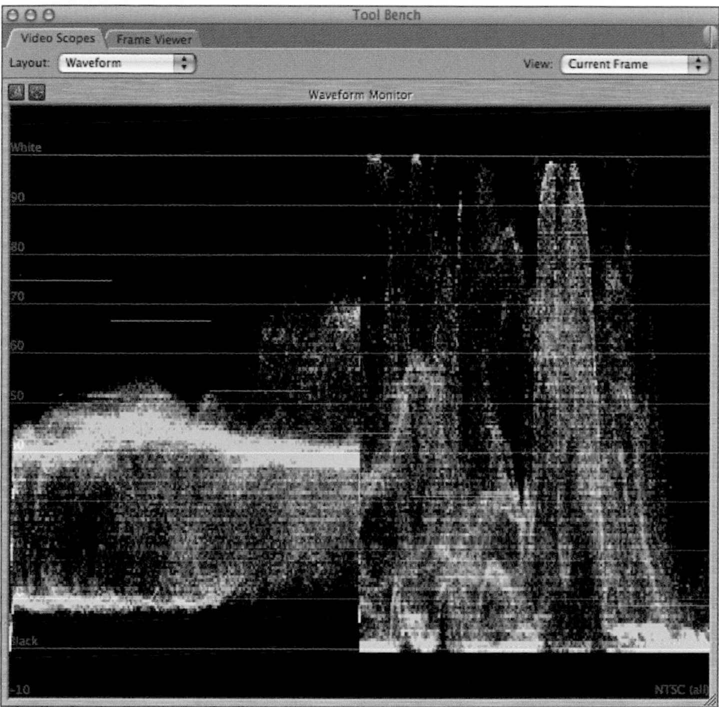

The graph in the Waveform Monitor is split just like the image in the Canvas, and you can see that the graph on the left side is not nearly as tall as the one on the right side.

Higher contrast ratios are not only more visually appealing; a low contrast ratio can later limit your ability to manipulate color in an image.

Comparing Low- and High-Contrast Images

Another way to view contrast is to consider how much of an image is found within the mids compared to how much of the image is in the blacks and whites. The balance between midtones and blacks-plus-whites is probably the most conventional way to describe contrast.

Images with large regions in the mids are considered *low contrast*. This results in an image that is fairly neutral, but in extreme cases, may result in an image that looks somewhat washed out.

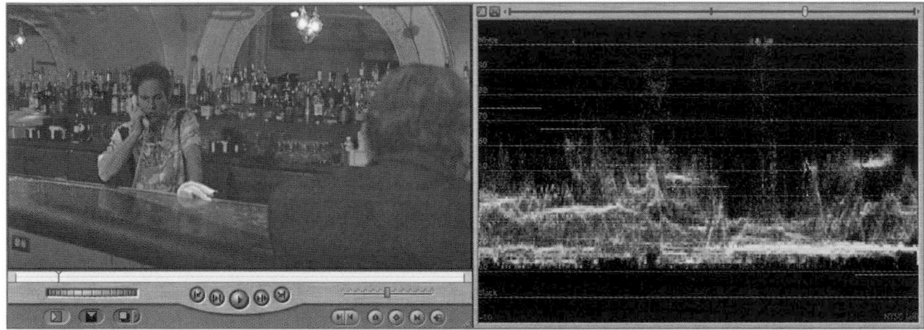

When the majority of the luminance values in an image are located in the whites and blacks, with few pixels in the mids, the image is considered *high contrast*.

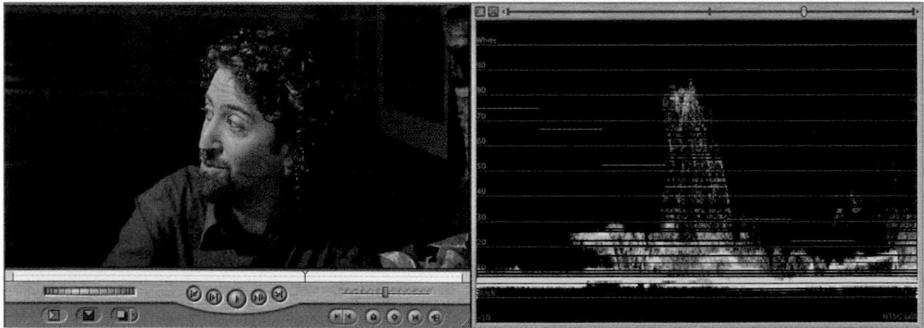

The borders between dark and light areas are usually perceived by viewers as edges, so higher-contrast images may be perceived as "sharper" than low-contrast images. On the other hand, extremes of black and white in very high-contrast images are typically harsher than we're used to seeing with the naked eye, so creating high-contrast images can lend a stylized look to a scene.

Whereas the *contrast ratio* of an image may be considered a simple qualitative issue (with higher contrast ratios able to bring out more image detail), whether or not the *perceived* contrast described in this section should be high or low remains primarily a matter of preference and artistic license.

Comparing High- and Low-Key Images

Another way to describe contrast is in terms of the lighting strategy used to shoot the image. Terms such as *high-key* and *low-key* (originally used to describe methods of lighting on the set) have carried over to color correction to distinguish different methods of lighting a scene for dramatic effect.

High-key generally describes images that are brightly and evenly lit. The lighting tends to be softer, with *fill light* eliminating harsh shadows. High-key images also happen to be low contrast. There may be black in the frame, but a look at the Histogram (which plots the bright and dark pixels of an image on a horizontal graph) will reveal that most luminance values are spread throughout the mids and the whites.

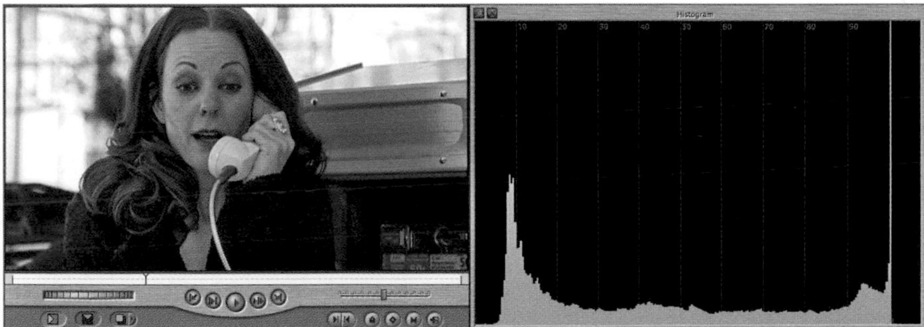

High-key images are often used to convey a light mood—the characters are happy, and all is well with the world.

Low-key images are the opposite. They are generally underlit, with deep shadows and plenty of them. As you've probably guessed, low-key images are also high contrast. Highlights tend to be harsh and bright compared to the blackness of the image. A look at the Histogram will often reveal large, wide swaths of values in the blacks, with few mids and perhaps a spike or two in the whites (though not in this example). Low-key lighting is often used to portray night, or a serious, dramatic moment. Think *film noir*.

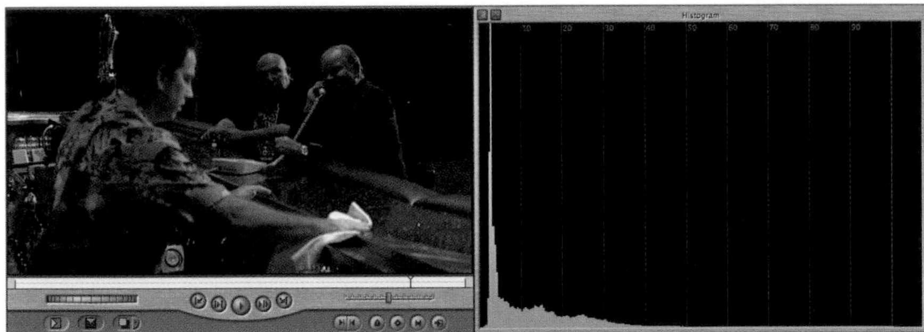

Why use these different ways to describe contrast? The description depends on who you're talking to, and what aspect of the image they're trying to describe. The director of photography may try to impress upon you the importance of preserving a high-key look, but the producer (who happens to be an amateur photographer) may counter that she thinks it should be low contrast—in reality, they're both describing a desire for the exact same look, they're just using different ways to describe it.

It's also worth pointing out that an image with a high contrast ratio, may not necessarily be a high-contrast, low-key image. Because the perceived contrast of an image is often dependent upon the amount of brightness and visible detail in the midrange of an image, it's completely possible to have a relatively low-contrast image with a high contrast ratio.

Now that you understand the basics of contrast, it's time for you to manipulate it to achieve specific goals.

Controlling Contrast Using the Color Corrector 3-Way Filter

The Final Cut Pro Color Corrector 3-way filter is the workhorse for all of the following exercises. It is one of two filters (along with the more simply-named

Color Corrector filter) that have a custom graphical interface with specific controls optimized for color correcting images.

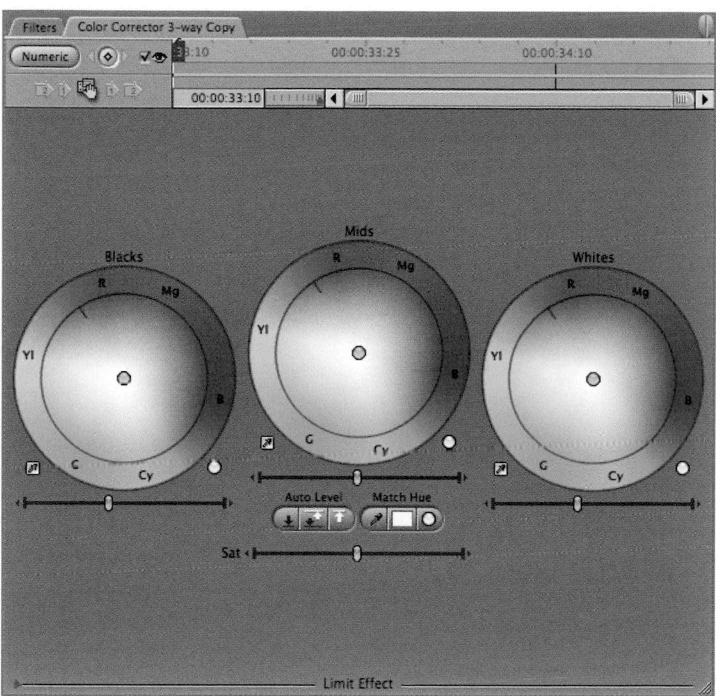

For now, you'll ignore the color wheels. With the three sliders underneath, you can push and pull the luminance values within an image using separate controls to target the image's black level, mids distribution, and white level.

In the following exercises, you'll use these three sliders to achieve complete control over the contrast in your images.

Adjusting the Black and White Points

Among its many virtues, the Color Corrector 3-way filter is able to play to an external monitor in real time, depending on your computer's configuration. Remember, you should *always* view the image you're manipulating on a broadcast monitor when preparing a program for broadcast in NTSC or PAL formats.

1 In the Browser, open the Exercise 02 - Controlling Contrast bin.

2 Double-click the *Controlling Contrast - Basics* sequence.

   The first clip in the sequence is a gradient generator. You'll notice that the default gradient is a ramp from 100 percent luminance (white) to 0 percent (black), with a direct correspondence to the diagonal graph shown in the Waveform Monitor.

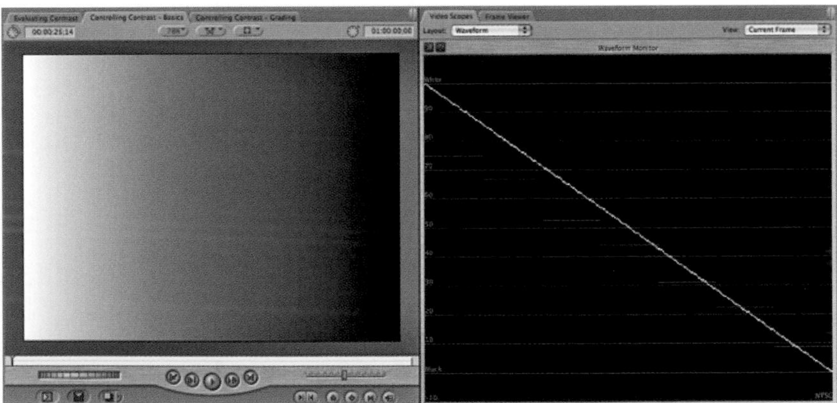

   This is an ideal test image to see how changes you make with the Color Corrector 3-way filter manipulate the balance of luminance in an image.

3 In the Timeline, select the **Gradient** clip, then choose Effects > Video Filters > Color Correction > Color Corrector 3-way.

4 In the Timeline, double-click the **Gradient** clip to open it into the Viewer.

Even though you've added a filter, you'll notice an additional Color Corrector 3-way tab at the top of the Viewer.

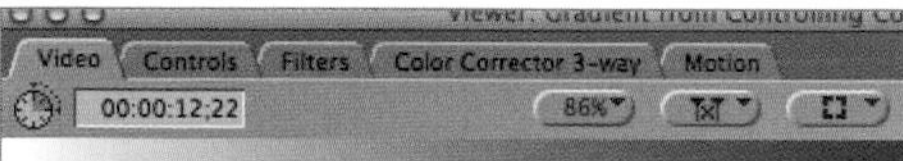

This tab contains a custom interface for the Color Corrector 3-way filter, providing explicit control over the characteristics of your image.

5 Click the Filters tab.

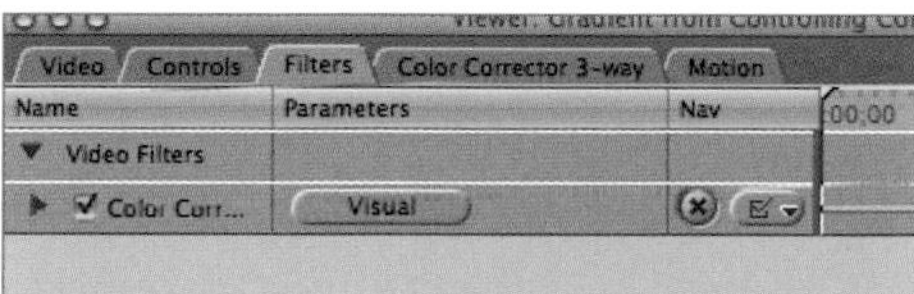

As you can see, the Color Corrector 3-way filter is present.

6 Click the disclosure triangle to the left of the filter name to view the filter's parameters.

A tall stack of parameters appears. Don't worry if you don't initially understand their functions. Every one of these parameters is represented by a graphical control in the Color Corrector 3-way tab.

Later, when you know what each parameter affects, you can adjust the sliders and dials in the Filters tab if you feel you need to make more finely detailed changes to the image than the graphical interface allows.

Also, color correction filters such as the Color Corrector 3-way filter cannot be removed or rearranged directly within the Color Corrector 3-way tab. Instead, these operations need to be performed in the Filters tab just as with any other video filter.

7 Click the disclosure triangle to close the parameters list, and click the Visual button to the right of the filter's name, or click the Color Corrector 3-way tab, to go to the Color Corrector 3-way graphical interface.

NOTE ► In the visual Color Corrector 3-way tab, you can click the Numeric button to go back to the Filters tab.

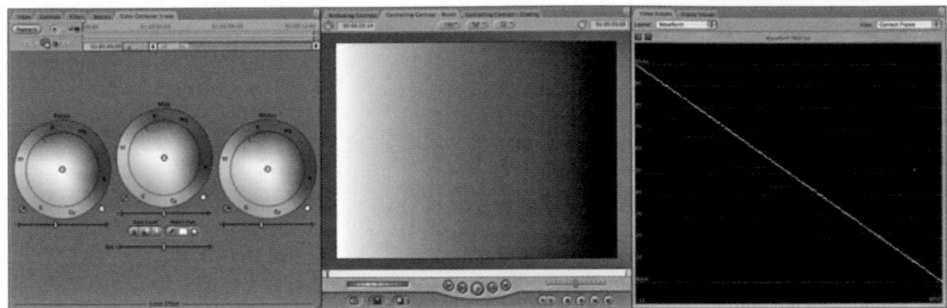

With the Color Corrector controls in view, and the Viewer, Canvas, and video scopes open side-by-side in the Final Cut Pro default Color Correction layout, you have all the tools you need for analyzing, adjusting, and monitoring your images.

Even though the three color wheels may be the biggest, brightest things on the screen, simply screaming to be manipulated, leave them alone for now. In this lesson, you are going to focus on the three slider controls beneath the wheels. These are the controls you'll use to manipulate contrast.

Each slider corresponds to one of the color wheels in providing control over the blacks level, mids distribution, and whites level. These sliders adjust the luminance of the image independent of the chrominance levels.

8 Drag the Whites slider to the left to lower the level of the whites.

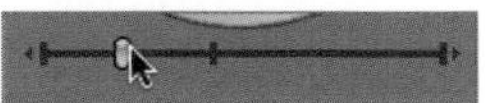

Two things happen. The light part of the image darkens to a deeper gray, and the graph redraws itself so the diagonal line lowers.

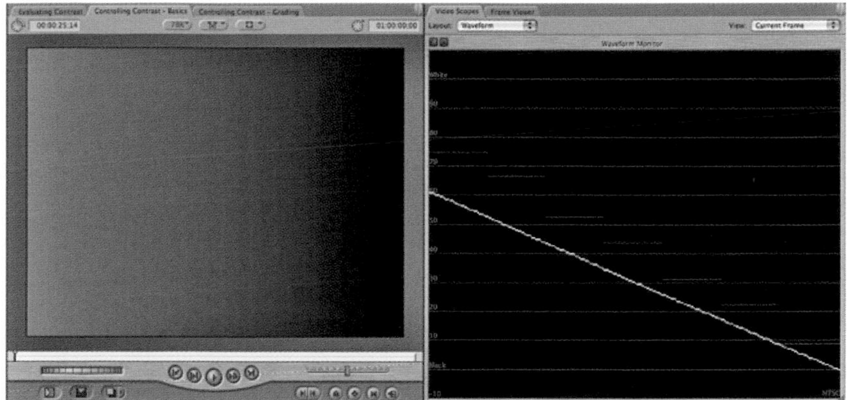

Notice, however, that the bottom of the graph didn't move. This is a vital characteristic of the three luminance controls in the Color Corrector 3-way filter. Changes to the whites leave the blacks untouched.

9 Drag the Blacks slider to the right to raise the level of the blacks.

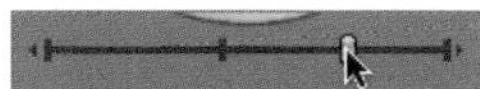

This time, you lightened the levels of the darkest parts of the image, which redraws the graph to reflect the new luminance distribution. Notice that, despite this second change, the whites level remains unchanged.

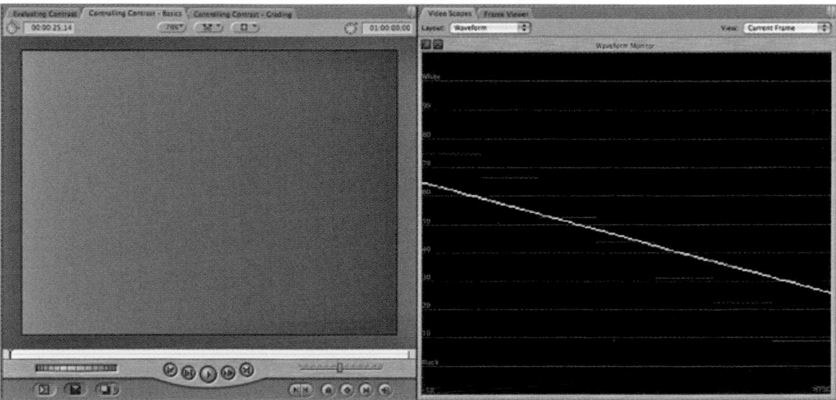

Incidentally, because you've just decreased the height from the blackest black to the whitest white, you've successfully lowered the contrast ratio of this image.

Changes you make to the blacks and whites levels are fairly easy to understand, because they essentially scale all of the image's luminance values linearly, relative to the opposite end of the graph.

Adjusting the Mids

The Mids slider provides control over the distribution of all values falling between the black and white points of your image.

1 In the Color Corrector 3-way tab, Shift-click any one of the Reset buttons to reset all of the parameters to their default values.

Ordinarily, clicking a Reset button resets only the parameters associated with that control, but Shift-clicking any color correction Reset button in the top control group resets everything except for the Limit Effects controls (which appear in the collapsed section at the bottom of the Color Correction tab). As a result, the image and the graph in the Waveform Monitor return to their original states.

2 Drag the Mids slider to the left.

Immediately, you'll notice a far different effect. The whites and blacks remain largely where they are (although more extreme changes do move the white point), but the range of grays in the middle of the image appear to move towards the left as the image progressively darkens.

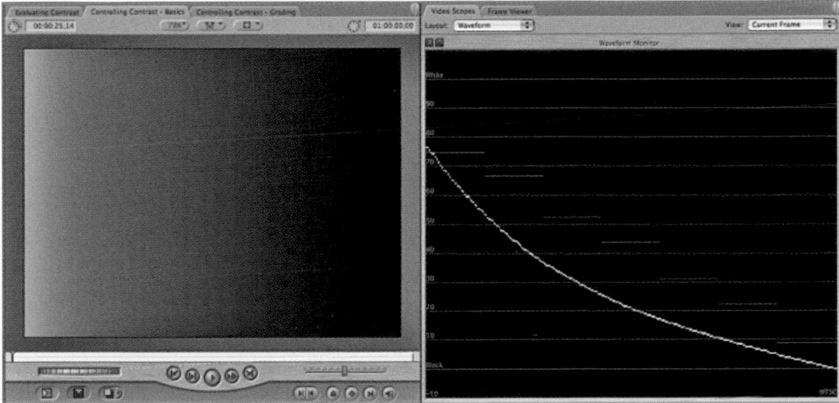

The result in the Waveform Monitor is even more dramatic. Changes to the blacks and whites resulted in a straight line in the graph, but lowering the mids had two effects: reshaping the graph into a downward curve, and moving down the white point.

3 Drag the Mids slider to the right.

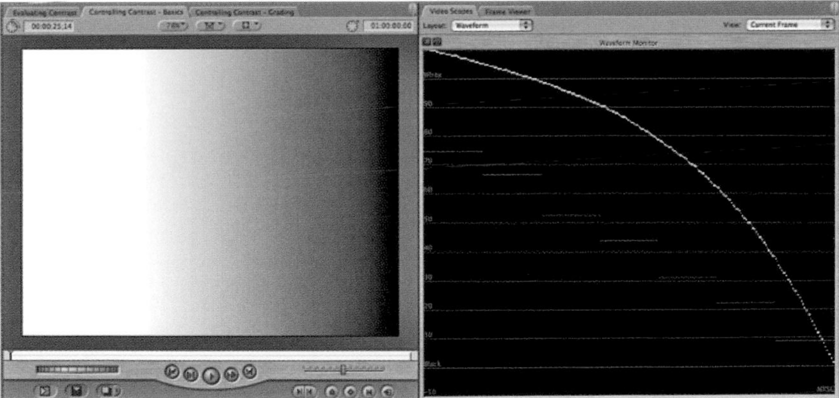

Predictably, this has the opposite effect, with the distribution of gray tones moving to the right as the image lightens, and the graph curving upward.

Basically, changes made to the mids redistribute the values falling between the white and black points of the image so the image can be lightened or darkened without muddying the blacks or whites. This change is nonlinear (as shown by the slope of the curve), which allows for subtle changes across the range of the image.

You can also see that the relationship between the mids and the whites is tricky. Changes made to one will require you to interact with the other.

Next, you'll see how adjusting the contrast in these three regions will enhance a real-world image. You'll also learn the proper sequence in which to approach these contrast corrections when using the Color Corrector 3-way filter.

Stretching Contrast in a Video Clip

The contrast sliders give you total control over the contrast ratio of any image by allowing you to adjust the distance from the brightest to the darkest value in the picture using the Blacks and Whites sliders. You can also control whether your image is high contrast or low contrast by redistributing the midtones that fall between using the Mids slider.

In the following exercise, you'll deal with one of the most common issues in video: murky-looking source footage with a low contrast ratio. You'll see how this is easily curable using the Blacks, Mids, and Whites controls.

1. Press the Down Arrow key to move to the first frame of the **Ski_Jump.mov** clip.

   You've seen this image before. It's the one with the blacks that are too high, and the whites that are too low, resulting in murky shadows and lackluster whites. You've probably already guessed what needs to happen based on the last exercise, but methodically going through this process will help you develop good habits for approaching the color correction process.

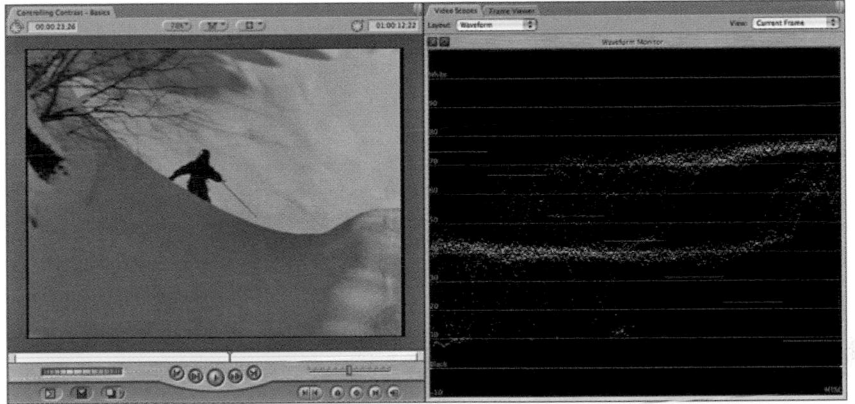

2 In the Timeline, select the **Ski_Jump.mov** clip, then choose Effects > Video Filters > Color Correction > Color Corrector 3-way.

3 In the Timeline, double-click the **Ski_Jump.mov** clip to open it into the Viewer, and click the Color Corrector 3-way tab to display the color correction controls.

NOTE ▶ If the Color Corrector tab from another clip is already open in the Viewer, opening a new clip into the Viewer leaves the Color Corrector tab open, as long as the new clip has one color correction filter applied to it. This saves you from having to constantly click the Color Corrector tab in the Viewer as you adjust numerous filters.

The first step in any color correction is to set the black levels. As you saw in the preceding exercise, the black point is unaffected by changes made to the whites or mids, so it serves as the baseline for all changes you make to the image.

TIP Get in the habit of setting the blacks first. If you make a change to the mids or whites first, and adjust the blacks last, the change in the blacks will definitely affect the distribution of mids and whites, resulting in more fiddling around on your part.

4 Examine the image in the Viewer.

You need to determine which parts of the image correspond to absolute black (0 percent) to make this adjustment. With few exceptions, most images should have at least a few pixels located at 0 percent. This results in deeper, richer blacks, which makes the lighter values pop out more by comparison.

One of the tricky things about this image is that the lighting is fairly diffuse, and the shadows of the trees aren't supposed to be that dark. However, there are some very dark shadows in the rocky outcropping at the left of the screen.

5 Look at the lower-left corner of the Waveform Monitor.

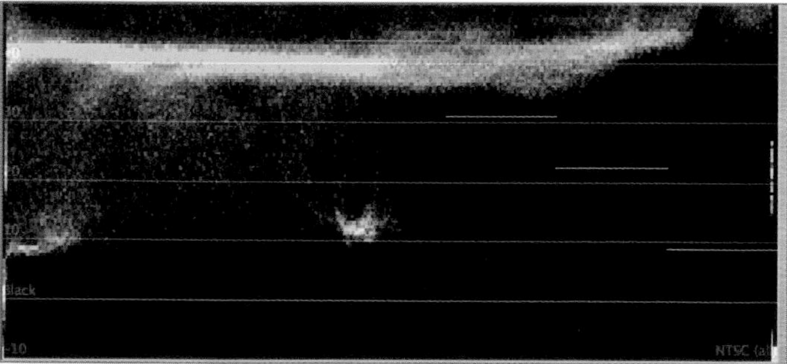

You can see a dip in the waveform graph that corresponds to the rocks. These levels seem low enough to qualify as the absolute black of the image, and, in fact, some of these pixels seem to be touching 0 percent black. Still, this image could benefit from a slightly deeper black level, although you don't want to make a big change.

6 To make a very slight reduction to the blacks, click the small arrow to the left of the Blacks slider five or six times.

TIP There are two good ways to use the mouse to make incremental adjustments with any effects slider: Click one of the little arrows at either end of the slider to nudge it in one-degree increments, or if you have a mouse with a standard scroll wheel, position the pointer at a slider and scroll upward to slide left or scroll downward to slide right. The scroll wheel technique is actually more accurate than dragging the slider itself.

You can also press the Command key while using a slider, forcing it to move slower, allowing finer adjustments.

As slight as this change is, you can see the graph in the Waveform Monitor stretch downward.

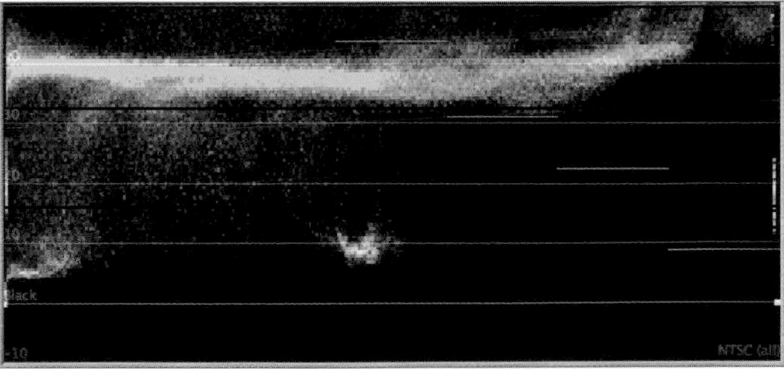

Although it's difficult to see, the dots at the bottom of the graph begin to bunch up at the black line. As more and more of the graph hits the bottom, the result is typically referred to as *crushing the blacks*. Crushing the blacks increases the deepness of the shadows, which can be pleasing, but comes at the expense of losing detail.

7 To see the result of severely crushed blacks, drag the Blacks slider farther to the left.

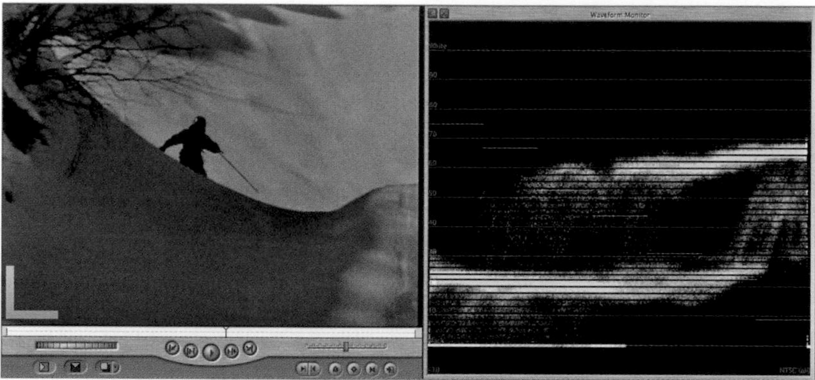

Notice that the dark areas of the image go completely black, and the bottom of the waveform graph bunches up. This is best way to tell if your blacks are crushed when it's difficult to determine in the Canvas.

Notice that the black levels never go below 0 percent. A value of 0 percent is the absolute bottom of the digital luminance scale. There is no way to create values that are "blacker than black." This is a very good thing when readying the video for broadcast because broadcast formats such as NTSC or PAL have regulations about black levels being lower than a certain amount. When working in Final Cut Pro, the values are simply digital percentages, so you don't have to worry about blacks being *unsafe*. This is true regardless of whether or not the source video was from a digital or analog format. Once digitized, all video is measured on a digital scale.

NOTE ▶ You need only be concerned with IRE black levels when outputting your program from digital to an analog format—and then it is simply a matter of properly setting up your video output hardware (and the software drivers that control it, if necessary) to the appropriate standard—0 or 7.5. There are no IRE settings internal to Final Cut Pro. The bottom line: when color correcting in Final Cut Pro, regardless of the system or format, always set blacks to 0 percent in the video scopes.

8 Press Command-Z to undo the last change.

Next, you'll address the biggest problem in this image—those dismal-looking whites in the snow. Adjusting the whites is generally the second step after adjusting the blacks, especially when the white level is so low.

9 Drag the Whites slider to the right to boost the whites until the top of the graph in the Waveform Monitor hits 100 percent.

The difference is huge, much more noticeable than the slight adjustment made to the blacks. The results of expanding the contrast ratio of this clip are immediately visible, almost as if you wiped a layer of grime off the monitor screen.

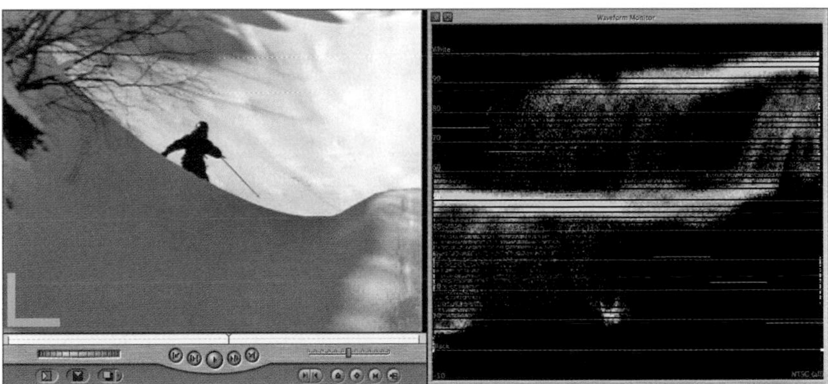

Incidentally, as you work it may be tempting to boost values into the super-white range (from 100 to 109 percent). Resist this urge. Although it may make your brights "whiter than white," you may also run into problems when you want to output your program to a broadcast format. Remember that when setting whites for broadcast, the levels should never rise above 100 percent.

Furthermore, even though the details are faint, there's still a lot of texture and detail in the bright regions of this image, and you want to avoid clipping them off and "flattening" the image.

Now that the black and white points of the image are set, check to see if you need to make any changes to the mids.

10 Play the clip.

As you get a third of the way though the clip, you should notice an immediate problem. The whites are practically glowing, and they appear strangely flat. Stopping playback reveals that the whites in the frame you were balancing were far too dark, but other whites later on in the clip are much brighter. In fact, the later whites are being clipped off at the top of the Waveform Monitor.

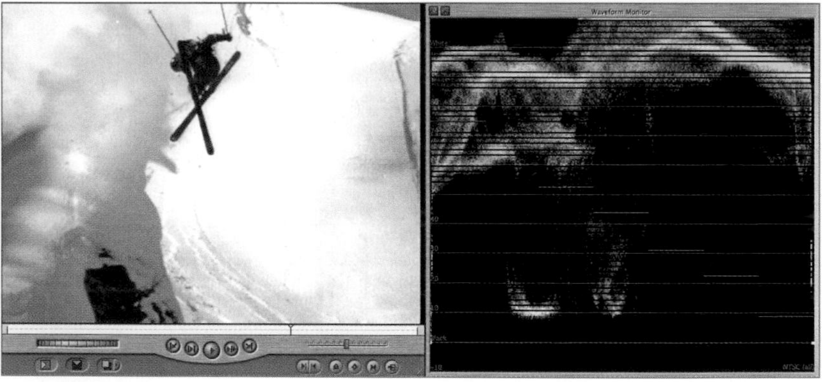

Unfortunately, the previous setting does not work throughout the entire clip, which brings up an important point. When you pick an image to color correct, you must evaluate it over its entire duration to account for changes in lighting that might happen later on in the shot.

11 Drag the Whites slider to the left to bring the white levels back to 100 percent.

This very nearly brings the white level back to its original level, and the whites, although legal, lose their snap. Because you've now determined that this is the widest possible contrast ratio for this shot, it's time to adjust the Mids to make this a higher-contrast shot.

12 Drag the Mids slider to the right.

This gives the desired whiter-looking whites, by making the midtones brighten up.

As you saw in the previous exercise, however, the whites have been pushed up, which you'll need to fix.

13 Drag the Whites slider to the left to bring the top of the graph back to 100 percent.

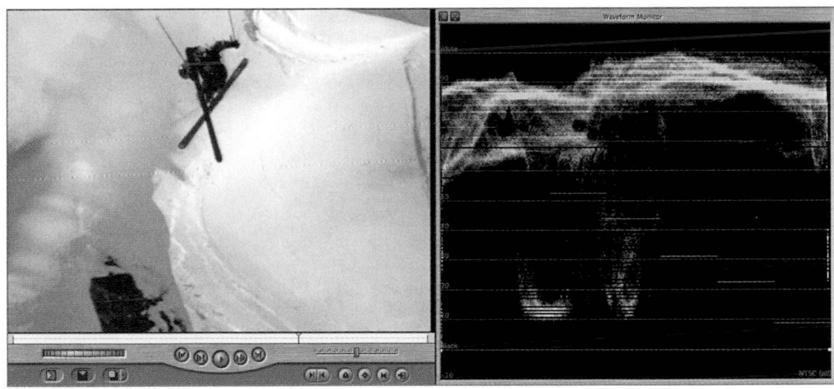

Ironically, this brings the Whites slider back to its default position. All of this effort illustrates that, oftentimes, adjusting the mids and whites is an interactive process of push and pull.

After all that, if you find yourself wondering whether this meddling has made any real improvement, you can perform a simple test to get a fast before-and-after look at the clip, to make sure you prefer the end result.

14 At the top of the Color Corrector 3-way tab, select and deselect the Enable Filter checkbox to toggle it on and off, comparing the two results.

As you've worked through this exercise, your eyes have gotten accustomed to the new contrast settings. Toggling the Color Corrector filter on and off is a good comparative tool you can use to see how much you've changed the initial look of the video.

Adjusting contrast is always the first step of color correction, and it comes before *any* changes you make to the clip's color. The process always begins by adjusting the blacks, then interactively making adjustments to the whites and mids until you've achieved the desired quality of contrast.

Setting Mood with the Mids

Adjusting the blacks and whites to establish the contrast ratio of an image is a fairly straightforward process. You want to provide the greatest contrast range for your image, and the only questions are which parts of the picture to map to absolute black, and which to absolute white.

Adjustments to the midtones, on the other hand, are much more subjective. Do you want a high-contrast look, or low-contrast? Is the picture supposed to be high-key, or low-key? There are no right or wrong answers, just what you and your client prefer.

The majority of the pixels in an image are generally found in the midtones. This is the luminance region with the most detail, and if the image is well-lit, it is also where faces are exposed. As a result, the distribution of midtones in an image goes a long way to defining the feeling of a shot.

For instance, by making simple adjustments to the midtones, you can influence the perceived time of day—is it midday, afternoon, or evening? Or, you can make sunlight look bright, or dark and overcast. These are all looks you can begin to define by adjusting the mids.

In this exercise, you'll make mids adjustments to a generally well-exposed image, in order to change the apparent time of day.

1 Open the *Controlling Contrast - Grading* sequence.

2 Scrub through the **Dance_Club.mov** clip and examine how the waveform changes over time.

   NOTE ▶ The best way to see how the video scopes change over the course of the clip is to scrub through the image by dragging the playhead in the Canvas or Timeline. While the clip is playing, the resolution of the scopes is reduced to a sampling of dots.

   As you can see, the contrast ratio of this clip is already as high as it can be, with many values at 0 percent, and several spikes at 100 percent.

3 Select the **Dance_Club.mov** clip, and choose Effects > Video Filters > Color Correction > Color Corrector 3-way.

4 In the Timeline, double-click the **Dance_Club.mov** clip to open the color correction filter into the Viewer. The Color Corrector 3-way tab updates to reflect the settings of the filter you just added.

As it is now, the quality of light in the image indicates afternoon, or an extremely well-lit evening. You'll first try to make this scene look more like an evening shot.

5 Drag the Mids slider to the left to lower the levels in the image.

This darkens the image, but now the highlights look dimmer. The Waveform Monitor confirms this observation by showing that the top of the graph has fallen to about 90 percent.

6 Drag the Whites slider to the right to return the top of the waveform graph to 100 percent.

It's a small change, but it puts the snap back into the highlights of the image, while keeping the rest of the room darker.

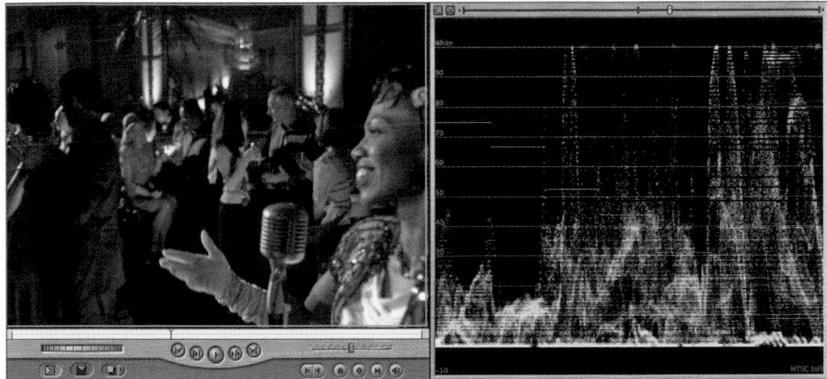

7 To compare the before-and-after results, select and deselect the Enable Filter checkbox.

Next, you'll reset the color correction controls and make the same clip look like it was shot closer to midday.

8 In the Color Corrector 3-way tab, Shift-click any of the Reset buttons to reset the default values.

9 Drag the Mids slider to the right to boost the levels and create the illusion of more light coming into the room.

As you make this adjustment, pay particular attention to the quality of the light in the background—this is the darkest area you need to boost.

As you've seen before, boosting the mids also boosts the highlights, and in this case, the mids adjustment is making the whites blow out well above 100 percent.

10 Drag the Whites slider to the left to bring the top of the waveform graph back down to 100 percent.

Now the image looks brighter, and the whites aren't blowing out any more.

It's not a bad range of options for using two simple sliders. Later on, you'll learn to combine contrast adjustments with color balance adjustments to create even more sophisticated looks. The important thing to remember is that adjustments to the contrast are the first, and sometimes only, adjustments you'll need to make.

Creating Artificially High Contrast

So far, you've been adjusting the contrast to create a natural look. However, you can use these same controls to create extremely stylized, high-contrast images. You might do this for a number of creative purposes: to enhance the separation of different elements within the frame, to hide a flaw in the exposure, or simply to create a distinctive look.

Creating a High-Contrast Look

In this exercise, you will treat the image you've been working with as high contrast.

1 In the Browser, open the Exercise 03 - High Contrast bin and double-click the *Higher Contrast - Finished* sequence.

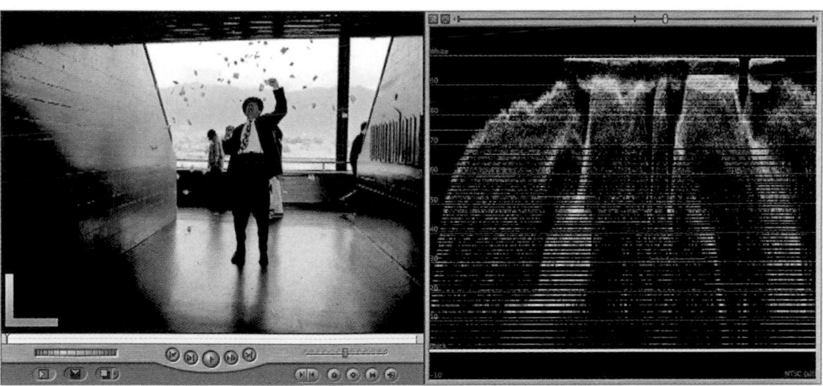

In order to create high contrast, you need to push up the midtones of the image towards white and down toward black, and away from the center, as you see in this image.

2 Open the *Higher Contrast - Beginning* sequence.

3 Select the **Winner.mov** clip, and choose Effects > Video Filters > Color Correction > Color Corrector 3-way.

4 In the Timeline, double-click the **Winner.mov** clip to open the color correction filter you've just added into the currently open Color Corrector 3-way tab in the Viewer.

The original image is very well exposed, with a high contrast ratio and detail throughout the entire range of luminance.

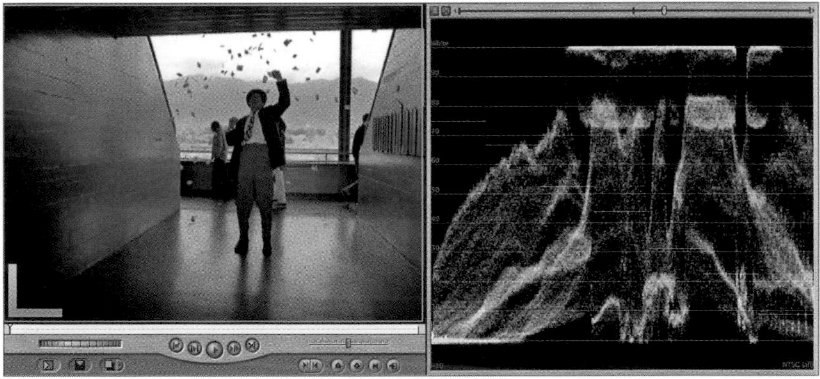

The first step you'll take toward creating a high-contrast look is to crush the blacks.

5 Move the Blacks slider to the left.

The farther you drag left, the more values get crushed to the bottom of the waveform graph, and the darker your image gets.

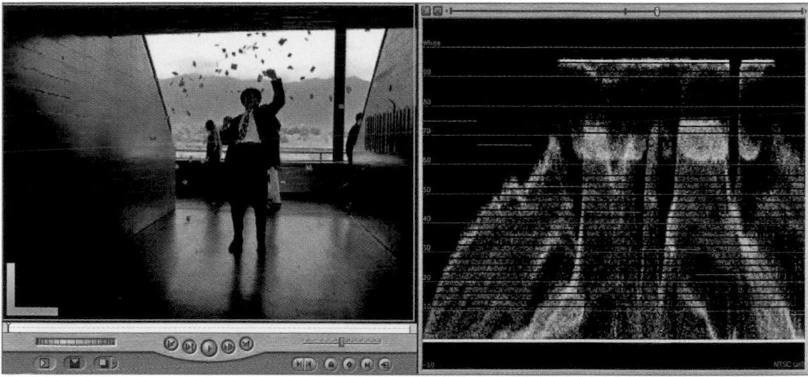

It's not high contrast yet, it's just dark. For truly high contrast, you need to boost the highlights back up. However, you're not going for a realistic look, so you can take a shortcut and crank up the mids first, without regard for where the highlights fall.

6 Drag the Mids slider to the right to redistribute the midtones up towards the whites. Don't be shy.

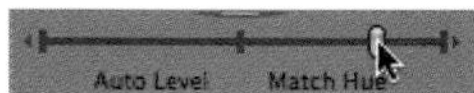

The result is definitely high contrast, but with whites that are outrageously overblown. Stylized or not, you cannot allow whites to go above 100 percent.

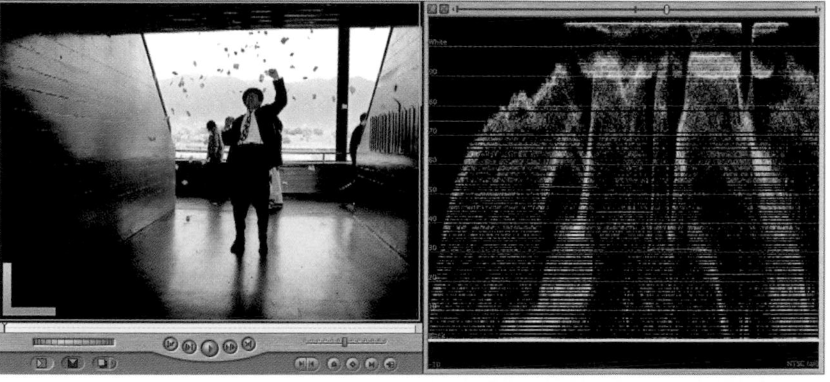

7 Drag the Whites slider to the left, until the top of the waveform graph sits at 100 percent.

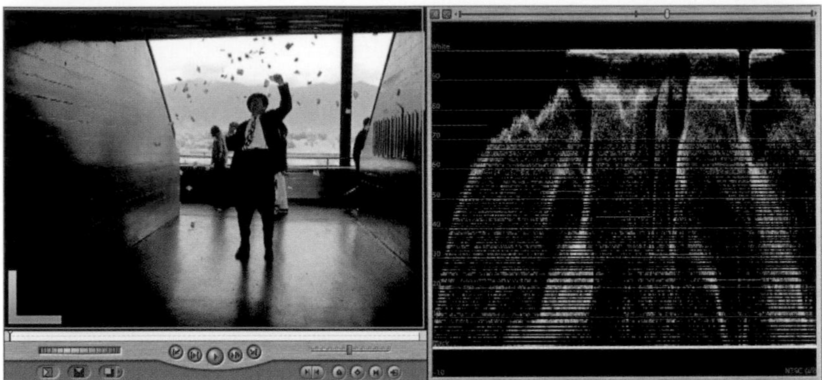

Now you have an extremely high-contrast image, with broadcast-legal luminance, and as an added bonus, you were able to retrieve some pleasing detail from the background.

Although this is not something you'd do to every image, it's good to know how to push the contrast to create more stylized effects.

However, suppose you didn't want to bring the whites back down in step 7. What if you wanted to blow out the whites, and leave them blown out? In the next exercise, you'll learn how to safely manage illegal values in an image—values that aren't broadcast safe—while getting the results you want.

Applying the Broadcast Safe Filter

Assume that you want to deliberately clip the whites in the previous exercise. Leaving illegal levels in a clip is never good practice, because they can cause innumerable problems later. In these instances, you can use the Broadcast Safe filter.

The Broadcast Safe filter limits the maximum allowable luminance and saturation levels. In this case, it is the perfect tool to help you extend the contrast of the clip by compressing the highlights to a broadcast-legal level.

1 Still working on the **Winner.mov** clip in the *Higher Contrast – Beginning* sequence, drag the Whites slider to the default center position, so that the whites blow out once again.

An examination of the Waveform Monitor confirms that the white levels are completely illegal.

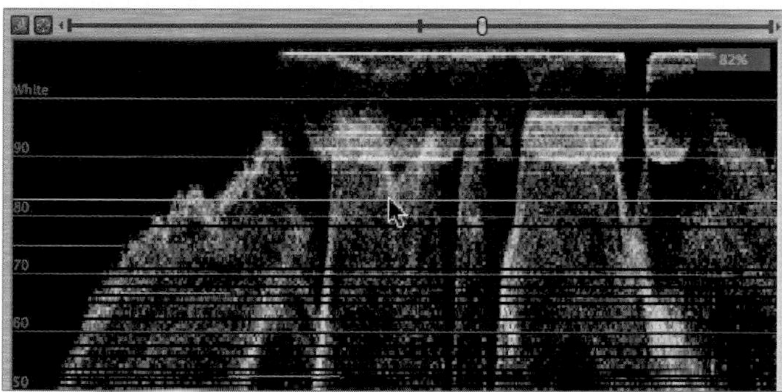

2 Select the **Winner.mov** clip in the Timeline, and choose Effects > Video Filters > Color Correction > Broadcast Safe to add the Broadcast Safe filter to the clip.

Instantly, you'll see that the illegal levels displayed in the Waveform Monitor have been compressed to a safe 100 percent, although the whites in the Viewer are still blown out.

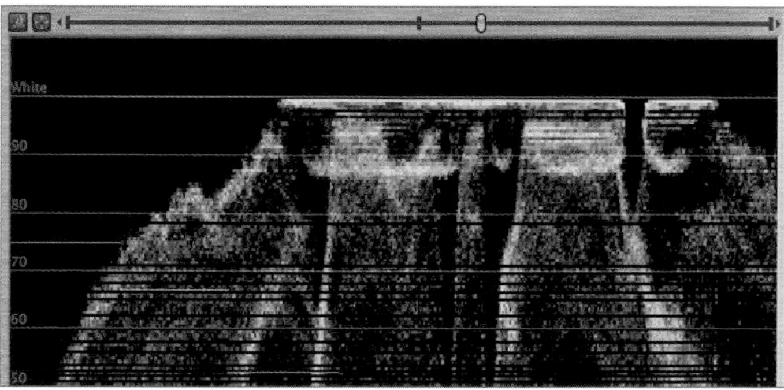

If you look at the image in the Canvas, you can see that a bit of detail has crept back into the image. You can just make out the faint outline of the mountain in the background.

This is because the broadcast monitor is *compressing* the illegal levels, or squeezing them all together, rather than *clipping* them, or cutting them off. The end result is still quite bright, but the effect is a little more pleasing.

3 Click the Filters tab.

Notice that the default mode of the Broadcast Safe filter is Conservative. This setting is recommended for most situations.

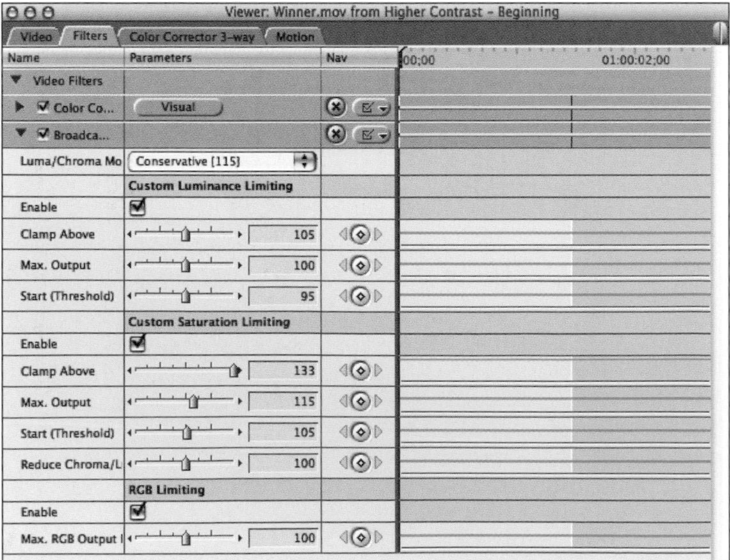

4 Click the Color Corrector 3-way tab.

5 Drag the Whites slider to the right so you can see how the Broadcast Safe filter is limiting the increased values.

As you continue to drag to the right, the values in the graph climb to 100 percent and then compress and bunch up.

The Broadcast Safe filter is good to use whenever you want to make a range of light values brighter but don't want to worry about going into unsafe luminance ranges.

6 Click the Filters tab.

7 In the Broadcast Safe filter, click the Luma/Chroma Mode pop-up menu to see the available choices.

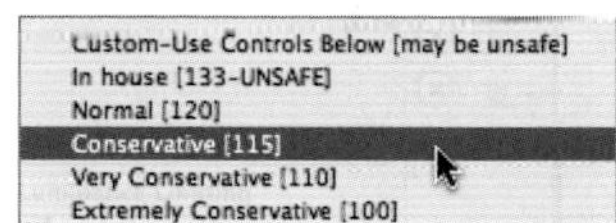

As a rule of thumb, you can use the default choice of Conservative, which limits values to 100 percent. The other choices, including the Custom option, set the top end of the luminance scale to better suit your needs.

NOTE ▶ When you're working in Custom mode, these controls are all manual. In choices other than Custom, the sliders have no effect.

A Note about Contrast and Grain

What is the result of all this pushing and pulling of the contrast? Whenever you expand the contrast range of an image, you're stretching a limited amount of color information across a wider range. Depending on the image format, and the amount of data in the original image, you may be able to make your changes without creating any discernable artifacts in the image.

However, in cases where you need to make extreme corrections, such as with underexposed or overexposed images, making contrast adjustments can result in unsightly artifacts. This is especially true when using highly compressed video formats such as DV that also lack color information.

In these cases, the process of increasing contrast can also bring out certain elements of the image that you would rather conceal. One of the most common problems is that increased contrast can make the image appear more grainy, by highlighting its grain (with film) or noise (with video). In these cases, you'll have to strike a compromise between the level of correction you need to make versus the amount of image noise you're willing to tolerate.

Lesson Review

1. What does contrast ratio describe?
2. What do the mids describe?
3. What's better, a higher contrast ratio or a lower contrast ratio?
4. Does a high contrast ratio automatically create a high-contrast image?
5. How do you maximize the contrast ratio of a clip using the Color Corrector 3-way filter?
6. How would you adjust the Mids slider to make an image seem like it's shot in the late afternoon?
7. What are two ways you can eliminate illegal whites in an image?

Answers

1. The distance between the blackest and lightest values in an image.
2. The range of values that falls within the middle tones of the image, between shadows and highlights.
3. Higher contrast ratios are generally better.
4. No. Contrast ratios and perceived contrast are different.

5. Adjust the Blacks slider so that the blackest part of the image is around 0 percent, and then adjust the Whites slider so that any highlights in the image are around 100 percent.
6. Drag the Mids slider to the left to lower the mids distribution.
7. You could use the Color Corrector 3-way filter and lower the whites, or you could apply the Broadcast Safe filter.

12

Lesson Files	Lesson Files > Lesson 12 > Color.fcp
Media	Color Correction Examples
Time	This lesson takes approximately 60 minutes to complete.
Goals	Identify color using a color wheel Manipulate color with hue, saturation, and luminance controls Incorporate color effects during grading Use video scopes to identify and manipulate color Use the Color Corrector 3-way filter Use color balancing to enhance the final scene Describe the color terms hue, saturation, color wheel, color space, primary, secondary, and complementary

Lesson **12**

Controlling Color

Lesson 11 was entirely focused on luminance and contrast. Once you've graded the contrast, the next step in the color correction process is to work on the color balance of the image.

Choosing the color balance is a creative, as well as corrective, endeavor. You may find yourself wanting to manipulate color to enhance an image, to alter the mood of a scene, or perhaps to create highly stylized color schemes for a title sequence or motion graphics segment.

Whatever your goals, you need to understand how to judge colors and which controls to use to create the desired effect. This lesson focuses on how you evaluate and manipulate color in Final Cut Pro. You will learn how to read and understand the color balance of an image and then use color correction to alter the color balance in that clip with total control.

Understanding Color Balance

Color balance refers to the relative amounts of red, green, and blue in an image. As the name implies, by controlling the balance of each color in relation to the others, you can change the hue and saturation of all the colors found within an image.

Final Cut Pro goes further by providing you with separate controls over the balance of the colors found in each of the three zones of luminance in an image, which allows you to make separate changes to the colors found in the blacks (such as shadows), those found in the mids (most of the image), and those in the whites (the bright areas and highlights). Each Color Balance control consists of a color wheel, at the center of which is a handle that allows you to make the necessary adjustments.

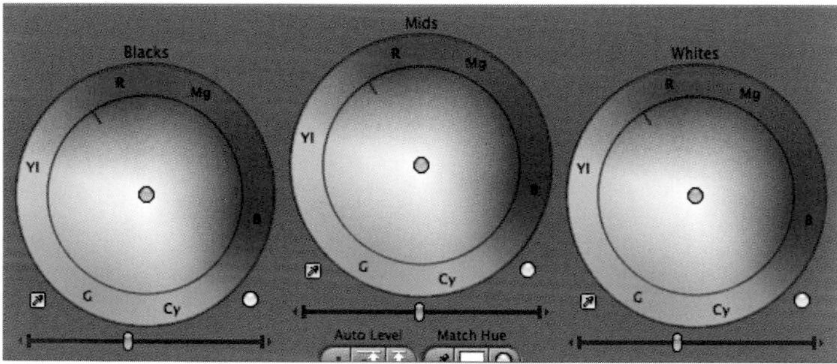

The contrast controls (the sliders beneath each wheel) help you ensure that the video is broadcast legal, but the Color Balance controls help you ensure that the colors in the image *look right*. For example, by manipulating the color balance within an image, you can make video shot with too much orange tint look more natural by neutralizing the tint.

Using Primary Color Correction

Ideally, color correction is an extension of the original cinematography. As a colorist, you are a collaborator in one step of the artistic process, and your ideas and contributions help shape the final look and emotional impact of the program. You will probably work with the director of photography (though not always) to establish a starting point for the color correction process, and the two of you may continue to finesse the images into their final form. It's also likely that the director or producer will have a say about the look of the program, and this input will weave its way into the creative process.

At other times, color correction may take the form of damage control, as you attempt to rescue footage that was shot under less than ideal conditions, or footage that was shot using an aesthetic that is no longer compatible with the project goals. Furthermore, the client may be relying on color correction to implement ideas that are too difficult or costly to execute on location.

Whatever the issues you need to address, color correction (also called *grading*), is generally broken down into two stages: *primary correction* and *secondary correction*. This lesson focuses on primary color correction, which involves adjusting the contrast and color balance of the overall image to achieve the desired look and feel. Secondary correction, when you isolate specific areas or colors in an image and modify them independently, is covered in *Apple Pro Training Series: Encyclopedia of Color Correction*.

In this lesson, you'll evaluate an image to determine *color casts* (hues affecting the overall image), one of the most common color issues you'll have to address. For example, this image may seem, at first glance, to be fine, but a closer examination will reveal a subtle blue cast from the shadows through the highlights.

Once you learn to identify a color cast in a clip, you'll work towards correcting it to create a clean, neutral look, where whites are pure and blacks are solid.

Whatever the overall look, the first, and sometimes only, step you need to take is to apply a single primary color correction.

Understanding the Color Balance Controls

Before you start pushing and pulling the color balance in your shots, take a few minutes to get a better understanding of the color wheel that's at the heart of the Color Balance controls. In doing so, you'll also learn how to better understand the Vectorscope, which displays a graph of the colors in your image against a backdrop of targets that are directly analogous to the color wheel.

In its various forms, the color wheel is an effective way to provide independent yet unified control over hue (color) and saturation (intensity of color). Once you understand how the color wheel represents the fundamental components of color, you can reliably predict and control the results of color adjustments.

Learning About the Color Wheel

The color wheel displays all of the possible hues around the outside of a circle. If you follow the edge of the color wheel, you can find the three *primary* colors: red, green, and blue.

The pure primaries are equally distant from one another, and they divide the color wheel into thirds.

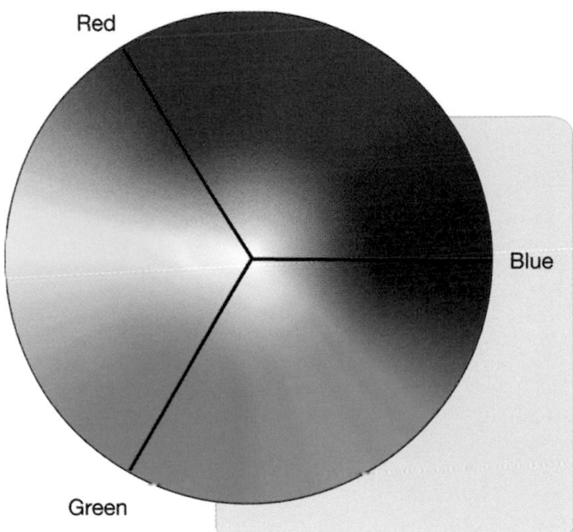

Video systems, regardless of the format, create color in an additive fashion, by mixing the three primaries together. The primary colors found on the color wheel correspond to the red, green, and blue components of a video signal; the red, green, and blue phosphors of a CRT display; and the red, green, and blue components of the pixels on a flat-screen monitor. (Incidentally, film also records color in three layers, or substrates, each of which is sensitive to red, green, and blue.)

By mixing these primary colors, any color of the rainbow can be displayed, and you can see this happening in the color wheel. As the primary colors blend together around the outer edge of the wheel, you can see other hues emerge.

An equal mixture of any two primaries creates the *secondary* colors on the color wheel. The three secondary colors are cyan, magenta, and yellow. For example, yellow (a secondary color) is a combination of green and red (both primaries).

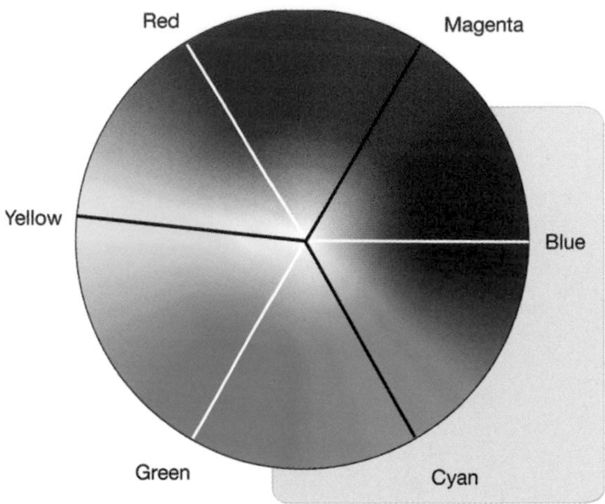

Notice that each secondary color falls directly opposite a primary color. Any two colors that are opposite one another—such as yellow and blue—on the color wheel are considered to be *complementary*.

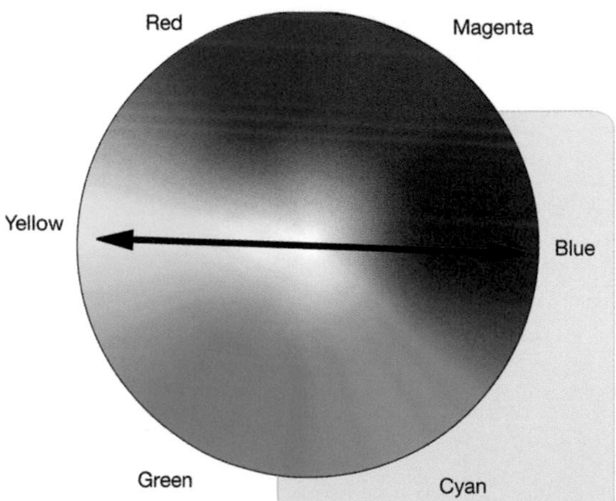

Combining any color with its complementary color on the wheel neutralizes it, effectively *desaturating* it. You can see this phenomenon represented in the color wheel—the outer edge of the wheel represents each hue at 100 percent saturation, and the center of the wheel has 0 percent saturation, which is represented by white.

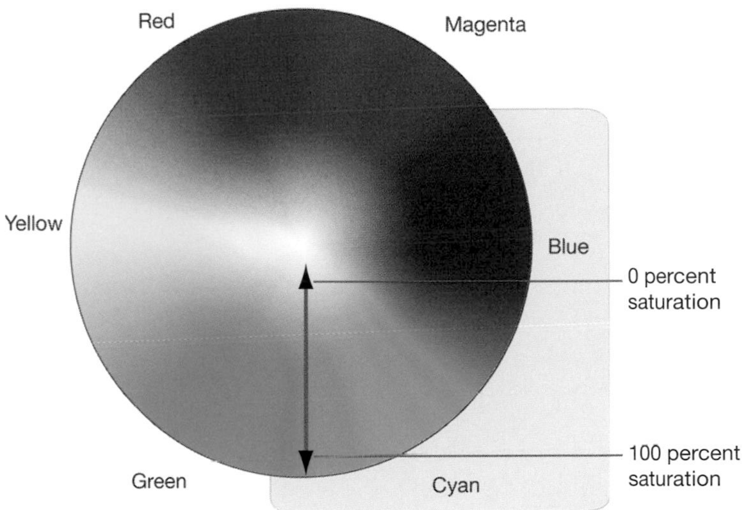

NOTE ► Even though 0 percent saturation is represented in the color wheel by white, it's important to remember that 0 percent saturation simply means an absence of color. Removing all saturation from an image does nothing to alter the luminance of the image, which may then consist of any shade of gray.

To effectively control colors with the Final Cut Pro color correction filters, you must understand the relationship between complementary colors, and the effect of blending them together.

Manipulating Color Channels with the Color Balance Control

This simple exercise will help you understand the color wheel's effect on an image and how those effects are displayed in the video scopes:

1 Open Lesson Files > Lesson 12 > **Color.fcp**.

   If it isn't already, set up your workspace to include the video scopes in the Tool Bench window.

2 Choose Window > Arrange > Color Correction to open the Video Scopes tab.

3 In the Layout pop-up menu, choose All to ensure all four scopes are visible.

4 Open the Exercise 01 - Color Wheel Basics bin.

5 Open the *Color Wheel Basics* sequence.

6 Double-click the first **Custom Gradient** clip in the sequence to open it into the Viewer. Then, at the top of the Viewer, click the Color Corrector tab.

   The first clip in the sequence is a custom gradient generator that's been set to a low, neutral gray. A Color Corrector filter has been applied to the clip, but all the parameters are still at their default, so it is not affecting the image.

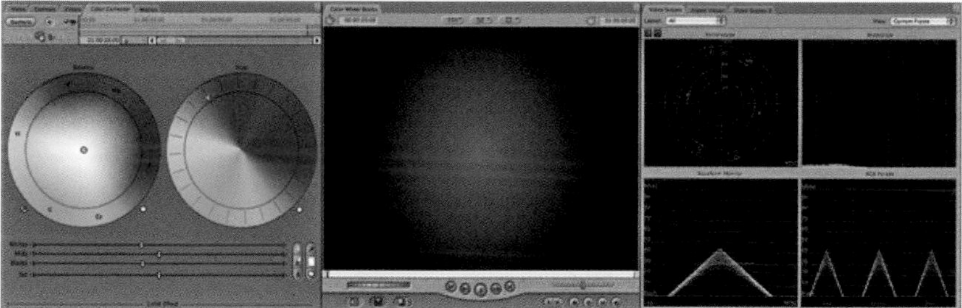

   The first thing you should notice in the Vectorscope is the lack of any graph whatsoever, which means that the image is completely desaturated. The second thing you should notice in the Parade scope is that each color channel is equally strong. This latter graph shows the additive nature of the red, green, blue primary color system—adding equal amounts of each color results in a neutral gray.

7 Click anywhere in the Color Balance control and drag toward the R (red) target.

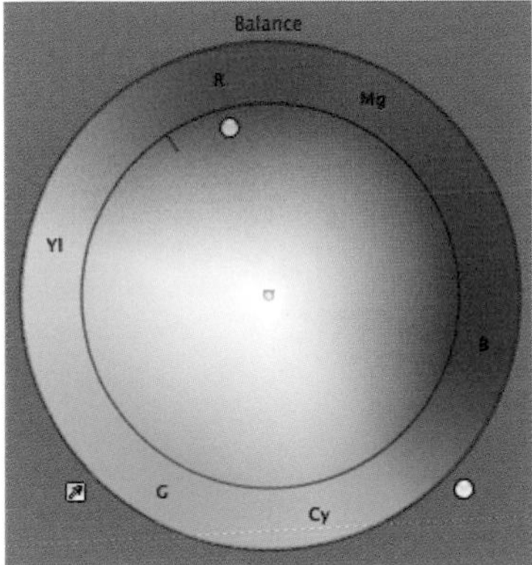

As you move the balance control handle, the image in the Canvas begins to turn red.

8 Control-click in the Vectorscope and choose Magnify from the shortcut menu.

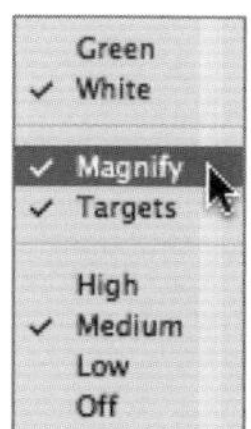

Because most adjustments you'll be making to an image happen close to the center of the Vectorscope, the Magnify setting lets you see the results in more detail.

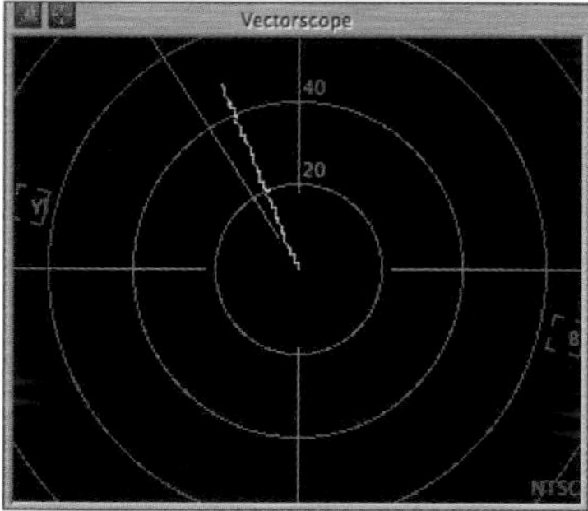

As you adjusted the Color Balance control, the graph in the Vectorscope stretched out in the same direction as the adjustment you made. The red channel, represented by the red graph in the Parade scope, also increased in intensity relative to the green and blue channels.

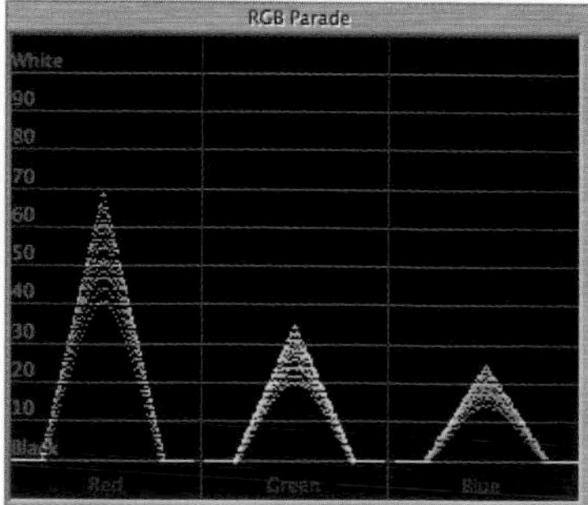

9 Click the Color Balance control and drag around the edge of the wheel towards the Cy (cyan) target. Watch the video scopes while you make the adjustment.

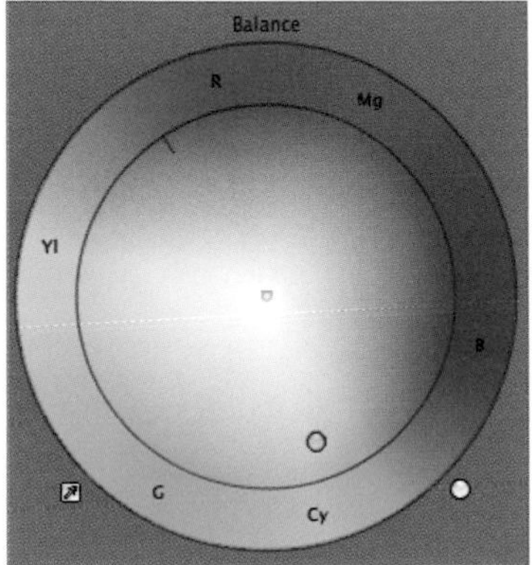

You can see the graph in the Vectorscope change to mirror the new direction of the balance control indicator. At the same time, you can see the three color channels in the Parade scope individually shift as you push and pull colors in each channel.

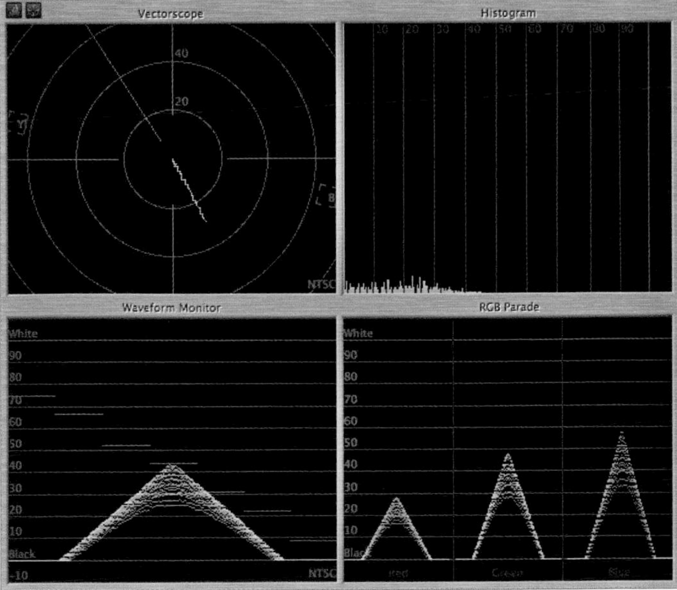

No matter what you do with the Color Balance control, and no matter how much the individual channel levels change in the Parade scope, the overall luminance of the image stays the same, as represented by the Waveform Monitor. This is an important concept. As its name implies, the Color Balance control lets you change the balance of colors in the red, green, and blue channels of an image, but the end result always has the same overall luminance.

More importantly, the Color Balance controls let you simultaneously rebalance the levels of all three color channels. This is an extremely powerful, and extremely fast, way to work.

10 Take a minute to make additional changes to the Color Balance controls, observing the changes in the picture and in the video scopes.

Adjusting Saturation and Neutralizing Colors with Their Complementary Colors

In this exercise, you'll use the Color Balance control to modify the saturation of a color and to neutralize any single color by adding it to its complementary color.

1 Press the Down Arrow key to navigate to the second clip in the *Color Wheel Basics* sequence. Double-click the second **Custom Gradient** clip to open it into the Viewer.

   This clip also has a Color Corrector filter applied.

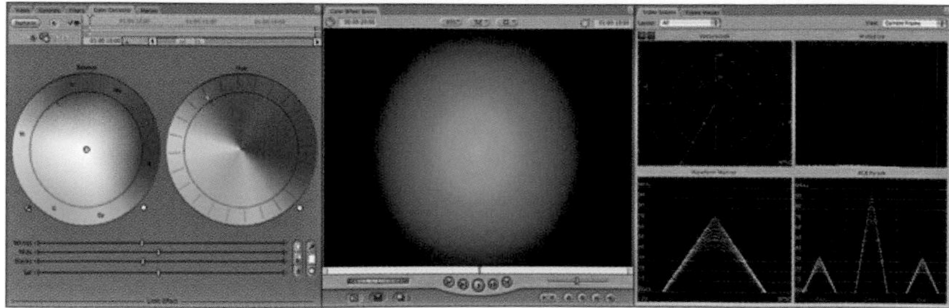

   This clip is a circular gradient, just like the first clip. However, this clip already has a clear green cast, which you can see in both the Vectorscope and Parade scope.

2 Click in the Color Balance control, and drag towards a point somewhere between the Mg (magenta) and B (blue) targets, so that the spike in the green channel of the Parade scope diminishes, while the blue and red spikes remain roughly the same height relative to one another.

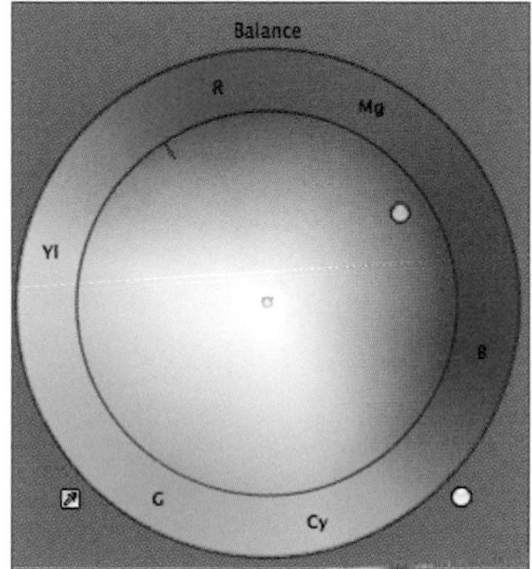

3 Stop dragging when the green has diminished but not quite faded completely, and look at the video scopes.

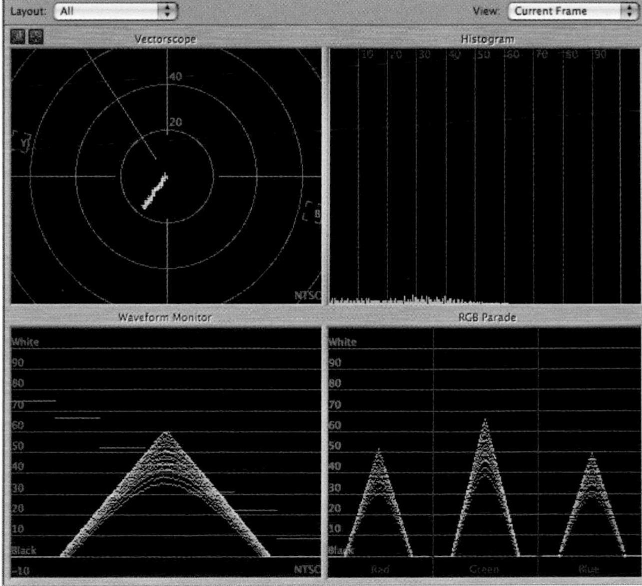

It's a little tricky to maintain the balance between the red and blue graphs in the Parade scope, while pulling down the green channel, but keep at it until you have roughly the result shown in the preceding figure.

By moving color balance in the opposite direction from the original green color, you've begun to desaturate the image, as you can see by the shortening of the graph in the Vectorscope. Because the balance between the red and blue spikes in the Parade scope is roughly equal, you can be sure that you're moving in the direction of purely neutralizing the image, rather than tinting it another color.

4 Immediately after you start to drag the balance control indicator to the right, hold down Shift and resume dragging, ever so slightly, until the three graphs in the Parade scope are the same height, and the graph in the Vectorscope is as close to the center as possible.

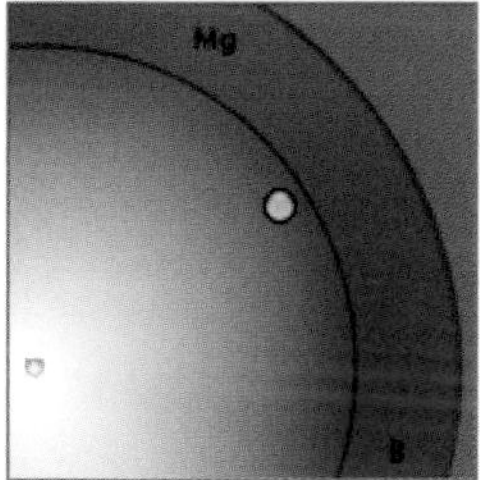

By Shift-dragging, you lock the angle of your adjustment. Because every hue is represented by an angle around the perimeter of the wheel, locking the angle lets you move the balance control indicator in and out from the center of the wheel to the edge, without changing its angle. This allows you to make saturation adjustments without also changing the hue of the image.

When you've made the adjustment, the gradient should appear nearly completely gray.

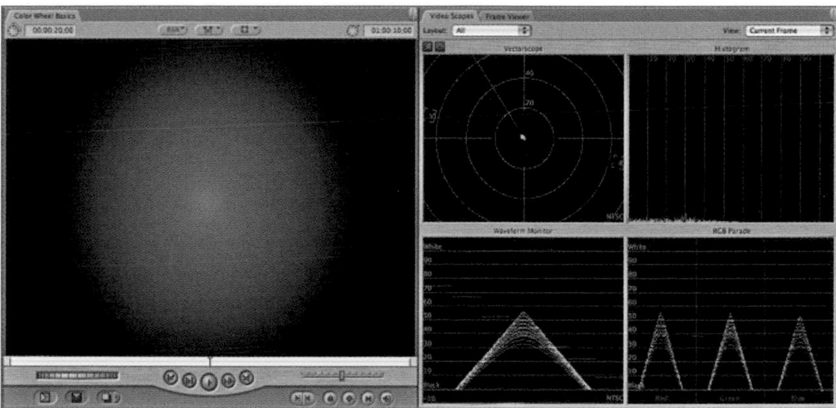

If the image is not gray, the channels as displayed in the Parade scope weren't balanced equally enough when you made the last change. Keep working at it until you've completely neutralized the color.

Feel free to continue experimenting with this last image until you get the hang of the technique. The most important thing to learn is that by moving a Color Balance control you can adjust each individual color channel of your image.

Even more important, the direction in which you rebalance colors with the Color Balance control is mirrored by the direction in which the graph moves in the Vectorscope. This direct relationship is a key element in your ability to predict necessary changes in color balancing.

Identifying and Correcting Color Casts

Have you ever taken a picture with a digital camera, or shot some video on vacation, only to get home and find that your footage is inexplicably orange, or blue, or green? What you're seeing is an incorrect white balance, often referred to as a *color cast.*

Every light source has a different *color temperature.* Each of the three types of light sources you'll typically encounter—incandescent (tungsten), fluorescent, and sunlight—produce light with spikes in different parts of the visible spectrum. Most of the time, you don't consciously notice these color temperatures, because the human eye is extremely adaptive and influenced by visual context. Generally, your perception of what is white and what is black is relative to the surrounding colors.

Film and video cameras are not usually so forgiving. Color casts are a result of the recording device not being correctly adjusted to interpret the color temperature of the dominant light source. With film, the film stock wasn't intended for the light source in use. With video, the white balance control was incorrectly set, or the automatic setting wasn't quite so automatic.

The results are sometimes obvious (The whites look orange!) and sometimes subtle (What's wrong with his face?); but, in any event, the colors in the image are not what was expected. No matter what your creative goals are for the color of an image, you generally want to begin with an image where the whites look white, the blacks look black, and faces look the way they're supposed to, instead of orange, or green, or blue.

For this reason, you must learn to spot a color cast, determine which color channel is creating a problem, and neutralize the cast using the Color Balance controls.

Identifying Color Casts

Colorists need to perceive nuances in color and color casts in an image, and know how to alter the colors to create a natural appearance. Although every colorist has subjective viewpoints on the use of color, finding a natural balance is often the first step to creating the final look of the video.

1. In the Browser, open the Exercise 02 - Auto Balance bin and double-click the *Auto Balance Exercise* sequence.

NOTE ▶ This lesson assumes that you are working on a calibrated external NTSC monitor. A computer monitor does not provide a true representation of the actual NTSC broadcast image. If your system is PAL, or you don't have an external monitor, you may complete this exercise using your computer's monitor, but be aware that it is not accurate for finishing purposes, and the resulting images will not look the same when output to broadcast video. If you have an SDI out from your video card and a DVI-D display, with the right adapter/converter, you can get a pretty reliable monitoring solution, although not 100 percent accurate.

2 In the Video Scopes tab, make sure that the Layout pop-up menu is set to All.

3 Before you do anything else, take a close look at the image in the Canvas.

Your first impression is extremely important. The longer you look at any image, the more your eyes adapt to the relative differences between the colors in the frame, and the less sensitive you'll be to a color cast in the picture.

You need to get into the habit of asking the following three questions:

- Do the shadows seem pure black, or are they slightly tinted?
- Do things that should be pure white seem properly desaturated?
- Do people's faces look healthy and natural, or do they look faded, tired, or motion-sick?

If the answer to these is a collective no, as it should be in this image, you need to quantify the problem. In this case, you may have noticed that the image has a slightly blue, cool quality to it. To confirm your suspicions, it's time to look at the video scopes to determine exactly what the problem is.

4 Look at the video scopes.

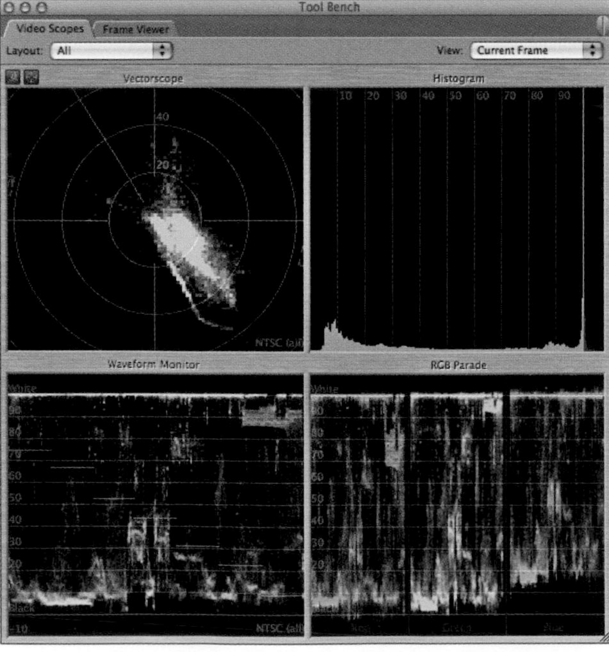

You'll notice that the image is well exposed, with a wide contrast ratio that stretches from 0 percent (black) all the way to 100 percent (white). Furthermore, there is an enormous amount of detail throughout the mids. From the clustering at the top of the Waveform Monitor, however, you can surmise that there's a bit of overexposure, and the huge spike to the right of the Histogram at the 100 percent line confirms that there's an excess of white in the image.

As far as color casts go, however, the scopes reveal two telltale signs that the image is too blue. Before going on to the next step, see if you can guess what they are.

5 From the Layout pop-up menu, choose Parade.

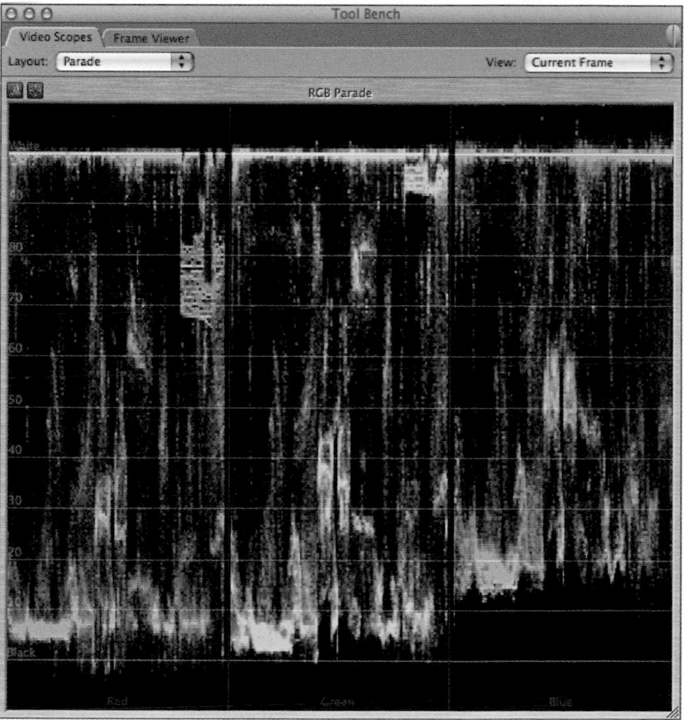

In many cases when there are abundant blacks and whites in the image, the three graphs that represent the red, green, and blue channels in the Parade scope look somewhat similar, in terms of their overall shape. Clearly, the mids will vary considerably, but because blacks represent an absence of all three colors, and whites represent the presence of all three colors, the tops and bottoms of each of the three graphs should fall roughly in the same places.

6 Carefully examine the top of the blue waveform.

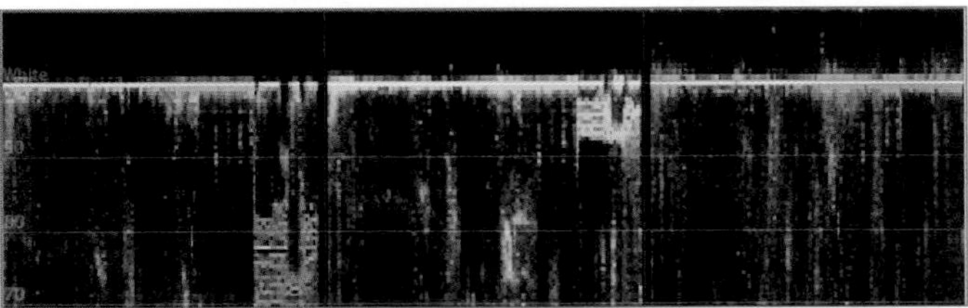

This confirms the problem. While the Waveform Monitor shows you the average luminance of all three color channels together, the Parade scope shows you that the blues in this image are considerably stronger than the reds and greens. The bottom of the Parade scope shows that the blue channel is lighter in the blacks, which explains why the blacks seem somewhat washed out, even though parts of the Waveform Monitor extend all the way to the bottom.

7 From the Layout pop-up menu, choose Vectorscope. Control-click the Vectorscope and deselect Magnify in the shortcut menu.

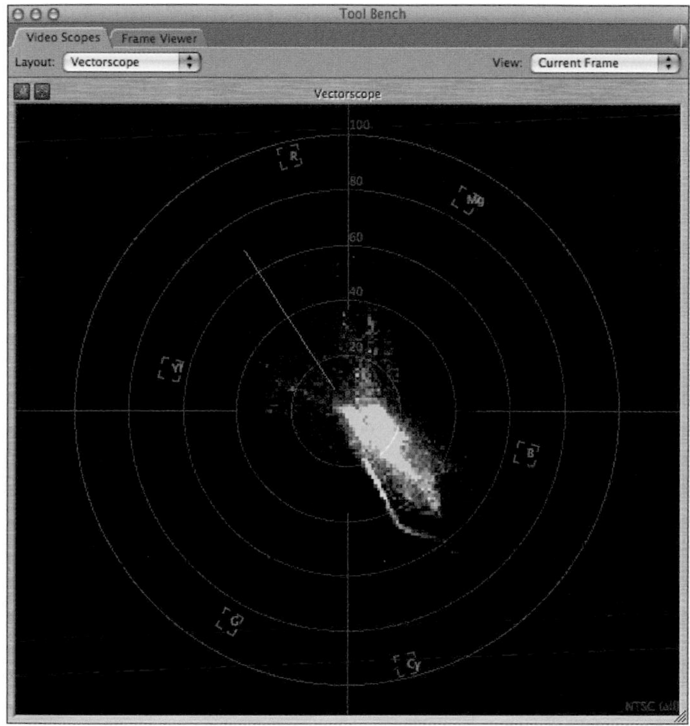

If you didn't have enough proof already, here's the smoking gun. In an image featuring three people, there are no traces clustered around the Flesh Tone line (the diagonal line in the upper-left quadrant) in the Vectorscope.

Furthermore, even though there is a lot of color in the Canvas (the reds and yellows in the clown's outfit and on the phone signage) the entire graph within the Vectorscope seems oddly uncentered, and in fact is offset in the direction of blue and cyan.

Although you can oftentimes identify a color cast by sight, the Parade scope and the Vectorscope are your best tools for correctly identifying the type, and severity, of a color cast in any image. Even though you may develop your eye to accurately spot the hue of a color cast, the scopes are still useful for revealing just how much correction you need to make, based on the numbers.

Correcting Color Casts with the Auto-Balance Eyedroppers

Now that you've identified an improper color cast, you'll want to eliminate it before taking any other steps. To expedite the process, the Color Corrector 3-way filter provides three Select Auto-balance Color buttons that can automatically rebalance an image to make the blacks and whites neutral and rich.

1 Open the **Phone_Call.mov** clip into the Viewer and click the Color Corrector 3-Way tab.

2 In the Video Scopes tab, choose All from the Layout pop-up menu.

You're now set to start correcting this clip. You'll notice a small eyedropper button at the bottom left of each Color Balance control in the Viewer. These are the Select Auto-balance Color buttons—one corresponds to each zone of luminance.

The most important of these buttons corresponds to the blacks and whites. Whenever you use the automatic balancing controls in Final Cut Pro, you want to start where the color cast is most noticeable. In this case, it's in the blacks.

3 Click the Blacks Select Auto-balance Color button so that it is highlighted.

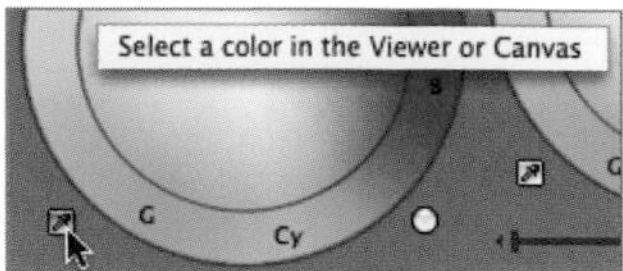

When you click the button, a tooltip appears with an instruction. What the instruction doesn't tell you is that you need to select an area that's supposed to be pure black.

This is an important decision, and it's not as easy as it may seem. You want to select an area that you think corresponds as closely to solid black as possible. In particular, because there's a color cast, you want to select an area that is *supposed* to be black, even if it doesn't appear to be so at first. In this image, there are several candidates: the woman's black dress, the shadow in the phone kiosk, or the color of the man's trousers. Each of these black areas is slightly different, however, and will yield different results.

4 Click in the shadows of the phone kiosk.

Immediately, three things happen. The most noticeable event is that the image immediately looks more natural.

If you look in the Color Corrector tab, you'll see that the balance control indicator in the Blacks Color Balance control has moved to the left, toward yellow. As you learned earlier, yellow is the complementary of blue, so this small adjustment neutralizes the cast in the blacks.

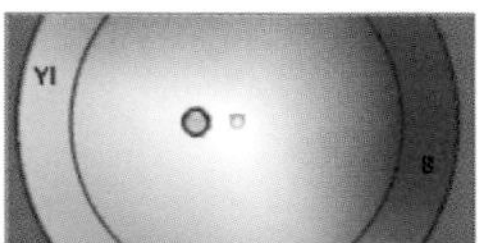

5 Look at the Parade scope.

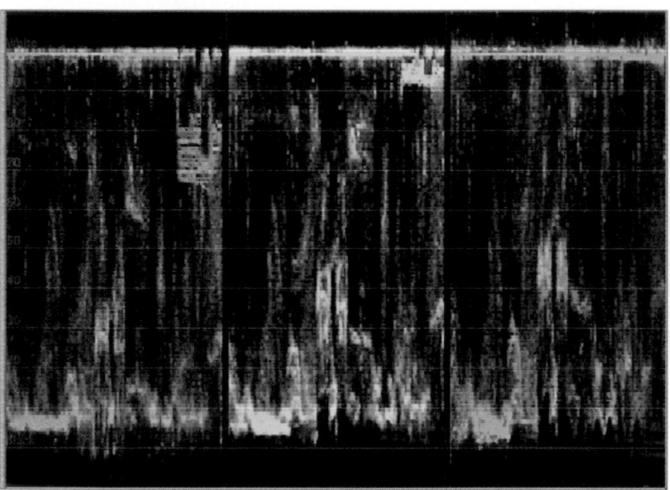

You should notice two things. First, the bottom of the blue graph now approximately matches the level of the red and green graphs. Second, the whites are still out of whack. Work remains to be done.

6 Click the Whites Select Auto-balance Color button to the left of the Whites Color Balance control.

Now, you want to click a region in the image that's supposed to be white. That seems easy enough, because there's plenty of white in the image.

7 In the Canvas, click the side of the white building.

Nothing happened! How can this be? The Parade scope clearly shows a blue cast in the whites. This situation illustrates an important rule you need to remember when you use the Whites Select Auto-balance Color button.

8 Press Control-Z to turn on luminance range checking in the Canvas (or choose View > Range Check > Excess Luma).

You now can clearly see that the area you tried to select is overexposed. When digital video is overexposed, the result is that all values over the maximum digital limit are clipped, and the resulting parts of the image are pure white. These areas will not have the color cast you're trying to correct because they're artificially white. Extreme whites that are likely to be overexposed—such as lens flares, glints, or hot highlights—are not good candidates for the Whites Auto-balance eyedropper.

You need to pick a new area of the picture. The shirt of the man standing next to the clown seems like a good choice. It's not overexposed, and it clearly looks like it has the blue cast you're trying to eliminate.

9 Press Control-Z to turn off luminance range checking in the Canvas.

10 Click the Whites Reset button to the right of the Whites Color Balance control.

11 Click the Whites Select Auto-balance Color button, and then click the man's shirt.

Immediately, you should see another unexpected problem.

Instead of correcting all of the whites in the image, it turns them unexpectedly sepia. If you look at the Parade scope, the balance has been horribly skewed. Apparently the shirt is supposed to have a slightly higher blue level. You need to find something else that is supposed to be white.

12 Click the Whites Reset button next to the Whites Color Balance control.

Next, try the phone logo on the side of the phone kiosk.

TIP Zoom in on the Canvas to make it easier to click smaller regions of white in an image. Press Z to select the Zoom tool, and click twice on the phone logo.

13 Click the Whites Select Auto-balance Color button, and then click the whitest group of pixels within the phone.

The result is a compromise. The building has become warmer, but this may be due to the quality of light at that time of day, or the fact that the paint on the building is a warmer shade of white. (In either case, a quick chat with the director of photography should clear that up.)

The important thing is that the faces, which seemed anemic before, are now looking a little healthier, which is confirmed by the graph in the Vectorscope. Unfortunately, in this example, there is no absolute benchmark for the accuracy of this correction, and it becomes a matter of preference and experience.

As you can see, the effectiveness of the Auto-balance eyedroppers is highly dependent on selecting the right pixels in the image. This process may involve some detective work on your part.

Sampling from the Mids

When correcting color casts, you typically need to adjust only two Color Balance controls to balance the image. Why? Because the Whites Color Balance control primarily affects the top 75 percent of the image. (The influence of this control falls off at this point, fading out around 10 percent luminance.) Everything from dark-gray shades of color up to white is affected.

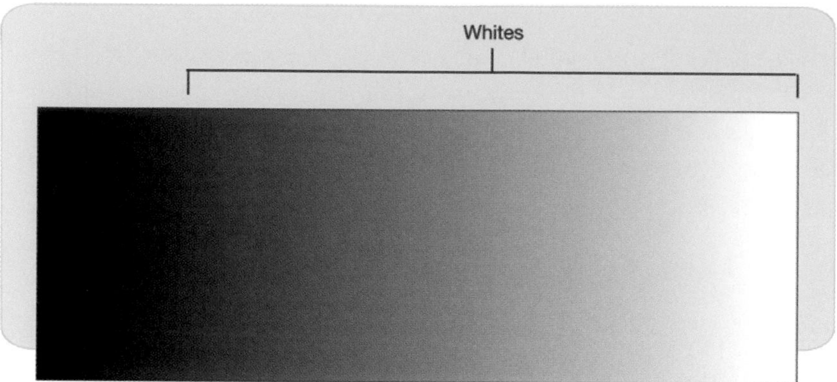

You probably noticed, however, that there are three eyedroppers, and so far you've ignored the one for mids.

In general, you should begin to color balance a scene by working in the whites or the mids to make the scene natural and realistic. Then, depending on the scene, additional adjustments may or may not be necessary.

If there is nothing white in the frame, your next best bet is to sample something that is as close to 50 percent gray as possible using the Mids Auto-balance eyedropper. The mids typically make up a large percentage of an image, and the Mids Color Balance control has influence over the colors falling between 10 percent and 90 percent luminance, with the maximum area of influence being the center 75 percent.

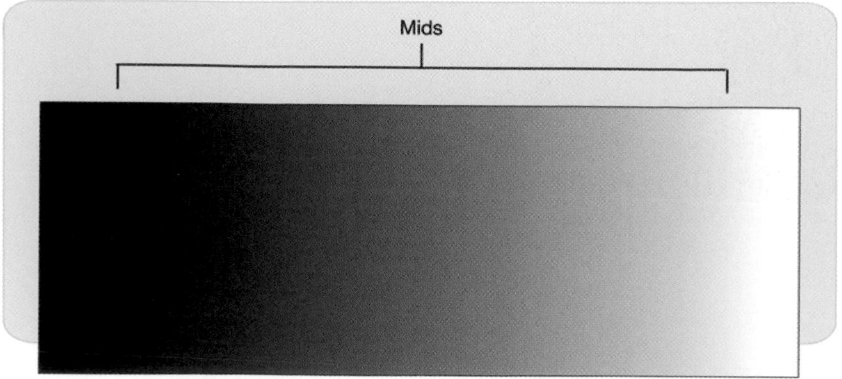

If the entire image is lit with light of the same color temperature, you may get away with balancing just the mids. The advantage of doing the primary color balancing with the mids is that you can avoid overly tinting the bright whites or deep blacks, if these regions are relatively free from color casts. This is, of course, highly dependent on the distribution of color throughout the three luminance zones of the image. Every image is different and requires a unique approach.

TIP When dealing with strong, saturated colors, the Whites Color Balance control has the strongest influence on yellow, cyan, and green. The Blacks Color Balance control has the strongest influence on red, blue, and magenta.

Manipulating Color Directly in the Blacks, Mids, and Whites

As you've seen, the Final Cut Pro color correction filters let you separately manipulate the colors in the blacks, midtones, and whites zones of an image.

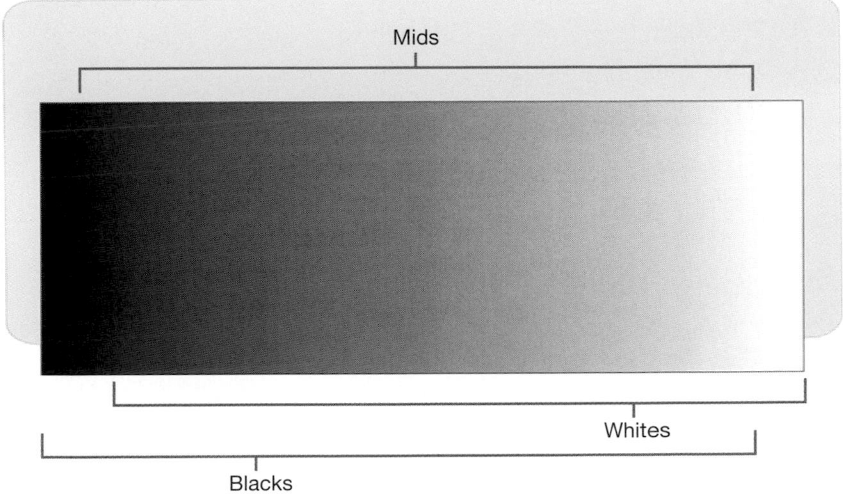

Any control that targets the blacks will affect only colors found in the shadows of the image, from full black up into the mid-gray tones.

Any control that targets the whites will affect only colors found in the highlights, from the mid-gray tones up to white.

Any control that targets the mids affects all the colors found in the midrange of the image, which constitutes the largest percentage of the viewing area.

These three zones have a great deal of overlap. For example, the controls that affect the mids extend their influence into the blacks and whites, but the effect tapers off before reaching the extreme blacks and whites, in order to preserve the ultimate black and white points you want to define.

Learning Each Color Wheel's Zone of Influence

Before moving to a practical example of color balancing, you'll do one last grayscale exercise. (It's the last one, we promise!) This time you'll explore the amount of overlap exerted by each color control.

1. In the Browser, open the Exercise 03 - Blacks, Mids, Whites bin.

2. Double-click the *Blacks, Mids, Whites* sequence.

3. Double-click the **Gradient** clip in the sequence to open it into the Viewer, and then click the Color Corrector 3-way tab at the top of the Viewer. (A Color Corrector 3-way filter has already been applied.)

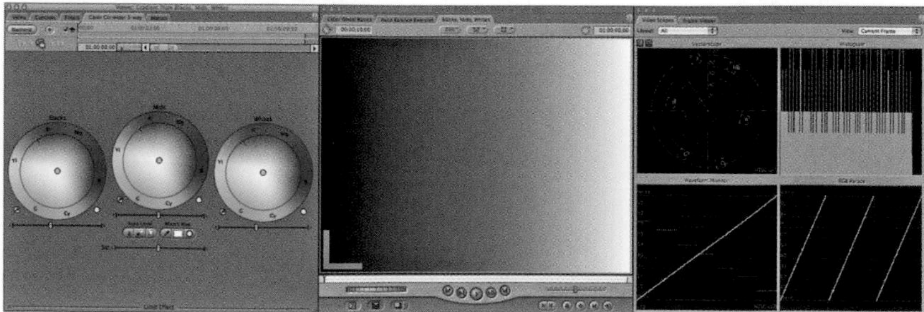

The clip you'll be working on first is another linear gradient generator, this time with the black on the left and the white on the right. It's an ideal way to see the effect each color control has on an image, stretching from absolute black to absolute white.

4 Click in the Blacks Color Balance control, and drag the balance control indicator in any direction to tint the blacks within the image. It's not necessary to drag all the way to the edge, just drag until the blacks are well tinted.

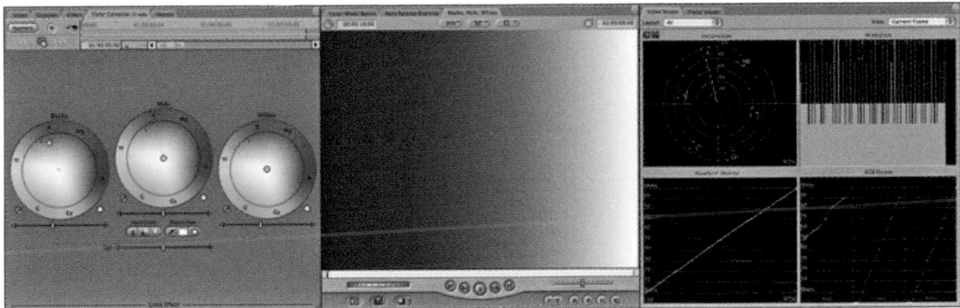

As you can see, the Blacks Color Balance control actually influences color well into mids. It's important to see, however, that this influence tapers off gently towards the end, so that by 80 percent luminance the control is barely having an effect, and this control has absolutely no effect on the upper 10 percent of whites.

5 Click the Blacks Reset button.

6 Drag the Mids balance control indicator in any direction.

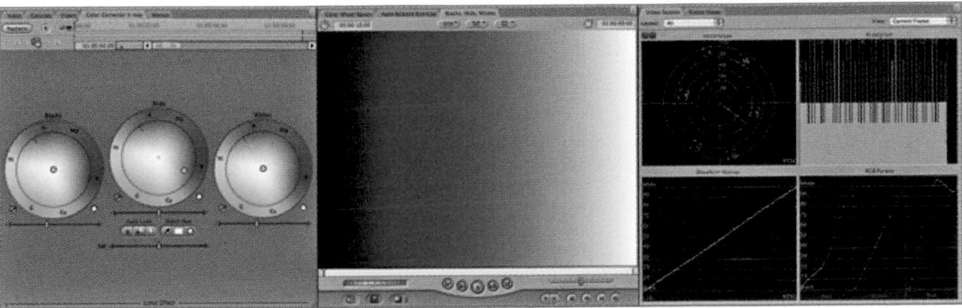

Predictably, you can see that the mids area of influence is strongest in the center region of luminance, tapering off at the blacks and whites, leaving them unaffected.

7 Click the Mids Reset button.

8 Drag the Whites balance control indicator in any direction.

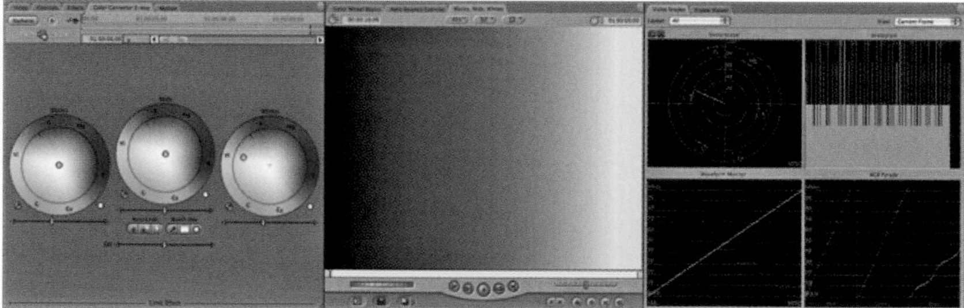

The effect of the whites adjustment is pretty much the inverse of the blacks, such that the lower 10 percent of the luminance range remains unaffected.

9 Take a minute to play around with all of the Color Balance controls at once, and observe how the colors mix together.

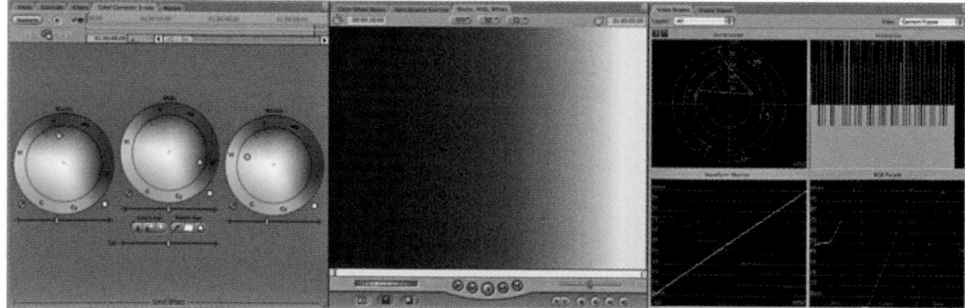

You can see that the blacks and whites both have a profound effect on the mids, yet a strong mids adjustment still manages to create a unique tint at the center of the gradient. Furthermore, you should also observe that the extreme blacks and whites remain unaffected by changes to either of the opposing controls.

You should now have a complete understanding of how the three Color Balance controls allow you to influence the color balance in each of the three zones of luminance. It's time for you to put this knowledge to a real-world test.

Color Balancing Zones of Luminance in an Image

Now you're going to use everything you've learned to color correct a shot manually, without using any automatic controls. In the process, you'll see that, with practice (and the help of the video scopes), it is often easier and faster to manually address color casts and other issues within an image.

1 Open the *Color Balancing Zones* sequence.

2 Double-click the **Phone_Call_CU.mov** clip in the sequence to open it into the Viewer, then at the top of the Viewer click the Color Corrector 3-way tab. (A Color Corrector 3-way filter has already been applied.)

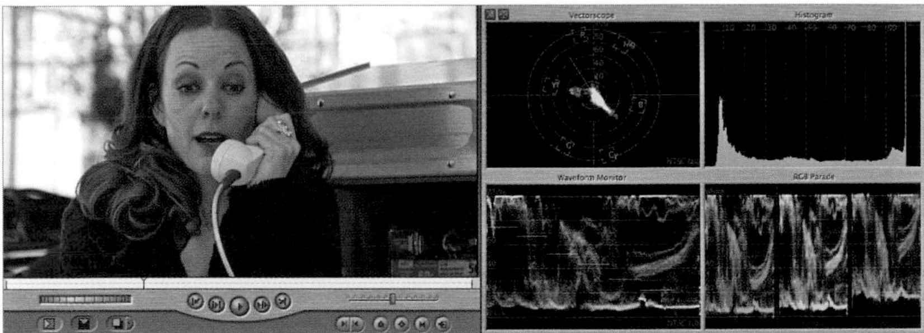

Ordinarily, you would first adjust the contrast with the Blacks, Whites, and Mids sliders. In this case, you're lucky, the shot has exactly the contrast the client wants, so you can skip this step.

3 Look at the Parade scope.

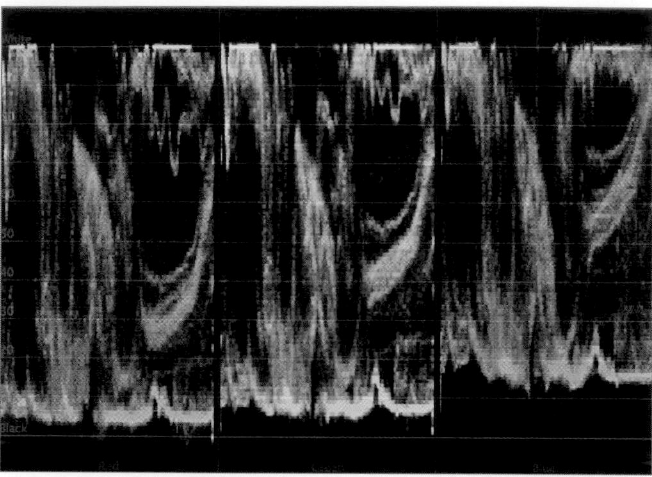

The Parade scope reveals that the blacks have abnormally high blue levels, so this is the first thing you'll need to address.

4 Look at the Vectorscope.

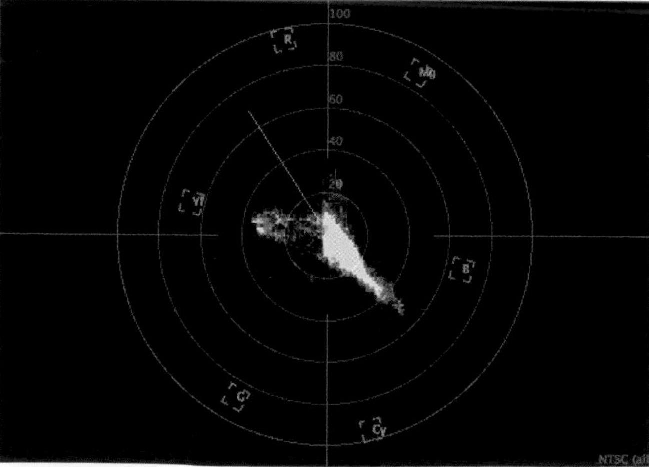

The scope reveals an offset into the blues. This provides you with a valuable clue about how to resolve the color cast issue.

5 Look at the Blacks Color Balance control, and find the direction of the complementary color to the biggest spike in the Vectorscope.

This tells you the direction in which you want to drag the Blacks balance control indicator to neutralize the color cast.

6 Drag the balance control indicator in the direction of the complementary color, in this case, somewhere between yellow and red.

Keep dragging, with one eye on your image, another eye on the Vectorscope (to keep track of the overall shift in hue), and a third eye on the bottoms of the three graphs in the Parade scope to make sure they become relatively balanced.

Don't worry if you don't drag the control very far. In real-world images, you'll typically find that very small changes in the Color Balance controls have a very big impact.

TIP At first, you may not notice any movement while dragging a balance control indicator. By default, the balance control indicators in the color correction filters move in very small increments, which is appropriate for most corrections. If necessary, you can Command-drag to make adjustments in larger increments.

When you're happy with the quality of the blacks, it's time to work on the whites.

7 Because the color cast in the whites is also in the blues, also move the balance control indicator towards a point between yellow and red.

This time, as you drag, keep your eye on the woman's skin color. Because of the large degree of overlap between the whites and mids, this is an opportunity to warm up some of the highlights on her face.

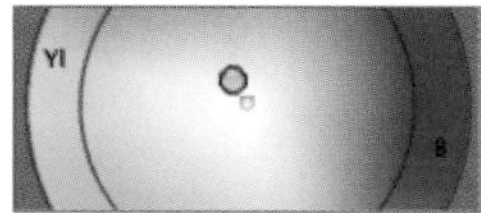

As you make this adjustment, you'll run into the same problem you saw earlier, when the building you thought was white began to turn sepia. It can be helpful to spot something else in the picture that is being affected by the whites color cast. This image has few whites, but there are some highlights on the ring on her finger that can serve as a rough guide.

Again, don't be surprised if you find yourself making a small adjustment to avoid severely tinting the background. In color correction, a little goes a long way. In any event, keep your change minimal, because there's one more step you can take.

8 In the Video Scopes tab, choose Vectorscope from the Layout pop-up menu.

For the last step in this procedure, you're going to boost the red channel in the mids to make the woman pop out a little more from the background. As you do this, keep a close eye on the Vectorscope, so you can keep track of how closely her adjusted skin tones come to the Flesh Tone line.

9 Drag the Mids balance control indicator in the direction of the complementary color, in this case, somewhere between yellow and red.

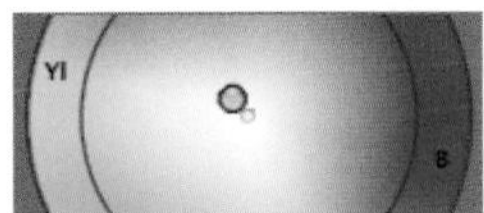

This will be your most subtle adjustment of all. You want to drag the balance control indicator out far enough to add more color to her face and some luster to her hair, but you don't want to move it out so far that the image turns brown.

NOTE ▶ If at any point you feel that you're doing more harm than good, don't get frustrated. It's easy for your eyes to get tired after looking at the same color shifts for a long time. Just click the Mids Reset button and start over.

As you drag the balance control indicator, keep your eye on the Vectorscope. You'll see her flesh tones near the Flesh Tone line, but they don't have to lie directly on the line. Indeed, if they did, she might look a little sallow. In this case, having the traces of the Vectorscope fall just above the Flesh Tone line seem to produce the most pleasing results, but this is a matter of interpretation.

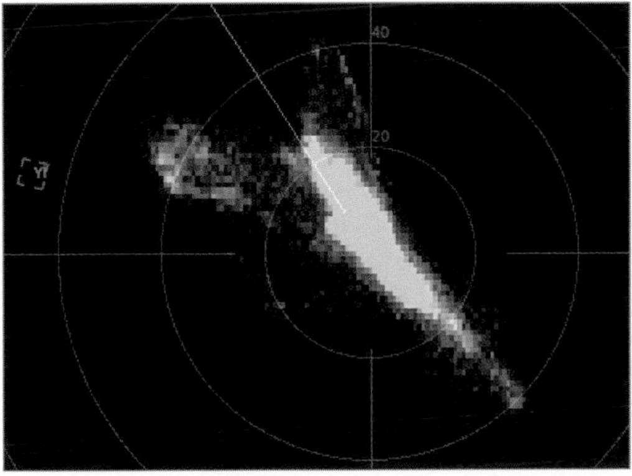

With this last adjustment, you're finished!

10 To see the before and after for this exercise (which is quite dramatic), select and deselect the Enable Filter checkbox beside the "eye" icon at the top of the Color Corrector tab.

In this lesson, you've learned how to perform the most common color correction task there is—identifying color casts in images and adjusting them. You've learned some of the most common ways of spotting problems in your images by using the video scopes, and you've learned precise methods of adjusting the different regions of an image, based on the luminance zone that a particular set of colors happens to fall into.

The **Color.fcp** project file contains a sequence called *Color Balancing Zones—Completed* that contains a finished version of this lesson. You can compare your own work to the color corrections in that version.

Lesson Review

1. What is primary color correction?
2. What is a color cast?
3. Which color channels does the Mids Color Balance control affect?
4. What happens when you mix a color with its complementary color?
5. If the traces in the Vectorscope extend all the way out to the 80 percent ring, what does that mean?
6. If the bottoms of the three graphs in the Parade scope are all around 0 percent, but they aren't lining up, which Color Balance control should you adjust to correct the apparent color cast?
7. Which two Select Auto-balance Color controls should you use first?
8. Do the areas affected by the Color Balance controls overlap?

Answers

1. The first adjustment of the contrast and color balance of the overall image.
2. An unwanted color that appears to tint the image.
3. Trick question. Each Color Balance control affects all color channels together.
4. They neutralize each other.
5. The image is very highly saturated.
6. The Blacks Color Balance control.
7. The Blacks and Whites.
8. Yes.

13

Lesson Files	Lesson Files > Lesson 13 > SceneContinuity.fcp
Media	Bar Scene
Time	This lesson takes approximately 120 minutes to complete.
Goals	Use comparison to aid in color matching Color correct a scene from beginning to end Learn a workflow for color matching Use Frame Viewer, Copy Filter controls, and playhead sync during color correction

Lesson **13**

Color Correcting for Scene Continuity

Now that you've learned the many methods of evaluating and correcting individual images, it's time to move on to the bigger picture—correcting an entire scene from beginning to end.

You will begin, as always, by correcting a single shot using the methods covered in the previous lessons. Then, to create a sense of visual consistency among each coverage shot, you'll use the same tools, with some new techniques, to match the look of the initially corrected shot to every clip in the scene.

Achieving Visual Harmony

In a dramatic program, most scenes portray an event that takes place at a single time, in a single place. As such, the general intensity and color of the lighting should be the same from shot to shot.

This is often at odds with the logistics of filmmaking, where the light may be quite different from one angle of coverage to another. It's especially true for projects shot outdoors using available light. If the scene took several hours to shoot, the quality of light in Actor 1's close-up may be very different from the quality of light filmed two hours later in Actor 2's reverse close-up.

When the lighting is different in two consecutive shots, the cut between those shots becomes noticeable. The audience may not understand why, but they'll notice a difference, and this will defeat the editor and filmmaker's goal of achieving seamless continuity. Any discontinuity in the look of consecutive images can be jarring and may take the viewer out of the moment as surely as a poorly timed edit.

Visual harmony is important for many types of programs. Reality TV, documentaries, and interview shows all aim to integrate footage shot in different lighting conditions into a coherent whole. Although there may be no real need to fool anyone into thinking that the shots happened at the same time and place, any unjustified change in lighting or color from one shot to the next can distract viewers from the flow of the program and the point you're trying to make.

Regardless of the lighting variances or the color of the source media, the color correction tools you use to make corrections to a single clip can also balance the colors of multiple clips in a scene. In this way, you can impose a seamless continuity that may be lacking in the original edit, so that every angle appears to be in exactly the same time and place, and every clip fits together.

Getting Started

1. Open Lesson Files > Lesson 13 > **SceneContinuity.fcp.**

   If your workspace isn't already set up to include the video scopes in the Tool Bench window, set this up now.

2 Choose Window > Arrange > Color Correction to arrange your layout to accommodate the Video Scopes tab.

Comparing Two Clips

It may sound obvious, but before you can correct one clip to match another, you must be able to compare both images in such a way as to quickly and accurately identify their differences. Before getting started with color correcting a scene, you'll spend a little time familiarizing yourself with clip comparison techniques in Final Cut Pro.

Toggling Between Images in the Canvas

The process of comparing two images is deceptively simple. It's always essential to judge the quality of an image using a calibrated broadcast-quality monitor, and not your computer's display, but it's even more critical when you start balancing the color of an entire scene.

For this reason, the most reliable and accurate method for comparing two images is also the simplest solution: flipping back and forth between two clips while watching the images change on your broadcast monitor.

The Show Edit commands allow you to temporarily jump to other edit points in the Timeline and then return to the frame at the initial position of the playhead:

- Show Previous Edit (Control–Up Arrow) toggles the last frame of the clip located immediately to the left in the Timeline.
- Show 2nd Prior Edit (Shift-Control–Up Arrow) toggles to the last frame of the second clip to the left in the Timeline.
- Show Next Edit (Control–Down Arrow) toggles to the first frame of the clip immediately to the right.
- Show 2nd Next Edit (Shift-Control–Down Arrow) toggles to the first frame of the second clip to the right.

- Show In Point (Control–Left Arrow) toggles the display of an In point only if you have defined an In point in the Timeline or Canvas.
- Show Out Point (Control–Right Arrow) toggles the display of an Out point only if you have defined an Out point in the Timeline or Canvas.

In this exercise, you'll practice using these keyboard shortcuts to compare shots in an edited sequence.

1 If you have an external broadcast monitor connected to your computer, make sure that it's set up properly, and that External Video is set to All Frames.

2 With the *Scene 1* sequence open, move the playhead to the third clip of the sequence, **Side Wide Angle (02).**

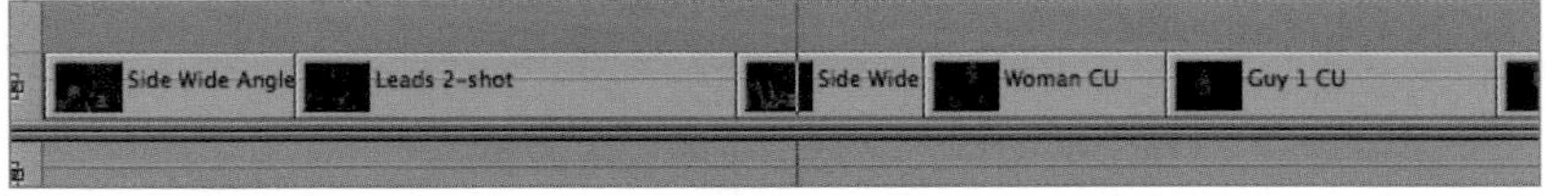

Its image appears simultaneously in the Canvas and in the broadcast monitor.

3 Hold down Control–Up Arrow.

The playhead immediately jumps to the last frame of the previous clip, showing you how the last image from the previous clip will segue into the current clip.

NOTE ► If the Show Edit keyboard commands don't respond, move the playhead off the first frame of the clip and repeat the command.

4 Release the keys you've been holding.

The playhead goes back to its initial position.

5 Press Control–Up Arrow a few times, and notice how you can flip back and forth between each image, getting an instant sense of the differences between color and brightness.

When you quickly jump back and forth between images, your eyes don't have time to adjust to each image, which makes it easier to spot variations.

As you flip between images, glance at the video scopes, and notice how they update with the image. You can use the Show Edit commands to compare images numerically, as well as visually, by flipping between their graphs on the scopes. This is an important technique that you'll be using often.

6 Hold down Shift-Control Up Arrow.

This time, the playhead jumps to the last frame of the second clip to the left. When correcting a scene with many angles of coverage, pressing Control–Up Arrow and Shift-Control–Up Arrow lets you quickly compare many different clips to get a sense of the colors throughout the scene.

7 Release the keys you've been holding, and press Control–Down Arrow and then Shift-Control–Down Arrow, to jump to the clips to the right of the current playhead position.

These commands are very useful when you're balancing shots that appear next to one another in a sequence. But if you want to balance clips that appear in entirely different parts of your program, you'll need to use the Show In Point and Show Out Point commands.

8 Set an In point at the current playhead position.

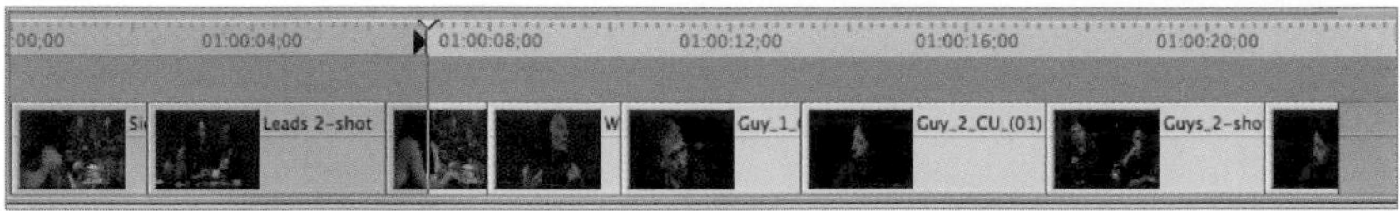

9 Park the playhead anywhere on the last clip in the sequence.

10 Hold down Control–Left Arrow.

The playhead jumps to the In point. This shortcut is useful for comparing two clips that are separated from one another in a sequence. It's also good for comparing the current frame with a specific frame in an adjacent clip, and not just In or Out points.

Making Side-by-Side Comparisons with the Frame Viewer

Another useful tool for comparing two images is the split-screen function found in the Final Cut Pro Frame Viewer.

As you have learned, the Frame Viewer lets you display other edit points relative to the current position of the playhead. The Frame Viewer also lets you compare two images *within the same frame* using a split-screen mode.

1 Move the playhead to the first clip in the sequence.

2 In the Tool Bench window, click the Frame Viewer tab.

By default, the Frame Viewer is set to a vertical split-screen mode, showing the current frame with filters on the left side of the frame, and the current frame without filters on the right. No filters are applied to the current clip, so there's no visible split in the image.

Like the View options in the video scopes, the Frame Viewer is flexible enough to compare a range of images in split-screen mode. The two pop-up menus underneath the image frame itself let you assign images to each part of the split-screen mode.

3 From the pop-up menu at the lower right of the Frame Viewer (next to the blue square), choose Next Edit.

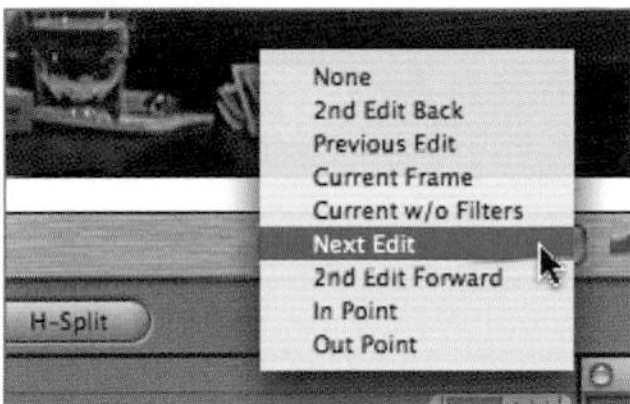

The left side of the Frame Viewer screen now displays the current frame, and the right side displays the first frame of the next clip to the right. As you saw in the menu, there are numerous options for comparing clips in your sequence, most of which correspond to the Show Edit commands you used previously.

If you look carefully at the corners that define the left half of the split screen, you'll see four square, color-coded handles. Each control and menu in the Frame Viewer is color-coded green or blue. These colors correspond to each of the two pop-up menus at the bottom of the Frame Viewer. The pop-up menus define which clips in the Timeline appear in each half of the frame, and they relate to the timecode values (at the top of the Frame Viewer) that show you which frames are being viewed.

In the current split-screen view, you can see that there is a color discontinuity between the two shots, but it may be difficult to make an "apples to apples" comparison because there is no single visual element shared by both images. Fortunately, you can customize the split between the two images.

4 At the bottom of the Frame Viewer window, click the H-Split button.

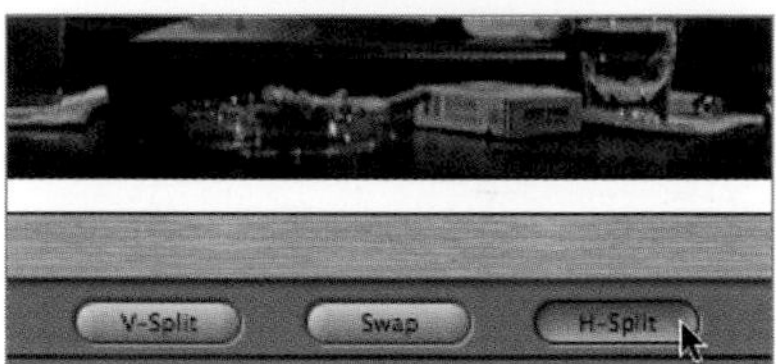

Now, instead of the vertical split screen, there is a horizontal split screen.

If you're ever confused about which clip is in which part of the screen, you can rely upon the color-coded handles that appear within the frame. In the current horizontal split, the four green corner handles in the bottom half of the screen correspond to the green icon next to the lower-left pop-up menu that's set to Current Frame. The blue half-handles, then, correspond to the icon next to the lower-right pop-up menu set to the Next Edit relative to the current frame.

At this point, you can compare the woman's shoulder in one shot to her arm in another, but it's still difficult to make an accurate comparison.

5 Click the Swap button.

The images are reversed on either side of the split, but it's still difficult to compare the lighting on her arm in each picture.

TIP You can also swap the two sides of a split screen by clicking the H-Split or V-Split buttons repeatedly, as long as you haven't customized the split rectangle.

6 Move the pointer to the lower-left edge of the split screen. When the pointer turns into a Resize pointer, drag the left edge to the right until you can see the woman's arm in each clip.

The Frame Viewer split screen is incredibly flexible because the split between both images is defined by a user-customizable rectangle. You can independently drag each of the four corner handles and each side of the split around the frame, so you can selectively compare any two areas of an image, regardless of their positions. Having made the adjustment, you can now compare the woman's arm in each clip, and the difference between each image is obvious.

There are several ways you can manipulate the split between two images.

7 Drag up the lower-right corner handle of the split screen so that the split area is a small square.

8 Move the pointer into the center of the split, and when the pointer becomes a hand, drag the split around in the frame.

By moving the split rectangle, you can easily compare different parts of both images.

9 Click the V-Split button to reset the Frame Viewer to a vertical split screen.

10 In the Timeline, move the playhead to the second clip.

The clips displayed in the Frame Viewer are always relative to the current playhead position. As you move the playhead around in your sequence, the Frame Viewer updates to display the appropriate images.

As you move around the sequence, however, you should notice one crucial thing. The only image that is displayed on your external broadcast monitor is *the current frame at the position of the playhead.*

The best time to use the Frame Viewer is after you make the first few corrections, flipping between clips and viewing the external monitor. Later, if you're having difficulty determining the difference between an uncorrected clip and another clip that has been corrected relative to the broadcast monitor, the split screen might give you more clues (particularly if flipping between both pictures and examining the video scopes graphs isn't revealing enough).

Split screen is also a good way to view your results as you begin learning how to correct a second shot to match a first, but you should always, always flip between both images on your calibrated broadcast monitor to finish the job.

Setting Up for Scene-by-Scene Color Correction

Several interface options make it easier to color correct a scene. In this section, you'll set up Final Cut Pro to take advantage of these options. Bear in mind that these settings are a matter of personal preference—what's good for one colorist may not work for another. Be aware that some Final Cut Pro features that have nothing directly to do with color correction can still provide numerous benefits to the colorist.

Setting Playhead Sync to Open

As you've seen, all color correction in Final Cut Pro is done with filters, and the color correction filters have custom controls in the Color Corrector 3-way tab of the Viewer. Opening another color-corrected sequence clip into the Viewer automatically reveals its Color Corrector parameters within the same tab, as long as the Color Corrector 3-way tab is already open.

You can use this behavior to automate opening clips into the Viewer by using the Open setting in the Playhead Sync pop-up menu in the Viewer or Canvas. As its name implies, the Open playhead sync setting automatically opens into the Viewer any clip that becomes visible in the Canvas.

If all of your clips have color correction filters applied, simply moving the playhead to another clip automatically opens its color correction controls into the Viewer. This saves you a few mouse clicks, and it ensures that you are always adjusting the color correction controls of the clip you are looking at.

> **NOTE ►** Although this is a useful way to work, you are advised to leave playhead sync set to Off while doing the exercises in this lesson, unless otherwise instructed.

1. Open the *Scene 1 - Finished* sequence.

2. In the Timeline, double-click the first clip to open it into the Viewer.

   All of the clips in this sequence have been color corrected, so they all have Color Corrector 3-way filters applied.

3. In the Viewer, click the Color Corrector 3-way tab to display the first clip's color correction controls.

4. From the Playhead Sync pop-up menu in the Canvas, choose Open.

   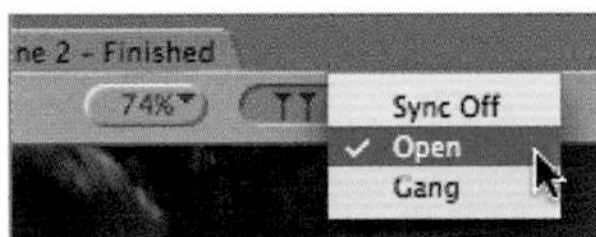

5. Drag the playhead through the Timeline from left to right, pausing briefly at each clip.

   As you scrub from clip to clip, you'll see how the Viewer window automatically displays the same image as the Canvas.

6. Move the playhead to the third clip in the sequence.

   The Open playhead sync mode even works with the Show Edit commands.

7. Select the Timeline, press Control–Up Arrow, then press Control–Down Arrow.

   Notice how the Color Corrector controls update every time the playhead moves. It might take a moment or two, but the Viewer always updates.

Although this style of working is convenient, there are many times you'll want to disable the behavior. For example, you must turn playhead sync off if you want to keep open the Color Corrector 3-way tab from one clip in order to scrub over to another section of the Timeline and drag that filter onto another clip, or when you're using the Match Hue controls.

If you routinely use the Open playhead sync mode, periodically check that Open is selected in the Playhead Sync pop-up menu, because it's fairly easy to accidentally deselect this mode.

Also note that Final Cut Pro always opens the clip on the highest track that has Auto Select enabled. If you have clips on multiple tracks, Option-click the Auto Select control to select just that track you want to color correct.

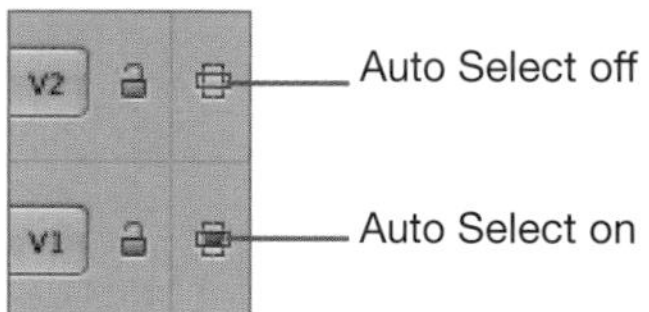

Choosing Timeline Options

There are several Timeline options you can set that make it easier to navigate and manage filters in a sequence. In this exercise, you'll set up the Timeline to take advantage of these options.

1 Open the *Scene 1* sequence in the Browser.

2 In the Browser, Control-click the *Scene 1* sequence and choose Settings from the shortcut menu.

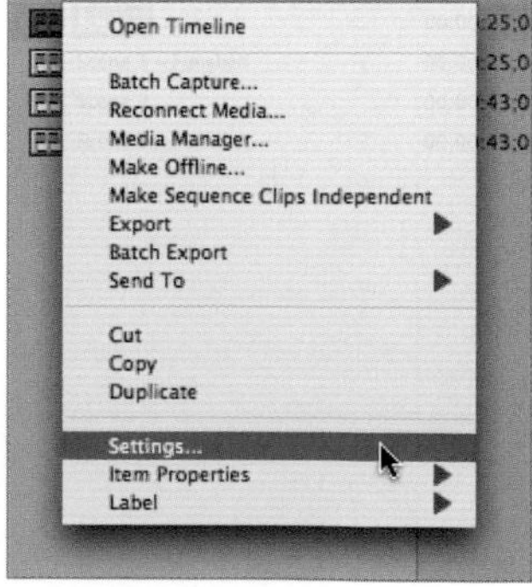

3 In the Sequence Settings window, click the Timeline Options tab.

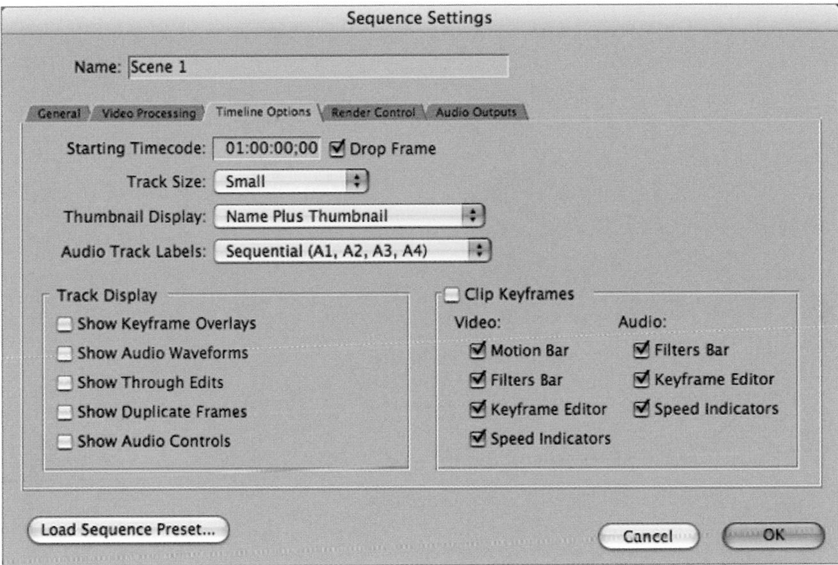

4 If it's not already set, from the Thumbnail Display pop-up menu, choose Name Plus Thumbnail.

Because you're not changing the edit points while you color correct a sequence, you don't have to worry too much about the computing overhead of redrawing the thumbnail images. In any event, thumbnails are incredibly useful for quickly spotting which clips come from the same angle of coverage, which facilitates copying filters among similar clips.

5 Turn on clip keyframes, and turn off everything within the Clip Keyframes section except for the Video: Filters Bar option.

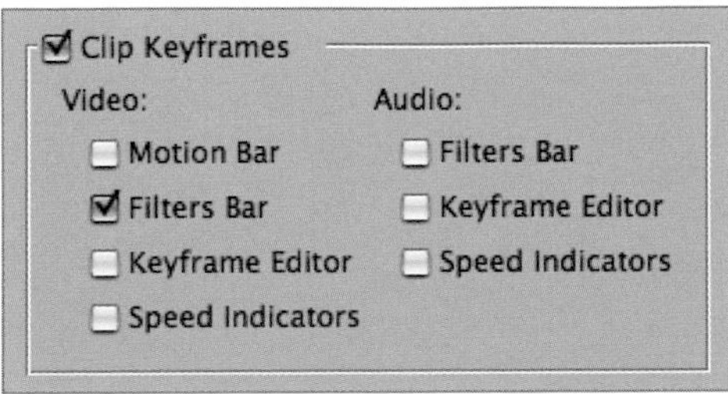

The Filters Bar option places a thin, gray area underneath each clip in the Timeline. Green stripes (filter bars) appear underneath every clip that has a filter applied, which enables you to determine, at a glance, which clips have color correction filters applied.

Filter applied No filter applied

6 Click OK to close the Sequence Settings window.

7 Move the pointer to the top of track V1 in the Timeline.

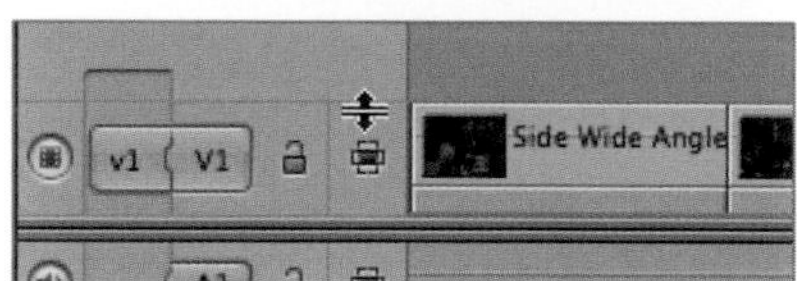

8 When the pointer turns into the Resize pointer, drag up the top of the track to make it taller.

As useful as the Timeline's clip thumbnails are, they don't do you any good if you can't see them.

If you're working on a sequence with a lot of video tracks, you might consider dragging down the border between the video and audio tracks, obscuring the audio tracks to make room for more video tracks.

TIP It's pretty typical for colorists to begin work on a program after the picture has been locked, so accidentally moving a clip, even a few frames, when you meant to just double-click it is a bad thing. If you lock all of the audio tracks of a sequence you're correcting, but not the video tracks, and keep linked selection turned on, you can minimize your risk of inadvertently nudging clips around.

Color Correcting a Complete Scene

Now that you've set up your window layout, learned how to compare images, and customized your Timeline, you can start working on an actual scene.

Choosing a Reference Shot

The first thing you need to do is determine which clip to use as the starting point for color correcting the scene. In general, you want to choose a reference shot that contains most of the characters that appear in that scene. If your scene features two characters, look for a two-shot that clearly shows both actors. If it's a group scene, find the widest shot that's representative, with as many people as possible clearly visible, which makes it easier to balance the skin tones in each individual's close-up with their skin tone in the corrected reference clip.

In any event, it's important to work on a reference clip that is an average shot from that scene, because after you've made your corrections and stylistic adjustments to that clip, you'll be comparing every other clip in the scene to that reference. If you pick a shot that's anomalous in any way (such as the only shot in which someone's in a spotlight, or standing in a shadow), you run the risk of incorrectly balancing all the other clips in that scene.

TIP It's always a good idea to communicate with the director and cinematographer to determine if they have an opinion about which shot most represents the intended look of the scene.

1 If it's not already open, double-click the *Scene 1* sequence, and choose Window > Arrange > Color Correction to reset the window layout.

2 Scrub through the first four clips in the Timeline, and see if you can pick the best one to use as a reference shot.

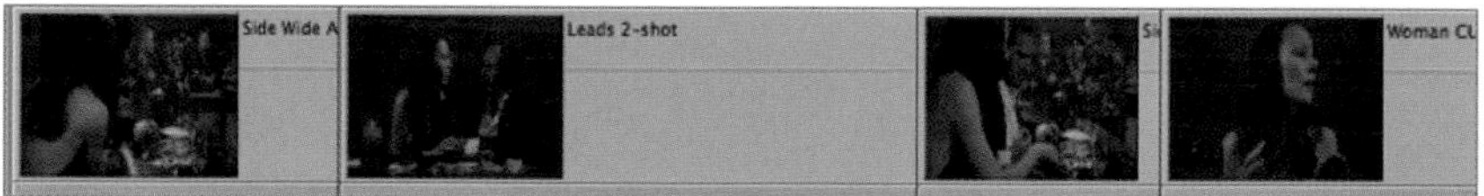

The fourth clip is the easiest to rule out. As a close-up, it shows the least amount of background, and it excludes all the other actors in the shot.

The first and third clips (both from the same angle of coverage), appear to fit the bill at first glance. They're wide shots, and they show every character in that scene. The problem is that the two most important characters (according to the director) are shown in profile, and we see only the back of the woman's head. On second thought, this is not an ideal starting point.

This leaves us with the second clip in the sequence, **Leads 2-shot**. It's the best shot of both lead actors, and it's wide enough to show a lot of the foreground, as well as the wall behind the actors. Correcting this shot will give you an excellent starting point for balancing this scene.

Developing the Scene's "Look"

One of the interesting things about being a colorist is that your job is one-third technician and two-thirds artist.

On the one hand, you have an obligation to provide a reasonably strong video signal, pleasingly visible detail, and minimal noise, and to keep your adjustments within the accepted broadcast limits.

On the other hand, you have an obligation to achieve your client's creative goals, to make shots darker or lighter, warmer or cooler, more saturated or less, depending on the aesthetic needs of the program. Assuming you have well-exposed footage, it's usually easy to strike a balance between both parts of the job.

Remember, as you correct this first shot, it's critical to view the output on a properly calibrated broadcast monitor.

> **TIP** This exercise provides only suggested changes. Feel free to veer off at any time and create your own look. To see the complete, color-corrected sequence, open *Scene 1 - Finished* from the Browser.

1 Locate the second clip in the sequence, the one you've chosen as the reference shot for the scene, and apply a Color Corrector 3-way filter.

  If you turned on clip keyframes earlier, a green filter bar appears underneath the second clip to show you that a filter is applied.

2 Open the second clip into the Viewer, and click the Color Corrector 3-way tab.

3 Press Control-Z to turn on Range Check > Luma.

  It's always a good idea to turn on range checking while you make adjustments, to give you an instant warning if you push anything too far.

4 Adjust the Blacks, Mids, and Whites sliders to set the black point of the graph in the Waveform Monitor at 0 percent and the white point for highlights at 100 percent. Watch the range-check icon at the top of the Viewer, as well as the Waveform Monitor, while you make this adjustment. Afterwards, lower the Mids slider just a few points to deepen the shadows.

NOTE ► If an image doesn't have any bright whites, or highlights, or any section that would plausibly go all the way up to 100 percent, it's neither necessary nor desirable to automatically boost the level of the brightest area in the image to 100 percent. In these cases, adjust the white point relative to how bright the lightest area in the picture would realistically be. This will keep the contrast from becoming artificially high. In other words, don't set someone's face to 100 percent white just because it happens to be the brightest element in a very dark picture.

5 Make any necessary adjustments to the Blacks and Whites Color Balance controls, using the Vectorscope and the Parade scope as your guide.

Neutralize the yellowish cast, and warm up the skin tones. To do that, add some cyan to the blacks to create true blacks, and add some blue to the whites to clean them up.

6 Add some red to the mids, to give some kick to the skin tones and create the impression of warmer lighting in the room.

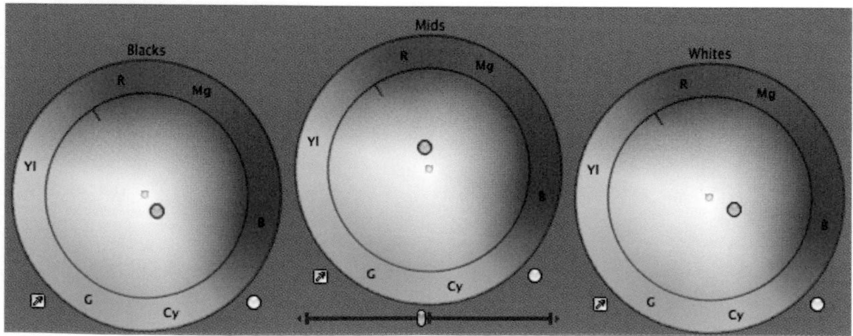

Next, you'll correct the other clips in this sequence so they match the tone and color you've achieved in your reference shot.

Matching Contrast Between Two Shots

The two clips that are adjacent to the **Leads 2-shot** reference clip are from the same angle of coverage, **Side Wide Angle**. You'll begin balancing the rest of the scene to the corrected reference clip by working on the first **Side Wide Angle** clip. As always, you'll begin this correction by adjusting the clip's contrast—in this case, to match that of the reference shot.

It's useful to note that the human eye is more sensitive to changes in brightness than in color, so you want to take particular care to make the contrast of all shots in a scene match as closely as possible.

1 Move the playhead to the beginning of the first clip in the sequence, **Side Wide Angle (01)**.

2 With the Timeline active, press Control–Down Arrow a few times, flipping between this clip and the previously corrected reference clip to its right. Examine the two clips for differences in contrast.

As you flip back and forth, make sure you check both the visual image and the graphs in the video scopes. When you're examining differences in contrast, the Waveform Monitor is a good guide.

In comparing the two waveform graphs, you should notice that the black point in the uncorrected clip to the left is not as low as in the corrected clip.

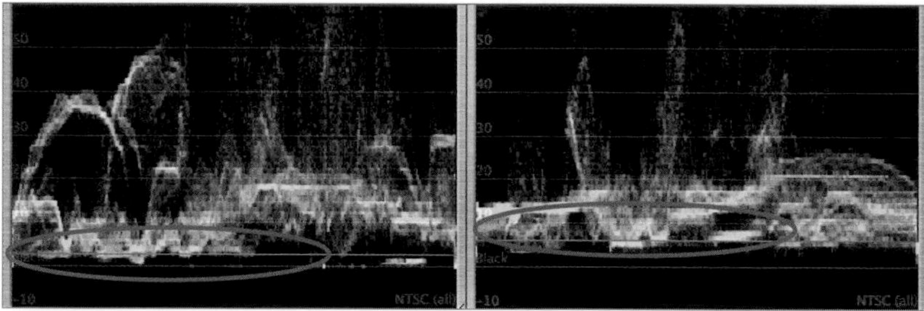

You should also notice that some of the distributions within the midtones are a little high, and the white point of the first clip's graph seems to match that in the second clip. In other words, the densest clump in the middle of the graph on the left (which is probably the cocktail bar surface) is about three percent higher than the densest clump in the graph on the right. This makes the **Side Wide Angle (01)** clip seem slightly brighter. This also tells you that you'll later be making an adjustment to the Mids slider.

There's a good way to measure these differences. Once you've spotted an identical feature in each graph, such as the cocktail bar, move the pointer within the Waveform Monitor, and an indicator appears. By dragging the indicator to line up with different features in the graph, you'll get a tooltip at the top of the Waveform Monitor that displays the digital percentage. The tooltip can help you determine how much correction you need to make.

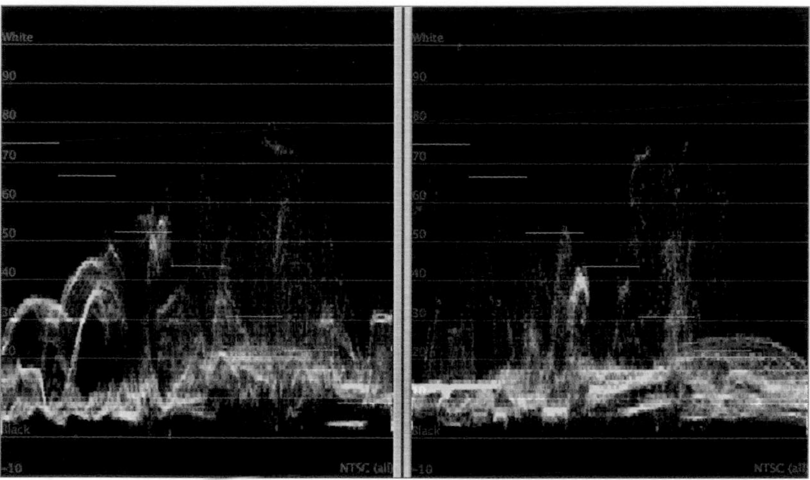

Side Wide Angle (01) Leads 2-shot

In this example, the first clip to the left measures the top of this feature at about 21 percent; the reference clip at the right measures the same feature at about 18 percent—a 3 percent difference, but enough to be noticeable.

Learning which parts of the graph correspond to which areas of each shot takes practice. Remember that the Waveform Monitor scans the entire image from left to right, drawing a graph based on the brightness of each vertical slice of the picture. Bright parts of the picture, such as the woman's arm, cause upward curves in the midtones at the middle of the graph. Highlights, such as the candles, cause spikes into the whites at the top of the graph. Dark areas, like the man's jacket sleeve and the bar surface, will cluster near the bottom of the graph.

TIP Sometimes it's easier to see how the graph corresponds to the image when the clip is moving. To ensure the scopes update while the sequence is playing, open the RT menu in the Timeline and choose Video Scopes Playback.

3 Add a Color Corrector 3-way filter to the **Side Wide Angle (01)** clip, and open it into the Viewer.

4 Adjust the Blacks slider so that the average distribution at the bottom of the Waveform Monitor graph for **Side Wide Angle (01)** approximately matches that of **Leads 2-shot**. This will be a very slight adjustment, so you may want to Command-drag the Blacks slider so it doesn't snap to the center position.

   If necessary, make the Timeline active and press Command–Down Arrow a few times to flip back and forth, comparing your results before making further adjustments.

5 Drag the Mids slider a few points to the left, lowering the mids so that the overall level of brightness in both clips appears to be the same and the relative distributions start to line up in the middle of the Waveform Monitor graphs.

   This will also be a slight adjustment—one that requires you to look at the image, in addition to watching the scopes.

   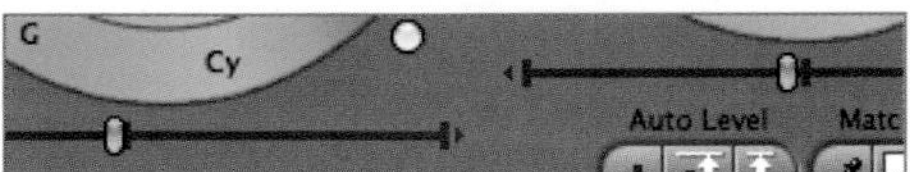

   It's important to realize that although the top and bottom of the waveforms are important, the distribution of values between them is even more important to the overall clip brightness. Even if the tops and the bottoms of the two graphs line up, the clips won't match if the inner distribution of values is significantly different.

6 To check the adjustment you've just made, make the Timeline active, and press Control–Down Arrow a few times, flipping between this clip and the reference clip, to make sure your correction matches. If it doesn't, keep making adjustments, checking the video scopes and flipping between images until you're satisfied that the shots match.

Matching Color Between Two Shots

Now that the contrast of the second clip has been set to match the reference shot, it's time to adjust the color.

1 In the Video Scopes window, from the Layout pop-up menu, choose Parade and make sure that View is set to Current Frame.

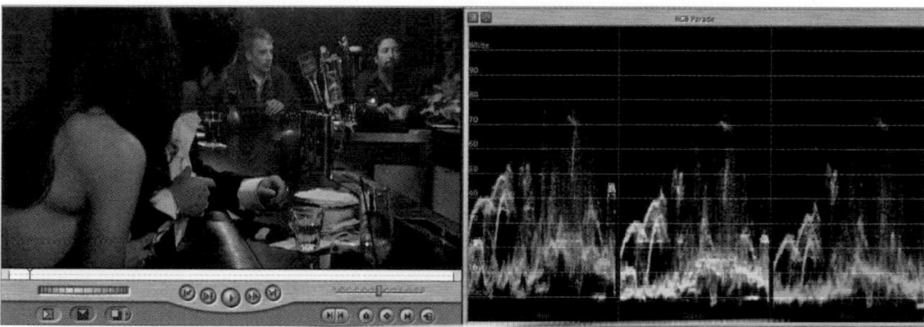

2 Make the Timeline active, and press Control–Down Arrow a few times, flipping between the **Side Wide Angle (01)** clip and the **Leads 2-shot** clip, comparing the images on the monitor and the graphs in the Parade scope.

The Parade scope shows you the balance of red, green, and blue in an image. When you're comparing two images, the Parade scope is a powerful tool for identifying exactly which color channels need balancing, and in which luminance zones.

As you toggle back and forth, look at the bottom of each graph. You should notice that, compared to the reference clip, the blues are too low and the reds are too high. This tells you what kind of adjustment you need to make to the Blacks Color Balance control.

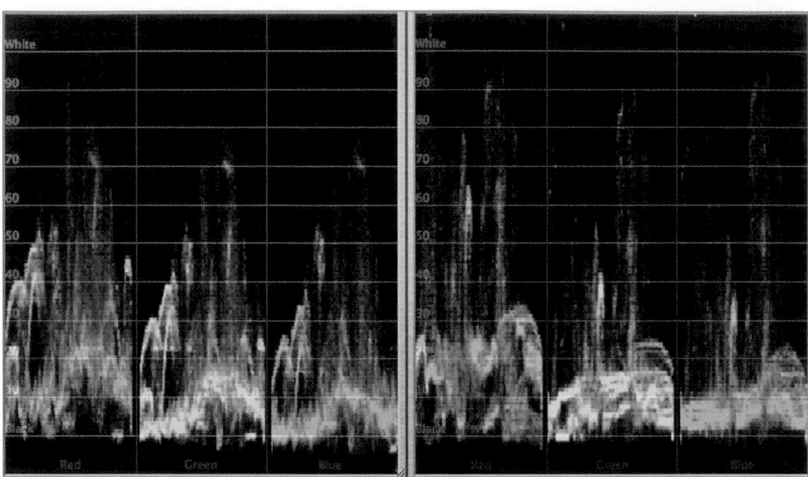

3 Drag the Blacks balance control indicator somewhere between the Cy (cyan) and B (blue) targets, until the bottoms of the red, green, and blue graphs match those of the reference clip.

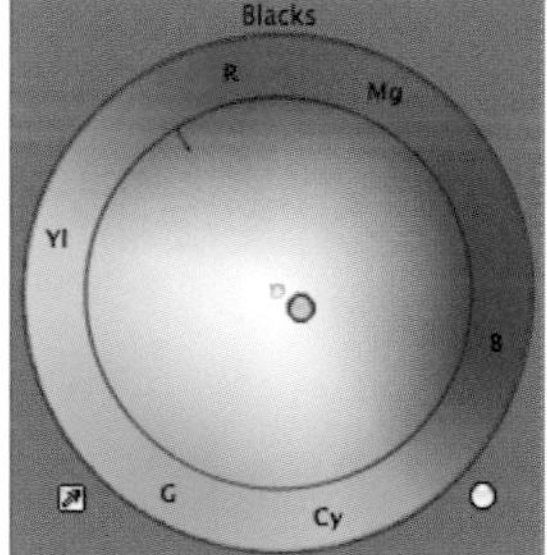

To check your work, make the Timeline active and press Control–Down Arrow a few times to compare the images and the graphs. Keep making adjustments until you're satisfied. When you're finished, the bottoms of the graphs should approximately line up.

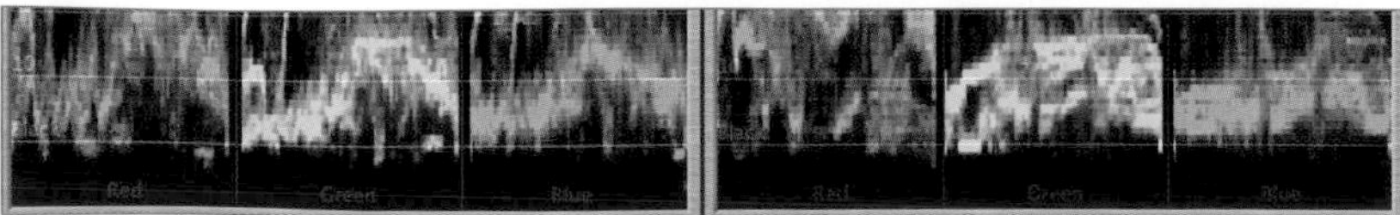

4 When you're finished, toggle between the images again, this time examining the tops of the graphs.

You should see that the first clip has much more yellow in the highlights of the skin tones than the reference shot. The tops of graphs in the Parade scope reveal this as green and blue channels that are too strong (remember that red + green = yellow).

5 Drag the Whites balance control indicator towards the B (blue) target to neutralize the yellowish cast in the highlights, but not so far as to overcompensate and tint the highlights blue.

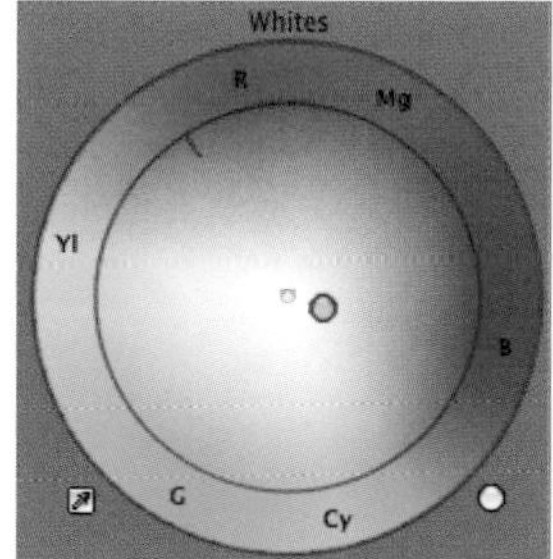

For this last adjustment, it's a bit difficult to accurately spot the tops of the red, green, and blue graphs, because there are so few values there. This would be a good time to increase the brightness of the traces.

6 In the upper-left corner of the Scopes window, click the Traces Brightness button.

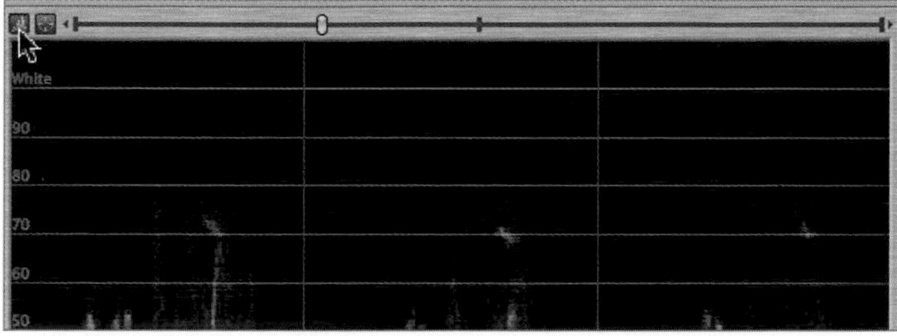

A slider appears next to the buttons.

7 Drag the slider to the right to increase the visibility of the video data.

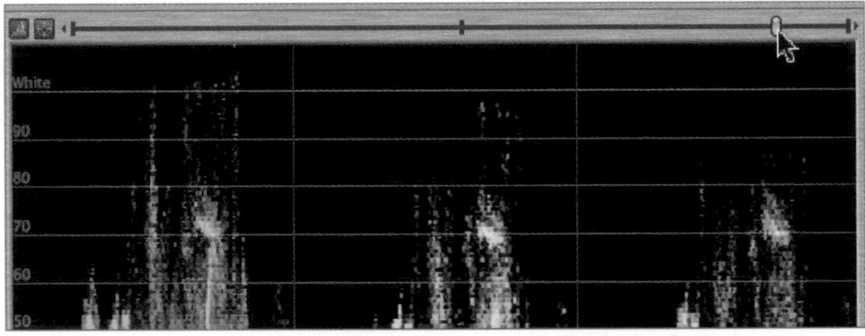

This makes it much easier to identify the color data in the brightest areas of the shot. When you're happy with the whites color balance setting, you may want to lower the brightness again to a more modest setting.

Now that the blacks are black, and the highlights are equally neutral to those in the reference image, it's time to adjust the mids to complete the match. For this last adjustment, you'll rely on the Vectorscope.

8 In the Video Scopes window, from the Layout pop-up menu, choose Vectorscope.

After you've matched the colors in the blacks and the whites, it often becomes difficult to see how the colors in the mids line up in the Parade scope. In these cases, the Vectorscope can give you a clearer picture of the differences between the overall color temperatures in two images.

9 Once again, make the Timeline active and press Control–Down Arrow a few times to compare the images and their graphs.

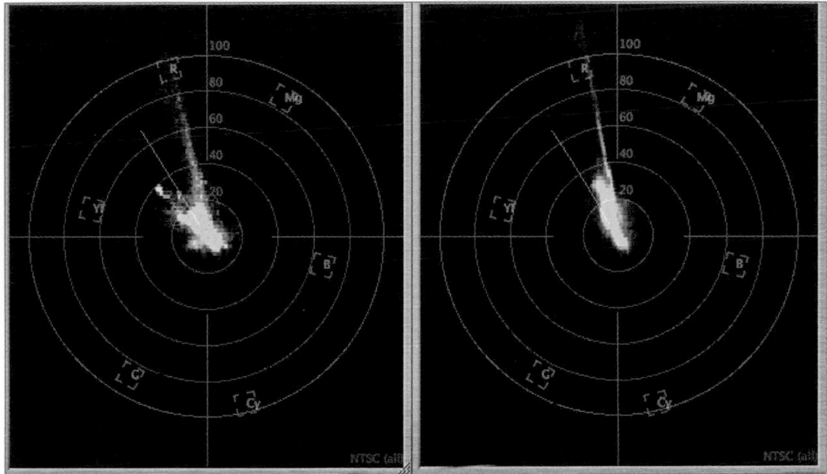

You should immediately see that the first clip doesn't have as much saturation towards the reds as the reference image. In particular, the cluster of values that fall just above the Flesh Tone line in the reference image's Vectorscope (to the right in the preceding figure) extends all the way up to about 33 percent, and the same cluster of values in the Vectorscope to the left is down around 18 percent—a large difference.

10 For **Side Wide Angle (01)**, drag up the Mids balance control indicator towards the Flesh Tone line until the cluster of values at the center of the Vectorscope matches those displayed by the reference clip. If necessary, make the Timeline active and flip back and forth, adjusting and comparing until you're satisfied you have a match.

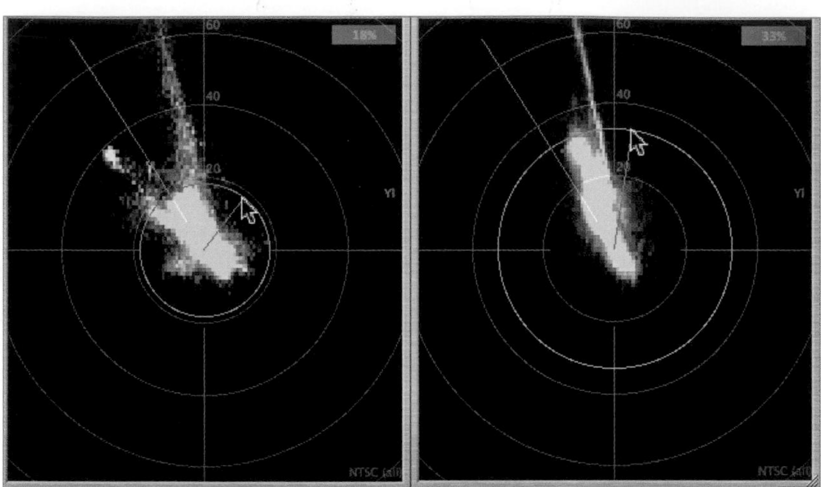

When you're finished, the shots should match just about perfectly. Play through both clips to make sure.

Copying Filters Forward to Other Clips from the Same Angle

Before you make any more manual adjustments to clips in this scene, it's time to ask yourself if there are any more clips featuring the same angles of coverage and with the same lighting. If so, you can copy the color correction filters from the corrected clips along with their settings, and apply them to other clips shot from the same angle.

It's very common for scenes to be constructed using repeated sequences of clips drawn from a few angles of coverage. For example, if there are three angles of coverage—shot A (a master shot of the room), shot B (a two-shot), and shot C (a close-up of actor 2)—the scene might be edited like this:

A–B–A–C

That's the situation in this scene. A quick look at the Timeline should reveal that the third clip is from the same angle as the first clip you corrected (**Side Wide Angle (02)**). So, you might as well copy the color correction filter forward to save yourself some work and guarantee consistency.

To facilitate this, each Color Corrector 3-way filter has a group of Copy Filter controls that let you copy the currently open filter and its settings and apply them to clips that follow it in the sequence.

Interestingly enough, the Copy Filter controls work similarly to the Show Edit commands. There is one control to copy the current filter forward to the next clip in the sequence, and a second control to copy it to the second clip forward. As in the hypothetical edited sequence (A–B–A–C), shots from the same angle rarely fall next to one another in narrative filmmaking, so these controls allow you to skip adjacent shots and apply the correction to the next instance of a shot from the same angle.

1 Make sure the color correction filter from the first clip in the sequence is open in the Viewer, and click the Copy to 2nd Clip Forward button.

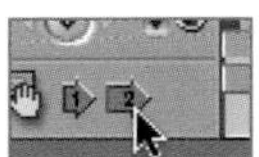

If you turned on clip keyframes in the previous exercise, a green filter bar appears underneath the third clip to show you that the filter has indeed been applied.

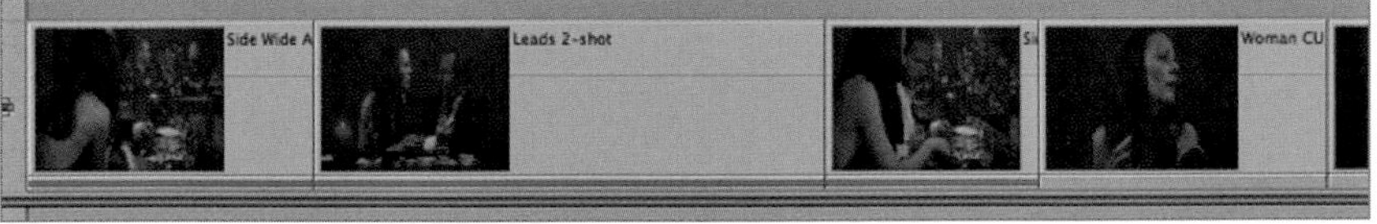

Playing through the sequence will show that all three clips are properly balanced. The ease with which color correction filters can be propagated through a sequence brings up an interesting issue—if you make a change to any of the filters that are applied to these clips, you'll need to copy that change to any other clips that have an identical correction.

This is because after you've copied a filter to another clip, its settings are completely independent of the original filter. However, the Copy Forward commands have an additional function to help you in this situation. If you use those commands to copy a color correction filter to another clip that already has a color correction filter applied, the settings of the filter in the second clip are overwritten to match those in the current filter.

2. Make sure the color correction filter from the first clip is open in the Viewer, and drag the Sat (saturation) slider to the left to noticeably desaturate the image.
3. Play through the sequence to verify that the first and third clips don't match.
4. Move the playhead back to the first clip and open the Color Corrector filter into the Viewer.
5. Click the Copy to 2nd Clip Forward button.
6. Play through the first three clips again and verify that the third clip has changed to match the first.
7. Press Command-Z twice to undo this change.

You'll notice that there are also buttons for copying color correction filter settings *from* color correction filters that are applied to the first and second clips behind the current clip (in the Timeline). For more detailed information on using the Copy Filter controls, see the Final Cut Pro documentation.

Matching Color with the Match Hue Controls

So far, you've learned how to manually adjust contrast and color to match shots. When you develop a facility with the tools, this is often the fastest way to proceed, and they certainly afford you the greatest amount of control in any possible color correction.

However, the color correction filters have another feature to make your life a bit easier: The Match Hue controls, found in the middle of the Color Corrector 3-way filter's custom controls, underneath the Mids controls.

The Match Hue controls automate the process of balancing a color within one zone of luminance to match a designated color in a different clip. It does nothing to adjust contrast; you must adjust that manually. However, it does provide a way to quickly and automatically adjust Color Balance controls to match a specific hue that you select, similar to the way Auto-balance eyedroppers work in the Color Balance controls.

Match Hue works well with clips that are from the same location, matching the color of a subject in one clip to the color of the identical subject in another clip. In the scene you're currently balancing, for example, the woman appears in every shot that's been corrected, and the location and situation is identical, even though the lighting varies from shot to shot. This is an ideal situation in which to use the Match Hue controls.

You can use the Match Hue controls in other situations, but your success will be completely dependent on your ability to accurately select analogous colors in each shot. For example, it's a mistake to assume that you can match the skin tone of any two people with similar skin color. Subtle differences in hue, even by a few percentage points, may result in significant deviations in the end result. Still, even in less than ideal situations, the Match Hue controls may provide you with a starting point if you're unsure how to proceed.

1 Move the playhead to the fourth clip in the sequence, **Woman CU**.

2 Apply a Color Corrector 3-way filter to the **Woman CU** clip, open it into the Viewer, and click the Color Corrector 3-way tab to view its controls.

This clip has a yellow/red cast similar to that found in other clips in this scene, but a closer examination reveals that it's different enough not to benefit from automatic application of any of the filters from the clips you've already color corrected. Because it's the same actor as in the reference shot, however, and because the clip is an insert shot (a close-up taken from the same angle as the wider two-shot), this is a perfect candidate for using Match Hue.

Before you do anything else, you need to adjust the contrast of this clip to match the reference clip. Otherwise, the Match Hue controls won't work as you expect.

3 Press Control-Shift–Up Arrow a few times to flip between the reference shot and the current shot, comparing the Waveform Monitor graphs.

4 Adjust the Blacks, Whites, and Mids sliders until the contrast ratio is identical, and the overall brightness in the midtones matches.

The adjustments will be fairly subtle, and you may see the value of relying on a comparison of the Waveform Monitor graphs. The yellow cast becomes a bit more pronounced when you brighten the image. You might find that making this adjustment visually would boost the brightness too high, because the color cast gives the illusion that the image is darker than it really is. The Waveform Monitor, however, provides a more objective reference.

With the contrast matched, you can use the Match Hue controls.

5 Click the Select Auto-balance Color button (the eyedropper).

A tooltip appears with the only instruction you'll ever need, an exhortation to choose a color to which you want to match the current clip—but neglecting to mention that it should be from a second reference clip.

It's important to understand that the Match Hue controls only make an adjustment to one of the three Color Balance controls, in an attempt to match a hue you select in a second reference image. The saturation and luminance of the selection are ignored. You can indirectly control which Color Balance control is adjusted—the Blacks, Mids, or Whites—by the area of the reference image you choose with the eyedropper.

The first thing you need to do is to identify a frame in the reference image containing clear highlights, midtones, and shadows in the subject you want to match.

6 Move the playhead back to the already-corrected **Leads 2-shot** clip that you've been using as the reference image, and scrub through the clip until you find a frame of the woman in profile, with a clear highlight visible on her forehead. (The first frame of the image is good.)

7 Because the entire image needs to be matched to the reference clip, and the location is identical, begin by clicking a highlight in the woman's forehead with the eyedropper.

Immediately, two things happen. First, the Match Color indicator is populated with the hue you just selected.

Second, the Whites Select Auto-balance Color button turned green.

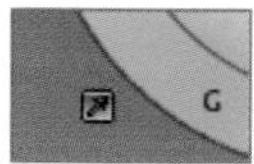

NOTE ▶ If the Whites Select Auto-balance Color button didn't turn green, and the Mids or Blacks Select Auto-balance Color button turned green instead, you didn't successfully pick a highlight. In the Match Hue controls, click the Select Auto-balance Color button again and try clicking the highlight in the reference image again.

At this point, the Match Hue controls are set up for you to make the match.

8 In the Color Corrector 3-way tab of the Viewer, click the now-highlighted Whites Select Auto-balance Color button.

9 Move the playhead back to the **Woman CU** clip, and scrub forward until you find a similar frame with the woman in profile that shows a clear highlight on her forehead matching the highlight you picked in the reference shot. (There's a suitable frame midway through the clip.)

10 Click the highlight with the eyedropper.

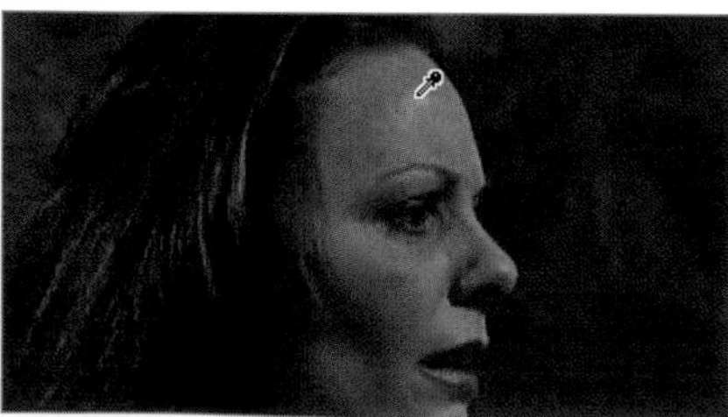

Immediately, the Whites Color Balance control is adjusted, and the highlights are rebalanced.

The success you have with the Match Hue controls is completely dependent upon which pixels you click with the eyedropper. If the result is significantly off, you probably mismatched a value in the whites with a value in the mids, or vice versa. For this reason, the Match Hue controls may sometimes appear to be more idiosyncratic than they really are. The bottom line is that you have to be very careful when choosing reference and match colors. If necessary, zoom in to the Canvas to better see which pixels you're selecting.

Next, you're going to match the hue of the blacks.

11 Reset the Match Hue controls by clicking the Reset Match Color button.

12 In the Match Hue controls, click the Select Auto-balance Color button (the eyedropper), move the playhead back to the first frame of the reference clip, and click in the shadow of her cheek.

If you chose the right part of the image, the Blacks Select Auto-balance Color button turns green.

13 Move the playhead back to the clip you've been correcting, scrub back to the frame range showing the woman in profile, then click the green Blacks Select Auto-balance Color button in the Color Corrector 3-way tab in the Viewer.

14 Click a shadow in her cheek that's similar to the first shadow you picked.

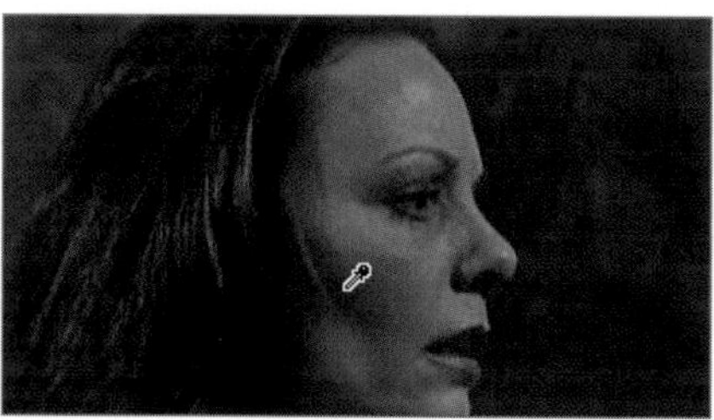

Again, you'll know you picked well if the image assumes a closer match. If it doesn't, you can click the Blacks Reset button and repeat steps 11 through 14, picking different areas of the image.

It still seems that there's a bit of a yellow cast to her face. The even distribution of the cast would indicate that it's time to use the Match Hue controls on the mids.

15 Reset the Match Hue controls, then click the Select Auto-balance Color button (the eyedropper). Move the playhead back to the first frame of the reference clip, and click a midtone color somewhere between the highlight and shadow.

If you've chosen well, the Mids Select Auto-balance Color button should turn green.

16 Return the playhead to the clip you've been correcting, scrub back to the frame range showing the woman in profile, then click the green Mids Select Auto-balance Color button in the Color Corrector 3-way tab in the

Viewer. Click a midtone on her forehead similar to the midtone you picked on the reference image.

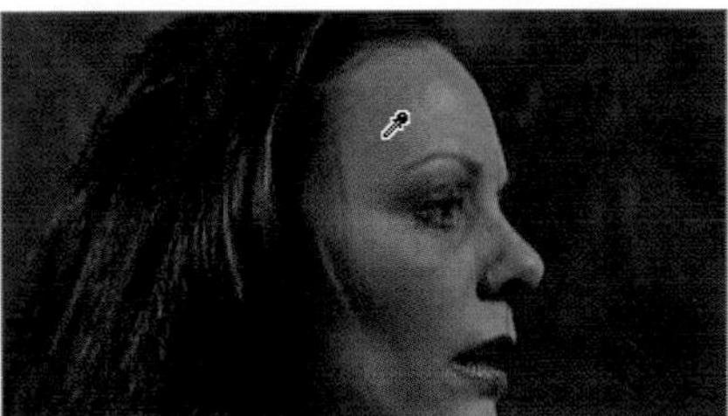

Assuming you chose good colors, the Mids Color Balance control is adjusted, and the image should now be a good match to the reference image.

As you can see, the Match Hue controls pack a lot of functionality into a minimal interface. To use Match Hue well, you need to have a solid understanding of how the colors of an image fall into the blacks, mids, and whites. The same criteria you would use to decide whether to adjust the Blacks, Mids, or Whites Color Balance controls manually also apply to the use of the Match Hue controls. In fact, you can elect to use Match Hue for only one or two of the Color Balance controls, adjusting the others manually.

There's one other thing you should know. Once the Match Color indicator and Blacks, Mids, or Whites Select Auto-balance Color buttons are set, these controls are available from every color correction filter in your sequence. This allows you to make the same adjustment in several different clips. To return to using the Select Auto-balance Color buttons for making regular blacks, mids, and whites balances, you must click the Reset Match Color button.

Choosing and Balancing a Second Group of Images with Different Contrast

The second half of this scene focuses on two people on the other side of the room. Because it's in the same scene, you'll want to match the color in these clips to the color in the clips you've just corrected. The lighting in the **Guys_2-shot** seems to closely match the lighting in the insert close-up shots that accompany it. If you focus on matching **Guys_2-shot** to the original reference shot for this scene, there's a chance you might also be able to apply that single correction to the insert shots, saving yourself more time and effort.

In any event, it's always good to start with a shot that has as many of the people in the scene as possible. Because the skin tones of people in any scene will vary slightly, finding the ideal look for the wide shot will provide you with a reference for each close-up insert shot.

1 In the Timeline, move the playhead to the first frame of the **Leads 2-shot** clip you've been using as a reference shot, and set an In point in preparation for flipping between this clip and the next one you'll be correcting.

2 Move the playhead to the **Guys_2-shot**, and scrub through to find a representative image.

3 Add a Color Corrector 3-way filter to the **Guys_2-shot**. Open that clip into the Viewer, and click the Color Corrector 3-way tab.

4 Press Control–Left Arrow a few times to flip between the reference clip and the current clip, getting a sense of the contrast corrections you'll need to make.

In this clip, the black level matches the reference clip, and the mids and whites also seem to be in the ballpark, but there's a noticeable difference in brightness between the two images. The **Guys_2-shot** appears darker on average than the reference. A closer examination of the bottoms of the scopes reveals that the dense cluster of values representing the shadows in the current clip is much narrower then the same cluster of values in the graph of the reference clip.

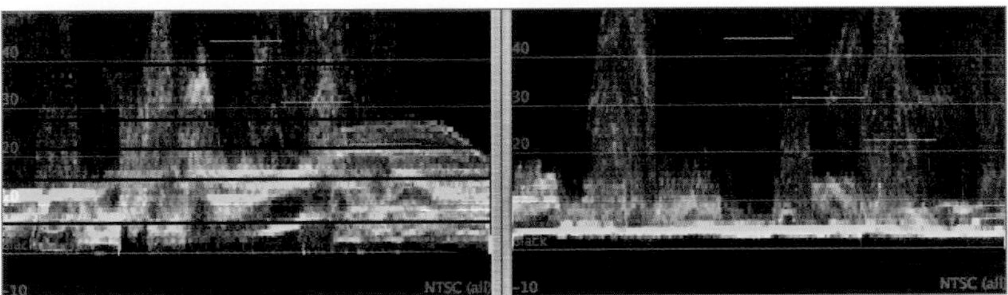

The shadows are being compressed without being crushed. This means that the shadows are so dark that you can't make out any detail, but there is detail there if you want to extract it. You can do this with a peculiar combination of settings.

NOTE ▶ It's also worth noticing that the highlights are considerably shinier in this shot than in the reference clip. This will be addressed by the same correction.

5 Drag the Mids slider to the right, stretching up the blacks so that the detail in the shadows approximately matches the reference image, while leaving the blacks pegged to the bottom.

Don't worry if this temporarily makes the highlights too bright; you will address them in a second step. For now, it's important to pull some detail out of the shadows.

6 Drag the Whites slider to the left, compressing the whites and bringing down the top of the waveform graph to match the highlights in the reference clip.

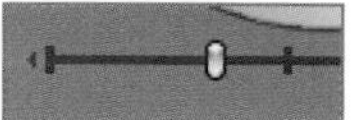

The end result of this somewhat unconventional correction is that you've brought some detail out of the shadows, and minimized the shine on the actor's faces, by selectively reducing the contrast in the clip—while boosting the overall brightness.

7 Select and deselect the Enable Filter checkbox a few times to see a before-and-after comparison.

8 Use whatever techniques you prefer to match the color balance in the blacks, whites, and mids in the **Guys_2-shot** clip to the reference clip.

You can do this manually by dragging the Color Balance control indicators, or you can try to use the Match Hue controls, even though there is no clearly analogous character in this shot. As you work, see if you can determine which of the two men has the pinker skin tone.

When you're finished, the resulting adjustments in the Color Balance controls should look something like this:

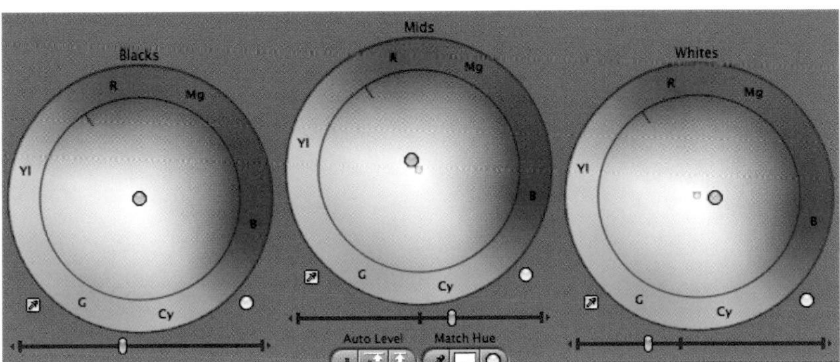

Dragging Filters onto Other Shots

In the preceding section, you corrected the two-shot so that you could apply the same correction to the two identically lit close-ups. One of the nice things about insert shots is that they're often lit with the same lighting setup. (Often, but not always, so don't count on it.)

If the lighting matches, your job is easy. If not, it's no big deal—you can still try using the first shot's settings as a starting point.

1 Make sure the color correction filter applied to the **Guys_2-shot** is open in the Viewer, and deselect the Enable Filter checkbox.

2 Press Control–Up Arrow and Control-Shift–Up Arrow a few times to compare the uncorrected waveforms of all three clips.

In this case, you've gotten lucky. The black point, white point, and mids distributions in the Waveform Monitor, and the color balance in the Parade scope, seem to match for all three shots.

This means you can copy the correction you've made to the **Guys_2-shot** clip to the other close-up shots. However, the distribution of clips is a little too awkward to use the Copy Filter controls, and besides, you want to apply this filter and its settings to three clips all at once. This is a good time to drag a filter from one clip to copy it to a selected group of other clips.

3 Click the **Guy_1_CU** clip, then Command-click the next two instances of the **Guy_2_CU** clips.

4 With these clips selected in the Timeline, click the Drag Filter button, and drag the filter onto one of the selected clips in the Timeline.

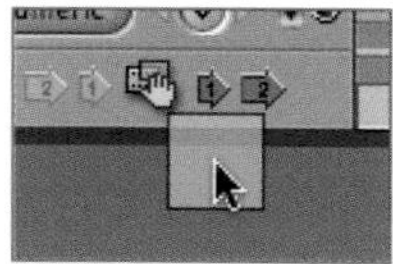

5 When the clips highlight, release the mouse button to apply the filter to all three selected clips.

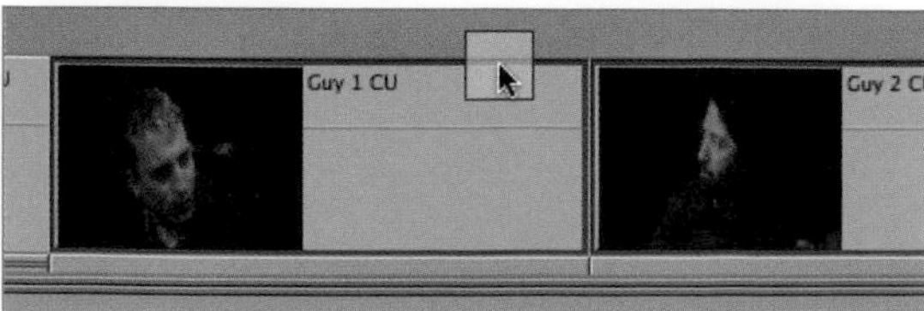

You're finished!

Project Tasks

Try removing the filters from Scene 1 with the Remove Attributes command and then rebalancing the entire scene with a different look.

Once you've exhausted the possibilities of the first scene, open **Scene 2-Extra Credit**, and see how fast you can balance the entire scene by copying filters among shots from identical angles of coverage.

1 Identify a reference shot to use as your starting point, and make your master correction.

2 Identify how many angles of coverage there are. In other words, mentally group all of the shots in the scene that have the same angle and lighting. Chances are, you can apply the same correction to all of them.

3 Work your way through the scene until it's finished.

Lesson Review

1. What are your principal goals when color correcting a scene?
2. What do you want to look for when choosing a reference shot to begin correcting?
3. When matching two shots, what's the first thing you do?
4. What are the Copy Filter controls for?
5. What is the Parade scope best at showing?
6. What are the Show Edit commands for?
7. What kind of clips can you usually use the same color correction filter settings for?

Answers

1. Maintain consistency in shots that appear in the same scene, that occur at the same time, and in the same location.
2. A shot that's representative of the scene, perhaps a wide angle that shows the actors and the environment, and ideally a clip that has most of the actors that appear within that scene onscreen at one time.
3. Match their contrast.
4. They copy a filter and its settings forward to other clips in the sequence.
5. Color balance in the blacks and whites.
6. Flipping back and forth between clips to compare them.
7. Clips with identical lighting, from the same angle of coverage.

Cameo

Reign Over Tape— Jeremy Roush

***REIGN OVER ME* WAS THE FIRST ALL-DIGITAL FEATURE FILM** edited on Final Cut Pro. But according to co-editor Jeremy Roush, that's wasn't the most important thing.

"The real story is that we achieved film quality through the whole process," says Roush. "It's so easy, really, to output a final film-res file now."

Released by Sony Pictures, *Reign Over Me* was shot with Panavision Genesis cameras in HDcamSR (1920 x 1080 pixels resolution) and edited on DVCProHD (1440 x 1080). Working with writer/director Mike Binder, Roush and co-editor Steve Edwards cut 120-plus hours of dailies at 1080p.

In an unusual move, the edit team did the final conform themselves, redigitizing at 4:4:4, 10-bit uncompressed video and decomposing those 10-bit QuickTime files to DPX frame sequences. Those sequences then went to a colorist for professional grading and to a CG house for background effects.

Finally, and even more unusually, Roush and assistant editor Michael Nouryeh went on to create the title sequence, closing scroll, fades, and dissolves on the final, graded frames using Final Cut Studio, Shake, and After Effects.

"There was a lot of shipping drives back and forth, but we saved hundreds of thousands of dollars," says Roush. "The actual film frames that went to the theaters were printed from the actual frames that we delivered."

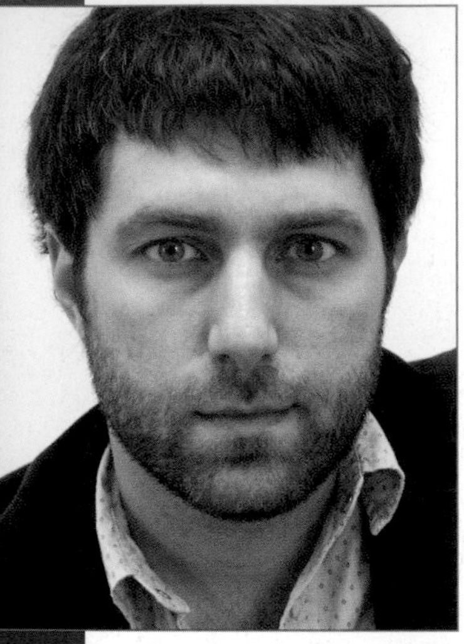

Roush says the experience gave him a new appreciation for how far technology has come, even in the past few years. “It’s easy to lose perspective on where we are today,” he says. “What people call film res is not actually more pixels per inch than what is captured by an 8-megapixel camera. In 1999, computers that could process 8 megapixels at 30 fps cost a million dollars. Now you can do it on a desktop for $2,000.”

All of which, says Roush, is good news for editors. “All these compromises we’ve been making for years in order to compensate for storage constraints and processor speeds—compressing the video and working with grainy visuals and rezzing files up and down—are no longer necessary even at the lowest budgets,” he says. “You can work at the highest resolution through the entire process.”

Roush says working in high-definition solves two key issues that plague editors in the offline/online workflow: focus and eyelines. “When you take film-quality frames and squeeze them down, often a shot will look in focus in SD, but when you get back to full res you realize it isn’t,” he says. “And when you’re working with compressed frames on a computer screen, it’s easy to misjudge the eyelines by just a fraction.”

Roush became a fan of the all-digital workflow while editing the title sequence for *Upside of Anger*. During the course of the edit, the movie was screened three times, which meant three trips to the online bay at a cost of about $35,000 each. “It was crazy. I said to Mike at the time, for the cost of onlining just the screenings, you could put together a four-workstation, 9-terabyte Xsan, including all the networking, and cut the whole film at full resolution.”

So for his next movie, *Man About Town*, Roush designed, spec’ed, and installed a nine-seat Xsan suite without any outside assistance . “I set up the whole Xsan and got it running by myself,” he says, “Just one guy and the manual. We did not have a single Xsan problem, no down time or lost time at all.” The team used the same suite for *Reign Over Me*.

The most important point for Roush is that the improved technology puts focus back on the people. “As computers get better, you don’t have to worry about the technical issues so much, and the talent of the individual is what you’re left with,” he says. “The artistry comes to the foreground.”

“My guess,” says Roush, “is that within two or three films , we’ll be able to upload the actual film directly from the artist to the theater. That’s the ride we’re on.”

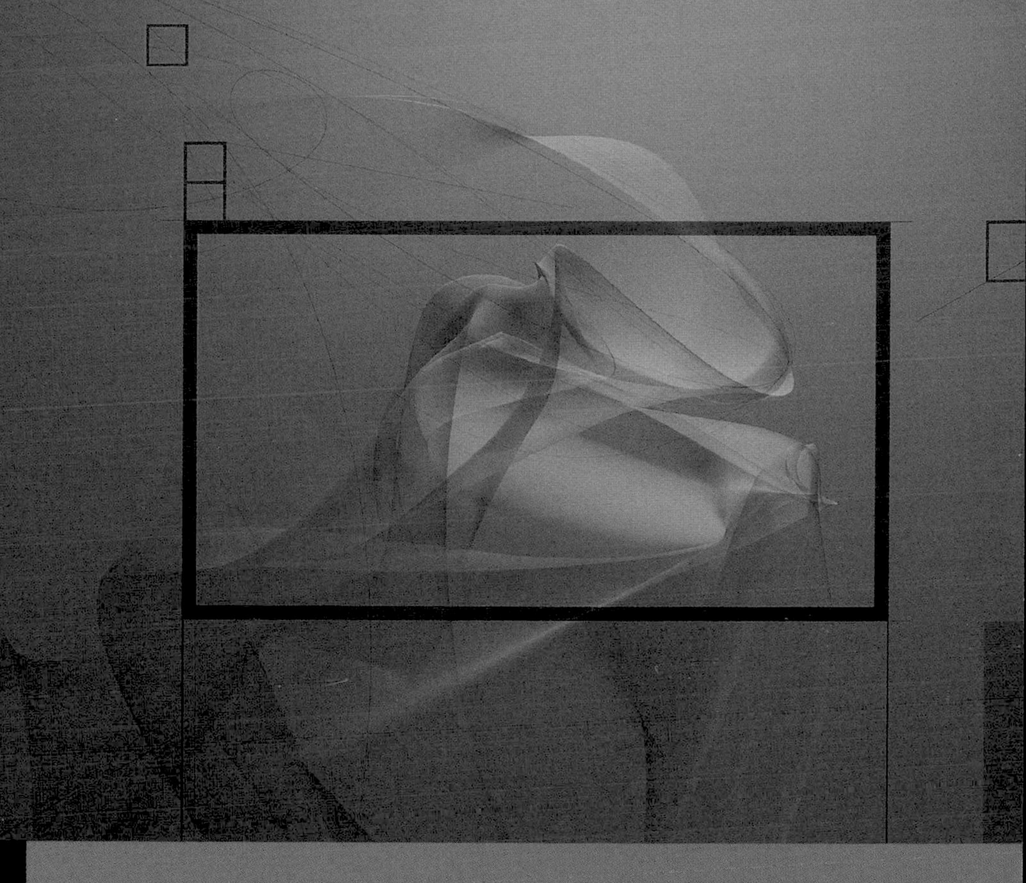

Project Management

14

Lesson Files	Lesson Files > Lesson 14 > Lessons Clip Management.fcp
Media	Poker, Gold Fever, and Misc
Time	This lesson takes approximately 150 minutes to complete.
Goals	Master the parameters associated with all clips Use complex Find commands to locate specific items Modify clip reel name and timecode Use auxiliary timecode fields Change reel numbers for a group of clips Sync audio and video from separate clips Create and modify merged clips Work with 16:9 media and sequences Understand workflows for 24p projects

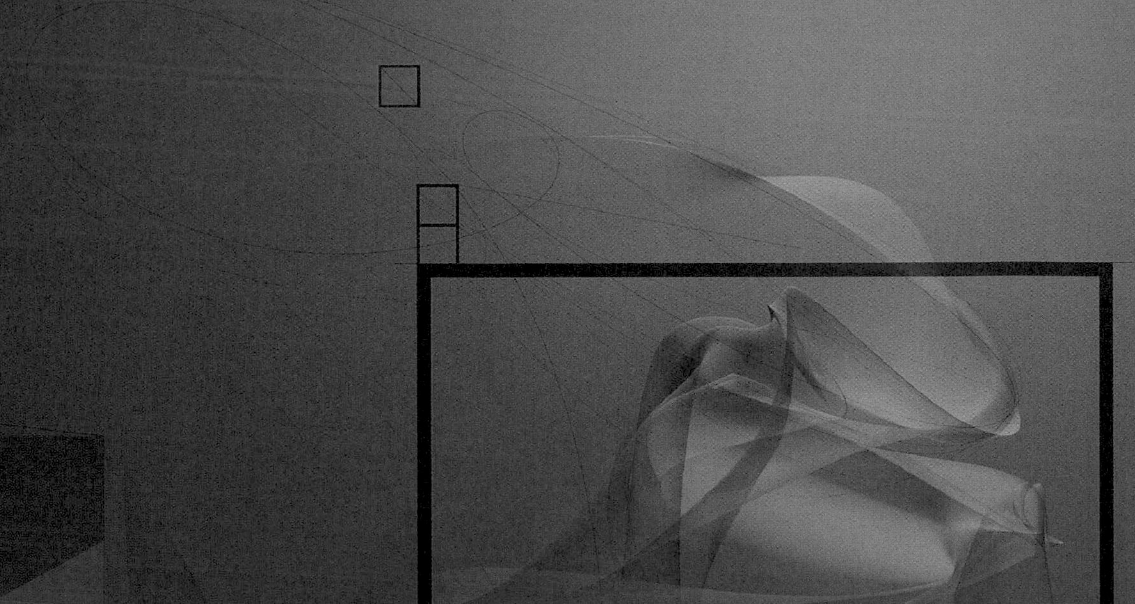

Lesson **14**

Advanced Clip Management

Good editing requires an organized workspace. Nothing is more important than managing the parameters, settings, and data associated with your clips. Even tiny errors can balloon into serious problems, including data loss, if you do not thoroughly understand how data is managed in Final Cut Pro and how to catch and correct problems.

Additionally, a solid understanding of the Final Cut Pro clip architecture can give you more flexibility in making editing decisions and can improve your productivity.

Using the Browser as a Clip Database

The Final Cut Pro Browser is actually an immensely robust database containing more than 75 different parameters for each clip or sequence. The first step in managing that database is to understand those parameters.

1 Open Lesson Files > Lesson 14 > **Clip Management.fcp.**

2 Expand the Browser window to fill your screen. Scroll through all of the columns.

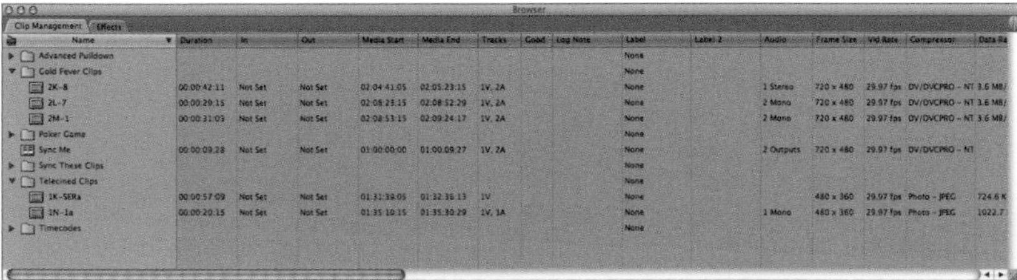

Although you can disregard many of the columns most of the time, it's important to know where to find this information when you need it.

3 Double-click the Poker Game bin.

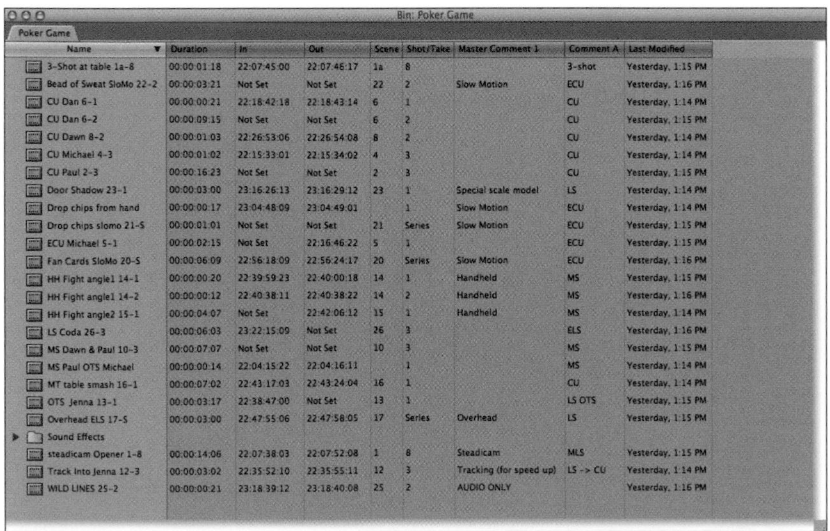

In this bin, most of the columns are hidden. Individual bins can have different column arrangements, and these are saved when you save the project.

4 Control-click the Comment A column header to open the shortcut menu.

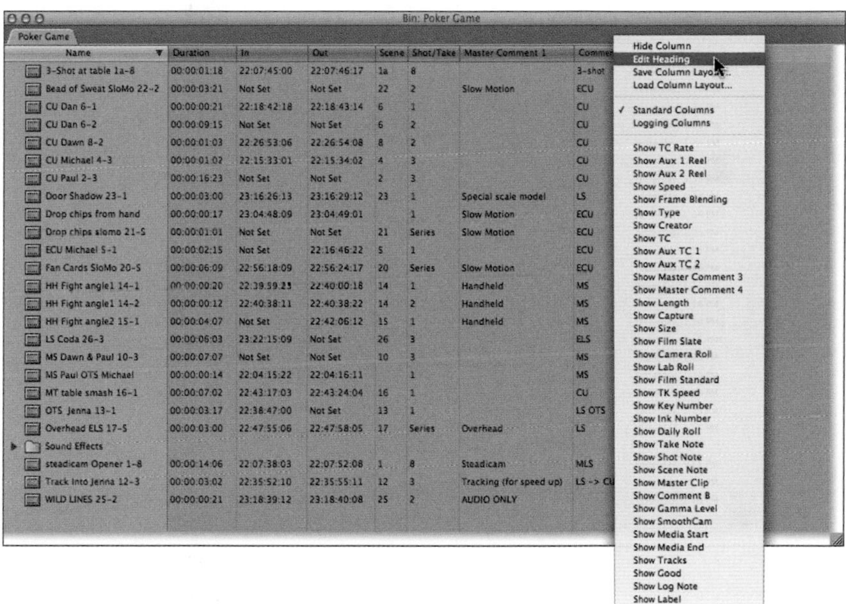

Name	Duration	In	Out	Scene	Shot/Take	Master Comment 1	Comme
3-Shot at table 1a-8	00:00:01:18	22:07:45:00	22:07:46:17	1a	8		3-shot
Bead of Sweat SloMo 22-2	00:00:03:21	Not Set	Not Set	22	2	Slow Motion	ECU
CU Dan 6-1	00:00:00:21	22:18:42:18	22:18:43:14	6	1		CU
CU Dan 6-2	00:00:09:15	Not Set	Not Set	6	2		CU
CU Dawn 8-2	00:00:01:03	22:26:53:06	22:26:54:08	8	2		CU
CU Michael 4-3	00:00:01:02	22:15:33:01	22:15:34:02	4	3		CU
CU Paul 2-3	00:00:16:23	Not Set	Not Set	2	3		CU
Door Shadow 23-1	00:00:03:00	23:16:26:13	23:16:29:12	23	1	Special scale model	LS
Drop chips from hand	00:00:00:17	23:04:48:09	23:04:49:01		1	Slow Motion	ECU
Drop chips slomo 21-S	00:00:01:01	Not Set	Not Set	21	Series	Slow Motion	ECU
ECU Michael 5-1	00:00:02:15	Not Set	22:16:46:22	5	1		ECU
Fan Cards SloMo 20-S	00:00:06:09	22:56:18:09	22:56:24:17	20	Series	Slow Motion	ECU
HH Fight angle1 14-1	00:00:00:20	22:39:59:23	22:40:00:18	14	1	Handheld	MS
HH Fight angle1 14-2	00:00:00:12	22:40:38:11	22:40:38:22	14	2	Handheld	MS
HH Fight angle2 15-1	00:00:04:07	Not Set	22:42:06:12	15	1	Handheld	MS
LS Coda 26-3	00:00:06:03	23:22:15:09	Not Set	26	3		ELS
MS Dawn & Paul 10-3	00:00:07:07	Not Set	Not Set	10	3		MS
MS Paul OTS Michael	00:00:00:14	22:04:15:22	22:04:16:11		1		MS
MT table smash 16-1	00:00:07:02	22:43:17:03	22:43:24:04	16	1		CU
OTS Jenna 13-1	00:00:03:17	22:38:47:00	Not Set	13	1		LS OTS
Overhead ELS 17-S	00:00:03:00	22:47:55:06	22:47:58:05	17	Series	Overhead	LS
Sound Effects							
steadicam Opener 1-8	00:00:14:06	22:07:38:03	22:07:52:08	1	8	Steadicam	MLS
Track into Jenna 12-3	00:00:03:02	22:35:52:10	22:35:55:11	12	3	Tracking (for speed up)	LS -> CU
WILD LINES 25-2	00:00:00:21	23:18:39:12	23:18:40:08	25	2	AUDIO ONLY	

This shortcut menu allows you to show and hide individual columns. There are quite a few columns to choose from. For now, do not add any additional columns.

5 Choose Edit Heading to rename the column header.

6 In the header area for the column, type *Shot Type*.

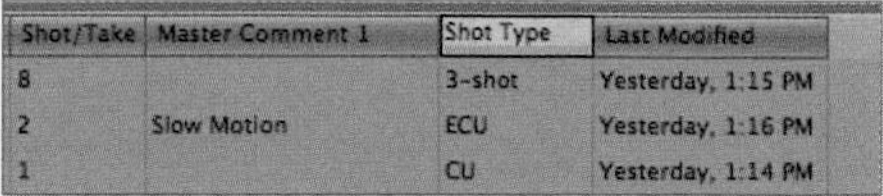

Shot/Take	Master Comment 1	Shot Type	Last Modified
8		3-shot	Yesterday, 1:15 PM
2	Slow Motion	ECU	Yesterday, 1:16 PM
1		CU	Yesterday, 1:14 PM

7 Control-click the column header area and choose Show Thumbnail from the shortcut menu.

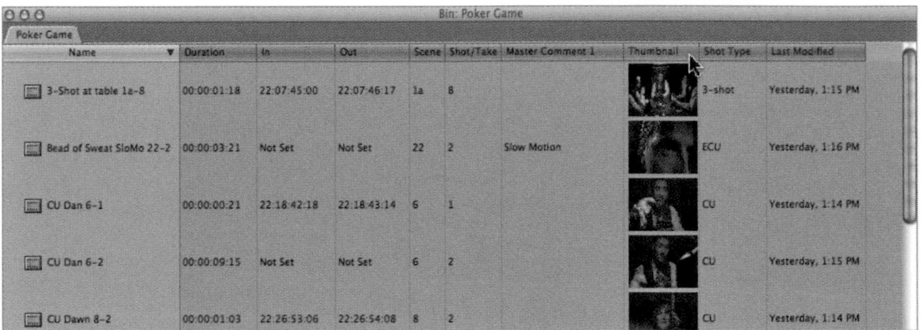

The thumbnail column appears. You can scrub through the thumbnail and even choose a new poster frame.

8 Find the clip called **Door Shadow 23-1**. Click the thumbnail and hold down the mouse button.

When you click a thumbnail, the pointer disappears, and you can drag to shuttle through the clip.

9 Drag to the right until you can see the shadow of the door open, then, holding down the mouse button, press Control, then release the mouse.

A new poster frame is set for the clip.

10 Drag the column header for Thumbnail to the left until it is the first column after Name.

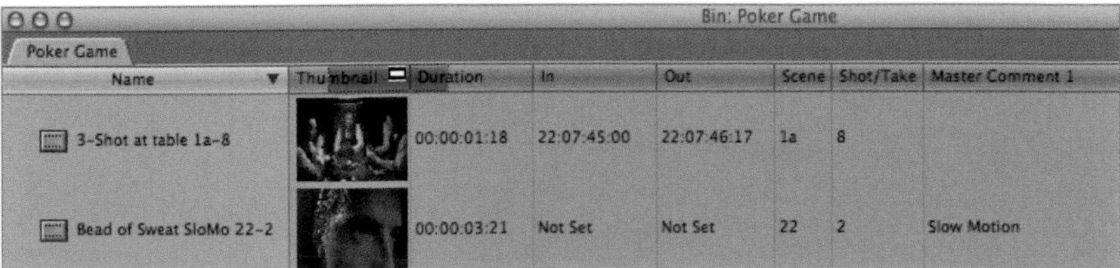

Saving and Sorting Columns

There is no right or wrong way to use the columns in the Browser. Different editing situations require that different columns are visible or hidden at any given time. If you create a set that you would like to reuse, you can save and restore that column layout.

1. Control-click the Browser column header area and choose Save Column Layout from the shortcut menu.

2. Name the layout and save it in the Column Layouts folder in the Final Cut Pro User Data folder.

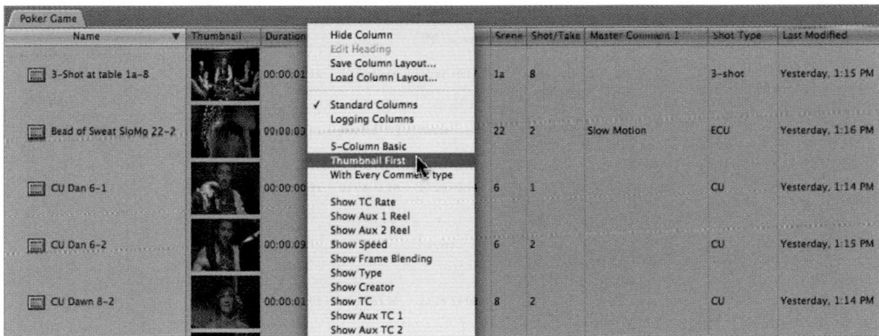

The first ten layouts stored in this folder will appear in the shortcut menu of every Browser or bin window. Choosing one will restore that layout to the current window.

3. Control-click the Thumbnail column header area and choose Hide Column from the shortcut menu.

You can also control the Browser view using sorting and secondary sorting.

4 Click the Scene column header.

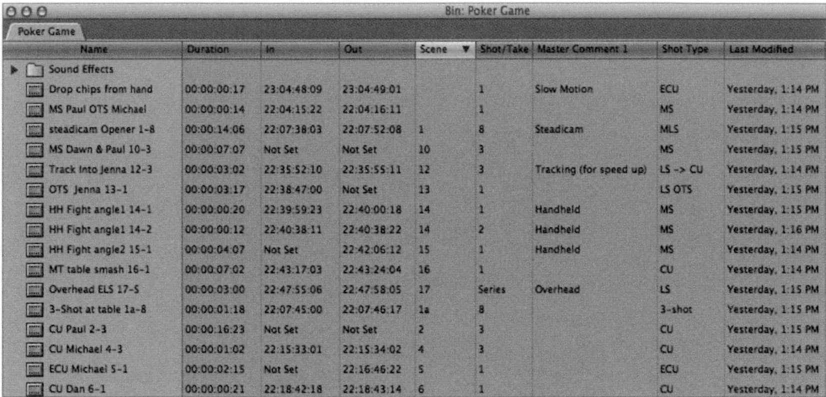

The clips are sorted on that column. A black sort arrow appears in the header. Note that without leading zeros, single digit numbers are not sorted in numerical order.

5 Click the header again.

The sort order is inverted.

6 Shift-click the Shot Type column header.

Now the clips are first sorted by scene and then by shot type. Each additional column that you Shift-click is added to the sort. You can identify the primary sort column because the primary sort arrow is black, and the secondary sort arrows are gray.

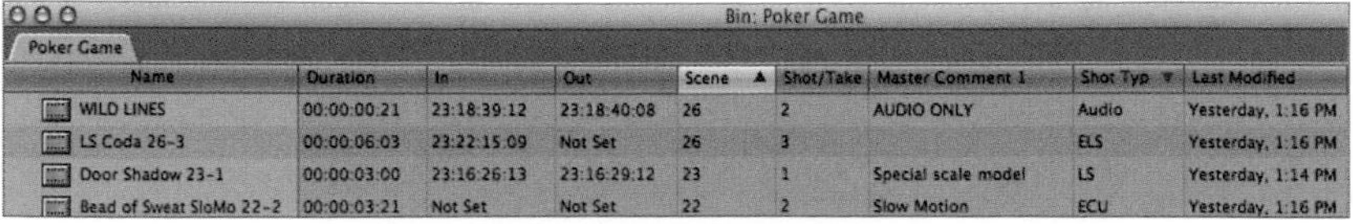

7 Click the Name column header to reset the sort.

Depending on the size of your monitor (and your vision), you might find that the text is a bit hard to read. Fortunately, you can enlarge it.

8 Choose View > Text Size > Medium.

The text in the Browser gets bigger. This affects all Browser windows and even the clip names in the Timeline.

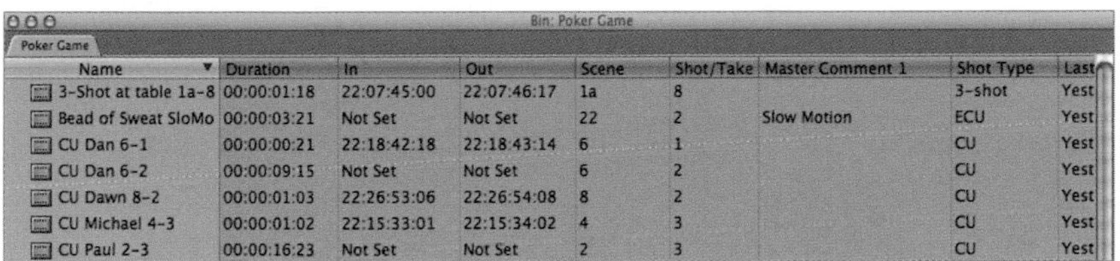

Bin: Poker Game

Poker Game

Name	Duration	In	Out	Scene	Shot/Take	Master Comment 1	Shot Type	Last
3-Shot at table 1a-8	00:00:01:18	22:07:45:00	22:07:46:17	1a	8		3-shot	Yest
Bead of Sweat SloMo	00:00:03:21	Not Set	Not Set	22	2	Slow Motion	ECU	Yest
CU Dan 6-1	00:00:00:21	22:18:42:18	22:18:43:14	6	1		CU	Yest
CU Dan 6-2	00:00:09:15	Not Set	Not Set	6	2		CU	Yest
CU Dawn 8-2	00:00:01:03	22:26:53:06	22:26:54:08	8	2		CU	Yest
CU Michael 4-3	00:00:01:02	22:15:33:01	22:15:34:02	4	3		CU	Yest
CU Paul 2-3	00:00:16:23	Not Set	Not Set	2	3		CU	Yest

When enlarging the text, you may need to adjust column widths to accommodate the larger font size.

9 Drag the right edge of the Name column to the right until all the words fit within the column.

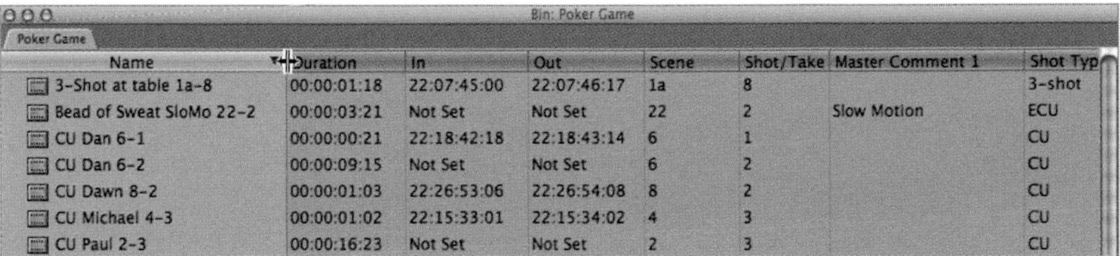

Bin: Poker Game

Poker Game

Name	Duration	In	Out	Scene	Shot/Take	Master Comment 1	Shot Typ
3-Shot at table 1a-8	00:00:01:18	22:07:45:00	22:07:46:17	1a	8		3-shot
Bead of Sweat SloMo 22-2	00:00:03:21	Not Set	Not Set	22	2	Slow Motion	ECU
CU Dan 6-1	00:00:00:21	22:18:42:18	22:18:43:14	6	1		CU
CU Dan 6-2	00:00:09:15	Not Set	Not Set	6	2		CU
CU Dawn 8-2	00:00:01:03	22:26:53:06	22:26:54:08	8	2		CU
CU Michael 4-3	00:00:01:02	22:15:33:01	22:15:34:02	4	3		CU
CU Paul 2-3	00:00:16:23	Not Set	Not Set	2	3		CU

Viewing a Clip's Item Properties

Another way to view the database contents is to view the Item Properties window of an individual clip or sequence.

1 Select the clip **CU Dawn 8-2**, and choose Edit > Item Properties or press Command-9.

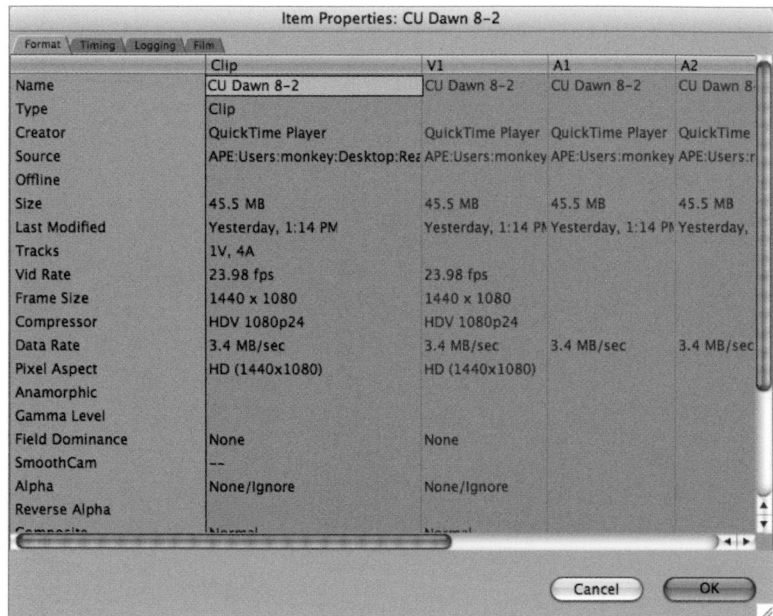

This window has four tabs that contain nearly all of the information found in the Browser columns. Because the data may be different for each of the audio or video tracks, each track is listed in its own column. Changes that you make in this window will update the Browser window, and vice versa.

2 Click OK to close the Item Properties window.

Using Complex Find Operations

You probably know how to use the Find command to locate a clip based on the text in its name, but that's only the beginning of the Final Cut Pro Find capabilities. Many more advanced Find operations are useful when you're working with a large, complex project.

Finding Unused Media

1 Choose Edit > Find, or with the Browser active, press Command-F.

The Find window appears.

2 From the For pop-up menu, choose Unused Media.

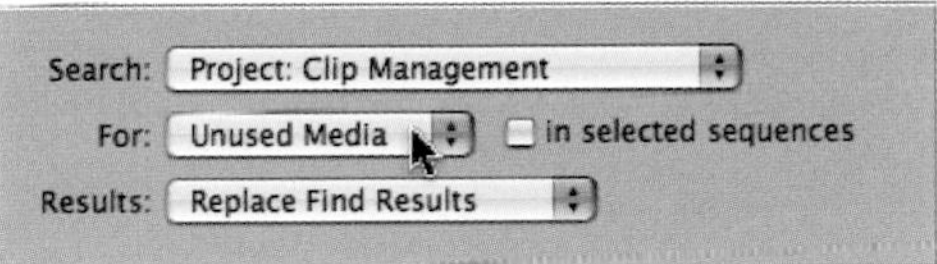

This instructs Final Cut Pro to search for clips that are not used in sequences. If you select the “in selected sequences” box, a search will only find clips not used in the currently selected sequences. If the box is deselected, a search will find clips that are not used in any sequences in the active project. With this setting selected, you do not need to choose anything in Search (although you can do so to further refine the search).

3 Deselect the “in selected sequences” box and click Find All.

The Find Results bin appears.

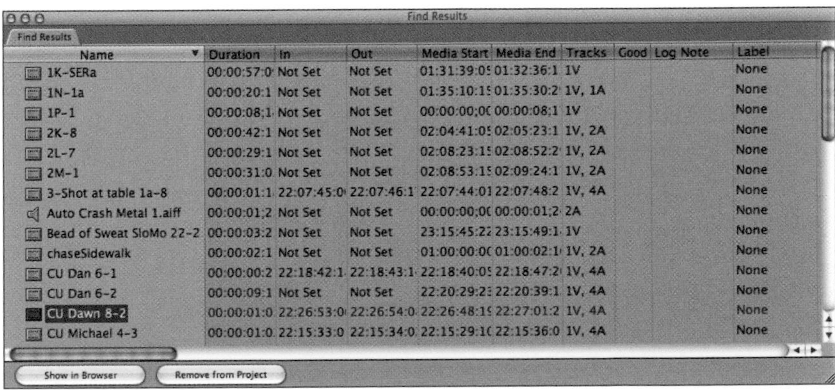

Name	Duration	In	Out	Media Start	Media End	Tracks	Good	Log Note	Label
1K-SERa	00:00:57:0	Not Set	Not Set	01:31:39:0	01:32:36:1	1V			None
1N-1a	00:00:20:1	Not Set	Not Set	01:35:10:1	01:35:30:2	1V, 1A			None
1P-1	00:00:08;1	Not Set	Not Set	00:00:00;0	00:00:08;1	1V			None
2K-8	00:00:42:1	Not Set	Not Set	02:04:41:0	02:05:23:1	1V, 2A			None
2L-7	00:00:29:1	Not Set	Not Set	02:08:23:1	02:08:52:2	1V, 2A			None
2M-1	00:00:31:0	Not Set	Not Set	02:08:53:1	02:09:24:1	1V, 2A			None
3-Shot at table 1a-8	00:00:01:1	22:07:45:0	22:07:46:1	22:07:44:01	22:07:48:2	1V, 4A			None
Auto Crash Metal 1.aiff	00:00:01;2	Not Set	Not Set	00:00:00;0	00:00:01;2	2A			None
Bead of Sweat SloMo 22-2	00:00:03:2	Not Set	Not Set	23:15:45:2	23:15:49:1	1V			None
chaseSidewalk	00:00:02:1	Not Set	Not Set	01:00:00:0	01:00:02:1	1V, 2A			None
CU Dan 6-1	00:00:00:2	22:18:42:1	22:18:43:1	22:18:40:0	22:18:47:2	1V, 4A			None
CU Dan 6-2	00:00:09:1	Not Set	Not Set	22:20:29:2	22:20:39:1	1V, 4A			None
CU Dawn 8-2	00:00:01:0	22:26:53:0	22:26:54:0	22:26:48:1	22:27:01:2	1V, 4A			None
CU Michael 4-3	00:00:01:0	22:15:33:0	22:15:34:0	22:15:29:1	22:15:36:0	1V, 4A			None

This search is a useful way to assess which clips in your project are not currently used in any sequences. Alternatively, you can search for only Used Media.

After you've done a Find All search and created a Find Results bin, you can further refine your results by searching within the Find Results bin.

4 Leave the Find Results bin open and press Command-F again.

When the Find Results bin is open, the Find command defaults to searching only within that bin, allowing you to refine your search.

5 From the For pop-up menu, choose All Media.

6 From the Column pop-up menu at the bottom of the window, choose Media Start and set the middle pop-up menu to Greater Than.

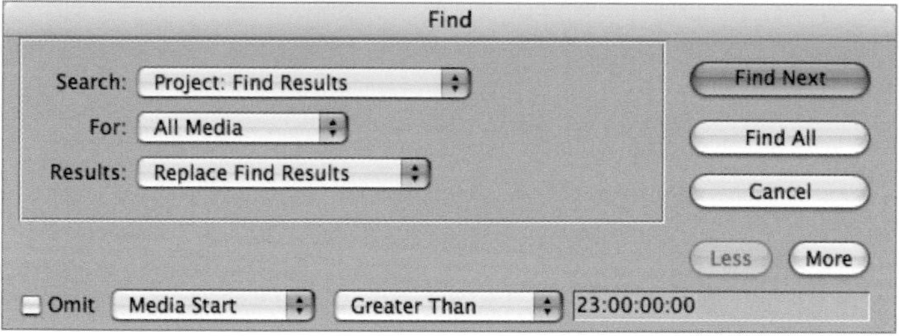

7 In the Search field, enter *23:00:00:00* and click Find All.

Be sure to type all zeros and colons for the best results.

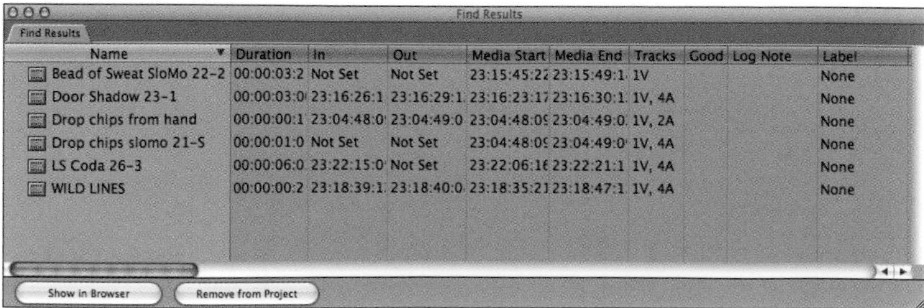

These search settings will find clips with a starting timecode later than the timecode you entered. This can be very helpful if you know the rough timecode number of a shot you're looking for. You can also search on the Media End column or combine both searches to find a specific timecode value.

You can further combine this search by adding more criteria to find clips of a certain name, from a particular reel, or based on the comment fields you may have filled out during logging.

You can even omit certain criteria. The example shown in the following figure is searching for clips with certain timecode and without "CU" in any column.

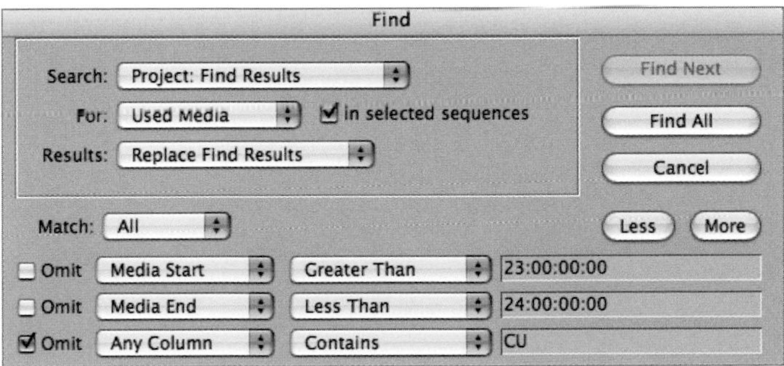

Working with Timecode

Among the most important properties of any clip are its reel number and timecode. This data is the only connection between the digitized clip and the source from which it was captured. If you modify this information, Final Cut Pro might not be able to recapture the clip. Further, if you want to move your sequence into another application (as you might do for color correction or other special effects), you will not be able to accurately reassemble it without the correct reel number and timecode.

Viewing Timecode

Timecode is displayed in a variety of formats based primarily on the frame rate and counting method of the clip. For example, a 24p clip has different timecode values than a clip recorded at 60i. Likewise, clips at 29.97 fps (standard NTSC video) can be represented in two different ways: drop frame and non-drop frame.

1. Close the Find Results bin and close the Poker Game bin.

2. Choose Window > Arrange > Standard or press Control-U.

3. Double-click **GoldFever Merged** to open it into the Viewer.

4. In the Viewer, click the View Settings button and choose Show Timecode Overlays.

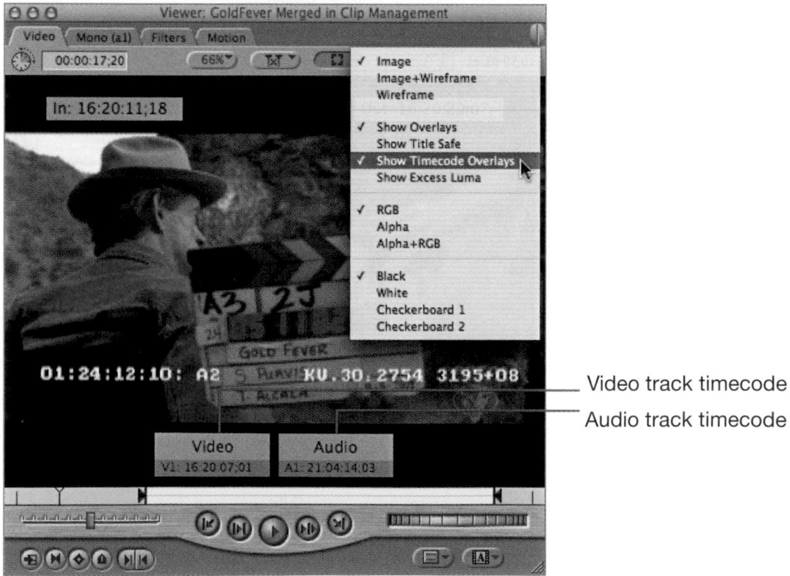

The Viewer shows the video and audio track timecodes on top of the image. Merged clips based on video and audio from different files show different timecodes for each track.

The timecode overlays disappear when the clip is playing.

You can also view a clip's timecode information in the Item Properties window.

5 Press Command-9 or choose Edit > Item Properties.

6 Click the Timing tab.

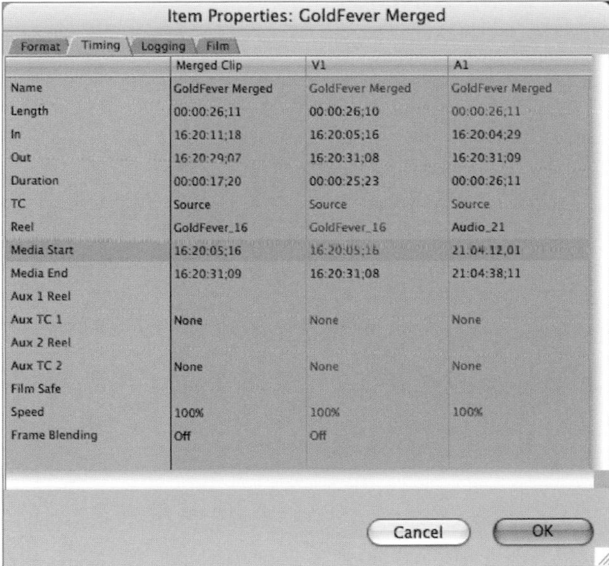

The timecode value for the first frame in the clip is shown in the Media Start row.

7 Click OK to close the Item Properties window.

Fixing a Bad Reel Number

There are occasions when you need to change the vital reel number information. One common mistake is to neglect to change the reel number when logging multiple tapes, resulting in clips with incorrect reel numbers.

1 Double-click the Gold Fever Clips bin to open it into its own window.

2 Scroll through the bin window until you can see the Reel column.

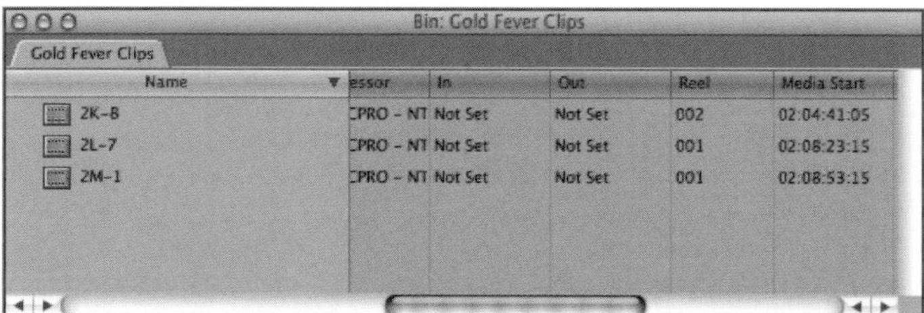

Often, you can identify clips with a faulty reel number based on the hours value in the timecode field. In this bin, the last two clips are marked reel 001, but their timecodes start with hour 02 in the Media Start column. Although this isn't a guarantee of a reel error, it can be a good indicator, because the hour indicator is often used to differentiate sequential tapes, especially those used in field production.

3 Select one of the clips with an incorrect reel number.

4 In the Reel column for the clip, enter *002* and press Return.

NOTE ► Changes made to a clip's reel number or timecode fields actually change the media file on disk. This means that every other clip that refers to the same media file will be updated to reflect the change. Even other applications that can read timecode will see this new information.

5 Click OK to accept the warning that you will be changing the file on disk.

6 Select the third clip in the Gold Fever Clips bin.

7 Control-click the Reel column and choose 002 from the shortcut menu.

8 In the dialog warning you about changing the file on disk, click OK.

Modifying Timecode

Occasionally, rather than fixing the reel number, you may need to change the timecode associated with a clip. Although you can view the clip's current starting timecode in the Media Start column, this information cannot be edited in the Browser or Item Properties window. You can modify only one clip's timecode at a time.

1 Open the Timecodes bin.

2 Double-click the clip **1P-1** to open it into the Viewer.

3 Choose Modify > Timecode.

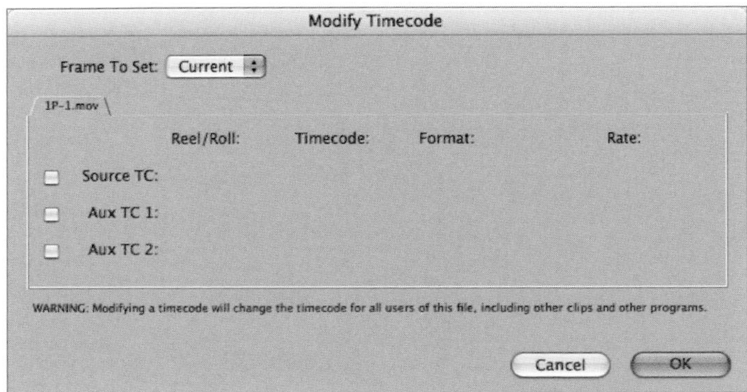

In this example, the clip's timecode was erroneously reset to 00:00:00:00. Fortunately, this clip has BITC (burned-in timecode) so you can use that to restore the correct timecode value.

4 Select the Source TC checkbox.

5 Make sure the Frame To Set pop-up menu at the top of the window is set to Current.

This ensures that the number you enter in this dialog is assigned to the current playhead position.

6 Move the window so you can see the Viewer and enter the timecode number from the BITC into the Source Timecode field to match the visible number.

If you did not adjust the clip in the Viewer, the timecode number should read 01:28:05:00.

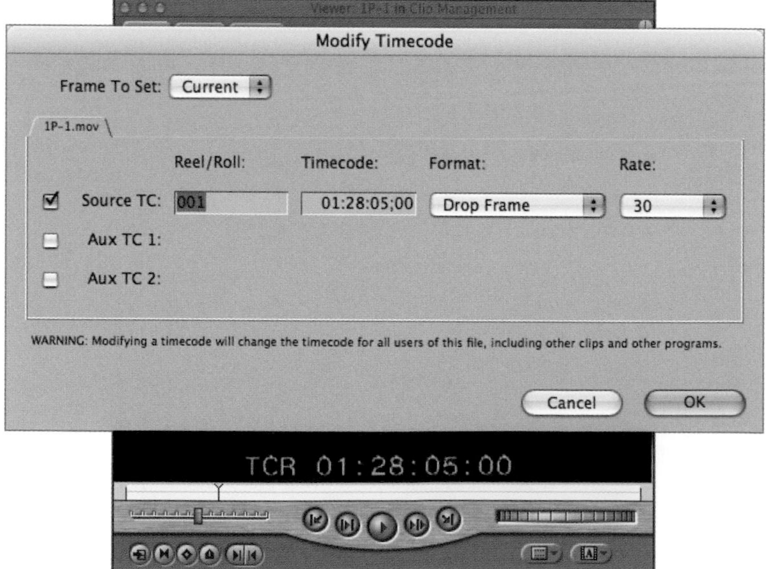

7 Choose Format > Drop Frame and leave Rate set to 30.

8 Click OK to close the dialog.

Now you can shuttle around the clip in the Viewer and see that the Current Timecode field always accurately matches the number burned into the video.

Using Auxiliary Timecode Tracks

In addition to the primary timecode track, Final Cut Pro allows you to assign two auxiliary reel numbers and timecode tracks. This information is also written into the media file, so once you add an auxiliary track, it will appear in any other clip that points to the same media file.

An auxiliary timecode track can be essential for clips shot at one frame rate (for example, 24 fps) and then transferred to another (such as 25 fps or 29.97 fps). Or, when you're using footage from multiple sources in a multiclip, you might have tape from three cameras, each with its own timecode, in addition to a smart slate that indicates the timecode from a music playback device. Each of the clips used in the multiclip needs to contain both sets of timecode.

You can keep the video's original timecode in the Source Timecode fields and use an auxiliary timecode field to store the version from the music. You can then use the auxiliary timecode value to sync up the clips in the multiclip, or if you're not using multiclips, you can compare the timecode values during editing to guarantee that the video is in sync with the prerecorded song.

1 In the Timecodes bin, open the clip **MCU in front of painter** into the Viewer.

2 Park the playhead on one of the first few frames, where you can see the timecode displayed on the smart slate.

3 Choose Modify > Timecode.

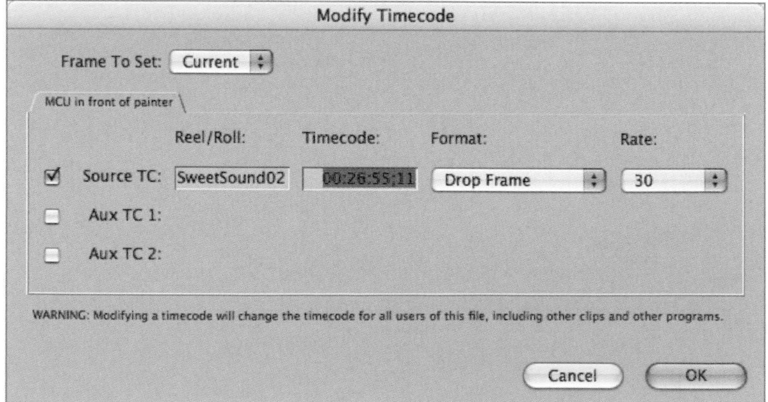

4 Select the Aux TC 1 checkbox to enable the auxiliary timecode fields.

5 Enter *DAT Playback TC* in the Reel field to indicate thc source of this timecode.

6 From the Frame To Set pop-up menu, choose Current and leave Rate set to 30.

7 In the Aux TC 1 Timecode field, enter the timecode number visible on the slate.

8 Click OK.

Now your clip has two timecode tracks assigned to it. You can choose which one you want to view in the Viewer and Browser windows.

9 In the Viewer, Control-click the Current Timecode field and choose Aux TC 1 from the shortcut menu.

All editing of this clip (including exporting edit decision lists [EDLs]) will now reference this alternate timecode value.

Viewing Alternate Timecode Formats

Final Cut Pro includes tools to view timecode in alternative ways to accommodate certain workflows with HD footage or with PAL footage that will be output to film. You can view 60 fps (or 59.94 fps) footage as 30 fps, and you can view 25 fps PAL footage as 24 fps.

You might want to view 60 fps material at 30 fps to match the display on some DVCPRO HD decks, or if you're going to finish the project on 30 fps SD (standard definition) video.

1 In the Timecodes bin, double-click **chaseSidewalk** to open it into the Viewer.

   This clip is a 60 fps DVCPRO HD clip. As you step through the clip, you can see that the Current Timecode field updates consecutive frames to 59 before rolling over to 00.

2 Control-click the Current Timecode field and choose 60 @ 30 from the shortcut menu.

This instructs Final Cut Pro to display each frame number twice, placing an asterisk next to the second instance of each number.

This does not change the file or the timecode associated with the file; it changes only the way the timecode is displayed in the Viewer.

NOTE ▸ The 60 @ 30 option is visible only on clips with 60 fps or 59.94 fps timecodes.

Similarly, you can choose to view 24 fps footage at 25 fps. This is commonly employed when 24 fps film material has been transferred onto 25 fps tapes (the standard PAL frame rate). This allows you to edit in a 25 fps sequence but generate a 24 fps EDL. Unlike the 60 @ 30 setting, 24 @ 25 is set in the Modify Timecode window rather than the Current Timecode field view settings.

Renaming Clips and Files

There are very few operations in Final Cut Pro that actually modify the file stored on disk. Changing the reel number or timecode has such an effect, and you can also change a file's name within Final Cut Pro.

Obviously, you could also just go to the Finder and rename a video file, the way you would change any other file, but doing that can cause Final Cut Pro to lose track of the file, and you could also lose track of the newly-renamed clip.

Often, clips get imported with nondescriptive names derived from scene and shot numbers, or even worse, sometimes clip names are auto-generated, such as clips imported from an XDCAM HD disc or P2 card. In cases like these, you may wind up with a folder full of clips with seemingly random names.

Fortunately, you can automatically rename a file based on the name of the clip in the Final Cut Pro Browser.

1 Select the clip **1P-1** from the Timecodes bin.

2 Rename the clip *Cutaway Clock* and press Enter to accept the new name.

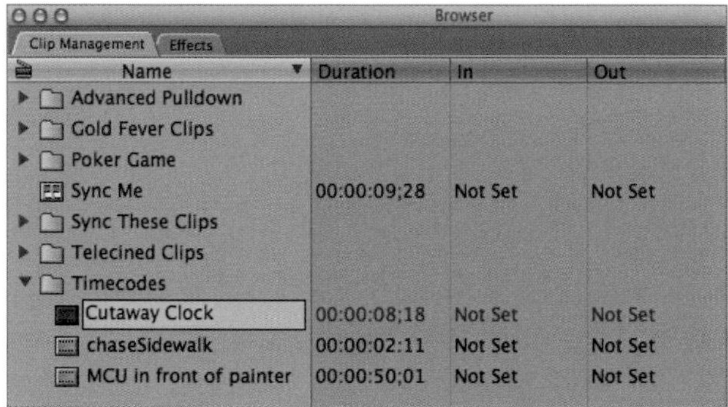

3 Choose Modify > Rename > File to Match Clip.

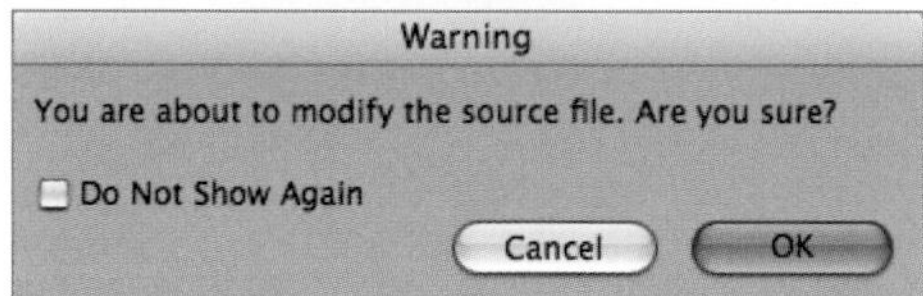

A warning appears because changing a file's name can affect clips in other projects or applications.

4 Click OK.

The file on disk is updated with the new name.

NOTE ▶ Open projects in Final Cut Pro will automatically relink to the newly-named file, but if the file is referenced in a project that is not currently open, clips will require manual relinking.

You can also perform the opposite action: renaming a clip in your project to reflect the name of the file on disk.

5 Select **chaseSidewalk** and rename it *Sidewalk Chase*.

Although there is no reason that you should refrain from renaming clips, you may occasionally want to restore the original name.

6 Control-click the clip and choose Rename > Clip to Match File from the shortcut menu.

   The clip name is restored.

Recording to Dual Systems

Often, your picture and sound will be recorded on separate media. This may be because the picture was recorded on film (which can't record audio), or because production logistics required recording the audio separately from the video, usually onto a DAT (digital audio tape) or hard disk recorder. This process is called dual-system recording because two devices are used (one for picture and one for audio).

If your footage was recorded in this way, an additional step is required before you can edit the footage. You must line up the audio so that lips and voices (and everything else) will play back in sync with the video.

Syncing Clips

In most cases, dual-system media are shot using a slate (sometimes called a clapboard) to provide a clear frame with which picture and sound can be easily synchronized.

1 From the Sync These Clips bin, open the clip **GoldFeverVideo**.

2 Find the exact frame where the clap stick on the slate closes, and set an In point at that frame.

   Although this is a timecode slate, in this case the numbers don't correspond with the timecode in your audio clip, so you should disregard them.

3 Open the clip **GoldFeverAudio**.

4 Find the frame where the sound of the clapboard can be heard (at 21:04:13;24).

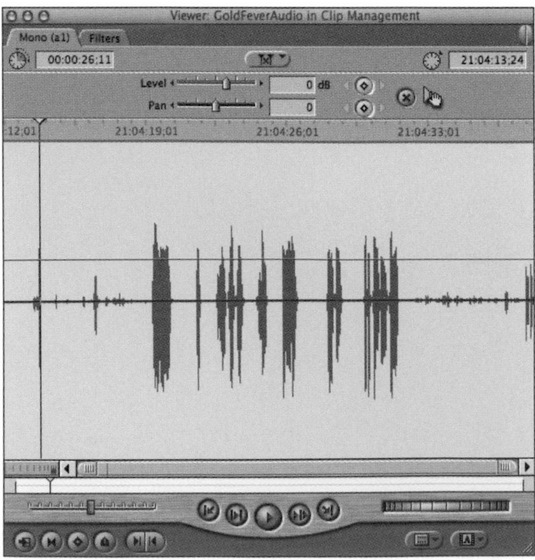

5 Set an In point at that frame.

You have now identified the same point in time on each clip.

Merging Clips

To combine these two clips into a single clip for editing, use the Merge Clips command.

1 Select the two clips in the Browser window.

2 Choose Modify > Merge Clips.

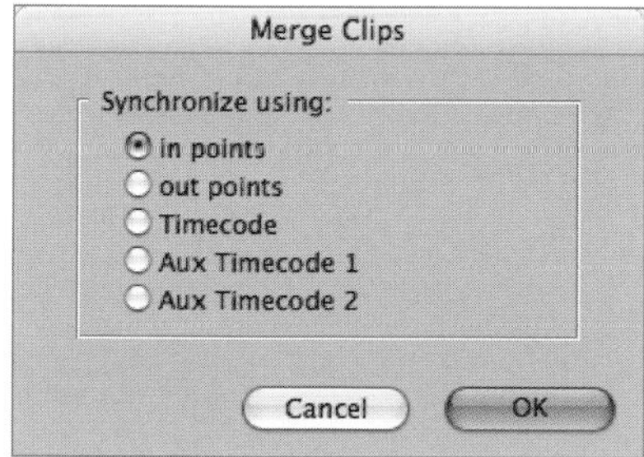

The Merge Clips dialog opens.

3 Set the clips to synchronize based on the In points you just set.

4 Click OK.

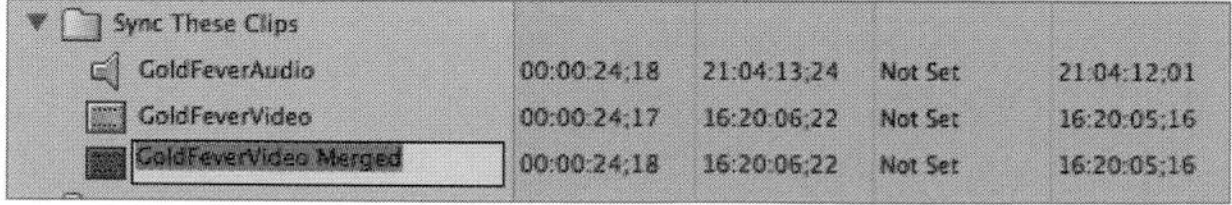

In the Browser, a new clip is created in the same bin as the other two clips. This merged clip points to the two separate media files on disk.

You can combine a single video track with up to 24 mono audio tracks or 12 stereo audio tracks to create a merged clip.

5 Double-click the new clip to open it into the Viewer.

Because the audio clip starts before the video clip, there are transparent frames at the beginning of the clip.

From this point on, you can edit with this merged clip, and the audio and video will remain in sync.

In some cases, you will not have a slate to assist you in syncing audio and video clips. You may, however, have identical timecode in the two clips. This can happen if the DAT player was slaved (synced) to the video camera on the set, or if another device was sending identical timecode to both the camera and audio recording device. In these cases, you can use Merge Clips to connect the audio and video files based on the timecode numbers in the clip, or enable one of the auxiliary timecode fields in the Modify Timecode window and enter the synchronized timecode numbers.

Then, set the Merge Clips dialog to merge based on that Aux TC field.

Syncing Clips Manually

If you have no timecode numbers or clapboard sound to help you sync audio and video, you'll have to do it manually. This may sound daunting, but experienced editors frequently face such situations and know how to handle them without fear.

1 From the Browser, open the *Sync Me* sequence.

This sequence contains audio and video from the same scene that need to be aligned.

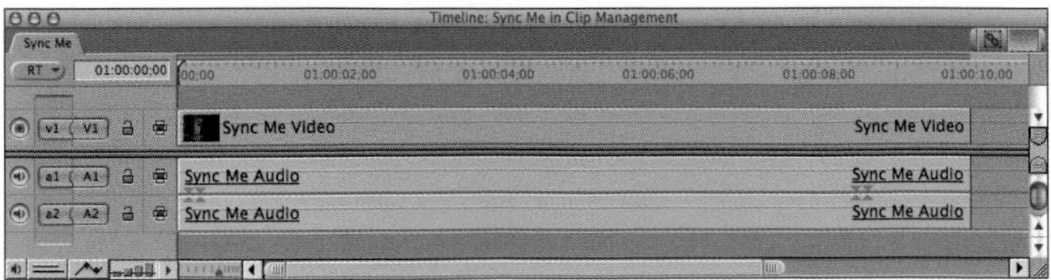

2 Play the sequence.

First, you must determine whether the audio is early or late compared to the video. In this case, it's easy to recognize that the audio is considerably earlier than the video. However, when you're only a few frames off, it can be very difficult to tell. The best thing to do is to find a section of the clip that features a percussive sound, or at least a plosive vocal sound (such as a p, b, or t).

3 Play the clip until approximately 8 seconds into the clip, when the bottle is put down.

This is a great place to find your sync because the glass makes a sharp sound.

4 Click the Timeline Layout pop-up menu and choose Show Audio Waveforms.

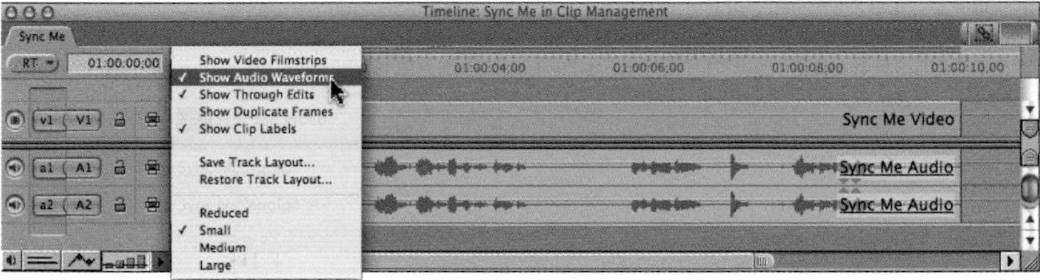

5 Locate the large burst in the audio waveform that corresponds to the bottle sound (around 07:00).

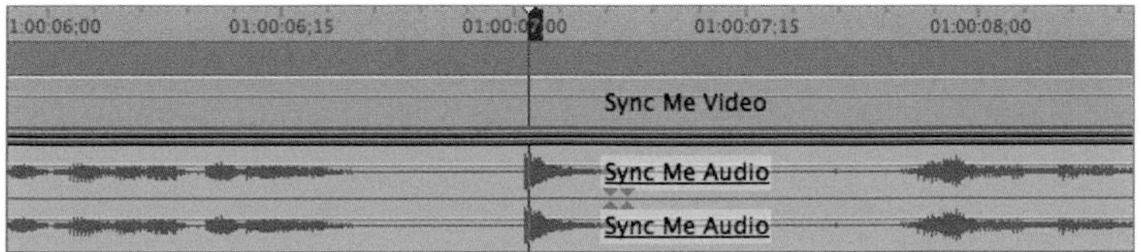

This indicates where the glass sound occurs.

6 Turn off the audio tracks by clicking the Audible control for tracks A1 and A2.

Turning off the audio allows you to find the video frame with which you're going to sync without distraction.

7 Play the sequence until you see the frame when the bottle is put down (at approximately 07:07).

8 Drag the audio clip so the waveform burst approximately lines up with the video frame you chose. Zoom in on the Timeline, if necessary.

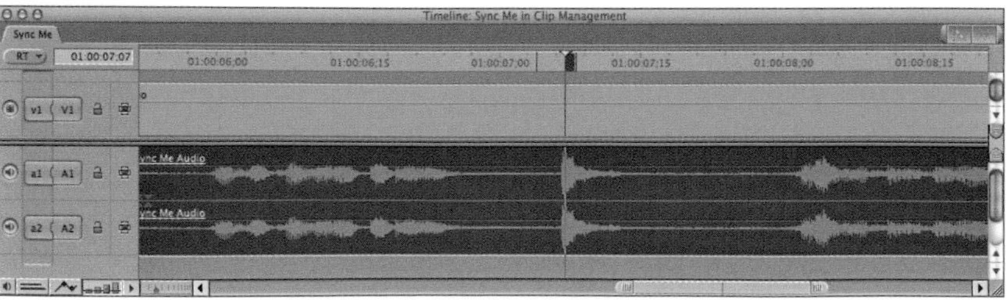

9 Turn the audio tracks back on and play around the area by pressing \ (backslash).

   Your audio and video should be in close synchronization, but you always want to make sure they're as exact as possible.

10 Select the audio clip and enter +3 (plus three).

   This will move the clip forward three frames.

11 Play around the area again.

   Does the sync appear better or worse?

12 Enter –6 (minus six) and play around the area again.

   How is it now? You've heard the sync three frames past and three frames before your original position. Which of the three positions sounds most accurate? If you can't tell, you may need to move the audio clip five frames in either direction instead of three, or find a better event to sync on.

   After you find the position you think is most accurate, move the audio clip +1 frame, and listen, then move it –2 frames and listen. Eventually you will find the position that seems in perfect sync.

   Before you merge the clips, watch the whole clip and look for other percussive or plosive sounds to make sure it all looks synchronized. The larger the monitor you use, the easier it usually is to identify correct sync.

13 Once the clips are in sync, select the clips, choose Modify > Link, then drag the new linked clip to the Browser.

With time, you will learn to recognize when clips are in or out of sync, and when they're out, you'll be able to guess pretty accurately how many frames off they are.

Understanding 24p Editing Basics

For many years, video makers have strived to simulate the characteristics of film to help bring their low-budget productions that high-budget cinematic flair. Film isn't inherently superior to video, but that "film look" carries with it the cachet and magic of the Hollywood dream factory.

One of the most noticeable and significant differences between film and video is the frame rate at which each is displayed. Video typically runs at 25 or 30 interlaced frames per second, but film is projected at 24 full frames per second.

Modern video formats now have the ability to operate at 24 full frames per second, commonly called *24p* (24 fps progressive). However, traditional video equipment—especially the hundreds of millions of televisions in use around the world—still operates at 25 or 30 interlaced frames per second.

Whether you're editing a show that originated on a 24p format (including 35mm film) or one that will be output to a 24p format, you should become a little familiar with how to navigate between the 24p world and the traditional interlaced worlds of NTSC and PAL formats.

Converting 24p to 29.97

Unless you have lots of hard drive space and special hardware, you will need to do your editing work at less than full film or high definition video resolutions. Most producers have their material transferred to standard definition video. The process of transferring film to video is known as *telecine.* HD material transferred to standard definition videotape is called a *downconvert.* In either case, how do you get 24 fps to play at NTSC's 30 fps rate and not have it look like a Keystone Cops comedy?

Although the NTSC video rate is often defined as 30 fps, it actually runs slightly slower. The slower rate became necessary when NTSC color television standards were developed and had to be compatible with black-and-white television standards. Never mind the actual details; what is important to know is that NTSC color footage runs at $30 \times 1000 \div 1001$, or 29.97 fps.

When film is run through a telecine machine or when 24p video is downconverted to NTSC, it also runs at slightly less than 24 fps. The adjustment, or *pulldown*, is 24 *x* 1000 ÷ 1001, or 23.976 fps (commonly referred to as 23.98). Most 24p video in NTSC countries is shot at this pulled-down speed, so no difference exists between the high definition and standard definition running times. Some new 24p DV camcorders also record at 23.98 fps.

To understand how pulldown works, let's pretend that video runs at 30 fps and film at 24 fps. How do you get 1 second of film (or 24p video) to equal 1 second of standard definition video? It doesn't make sense at first, because it doesn't divide up evenly: 30 divided by 24 equals 1.25.

The trick is that NTSC video consists of two fields per frame, or 60 fields per second. In the early days of television, a cathode-ray gun was used to project the image onto the phosphorous surface of the screen, but the picture would flicker when displayed at 30 fps. The solution was to draw every other line in one pass, known as a *field*, then fill in the remaining lines on the second field pass. So we think of NTSC video running at 60 fields per second. Does this help our mathematical dilemma? Not really: 60 divided by 24 equals 2.5, and you wouldn't want to cut frames in half. However, if we alternate between copying each frame of film (or 24p video) to two fields and then three fields of NTSC video, we can successfully compensate for the frame rate/field rate ratio.

This is known as 3:2 pulldown, although it would be more accurate to call it 2:3:2:3 pulldown, because that is what is really going on. The start of this 2:3:2:3 pattern (or *cadence*) is called the A frame, and this is copied to two NTSC video fields. Next comes the B frame, which goes onto the next three video fields. At this point we don't have a complete video frame, so we need to copy the next, or C, frame to two video fields. Finally, the D frame is copied onto the remaining three video fields. Now we have four frames of film, or 24p video, conformed to five whole frames (that's 10 fields) of NTSC video; 10 divided by 4 equals 2.5.

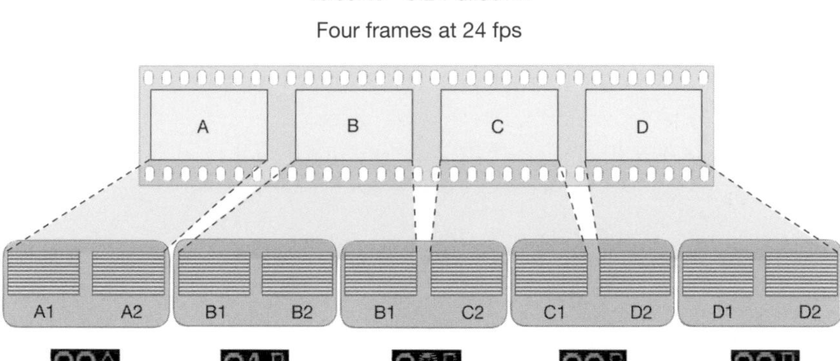

Understanding Timecode and A Frames

The relationship between 24 fps media and 30 fps video becomes even more important when working with timecode. Telecine and downconverting use 30 fps non-drop frame timecode. Every A frame—the start of the 2:3:2:3 pattern—must land on a timecode frame that ends with either a 0 or a 5. In other words, an A frame should show up on video frames where the timecode ends on 00, 05, 10, and so on. It is also important to start every clip on an A frame. If you reverse telecine a batch of clips with Cinema Tools (converting from 30 fps back to 24 fps), it looks for the A frame using timecode, and if any clip doesn't start on an A frame, it trims a few frames off the head so that it does start on an A frame.

The importance of starting every clip on an A frame is maintained through Final Cut Pro when the Film Safe option is selected in the Browser. This way, if the sequences are run through the Media Manager, and the clips are trimmed, they will always start on an A frame.

Viewing Edge Code and Timecode

You may have seen clips with numbers all over the image area. These numbers provide a look at what is normally invisible—the film edge code, and the video and audio timecodes. Having timecode and edge codes burned onto the image area helps you see that the logs and lists for the offline edit match up to the original media.

Sound for film and 24p video shot for theatrical release is usually recorded on a separate recorder. This requires tracking yet another set of timecode numbers associated with the audio recorder.

Working with film requires tracking even more numbers. During the manufacturing process, numbers and bar codes are exposed on the edge of the film. When the film is developed, these become visible and are used to match the negative to the final edit. These numbers are called keynumbers, or keycode. And if a positive workprint for projection is made, it may have another set of numbers applied between the sprocket holes with a special numbering machine. These numbers are known as ink numbers, or Acmade code, named after a popular film-numbering machine. Although keynumbers are added by the manufacturer and are arbitrary, ink numbers can represent daily rolls, scenes, or other specific information that helps bring order to the otherwise chaotic mix of codes and numbers used in film editing.

Working with so many numbers covering the image might seem distracting, but they are considered essential in film and 24p offline editing. Traditionally, this information is burned into the video image during the telecine or down-convert process, but Final Cut Pro offers another option.

You can enter the information into the Cinema Tools database and view it overlayed on the video images. This allows you to hide all those codes when you're concentrating on the story, and display them when you need to verify that all the numbers are lining up correctly.

1 Open the Gold Fever Clips bin and double-click **2K-8**.

2 Turn on video overlays by choosing View > Show Overlays or pressing Control-Option-W.

3 Turn on the keycode overlays by choosing View > Timecode Overlays > Keycode.

NOTE ▸ This clip does not have any embedded ink numbers, so turning on the ink numbers has no effect.

The overlays now display all of those crazy numbers so you can verify that your edit lists are accurate.

Editing 24 fps Originals at 29.97 fps

Film and 24p video can be edited in a 29.97 fps NTSC video project. This process is known as *matchback*. For film, videotape numbers and timecode are matched back to camera rolls and keynumbers. In the case of 24p video, the 30 fps timecode from the downconverted video is matched back to the original 24 fps timecode. Although considered inferior to editing at 24 fps, hundreds of made-for-cable movies as well as theatrically-released films have been successfully finished this way.

One problem when editing a matchback project is that the 3:2 cadence is often changed during editing. This means that the predictable AA BB BC CD DD pattern can break. For example, when you make an edit, the outgoing frame of the last shot may be a DD frame, and the incoming frame of the next shot might start on a BC frame. This makes it difficult to figure out where the original frames should start and end.

Another problem is that the software must check the running time and make adjustments to keep from drifting out of sync. This is usually noted in the cut list as a one-frame adjustment, but it is not always apparent.

There have been many attempts at improving the process, but the fact that so many matchback projects are finished without major problems attests to its effectiveness. Successful matchback projects can often be credited to the skill of negative cutters and to online editors who faithfully match the offline edit as closely as possible.

Using Film-Safe Editing

The Film Safe feature is actually used for any 24 fps material edited in a 30 fps sequence, whether it originated on film or video. For example, footage shot on 24p HD is often dubbed to 30 fps SD NTSC tape for editing. After you've made your editing decisions, an EDL is created, and the original HD footage is conformed to match the edit, creating a 24p master for broadcast, duplication, or printing to film.

Because there are duplicate frames in the NTSC version (added during the 24-fps-to-30-fps conversion process), it is possible for you to make edits on these new *imaginary* frames (that don't exist in the 24p original). This can cause problems when trying to conform the HD footage. However, you can prevent this by activating the Film Safe setting for your clips.

1 Select the three clips in the Gold Fever Clips bin.

2 Scroll through the Browser columns horizontally until the Film Safe column is visible (in the last column).

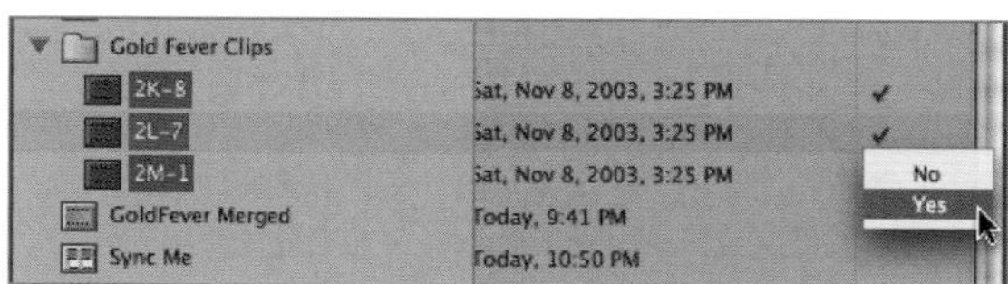

3 Control-click the Film Safe column and choose Yes from the shortcut menu.

A checkmark appears in that column for all of the selected clips.

Although Final Cut Pro will let you make edits on these imaginary frames, when you perform a Media Manager trimming operation on your completed sequence, the Film Safe setting ensures that the trimmed clips will always begin and end on real frames, not imaginary ones.

Returning 29.97 fps to 24 fps

As you saw, it takes some doing to get film telecined or to get 24p HD video downconverted to standard definition NTSC video. Now, in order to work at 24 fps, you need to undo all that.

During capture, Final Cut Pro can remove the extra video fields (added during the telecine process) when using special video hardware like the Aurora Film IgniterX and AJA KONA video cards. It can also capture directly to 23.98 fps from digital video if it was recorded using the advanced 2:3:3:2 pulldown setting found in some Panasonic cameras (see "Using 2:3:3:2 Advanced Pulldown (Panasonic 24p)" later in this lesson).

Alternately, Final Cut Pro (with the help of Cinema Tools) can reverse telecine 30 fps clips to their original 24p state, accurately disassembling and reassembling the frames.

1 Select both clips in the Telecined Clips bin.

2 Choose Tools > Cinema Tools Reverse Telecine.

   That's it. You have now converted both of those 29.97 fps clips into 24 fps clips. You can verify that by looking at the timecode for those clips.

3 Select one of the clips in the Telecined Clips bin.

4 Choose Edit > Item Properties > Format, or press Command-9.

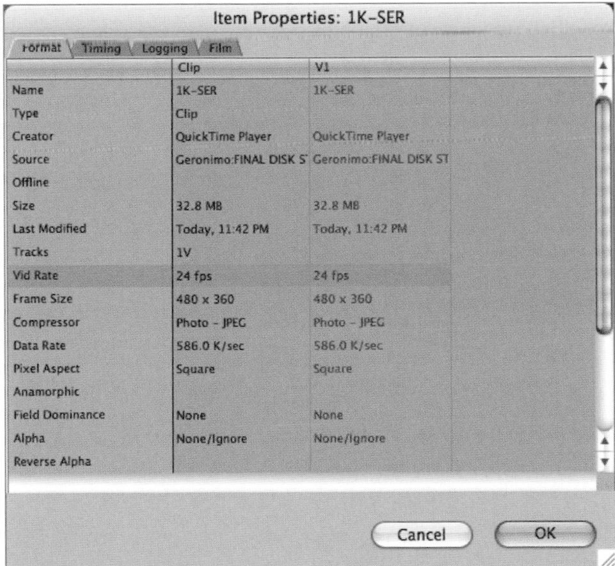

   The Vid Rate column now reads 24 fps.

5 Click OK to close the Item Properties window, and choose Modify > Timecode.

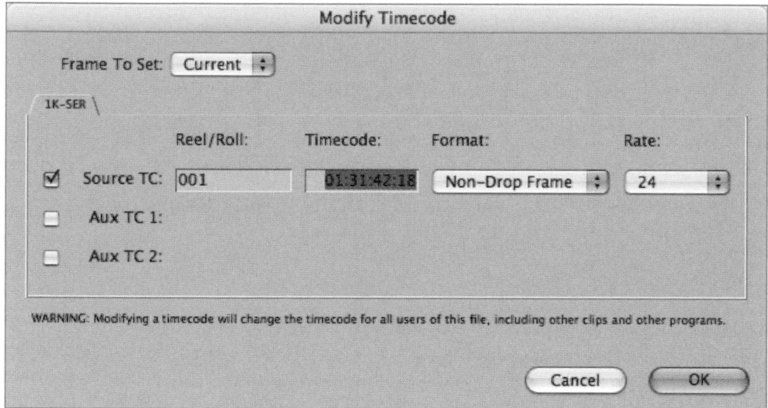

The custom timecode associated with the clip is still there, but it has been converted into 24 fps timecode.

WARNING ▶ This operation is not reversible. It permanently alters the media files on your disk! This is potentially one of the most destructive commands in Final Cut Pro, and what's more, there's no confirmation dialog. Also, this command will reverse telecine files that were never telecined in the first place. Any 30 fps file will be modified, and data will be lost! You have been warned!

If you want more control over the reverse telecine process, you can use Cinema Tools. In that application, you can make new clips (instead of changing the 29.97 fps originals) and reverse telecine to 23.98 fps instead of 24 fps.

Using 2:3:3:2 Advanced Pulldown (Panasonic 24p)

To convert 3:2 pulldown material to 24 fps QuickTime files, you have to take apart and reassemble video frames to recover the original film or 24p frames. In the case of DV, this involves uncompressing video frames, separating the frames into individual video fields, rebuilding new frames, and finally recompressing the video. All this takes time, and there is a chance of image degradation, although due to the quality of the Apple DV codec, you will probably never notice it.

The 2:3:3:2 pulldown used on Panasonic 24p cameras (also called *advanced pulldown*) does not straddle the C frame between two video frames. Only the BC video frame needs to be removed during reverse telecine. This avoids the need to reassemble frames to get to the original progressive frames. An added benefit is that Final Cut Pro can capture directly to 24 fps. Even if you need to postprocess the clips in Final Cut Pro or Cinema Tools, doing so is faster than working with 3:2 pulldown material.

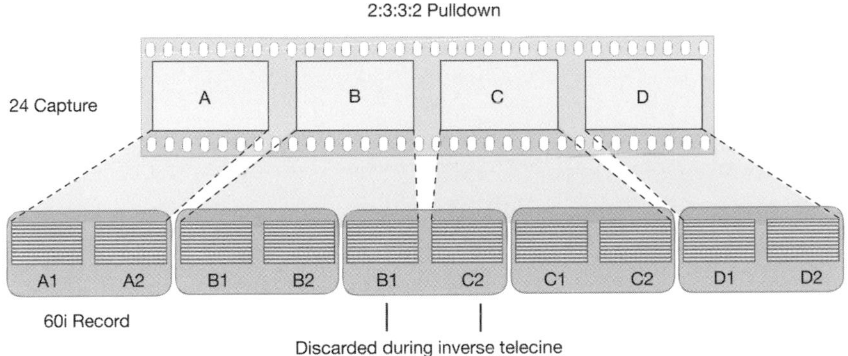

There is one disadvantage to 2:3:3:2 pulldown: a somewhat greater amount of visible motion jitter compared to 3:2 pulldown. However, 3:2 material and even film projected in theaters shows motion jitter on certain camera pans and other movement. Furthermore, most people can't see the difference between 3:2 and 2:3:3:2 video.

NOTE ▶ The Cinema Tools Reverse Telecine command will automatically detect 2:3:3:2 files and reverse telecine them correctly.

Capturing to 24p with Final Cut Pro

Choosing the settings for capturing 2:3:3:2 media is relatively easy. If you don't already have a capture setting, simply modify one of the DV capture settings and check the "Remove Advanced Pulldown (2:3:3:2) From DV-25 and DV-50 Sources" checkbox in the Capture Preset Editor. Final Cut Pro will identify the BC frames and remove them before writing the QuickTime movie at 23.98 fps.

If you have already captured 2:3:3:2 advanced pulldown clips at 29.97, you can use Final Cut Pro to remove the pulldown.

1 Select the clips in the Advanced Pulldown bin.

2 Choose Tools > Remove Advanced Pulldown.

   The clips are automatically converted to 23.98 fps. This command will not modify clips that do not contain the 2:3:3:2 advanced pulldown.

   WARNING ▶ This command modifies the actual media files on disk and throws away data from the original file. Use with caution!

Audio Issues with Reverse Telecine

Typically, projects that will be finished on film are edited at 24 fps, whereas projects to be finished on 24 fps HD are edited at 23.98. Final Cut Pro and Cinema Tools can accommodate either speed, but special consideration should be given to audio.

When Cinema Tools reverse telecines the clips to 24 fps, it pulls up the audio to maintain sync. This means that the audio on 24 fps clips that were synced in telecine will have a sampling rate of 48,000 *x* 1001 ÷ 1000, or 48,048 Hz. However, if the original production audio is synchronized separately from telecine in Final Cut Pro, it must remain at the original 48 kHz sampling rate.

Mixing these sampling rates shouldn't present any problems, though it does add some load to the processor. The playback quality should be set to low, or the audio may need to be rendered. Don't worry about low-quality audio on your finished project; Final Cut Pro resamples and mixes down in high quality when outputting to tape or QuickTime files.

What About PAL?

To the user, working in PAL is almost exactly the same as working in NTSC, though the required math is quite different. Also, you must use different settings to account for the other ways that PAL differs from NTSC.

Getting from 24 fps to 25 fps

When 24 fps material such as film is telecined or downconverted to 25 fps PAL video, it is usually done at a pulled-up speed of 25 divided by 24, which results in everything running approximately 4 percent fast. Although this is barely noticeable visually, it can often be detected by the pitch shift that occurs in the audio. Some telecine machines can automatically compensate for this pitch shifting.

Alternately, the telecine can maintain the original 24 fps frame rate. It involves inserting an additional video field every 12 frames and is known as a *24&1 transfer*. However, cut lists on 24&1 transfers can be accurate to only plus or minus one frame, and you cannot use reverse telecine to get rid of the extra fields. This method is seldom used.

Editing 24 @ 25

If you plan to edit your footage at 25 fps, but at a later time you're going to want to matchback to the 24 fps master (whether it's on film or 24p HD), you must edit with the correct sequence preset.

1. Create a new sequence.

2. Choose Sequence > Settings.

3. Click the Load Sequence Preset button at the bottom of the window.

4. From the pop-up menu, choose DV PAL 48 kHz - 24 @ 25 and click OK.

   This sequence will appear to have a 24 fps frame rate, but all the timecode windows (and EDLs) will display at 25 fps. This allows you to edit in 24 fps, but the timecode will always match the 25 fps timecode on your PAL source tapes.

Getting from 25 fps to 24 fps

Final Cut Pro and Cinema Tools can convert PAL clips back to 24 fps, although, instead of performing a reverse telecine in which the fields are deconstructed and reconstructed, the clips are *conformed*. Conforming a clip means that each frame is given an equal duration (in fractions of seconds) based on the frame rate you specify. For example, if you conform a 480-frame clip to 24 fps, each frame is assigned a duration of 1/24th of a second, and the clip becomes 2 seconds long. This changes the duration of the clip, thereby undoing the four percent change that occurred during the telecine.

Outputting 24 fps Footage to a PAL Monitor

Just as when outputting 24fps video to an NTSC monitor, Final Cut Pro must add in extra frames to make the video play back on an external PAL monitor. You can choose quality or performance using the Pulldown setting in the Playback tab of the System Preferences window.

1. Choose Final Cut Pro > System Settings.
2. Click the Playback Control tab.
3. Set the Pulldown Pattern pop-up menu to 24@25 Pulldown for the smoothest-looking playback, or set the Pulldown Pattern pop-up menu to 24@25 Repeat for better performance.

Lesson Review

1. How do you customize the name of a Browser column?
2. How do you sort a bin by more than one column?
3. How many timecode tracks can a clip have?
4. What is 60 @ 30 timecode?
5. How do you sync clips whose video and audio are in different files?

6. How can you change the name of a file on disk to match a clip name?
7. How is 24p material converted to 29.97?
8. How is 29.97 material converted back to 24p?
9. What is the purpose of Film Safe editing?
10. What is advanced pulldown?

Answers

1. Control-click the column header and choose Edit Heading from the shortcut menu (only available on Comment fields).
2. Shift-click additional column headers to perform a secondary sort.
3. Three: one source timecode and two auxiliary timecode tracks.
4. A way to view 60 fps timecode at 30 fps. Every frame number is doubled, and the doubled frame contains a trailing asterisk.
5. Use the Merge Clips command.
6. In the Browser, select the renamed clip and choose Modify > Rename > File to Match Clip.
7. Each frame is spread across multiple fields in one of several cadences.
8. The cadence is identified, and the duplicates removed. This is called reverse telecine.
9. Film Safe editing prevents you from making edits on imaginary frames.
10. Advanced pulldown is specific to Panasonic 24p cameras and is an alternate cadence that is especially easy to reverse, at the expense of a minor quality loss.

15

Lesson Files	Lesson Files > Lesson 15 > Media.fcp
Media	Blind Date
Time	This lesson takes approximately 45 minutes to complete.
Goals	Use the Make Offline command Resolve offline files with the Reconnect Media command Identify a clip's media file using the Source column Use Reveal in Finder to find a clip in the Finder Consolidate media to move a project between computers Trim a sequence to delete unneeded media

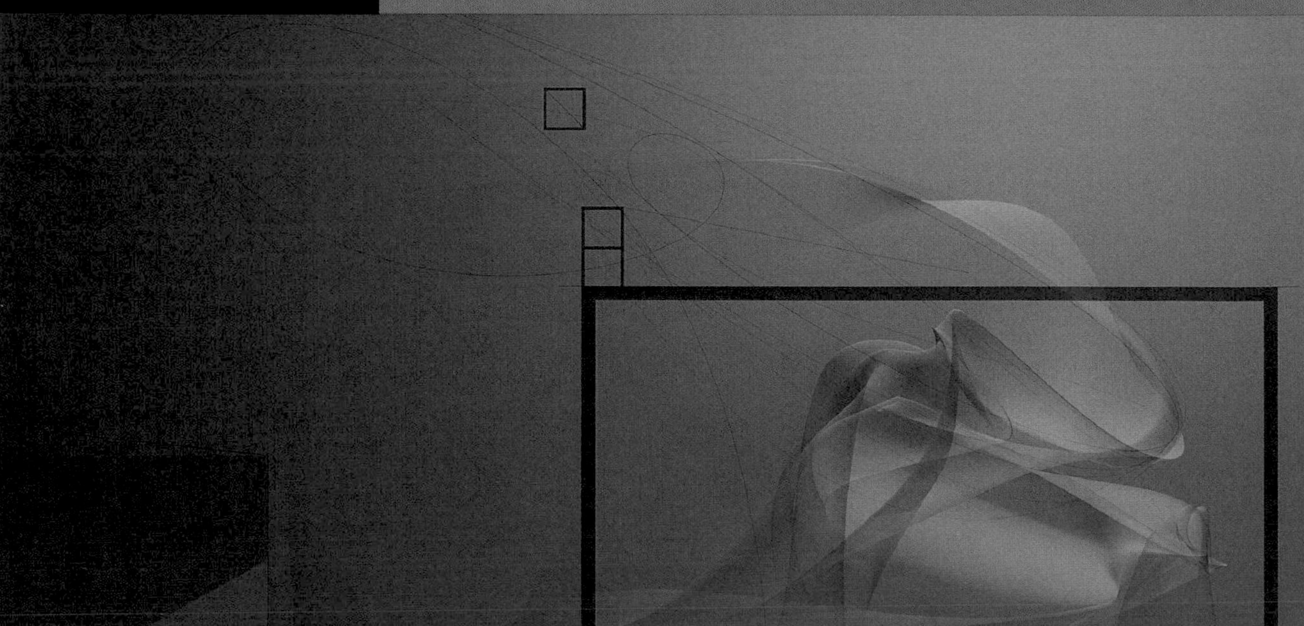

Lesson **15**

Managing Media

One of the most satisfying things about working in a nonlinear editing system such as Final Cut Pro is that you almost never have to think about the physical realities of film and tape. Inside Final Cut Pro, you can rename clips, reuse them, cut them up, and even combine and distort clips using special effects. Because Final Cut Pro is entirely nondestructive, nothing ever happens to the weighty media files in your Capture Scratch folder. They remain intact and safely backed up on your original source tapes.

But sooner or later you're going to have to face those files to make room for a new show, to move your project from one system to another, or perhaps to take advantage of the offline/online model of editing.

Understanding the Relationship Between Clips and Media

Media files are usually just QuickTime movies stored on your hard drive. There's nothing to stop you from moving them around or deleting them in the Finder, but it's not a good idea to do so. Your Final Cut Pro project relies on those media files, and if you move them around or manipulate them outside of Final Cut Pro, you may be in for a surprise. Whenever Final Cut Pro opens a project (or whenever you return to an open project in Final Cut Pro from another application), the program scans your hard drive to verify that all of the files referenced by that project are available. It also verifies that those files are the same size and shape that they were in the last time you opened the project. If any files are missing or have been changed, Final Cut Pro displays a warning message:

You are given the choice to ignore some files (by selecting checkboxes in the Forget Files section), reconnect the missing files, or continue with the project while the files remain offline. For clips used in a sequence, the Timeline displays offline clips in white; in the Browser, offline clips' icons have a slash through them.

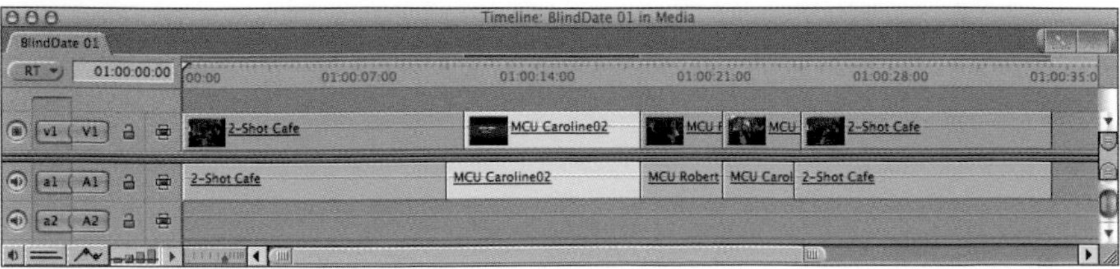

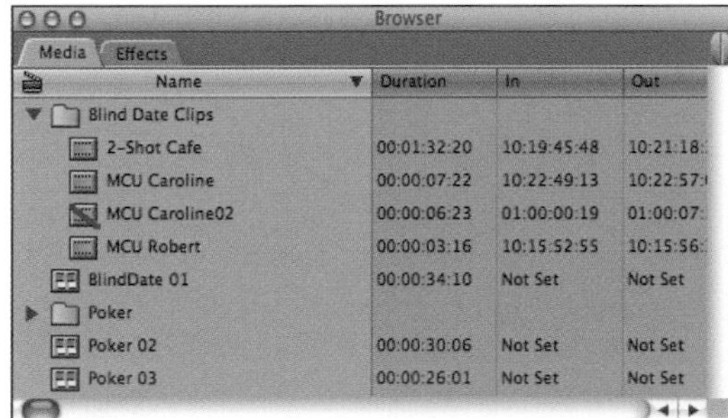

You can continue to edit your project and ignore the missing files. This is your only choice if the needed files are on a disk that is temporarily unavailable and you plan to reconnect or recapture them later. However, playing across an offline clip shows the following offline screen in the Canvas or Viewer.

Using Search Folders

You can specify folders that Final Cut Pro will search automatically whenever it can't find a file. If you're a mobile editor, frequently working on different systems, this may not be very helpful; but if you work mainly on one Mac and organize your media intelligently, this can keep you from seeing that Offline Files dialog.

1 Choose Final Cut Pro > System Settings.

2 Click the Search Folders tab.

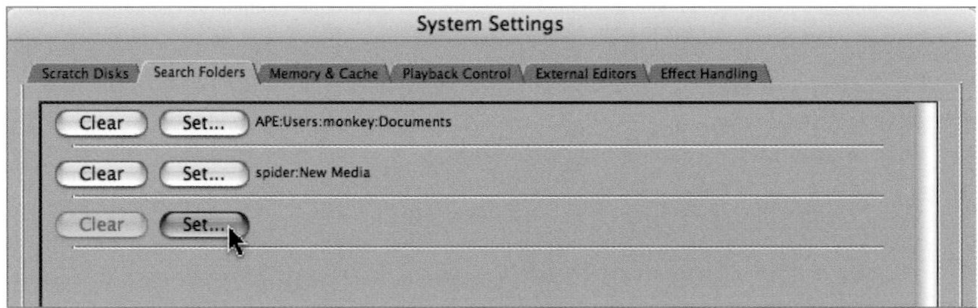

3 Click the Set button.

4 Navigate to a folder where you store your media (for example, your Documents folder, or the root of your media drive) and click Choose.

   You can add as many search folders as you like. Whenever you open a project and the files are not in the same locations as when you last closed the project, Final Cut Pro will search these folders first before bothering you with the Offline Files dialog.

5 Click OK to close the System Settings window.

Forcing Clips Offline

There are some occasions when you will want to place clips offline deliberately. For example, if you have an effects shot that is being re-delivered from your compositor, you might want to take the previous version offline.

1 Open Lesson Files > Lesson 15 > **Media.fcp**.

2 Open the *BlindDate 01* sequence and play it.

3 In the Timeline, select **MCU Caroline02.**

4 Choose Modify > Make Offline.

The Make Offline dialog appears.

You are presented with the choices to leave the media file where it is on the disk, to move it to the Trash, or to delete it.

WARNING ▶ Be very careful with this function! If you delete files this way, they will be gone forever. Also, if there are other affiliate clips in your project that point to the same media file, they will be placed offline as well.

5 Select "Leave Them on the Disk" and click OK.

The offline clip remains selected in the Timeline, but it is now colored white, and the affiliate clip in the Browser has a red slash through it.

Reconnecting Offline Files

You can repair or reconnect an offline file at any time (provided that the corresponding media file exists on your disk) using the Reconnect Media command.

1 In the Browser, select the offline clip **MCU Caroline02**.

2 Choose File > Reconnect Media.

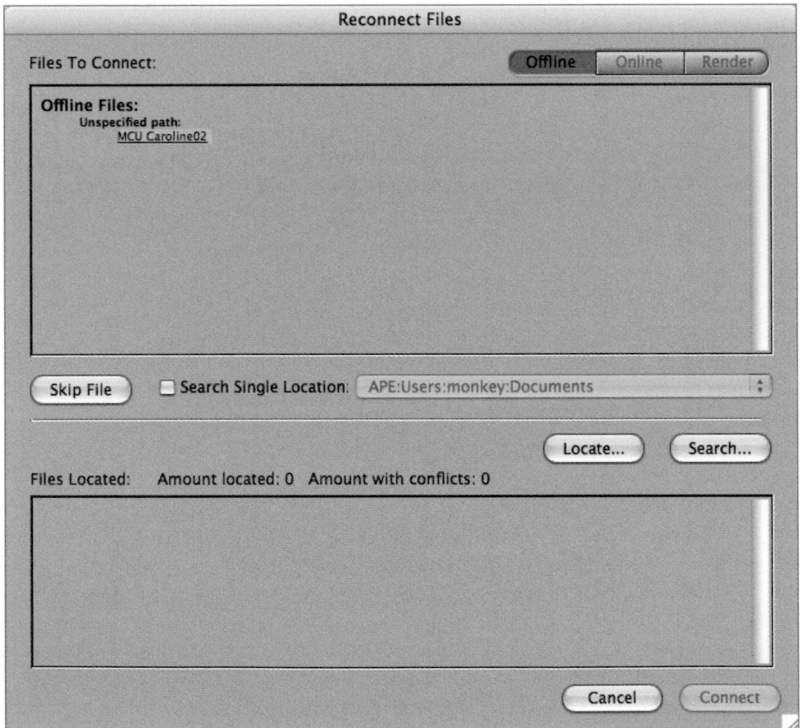

Examine the three buttons at the top of the dialog. These buttons allow you to ignore or reconnect your offline, online, and render files separately. This project doesn't include any online or render files, so those buttons are dimmed.

The upper pane in the dialog lists the missing files, grouped by their last known locations. The first file in the list is highlighted, and you can choose to skip, locate, or search for this missing file.

If you click the Search button, Final Cut Pro will scan the disks identified in the Search Location pop-up menu and attempt to locate the missing file. If you click the Locate button, you can manually navigate to the files.

3 Deselect Search Single Location.

NOTE ▶ It is easy to forget to deselect the Search Single Location setting, which means that the search feature may not find files that you are sure are on your disk. Don't fret; just deselect the checkbox and search again.

4 Click the Locate button.

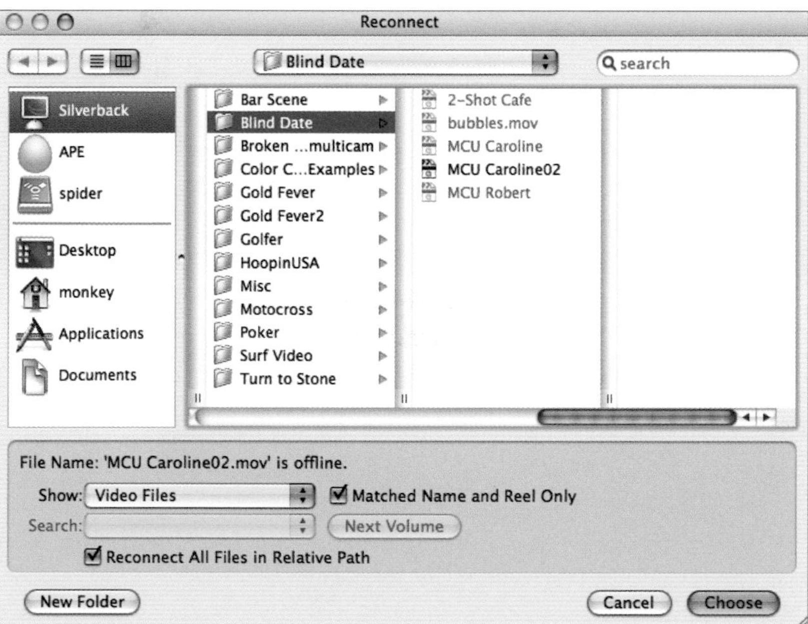

The Reconnect dialog appears, allowing you to manually search your disks for the file.

Ordinarily, the "Matched Name and Reel Only" setting is selected, so all files without identical names (and reel numbers) to the original files will be filtered out, preventing you from selecting them by mistake. But in this case, you are deliberately relinking the clip to a new piece of media with a different name—one with a graphic element added.

5 Deselect "Matched Name and Reel Only."

6 Navigate to the Blind Date folder and select the **bubbles.mov** file, then click Choose.

7 If you encounter a File Attribute Mismatch warning, click Continue, then in the Reconnect Files window, click Connect.

In the Browser, the offline clip **MCU Caroline02** is now reconnected to the **bubbles.mov** clip. The red slash is gone, and the affiliate clip in the sequence **BlindDate 01** is updated as well.

8 Play the sequence again.

The thought bubble graphics have been added to the clip.

9 Control-click the clip in the Browser and choose Rename > Clip to Match File from the shortcut menu.

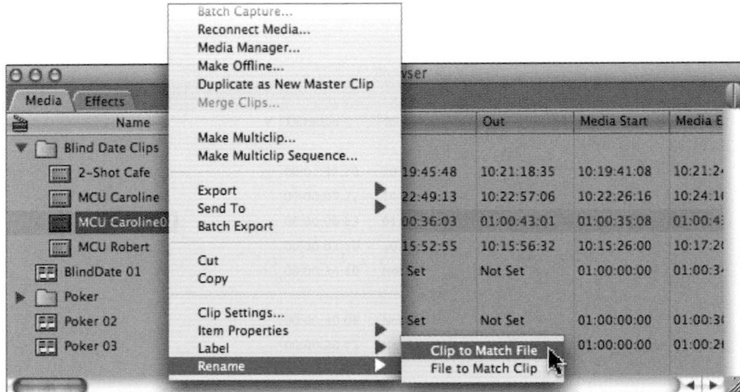

The clip name is updated to reflect the file on disk. Notice that the affiliate clip in the Timeline is also updated.

Reconnecting Online Clips in One Step

Another way to complete this same procedure would be to simply select the original online clip and choose Reconnect Media without first making it offline.

You performed the task in two steps in the previous exercise to illustrate all of the available options.

Deleting Media for Unused Clips

Another reason you might choose to make clips offline is to save disk space. If your project includes unused clips, you can delete the media files associated with them to recover storage space or just to tidy up your hard disk. Although you can just delete files in the Finder, it may be difficult to determine exactly which files are safe to remove. In the next exercise, you learn a procedure that prevents you from accidentally deleting a file used in your show.

1. Select the *Poker 02* and *Poker 03* sequences in the Browser.

2. Perform a Find by pressing Command-F or choosing Edit > Find.

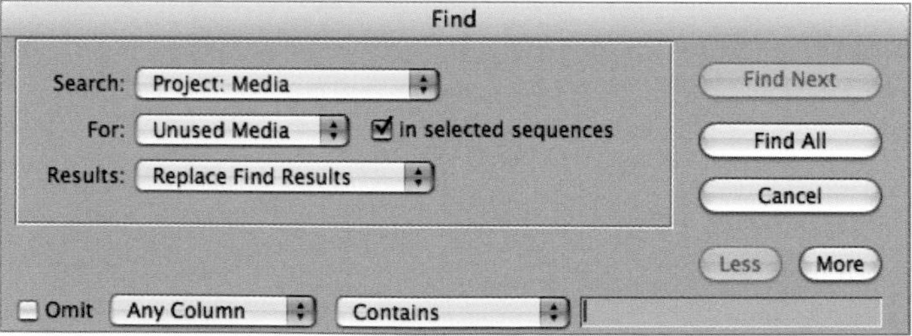

3. In the Find dialog, choose Unused Media from the For pop-up menu and select the “in selected sequences” checkbox. Click Find All.

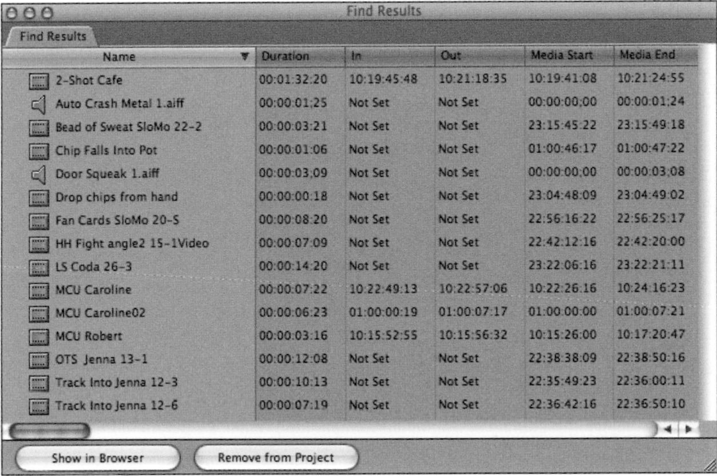

Find Results

Name	Duration	In	Out	Media Start	Media End
2-Shot Cafe	00:01:32:20	10:19:45:48	10:21:18:35	10:19:41:08	10:21:24:55
Auto Crash Metal 1.aiff	00:00:01;25	Not Set	Not Set	00:00:00;00	00:00:01;24
Bead of Sweat SloMo 22-2	00:00:03:21	Not Set	Not Set	23:15:45:22	23:15:49:18
Chip Falls Into Pot	00:00:01:06	Not Set	Not Set	01:00:46:17	01:00:47:22
Door Squeak 1.aiff	00:00:03;09	Not Set	Not Set	00:00:00;00	00:00:03;08
Drop chips from hand	00:00:00:18	Not Set	Not Set	23:04:48:09	23:04:49:02
Fan Cards SloMo 20-S	00:00:08:20	Not Set	Not Set	22:56:16:22	22:56:25:17
HH Fight angle2 15-1Video	00:00:07:09	Not Set	Not Set	22:42:12:16	22:42:20:00
LS Coda 26-3	00:00:14:20	Not Set	Not Set	23:22:06:16	23:22:21:11
MCU Caroline	00:00:07:22	10:22:49:13	10:22:57:06	10:22:26:16	10:24:16:23
MCU Caroline02	00:00:06:23	01:00:00:19	01:00:07:17	01:00:00:00	01:00:07:21
MCU Robert	00:00:03:16	10:15:52:55	10:15:56:32	10:15:26:00	10:17:20:47
OTS Jenna 13-1	00:00:12:08	Not Set	Not Set	22:38:38:09	22:38:50:16
Track Into Jenna 12-3	00:00:10:13	Not Set	Not Set	22:35:49:23	22:36:00:11
Track Into Jenna 12-6	00:00:07:19	Not Set	Not Set	22:36:42:16	22:36:50:10

Show in Browser | Remove from Project

NOTE ► If your Find dialog still has active search criteria from a previous search, click the Less button to disable the additional criteria and return the dialog to its default state.

4 Select all of the clips in the Find Results bin.

5 Choose Modify > Make Offline.

To delete the clips, you could choose either Delete from Disk or Move to Trash. In either case, the offline clips remain in your project, along with the timecode information necessary to recapture the media, but attempting to play them will invoke the Offline Media screen.

6 Click Cancel and close the Find Results bin.

Locating a Clip's Media File

The procedures described so far have focused on modifying the relationship between a clip and its media file. Sometimes you may want to simply identify a clip's media file on disk.

This can be useful for both offline and online clips. When you encounter offline clips in your project, you may not know why those files are not available. Sometimes, an external hard drive containing the media might not have been mounted, or a file or folder may have been renamed or moved. When moving a project from one location to another, it is fairly common to encounter clips that have lost links to their corresponding media files.

One trick that can help you track down the correct media for an offline clip is to check the Source column in the Browser.

1 Control-click the Browser column header area and choose Show Source from the shortcut menu.

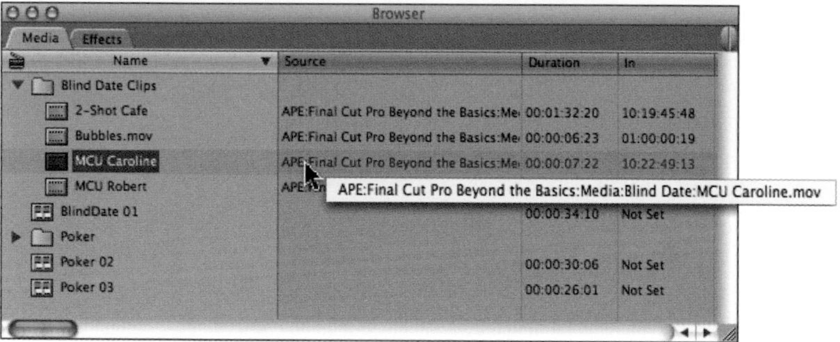

This column provides the path to the media file associated with the clip. If you pause the pointer over any clip, a tooltip displaying the entire path will appear. (You can also drag the right edge of the column header to widen it.)

If the clip is missing, this column provides the path to the last known location of the file. If you forced the clip offline manually, it will simply report that the clip is offline. Still, for missing clips, this might help identify what disk is unmounted or provide other clues to the proper media file.

If you want to find on a disk the file associated with any clip (online or offline), the Reveal in Finder command gets you there in a hurry.

2 In the Browser, Control-click **bubbles.mov** and choose Reveal in Finder from the shortcut menu, or choose View > Reveal in Finder.

The Finder window containing the selected clip is brought to the front.

This command also can be used on offline clips, but if the media file can't be found, nothing happens at all.

NOTE ▶ Reveal in Finder may give unexpected results when used with merged clips or multiclips.

Using the Media Manager

The Final Cut Pro Media Manager is a versatile and comprehensive media manipulation tool.

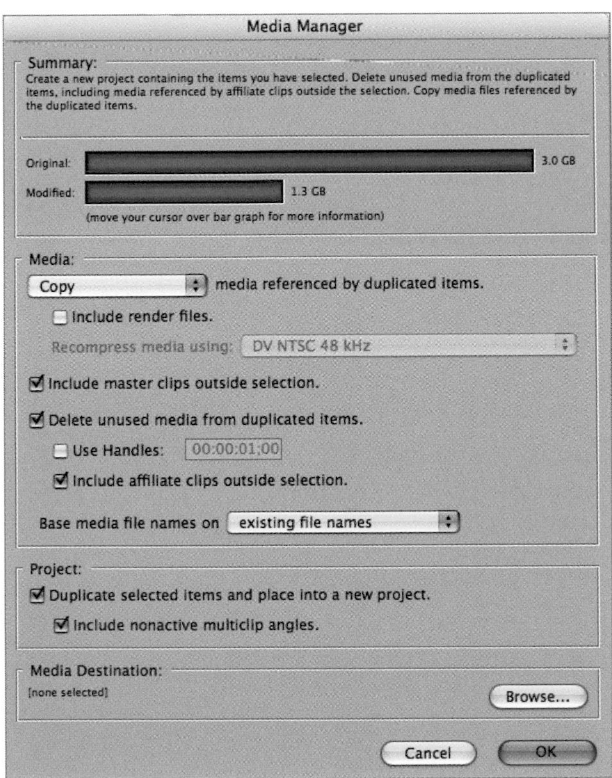

Whether you are moving your project from one computer to another, trying to eliminate clips and files you're not using, preparing a sequence for output, or even recompressing a group of files from one codec to another, the Media Manager is your one-stop shop.

Consolidating Media

When you need to move a project from one computer to another, you may not know where all of your media resides. Although most files are probably in your Capture Scratch folder, a graphic or still image may be in another location. Sound effects files may be stored in yet another location. Rather than manually scouring your disk for related files, you can use the Media Manager tool to be sure you won't miss anything (and to avoid grabbing files you don't need).

1 Press Command-A to select everything in your Browser.

2 Choose File > Media Manager.

3 In the Media section, choose Copy from the pop-up menu.

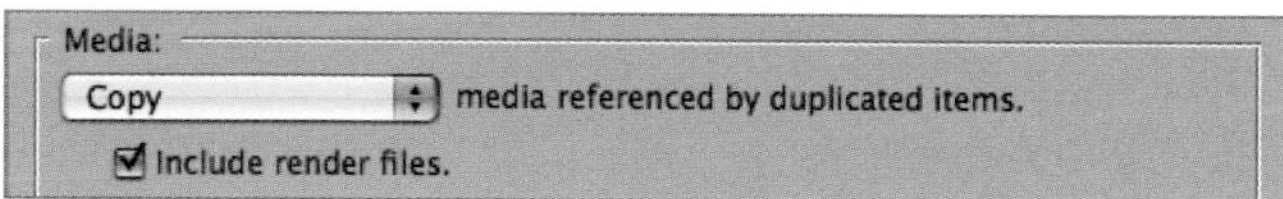

This will duplicate all the media associated with the selected items (in this case, the entire project) and place it in a new location.

4 Select the "Include render files" checkbox.

5 In the Media Destination section, click the Browse button and select a disk location for the copied files. Create a new folder for the copied media.

To move your files from one computer to another, you typically would want to set this destination to a removable or external hard disk that you could move to a new edit station.

6 In the Media section, deselect "Delete unused media from duplicated items."

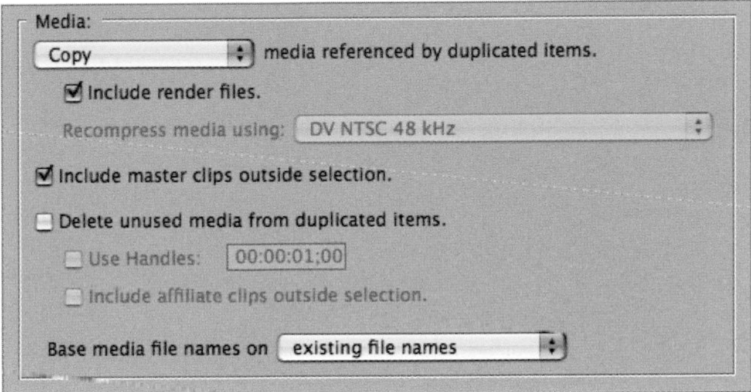

This setting usually has a dramatic impact on the green bars in the Summary section. In this example, you want the project on the new computer to be identical to the previous version, so you do not want to delete anything.

The summary at the top of the window details your operation. The size of the bars indicates the relative amount of disk space your media is occupying. The top bar is the current state, and the bottom bar shows what will happen after you complete the Media Manager operation. Because in this example you are not deleting anything, the two bars are identical.

7 Leave the "Base media file names on" pop-up menu set to "existing file names."

8 In the Project section, be sure "Duplicate selected items and place into a new project" is selected.

This last setting creates a new project on your destination volume that points to the new versions of the media files. Although this step is not required (you could manually copy your existing project file in the Finder), this ensures that the new project will not have any offline files, and you won't have to reconnect media when the project gets to the new workstation.

9 Click OK.

Immediately, you are prompted with a Save dialog, asking you to name and save the new project file. Save it on the same disk as the new media.

10 Click Save.

The program will then perform the Media Manager operation and open the new project in the Browser.

11 In the new project, open the sequences and clips to confirm that the new project is an identical copy of the old project. Then close the new project.

Moving Media

If you have limited disk space, or you are consolidating media onto a single disk (as you might do when preparing a project for backup to DVD), you can choose Move instead of Copy in the Media Manager.

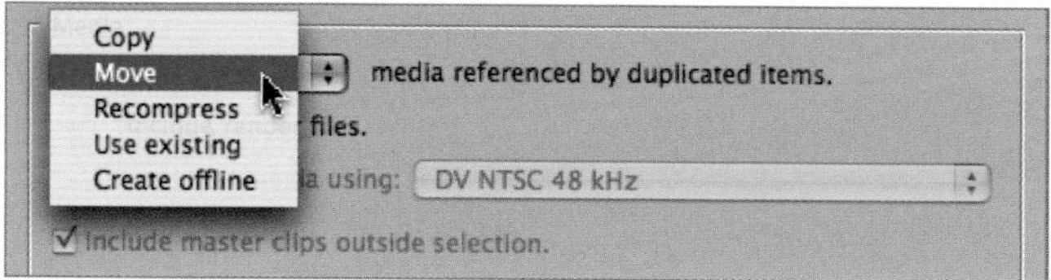

With this setting, all the files used in your project will be copied to a new location, and the originals will be deleted. You will not wind up with duplicate copies of your files.

Trimming Sequences in Media Manager

This type of trimming has nothing to do with adjusting edit points, but rather it is a way to eliminate excess media after your sequence has been completed. Usually, you shouldn't do this until you have completely finished making major editorial changes.

1 Select sequences *Poker 02* and *Poker 03*.

The operation will be applied only to the media referenced in these two sequences.

2 Control-click the selected items and choose Media Manager from the shortcut menu.

3 In the Media pop-up menu, choose Copy.

WARNING ▸ Although Final Cut Pro will not prevent you from choosing Move or Use Existing, doing so when trimming clips is extremely dangerous. If a power failure or crash occurs during the operation, your files could be left in an unusable state, requiring you to recapture all of your media. When trimming, always create new files. After the operation is complete, you can delete the original media manually.

4 Select "Delete unused media from duplicated items."

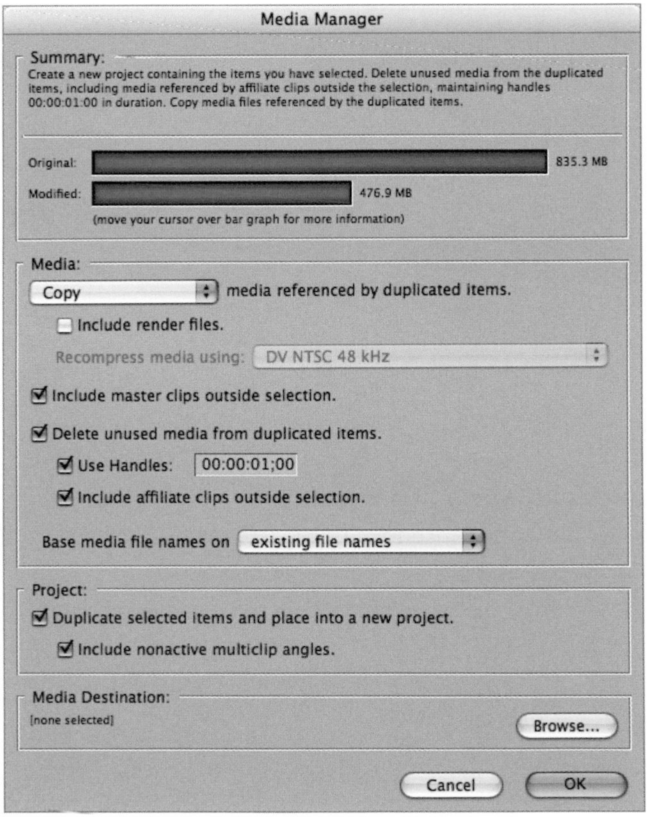

When you select this option, the summary section at the top of the dialog changes dramatically. Now, the Modified media bar is much smaller than the Original. This difference reflects the media outside the In and Out points of the clips used in the two selected sequences.

5 Select Use Handles and set the value to *1:00*.

Although presumably you are completely done editing, there could be an emergency or problem that might require a tiny adjustment to your edit. Adding a little bit of wiggle room is a good way to accommodate such an unforeseen issue if one should arise after this operation is completed.

6 Deselect "Include affiliate clips outside selection."

If this option is selected, the Media Manager will scan the rest of your project for any other uses of the clips contained in the selected sequences. If such clips exist, and they have In or Out points set, the Media Manager will include that section in the newly created clips. This means that you will not save as much space as you would by ignoring those clips.

Because you specified Copy for this operation, there is no harm in ignoring this additional media. If you had specified Move or Use Existing (instead of Copy), then you would be permanently deleting the media that you might be planning to use in another sequence.

7 Select "Duplicate selected Items and place into a new project."

This will create a new project containing only the selected sequences and pointing to the new, trimmed media.

8 Set your destination and click OK.

9 Name the new project and click Save.

After the files are processed, the new project is automatically opened. If you do not plan to make any additional changes or use any of the media from the old project, you can select all the items in the old project and use the Make Offline command to delete the media files from your disk.

Lesson Review

1. What are the two most likely causes of an offline clip?
2. What is a search folder and how is one created?
3. What is the difference between the Locate and Search buttons in the Reconnect Media window?
4. Why would you choose to use the Locate button instead of the Search button?
5. How can you find the media associated with a clip on your disk?
6. What does it mean to trim a sequence?
7. Why would you want to trim a sequence?
8. When would you trim a sequence?
9. How do you trim a sequence?

Answers

1. A hard disk that is turned off or not connected to the computer, or a project that was created on a different system for which you don't have the media files.
2. Search folders are hard disk locations that Final Cut Pro will automatically search for offline clips. You can assign any folder as a search folder in the System Settings window.
3. The Locate button allows you to manually choose the directory; the Search button automatically finds the file for you.
4. You would use the Locate button if you had more than one version of the file, and you wanted to control which version was linked to the clip in your project.
5. Choose the Reveal in Finder command, or look at the Source column in the Browser or Item Properties window.
6. Creating a copy of the sequence where only the media between the clips' In and Out points is kept, and the excess media is discarded.
7. Generally to save disk space or to create a streamlined backup of your sequence for later recapture.
8. Only after editing was completely finished.
9. Use the Media Manager and select the "Delete unused media from duplicated items" setting.

16

Lesson Files	Lesson Files > Lesson 16 > Tapeless.fcp
Media	Surf Video and Surround Mix
Time	This lesson takes approximately 90 minutes to complete.
Goals	Ingest media from Panasonic P2 cards Create MPEG and H.264 files for DVD using Compressor Create droplets for automatic drag-and-drop encoding Export QuickTime reference and self-contained files Export audio and OMF audio

Lesson **16**

Tapeless Importing and Outputting

While the most rewarding part of the editing process is the storytelling aspect, nothing can beat the sense of satisfaction that comes from the two primary milestones that begin and end your work. When shooting is complete, you mark that accomplishment by engaging in the ritual of moving the footage from the camera into the computer. And when editing is complete, you celebrate by outputting the video for audience consumption. As video technology has evolved, these tasks have changed significantly from an analog tape-based process to an entirely digital, file-based process.

In this lesson, you will ingest video clips from a Panasonic P2 card and output a finished sequence suitable for distribution on DVD, on the web, or with third-party applications. You will use Compressor to encode MPEG-2 files for use in DVD authoring and for MPEG-4 files suitable for the web. You will export audio using Open Media Format (OMF), and export a QuickTime reference file for use in other applications.

Ingesting Tapeless Clips

One of the benefits of shooting on a tapeless format such as the Panasonic P2 is that clips are stored right in the camera as digital files. Panasonic uses the DVCPRO HD codec and saves the data in a media container format called MXF (material exchange format). MXF files can be converted losslessly into QuickTime movies for editing in Final Cut Pro 6 using that program's Log and Transfer function. (Earlier Final Cut Pro versions utilize a similar function called Import P2.)

With the Log and Transfer function, you can ingest files directly from a P2 card, a P2 store, or from any folder containing MXF files.

You can ingest entire clips or mark In and Out points to ingest only a portion of a clip. The files you ingest are transferred in the background and imported directly into your Final Cut Pro project.

1 Open the **Tapeless.fcp** project and choose File > Log and Transfer (or press Shift-Command-8).

The Log and Transfer window opens.

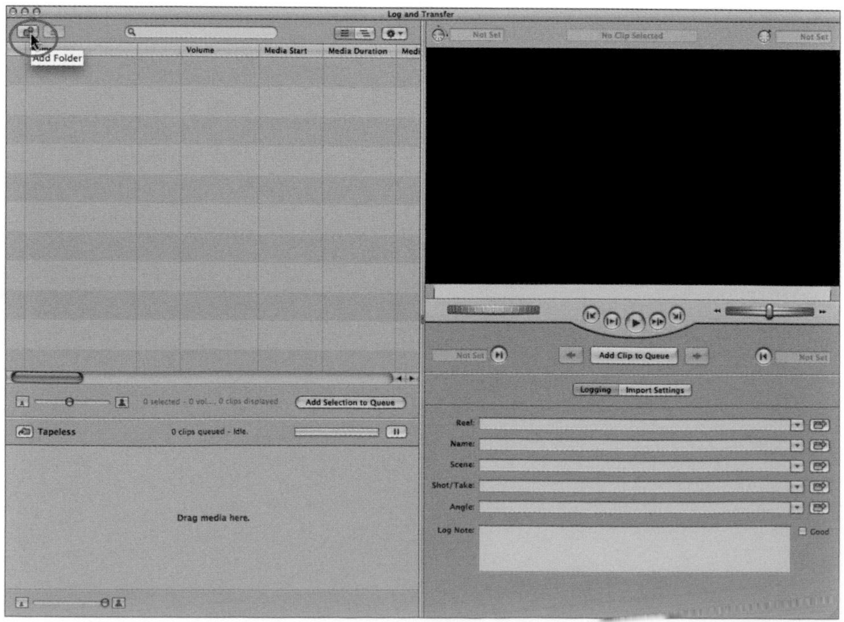

2. Click the Add Folder button.

   A File Open sheet appears. If you have a P2 device mounted on your computer, you can navigate directly to it. In this case, you will navigate to a folder containing the contents of a P2 card.

3. Navigate to Media > P2 Footage and click Open.

   NOTE ▶ Do not select the Contents folder inside the P2 Footage directory.

	Name		Volume	Media Start	Media Duration
○	0001WT		P2 Footage	01:24:15:10	00:00:06:23
○	00027H		P2 Footage	01:24:22:03	00:00:07:15
○	00035D		P2 Footage	01:24:29:18	00:00:06:16
○	00044Y		P2 Footage	01:24:36:04	00:00:00:19
○	00053S		P2 Footage	01:24:36:23	00:00:08:12

   The clips stored on the P2 card are loaded into the Log and Transfer window. If you have a large number of clips, you can reduce the thumbnail size to view more clips in the list.

4. Use the slider beneath the list to adjust the size of the thumbnails.

5. Click the first clip in the list.

The clip appears in the viewer area on the right side of the window. You can play the clip using all of the familiar playback controls, including the J-K-L shortcut keys.

6 Play the clip. Mark an In point just before the man appears and mark an Out point after he exits the frame.

7 Name the clip *MS walk path*, set the Scene number to *21*, and enter any other logging data, or metadata, you would like to add.

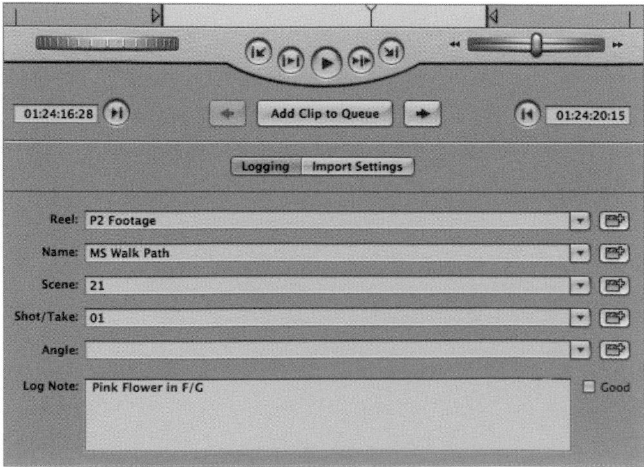

8 Click the Add Clip to Queue button.

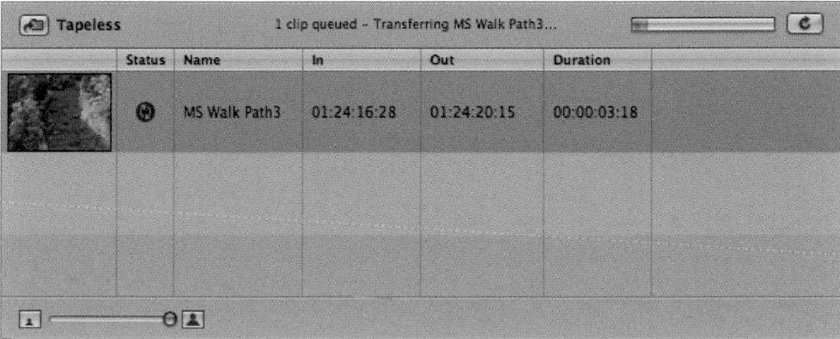

The clip is moved to the queue area and is immediately converted to a QuickTime file, saved in your Capture Scratch folder, and automatically imported into the active Final Cut Pro project.

Once you add an item to the queue, the conversion and importing process occurs in the background, so you can continue to log clips.

9 Click the Next Clip button.

The next clip is loaded into the viewer area. Because this is another take of the same scene, you can use the shortcut menus in the logging area to load the information.

10 From the Name pop-up menu, choose MS Walk Path. Because you don't want the clip to have an identical name to the previous clip, click the Auto-increment button to the right of the Name field.

11 Fill in any additional logging information you desire.

If you don't add the clip to the queue at this point, all the logging information will stay with the clip. This allows you to review and compare several clips at once before committing to the logging information you want to retain.

12 Click the Next Clip button to load the next clip, and play it.

This is a close-up of one footstep, obviously from the same scene.

13 Name the clip *CU Foot* and enter any additional logging info you desire.

The list of clips on the left side of the window is updated automatically. When looking at this list, you can often detect some shots that you probably won't want to import. Short *bumps*—when the camera was accidentally turned on and off—can be easily detected by looking at the Media Duration column.

14 Note the media duration for the fourth clip.

○	MS Walk Path1		P2 Footage	01:24:22:03	00:00:07:15	01:24:29:17	No
○	CU Foot		P2 Footage	01:24:29:18	00:00:06:16	01:24:36:03	No
○	00044Y		P2 Footage	01:24:36:04	00:00:00:19	01:24:36:22	No
○	00053S		P2 Footage	01:24:36:23	00:00:08:12	01:24:45:04	No

It is only 19 frames long. In this case, the cameraman was just focusing, and accidentally turned the camera on and off, creating a clip.

15 Select the fourth clip and press Delete.

A warning appears.

If you delete the clip, it will be gone forever, so you should do this only when absolutely necessary. It's usually safer to leave the clip alone, especially in this case because it is so short and not taking up much space.

16 Click Cancel to reverse the choice to delete the clip.

TIP You can sort the clips in the Log And Transfer window by their duration, thereby grouping all of the "shorties" together. This makes it easy to quickly review and optionally delete them all at once.

Viewing Additional Metadata

Among the other advantages of working with file-based acquisition formats is that you can add metadata to clips in the field and access it in the editing suite. Each camera model allows different types and amounts of metadata to be attached to a clip. Final Cut Pro can display metadata in the Log and Transfer window.

1 In the clip list, Control-click the column header area.

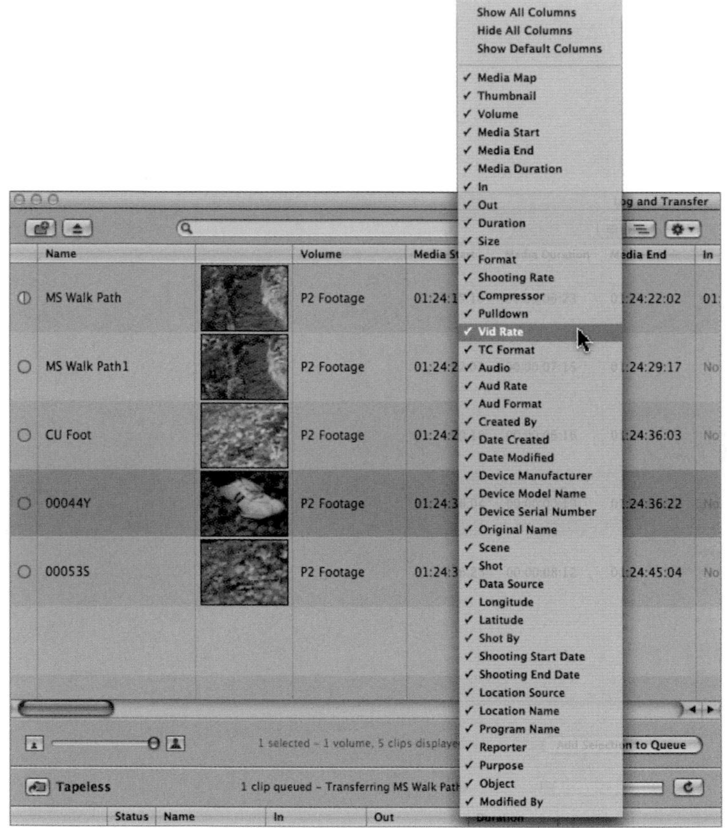

A large list of columns appears, representing all the data that might be embedded in the clip or added during the logging process. This list differs significantly from the Browser list you may be familiar with because it contains many elements available only in certain cameras.

2 Choose Show All Columns and scroll through the window.

All of the columns are displayed in the file list area. You can resize and rearrange the columns, and use them to sort data just like the columns in the Browser.

You can also search the contents of the clip list with the search field at the top of the window.

3 Enter *walk* into the search field.

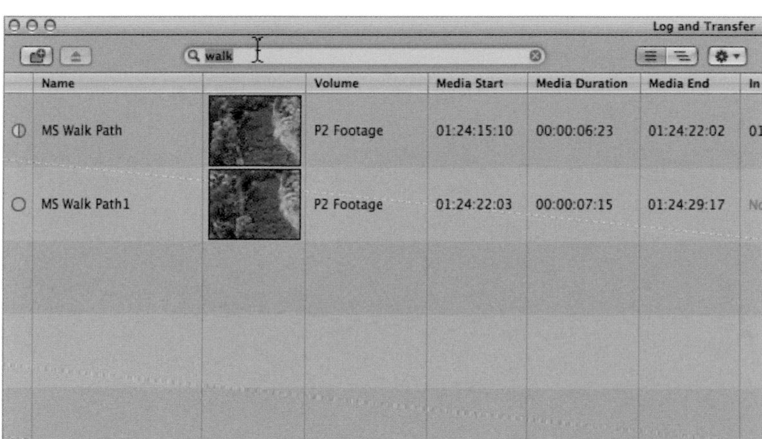

The list is filtered to include only those clips containing that information.

4 Click the circled X button at the right edge of the search field to clear it.

5 Command-click the second and fourth clips to select them, then click Add Selection to Queue.

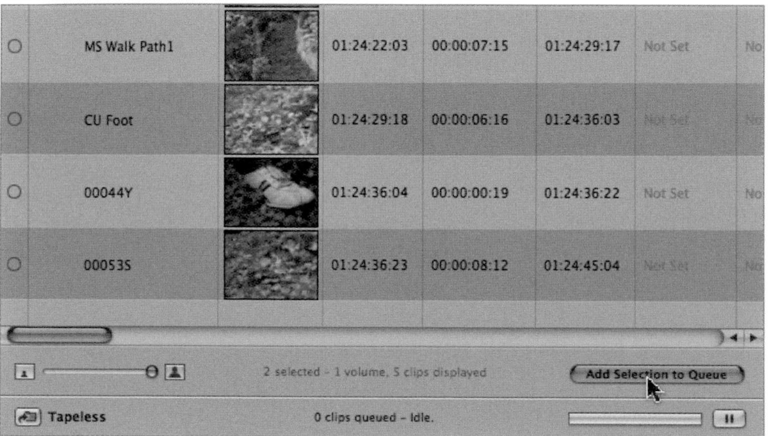

The clips are added to the queue and automatically ingested. Because the last clip was never logged, the entire media will be ingested, and its name will retain the auto-generated code.

6 Close the Log and Transfer window.

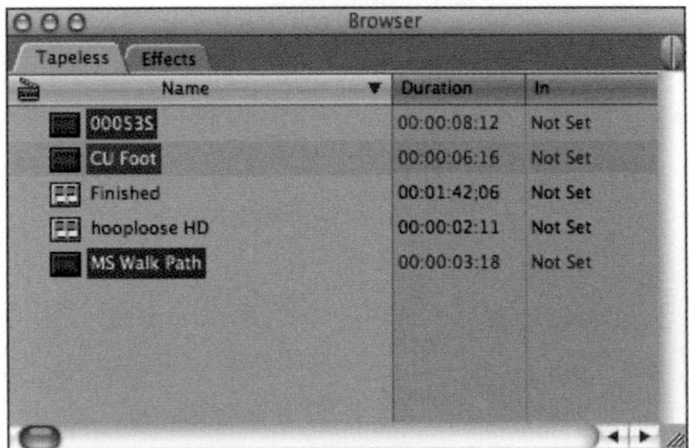

All of the clips now appear in your Final Cut Pro project, ready for editing.

Outputting Content for DVD

When you have completed a movie, you typically will output it to a distribution medium. Currently, DVD is the most popular format for distributing high-quality video; but once you choose that format, you must still set your DVD's aspect ratio (4:3 or 16:9) and choose its frame rate. Furthermore, video for DVD must be converted into the MPEG-2 format, which has many parameters that control quality, encoding speed, and playback versatility.

Compressor, included in Final Cut Studio, simplifies this encoding process by providing many encoding presets and the ability to batch encode content to multiple formats and versions.

Exporting to MPEG-2 Using Presets

You can export an MPEG-2 file directly from Final Cut Pro, although Compressor will do most of the work. Compressor contains presets that reduce the enormously complex compression choices to a few relatively easy questions.

1 In the Browser, select the *Finished* sequence.

2 Choose File > Export > Using Compressor.

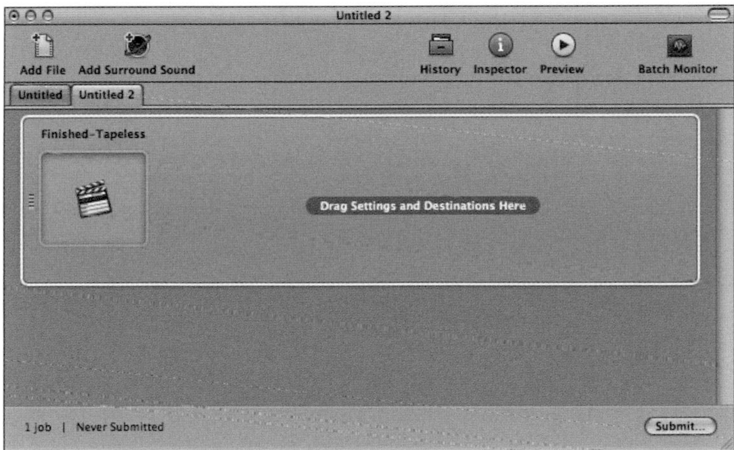

Compressor opens, and your sequence is opened into a new batch list.

3 In the Settings window, click the disclosure triangle to view the DVD group.

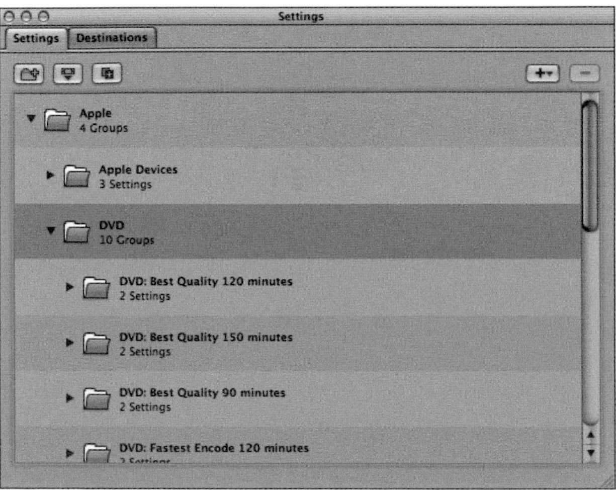

A list of subfolders is displayed containing preset groups intended for DVD encoding.

The first thing to decide is whether you want to choose a group for Best Quality (two-pass encoding) or Fastest Encode (one-pass encoding). Obviously, using a Best Quality preset group will usually result in better-looking video, with few, if any, compression artifacts; but its two-pass encoding process can take much longer than using a comparable Fastest Encode preset. For this lesson, you'll choose one of the Fastest Encode presets.

Next, you need to consider how much video you will be fitting onto the disk. The presets give you three duration options: 90 minutes, 120 minutes, and 150 minutes. This choice is important because the less video you set out to store on the DVD, the higher the visual quality. So, if you have less than 90 minutes of video, choose the 90-minute preset. However, in order to fit 145 minutes of video on the disk, you will have to use the 150-minute setting, which will use a lower bit rate that slightly reduces image quality.

It's also important to understand that these duration values refer to the *total* minutes of video you plan to include on the DVD, not just the length of the current file. For example, you might be making a DVD that includes five 20-minute movies (for a total of 100 minutes). If you encoded each of them at the 90-minute setting, they would very likely occupy too much space, and you couldn't fit all of them on the DVD.

4 Click the disclosure triangle next to the "DVD: Fastest Encode 90 minutes" folder.

   Inside the folder are two settings: one for video and one for audio in the AC3 format. You must use both settings to encode the audio and video components of your show for the DVD. You apply both settings at once by dragging the group folder to your video.

5 Drag the "DVD: Fastest Encode 90 minutes" folder from the Batch window to the Finished – Tapeless batch item.

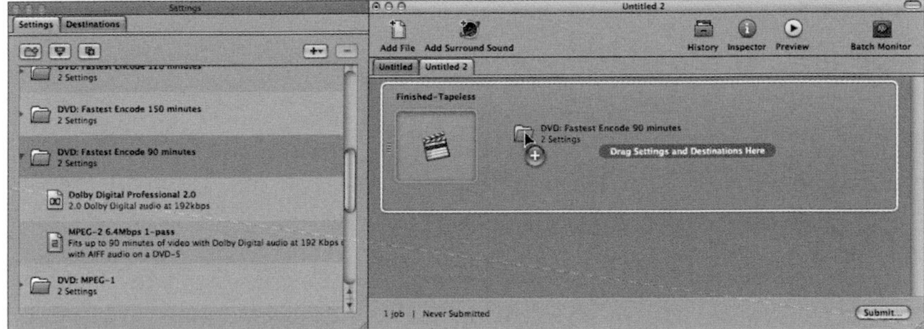

Two jobs appear in the Batch window, one for each preset.

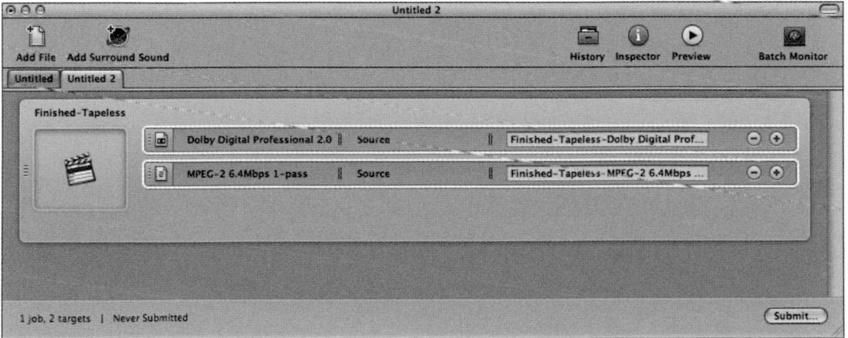

Setting the Destination and Filename

Before submitting the batch, it's important to check the name of the files you are exporting and the location where it will be stored on your disk.

The preset displays the intended destination in the middle area and displays the filename on the right.

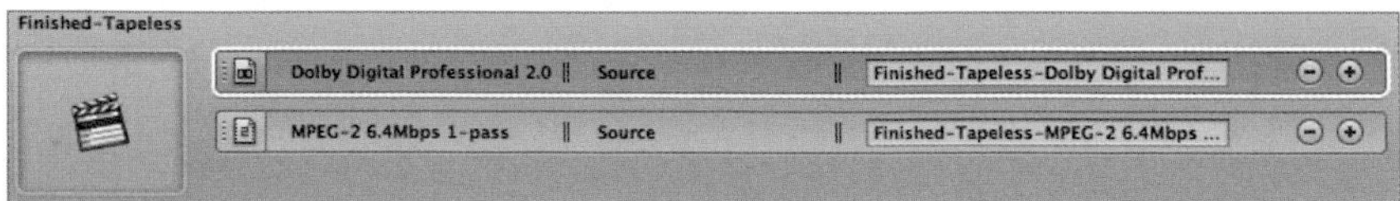

By default, the destination is set to Source, so newly-created files are stored in the same location as the original file. However, in this case you are exporting from a sequence within a Final Cut Pro project. Technically, no source file exists, so Compressor will save the file to the root directory of your disk, where you're unlikely to find it.

Although exporting from a Final Cut sequence is by far the most common workflow, you rarely would want to save a file to this Source destination, so it's advisable to change the destination before beginning the encode. Fortunately, doing so is relatively straightforward.

1 Control-click the first job listed and choose Destination > Other from the shortcut menu.

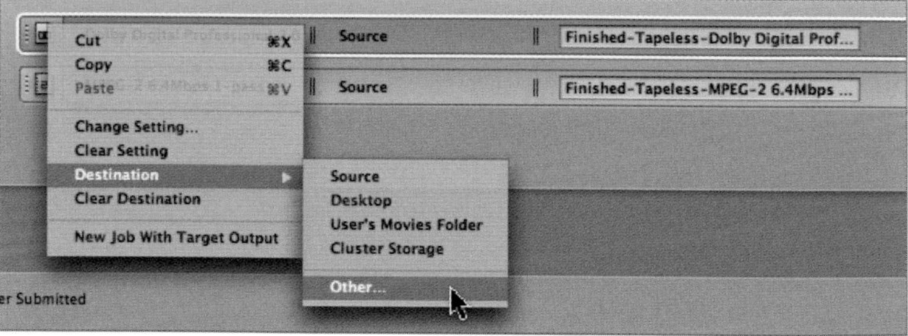

A few preset destinations appear in the list, allowing you to quickly set the clip to be saved to the Desktop, your Movies folder, or to a preset Cluster Storage setting. Or, you can choose Other to set a custom location.

2 Navigate to ~/Documents/Final Cut Pro Documents.

3 Click the New Folder button, name the folder *Compressor Output*, then click Create.

4 Click Open to choose that folder as your new destination.

5 Use this same technique to set the same destination for the other preset.

TIP Compressor also allows you to create custom destinations that will automatically appear in the submenu of the shortcut menu for all jobs.

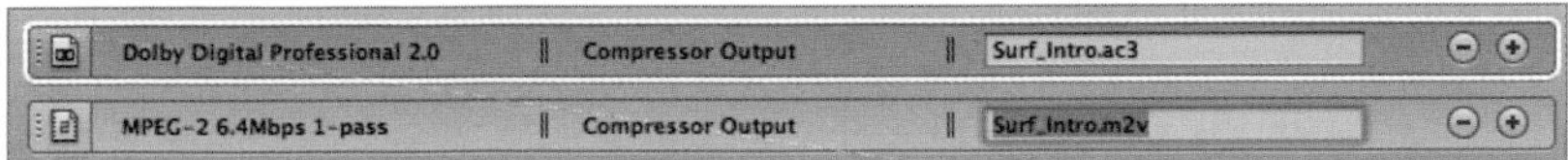

6 Click the name area for the MPEG job and rename the output file *Surf_Intro.m2v*.

7 Rename the Dolby job output *Surf_Intro.ac3*.

TIP Use identical names for matching audio and video output, which enables DVD authoring software to automatically link the files.

Customizing Compression Settings

The Compressor presets are great starting points, but video compression is notoriously fickle. Compression settings that produce amazing results with one scene might create a blocky, smeary mess with another. Many individual parameters can be adjusted individually to optimize your settings for a specific video. Unfortunately, good results almost always require a fair amount of trial and error, and encoding video can be a pretty slow process. For best results, you should identify and test a short section of your show that is likely to challenge the compression method. Look for a section with fast cutting, fast horizontal pans, grainy images, and so forth, and compress just that section using a variety of settings.

Fortunately, customizing settings in Compressor is quite easy.

1 In the Settings window, click the New Setting button and, from the pop-up menu, choose MPEG-2.

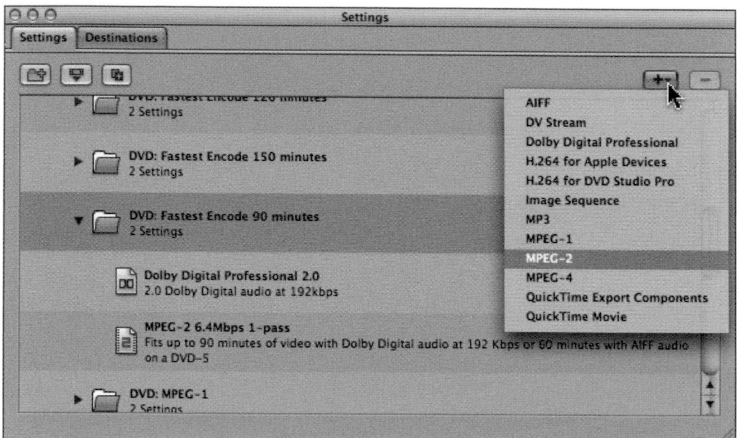

A new preset is added to the custom folder in the Settings window.

2 In the Inspector, name the preset *Custom SD DVD*.

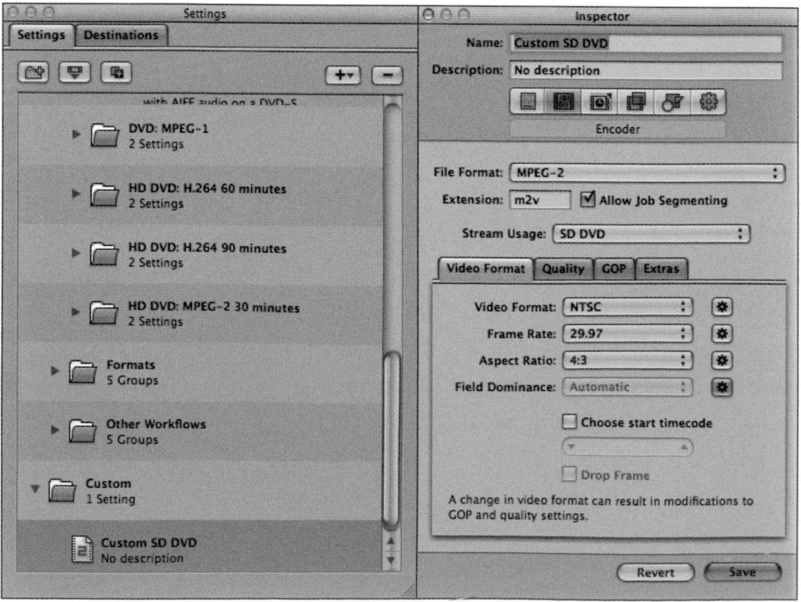

The file format will automatically be set to MPEG-2.

3 Set the Stream Usage to SD DVD, and click the automatic button to the right of the Video Format, Frame Rate, and Aspect Ratio fields to enable automatic format detection for all three parameters.

When these parameters are set to Automatic, Compressor will assign the appropriate settings based on the nature of the source footage. This allows you to use the same preset for a variety of source material.

4 Click the Quality tab.

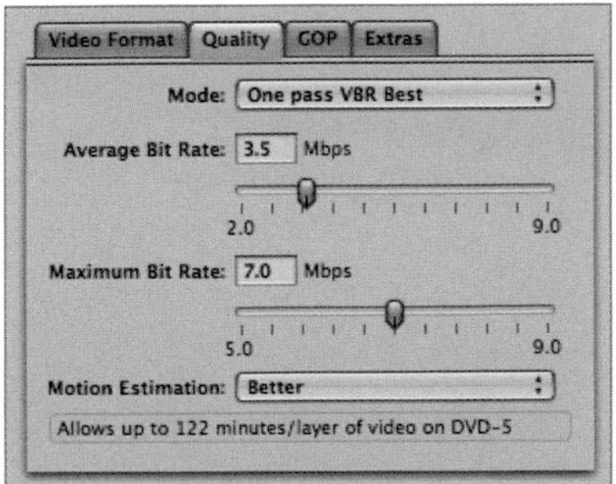

In the Quality tab, you can set the bit rate of the compressed file, as well as choose the encoding method (or mode).

5 From the Mode pop-up menu, choose "Two pass VBR."

VBR (variable bit rate) is a superior way to encode MPEG-2 content. It encodes complex scenes that include fast motion and rapid cuts at a higher data rate than it encodes scenes with few edits and less motion in the shots. This reduces overall file size, allowing you to fit more content on your DVD.

Two-pass VBR further improves image quality by performing the encoding twice. The first pass assesses which scenes in the show will need higher data rates and which scenes can be reproduced accurately with a lower data rate. Of course, the downside is that a two-pass VBR preset takes twice as long to compress as a one-pass preset.

6 Set Average Bit Rate to 3.5 and Maximum Bit Rate to 7.0.

In general, the higher your average bit rate, the less important it is to use the two-pass method. Typically, two-pass encoding provides significant improvement at data rates below 3.5 Mbps.

7 Set the Motion Estimation to Better, the middle setting.

Motion Estimation detects movement within the frame. The higher the setting here, the better Compressor will encode that motion without turning the video into a blocky mess. Of course, the higher the quality setting is, the longer the encode time. A good rule of thumb is to use the Good setting when using one-pass mode, and use the Best setting only when using the one- or two-pass VBR Best modes.

8 Click the GOP tab.

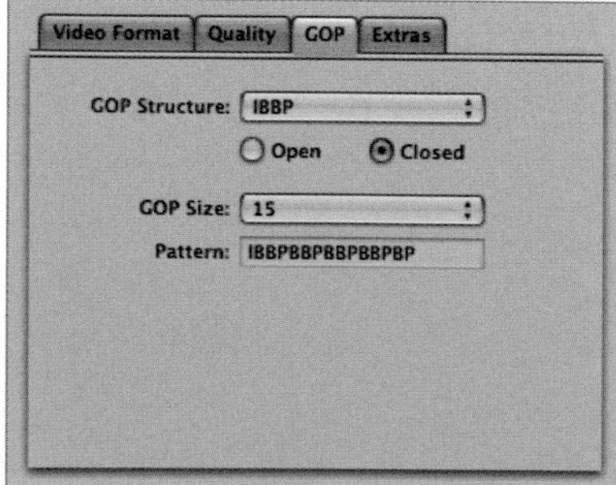

GOP stands for *group of pictures*; this tab helps you control the size of the chunks in which your MPEG-2 stream will be encoded. This is part of the magic that helps make MPEG-2 video look so good. MPEG-2 is far more sophisticated than other keyframe-based compression formats, and Compressor lets you fine-tune the GOP structure to optimize picture quality.

Consult the Compressor Help file for more information on customizing GOP structure.

Other GOP Patterns

If your video contains many sections of very fast cutting, or lots of motion within the frame, you may find that the quality of your video degrades significantly between keyframes (I-frames). In this case, try setting the GOP structure to IBP or IP.

These settings will create many more keyframes, which will make your video look better, but it will require significantly higher data rates (and will occupy more space on the DVD). Typically, IBP requires at least 6 Mbps, and IP requires 8 Mbps, to realize adequate image quality.

Similarly, the smaller the size of the GOP, the more groups you'll have and the more keyframes you'll have. This results in higher-quality video, but at the expense of a higher data rate.

Open GOPs allow P and B frames to reference keyframes from other GOPs. Closed GOPs always begin with their own I-frames, and any P- or B-frames in that GOP can only reference keyframes within that GOP. Open GOPs can achieve lower data rates by requiring fewer I-frames; however, open GOPs cannot be used on mixed-angle or multiple-angle DVDs.

Also, chapter markers must be set on I-frames, so closed GOPs allow for more accurate placement of chapter markers. (With open GOPs, your marker may be as far as half a second away from the frame in which your scene begins.) In general, use closed GOPs unless you're really hurting for disk space and are not using frequent chapter markers.

9 Click the Extras tab to examine the remaining settings for your custom preset.

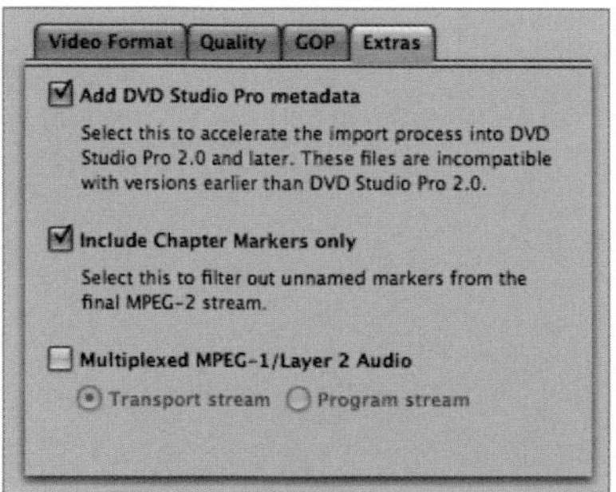

10 Make sure that the "Add DVD Studio Pro metadata" checkbox is selected.

This setting significantly reduces the time DVD Studio Pro requires to open and parse the video files you create.

11 Select the "Include Chapter Markers only" checkbox.

This will instruct Compressor to ignore any extraneous markers that may be in your Final Cut Pro sequence when the file is encoded.

The last checkbox in the Extras tab is used only for special cases when your MPEG stream is intended for direct broadcast instead of DVD.

12 Click the Save button in the lower-right corner of the Inspector.

Customizing Additional Settings

Compressor allows you to perform a wide range of modifications to your footage during the encoding process. These modifications can include transforming the frame size or frame rate, changing interlacing settings, or adding filters.

1 In the Frame Controls section, deselect the Frame Controls Automatic button to unlock the pop-up menu.

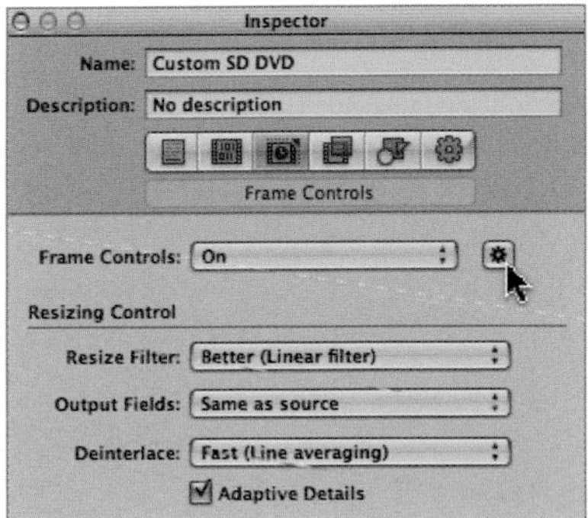

2 Set Frame Controls to On and leave the remaining settings at their defaults.

These settings allow you to control the quality level used when footage must be converted between frame sizes or rates. Be aware that using the Best quality settings can be very processor intensive.

3 Click the Filters button.

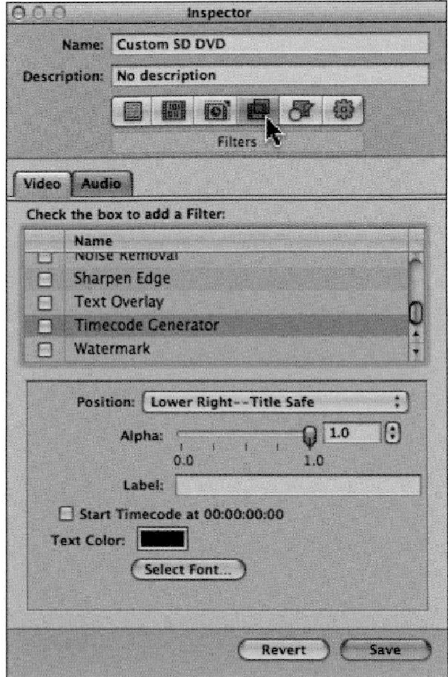

This pane allows you to add filters to the video. If you scroll through the list, you'll see that it contains many useful filters, including a Timecode Generator to create a BITC (burned-in timecode) version of your video, as well as a Watermark filter, which allows you to add a *bug* or other semi-transparent logo over your clips. You can even use a Motion project to create an animated watermark.

4 Click the Geometry button.

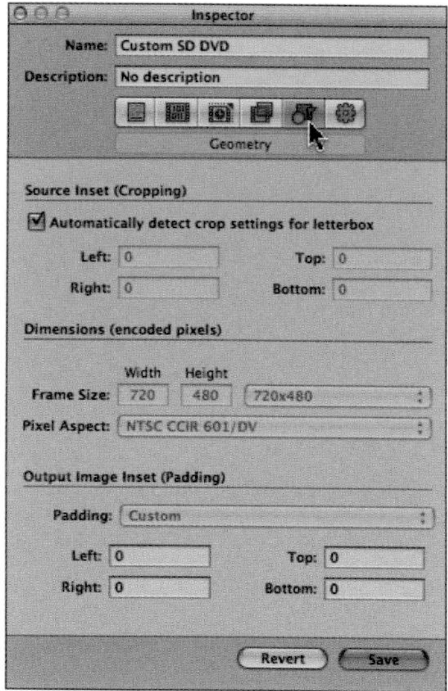

This pane allows you to crop, pad, or define a new frame size for your output. Cropping will not change the size of your output movie but will zoom in on your original by the number of pixels you specify. If you have a letterbox you want to remove, you can select the "Automatically detect crop settings for letterbox" checkbox, but be aware that if you don't also change the frame size settings, this option may cause your original video to appear stretched.

If you want your output movie to fit a widescreen aspect ratio, you must modify the output dimensions accordingly. To ensure you are creating a frame size with the correct aspect ratio, choose from the presets in the pop-up menu to the right of the Frame Size data fields.

NOTE ▶ In many cases, the Dimensions section will be dimmed due to settings in the Encoder tab. For example, MPEG-2 files for SD DVDs have a preset frame size that cannot be altered.

Padding will add a black border around your original video, adding a letterbox using one of the preset sizes or based on custom pixel settings. Padding will not stretch or squeeze the original video, and it will observe the output frame size defined in the Dimensions settings above it.

All of these settings affect one another, so, for example, if you both crop and pad a clip, the edge pixels of the original will be cropped out, and a black border will be added around the newly cropped image.

Saving and Applying Custom Presets

Once you have successfully set all of your parameters, your preset can be used like any of the presets built into Compressor.

1 In the Inspector, click the Save button.

The preset is updated and saved.

2 Drag the custom preset from the Custom bin in the Settings window onto the item in the batch list.

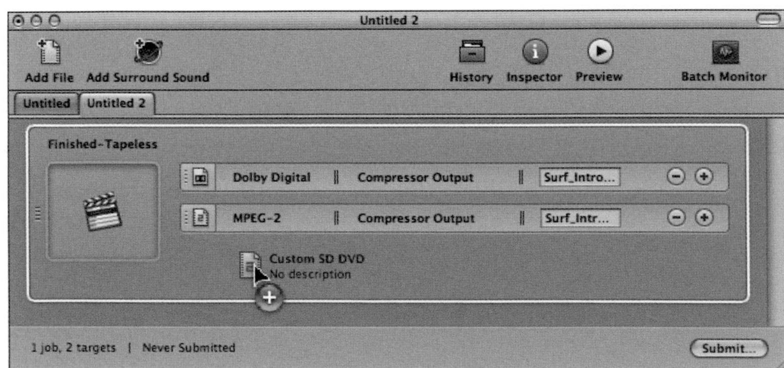

The job is added to the list.

3 Set the Destination to the Compressor Output folder, as you did earlier in this lesson.

Now, you have two MPEG-2 compression settings in your queue. You can choose to compress them both, and compare the resulting quality, or you can delete one from the list by selecting it and pressing Delete.

4 In the Batch window, click the Submit button.

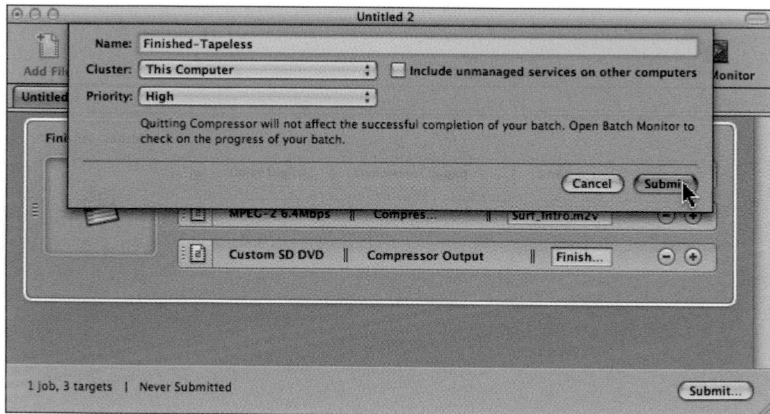

The Confirmation window appears.

5 Click Submit again.

Compressor will begin encoding all of the files.

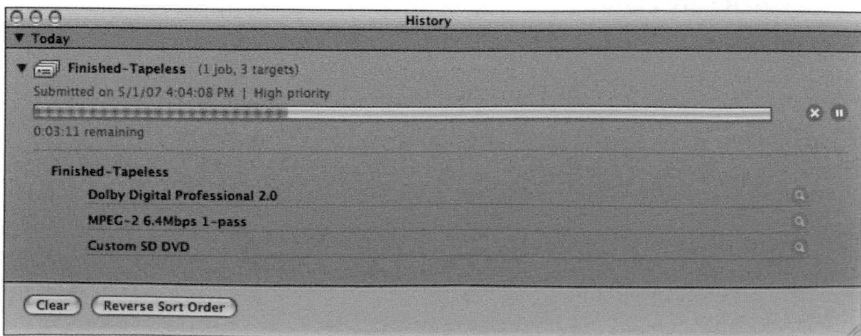

You can view the status of the encoding in the History window.

Creating Video for HD DVDs

DVD Studio Pro can encode content for HD DVDs using the H.264 codec. You can encode HD DVD video files in Compressor just as you created MPEG-2 streams for standard definition DVDs, except that you use different presets.

1 In Final Cut Pro, select *hooploose HD*.

 This is a 960 x 720 HD sequence running at a frame rate of 60i.

2 Choose File > Export > Using Compressor.

 Compressor appears (or opens), and the sequence is added to the batch.

3 From the Settings window, drag the "HD DVD: H.264 60 minutes" folder onto the hooploose HD – Tapeless item in the batch list.

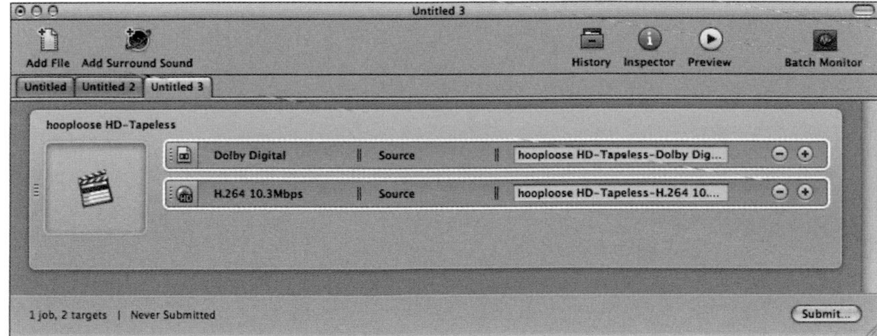

Two entries are added to the batch list: one for audio and one for video.

You could click the Submit button now to begin encoding, but instead, you will create a custom HD compression setting.

Using Custom H.264 Settings

Compressing for HD is similar to compressing for SD, but some of the settings have different names and slightly different functions. Like all compression, the generic settings rarely give optimal results for all footage. To make your footage look its best, you should get in the habit of experimenting with a variety of settings to see which provide the best quality at the lowest file sizes.

In this exercise, you will modify the preset and save it as a new, custom setting. Custom settings can also be created by clicking the Add Custom Setting button in the top left corner of the Settings window.

1 In the Batch window, double-click the H.264 10.3Mbps preset.

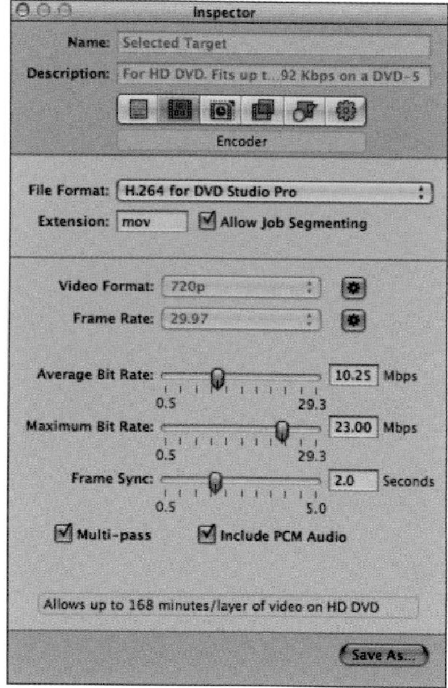

The Inspector displays the preset's settings.

2 In the Inspector, set the Average Bit Rate to about 7.5 Mbps.

The H.264 compression algorithm is nearly twice as efficient as the MPEG-2 codec, so you can expect higher quality at a lower bit rate. However, keep in mind that the larger your video frame is, the higher the required bit rate. Because this sequence is the smaller 720p frame size, you can conserve space by lowering the bit rate without compromising quality.

3 Set the Frame Sync slider to 1.0 seconds.

The Frame Sync setting controls how often automatic keyframes are added to your compressed movie. The higher the setting is, the less frequently keyframes are added, which reduces file size but may compromise quality. The ideal setting will depend on how dynamic your show is.

4 Make sure the Multi-pass checkbox is selected.

This is equivalent to using the two-pass VBR mode in the MPEG 2 settings. Multi-pass takes twice as long, but it ensures a better distribution of bits and can significantly improve visual quality, especially at lower data rates.

5 Deselect the Include PCM Audio checkbox.

In most cases, as in this example, you will encode your audio into the Dolby AC3 format as a separate item in the batch list, which makes this setting redundant.

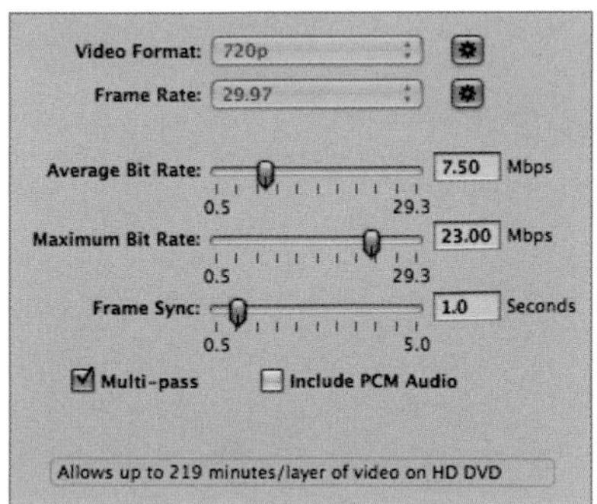

6 Click Save As to save your custom preset.

The Save Setting dialog opens.

7 Name the preset *Custom HD for DVD* and click Save.

8 In the batch list, Control-click the H.264 10.3Mbps preset and choose Change Setting from the shortcut menu.

A sheet appears containing all of the folders and settings from the Presets window.

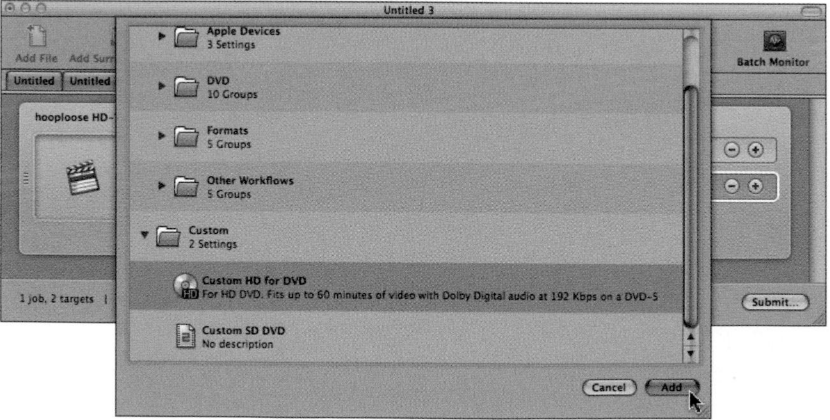

9 Expand the Custom folder and select the Custom HD for DVD setting, then click Add.

10 Click Submit to begin compressing the HD video file.

Encoding Video for Other Devices

Compressor can also export video suitable for iPods, iPhones, Apple TV, other cell phones, podcasting, or websites. Creating such files is as simple as choosing the appropriate Compressor preset.

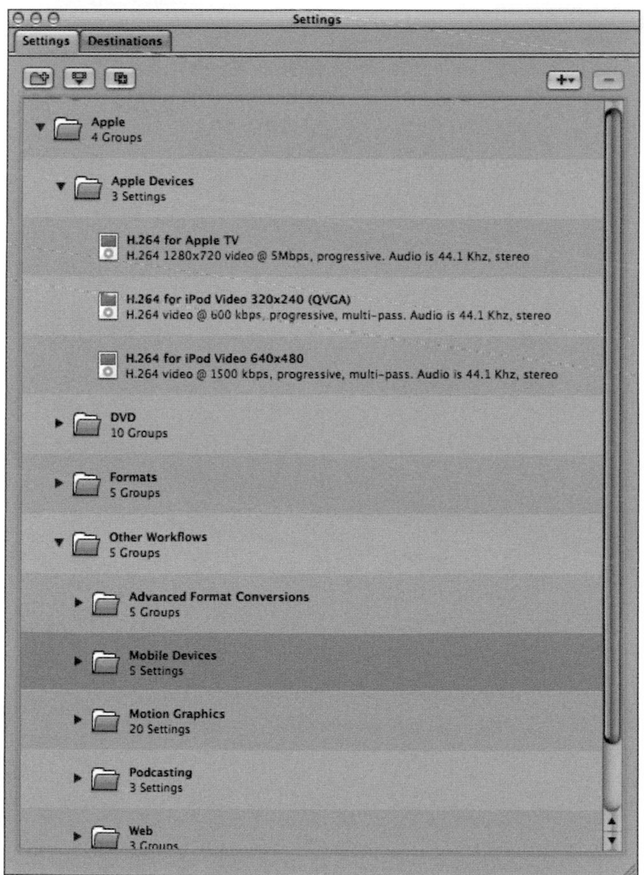

For more information on using these specific presets and how to best customize them for your specific projects, please see the Compressor User's Manual or Peachpit Press's *Apple Pro Training Series: Compressor Quick-Reference Guide* by Brian Gary.

A Note about Web Video

There are countless video formats currently in use on the web. Final Cut Pro Studio 2 includes presets for two popular codecs: MPEG-4, a high-quality, low-bandwidth, widely compatible codec; and H.264, which produces excellent results at low-bandwidth settings but requires QuickTime 7 or higher for playback. Technically, H.264 is a variant of the MPEG-4 codec, but it is not playable on some older devices that can play MPEG-4 video, such as cell phones.

After choosing which codec you want to use, you must additionally choose whether your file should use streaming or progressive download. Typically, shows shorter than 10 minutes are ideal for progressive download, whereas streaming is appropriate for longer shows. However, streaming files require special streaming software on your web server, whereas progressive download files can be embedded into any web page without requiring additional software.

Exporting Audio

Final Cut Pro can export audio in a wide variety of formats, each tailored for a specific workflow. Final Cut Pro can accommodate your workflow whether you are finishing your audio mix in Soundtrack Pro, Digidesign's Pro Tools, or another dedicated audio tool; recording multiple channels directly to a multichannel recorder (using special audio I/O hardware); or outputting tracks to be encoded for multichannel surround sound.

Setting AIFF Options

The simplest type of audio output is a simple stereo mix. This will generate a two-channel AIFF file that can be played back in any stereo-capable software or hardware.

1 In Final Cut Pro, select the *Finished* sequence.

2 Choose File > Export > Audio to AIFF(s).

The Save dialog appears.

3 Name the file *StereoOutputTest* and set Where (the destination) to Desktop.

4 Set the Rate pop-up menu to 48 kHz, Depth to 16-bit, and Config to Stereo Mix.

NOTE ▶ Final Cut Pro can output audio up to 24-bit and 96 kHz for maximum quality; however, there is no advantage to exporting to a quality setting higher than the source audio.

5 Click Save.

The stereo audio file is saved to your desktop.

Exporting Channel Groups

In addition to exporting a stereo mix, Final Cut Pro can also export audio as channel groups. This option exports multiple mono or stereo AIFFs based on the audio channel settings in your sequence. This can be useful if you plan to modify the individual channels in another program or even to import later into another Final Cut Pro project.

1 Double-click the *Finished* sequence to open it.

2 Choose Sequence > Settings to open the Sequence Settings window.

3 Click the Audio Outputs tab.

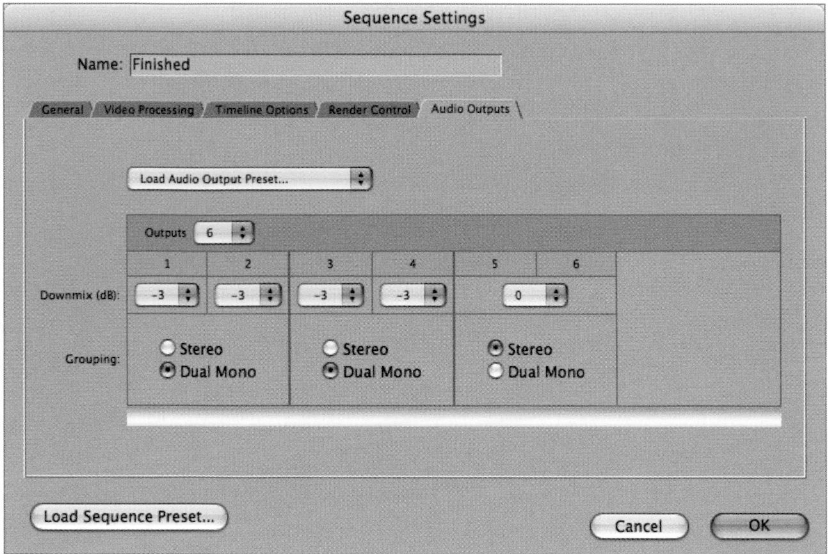

This sequence has six outputs: four mono channels and one stereo pair.

4 Click OK to close the Sequence Settings window.

NOTE ▶ You will probably see a warning dialog indicating that the current audio device doesn't have enough outputs to play the sequence correctly. This sequence requires special audio hardware. To complete this exercise, do not select the Downmix checkbox. Click OK to close the Warning message.

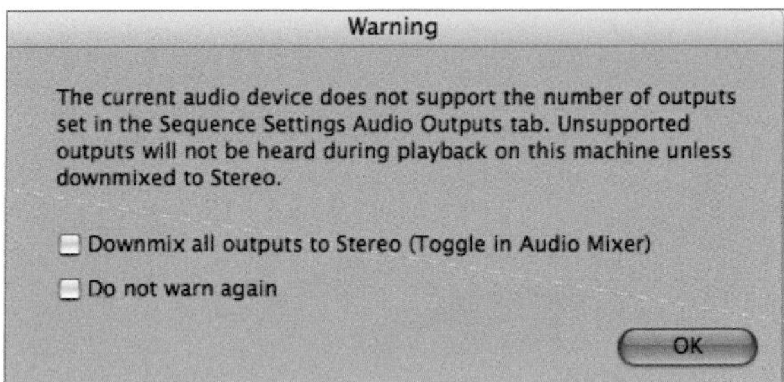

5 Choose File > Export > Audio as AIFF(s).

The AIFF Export Save dialog opens.

6 From the Config pop-up menu, choose Channel Grouped.

7 Set the desired destination for your output files and click Save.

NOTE ► Because the Channel Grouped setting will create as many files as you have audio outputs, each file will be based on the name you enter in the AIFF Export dialog with an incrementing digit appended to the end (such as xxx-1, xxx-2, xxx-3 and so on).

Making a Multichannel QuickTime Movie

It is also possible to export a single QuickTime file with as many audio channels as you have set in your Final Cut Pro sequence. This would be used in similar situations as the channel group export, but all the audio is stored in a single file, making it extremely portable and convenient. Importing such a clip back into Final Cut Pro would result in a clip with many audio tabs.

1 Choose Sequence > Settings or press Command-0.

   The Sequence Settings window opens.

2 In the General tab, make sure the Audio Settings: Config pop-up menu is set to Discrete Channels.

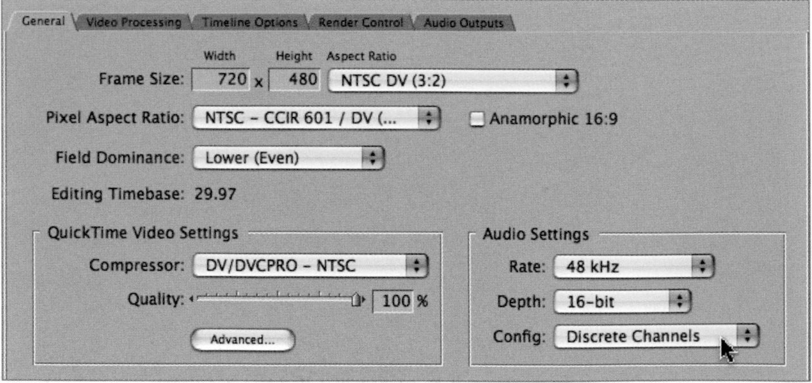

   The other two choices in this menu are identical to the Stereo Mix and Channel Grouped options discussed earlier in this lesson.

3 Click OK to close the Sequence Settings window.

   If the Audio Output warning dialog appears again, click OK to close it.

4 Choose File > Export > QuickTime Movie.

   The Export to QuickTime Movie Save dialog appears.

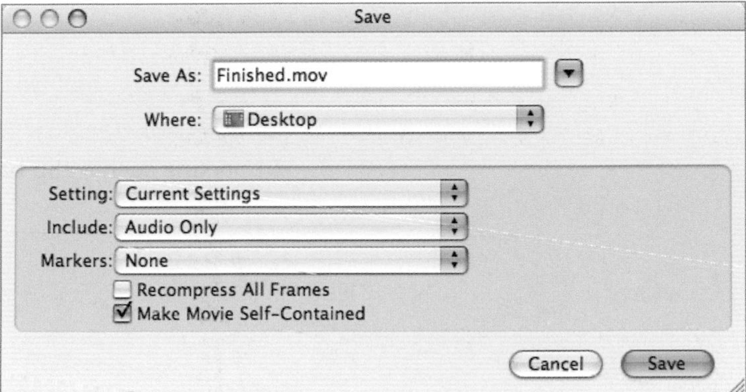

5 From the Include pop-up menu, choose Audio Only, and select the Make Movie Self-Contained checkbox.

6 Set a destination for your output and click Save.

A QuickTime movie will be created with six audio tracks, corresponding to the six tracks in your Final Cut Pro sequence.

Exporting Audio to OMF

Many filmmakers prefer to perform their final audio mix using Digidesign's Pro Tools or another dedicated audio workstation. You can export audio from a Final Cut Pro sequence to an interchange format called Open Media Format (OMF) that can be imported into Pro Tools and other software. An OMF file contains all of the audio data from all of the tracks in a Final Cut Pro sequence. It also maintains the arrangement of individual clips and tracks, so when the OMF file is opened in another program, the audio portion of your Final Cut Pro sequence is faithfully reproduced. Be aware, however, that audio filters and effects will not be included in the OMF file.

1 Choose File > Export > Audio to OMF.

The OMF Audio Export dialog opens.

Although you can modify the sample rate and bit depth, it is usually best to leave those settings unaltered so that they match the audio in your sequence and source footage.

2 Set Handle Length to 5 seconds (00:00:05:00).

Adding handles is especially important for audio clips. The engineer who will import your OMF will likely be adding fades to the beginning and end of every single audio element in your show. The more extra footage you provide, the more flexibility the audio editor will have.

3 Leave the Include Crossfade Transitions checkbox selected and the Include Levels and Include Pan checkboxes deselected. Click OK.

TIP Most audio editors prefer to set their own audio levels rather than import the level you set during your rough cut. Always check with your audio mixer about the settings they prefer.

The OMF Save dialog appears.

4 In the lower-left corner of the window, deselect the Hide Extension checkbox.

NOTE ▶ You may need to expand the window to see the Hide Extension checkbox.

The .omf extension is added to the filename. Because the file may be going to a Windows-based workstation, it's best to leave the .omf extension visible.

5 Choose a destination for your OMF file and click Save.

Delivering Corresponding Video

If you're creating your audio mix in a separate application, it's very important to lock your picture before exporting an OMF. If you make editorial changes in Final Cut Pro after handing off the audio to a sound editor, you could create sync problems that will be difficult to fix.

Typically, in addition to the OMF, you will also deliver to your sound editor a QuickTime movie of the corresponding picture with BITC that matches the timecode in the OMF (which is based on the timecode in the exported sequence).

It's essential that the picture and sound are exactly the same length. It's also a good habit to provide a sync beep at the head and tail of your show.

TIP A one-frame clip of Bars and Tone serves as an effective sync beep.

You can see an example of sync beeps at the head and tail of the *Finished* sequence (note that they appear in every track). Also notice that the timecode for the sequence begins at 23:58:30:00, and the first frame of picture begins at exactly 00:00:00:00.

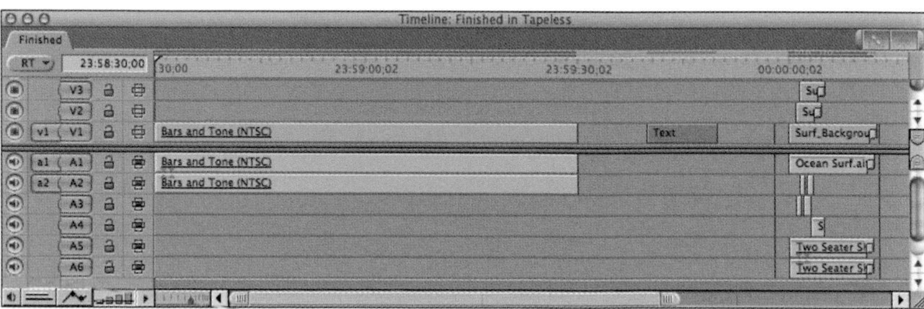

Exporting to Dolby AC3 Format

If you are preparing your audio for DVD, the best format to use is Dolby AC3. This format is compressed, so it takes less space and less bandwidth on the DVD, plus it has the added benefit of being able to store multiple channels for surround sound. You can encode AC3 in a wide variety of formats from a single mono channel all the way up to 6.1 channels (left, center, right, left surround, center surround, right surround, and low-frequency effects).

To create surround sound AC3 files, your audio must be mixed into separate tracks for the multiple channels. This could be one QuickTime movie with multiple tracks, or it could be separate files for each channel.

> **NOTE ►** All audio to be compressed to AC3 needs to be sampled at 48 kHz, and all files need to be the same length, or Compressor will add silence to the end of shorter tracks to force them all to the same duration.

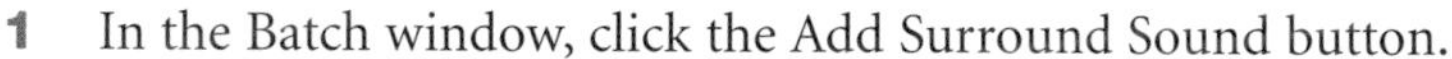

1 In the Batch window, click the Add Surround Sound button.

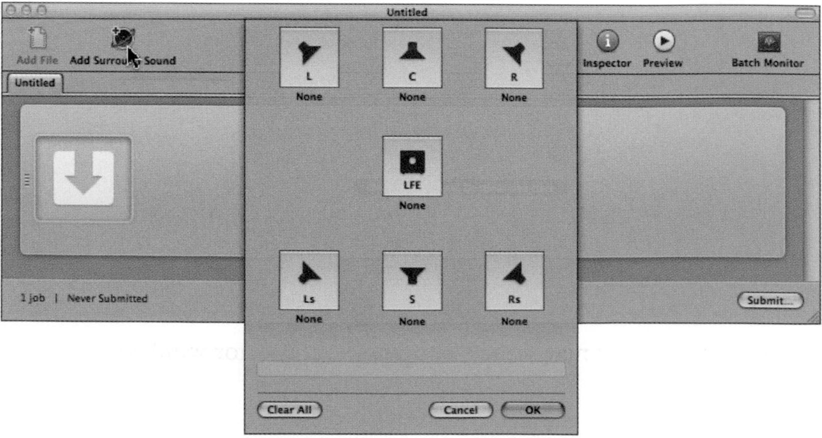

The channel assignment interface appears.

2 In the upper-left corner, click the L icon.

3 Navigate to Media > Surround Mix and open **FinalMix.L**.

This opens the audio file that will go into the front left channel.

4 Click the center box, and open **FinalMix.C**.

5 Follow the same process to assign the right, left surround, right surround, and low-frequency effects channels. (This example does not have a center surround channel.)

FinalMix.R is the right channel, **FinalMix.Ls** is the left surround, **FinalMix.Rs** is the right surround, and **FinalMix.LFE** is the low-frequency effects channel. Leave the S channel unassigned.

6 When all the channels are assigned, click OK to add the group to the batch list.

7 From the Settings window, Navigate to Formats > Audio, and drag the Dolby Digital Professional 5.1 preset to the Surround – FinalMix item in the Batch window.

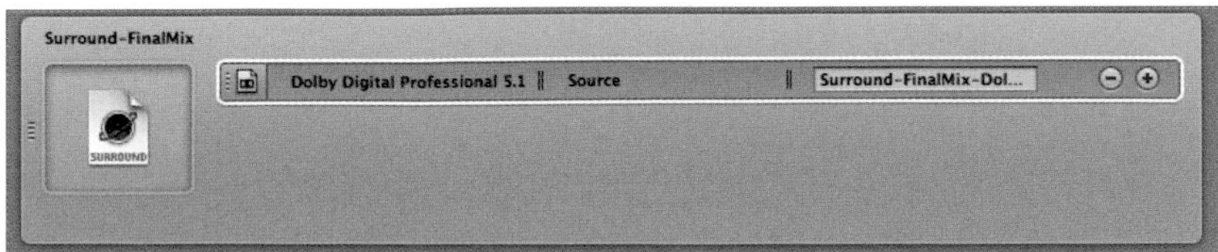

8 Double-click the new setting to open the Inspector window.

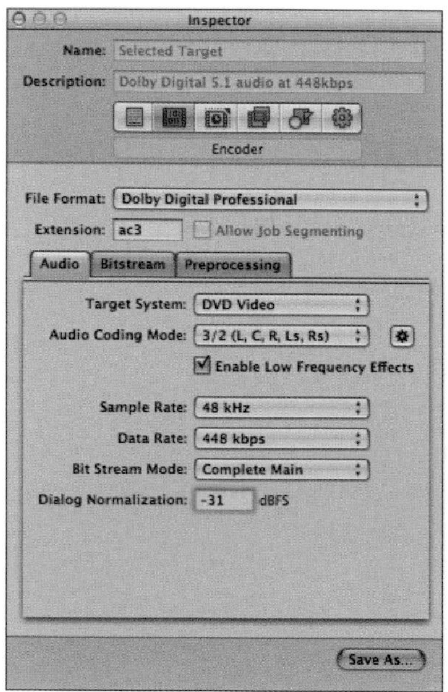

9 Set Audio Coding Mode to 3/2 and select the Enable Low Frequency Effects checkbox (if it's not already selected).

10 You can adjust the Data Rate for higher or lower compression quality, but the default 448 kbps is sufficient for most 5.1 streams.

The Audio Coding Mode setting determines which Data Rate settings are available. For example, five channels require more bandwidth than two channels, so Data Rate must be set higher.

11 Set Dialog Normalization to *–31*.

This will ensure that the audio will not be modified during encoding or on playback. Other settings may cause the center channel volume to be attenuated during playback to permit louder sounds in the other channels.

All of the other settings may be left at default for this exercise.

12 Go back to the Batch window and click Submit to begin the batch processing.

NOTE ▶ You can also use Soundtrack Pro to create and export surround sound mixes. For more information, see the Soundtrack Pro User's Manual or Martin Sitter's *Apple Pro Training Series: Soundtrack Pro 2.*

Exporting QuickTime Files

When your show is finished, you will likely want to export your show in many output formats. You've already learned how to create a file for DVD or web use. There are reasons you may want to create a full-resolution QuickTime movie as well.

A QuickTime movie is a good archive of a finished project (along with your precious project file, of course). You can save a single file that contains your whole movie in its native resolution, so you can archive or delete the bulky media files referenced by your project. You can use that file in Compressor or any other QuickTime-compatible program to create more MPEG or H.264 files, or files in any other formats.

You can output that file to tape, just as you would output directly from your edited sequence. Effects will never become unrendered, and you will enjoy the convenience of having all the data in one safe place rather than in a reference movie that links to myriad files all over your disk(s).

You might also want to deliver a full-resolution copy of your show to another editor or use it yourself in a new project. For example, you might want to generate a trailer or promo spot based on the finished show, or you might want to include a section in a show reel.

1 In the Browser, select the *Finished* sequence.

2 Choose File > Export > QuickTime Movie.

The QuickTime movie export Save dialog appears.

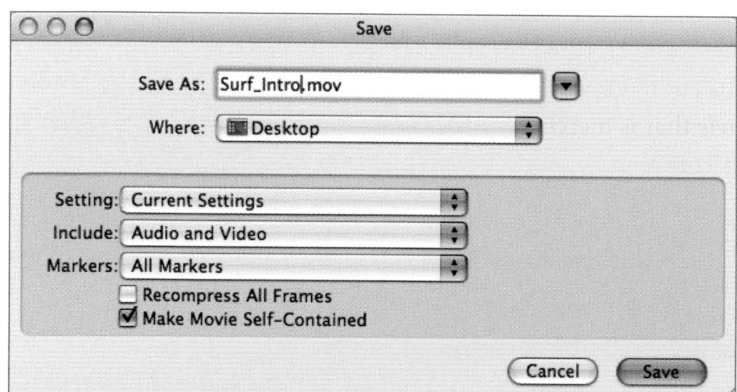

3 Name the new file *Surf_Intro.mov* and navigate to your desired destination.

By default, the Setting pop-up menu is set to Current Settings, which means the exported movie will have the same frame size, frame rate, audio, and compression settings as the sequence. The source footage that matches those sequence settings is displayed in gray in the Timeline render bar, and it will not be recompressed, thus preserving the highest possible quality.

In nearly all cases, you will leave the Setting pop-up menu unchanged. However, if you ever want to transcode your sequence into a different sequence preset, you could do that by changing this setting. In most cases, there is a better way to transcode: editing the clips into a sequence with the desired settings within Final Cut Pro, or using Compressor.

4 From the Include pop-up menu, choose Audio and Video. From the Markers pop-up menu, choose All Markers.

The Markers pop-up menu allows you to control which types of markers are included in the QuickTime movie. Many of the marker types are readable by other software, such as DVD Studio Pro or Soundtrack Pro.

5 Select the Make Movie Self-Contained checkbox and click Save.

Creating Reference Movies

The Make Movie Self-Contained checkbox is a very powerful setting. It determines whether your exported movie is a huge file containing a copy of all of the video and audio clips used in your sequence, or whether you get a tiny *reference movie* that is merely a pointer to all of those files, wherever they may exist on your computer.

Reference movies are great. They're much quicker to make than regular movies, they're very small, and you can use them in Compressor just like a regular QuickTime movie or any other QuickTime-compatible program. However, if you move, modify, or delete any of the video files that were used in the sequence from which you exported, the reference movie will no longer work. If that happens, opening it in any application may yield an error message and a search dialog (similar to the Final Cut Pro Offline Files dialog) asking you to locate the missing file.

Final Cut Pro reference movies contain all of the audio data from the sequence, plus any frames that needed to be rendered at the time of the export. But raw video will be pulled from the files in your Capture Scratch folder, and sections of the sequence that were previously rendered are pulled from the files in your Render Files folder. If any of those files are altered, the reference movie will become unplayable.

Reference movies are fine as long as you have no intention of taking them off the computer, and you don't plan to make changes to the files they're based on (such as re-rendering a portion of your sequence).

1. Select the *Finished* sequence.

2. Choose File > Export > QuickTime Movie.

   The QuickTime movie export Save dialog appears.

3. Name the new file *SurfIntroRef.mov* and navigate to your desired destination.

4 Set the Setting pop-up menu to Current Settings, the Include pop-up menu to Audio and Video, and the Markers pop-up menu to All Markers.

5 Deselect the Make Movie Self-Contained checkbox and click Save.

The exported file will be a reference movie.

Lesson Review

1. How do you export MPEG-2 files for use in DVD Studio Pro?
2. What is a GOP?
3. What codec is most commonly used in Compressor for HD DVD encoding?
4. Name ways to export audio data from a Final Cut Pro sequence.
5. What should always accompany an OMF export?
6. What is a reference movie, and how do you make one?

Answers

1. In Final Cut Pro, choose Export > Using Compressor and choose an MPEG-2 preset or create a custom preset.
2. GOP stands for *group of pictures* and describes the arrangement of keyframes and non-keyframes within an MPEG stream.
3. HD DVDs are usually encoded in Compressor using H.264 format at high data rates.
4. As a mixed stereo AIFF, as a channel grouped AIFF, as a multitrack QuickTime movie, as an OMF, and as a compressed AC3 file.
5. OMF exports should always be delivered with a corresponding video file, preferably with BITC that matches the timecode in the OMF.
6. A reference movie is a tiny QuickTime file containing pointers to the media contained in the clips used in a sequence. You create one by deselecting the Make Movie Self-Contained checkbox in the QuickTime Movie Save dialog.

Index

D

G

N

O

P

Q

R

V

W

X

ONE SIX RIGHT

THE ROMANCE OF FLYING

Footage used in this book is from the feature documentary "One Six Right".
Learn more about this independent film's journey from conception to distribution at:
www.apple.com/pro/profiles/terwilliger

W W W . O N E S I X R I G H T . C O M

The Apple Pro Training Series

The best way to learn Apple's professional digital video and audio software!

The Apple Pro Training Series is the official training curriculum of the Apple Pro Training and Certification program. Upon completing the course material in these books, you can become an Apple Certified Pro by taking the certification exam at an Apple Authorized Training Center.

To find an Authorized Training Center near you, visit:
www.apple.com/software/pro/training

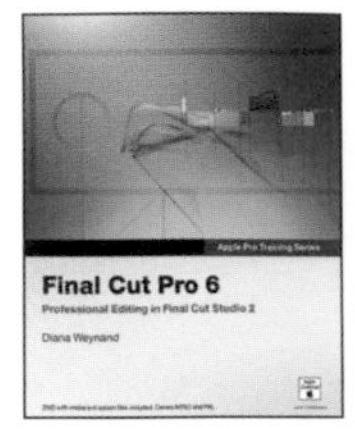

Final Cut Pro 6
0-321-50265-5 • $54.99

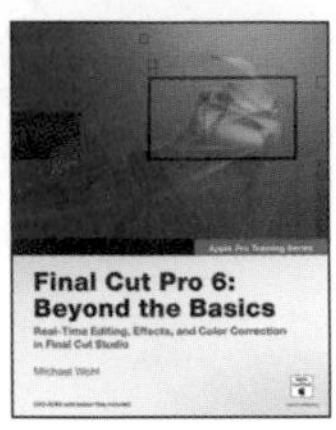

Final Cut Pro 6: Beyond the Basics
0-321-50912-9 • $54.99

The Craft of Editing with Final Cut Pro
0-321-52036-X • $54.99

Motion Graphics and Effects in Final Cut Studio
0-321-50940-4 • $54.99

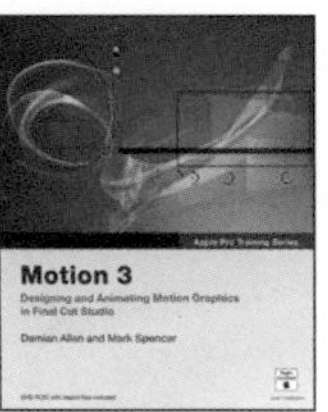

Motion 3
0-321-50910-2 • $54.99

Soundtrack Pro 2
0-321-50266-3 • $54.99

Color
0-321-50911-0 • $54.99

DVD Studio Pro 4, Second Edition
0-321-50189-6 • $54.99

Apple Pro Training Series: Logic Pro 7 and Logic Express 7
0-321-25614-X • $49.99

Apple Pro Training Series: Advanced Logic Pro 7
0-321-25607-7 • $49.99

Encyclopedia of Visual Effects
0-321-30334-2 • $54.99

The Apple Training Series

The best way to learn Apple's hardware, Mac OS X, and iLife applications.

iLife '06
0-321-42164-7 • $34.99

iWork '06 with iLife '06
0-321-44225-3 • $34.99

Desktop and Portable Systems, Third Edition
0-321-45501-0 • $59.99

Mac OS X Support Essentials
0-321-33547-3 • $54.99

To order books or view the entire Apple Pro Training Series catalog, visit: **www.peachpit.com/appleprotraining**